The Handbook for TEACHING LEADERSHIP

The Handbook for TEACHING LEADERSHIP

Knowing, Doing, and Being

Edited by

Scott Snook
Nitin Nohria
Rakesh Khurana

Harvard Business School

SAGE

Los Angeles | London | New Delhi
Singapore | Washington DC

SAGE

Los Angeles | London | New Delhi
Singapore | Washington DC

FOR INFORMATION:

SAGE Publications, Inc.
2455 Teller Road
Thousand Oaks, California 91320
E-mail: order@sagepub.com

SAGE Publications Ltd.
1 Oliver's Yard
55 City Road
London EC1Y 1SP
United Kingdom

SAGE Publications India Pvt. Ltd.
B 1/I 1 Mohan Cooperative Industrial Area
Mathura Road, New Delhi 110 044
India

SAGE Publications Asia-Pacific Pte. Ltd.
33 Pekin Street #02-01
Far East Square
Singapore 048763

Senior Executive Editor: Lisa Cuevas Shaw
Assistant Editor: MaryAnn Vail
Editorial Assistant: Mayan White
Production Editor: Eric Garner
Typesetter: C&M Digitals (P) Ltd.
Proofreader: Theresa Kay
Indexer: Sheila Bodell
Cover Designer: Gail Buschman
Marketing Manager: Helen Salmon
Permissions Editor: Karen Ehrmann

Printed in the United States of America

Library of Congress Cataloging-in-Publication Data

The handbook for teaching leadership : knowing, doing, and being / Editors, Scott Snook, Nitin Nohria, Rakesh Khurana.

p. cm.
Includes bibliographical references and index.

ISBN 978-1-4129-9094-3 (cloth : acid-free paper)

1. Leadership—Study and teaching 2. Leadership. I. Snook, Scott A., 1958- II. Nohria, Nitin, 1962- III. Khurana, Rakesh, 1948-

HD57.7.H3562 2012
658.4′07124—dc23 2011031173

This book is printed on acid-free paper.

11 12 13 14 15 10 9 8 7 6 5 4 3 2 1

CONTENTS

ACKNOWLEDGMENTS

This Handbook grew out of a leadership colloquium convened at Harvard Business School in June of 2009. Over 100 experienced leaders, teachers, students, scholars, consultants, and executives gathered along the banks of the Charles River to share their thoughts on the question: *How can leadership be taught?* We thank Harvard Business School and Dean Jay Light for their unflagging support of this ambitious undertaking. A special thanks goes out to our dean of the Division of Research, Srikant Datar, without whose generous intellectual and financial resources we would have never even attempted such a project. Behind the scenes worked a magician. The über-creative presence of Maurizio Travaglini created the physical and spiritual holding environment from which all good things came. Finally, we can't say enough about the tireless efforts of Deborah Bell, our conference coordinator. Without Debby's patience, persistence, and attention to detail, nothing would ever have gotten done. Such is both the blessing and the curse of having three professors trying to lead a project about leading.

Organizing a conference is one thing, pulling together an edited volume is quite another. To this end, we are indebted to Tony Mayo and his crew at the Leadership Initiative—an interdisciplinary enterprise dedicated to stimulating leadership research and teaching across the HBS community. In particular, we are especially grateful to Amanda Pepper who singlehandedly coordinated the monumental effort to assemble the individual inputs of over 50 authors into the collective output of a Handbook. True leadership! A heartfelt thanks also goes out to our Seal Team 6 of copyediting, Steven Shafer and Caitlin Anderson, both of whom copyedited each chapter to ensure consistency in style without compromising the voices of each author.

At a time when the traditional publishing world is turning upside down, when edited volumes and handbooks embody some of the most difficult challenges to leaders in this turbulent industry, our editor at SAGE, Lisa Shaw, had the courage to support this ambitious project. From the start, she saw the promise in our idea. At times perhaps even more than we did, she understood the obligation we have to develop better leaders by sharing the collective wisdom of those who have been teaching the subject for years. This was a risky venture. We are forever grateful to Lisa and her entire editorial team at SAGE—MaryAnn Vail, Mayan White, and Eric Garner—for their boundless flexibility and good cheer. For us, they truly modeled the role of any good leader: inspire, challenge, and support. We were blessed to have them as true partners in this work.

As always, we owe a heartfelt debt to our families, without whose generous love and support none of this would have been possible or even worth doing. In particular, we'd like to publicly acknowledge our wives—Kathleen Snook, Monica Chandra, and Stephanie Khurana—a trio of truly amazing women. Accomplished professionals in their own right, in countless ways everyday, each of them reminds us how much we can learn from our responsibilities as partners, parents, teachers, and leaders—four important roles in society with a great deal of overlap, with a great deal to say to each other, if only we can find a way.

Leadership is a collective endeavor; teaching it, perhaps more so. Therefore, we'll end where we started, by paying tribute to the main cast: our conference participants, our authors, and our students. To our growing community of leadership scholars, thank you for joining us on this journey. Without your passion, intellect, and commitment to developing better leaders, we never could have imagined what we might accomplish together. To our authors, we know how busy you are. And yet when we asked, you said yes. Such is your dedication to this nascent field and to sharing your wisdom, the collective sum of which is now captured in this foundational handbook. Finally, we must thank our students. Just as none of us are leaders without followers; none of us are teachers without students. And yet as we grow more experienced, we increasingly recognize how these lines blur; followers lead and students teach. This Handbook is dedicated to all students of leadership, those we've learned from in the past, those who are in it with us today, and perhaps most importantly, those who will lead us into the future.

TEACHING LEADERSHIP

Advancing the Field

◆ Scott A. Snook, Rakesh Khurana, and Nitin Nohria

Harvard Business School

It has been more than twenty-five years since a handful of intrepid associates in West Point's Department of Behavioral Sciences and Leadership published their pioneering work, *Leadership in Organizations* (1985), widely considered to be the first formal textbook specifically designed to "teach leadership." Since then, the field of leadership has exploded. A simple Google search of "leadership books" returns more than 84 million hits. Not surprisingly, as overall interest in leadership has grown, so has the demand for courses on the topic. Scan the mission statements of most major universities and professional schools and you'll find that "educating leaders" is the common thread.[1] Search the catalogues of almost any college and you'll find dozens of courses with the word "Leadership" in their titles.

---

[1]Many universities, especially in their graduate programs of business administration, law, medicine, education, public health, and public policy, claim that their mission is to educate leaders who will advance the well-being of society in their respective fields. Here, for example, are the mission statements of some leading business schools:

The mission of the ________ Business School is to . . .

. . . ***educate leaders*** *for business and society. (Yale)*
. . . ***educate leaders*** *who make a difference in the world. (Harvard)*
. . . ***develop*** *principled, innovative* ***leaders*** *who improve the world . . . (MIT)*
. . . ***develop*** *innovative, principled, and insightful* ***leaders*** *who change the world. (Stanford)*
. . . ***prepare*** *business* ***leaders*** *who fuel the growth of industries and economies. (PENN)*
. . . *improve society by* ***developing leaders*** *in the world of practical affairs. (UVA)*
. . . ***educate and develop leaders*** *and builders of enterprises . . . (Columbia)*
. . . *offer the world's best business* ***leadership education.*** *(Dartmouth)*

And yet, if you were charged with *teaching* a course on leadership today, where would you start? Where would you turn to learn about the incredible array of approaches to teaching this ill-defined, yet important topic? How would you go about tapping into the wealth of practical experience in order to benefit from the hard-won lessons of those who have gone before you? What are the various theoretical assumptions and pedagogical techniques you might consider in the process of designing and delivering a course in this underdeveloped and undisciplined (in both the literal and practical sense of the word) field? How should one even "think about" the challenge of "teaching leadership"? This *Handbook* is intended to be a foundational reference for educators who teach primarily in traditional classroom settings and who find themselves facing this increasingly important, but daunting challenge.[2]

The teaching of any subject is many-sided. However, discharging the responsibilities of a university educator is particularly complex. Teaching is only one of many activities expected of a typical faculty member. There is also an expectation that what is taught should be grounded in research. Even for teachers who do relatively little leadership research, it is still assumed that what they convey to students represents the most important research relevant to the field. Moreover, when it comes to the subject of teaching leadership, university educators must also recognize that they are members of a larger community of academics responsible for shaping society's future leaders. Therefore, academics involved in teaching leadership must consider a broader context that often extends beyond the traditional boundaries of their home discipline and intellectual community. Finally, those of us who teach leadership must also acknowledge an increased responsibility to our larger community. If we are successful as teachers, by definition then, our students—that is, future leaders—will play a disproportionate role in shaping the future of society. This is an obligation we should not and cannot take lightly.

If the teaching of leadership comes with unique obligations for the instructor, it also begs similarly important questions about the nature and quality of what is taught. Teaching languishes if it is not rooted in a solid understanding of pedagogy and grounded in quality research. University educators are expected to have a more intricate knowledge base—in both breadth and depth, more fundamental and more strictly criticized and tested—than is available to a layperson. Teaching in a university places a special obligation on an educator. In particular, what is asserted to be knowledge about leadership must be true. This is particularly challenging when it comes to leadership. Because when an academic makes an assertion in

[2]Clearly there is no shortage of books on leadership. So why add another? There are literally thousands of "classic books" on the general topic of leading (Bass & Stogdill, 1974; Bennis, 1989; Burns, 1978; Gardner, 1993; McCall, 1998) and another couple hundred popular books that offer advice on becoming an effective leader (Covey, 1990; George & Sims, 2007; Goldsmith, 2006; Kotter, 2008; Kouzes & Posner, 2007). As a result, one popular option currently available to leadership educators is to select one or more of these classic or popular books and design a course around it. Or, if you subscribe to a broader view of development (Avolio, 2005; Paulus & Drath, 1995; Quinn, 1996), the Center for Creative Leadership publishes a *Handbook of Leadership Development*, currently in its third edition (van Velsor, McCauley, & Ruderman, 2010). Alternatively, there are dozens of source books that offer scores of innovative resources, exercises, cases, and instruments, all published to support the design and delivery of leadership programs (Giber, Carter, & Goldsmith, 2000; Schwartz, Axtman, & Freeman, 1998; Schwarz & Gimbel, 2000). Finally, there are a handful of respected leadership textbooks (Northouse, 2010; Yukyl, 2009) that have stood the test of time (both currently in their 5th & 7th editions, respectively) that offer comprehensive surveys of major theories and research *about* leadership.

the field of leadership and communicates knowledge to students, engages students in the practical application of that knowledge or imbues the identity of leadership on that student, the educational outcomes need to adhere to the criteria of veracity and accuracy we hold for any other field taught in a university setting. Moreover, academics must do this while adhering to societally expected commitments to scholarly, detached, and dispassionate judgment. Without such a commitment, academics and the subjects they teach are in danger of being discredited.

It is far too easy to enumerate flaws in the current state of leadership education: course content rarely conforms to the norms of the scientific method (Bennis & O'Toole, 2005); teachers employ casual and often self-serving empirical evidence (Ghoshal, 2005); approaches are rarely grounded in well-established theoretical traditions (Doh, 2003); there are as yet few credible communities of practice dedicated to developing and sharing best practices; and there is scant empirical evidence that any of these approaches really work (Pfeffer & Fong, 2002; Mintzberg, 2004). In short, the current state of leadership education lacks the intellectual rigor and institutional structure required to advance the field beyond its present (and precariously) nascent stage.[3]

In our opinion, the field of leadership education has reached a critical stage. After several decades of experimentation, with scores of teachers having developed and delivered a wide range of courses on the topic, we believe that the time is right to take stock and share our collective experience. Just spend some time with a group of people who are currently teaching leadership and you will come away with a few inescapable conclusions.[4] First, individually we have learned a great deal. Over the past twenty-five years, largely on our own, in various classrooms scattered throughout the globe, thousands of educators have accumulated an impressive wealth of individual wisdom. Unfortunately for the field, we rarely talk to each other, and surprisingly little gets shared. Second, with few exceptions, most of us are extremely passionate about what we do. The demand for improving the practice and quality of leading has never been greater and for those responsible for preparing future leaders, the sense of urgency and commitment is palpable. Third, after spending only a few minutes with such a group, you quickly discover that there clearly is no consensus on *the one best way* to teach leadership. There are currently as many ways to teach the topic as there are definitions of it (Rost, 1991), each proponent as enthusiastic as the next about his or her favored approach. And finally, we have learned that most experienced teachers are not only happy to share what they have learned, but equally eager to discover what others have been up to as well.

Unfortunately, unlike some of the more well-established academic disciplines, there are few institutional resources available to support this increasingly important and motivated community of educators whose academic homes are widely scattered across traditional disciplinary boundaries. To us, the implications were clear. Such a

[3]For an attempt at furthering this movement, see Nohria and Khurana (2010), *Handbook of Leadership Theory and Practice: An HBS Centennial Colloquium on Advancing Leadership*.

[4]To address this shortcoming, we convened an ambitious conference at the Harvard Business School in June 2009 titled, "How can leadership be taught?" The purpose of this colloquium was to share best practices, increase our collective understanding of the current state of the field, and to further strengthen an emerging community of practice within the academy centered on the teaching of leadership. To accomplish this goal, we invited a highly select group of educators with well-established reputations for having developed and taught courses on leadership that have a demonstrated history of success. The response was overwhelming. Following the conference, there was a groundswell of support for publishing a handbook on the topic to share, consolidate, and improve the practice of teaching leadership.

wide-ranging collection of promising, yet unorganized, individual experience demanded an equally impressive collective effort to take stock and consolidate. As a result, we offer this handbook with the following three goals in mind:

1. **Take Stock and Consolidate Progress.** Our primary goal is to share what we have learned after almost three decades of accumulated experience teaching leadership. To do this, we cast a wide net. Leadership educators from a broad range of disciplines and in a wide range of settings have experimented with a dizzying array of pedagogical approaches. Upon closer scrutiny, it is clear that some of us have been largely teaching *about* leadership (informing our students about the nature of the phenomenon); others have been teaching *how to* lead (equipping students with a set of skills and capacities enabling them to lead more effectively); and still others have focused primarily on helping our students actually *become* leaders (assisting students to gain access to and acquire the identity of a leader). These are but a few of the fundamental distinctions in an emerging field that have significant implications not only for design and delivery, but also for assessment. As a result of such conceptual disarray and interdisciplinary diffusion, solid data on outcomes assessment and theoretical grounding have lagged significantly. It is clear that a comprehensive volume is needed at this point in order to take stock and consolidate what we have learned.

2. **Establish a Foundational Reference for Teaching Leadership.** It was also clear that fresh theoretical approaches to teaching leadership abound, but no central clearing house currently existed to consolidate and share such potential. Exciting advances in related fields such as brain research, identity, ethics, adult development, communications, positive psychology, human intelligence, and educational theory require a single source for educators to consult if we are to have any hope of realizing our potential for improving the practice of teaching leadership. The explosive and yet undisciplined field of leadership education has reached a critical mass where a comprehensive volume is required not only to share novel ideas but also to help establish conceptual boundaries and shape the future contours of this emerging field. With a steadily increasing number of schools committed to developing leaders as a central goal, and with more and more educators entering the field from an increasingly wide range of disciplinary backgrounds, the time is right to consolidate what we have already learned and to establish a foundation upon which intelligent progress can be made. We hope to address this need by providing leadership educators with a single reference that not only shares current best practices, but does so within a broad conceptual framework that encourages greater theoretical rigor.

3. **Build a Respected Community of Practice.** With the demand for courses on leadership growing exponentially, the need to establish a respected community of dedicated scholars and practitioners is more important than ever. As a nascent field, leadership education is currently populated by a loosely coupled collection of wildly diverse, well-intentioned, but poorly organized gaggle of scholars and practitioners who are largely left to their own devices when it comes to deciding how best to teach leadership. From college classrooms to corporate universities to snake doctors, the field is littered with unsubstantiated yet flourishing responses to the seemingly endless demand to grow better leaders. Despite leadership being so central to the core mission of many schools, there is surprisingly little serious scholarship on how to teach it in any of these institutions. Indeed, research on leadership education falls at best on the periphery rather than at the center of most schools that profess to educate leaders as their animating purpose. Many of today's most popular leadership courses are delivered by external consultants, senior lecturers,

and adjunct faculty, all largely marginalized members of the academy who were either denied tenure or had broken ranks with their "more academic colleagues" in order to teach leadership. More still are being taught by former practitioners who attained iconic status as successful leaders and now want to share their wisdom, secure their legacies, or cash in on their success.

If we continue to allow leadership education to be framed, defined, and sustained by such an ad-hoc approach, we open ourselves to an entire range of potentially grave risks: Will students continue to take university mission statements seriously? How long before students recognize the yawning gap between espoused aspirations and reality in our classrooms? And perhaps most importantly, how long can society survive without growing a stronger field of emerging leaders?

Organizing Framework: Knowing, Doing, Being

As editors, we recognize that this volume will rarely be read straight through. If you are like us, many of you started with a brief scan of the table of contents and are now following up with a cursory look at the introduction and its organizing framework, before seeking out chapters penned by your favorite authors. As a result, before summarizing each chapter, we want to first offer a simple conceptual framework to help organize your "thinking about" teaching leadership.

Most learning experiences can be analyzed along the dimensions of content, process, and structure. Leadership education is no different. Here we present three models that not only help us frame our thinking about the field, but also inform the structure of our handbook.[5]

Content. All teaching involves planned change, and yet few leadership programs clearly articulate the intended *content* of change. When teaching leadership, the first question should be: *What* is changing (the substance)? Building on a framework found at the heart of the US Army's leadership development doctrine, we present a content model of change known as BE, KNOW, and DO (see Figure 0.1).[6] To be successful, there are certain things leaders must know (knowledge), certain things they must be able to do (skills), and certain ways they must be (character, identity, world view). We apply this content model of change to organize the first three major sections of our handbook.

Section I: Knowing, contains various approaches to teaching leadership that emphasize the cognitive domain. The unifying assumption here is that knowing *about* leadership helps prepare future leaders for

[5]For a detailed description of these models, see Snook (2008), *Leader(ship) Development.* Boston, MA: Harvard Business Press. Case no. 408–064.

[6]This model is adapted from the US Army's leadership doctrine as originally outlined in Department of the Army (1999), *FM 22-100, Army Leadership: BE, KNOW, DO.* For more detailed descriptions of how this model has been adapted to the business world, see *BE, KNOW, DO: Leadership the Army Way,* with an introduction by Frances Hesslebein and General Eric Shinseki (2004). See also Khurana and Snook (2004), "Developing Leaders of Character: Lessons From West Point." The central components of this model are rooted in the three traditional domains of psychology: cognitive (KNOW), behavioral (DO), and affective/attitudinal (BE). For a sophisticated treatment of domains of growth, see Mentkowski and Associates (2000), *Learning That Lasts.* In this book, Mentkowski distinguishes development as being "characterized by deep, enduring structures of the self: how the learner engages issues of personal integrity and purpose. It entails a view of the self in process and a focus on the ethical or spiritual dimensions of life. Many educators regard it as the most crucial goal of higher education" (Mentkowski & Associates, 2000, p. 187). In one of the earliest studies of leadership development programs, Conger (1992) uncovered four key approaches that also roughly map onto our content model: (1) personal growth (BE), (2) conceptual analysis (KNOW), (3) skill development (DO), and (4) feedback (all three).

Figure 0.1 Content Model of Change

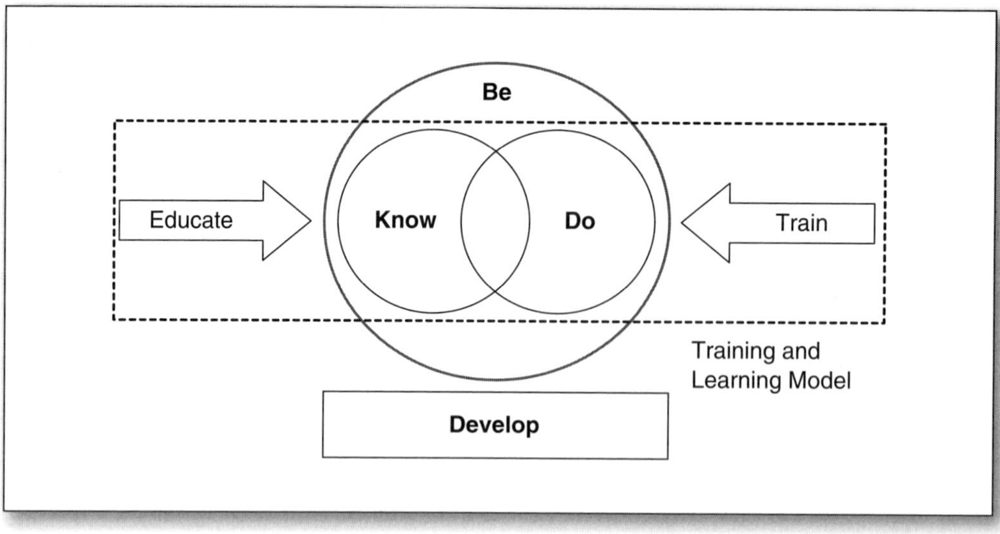

the effective practice of leading. Whether this knowledge comes from relevant social science concepts and theories or classic works of literature, the common theme here is to better understand leadership from a fundamentally analytical perspective. Section II: Doing, examines key behavioral aspects of leading. Critical skills, leader performance, and experiential learning lie at the heart of this section. While sections I and II focus on the acquisition of relevant knowledge and skills—producing leaders who are better *in*-formed and behaviorally competent—Section III: Being, contains essays that focus primarily on the identity of leaders, their character, their values, who they *are* as human *be*ings. Approaches here take on a decidedly clinical (v. analytical) and ontological (v. epistemological) flavor, with explicit goals to trans-form (v. in-form) students. Finally, Section IV: Context, expands our horizons beyond traditional university classroom settings to sample a few of the more innovative approaches in the field where unique contextual considerations play a significant role in the design and delivery of leadership education.

In theory, categorizing various approaches to leadership education by content domain helps us better frame our thinking about the art and science of teaching leadership. In practice, however, there is often considerable overlap across content domains. In fact, few of our authors are entirely comfortable with having their approach to this complex topic slotted into only one section of our book. However, the fundamental insight remains: As leadership educators, we must start with a clear sense of the type of change we hope to achieve in our students. Not surprisingly, learning how to Know, Do or Be requires a significantly different approach to educational design and delivery. After you've settled on the fundamental content of change, it is time to consider basic questions of process.

Process. How does it happen (the method)? Issues of process focus on fundamental mechanisms of change. For example, in the "Knowing" section you'll find approaches based on various cognitive processes: some emphasize conceptual understanding; others use cognitive modeling, framing, and critical thinking; and still others rely on participant-centered, case-based learning. In the "Doing" section you'll hear from teachers that employ acting, repetition, action-learning, and behavioral checklists to drive their unique approaches to teaching leadership. In Section III ("Being"), you'll learn about ontological processes that draw heavily from clinical and phenomenological traditions. Some of these processes include biofeedback, structured reflection, playfulness, transference, and the Socratic method. In the final section on "Context," each author relies on a range of powerful processes, largely determined by the unique developmental demands of their particular setting. Some of the more novel mechanisms include peer-to-peer learning, cross-disciplinary collaboration, social entrepreneurism, and cultural immersion.

While each chapter addresses key mechanisms for change, there is more to the process component than simply identifying central pedagogical methods. Based on a traditional engineering model of input, throughput and output (with feedback loops), we offer the following process model of change to emphasize what we've come to call the underappreciated "bookends of development" (see Figure 0.2).

In our experience, most leadership educators spend the bulk of their time in the middle, designing and executing the actual experience. Whether it's a class, a course, simulation, exercise, or an entire program, when teaching leadership, it's the planned *experience* (or event) that gets most of our attention. Based on years of research and assessment, we argue for paying greater attention to the oft-neglected bookends of *readiness* (How open and ready are students for the experience?) and *reflection* (What will they do with the experience? How will they apply what they have learned in the classroom to practice? How can we increase the likelihood that our intended changes will "stick"?).

With just a bit of thought, we've discovered a few novel ways to "extend the classroom" in both directions. For example, when advertising a course for Authentic Leadership Development (see Chapter 20) in our School's elective bulletin, we take great pains to craft the course description so as to dramatically increase the likelihood that we will get the kind of students who are "developmentally ready" for the type of deep introspection required in our course. For example, "Do NOT take this course if you are unwilling to share personal life experiences in a small group setting." Requiring students to write an "admissions essay"—*Why I want to take this course*—prior to enrollment is also a relatively simple but powerful way not only to weed out potentially "unready" students but also as a way to increase commitment and start the process of learning long before the first class meets. Similarly, with just a bit of effort and imagination, we can extend the learning on the backend as well. Many leadership educators integrate reflective essays into their curriculum as a means of deepening and extending the experience beyond the classroom. Others rely on innovations in the structural component of course design to help them address the underappreciated bookends of development.

Figure 0.2 Process Model of Change

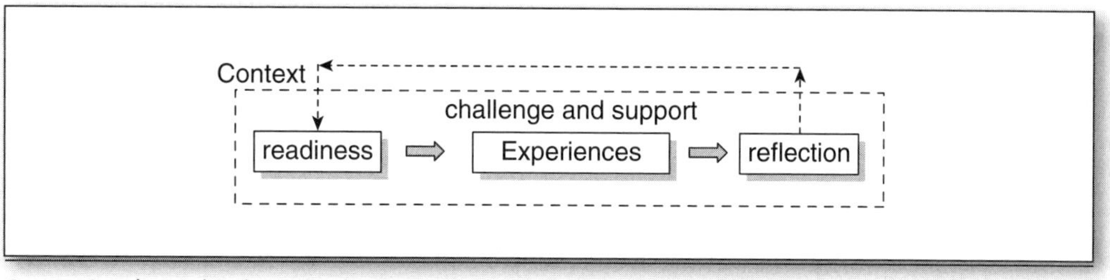

Source: Snook, *Leader(ship) Development,* case no.9-408-064. Copyright ©2008 by the President and Fellows of Harvard College. Reprinted by permission of Harvard Business School Publishing.

Structure. Under what conditions does change take place? (Where? When? How often? By whom? For whom? With whom? In what order?) Explicitly examining issues of sequence, setting, organization, culture, purpose, history, physical surroundings, and demographics completes our introductory framing of how to think about teaching leadership. While we've asked each of our contributors to "set the stage" by describing relevant structural dimensions in each of their chapters, we'll briefly outline what we mean by the structural component of leadership education here not only to help you better understand the following essays but also to help you think more deeply about your own design decisions. Finally, because of its practical and theoretical importance, we selected one particularly important dimension of structure—*context*—as the organizing concept for the final section of our book.

Most educators typically find fundamental notions of "content and process" to be fairly intuitive. For some reason, however, many teachers find the idea of "structure" a bit more problematic. Perhaps one source of this confusion springs from the relatively few "degrees of structural freedom" many of us experience in a traditional university setting. For some, most issues of structure feel like "givens," or school policies dictated to us by the curriculum czar: There is a standard class length. You will teach in a traditional classroom setting. A "course" has to consist of so many class meetings per semester, so many contact hours per credit hour, so many students per class, etc. The age and demographic mix (readiness) of our students is largely a given as well, as is the history and physical and cultural surrounding of the broader educational setting.

While a few of these structural constraints may indeed represent actual limits, it's been our experience that many of these restrictions are self-imposed. Once again, with a bit of imagination and initiative, we have learned that much greater freedom and flexibility exists in the structural component than we had originally thought. As we survey the field, we are heartened to learn that we are not alone in this regard. Many leadership educators have found innovative workarounds, adaptations, and down-right frame-breaking ways to better align structure with content and process in ways that dramatically improve their impact on future leaders. We are confident that you can do the same.

To illustrate how this can happen, we will highlight a personal example close to home, a second-year elective course we offer MBA students at the Harvard Business School (HBS): Authentic Leadership Development (ALD). Based on his experience as a successful business leader and extensive interviews with top leaders, a colleague of ours named Bill George developed a novel approach to leadership summarized in the following assertion: "When you follow your internal compass, your leadership will be authentic, and people will naturally want to associate with you. Although others may guide or influence you, your truth is derived from your life story, and only you can determine what it should be" (George & Sims, 2007, p. xxiii).

While you'll learn much more about this course in Chapter 20, we just want to highlight a few of the most important structural components of its design here, many of which required significant departures from the standard HBS class design and school policy. First, to accommodate the high levels of personal interaction required by his theory, class size was reduced below its most economical limit of 90. Next, student sections are further divided into six-person leadership development groups (LDGs) that meet once a week in small group seminars to share personal experiences. (HBS has limited space to meet in small groups; classrooms are designed to support a standard section size of 90.) LDGs are student-facilitated and meet with no teachers present. (Half of the entire course is spent in LDGs, without a faculty member present. You can imagine the concerns this structural issue raised!) Each LDG meeting is followed by mandatory reflective essays uploaded and read by ALD faculty. (This innovation helps keep faculty in the developmental loop without violating the trust and intimacy required for work in LDGs.) Because of the highly personal nature of class discussions, no visitors are allowed and students draft and sign their own contracts of confidentiality. Our point here is not to tout ALD, although most students report it to be one of the most transformational experiences during their time at HBS. Our point here is to highlight the potential, and often untapped, power of the structural component of design.

Book Structure

Based on our collective experience researching and teaching leadership, we have organized a tour of the topic that we hope you will find both practical and intellectually honest. Consistent with our assessment of the nascent and somewhat inchoate state of leadership education as a field, we decided to organize the *Handbook* not around the familiar hierarchy of research, theory, and practice (we're just not there yet), but rather around our content model of change. Section I contains eight chapters whose approach to teaching leadership emphasizes *Knowing* (cognition). Section II contains an additional seven chapters, all with an experiential focus on *Doing* (behavior). All of Section III's authors teach leadership by targeting *Being* (identity). While most contributions in the first three sections are written by educators who teach college students primarily in traditional classroom settings, in our final section we intentionally sample from a broad range of target audiences who teach in nontraditional educational contexts.

While we've attempted to impose some structure on the field by slicing it by primary domains of change, clearly these conceptual categories are artificial and no approach to teaching focuses solely on a single domain. No doubt many of our contributors would argue strongly with the label we've inflicted on their work. However, we hope that you'll find this structure useful, if for no other reason than to sharpen your own thinking: What type of change am I targeting when I teach leadership?

As you'll see, each chapter is unique, each author's voice distinct. Since leadership education "as a field" is quite young, we were particularly sensitive not to overreach and impose more structure or imply more answers than currently exist. However, we did ask each of our contributors to address the following three questions:

1. ***Description***: *What is the essence of your particular approach to teaching leadership?* Each chapter contains a thick description of the experience, emphasizing distinctive aspects that make their approach particularly unique or powerful. To help readers appreciate issues of generalizability, each chapter also addresses relevant structural issues such as context, history, and audience as our authors describe their individual methods (design and delivery) of teaching leadership.

2. ***Theory***: *What are the conceptual, theoretical, and disciplinary roots upon which you base your approach to teaching leadership?* What are your basic assumptions about leadership, teaching, and change that support such an approach? All of us have at least implied theories behind our attempts at teaching leadership. This question was designed to encourage our contributors to be more explicit about the conceptual underpinnings of their particular approaches.

3. ***Assessment***: *What are the inherent strengths and weaknesses of your approach?* Each author is asked to share any evidence they might have for evaluating the effectiveness of their particular approach to teaching leadership. What are the specific goals of your course or program? How do you know if you have achieved them? We recognize outcomes assessment as a current weakness in the field and challenged our

authors to share whatever progress they've made in addressing this difficult issue.

Section I. Teaching Leadership: Approaches That Emphasize Knowing

Contributors to Section I primarily emphasize the more classical and cognitive domain of knowing. Each chapter in this section defines and delimits the body of knowledge, frameworks, and concepts that are argued to be essential to an effective leader's cognitive toolkit. While these chapters are interdisciplinary in character and far from exhaustive, they do establish the fundamental behavioral and social scientific character of the knowledge that leaders should understand.

Ancona argues that a core cognitive skill of effective leadership is the ability to analyze the context within which leaders operate. Based on the "4 Capabilities Leadership Framework" that underpins MIT's MBA and executive education leadership training, Ancona elaborates on the social psychological process of "sensemaking" and how it can be taught in the classroom. Sensemaking takes place specifically through the construction and explicit outlining of individual mental maps (or narratives) of the external context, even though that map has to change when the world changes. Based on work with Sloan Executive Program participants, Ancona's research suggests that sensemaking has had the greatest impact on how participants change their own leadership behavior going forward.

Mumford, Peterson, Robledo, and Hester examine the impact of one of the most widely used methods in business education—case studies—and consider the impact of such discussion-based approaches on leadership training. The authors argue first that case-based instruction is attractive, in part, because case-based knowledge provides the basis for leader cognition. Subsequently, this chapter reviews available evidence on case-based knowledge and, based on that review, describes some key considerations to be taken into account when cases are used for teaching leadership. Finally, our authors discuss the implications of these observations for improving leadership development and leadership education programs.

Kellerman's contribution outlines a "new, old approach" to teaching leadership that is grounded in the liberal arts tradition, and that derives its content from the great leadership literature. Kellerman describes a course she developed at Harvard's Kennedy School (and has since also taught to undergraduates at Dartmouth) called Leadership Literacy. It is designed to provide all students a fundamental familiarity with the seminal texts on power, authority, and influence that constitute the classics of the leadership literature. This chapter contributes to the debate about what it is that leaders need to know by arguing that there is in fact a leadership canon, that this body of work lends a necessary heft and depth to the field of Leadership Studies, and that for this reason alone it can and should constitute a core curriculum for all serious students of leadership.

Next, Alvarez addresses the question of how academics, who are not primarily oriented to action, can teach future leaders about the exercise of power, which he defines as "leadership's means of production." Alvarez summarizes what political scientists have learned about power and then argues for the case method, which goes beyond mere analysis but stops short of purely experiential methodologies, as the best way to develop the "imagination for action" necessary for political actors. After recommending specific practices for teaching the exercise of power and influence, the author addresses the ethical implications of the subject, a topic that the present economic crisis—one grounded in the character of elites as well as in finance—has brought once again to the forefront.

How do you influence individuals, groups, and organizations whose cultural, political, and institutional backgrounds are different from the leader's? This is the challenge of "global leadership," an increasingly common and important contextual dimension for leaders today. Based on years of research on cross-cultural and global leadership, Javidan argues that the answer to the global leadership challenge is to develop something he calls "Global Mindset." There are three critical dimensions to this mindset: individual, psychological, and social capital. Javidan proposes a curriculum consisting of a multilayered sequence of learning experiences that are designed to increase one's global mindset and hence increase the likelihood of being a successful Global Leader.

Starkey and Hall challenge the "economic narrative" of management and leadership education that dominates business schools. Their essay first examines the economic model and why it has grown to become so powerful, despite faulty and one-sided assumptions about individuals, business, and society, and the narrow view of leadership it generates. In its place, they propose a more complex "social narrative" of leadership based upon richer, more inclusive understandings of the self, business, and society, one that promotes reflection on the nature of identity, humanity, and community. Envisioning management as a complicated balancing act and project of identity construction, Starkey and Hall explicitly promote in their teaching the development of a learning community and a capacity for self-reflection that challenges the individualism that often accompanies power and wealth. Emphasizing dialogue, relationships, and intercultural awareness rather than a narrow focus on markets and the bottom line, their model is rooted in values such as compassion and empathy rather than the dominant discourse of rationality.

The contribution from DeLong and Hill explores in close detail the Leadership and Organizational Behavior Course (LEAD) at the Harvard Business School. LEAD addresses several fundamental aspects of managing and leading people, including ways of understanding and influencing group behavior and performance; how to work with and manage people on a one-on-one basis; and strategies for leading, motivating, and aligning people behind a common vision or direction. In addition, LEAD confronts some of the basic choices and strategic questions involved in learning to lead and in managing one's career. Finally, LEAD attempts to help students make the transition from individual contributor to manager/leader and to build a career over time that leverages their unique individual capabilities. This course operates on the assumption that the industry, country, or specific function or size of an organization matters much less than how students make a difference within any given organizational context.

Finally, Useem's chapter argues that one effective way to overcome the gap between leadership knowledge and leadership action is to develop and instill a "leadership template." A leadership template is a device for suggesting and then triggering action for those in leadership positions by setting forth a set of essential principles that are generic enough to apply to a variety of circumstances, but specific enough to provide tangible guidance. Useem goes on to describe the key qualities of such a leadership template (it should be simple, customized, aware of its limitations, and derived from the practice and experience of leaders); suggests ways to develop one; and identifies methods for ensuring that it effectively informs managerial actions. He also explores various means of instilling a leadership template, including the self-directed study of other leaders, mentoring and coaching, stretch assignments, learning from setbacks and crises, and knowledge drawn from after-action reviews.

In total, we believe these chapters as a section assemble, codify, and thereby advance knowledge about one of the most critical arenas of leadership education—what leaders ought to Know.

Section II. Teaching Leadership: Approaches That Emphasize Doing

Contributors to Section II emphasize the behavioral aspects of leading by focusing primarily on experiential approaches to development.

The work of Halpern and Richards attempts to answer two questions: What specific elements of actors' training are useful in teaching leadership? How can the context of the theater create an environment where transformative learning can occur and extend beyond the classroom? Halpern and Richards concentrate on the development of "leadership presence," the ability to forge meaningful connections with others in order to motivate and inspire them toward a desired outcome. The chapter discusses the PRES—Presence, Reaching out, Expressiveness, and Self-knowledge—model of leadership presence that the authors have developed for use in theater-based leadership seminars. They argue that experiential learning through theater develops this leadership presence by helping individuals, through participation in the types of introspective and interactive exercises used by actors to prepare for their roles, better to understand themselves and improve their ability to connect with others.

Next, Goffee and Jones apply a sociological approach to leadership and describe a method of teaching that is organized around three conceptual axioms: Leadership is situational, relational, and non-hierarchical. The first axiom accounts for the difficulties in establishing universals for good leadership, while the second reminds us that leaders have followers and that the management of social distance is a vital skill for leaders. The third warns against assuming that those in senior positions within organizations will inevitably act as leaders; rather, it is distinctive personal attributes that define leadership more than attributes of position. In sum, Goffee and Jones urge executives to "Be yourself—more—with skill," thus reminding us that leadership is about knowing and selectively showing one's true self, combined with the skillful application of individual strengths to particular situations.

Meikle's chapter describes the Elkiem High Performance Masterclass, which applies the results of research into some of the world's highest performing organizations—the Julliard School of Music, elite academic institutions, and Military Special Forces units. In keeping with the active nature of high-performance leadership, Meikle insists that those who participate take action, stimulate and maintain momentum, and demand high standards of execution. Based on the linked assumptions that people change when their circumstances change, that certain changes in circumstances will stimulate improved performance, and that leadership involves creating those changes in circumstances, the Masterclass focuses on teaching leaders how to create circumstances that generate higher performance from those they lead.

The contribution from Anderson and Kole examines Leadership Effectiveness and Development (LEAD), the only required course in the MBA program at the University of Chicago's Booth School of Business. The authors describe the research foundation for the course, examine the specific content that combines the *knowing* and *doing* aspects of leadership education, and provide representative experiences from selected course participants. This chapter shows how the course, which inculcates self-awareness and teaches students how to extract the "right" lessons from experience, combines classroom instruction, experiential learning, and one-on-one coaching. The goal of LEAD is to enable students to develop an accurate view of both their strengths and areas in need of development, and to learn how to gain usable insights from experience in an objective and replicable way.

Mintzberg's chapter describes a family of programs that aim to transform the development of managers. These programs are based on an understanding of organizations as "communities of human beings" rather than "collections of human resources," and employ a vision of management as engagement rather than heroic leadership. One such program links management education to management development by encouraging practicing managers to reflect on their own experience and share that reflection with others. Another program is designed to promote organizational development by allowing teams of managers from different companies to engage in "friendly consulting" with one another. Still another program targets leaders in health care and encourages social development by encouraging participants to bring major issues of community concern into the classroom for discussion. A final program fosters self-development by bringing together small groups of managers, without faculty or facilitators, to explore the development of themselves and their organizations. Together, Mintzberg contends, these programs point to an entirely new direction in management and organizational development.

Csoka's chapter shifts our focus to performance. He does this by drawing from the burgeoning fields of sports psychology and new brain science to create a unique approach to leadership education that focuses on developing leaders who can operate at their very best, when it matters the most. In today's world, this often means leaders who can think effectively and act with confidence and precision under conditions of extreme stress and uncertainty. Csoka identifies a suite of skills that are essential for developing greater self-control under extreme conditions. Using advanced biological and neurofeedback technologies, leaders learn to master control over key mental and physiological responses that often inhibit performance in several areas critical to leadership effectiveness. These areas include goal setting, adaptive thinking, stress and energy management, attention control, and mental imagery. With time and practice, these skills become an essential part of who we are as leaders.

Finally, LeBoeuf, Emery, Siang, and Sitkin describe an approach used by Duke University's Fuqua School of Business to build a holistic leadership development process. This program is built around three key design principles: a leadership model with a 360-degree feedback process, an "end-to-end" perspective rooted in personal and leadership development experiences, and an emphasis on the integration of all student activities. This structural design helps Fuqua to fulfill the important role that business schools play in preparing their MBA students to become not just competent business managers but also responsible leaders, by leveraging students' educational experience to form in them a specific leadership identity characterized as "a leader of consequence."

Section III. Teaching Leadership: Approaches That Emphasize Being

This section contains seven approaches to teaching leadership that focus primarily on students' identity (who they are, their character, their values). At some base level, the content of leadership education can be distilled down into two words: competence and character.[7] Chapters in Sections I and

[7]This notion of "competence and character" is taken from a speech delivered by General Norman Schwarzkopf to the United States Corp of Cadets at West Point on the May 15, 1991. After successfully commanding coalition forces in Operation Desert Storm, Schwarzkopf visited his alma mater to share his thoughts about what it would take to lead in the twenty-first century. Distilling more than thirty-five years of personal leadership experience, the general summarized the essence of leadership in two words: competence and character. No one follows a leader for long if they don't know what they are doing, if they are not tactically and technically competent. Equally important, however, is character. "Give me someone who has that piece right and I can teach them to do anything."

II focus largely on competence, how to help students acquire the relevant knowledge and skills of leadership. Authors in this section target a much deeper, and in many ways more mysterious, component of leadership education: character and identity.

Most experienced teachers are fairly comfortable teaching *about* leadership. After all, in most university settings, the successful acquisition of technical knowledge and skills is the central goal of education. Even more importantly, perhaps, we know *how* to do this. We know how to inform; we know how to "transfer knowledge"; we know how to train skills. Most of us have spent much of our adult lives either learning or teaching important conceptual knowledge and technical skills. In fact this process forms the very heart of most educational experiences in traditional classroom settings. However, what is the equivalent of teaching knowledge and training skills in the BE domain of leadership education? How does one create a learning experience that targets students' identity, shapes their values, or uncovers their passions? How does one teach leadership in a way that not only *informs* them *about leadership* but also *transforms* them into actually *being leaders*? In this section, several authors share courageous and often unconventional approaches to teaching that target the very essence of who we are, the BE component of leadership education.

Erhard, Jensen, and Granger anchor this collection by taking dead aim at the BE component. In a highly provocative chapter titled "Creating Leaders," this eclectic group of scholars argues for adopting a decidedly ontological approach to leadership education that promises to leave students actually *being* leaders. Contrasting their ontological approach—described as being and action as experienced "on the court"—with more traditional perspectives where leadership is observed and commented on "from the stands," this chapter presents a rigorous theory of leadership education that begins and ends with the following bold promises to students:

- You will leave this course being who you need to be to be a leader.
- You will leave this course with what it takes to exercise leadership effectively.

For these authors, integrity, authenticity, and being committed to something bigger than oneself form the base of "the context for leadership," a context that once mastered, leaves one actually being a leader. It is not enough to know about or simply understand these foundational factors, but rather by following a rigorous, phenomenologically based methodology, students have the opportunity to create for themselves a context that leaves them actually being a leader and exercising leadership effectively as their natural self-expression.

Kets de Vries and Korotov add a clinical voice to the conversation. Drawing from their extensive experience creating transformational leader development programs, these authors describe how to create powerful "transitional spaces" where self-learning, reflection, and playfulness rule the day. Consistent with a clinical approach, participants are challenged to confront their illusions of rationality by exploring their pasts and examining the potentially powerful roles that emotions, transference, countertransference, and motivational need systems play in everyday human functioning. There are no quick fixes or instant solutions to this type of leader development. Creating long-term sustainable change is all about process, and experiencing such deep process takes time. At its core, such a clinical approach involves the "ability to use oneself as an instrument, the capacity to reflect and (when necessary) to go deep into oneself and explore the effect of our inner world on our behavior and that of others."

Originally trained as a social anthropologist, O'Toole invites us to join him on a personal journey: how he discovered (and still teaches) what he eventually came to know as "values-based leadership"—a fusion of practicality and morality. Approaches that emphasize being inevitably bump into fundamental questions of values and character. O'Toole addresses these thorny issues head-on by adopting the role of "Platonic mid-wife." Employing the Socratic method, he attempts to "educe" from students their own personal, implicit theories of leadership; to surface and then rigorously test what they already know about the topic by studying historical leaders such as Gandhi, Lincoln, and Mandela, as well as more contemporary leaders found in the business world. All the while, O'Toole continually encourages his students to assess the moral and ethical components of whatever approach they might choose. In the end, what ultimately sets values-based leaders apart from all the others is that they "create followers by enabling them to see clearly—and to achieve effectively—that which *they* hold dear."

Petriglieri argues that much of what goes on under the banner of "leadership development" today is limited to the acquisition of abstract knowledge and behavioral competencies. And yet, "requests for support in crafting identities seldom lie far below the surface of organizations' or individuals' interest in leadership programs." Unfortunately, the growing psychological distance between work organizations and their employees has resulted in managers turning to business schools in general, and leadership programs in particular, to fulfill the role of identity workspaces. Petriglieri explains how leadership courses in today's business schools function as holding environments for identity work—workspaces that facilitate the process of consolidating existing identities and crafting new ones: "What does leading mean? Who am I as a leader?" He goes on to describe a set of unique learning processes and design principles that enable such programs to successfully fulfill this function.

In the next chapter of this section, George describes a novel identity-based approach he calls "Authentic Leadership Development." His theory is based on the fundamental premise that "leaders are most effective when they follow their True North—their beliefs, values, and principles." The central challenge then is to help students discover their True North. To do this, George has designed a multilayered, highly personal experience that consists of course readings, personal exercises, facilitated case discussions, and intimate small-group work. The entire process is highly introspective and designed to increase students' clarity about who they are, their core values, motivated capabilities, and ultimately their leadership purpose. A successful business leader himself, George illustrates what it takes to teach this course by sharing intimate details of his own developmental journey throughout the chapter.

The chapter by Moldoveanu introduces an approach to leadership development based on "self-understanding and self-transformation." This approach employs sophisticated models of a person's modes of being as tools that the trainee uses to understand his or her own behaviors and to effect purposive and lasting changes in these behaviors. Moldoveanu takes the reader through several detailed case studies of transformation-oriented interventions that were guided by precise and detailed models of the behavioral pattern that a trainee was attempting to modify. The essay then emphasizes the relevance of this approach for the broader field of leadership development.

Finally, the chapter by Ganz and Lin argues for a pedagogy of practice that aligns the content of what is taught with the method of instruction. This pedagogy teaches leadership by practicing leadership. The essay describes the principles of this approach, shares a curricular framework, and provides examples drawn from a variety of contexts. Predicated on a definition of leadership that emphasizes the role of the leader in enabling others to achieve shared purpose under conditions of uncertainty, this method requires students to take leadership of a project that is rooted in their values, designed to achieve a specific goal, and requires that they secure the support and commitment of others. An additional benefit of this pedagogical approach, they argue, is that it develops new leadership capacity through cascaded learning; just as leadership creates not followers but new leaders, this approach creates new teaching capacity among its students.

Taken together, these chapters suggest that leadership education involves more than teaching knowledge and skills. While important, teaching *about* leadership and *how* to lead simply isn't enough. To be effective, we must also think deeply about issues of identity and character. What does it mean to actually *be* a leader? Followers respond not only to leaders' technical competence (what they know and can do) but also to who they are. As a result, creative approaches that emphasize being, such as those offered in this section, should be considered an essential component to any holistic approach to educating leaders.

Section IV. Teaching Leadership: Approaches That Emphasize Context

Contributors to Section IV are distinguished by their sensitivity to unique contextual aspects of their participants (post-post graduates, junior officers in the Army, transitioning executives, and inner-city youth). Most chapters in Sections I–III address content and process issues within traditional classroom settings. The context is typically MBA or executive education students in a formal classroom. Here, we intentionally relax this structural constraint and cast our net widely to sample innovative approaches to teaching leadership in different contexts. In some of these approaches what changes in the context is the nature of the participants (more youthful and more experienced, in business and in other fields) and how they are engaged. In other approaches, what is different is not just the students, but the context itself; the focus is on leadership development in situ—in organizations and in the field. In yet other cases, the question is how might leadership development be different depending on the country or broader societal culture in which it is embedded. As a result, we learned a great deal from this distinguished list of leadership entrepreneurs and we hope that you will as well.

Ringleb and Rock introduce this section by asking us to consider the provocative question, How would you design a leadership development intervention if you could actually measure emotion? Operating at the intersection of neuroscience and social psychology, Ringleb and Rock describe an exciting new learning environment at CIMBA, an international MBA program located in Italy and headed by the University of Iowa. Applying recent developments in brain-imaging technology, students at CIMBA receive real-time feedback on critical neurophysiological responses that allow them to gain powerful and personalized insights into the relationship between cognition and emotion as it relates to the learning and practice of leading. Dramatic advances in neuroscience are impacting virtually every major discipline in the academic world. Teaching leadership shouldn't be the last to tap into this exciting potential.

In the next chapter, Burgess breaks the frame of a traditional classroom by asking, How would you teach leadership if your "students" were several thousand geographically- dispersed US Army company commanders whose best "teachers" might actually be each other? He then shares the story of how he and a small band of dedicated junior officers, on their own, purchased a URL and developed one of the most innovative and far-reaching approaches to teaching leadership the Army has seen in years. Their name is CompanyCommand .com; their innovation is peer-to-peer leadership development. There are many lessons in this chapter. Perhaps the most powerful one is that leadership can be taught outside the formal organizational structure, through a grass-roots learning network, by peers sharing their experience in vibrant professional forums. What shape might this insight take in your organization?

From the brain, to the battlefield, to the inner city, dramatic shifts in context demand equally dramatic innovations in how to teach leadership. In his chapter, Klau presents the comprehensive leadership development model employed by City Year, a national service organization that engages young adults of all backgrounds, ages 17–24, in a demanding year of full-time citizen service. Titled The Flame of Idealism, this program is designed to unleash the full potential of a challenging long-term service experience by transforming idealistic young adults into effective, engaged, and inspiring civic leaders. Inspired by a fundamental belief in the transformational power of idealism—a belief that you can change the world—City Year not only recognizes the interconnected nature of social change (the outer world) and individual transformation (the inner world) but uses this powerful interaction to grow young leaders.

Dickson, Lelchook, Sully de Luque, and Hanges tackle the thorny issue of teaching leadership across cultures. After presenting a summary of Project GLOBE—the largest study of leadership across cultures to date—these authors go on to unpack what they see as "the big question" in this domain: Is there a relationship between specific cultural values and preferred styles of leading? When looking across cultures, what approaches to leadership appear to be universal and which are culturally contingent? They end by offering a number of suggestions for how we might all use GLOBE data to facilitate the teaching of leadership across cultures.

Chatterjee, Friedman, and Yardley take us to the heart of Wall Street by describing the origins and development of the Leadership Acceleration Initiative (LAI) at Goldman Sachs. They also provide an assessment of its strengths and weaknesses. The LAI emerged in response to the need to develop leaders for strategically important roles within the firm and to do so in a way tailored to the unique demands of its audience of managing directors in a fast-changing industry with little time to spare. Since its origin in 1999, the flexible structure of LAI has enabled Goldman Sachs to meet the firms' leadership needs by serving as a means for leaders to connect with one another, contribute to the firm's objectives, and develop both their commercial instincts as well as their leadership impact.

The next chapter focuses on one particularly knotty contextual variable: interdependence. In fact, Palus, McGuire, and Ernst begin by boldly calling for a *declaration of interdependence*, arguing that all of the most important challenges leaders face today—climate, war, disease, prosperity, justice—are by their very nature interdependent: "They can only be solved by groups of people working collaboratively across boundaries." Based on years of research and teaching at the Center for Creative Leadership, these authors offer four "practical arts" for teaching the kind of interdependent leadership required to succeed in today's highly connected world. Behind these four arts is a novel conceptualization of leading, one that moves us through dependence and independence to interdependence by embracing three essential leadership outcomes: shared direction, alignment, and commitment.

Staying on point, McGaw calls for us to "pay far greater attention to the interdependency of business success and social progress." Leading at this powerful intersection is an emerging community of social intrapreneurs—high-potential business leaders who are helping their companies grow in ways that both produce financial results *and* contribute to our collective well-being. McGaw describes a recent Aspen Institute initiative called the First Movers Fellowship Program, which was designed specifically to strengthen the capacity of these unique leaders to innovate and lead change in their companies and communities.

We end on a positive note. In many ways, our final chapter brings us full-cycle. We began this journey by sampling from a broad array of approaches to teaching leadership across multiple content domains. The context for most of them was a standard classroom, in a traditional university setting. Our final section takes us off-campus to explore contexts and challenges as far ranging as the brain, battlefields, inner-city youth, globalization, interdependence, and social intrapreneurs. Finally, we return home, back to where we started. In a provocative essay titled "Re-Developing Leaders," Kanter reminds us that a university's promise to support "life-long learning" need not be a hollow one, particularly when it comes to leading. We know what undergraduate schools look like; we also know what graduate and professional programs do. However, with increasing life expectancies in the developed world now stretching our productive years far beyond what our schools' founding fathers ever imagined, perhaps it is time to imagine what a university might offer to already-accomplished leaders. What would a "third-stage school" look like? How would you design a leadership re-development program for experienced leaders who wish to tackle societal and global problems in the next phase of their lives?

These were the animating questions that led a small group of faculty at Harvard to launch a university-wide experiment called "The Advanced Leadership Initiative." Drawing from her extensive background in leading change, Kanter shares a story of what it was like to create a life-stage-appropriate leadership development program within and across a university setting not known for its interdisciplinary, cross-sector collaboration and ownership. Not surprisingly, it's a story within a story—not only about how to help late-stage leaders remain relevant and lead change, but also how to help late-stage universities do the same.

Teaching Leadership—Seriously

While leadership is an easily recognized phenomenon, it is still neither an easily recognized field of inquiry nor an enterprise characterized by well-accepted or well-understood approaches for teaching and development. What is unique about the situation today is that for the first time ever, mainstream academic institutions have begun to recognize the importance of leadership as a legitimate field of scholarly inquiry and teaching. In particular, those graduate schools that purport to educate and train leaders are at an inflection point with respect to taking seriously the teaching of leadership. With this volume, we attempt to define the general contours of this nascent field by sharing the wisdom of some of our more experienced colleagues and by placing their work within an admittedly broad conceptual architecture designed to help others make better sense of what we've all been up to. While we recognize that leadership as a serious subject of scholarly research and as a subject that can be effectively taught to our students has a significant way to go, we hope that by consolidating years of hard-won experience in this handbook we can now at least imagine a future in which the gap between the espoused mission of many of our educational institutions and what is actually done in them can be narrowed. We are hopeful this volume might be one small step in that journey.

References

Associates, Department of Behavioral Sciences & Leadership, United States Military Academy (1985). *Leadership in organizations.* Garden City Park, NY: Avery Publishing Group.

Avolio, B. J. (2005). *Leadership development in balance.* Mahwah, NJ: Erlbaum Associates.

Bass, B. M., & Stogdill, R. M. (1974). *Handbook of leadership*. New York: The Free Press.

Bennis, W. (1989). *On becoming a leader*. New York: Perseus Books.

Bennis, W., & O'Toole, J. (2005). How business schools lost their way. *Harvard Business Review,83*(5), 96–104.

Burns, J. M. (1978). *Leadership*. New York: Harper & Row.

Conger, J. (1992). *Learning to lead*. San Francisco, CA: Jossey-Bass.

Covey, S. R. (1990). *Principle-centered leadership*. New York: Fireside.

Department of the Army. (1999). *FM 22-100, Army leadership: BE, KNOW, DO*. Washington, DC: US Government Printing Office.

Doh, J. P. (2003). Can leadership be taught? Perspectives from management educators. *Academy of Management Learning and Education, 2*(1), 54–67.

Gardner, J. (1993). *On leadership*. New York: The Free Press.

George, B., & Sims, P. (2007). *True north*. San Francisco, CA: Jossey-Bass.

Ghoshal, S. (2005). Bad management theories are destroying good management practice. *Academy of Management Learning & Education, 4*(1), 75–91.

Giber, D., Carter, L., & Goldsmith, M. (2000). *Linkage Inc.'s best practices in leadership development handbook*. San Francisco, CA: Jossey-Bass/Pfeiffter & Linkage Inc.

Goldsmith, M. (2006). *Global leadership: The next generation*. Upper Saddle River, NJ: Prentice Hall.

Hesslebein, F., & Shinseki, E. (2004). Introduction. In *BE, KNOW, DO: Leadership the army way*. San Francisco, CA: Jossey-Bass.

Khurana, R., & Snook, S. (2004). Developing leaders of character: Lessons from West Point. In R. Gandossy & J. Sonnenfeld (Eds.), *Leadership and governance from the inside out* (pp. 213–232). Hoboken, NJ: John Wiley & Sons.

Kotter, J. (2008). *A sense of urgency*. Boston, MA: Harvard Business Press.

Kouzes, J. M., & Posner, B.Z. (2007). *The leadership challenge* (4th ed.). San Francisco, CA: Jossey-Bass.

McCall, M. W. (1998). *High fliers*. Boston, MA: Harvard Business School Press.

Mentkowski, M., & Associates. (2000). *Learning that lasts*. San Francisco, CA: Jossey-Bass.

Mintzberg, H. (2004). *Managers not MBAs: A hard look at the soft practice of managing and management development*. San Francisco, CA: Berrett-Koehler.

Nohria, N., & Khurana, R. (Eds.). (2010). *Handbook of leadership theory and practice: An HBS centennial colloquium on advancing leadership*. Boston, MA: Harvard Business School Publishing.

Northouse, P. G. (2010). *Leadership: Theory and practice* (5th ed.). Thousand Oaks, CA: Sage Publications.

Paulus, C. J., & Drath, W. H. (1995). *Evolving leaders*. Greensboro, NC: Center for Creative Leadership.

Pfeffer, J., & Fong, C. T. (2002). The end of business schools? Less success than meets the eye. *Academy of Management Learning & Education, 1*(1), 78–95.

Quinn, R. E. (1996). *Deep change: Discovering the leader within*. San Francisco, CA: Jossey-Bass.

Rost, J. C. (1991). *Leadership for the 21st century*. New York: Praeger.

Schwartz, M. K., Axtman, K. M., & Freeman, F. H. (1998). *Leadership education: A source book of courses and programs* (7th ed.). Greensville, NC: Center for Creative Leadership.

Schwartz, M. K., & Gimbel, K. J. (2000). *Leadership resources: A guide to training and development tools*. Greensboro, NC: Center for Creative Leadership.

Snook, S. A. (2008). *Leader(ship) development (9-408-604)*. Boston, MA: Harvard Business School Publishing.

Van Velsor, E., McCauley, C. D., & Ruderman, M. N. (2010). *The Center for Creative Leadership handbook of leadership development* (3nd ed.). San Francisco, CA: Jossey-Bass.

Yukyl, G. (2010). *Leadership in organizations* (7th ed.). Englewood Cliffs, NJ: Prentice Hall.

SECTION I

KNOWING

1

SENSEMAKING

Framing and Acting in the Unknown

◆ Deborah Ancona
MIT-Sloan School of Management

This chapter introduces "sensemaking" as a key leadership capability for the complex and dynamic world we live in today. Sensemaking, a term introduced by Karl Weick, refers to how we structure the unknown so as to be able to act in it. Sensemaking involves coming up with a plausible understanding—a map—of a shifting world; testing this map with others through data collection, action, and conversation; and then refining, or abandoning, the map depending on how credible it is.

Sensemaking enables leaders to have a better grasp of what is going on in their environments, thus facilitating other leadership activities such as visioning, relating, and inventing. This chapter outlines ten steps to effective sensemaking, grouped under enabling leaders to *explore the wider system*, *create a map of that system*, and *act in the system* to learn from it. It illustrates how rigidity, leader dependence, and erratic behavior get in the way of effective sensemaking, and how one might teach sensemaking as a core leadership capability. The chapter ends with a student manual on sensemaking from an MBA leadership class.

❖ ❖ ❖

At the MIT Sloan School of Management we teach the "4-CAP" model of leadership capabilities. The four capabilities include sensemaking, relating, visioning, and inventing (Ancona, Malone, Orlikowski, & Senge, 2007).

While participants in our leadership workshops and classes are reasonably comfortable with the idea that *relating* is about building trusting relationships among people and across networks, *visioning* involves painting a compelling picture of the future and what is possible, and *inventing* means creating the structures and processes needed to move toward the vision, most scratch their heads at the term *sensemaking*. And yet our 360-degree survey data reveal that sensemaking is highly correlated with leadership effectiveness—even more than visioning. In addition, when people finish our programs—and even five years later—they report that sensemaking was one of the most valuable concepts and skills they have learned. "Sensemaking" lingers in organizational vocabulary long after our courses are over.

So what is "sensemaking," and why is it so central to effective leadership?

What Is Sensemaking?

Karl Weick, the "father of sensemaking," suggests that the term means simply "the making of sense" (Weick, 1995, p. 4). It is the process of "structuring the unknown" (Waterman, 1990, p. 41) by "placing stimuli into some kind of framework" that enables us "to comprehend, understand, explain, attribute, extrapolate, and predict" (Starbuck & Milliken, 1988, p. 51). Sensemaking is the activity that enables us to turn the ongoing complexity of the world into a "situation that is comprehended explicitly in words and that serves as a springboard into action" (Weick, Sutcliffe, & Obstfeld, 2005, p. 409). Thus sensemaking involves—and indeed requires—an articulation of the unknown, because, sometimes trying to explain the unknown is the only way to know how much you understand it.

Finally, sensemaking calls for courage, because while there is a deep human need to understand and know what is going on in a changing world, illuminating the change is often a lonely and unpopular task. The leader who demonstrates that an organization's strategy has not been successful, for example, may clash with those who want to keep the image of achievement alive.

In the realm of business, sensemaking can mean learning about shifting markets, customer migration, or new technologies. It can mean learning about the culture, politics, and structure of a new venture or about a problem that you haven't seen before. It can mean figuring out why a previously successful business model is no longer working. Sensemaking often involves moving from the simple to the complex and back again. The move to the complex occurs as new information is collected and new actions are taken. Then as patterns are identified, and new information is labeled and categorized, the complex becomes simple once again, albeit with a higher level of understanding.

Sensemaking is most often needed when our understanding of the world becomes unintelligible in some way. This occurs when the environment is changing rapidly, presenting us with surprises for which we are unprepared or confronting us with adaptive rather than technical problems to solve (Heifetz, 2009). Adaptive challenges—those that require a response outside our existing repertoire—often present as a gap between an aspiration and an existing capacity—a gap that cannot be closed by existing modes of operating.

At such times phenomena "have to be forcibly carved out of the undifferentiated flux of raw experience and conceptually fixed and labeled so that they can become the common currency for communication exchanges" (Chia, 2000, p. 513). As such, sensemaking is about making the intractable actionable. But action is not a separate and later step in sensemaking. Rather, acting is one more way of understanding the new reality, providing additional input for us to bracket and assign meaning (Weick et al., 2005).

Thus, sensemaking involves coming up with plausible understandings and meanings; testing them with others and via action; and then refining our understandings or abandoning them in favor of new ones that better explain a shifting reality.

Brian Arthur (1996) uses a gambling casino analogy to illustrate the kind of profound uncertainty we currently face that creates a great need for sensemaking:

> *Imagine you are milling about in a large casino with the top figures of high tech. . . . Over at one table, a game is starting called Multimedia. Over at another is a game called Web Services. There are many such tables. You sit at one.*
>
> *"How much to play?" you ask.*
>
> *"Three billion," the croupier replies.*
>
> *"Who'll be playing?" you ask.*
>
> *"We won't know until they show up," he replies.*
>
> *"What are the rules?"*
>
> *"These will emerge as the game unfolds," says the croupier.*
>
> *"What are the odds of winning?" you wonder.*
>
> *"We can't say," responds the house. "Do you still want to play?"*

Sensemaking in such an environment involves "being thrown into an ongoing, unknowable, unpredictable streaming of experience in search of answers to the question, 'What's the story?'" (Weick, Sutcliffe, & Obstfeld, 2005). It means looking for a unifying order even if we are not sure if one exists. It requires figuring out how best to represent this order and continuing to play the game indefinitely even if we never know if we have found the order. This, according to Joseph Jaworski and Claus Otto Scharmer (2000), is the moral of Brian Arthur's casino analogy. "What distinguishes great leaders from average leaders is their ability to perceive the nature of the game and the rules by which it is played, as they are playing it" (p. 2).

Seen from this perspective, sensemaking is an emergent activity—a capacity to move between heuristics and algorithm, intuition and logic, inductive and deductive reasoning, continuously looking for and providing evidence, and generating and testing hypotheses, all while "playing the game." As such sensemaking requires that leaders have emotional intelligence, self-awareness, the ability to deal with cognitive complexity, and the flexibility to go between the "what is" of sensemaking and the "what can be" of visioning. Perhaps equally important, it also requires that leaders be able to engage others in their organizations in figuring out how to play the game.

How critical is sensemaking in today's world? We are certainly in the midst of enormous global change, whether we consider politics, economics, climate change, resource depletion, or dozens of other arenas. In the sphere of business, John Chambers, the CEO of Cisco, believes that "from a business model and leadership perspective, we're seeing a massive shift from management by command-and-control to management by collaboration and teamwork. You could almost say this shift is as revolutionary as the assembly line" (Fryer & Stewart, 2008, p. 76). Questions abound: How will global competition play out? Will China and India dominate this century? Is the economic crisis over? How will terrorism impact international trade relations?

But sensemaking is not limited to such cosmic problems. At an organizational level, leaders need to engage in sensemaking to understand why their teams are not functioning, why their customers are leaving, and why their operations are falling short on safety and reliability. At a personal level, sensemaking can help in understanding why you have not lived up to your own expectations as a leader, or why you don't seem to be getting along with your new boss. We teach sensemaking to undergraduates, MBAs, mid-level executives, and top management teams since the ability to understand a changing context is needed at every level.

How Does Sensemaking Help?

So yes, sensemaking is an extremely useful skill, but how exactly does it work? Weick (2001) provides one answer, by likening sensemaking to cartography. Maps can provide hope, confidence, and the means to move from anxiety to action. By mapping an unfamiliar situation, some of the fear of the unknown can be abated. By having all members of a team working from a common map of "what's going on out there," coordinated action is facilitated. In an age where people are often anxious about their circumstances, mapmaking becomes an essential element of sensemaking and leadership. In a world of action first, sensemaking provides a precursor to more effective action.

As we try to map confusion and bring coherence to what appears mysterious, we are able to talk about what is happening, bring multiple interpretations to our situations, and then act. Then, as we continue to act, we can change the map to fit our experience and reflect our growing understanding.

It is important to note that in this sense of the word, there is no "right" map. Sensemaking is not about finding the "correct" answer; it is about creating an emerging picture that becomes more comprehensive through data collection, action, experience, and conversation. The importance of sensemaking is that it enables us to act when the world as we knew it seems to have shifted (Weick, Sutcliffe, & Obstfeld, 2005). It gives us something to hold onto to keep fear at a distance.

This use of sensemaking can be illustrated through a story (articulated in a poem by Holub, 1977) and elaborated here for illustrative purposes. A small military unit was sent on a training mission in the Swiss Alps. They did not know the terrain very well, and suddenly it began to snow. It snowed for two days. There were large drifts everywhere, and it was hard to see through the clouds and blowing snow. The men considered themselves lost. They were cold and hungry, and panic began to spread through the unit as they thought of what would become of them. But then one of them found a map in his pocket. Everyone crowded around trying to figure out where they were and how they could get out. They calmed down, located themselves, and plotted a route back to their base.

They pitched camp, lasted out the snowstorm, and moved into action. Of course they didn't always hit the landmarks they thought they would, so getting back involved still more sensemaking. They got help from villagers along the way, and shifted their path when faced with obstacles. And then, when they finally got back to base camp, they discovered that the map they had been using was actually a map of the Pyrenees and not the Alps.

The moral of the story? When you're tired, cold, hungry, and scared, any old map will do (Weick, 1995).

When I use this story with students, they protest that a bad map can be a disaster—especially when you are wandering around in the mountains in the middle of a blizzard—and of course that's true. Given a choice, we would all choose the best map possible. Yet the soldiers in the story were able to survive using a bad map because they acted, had a purpose, and had an image of where they were and where they were going, even though they were in many ways mistaken. The point is that in sensemaking, the map is only a starting point. One then has to pay attention to cues from the environment, incorporate new information, and in so doing turn what may be a poor map into a useful sensemaking device (Weick, 1995).

There are many reasons why a poor map may be "good enough." First, a poor map may actually enable leaders and teams to move ahead with assurance toward goals that might seem unattainable if their view of the world was actually more accurate. Under some circumstances, accuracy may immobilize, while partial reality may motivate. Indeed, the very idea that accuracy is possible pertains more to the "object" world where situations are constant, than to the flow of organizational life in a shifting context. Second, enabling people to get some sense of a situation, calm down, and act may be more important than finding "the" right answer, which we can never find anyway. Third, in a rapidly changing environment speed may trump accuracy. And finally, it is very difficult to know whether our perceptions will prove accurate or not, because these perceptions and the actions they promote will themselves change our reality, and because different perceptions can lead to the same actions.

In short, plausibility as opposed to accuracy is more important in sensemaking—stories and maps that explain and energize, that invite people to discuss, act, and contribute ideas trump those that are more exclusively focused on trying to achieve the best possible picture of a reality that is changing and elusive (Weick, 1995).

How Does Sensemaking Connect to Other Leadership Capabilities?

Once we have a better grasp of what is going on in our world through sensemaking, then we have a much clearer idea of how to engage our other leadership capabilities of visioning, inventing, and relating. With a clearer sense of the external terrain, our visions and execution capabilities improve because they "fit" current circumstances. With the focus and energy that come with a plausible map, relating, visioning, and inventing can flourish. With a greater understanding of the people with whom we work, communication and collaboration proceed more smoothly. In a society that values action, effective leaders must rely on and reward the sensemaking that helps direct and correct that action. On the other side, a vision for the future helps to focus sensemaking on areas of importance to the organization; inventing provides more data for sensemaking; and relating provides the interactive network through which sensemaking can occur.

For example, Victor Fung, the Chairman of the Li & Fung Group, a global sourcing, distribution, and retail enterprise, engages the company in a planning process every three years. The unique element of this process is that once the plan is set, it does not change for the three-year period. This allows the company to focus on results with a long enough runway to achieve significant stretch goals over the plan period.

Given the uncertainty in the current environment, prior to the planning process for 2011–2013, twenty-six manager teams were formed to engage in sensemaking and inventing new directions for the firm. Some looked at trends in the Chinese economy, some benchmarked best practices in HR and IT in companies around the world, some looked at better ways to collaborate globally to serve customers, while others re-examined internal cultural artifacts to determine their fit with changed conditions. Through shared sensemaking in teams including people from different geographies and parts of the organization, new ideas emerged and pilot projects were tested and fed—real time—into the planning process. The result: a new three-year plan better suited to changed external conditions.

How Do You Do Effective Sensemaking?

While sensemaking is quite a complex concept, it can be broken down into three core elements: exploring the wider system (steps 1 to 4), creating a map of the current situation (steps 5 and 6), and acting to change the system to learn more about it (steps 7 to 9). Each element can be further broken down into a set of suggested behaviors.

Explore the Wider System

This aspect of sensemaking is perhaps best captured in the words of Marcel Proust: "The real voyage of discovery consists not in seeking new landscapes but in having new eyes." The key here is to work with others to observe what is going on, to tap different data sources and collect different types of data, and to keep prior biases from interfering with your perceptions. Some helpful tips include the following:

1. *Seek out many types and sources of data. Combine financial data with trips to the shop floor, listen to employees as well as customers, and mix computer research with personal interviews.*

We learn the most about events or issues when we view them from a variety of perspectives. While each may have its own particular flaws, when the different modes of analysis reveal the same patterns, we can feel more confident as we converge on an interpretation of what is really going on (Weick, 1995).

At IDEO, a product design company, this aspect of sensemaking is a key ingredient in innovative design. One team that was redesigning a hospital emergency room put a camera on the head of a patient and left it on for ten hours to add some visual data from a key stakeholder to the other information they had. The result: ten hours of ceiling! This new perspective completely changed the mental models of the designers, who up to this point had not fully considered the patient experience. Armed with this new mindset they shifted the design to include writing on the ceiling and other spaces most visible to patients. Without the additional data, which greatly enriched the designers' understanding of what was really happening in the ER environment, the final design would have been far less effective.

2. *Involve others as you try to make sense of any situation. Your own mental model of what is going on can only get better as it is tested and modified through interaction with others.*

Sensemaking is inherently collective; it is not nearly as effective to be the lone leader at the top doing all the sensemaking by yourself. It is far better to compare your views with those of others—blending, negotiating, and integrating, until some mutually acceptable version is achieved. Soliciting and valuing divergent views and analytic perspectives, and staying open to a wide variety of inputs, results in a greater ability to create large numbers of possible responses, thus facilitating resilient action (Sutcliffe & Vogus, 2003).

In a recent sensemaking exercise, the members of a team charged with determining how much the economic downturn had affected their firm all started out with very different estimates. All of these estimates suffered from a lack of knowledge about certain parts of the business. By listening to the input of the finance, HR, engineering, and marketing groups, and discussing the very different assumptions and data sources of each group, the team eventually converged on an estimate and a cooperative response across functions.

3. *Move beyond stereotypes. Rather than oversimplifying—"Marketing people are always overestimating the demand"—try to understand the nuances of each particular situation.*

"Seeing with new eyes" requires that we look at each new situation with an open mind, understanding it in all of its unique aspects. Relying on stereotypes is the opposite of this approach, attributing qualities to the situation that belong to a stereotype but are not really present in the situation itself. Our political process, for example, seems to be stalled at the moment by the inability of many politicians (and citizens) to understand and respect other points of view. Rather than see with new eyes, people rely on labels ("Democrat," "Republican," "liberal," etc.) as if these stereotypes alone represent the views, policies, and solutions of all members of the other group. The result, ultimately, is an inability to come up with fresh and widely acceptable solutions to our very real problems.

4. Be very sensitive to operations. Learn from those closest to the front line, to customers, and to new technologies. What trends do current shifts portend for the future? What's behind the trends that we see recurring in different parts of the world?

Andy Grove, the former CEO and chair of Intel, believed in being "paranoid." By that he meant that you always have to be worried about new trends that can destroy or enhance your business, and new competitors that can win in the market. So he designed Intel to monitor many trends—to do ongoing sensemaking. This involves watching what customers are buying and where they go if they drop Intel, finding out what new research is being done at key universities, continuously tracking quality, and checking constantly that this information is accurate and up to date. Why? Because in his industry it is important to respond to changes in markets and technologies early, not when others have already captured a competitive advantage.

CREATE A MAP OR STORY OF THE SITUATION

As mentioned earlier, sensemaking can be likened to cartography. The key is to create a map/story/frame that—at least for a brief period of time—adequately represents the current situation that an organization is facing. Furthermore, it is not really useful for each person to have his or her own map; a team or organization needs to have a shared map to enable shared action.

5. Do not simply overlay your existing framework on a new situation. The new situation may be very different. Instead, let the appropriate map or framework emerge from your understanding of the situation.

Despite telling people that they have to let a map emerge, in many subtle ways old maps reassert themselves. If you go to an interview with a set of fixed questions, those questions will frame and in some ways restrict the information you obtain. Contrast that with an open-ended question, such as "What do you think about x?" In this case you are more likely to uncover unanticipated and potentially valuable viewpoints and information.

Take, for example, the leaders of a large global company operating in China. Because they had always understood their competitors to be other large global companies, they could not understand their falling profits and loss of market share. After all, their competitors were not gaining market share, so what was happening? It was only after local operators explained that small, local, Chinese companies were exploding on the scene and taking away business that they understood. These competitors had not even been on the company's radar screen, despite having been on the scene for a number of years. The established pattern of sensemaking remained limited to the large, global players.

Or consider Costco managers who viewed their scope of responsibility to be sales, marketing, and distribution. Issues of the myriad players in the supply chain were just not part of the picture. However, as managers came to be increasingly worried about reliability of supply, this old, and in many ways limited, framework no longer seemed to work. Suddenly, as they saw for the first time their connection to all points along the supply chain, the managers found themselves concerned with the sustainability of bean-grower communities on the other side of the world. Their mental model had changed and they were better prepared to act.

6. *Put the emerging situation into a new framework to provide organizational members with order. Use images, metaphors, and stories to capture the key elements of the new situation.*

It is not always easy to move from a complex and dynamic situation to a singular image or metaphor. "To consolidate bits and pieces into a compact, sensible pattern frequently requires that one look beyond those bits and pieces to understand what they might mean" (Weick et al., 2005). Often it is necessary to move outside a system in order to see the patterns within. When John Reed, the retired chair of Citigroup, was in charge of the back office he came to categorize their operations as more of a "factory" than a "bank." This new image became a reality as he hired managers from car companies, reorganized work in assembly lines, and consequently greatly improved efficiencies.

Or consider the experience of Gandhi when he left South Africa and came to India. When asked to join the Indian Independence Movement, he refused, saying that he knew nothing about India. His mentor then suggested that he get to know India, so he spent months riding the trains from village to village. When he returned he told the Indian National Congress that they did not understand the "real India," which was not made up of lawyers and merchants in Delhi, but "700,000 villages" with millions of people that "toil each day under the hot sun." Then Gandhi courageously told the party leaders that they were not so different from their British rulers, that they needed to discard their limited maps and substitute one based on a new picture of India based on real information about the common man, not the privileged few.

Of course, there is always more than one metaphor that can capture a situation, which means that any given metaphor is likely to be contested. In Egypt, for example, the battle between government leaders and the crowds in Cairo's Independence Square involved competing metaphors: were those occupying the square traitors who should be punished or patriots fighting for freedom and democracy who should be celebrated.

ACT TO CHANGE THE SYSTEM TO LEARN FROM IT

People learn about situations by acting in them and then seeing what happens (Weick, 1985). Children often learn the rules in a family by pushing boundaries and then looking for the point at which they get reprimanded. Doctors sometimes learn what is wrong with a patient by starting a treatment and seeing how the patient responds. In short, directed action is a major tool with which we learn about situations and systems.

7. *Learn from small experiments. If you are not sure how a system is working, try something new.*

While action is a key sensemaking tool, it is often wiser to begin with—and learn from—small experiments, before broadening the action to drive change across the larger system. Sensemaking involves "acting thinkingly," which means that people "simultaneously" interpret their knowledge with trusted frameworks, yet "mistrust those frameworks by testing new frameworks and new interpretations. . . . " Or, put another way, "[A]daptive sensemaking both honors and rejects the past" (Weick et al., 2005, p. 412).

Several companies we work with at the MIT Leadership Center have had business models in which they sell products, services, or technology to organizations that then brand and sell them to the ultimate customer. In many cases, the companies eventually decided that they could make the finished products or services themselves and sell them at much higher margins. But this new business model would put the companies in direct competition with their own customers—a risky move and a whole new way of acting in the marketplace. The solution: small experiments. Try the new approach in one product domain, see what happens, determine what works and what doesn't work, and then expand to other product domains, operating with a much greater sense of what it actually means to work under this new business model.

8. *People create their own environments and are then constrained by them. Be aware and realize the impact of your own behavior in creating the environment in which you are working.*

Sensemaking involves not only trying out new things but also trying to understand your impact on a system as you try to change it. In one organization, for example, the leaders launched a new initiative to encourage lower-level employees to offer suggestions and ideas for new ways of working. They toured the plants, held meetings, and approached employees in informal settings. However, these actions were read differently by the employees. One employee, for example, explained that when a meeting is held in a conference room with arranged seating, the formal atmosphere prevents people from speaking up. Others explained that an apparently informal conversation with a leader is viewed as a "test," not a true inquiry. In other words, the leaders' attempts to listen to the voice of the employee were seen by the employees through an "authority-ranking social frame," and hence they did not have the desired effect (Detert & Treviño, 2010). For their part, the leaders in this example did not really examine the impact of their new role as "empowering leaders," and did not do the necessary sensemaking to understand how employees really felt. Hence a well-intentioned attempt at empowerment actually increased the sense of centralized control, with neither party realizing how their conditioned thinking impacted the system and inhibited change.

The ideas outlined above can help a leader improve his or her sensemaking skills, but leaders should never forget that sensemaking is not a one-and-done activity. Operating in a complex and uncertain world means needing to course-correct quickly when (not if) things go wrong. This means that you have to detect, contain, and bounce back from errors. You need to improvise solutions to problems as they appear rather than letting them escalate and get out of hand. Thus, sensemaking in a new situation can help you understand and act in that situation, but rapid sensemaking is also needed when your actions do not have the predicted consequences or when what you thought was coming around the corner is not there at all. Systems that are better able to deal with these surprises do not get bogged down in finding blame or wishful thinking about what might have been. Instead they work to restore, invent, improvise, and recover in creative ways (Sutcliffe & Vogus, 2003).

What Gets in the Way of Effective Sensemaking?

If sensemaking is such an important leadership capability in a world of complexity, uncertainty, and continuous change, then why is it that we stumble at doing it at all, much less doing it well? Part of the answer lies in the fact that sensemaking may be most needed when we feel under threat or crisis, and the very mechanisms that get engaged to deal with fear are the ones that can hamper sensemaking. Thus far this chapter has emphasized that sensemaking involves exploring our changing world through multiple kinds and sources of data, selecting new frameworks and new interpretations to form new maps and mental models that offer plausible explanations of the changes going on, then acting with resilience, verifying and updating our maps as needed to better our understanding and achieve more desirable outcomes. Yet if sensemaking is most often needed when our understanding of the world seems inadequate and we are surprised by events, then such times are also moments of threat and fear that may reinforce existing maps and mental models, increase our reliance on old information, and inhibit action. Threat and fear are associated with rigidity, a need for direction, and erratic behavior—which work against effective sensemaking.

RIGIDITY

Ever since the classic article by Staw, Sandelands, and Dutton (1981) it has been shown that threat and fear lead to rigidity. Thus, in individuals, teams, and organizations, threat often results in the consideration of fewer external cues and a reliance on tried and true modes of operating. As a result, threat is often more associated with inertia, protection of the status quo, and sometimes even inaction—the deer in the headlights syndrome. Threat is seen as the time to batten down the hatches, keep outsiders away, and get back to business as usual. Yet, threat conditions are when high levels of sensemaking and change are most needed. Thus, leaders at all levels within an organization need to fight against this rigidity in order to enable active sensemaking and inventing.

The evidence is clear: Companies that make changes during economic downturns, that offer new products and services for a new set of circumstances, and that prepare for the moment when things will change in a more positive direction are the ones that not only survive but prosper. For example, right now many companies are coming out with less expensive versions of products in the United States and looking to move more of their sales to countries such as China, India, and Brazil where economies are still growing at high rates. But seeing what changes are actually taking place and knowing which actions will be most useful requires sensemaking and an ability to push against the rigidity that comes with threat.

DEPENDENCE ON DIRECTION

Threat and fear also can result in constriction of control and a felt need for direction (Meindl, Ehrlich, & Dukerich, 1985; Staw, Sandelands, & Dutton, 1981). In the face of uncertainty, people look to others to show them the way. When people are afraid, they look for direction and reassurance. In such instances leaders do need to be reassuring, to communicate what they know and what they don't know, and to show care and concern. They also need to indicate how they plan to move ahead and mobilize for the new times ahead. However, the last thing that leaders should do is to treat their employees like children, dependent upon the one leader—even if there is a pull to do so.

People need to be treated as capable adults. If sensemaking is inherently social, and if more and different kinds of data are important, especially from the front lines during times of threat, then leaders at the top of the organization need to encourage others further down in the organization to assist in ongoing sensemaking. For example, at Best Buy it wasn't top management, but a young marketing manager, who began to see what a lack of communication was doing to relationships with employees. She decided to use social media technologies to get employees (there are 160,000) to participate in polls, brainstorm new ideas, and attend town-hall meetings with management. The result was a greater level of dialogue, more new ideas for increased sales, and a 32 percent drop in turnover (Tucker, 2010).

ERRATIC BEHAVIOR

Threat and fear can also result in erratic behavior as leaders try one solution and then another in a frantic search for something that works. However, such dramatic shifts in behavior make it very difficult to engage in effective sensemaking. In order to assess if action in a new environment is working, you need to have time to determine the outcomes of your actions and to examine key feedback loops as multiple factors play out over time.

In medical crisis simulations new interns attempted to diagnose patients with symptoms that did not conform easily to clear-cut diseases. Some displayed rigidity responses, leaping to the most likely diagnosis and ignoring signals that the diagnosis was incorrect. Others engaged in erratic behavior, trying new treatments but never holding to them long enough to determine if they were working. The most successful doctors engaged in effective sensemaking by paying attention to the cues that a treatment was not working and then trying the next one long enough to determine if it might work (Rudolph, Morrison, & Carroll, 2009). Thus, leaders need to help themselves and others to act and limit the effects of rigidity and dependency, while avoiding erratic action where learning is minimized.

Of course it is not only threat and fear that inhibit effective sensemaking. In a globally competitive environment our reward structures are geared toward rewarding immediate action and hence we may be signaling that sensemaking is not a valued activity. Also, while the leadership literature and leadership training tend to concentrate on interpersonal skills, negotiating, visioning, execution, decision-making, charisma, and collaboration, sensemaking is seldom seen on the list. If organizations want to see more effective sensemaking then they will have to create the kinds of practices, structures, vocabulary, and rewards that encourage it.

TEACHING SENSEMAKING AS A LEADERSHIP CAPABILITY

Any program or class that includes sensemaking as a leadership capability should use multiple teaching modes to bring this complex concept to life and create capacity in this domain. Combining theory, role models, action learning, feedback, and class assignments can result in a rich curriculum that students will enjoy. At MIT, we teach sensemaking as one of four leadership capabilities so that students can see how it is intricately interwoven with creating connections, building a vision, and implementing change.

We have also found that providing a safe environment for students to learn about leadership theory, get feedback on their capabilities, practice new skills, reflect, and plan is best done outside the framework of regular classes. With this in mind, we believe that a workshop format—one to three full days—works best. If this format is not possible, we have taught this sequence in three-hour blocks once a week.

THEORY

Since students seldom have an existing knowledge base on sensemaking, some theoretical introduction is necessary. While there are a number of excellent books on the subject (see the reference list at the end of the chapter) we find it more productive to provide short lectures on sensemaking coupled with some of the other learning modes. Lectures often follow the format of this chapter: They start with a brief discussion of the core concepts, describe the role of sensemaking in today's world, then provide an overview of what makes for effective sensemaking and what gets in the way.

To give concepts more meaning, we ask our students to think of an instance when they had to engage in active sensemaking—starting a new job, moving to a new city, or trying to do economic forecasts in a recessionary environment. Students also meet in groups to discuss leaders they have seen who do sensemaking well or poorly, and probe for what these leaders actually did in their sensemaking. They can then apply the concepts to their own experiences.

ROLE MODELS

One of the most effective ways to learn about sensemaking is either to listen to current leaders talk about their own sensemaking activities, or watch videos of leaders in action and analyze their sensemaking activities. In either case, students should be encouraged to push for specifics: How did the leader know that sensemaking was needed? What types of data did he or she collect? Who else was engaged? What forms did exploration and mapping take? What experiments were run?

In terms of media as opposed to "live" presentations, commercial films sometimes provide excellent examples of sensemaking and other leadership capabilities. In the movie *Gandhi,* for example, Gandhi must engage in sensemaking when he goes to South Africa and has to try to understand a new culture, when he goes to India and must prepare for the fight for independence, and when he must strategize about how to deal with setbacks to his goals for the country. Whether traversing India on the roof of a train, talking to people of all walks of life, figuring out not only conditions within India but the aspirations and weaknesses of the British colonial rulers, Gandhi's sensemaking is constant and critical to his relating, visioning, and inventing.

The movie *Apollo 13* has a wonderful sensemaking sequence as both the astronauts and mission control try to make sense of what has gone wrong with the mission when it is rocked by explosives. Pitting old mental models—you can't have such a failure, it must be instrument error—against incoming data—alarms going off, the rocket shaking, gas leaking—the film shows the difficulties of effective sensemaking during a crisis. A more recent film, *Social Network,* provides an outstanding picture of ongoing sensemaking by the various players in the unfolding drama of the Facebook phenomenon.

In the absence of guest speakers or videos, current news stories can be analyzed. Examining the sensemaking of President Obama as new crises emerge, or the Secretary of the Treasury during the economic crisis, or the marketing group of a global company as they see China, India, and Brazil emerging as economic powerhouses can all help students understand the concept.

ACTION LEARNING

While it is valuable to analyze the sensemaking of others, the best way to learn sensemaking is to actually do it. One way to accomplish this is by having students pretend they are about to take over another person's job. The students can each put together a plan for sensemaking about the job and then compare their plans to those of others, discuss the differences, and combine approaches to improve their sensemaking approach. They can then interview the person to test how their approach worked.

Students might also do the sensemaking necessary to decide if a particular venture capital company should buy a new start-up and then ask a member of the company to comment about how his sensemaking differed from theirs.

Sensemaking, however, is done best in the context of real world projects, and at the team level where the social aspect of sensemaking becomes apparent. In some of our projects we challenge students to come up with a consulting plan or design a new product. The students are formed into x-teams (Ancona & Bresman, 2007)—externally oriented teams that must build connections outside of the team as well as inside—and asked to first explore their environment. They investigate their own capabilities; the organizational terrain; the organizational strategy; potential allies and adversaries; customers and competitors; and current trends that might affect their success. They interview each stakeholder in the project and try to understand expectations for the team and its product, desired outcomes, and his or her view of the situation. After this exploration phase, they create a map of what they have discovered and begin to act to assess if the map is plausible. As they go through this process, team members are asked to keep track of their initial assumptions and whether those assumptions are confirmed or negated. Workbooks are used to guide these activities. Finally, they move into actually doing the project. Such projects result in students having a real appreciation as to how they might incorporate sensemaking into their own leadership toolbox.

FEEDBACK

Many of our students participate in our 360-degree feedback process using the 4-CAP leadership framework. The sensemaking segment asks raters from the students' former employers to evaluate the student on *exploring the wider system,* e.g., uses a broad array of types of data and analytic lenses; *mapping,* e.g., is able to consolidate bits and pieces into a coherent whole; and *acting in the system,* e.g., tries small experiments to determine if they understand the organization. Students get feedback on how their sensemaking was viewed by managers, peers, subordinates, and possibly other outside groups such as customers and suppliers. After examining the feedback, students are coached on what the data might mean and they are asked to put together an action plan on how they can continue to hone their skills and improve on their weaknesses. In addition, their sensemaking capabilities are compared to the other capabilities to determine its relative strength in the student's repertoire of skills and behaviors. Through this external assessment and self-evaluation and planning, students develop a better sense of who they are as leaders and how they can move forward in their leadership development.

ASSIGNMENTS

Another assignment that helps students learn about sensemaking is to have them consolidate everything they have learned into a "leadership change manual." The goal is to create a pragmatic tool for carrying out organizational change—a tool that must include a section on sensemaking. An example of a student change manual can be found in Figure 1.1.

Another assignment asks students to describe their "leadership signatures" or their unique way of leading. One section of this assignment is focused on how students actually engage in sensemaking—for example, Are they over-reliant on computer search and not so good at face-to-face communication? Are they good at analysis but not so good at action?—and includes a section on how to hone strengths and improve on weaknesses.

By linking theory, role models, action learning, feedback, and assignments in class, students can and do improve their ability to carry out effective sensemaking.

Conclusion

In a world that is growing "smaller" but ever more complex, where unpredictable events and shifting political, economic, environmental, and social conditions challenge us at every turn, we all need to make better sense of what is going on. We should all explore the wider system, create maps that are plausible representations of what is happening, and act in the system to improve our understanding of reality. We will never capture it all, and never know how close we are. The best we can do is to make sensemaking a core individual, team, and organizational capability so that we can break through our fears of the unknown and lead in the face of complexity and uncertainty.

Figure 1.1 Example of a Student Change Model

2.0 *Sensemaking: Identifying Specifications*

Sensemaking can be thought of as the process by which leaders gather data about the problem facing the organization, much like engineers gather information about a technical problem by soliciting engineering specifications.

Sensemaking is often one of the first steps managers take to help understand the context in which a company and its people operate. Sensemaking partners closely with relating, and together they form the Axis of Enablement. In a dynamic business environment, sensemaking efforts must be continually updated throughout the change process.

Cut out and keep

Installation Hints:

- ❑ Get data from multiple sources
- ❑ Pursue opinions that differ from your own
- ❑ Test your assumptions with experiments
- ❑ Seek out multiple perspectives
- ❑ Iterate, but also remember to act on your data

Troubleshooting:

- ❑ Build credibility by Relating in interviews
- ❑ Don't be afraid to talk to people outside the company/industry for advice

Installation Steps

To conduct effect sensemaking, a leader must:

Explore the wider system

It is important to listen and broadly question all internal and external stakeholders that have been identified. If the nature of the problem or change is not already explicit, then it is important to use this information to help define the issue. Formal and informal interviews, reports, social media and other online content are all valuable sources of information that can be leveraged. The data gathering process dovetails closely with relating and so provides an early opportunity to build rapport with employees.

Pursue opinions that differ from your own

Leaders must keep an open mind when building a sensemaking map. An important part of this is to quickly identify your own mental models and assumptions and realize how these may bias your approach to data collection. Questioning these underlying assumptions is also critical to ensuring that cognitive biases do not interfere with your sensemaking process. Leaders should delay the formation of opinions until sufficient data has been gathered, including information from those that may disagree with his/her perspective. Never be afraid to ask, "What am I missing here?"

Test your assumptions

Sensemaking is an iterative process and because of this, leaders will need to evaluate their progress periodically to see if they are headed in the right direction. This is especially important when confronted with adaptive, rather than technical changes, as the nature of the solution may need to change over time as the environment changes. Once enough balanced data is gathered to form an initial hypothesis, leaders should 'learn by doing' through low-risk experiments to test their understanding and add the data gathered from these trials to their sensemaking map.

Adopt multiple perspectives

Try to see the issues from multiple perspectives. If a leader has reached his/her conclusions independently and the conclusions seem 'too easy' then the leader's ideas may simply be reiterating organizational stereotypes. Leaders should make use of teams and committees of key stakeholders comprising those with power, those in opposition to the change, and also those without authority (but who will be affected), to ensure their initiatives incorporate multiple perspectives. Viewing the issues from only one or two perspectives is unlikely to capture enough information for complex changes.

Iterate and Act

Sensemaking is an ongoing process that extends beyond just initial data gathering and implementation, but also captures feedback on the change's success after completion. As more data is obtained, a leader must update his/her map of the organization or issue and the leader's vision or invented options also refined. However, it is important for a leader not to be paralyzed by masses of data such that no action or progress is made and the initiative stalls. Therefore, once sufficient balanced information is gathered it will be time to take action and secure those early victories to help the change process gain momentum.

Troubleshooting Tips

The sensemaking process can be daunting as data becomes overwhelming and initially unknown gaps in understanding are illuminated. Leaders should keep in mind the following tips to facilitate the sensemaking process.

Build credibility

If a leader is brought in to turn around a new group or section, then there is a strong chance that any past credibility they have built up, may not travel directly with them to the new group. However, the sensemaking process provides an excellent opportunity to establish rapport, find out about employees' concerns, and also to explain and advocate the purpose of the change. Listening to employees, showing empathy and understanding, and demonstrating that their views have been heard and incorporated can help enormously. Noting down salient points

(Continued)

Figure 1.1 (Continued)

during interviews can not only help leaders to recall facts later, but also demonstrate their commitment to listening. Through the sensemaking and relating processes, leaders can often build credibility by demonstrating trustworthiness, competence, and dynamism.

Identify who to talk to

Leaders should try to map out likely stakeholders and include a balance of those that may support, oppose or be indifferent to the change initiative. During these initial interviews seek recommendations from each of these people regarding whom to talk to next. However, leaders should be aware that these referrals may be designed to reinforce the stakeholder's own positions. If possible, leaders should talk to others that have been in similar situations, perhaps outside of their companies and ask experts what sources of information they found most valuable.

Real World Example: Chuck Vest's Leadership as President of MIT

When Charles Vest was appointed as President of MIT he inherited a complex organization that required considerable sensemaking to navigate. One particular organizational change he implemented centered on ensuring gender equally at MIT. While a committee of female faculty members highlighted the need for change, Mr. Vest set about conducting hundreds of interviews, often by referral, to help build his map of the institution. When he heard that women were discriminated against within the faculties he reviewed the data and addressed the problem in a "just do it" fashion that helped him secure an early and meaningful victory to build upon.

References

Ancona, D., & Bresman, H. (2007). *X-Teams: How to build teams that lead, innovate and succeed.* Boston, MA: Harvard Business School Press.

Ancona, D., Malone, T., Orklikowski, W., & Senge, P. (2007). In praise of the incomplete leader. *Harvard Business Review,* 85(2), 92–100.

Arthur, W. B. (1996). Increasing returns and the new world of business. *Harvard Business Review, 74(4),* 100–109.

Chia, R. (2000). Discourse analysis as organizational analysis. *Organization, 7(3),* 513–518.

Detert, J. R., & Treviño, L. K. (2010). Speaking up to higher ups: How supervisors and skip-level leaders influence employee voice. *Organization Science, 21,* 249–270.

Fryer, B., & Stewart, T. A. (2008). Cisco sees the future: An interview with John Chambers. *Harvard Business Review, 86(11), 72–79.*

Heifetz, R., Grashow, A., & Linsky, M. (2009). *The practice of adaptive leadership: Tools and tactics for changing your organization.* Boston: MA: Harvard Business Press.

Holub, M. (1977). Brief thoughts on maps. *Times Literary Supplement,* 4 February, p. 118.

Jaworski, J., & Scharmer, C. O. (2000). Leadership in the new economy: Sensing and actualizing emerging futures (Working paper). Cambridge, MA: Society for Organizational Learning and Generon.

Meindl, J. R., Ehrlich, S. B., & Dukerich, J. M. (1985). The romance of leadership. *Administrative Science Quarterly, 30,* 78–102.

Rudolph, J. W., Morrison, J. B., & Carroll, J. S. (2009). The dynamics of action-oriented problem solving: Linking interpretation and choice. *Academy of Management Review, 34,* 733–56.

Starbuck, W. H., & Milliken, F. J. (1988). Executives' perceptual filters: What they notice and how they make sense. In D.C. Hambrick (Ed.), *The executive effect: Concepts and methods for studying top managers* (35–65). Greenwich, CT: JAI.

Staw, B. M., Sandelands, L. E., & Dutton, J. E. (1981). Threat-rigidity effects in organizational behavior: A multilevel analysis. *Administrative Science Quarterly, 26,* 501–524.

Sutcliffe, K. M., & Vogus, T. (2003). Organizing for resilience. In K. S. Cameron, J. E. Dutton, & R. E. Quinn (Eds.), *Positive organizational scholarship* (94–110). San Francisco, CA: Berrett- Koehler.

Tucker, R. B. (2010, March 11). Listening to employees is a Best Buy. [Web log post]. Retrieved from www.business-strategy-innovation.com/2010/03/listening-to-employees-is-best-buy.html

Waterman, R. H., Jr. (1990). *Adhocracy: The power to change.* Memphis, TN: Whittle Direct Books.

Weick, K. E. (1985). Cosmos vs. chaos: Sense and nonsense in electronic contexts. *Organizational Dynamics, 14(2),* 51–64.

Weick, K. E. (1993). The collapse of sensemaking in organizations: The Mann Gulch disaster. *Administrative Science Quarterly,* 38, 628–652.

Weick, K. E. (1995). *Sensemaking in organizations.* Thousand Oaks, CA: Sage.

Weick, K. E. (2001). *Making sense of the organization.* Oxford: Blackwell.

Weick, K. E., & Roberts, K. H. (1993). Collective mind in organizations: Heedful interrelating on flight decks. *Administrative Science Quarterly, 38,* 357–381.

Weick, K. E., & Sutcliffe, K. M. (2007). *Managing the unexpected* (2nd ed). San Francisco, CA: Jossey-Bass.

Weick, K. E., Sutcliffe, K. M., & Obstfeld, D. (2005). Organizing and the process of sensemaking and organizing. *Organization Science, 16(4),* 409–421.

2

CASES IN LEADERSHIP EDUCATION

Implications of Human Cognition

◆ Michael D. Mumford, David Peterson, Issac Robledo, and Kimberly Hester

University of Oklahoma

Case-based instruction represents one of the most widely used techniques in leader education. In the present effort we argue that case-based instruction is attractive, in part, because case-based knowledge provides the basis for leader cognition. Subsequently, the available evidence on case-based knowledge is reviewed. Based on this review, some key considerations should be taken into account when cases are used in leadership education: Instructors should familiarize students with prototypic cases before exceptional cases are presented, and they should be sure to engage existing or naïve frameworks for organizing cases. Instructors should be consistent in the mental models they provide for organizing the cases they teach, and be aware that advanced leaders better handle complex cases than less experienced ones. Further research is required for the optimum development and application of cases in leadership education.

❖ ❖ ❖

Many techniques have been employed in the education of leaders. For example, some instructional programs employ a behaviorally based approach (e.g., Dvir, Eden, Avolio, & Shamir, 1999). Here the key dimensions implied by a leadership theory are described, along with relevant behaviors, and people are provided with practice in executing these behaviors. Other instructional methods seek to prepare leaders for their next position (e.g., Jacobs & Lewis, 1992). In this approach key transition points are identified and leaders are presented with exercises to help them address the problems likely to be encountered in the next phase of their career. Still other approaches attempt to develop leadership potential by teaching self-management strategies (Sims & Lorenzi, 1992).

These and a number of other techniques all have some potential value as interventions that might be used in leadership education (Yukl, 2010). However, embodied in many, if not all, of these instructional programs is the use of a particular instructional technique. More specifically, most leadership educational interventions present cases—either written or video illustrations of past incidents of leader performance. Our intent in the present chapter is twofold: first, to examine what is known about the acquisition and application of case-based knowledge; second, to examine the implications of our current understanding of case-based knowledge for leadership education.

Leadership Cognition

CONTEXT

At the outset, it should be recognized that not all leadership education programs require acquisition of case-based knowledge. For example, some programs might seek to teach leaders to recognize key attributes of decision strategies (Vroom & Jago, 1988). Other educational programs might seek to teach leaders to recognize follower emotions (Côté, Lopes, Salovey, & Miners, 2010). These and many other educational programs do not demand case-based instruction although cases might be used to illustrate key points in these educational programs.

Providing case-based knowledge, however, will prove more critical when the goal of the instructional program is development of the cognitive skills underlying leader performance (Lord & Hall, 2005; Mumford, Friedrich, Caughron, & Byrne, 2007). Attempts to develop leaders' cognitive skills are held to be critical when leaders must address crisis situations. The available evidence indicates that people are more likely to seek leaders and leaders will have a greater impact on performance under crisis conditions (Bligh, Kohles, & Meindl, 2004; Halverson, Holladay, Kazma, & Quinones, 2004; Hunt, Boal, & Dodge, 1999). Crisis situations are significant with regard to the need for cognition for four reasons.

First, crises present novel events, or problems, where cognitive analysis of the problem and its implications is critical (Connelly, Gilbert, Zaccaro, Threlfall, Marks, & Mumford, 2000). Second, crisis situations tend to be ill-defined or poorly structured. Ill-defined problems typically require cognitive appraisal of the situation and its implications (Doerner & Schaub, 1994). Third, crises emerge rapidly with high-stakes outcomes being attached to actions for both the leader and their followers—outcomes that demand analysis (Bluedorn, Johnson, Cartwright, & Barringer, 1994). Fourth, effective leadership in crisis situations requires sensemaking and sensegiving on the part of leaders (Drazin, Glynn, & Kazanjian, 1999; Weick, 1995). Sensemaking and sensegiving, however, are based on leaders' understanding of the situation, its demands, and the needs of followers.

In crisis situations the need for sensemaking implies that leaders must forecast the effects of alternative courses of action. In keeping with this observation, Shipman, Byrne, and Mumford (2010) asked undergraduates to create a vision for leading a new experimental school. The quality, utility, and emotional impact of these vision statements were assessed along with the forecasting activities engaged in during vision formation. Specifically, the extensiveness of forecasting, forecasting resource requirements, forecasting negative outcomes, and forecasting time frame were assessed. It was found that the extensiveness of forecasting activities was correlated in the .40s with vision quality, utility, and emotional impact.

What should be recognized here, however, is that forecasting is a contextually based form of cognition (Noice, 1991; Xiao, Milgram, & Doyle, 1997). More specifically, in forecasting people use incidents of prior experience to identify critical attributes of the situation at hand (Patalano & Siefert, 1997) and anticipate the likely effects of alternative courses of action (Langholtz, Gettys, & Foote, 1995). Thus the basis for forecasting is held to lie in leaders' case-based, or experiential knowledge (Hedlund, Forsythe, Horvath, Williams, Snook, & Sternberg, 2003; Mumford et al., 2007). With forecasting it becomes possible for leaders to engage in the sensemaking and sensegiving held to be critical to performance under crisis conditions.

In fact both qualitative and quantitative studies tend to support this proposition. For example, Isenberg (1986), in a qualitative study, asked experienced managers and business students, their less experienced counterparts, to think aloud as they developed a plan to address a leadership problem. The obtained findings indicated that more experienced leaders, senior managers, differed from business students based on their application of prior cases and analysis of conditions bearing on selection of appropriate cases for use in solving this leadership problem. Other qualitative studies by Berger and Jordan (1992) and O'Connor (1998) also suggest that use of case-based knowledge is critical to leaders' problem-solving efforts.

In a quantitative study, Strange and Mumford (2005) asked undergraduates to formulate a vision for directing a new experimental school. These vision statements, presented as speeches, were appraised by students, parents, and teachers for utility and emotional impact. Prior to preparing these visions, however, study participants were presented with good or poor case models and they were asked to analyze these cases with respect to causes, goals, both, and neither. It was found that the strongest vision statements were obtained when good cases were analyzed with respect to causes and poor cases were analyzed with respect to goals. In another quantitative study, Hedlund et al. (2003) assessed individual differences in available case-based or tacit knowledge and found that greater case-based knowledge correlated in the .40s with indices of performance in a sample of army leaders.

CASE-BASED KNOWLEDGE

Taken as a whole, the studies reviewed above imply a clear conclusion: Case-based knowledge is apparently critical to leader performance. This straightforward observation, however, brings to the fore two other questions. First, what is the content of case-based knowledge? Second, how is this knowledge stored and retrieved from memory for use in problem-solving?

Case-based, or experiential knowledge appears to be relatively easily acquired by people (Kolodner, 1997), with people acquiring this knowledge either through direct personal experience or narratives that present actors engaged in problem-solving. Thus case-based knowledge may be required through written vignettes, videos, stories, or personal experience. It does not appear difficult, relative to other types of knowledge, for people to acquire and apply case-based knowledge (Hunter, Bedell-Avers, Ligon, Hunsicker, & Mumford, 2010).

However, case-based knowledge, while readily acquired, appears unusually complex. Thus Hammond (1990), in a study examining the use of case-based knowledge in planning and forecasting, found that these knowledge structures included an unusually wide array of information. More specifically, information was included in these knowledge structures bearing on causes, resources, contingencies, restrictions, actors, actions, affect, systems, and outcomes. What should be recognized here is that the complex content of case-based knowledge implies strong processing demands whenever this knowledge is applied in problem-solving. Thus people typically work with a limited number of cases, drawing pieces of information from these cases in a sequential fashion to minimize processing demands (Scott, Lonergan, & Mumford, 2005).

Cases are held to be stored, and recalled, from memory through use of a library system (Bluck, 2003; Habermas & Bluck, 2000). In this library system, cases are held to be indexed against significant, psychologically salient, aspects of the situation such as goals, outcomes, key performance demands, and affective states. Within this indexed set of cases a subset, a small subset, of prototypical cases applying in the situation at hand are identified (Hershey, Walsh, Read, & Chulef, 1990). Associated with these prototypic cases are commonly encountered exceptions to case prototypes that are marked as exceptions and tied to diagnostics indicating the likely relevance of these common exceptions. Cases are recalled based on matching of the cases to the situation at hand with prototypic cases being recalled and applied unless active monitoring of diagnostics implies an exception should be applied.

With activation of a case, or a small set of related cases, people can begin to access the information stored in cases. However, to use this information in forecasting, sensemaking, and problem-solving, people must actively work with elements of a case, causes, resources, restrictions, actions, actor affect, in envisioning potential outcomes and actions that might be taken to effect these outcomes (Scott et al., 2005). Thus, the information a person chooses to work with and the sequence, and/or weights, assigned to different pieces of information will have a powerful influence on how people apply case-based knowledge in problem solving, in general, and leadership problem solving, as a case in point (Hunt, 2004; Mumford, Friedrich, Caughron, & Antes, 2009; Vessey, Barrett, & Mumford, 2011).

Cases in Leadership Education

Our foregoing observations about case-based knowledge structures are noteworthy because they have a number of implications bearing on how cases are used in leadership education. More specifically, the nature of case-based knowledge has implications for (1) case content, (2) case analysis, (3) case organization, and (4) case application. In addition, the nature of case-based knowledge and the instructional methods applied have implications for how evaluation of these educational programs should occur. In the following section we will examine each of these issues in turn.

CASE CONTENT

Perhaps the most straightforward implication of the nature and structure of case-based knowledge arises from how this knowledge is organized. Earlier, we noted that case-based knowledge was organized on a prototype plus exception basis (Bluck, 2003). This observation, in turn, implies that leadership education, especially when students are unfamiliar with the topic at hand, is most likely to prove effective when prototypic cases are initially presented. In other words, exceptional or unusual cases should be presented only after students have mastered case prototypes. Moreover, given that basic case prototypes provide the foundation for case-based knowledge structures, it seems reasonable to assume that more time should be spent in presentation and elaboration of case prototypes as opposed to exceptional cases.

With regard to presentation of case prototypes, however, three further points should be borne in mind. First, people tend to select and apply cases based on key diagnostics applying to the situation at hand. Moreover, poor performers often tag cases to superficial features of the problem at hand such as goals or actor power (Kaizer & Shore, 1995). This observation, in turn, implies that presentation of case prototypes will prove most effective when "deep structure" diagnostics bearing on case application are presented such as critical causes, resource requirements, or actor affect (Marcy & Mumford, 2010). Thus, not only should case-based instruction elaborate prototypic cases, the conditions under which these cases can, or should, be applied must be described.

Second, leadership, as a phenomenon, is not a new concept for most people. As a result, people can be expected to possess case-based knowledge of prior leaders they have been exposed to or incidents of leadership in which they have engaged. The problem that arises in this regard is that new case prototypes being presented may be organized and understood in terms of extant personal prototypes. Indeed, Ligon, Hunter, and Mumford (2008) have provided evidence indicating that extant personal cases may be used to organize a variety of leadership experiences. Thus, those teaching leadership must differentiate the material being taught from personal life experience or, alternatively, seek to embed this material within extant prototypes. Although this latter instructional approach may, from time to time, prove viable, its likely success will be limited by the range of prototypic conceptions people might apply based on personal history.

Third, in presenting case prototypes, one may describe the case in great detail or one may describe the case globally. Typically, more experienced leaders prefer to work with more global descriptions of case material, especially when they are given the opportunity to seek additional information as necessary (Thomas & McDaniel, 1990). For novices, however, excessively detailed case information may prove overwhelming (Ericsson & Charness, 1994). As a result, it appears case material should be presented at a moderate level of depth where instructors seek to stress critical aspects of the case as they apply to how events unfold.

Our foregoing observations indicate that case-based instruction should focus on prototypic cases where cases are distinguished from stereotypic conceptions of leadership and the cases are presented at moderate levels of complexity where diagnostics are noted. Although these observations are plausible, in general, little has been said about how exceptional, or deviational, cases (with respect to case prototypes) should be presented. To begin, it appears that people do not retain a large number of exceptions to case prototypes—typically not more than seven. Thus a large number of deviations, or exceptional cases, should not be presented in leadership education. The limited number of exceptional cases that can be stored, and recalled, by most individuals, in turn, implies that the case exceptions provided must be selected to reflect the most commonly encountered exceptions to case prototypes.

When instruction focuses on providing leaders with exceptions to case prototypes three additional steps should be taken. First, when deviant, or exceptional, cases are presented they should be presented *after* familiarization of leaders with case prototypes. Second, the key features of exceptional cases that differentiate deviational cases from relevant case prototypes should be explicitly noted. Third, the diagnostics or attributes of the situation that call for application of exceptional cases should be clearly articulated. The need for explicit delineation of diagnostic markers derives from people's bias to apply prototypic cases unless a clear reason exists for application of exceptions (Holyoak & Thagard, 1997). Thus providing students with exceptions must be built on the scaffold provided by case prototypes and relevant diagnostics.

CASE ANALYSIS

Providing case prototypes, and major exceptions to these prototypes, is only one activity involved in case-based leader instruction. As noted earlier, case-based knowledge structures subsume a large amount and a wide variety of information. One implication of this observation is that leaders will typically not apply a large number of cases in problem solving (Scott et al., 2005). Another implication is that leaders will work with different pieces of information embedded in these cases—often working with multiple pieces of information in a sequential fashion (Mumford, Schultz, & Osburn, 2002). Thus leaders may work with cases using causes to identify requisite actions or actors to draw implications about follower affect. The implication of this observation is straightforward: Case-based instruction must also provide leaders with strategies for working with case-based knowledge.

In one study along these lines, Marcy and Mumford (2010) asked undergraduates to work on an educational leadership task—directing a large university. Prior to starting work on this computer simulation, participants were given training in various strategies for working with case-based knowledge. It was found, in keeping with the observations of Mumford and Van Doorn (2001), that when leaders abstracted key causes from cases better performance was observed especially when leaders were confronted with high complexity problems. Thus having leaders identify powerful causes, causes affecting multiple outcomes, causes having direct effects, and causes under the individual's control, all might prove valuable in helping leaders work with causes (Marcy & Mumford, 2007).

What should be recognized in this regard is that the type of information drawn from case-based knowledge and the strategies appropriately employed in working with this knowledge will vary as a function of problem type. This point was illustrated in a series of studies by Vessey, Barrett, and Mumford (in press) and Barrett, Vessey, and Mumford (2011). In the first of these studies individuals working in leadership roles were presented with an objective, depersonalized problem while in the second study a more personal, affectively oriented leadership problem was presented. In both studies participants were provided with training in strategies for working with different types of case-based information.

For example, the strategies trained included (1) causes (work with causes having direct effects), (2) resources (identify critical resource requirements), (3) affect (identify affective reactions of key actors), and (4) goals (work toward high payoff synergistic goals). The findings obtained in these studies indicated that when problems and activated cases were social in nature, training in affective, or goal-oriented strategies was particularly helpful with regard to leader performance. When the problem was more objective, or less personal, training in causal analysis and resource utilization strategies resulted in the best leader performance.

The findings obtained in these studies are noteworthy for three reasons. First, optimal case-based instruction requires training strategies for working with case-based knowledge as well as providing cases. Second, different problem types, and different cases, will call for the use of different strategies by leaders in problem solving. Third, leader performance was most likely to improve with training when multiple high value strategies for working with cases were provided. Thus, it is not sufficient in case-based instruction just to provide cases. Viable strategies for working with the information embedded in these cases must also be provided.

At one level these conclusions are straightforward. However, when one considers these findings with respect to leader education a few somewhat more subtle, albeit critical, conclusions emerge. To begin, in selecting cases or developing case material, cases should be selected that not only provide requisite knowledge but also illustrate appropriate strategies for working with this knowledge. Thus, effective case-based instruction should stress both content—the case—and process—strategies for working with this content (Reeves & Weisberg, 1994). Moreover, viable cases should provide material illustrating when, how, and why application of a particular strategy, or set of strategies, is useful.

A related point bears on acquisition of appropriate strategies. Typically, in strategy acquisition people prefer to apply more concrete, outcome-oriented strategies in problem-solving (Mumford, Blair, Dailey, Leritz, & Osburn, 2006). Thus, if working with causes, they will default to working only with causes that have large, direct effects. However, skilled leaders often apply more subtle strategies—for example, working with causes not subject to restrictions or working with causes affecting multiple outcomes (Mumford & Van Doorn, 2001). Thus, effective instruction, especially for more experienced leaders, should provide more complex and abstract strategies for working with certain types of case-based information illustrating when and how those strategies might be used to improve leader performance.

Implied by our foregoing comments, of course, is another noteworthy point. Many strategies might be applied to a variety of types of information when case-based knowledge is being used as a basis for problem-solving. To complicate matters even further, complex interactions, or interdependencies, will emerge as strategies are executed in a complex sequence of operations. These observations are noteworthy because they suggest that meta-cognitive skills training should often accompany strategy training in leadership education (Mumford, Zaccaro, Harding, Jacobs, & Fleishman, 2000).

Finally, it should be recognized that while people acquire case-based knowledge quickly, strategies for working with this knowledge are often acquired more slowly (Mobley, Doares, & Mumford, 2002). Moreover, a variety of strategies are available for working with each type of information, and application of these strategies must often occur in a dynamic, albeit interdependent, fashion. Unless the leadership education program is lengthy, it is unlikely that all these issues can be fully addressed in a course of instruction. Thus in leadership education, especially leadership education based on a case approach, it is critical to provide self-reflection and learning to learn skills (Manz & Sims, 1981; Mumford et al., 2007). It can be expected that self-reflection and learning to learn skills will prove most beneficial when they focus on analysis of success in strategy application vis-à-vis the case information being applied and the problem at hand (Dailey & Mumford, 2006).

CASE ORGANIZATION

Earlier we noted that case-based knowledge structures are organized in a library system. Appropriate organization of cases not only facilitates retrieval of case-based knowledge, it also permits this knowledge to be applied more effectively in addressing leadership issues. In keeping with this proposition, Connelly et al. (2000) presented leaders with a set of leadership tasks that they were asked to organize by grouping related tasks together. It was found that more effective leaders, as assessed by awards and critical incident performance, employed better organizing structures for leadership knowledge.

Accordingly, one key activity of case-based instructional programs is providing a set of principles, or a mental model, for organizing case-based knowledge. Thus when cases are presented, variables or attributes for organizing these cases should be presented as part of instruction. What should be recognized here, however, is that a variety of frameworks are available for organizing case-based knowledge (Hmelo-Silver & Pfeffer, 2004). For example, cases might be organized based on theory, they might be organized based on certain aspects of case content (e.g., causes, goals, actors), or they might be organized based on attributes of the situation (e.g., task, time-pressure, risk).

The availability of a variety of frameworks for organizing case-based knowledge is noteworthy with regard to leadership education for three reasons. First, in effective case-based programs a consistent organizing framework should be presented throughout instruction. Thus instructors should not organize cases by causal content in one set of classes and situational markers in another set of classes. Second, case prototypes presented should clearly articulate critical organizing principles relevant to the framework being applied. For example, if initiating structure and consideration are being used as organizing frameworks, prototype cases presented should clearly illustrate either initiating structure or consideration. Third, the frameworks used to structure or organize cases in leadership education should typically be valid, generalizable, and capable of being adapted by leaders for use in real-world settings. This observation is noteworthy because it suggests that a substantial investment must be made in the development of appropriate structures for organizing the cases to be presented in leadership education courses.

What should be recognized in this regard is that people have implicit theories, or extant mental models, available for organizing their experiences of, and their experiences as, leaders (Lord & Hall, 2005; Lord & Maher, 1990). What should be recognized here is that these naïve or implicit theories, and the variables drawn from these theories to organize case-based knowledge, may not be consistent with the organizing structure provided in leadership education courses. This observation is noteworthy because it implies that in leadership education both sense-breaking and sense-making exercises (Gioia & Thomas, 1996) should be provided to allow students to both discount their extant organizing structures (e.g., mental models or implicit theories) and adopt the organizing structures being taught in the leadership education program at hand.

In this regard it is important to bear in mind a key characteristic of the mental models or implicit theories used as organizing structures. These organizing structures are formulated based on people's use of knowledge, including case-based knowledge, in real-world problem-solving. Thus Hmelo-Silver and Pfeffer (2004) found that hobbyists, biologists, and novices all employed different models, or variables, for understanding operations of an aquarium. Notably, hobbyists' and biologists' models differed with respect to variables relevant to application of their knowledge. This finding is noteworthy because it suggests that effective leadership education programs will base presentation of cases with regard to variables, or organizing principles, commonly held to guide practical application of knowledge in real-world settings.

What should be recognized in this regard, however, is that practical demands, and thus relevant organizing structures, change as leaders move through their careers (Jacobs & Jaques, 1991). Thus Mumford, Marks, Connelly, Zaccaro, and Reiter-Palmon (2000) found that mid-career leaders stress idea generation while more senior leaders stress contextual evaluation of ideas. Because similar findings have been obtained by Mumford, Campion, and Morgeson (2007), it seems reasonable to conclude that the organizing structures provided for cases through theory, case elements applied, or situational features will change as people gain experience and move through their careers as leaders. Thus organizing structures should not be viewed as fixed when cases are providing a basis for leader education.

CASE APPLICATION

Above we noted that the way case-based knowledge is organized depends on how it is applied. Moreover, acquisition of case prototypes and exceptions appears to improve when case-based knowledge is actively applied in real-world problem-solving (Kolodner, 1997). Further, it appears that acquisition of strategies for applying case-based knowledge is facilitated through application of select case content, and strategies, for applying this content in solving the problems presented to people (Scott et al., 2005).

In one study along these lines, Marcy and Mumford (2010) provided leaders with training in applying causal content of case-based knowledge in solving problems arising in university leadership positions. Not only were strategies for working with case-based knowledge bearing on causes provided, but participants were provided with practice in applying these strategies in solving a set of practice problems. And, consistent with the earlier findings of Marcy and Mumford (2007), practice applying these causal analysis strategies contributed to leader performance. Similarly, in presenting prototypic cases, it appears practice applying those prototypes to performance in real-world settings is generally valuable (Kaufman & Baer, 2006).

What should be recognized in this regard, however, is that practice applying case-based knowledge or associated strategies and organizing principles need not necessarily involve actual real-world experiences. For example, Shipman et al.'s (2010) findings with regard to forecasting—for example, forecasting the effects of changing causes or forecasting the effects of changing actors—might provide one set of problems that would provide people with practice in applying case-based knowledge. Another approach that might be used in leadership education, especially when working with experienced leaders, is to have leaders describe and discuss case prototypes, major exceptions to this prototype, and strategies by which they worked with this case-based knowledge in problem-solving. In fact, Avolio, Reichard, Hannah, Walumbwa, and Chan (2009) and Yukl (2010) have provided evidence indicating that discussion of cases and case attributes provides another potentially viable approach for supplying people with practice in applying case-based knowledge. Still another classroom approach that might be employed is to ask students to participate in classroom exercises where feedback with regard to peers, or instructors, is given concerning their use of cases, case organization, and strategies (Taggar, 2002).

Of course, other techniques might be proposed and prove effective in encouraging students to apply case-based knowledge in leadership education. What should be recognized here, however, is that it is critical that leader education include a set of low-fidelity simulation exercises (Motowidlo, Dunnette, & Carter, 1990) that allow for application of cases, strategies, and organizing structures. What is critical in these low-fidelity simulations is that they are structured in such a way that feedback can be provided concerning application of cases, case content, analytic strategies, and case organization (Goldstein & Ford, 2002). Thus in case exercises the issue at hand is not overall performance but rather effective application of case-based knowledge.

Our foregoing observations are noteworthy because they point to some conclusions that might arise from another technique that has been used to encourage application of case-based knowledge. More specifically, leaders might be asked to apply case-based knowledge in addressing real-world problems arising on their jobs. Although this kind of real-world intervention strategy might prove attractive, in part, because it demonstrates the utility of education, it is likely to prove problematic for two reasons. First, people do not analyze cases, case content, strategies, and case organization as they act in the real world (Gollwitzer, 1999)—thereby undermining learning. Second, when asked to apply cases in real-world settings people typically apply only poorly mastered prototypes focusing on prototypic cases that seem relevant to achieving stated goals (Nutt, 1984). Both of these trends will undermine case-based learning in real-world settings. However, it is possible that these trends might be offset by coaching or after action reviews where the actions taken in the real world are treated as case-events to be analyzed with respect to prototypicality, content, strategy, and organization (Mumford et al., 2007). Typically, such after-action reviews will prove most effective when they are systematic and facilitated by experts in leadership education.

Conclusions

In the present effort, we have presented an argument that the type of knowledge used by leaders in solving the problems they are presented with is case-based, or experiential, knowledge (Mumford et al., 2007). Case-based, or experiential, knowledge allows leaders to make sense of complex, unfolding situations, understand the expectations of followers, and formulate viable visions (Strange & Mumford, 2005). Recognition of leaders' reliance on case-based knowledge has led cases to be widely employed leader education.

Cases are, by virtue of their realism, engaging to those being prepared for positions of leadership (Goldstein & Ford, 2002). By the same token, however, case-based knowledge, although readily acquired, is complex (Hammond, 1990). The complex nature of case-based knowledge, in turn, makes the use of cases in leader education an unusually difficult method of instruction. It is not enough simply to present, or encourage students to discuss, a case. Rather, prototypic cases and key exceptions must be presented. The diagnostics marking the relevance of these cases must be noted. The cases must be presented in such a way as to build organized knowledge structures. Those being educated for leadership positions must also be provided with strategies that will allow them to work with certain types of information embedded in cases. And, they must be provided with practice and feedback in applying these cases in solving leadership problems.

At a global level, these conclusions seem difficult to debate. However, our foregoing observations also point to a number of ambiguities that surround application of cases in leader education. For example, what are the merits of stressing causes as opposed to restrictions as opposed to actors and actor capabilities in leadership education? How much emphasis should be given to providing leaders with exceptions to case prototypes? How should prototypic cases be identified? And, what strategies will prove most useful for leaders operating at different levels for applying case-based knowledge?

What should be recognized here is that with regard to these, and a number of other questions, a strong body of evidence is not available to guide the development and application of cases in leadership education. At one level, this observation suggests we need a more systematic stream of research examining how cases should be presented in leadership education. At another level, these observations suggest we need to take a more systematic approach in developing the cases we apply in leader education. We hope that the present effort will serve as an impetus for future work, both laboratory and classroom work, intended to provide a more in-depth understanding of how cases should be applied in leadership education. We believe that such work will prove of critical importance, in part, because case-based knowledge provides the foundation for leaders thinking about the critical, complex problems they will be presented with as they seek to advance our institutions and our world.

References

Avolio, B. J., Reichard, R. J., Hannah, S. T., Walumbwa, F. O., & Chan, A. (2009). A meta-analytic review of leadership impact research: Experimental and quasi-experimental studies. *The Leadership Quarterly*, *20*, 764–784.

Barrett, J. D., Vasey, W. B., & Mumford, M. D. (2011). Getting leaders to think: Effects of training, threat, and pressure of performance. *The Leadership Quarterly, 22, 729–750.*

Berger, C. R., & Jordan, J. M. (1992). Planning sources, planning difficulty, and verbal fluency. *Communication Monographs, 59,* 130–148.

Bligh, M. C., Kohles, J. C., & Meindl, J. R. (2004). Charisma under crisis: Presidential leadership, rhetoric, and media responses before and after the September 11th terrorist attacks. *The Leadership Quarterly, 15,* 211–239.

Bluck, S. (2003). Autobiographical memory: Exploring its functions in everyday life. *Memory, 11,* 113–123.

Bluedorn, A. C., Johnson, R. A., Cartwright, D. K., & Barringer, B. R. (1994). The interface and convergence of the strategic management and organizational environment domains. *Journal of Management, 20,* 201–263.

Connelly, M. S., Gilbert, J. A., Zaccaro, S. J., Threlfall, K. V., Marks, M. A., & Mumford, M. D. (2000). Exploring the relationship of leadership skills and knowledge to leader performance. *The Leadership Quarterly, 11,* 65–86.

Côté, S., Lopes, P. N., Salovey, P., & Miners, C. (2010). Emotional intelligence and leadership emergence in small groups. *Leadership Quarterly, 21,* 409–508.

Dailey, L., & Mumford, M. D. (2006). Evaluative aspects of creative thought: Errors in appraising the implications of new ideas. *Creativity Research Journal, 18,* 367–384.

Doerner, D., & Schaub, H. (1994). Errors in planning and decision making and the nature of human information processing. *Applied-Psychology: An International Review, 43,* 433–453.

Drazin, R., Glynn, M. A., & Kazanjian, R. K. (1999). Multi-level theorizing about creativity in organizations: A sensemaking perspective. *Academy of Management Review, 24,* 286–329.

Dvir, T., Eden, D., Avolio, B. J., & Shamir, B. (1999). Impact of transformational leadership on follower development and performance: A field experiment. *Academy of Management Journal, 45,* 735–744.

Ericsson, K. A., & Charness, W. (1994). Expert performance: Its structure and acquisition. *American Psychologist, 49,* 725–747.

Gioia, D. A., & Thomas, J. B. (1996) Institutional identity, image, and issue interpretation: Sensemaking during strategic change in academia. *Administrative Science Quarterly, 41,* 370–403.

Goldstein, I.L., & Ford, J.K. (2002). *Training in organizations.* Belmont, CA: Wadsworth.

Gollwitzer, P. M. (1999). Implementation intentions: Strong effects of simple plans. *American Psychologist, 54,* 493–523.

Habermas, T., & Bluck, S. (2000). Getting a life: The emergence of the life story in adolescence. *Psychological Bulletin, 126,* 748–771.

Halverson, S. E., Holladay, C. C., Kazma, S. M., & Quinones, M. A. (2004). Self-sacrificial behavior in crisis situations: The competing roles of behavioral and situational factors. *The Leadership Quarterly, 15,* 211–240.

Hammond, K. J. (1990). Case-based planning: A framework for planning from experience. *Cognitive Science, 14,* 385–443.

Hedlund, J., Forsythe, G. B., Horvath, J. A., Williams, W. M., Snook, S., & Sternberg, R. J. (2003). Identifying and assessing tacit knowledge: Understanding the practical intelligence of military leaders. *The Leadership Quarterly, 14,* 117–142.

Hershey, D. A., Walsh, D. A., Read, S. J., & Chulef, A. S. (1990). Effects of expertise on financial problem-solving: Evidence for goal-directed, problem-solving scripts. *Organizational Behavior and Human Decision Processes, 46,* 77–101.

Hmelo-Silver, C. E., & Pfeffer, M. G. (2004). Comparing expert and novice understanding of a complex system from the perspective of structures, behaviors, and functions. *Cognitive Science, 28,* 127–138.

Holyoak, K. J., & Thagard, P. (1997). The analogical mind. *American Psychologist, 52,* 35–44.

Hunt, J. G. (2004). Consideration and structure. In J. M. Burns, G. R. Goethals, & L. Sorenson (Eds.), *Encyclopedia of leadership* (pp. 196–204). Great Barrington, Massachusetts: Berkshire/Sage.

Hunt, J. G., Boal, K. B., & Dodge, G. E. (1999). The effects of visionary and crisis-responsive charisma on followers: An experimental examination of two kinds of charismatic leadership. *The Leadership Quarterly, 10,* 423–448.

Hunter, S. T., Bedell-Avers, K. E., Ligon, G. S., Hunsicker, C. M., & Mumford, M. D. (2008). Applying multiple knowledge structures in creative thought: Effects on idea generation and problem-solving. *Creativity Research Journal, 20,* 137–154.

Isenberg, D. J. (1986). Thinking and managing: A verbal protocol analysis of managerial problem solving. *Academy of Management Journal, 29,* 775–788.

Jacobs, T. O., & Jaques, E. (1991). Executive leadership. In R. Gal & D. A. Mangelsdorff (Eds.), *Handbook of military psychology.* Oxford, England: John Wiley & Sons.

Jacobs, T. O., & Lewis, P. (1992). Leadership requirements in stratified systems. In R. L. Phillips & J. G. Hunt (Eds.), *Strategic leadership: A multiorganizational-level perspective* (pp. 15–25). Westport, CT: Quorum Books.

Kaizer, C., & Shore, B. M. (1995). Strategy flexibility in more and less competent students on mathematical word problems. *Creativity Research Journal, 8,* 77–82.

Kaufman, J. C., & Baer, J. (2006). *Creativity and reason in cognitive development.* New York: Cambridge University Press.

Kolodner, J. L. (1997). Educational implications of analogy: A view from case-based reasoning. *American Psychologist, 52,* 57–66.

Langholtz, H., Gettys, C., & Foote, B. (1995). Are resource fluctuation anticipated in resource allocation tasks. *Organizational Behavior and Human Decision Processes, 64,* 274–282.

Ligon, G. M., Hunter, S. T., & Mumford, M. D. (2008). Development of outstanding leadership: A life narrative approach. *The Leadership Quarterly, 19,* 312–334.

Lord, R. G., & Hall, R. J. (2005). Identity, deep structure and the development of leadership skill. *The Leadership Quarterly, 16,* 591–615.

Lord, R. G., & Maher, K. J. (1990). Alternative information-processing models and their implications for theory, research, and practice. *Academy of Management Review, 15,* 9–28.

Manz, C. C., & Sims, H. P., Jr. (1981). Vicarious learning: The influence of modeling on organizational behavior. *Academy of Management Review, 6,* 105–113.

Marcy, R. A., & Mumford, M. D. (2010). Leader cognition: Improving leader performance through causal analysis. *The Leadership Quarterly, 21,* 1–19.

Marcy, R. T., & Mumford, M. D. (2007). Social innovation: Enhancing creative performance through casual analysis. *Creativity Research Journal, 19,* 123–140.

Mobley, M. I., Doares, L., & Mumford, M. D. (1992). Process analytic models of creative capacities: Evidence for the combination and reorganization process. *Creativity Research Journal, 5,* 125–156.

Motowidlo, S. J., Dunnette, M. D., & Carter, G. W. (1990). An alternative selection procedure: The low-fidelity simulation. *Journal of Applied Psychology, 75,* 640–647.

Mumford, M. D., Blair, C., Dailey, L., Lertiz, L. E., & Osburn, H. K. (2006). Errors in creative thought? Cognitive biases in a complex processing activity. *The Journal of Creative Behavior, 40,* 75–109.

Mumford, M. D., Friedrich, T. L., Caughron, J. J., & Antes, A. L. (2009). Leadership development and assessment: Rethinking the state of the art. In K.A. Ericsson (Ed.), *The development of professional expertise: Toward the measurement of expert performance and design of optimal learning environments* (pp. 84–107). Cambridge, UK: Cambridge University Press.

Mumford, M. D., Friedrich, T. L., Caughron, J. J., & Byrne, C. E. (2007a). Leader cognition in real-world settings: How do leaders think about crises? *The Leadership Quarterly, 18,* 515–543.

Mumford, M. D., Marks, M. A., Connelly, M. S., Zaccaro, S. J., & Reiter-Palmon, R. (2000). Development of leadership skills: Experience, timing, and growth. *The Leadership Quarterly, 11,* 87–114.

Mumford, M. D., Schultz, R. A., & Osburn, H. K. (2002). Planning in organizations: Performance as a multi-level phenomenon. In F. J. Yammarino & F. Dansereau (Eds.), *Research in multi-level issues: The many faces of multi-level issues* (pp. 3–63). Oxford, England: Elsevier.

Mumford, M. D., & Van Doorn, J. R. (2001). The leadership of pragmatism: Reconsidering Franklin in the age of charisma. *The Leadership Quarterly*, *12*, 279–310.

Mumford, M. D., Zaccaro, S. J., Harding, F. D., Jacobs, T. O., & Fleishman, E. A. (2000). Leadership skills for a changing world: Solving complex social problems. *The Leadership Quarterly, 11*, 11–35.

Mumford,T. V., Campion, M. A., & Morgeson, F. P. (2007). The leadership skills strataplex: Leadership skill requirements across organizational levels. *The Leadership Quarterly, 18*, 154–166.

Noice, H. (1991). The role of explanations and plan recognition in the learning of theatrical scripts. *Cognitive Science, 15*, 425–460.

Nutt, P. (1984). Types of organizational decision processes. *Administrative Science Quarterly, 29*, 414–450.

O'Connor, G. C. (1998). Market learning and radical innovation: A cross case comparison of eight radical innovation projects. *Journal of Product Innovation Management, 15*, 151–166.

Patalano, A. L., & Siefert, C. M. (1997). Opportunistic planning: Being reminded of pending goals. *Cognitive Psychology, 34*, 1–36.

Reeves, L., & Weisberg, R. W. (1994). The role of content and abstract information in analogical transfer. *Psychological Bulletin, 115*, 381–400.

Scott, G. M., Lonergan, D. C., & Mumford, M. D. (2005). Conceptual combination: Alternative knowledge structures, alternative heuristics. *Creativity Research Journal, 17*, 79–98.

Shipman, A. S., Byrne, C. L., & Mumford, M. D. (2010). Leader vision formation and forecasting: The effects of forecasting extent, resources, and timeframe. *The Leadership Quarterly, 21*, 439–456.

Sims, H. P., Jr., & Lorenzi, P. (1992). *The new leadership paradigm: Social learning and cognition in organizations.* Newbury Park, CA: Sage.

Strange, J. M., & Mumford, M. D. (2005). The origins of vision: Effects of reflection, models, and analysis. *The Leadership Quarterly*, *16*, 121–148.

Taggar, S. (2002). Individual creativity and group ability to utilize individual creative resources: A multilevel model. *The Academy of Management Journal, 45*, 315–330.

Thomas, J. B., & McDaniel, R. R. (1990). Interpreting strategic issues: Effects of strategy and the information–processing structure of top management teams. *The Academy of Management Journal, 33*, 286–306.

Vessey, W. B., Barrett, J., & Mumford, M. D. (in press). Leader cognition under conditions of threat: "Just the facts." *The Leadership Quarterly.*

Vroom, V. H., & Jago, A. G. (1988). *The new leadership: Managing participation in organizations.* Englewood Cliffs, NJ: Prentice–Hall.

Weick, K. E. (1995). *Sensemaking in organizations.* London: Sage.

Xiao, Y., Milgram, P., & Doyle, D. J. (1997). Planning behavior and its functional role in interactions with complex systems. *IEEE Transactions on Systems, Man and Cybernetics, Part A: Systems and Humans, 27*, 313–324.

Yukl, G. (2010). *Leadership in organizations* (7th ed.). Upper Saddle River, NJ: Prentice Hall.

Acknowledgments

We would like to thank Jerry Hunt, Tamara Friedrich, Jay Caughron, and Alison Antes for their contributions to the present effort. Correspondence should be addressed to Dr. Michael D. Mumford, Department of Psychology, The University of Oklahoma, Norman, Oklahoma, 73109 or mmumford @ou.edu.

3

BECOMING LEADERSHIP LITERATE

A Core Curriculum

◆ Barbara Kellerman
Harvard Kennedy School of Government

The chapter describes a new approach to teaching leadership that draws on old insights. The approach is grounded in the tradition of the liberal arts and derives its content from classic texts that treat the topic of leadership. More particularly, the chapter describes a course developed at the Harvard Kennedy School of Government (and since also taught to Dartmouth College undergraduates) titled "Leadership Literacy." It is designed to give students a fundamental familiarity with timeless and seminal texts on power, authority, and influence. These texts constitute a leadership canon. The discussion is embedded in the larger debate about what it is that leaders need to know. The position here is (1) that there is in fact a great leadership literature, (2) that this body of work lends a necessary heft and depth to the field of Leadership Studies, and (3) that it can and should constitute a core curriculum for all serious leader learners.

❖❖❖

The field of leadership does not suffer a dearth of pedagogical pointers. As is pointed out elsewhere in this volume, the interest in learning leadership has exploded in the last few decades and along with it has come a similar explosion of related books, articles, and other artifacts.

Notwithstanding this flood of recent resources, it seems clear even now that relatively few of the written works will stand the test of time. Relatively few will prove so significant, and so obviously universal in their application, that fifty years from now they still will be read.

What does this say about the field per se, about Leadership Studies? Does this mean that there are no leadership classics? Is there no body of great leadership literature that could reasonably be said to constitute a core curriculum for anyone, anywhere, at any level, with any interest in leadership?

These are the questions to which for the last decade or so I sought an answer. These are the questions to which I finally responded by developing a course at the Harvard Kennedy School titled "Leadership Literacy." These are the questions that led to my most recent book, *Leadership: Essential Selections on Power, Authority, and Influence*. And these are the questions that I will address in this chapter, in four successive sections: Context, Concept, Content, and Conclusion.

Context

The Harvard Kennedy School is a graduate school that is considered to be, and considers itself to be, a professional school. As the current dean, David Ellwood, put it, the School's mission is to "train enlightened public leaders and generate ideas that provide solutions to our most challenging public problems." So far as leadership is concerned, then, the School is seen as a training ground that develops public leaders and prepares them for the tasks that lie ahead. As a result of this emphasis on the practice of leadership and management, a high percentage of Kennedy School students take courses explicitly directed toward this goal. In fact, during the last decade, after the School established its Center for Public Leadership, the popularity of such courses increased exponentially.

For obvious (and some not so obvious) reasons, most students are interested primarily in those classroom experiences that promise to provide skills and knowledge that teach how to lead. Overwhelmingly, in other words, in keeping with the temper of the times, students are keen on *being* and *doing*, on learning the professional practice of leadership, and on securing answers to what they consider the significant questions: (1) Who exactly am I at this point in my life? (2) Why exactly should I create change? And, (3) How exactly do I create change—how can I lead? Their passion is not, in other words, for *knowing*—for knowing leadership theory, or leadership research, or leadership as the stuff of, for example, history, philosophy, sociology, not to speak of leadership as a literary exercise. Nor, I might add, are students interested in any obvious way in leadership as being, equally, about followership.

So I had a dilemma. The longer I was involved with leadership in the confines of the academy, the more persuaded I was that it was important to provide the sense that there was a "there" there. It was important to convey to various audiences first that the interest in leadership should be viewed not merely as a passing fad or fancy, and second that the field per se was other than trivial or superficial. Rather, leadership and followership have and always have been of critical importance to the course of human history, and as a subject of study it does have a center, a core curriculum that testifies to its coherence in matters of dominance and deference.

Who exactly were the audiences that I sought to address? Broadly speaking, they can be divided into two groups: external and internal. The external audience includes skeptics, such as those in academe, who more often than not, even now, remain less than fully persuaded—to put it politely—that Leadership Studies is a serious field of study, one worthy of being included in graduate or undergraduate curricula. The external group further includes clients, customers of various sorts, who buy what those of us in the leadership field (elsewhere I call it the leadership industry) have to sell. They range from young students to senior executives, who deserve to be certain that what we do is legitimate, worth their time and money. My claim is simply this: that what we do is defensible at least in part because our work is intellectually grounded. It is grounded in a body of work—the leadership canon—that does, or should, constitute a core curriculum.

The internal audience consists of those of us in leadership who occasionally question the rigor and coherence of the work we undertake. Signs of uncertainty are everywhere, including in the proposal for the present book, which stated frankly that, "Unfortunately, unlike some of the more well-established disciplines, there are few institutional resources available to support [leadership] teachers whose academic homes are widely scattered across traditional disciplinary boundaries." In other words, in addition to the more obvious concerns associated with teaching leadership, such as inadequate evaluation of what we do, the lack of an intellectual center or academic core continues to be a significant problem. It troubles those on the outside—and some of us on the inside as well.

It's fair to say, then, that the course I titled "Leadership Literacy" was intended to address a theoretical problem, notwithstanding the practical context within which I was manifestly embedded. Put another way, notwithstanding the practical, professional context within which I was embedded—or perhaps precisely *because* of it—I set out to develop a learning experience that was *other* than obviously practical and professional. I set out to develop a course in the tradition of the liberal arts that contributed to leadership learning not directly but *in*directly. In support of this contrarian approach, I turn to Stanley Fish, an esteemed academic gadfly, who insists that "higher education, properly understood, is distinguished by the *absence* [italics mine] of a direct and designed relationship between its activities and measurable effects in the world."

It turns out—and I myself was not certain at the start—that there *is* a great leadership literature. There is a great literature *about* leadership. There is a great literature that is, itself, an *act* of leadership. And there is a great literature, intended originally to be read aloud, generated by *leaders themselves.* I should add that I use the word *literature* expansively; not every great leadership text is a literary masterpiece. Many foundational texts in the social sciences and humanities belong in this leadership canon.

What I could not know until the waters were tested is whether anyone would be interested. Would students at the Harvard Kennedy School, who came in large numbers to be "trained" as leaders, have an interest in exploring leadership as an area of intellectual inquiry? Would students be willing to invest their time in studying leadership qua leadership, "in the absence of a direct and designed relationship" between what they did in the classroom and what they did outside? As I asked elsewhere: "If you want to be a real-world leader, what's the point of Plato? If you want to be a twenty-first-century leader, why consider Elizabeth I? If you want to be a business leader, why take time with Gandhi? Or for that matter, if you want to be a political leader, why invest as much as a minute in Mary Parker Follett?"

In the beginning, the numbers were small. The first time I offered Leadership Literacy only a few students showed up—sixteen, as I recall. But then the numbers grew and as time went on the course became popular, freely selected by intellectually curious students who had nothing that was obviously professional to gain from taking a course that was in no obvious way about their being or becoming a leader. (Of course, my contention is that Leadership Literacy is all about being and becoming a leader, though the connection is other than obvious. It's Fish-like.) Let me be clear: At the Harvard Kennedy School, Leadership Literacy is an elective that students select from a sea of other courses, many of which are required. So the number of students who choose to take Leadership Literacy has never been huge. But in a world where size matters (the more students faculty attract, the more generally they are rewarded), it's worth pointing out that there is a considerable market for a leadership course that is, more than anything else, about the life of the mind.

Moreover, there is a market for a course of this type among a very different student population. In Fall 2010 I was Visiting Professor of Leadership at Dartmouth where I taught a similar course based on Leadership Literacy to undergraduates. (At Dartmouth the course was titled "Foundations of Leadership—and Followership.") Some sixty students enrolled and, based on my observations, were overwhelmingly satisfied and grateful for a place to play with ideas about being powerful and powerless.

Concept

The question with which I began to develop the course was, "What do leaders need to know?" For that matter, "What do any of us need to know?" What, in other words, in this day and age is the mark of a good education?

The answers are not immediately apparent. In fact, the subject is now and arguably always has been a bone of contention. There never was widespread agreement on what we should learn and how. Nor is there current agreement on what should be the purpose, not to speak of content, of higher education in the twenty-first century. Broadly speaking, on the one side are those who favor the traditional liberal arts: those who believe that in the present as in the past it is the liberal arts that undergird a good education. On the other side are those who insist (especially when jobs—good ones—seem scarce) that twenty-first-century learning needs to be more purely practical. They argue that undergraduates stand to benefit more from taking a course in, say, accounting as opposed to Aristotle, in budgeting as opposed to Bach. Given the seriousness of this divide, and the new skepticism about the old virtues and verities, traditionalists are on the defensive. Even Drew Gilpin Faust, president of Harvard, has felt obliged to defend the benefits of a liberal arts education, which at the undergraduate level is what Harvard does best. "Human beings," she said, "need meaning, understanding, and perspective, as well as jobs." (Incidentally, Faust's point is not one that has to be made to adult learners. Continuing education courses that focus on the arts and humanities are thriving, experiencing growing enrollments even in [because of?] hard times.)

So far as learning leadership is concerned, it is nothing if not in keeping with the temper of the times. As I wrote in *LEADERSHIP: Essential Selections on Power, Authority, and Influence,* in the main, "twenty-first-century leadership education and development are about practice, not theory; about the present, not the past; about prose, not poetry; about evaluation, not meditation; about the real world, not the world of the imagination. Put directly, twenty-first-century leadership learning excludes the liberal arts almost entirely . . . in favor of a focus on a practical purpose."

The course, Leadership Literacy, is, then, a glaring exception to the general rule which, particularly at the graduate level, favors the specialist over the generalist. It is a throwback, if you will, to a time when the mark of a good education included at least some familiarity with great works of literature, particularly such great works as pertained directly to the learner's area of endeavor. What I am describing, in short, is a course intended for those with an intellectual curiosity about leadership and followership, whether or not they are, or intend to become, leaders themselves.

Think of it this way. The idea of this particular learning experience is to familiarize students with the great literature on power, authority, and influence. In other words, I include in the course classics whose content contributes (1) to an intellectual understanding of leadership and followership and (2) to the exercise of leadership, indirectly if not directly. But there is an additional benefit. The great literature on leadership is extraordinary not only because of *what* is written, but, sometimes, because of *how* it is written. Put directly, more often than not, the great leadership literature is, of itself, great *literature*.

When I first started teaching the course the syllabus was long—too long. I could not bring myself to exclude works I deemed classics of the genre. But, over time, I understood the need for pruning, both for the sake of the students and for the collection that now stands as a book. So, inevitably, the question arose: How to decide what to put in and what to leave out?

First I had to settle the issue of what exactly constituted a leadership classic. Was it enough to define the work simply as seminal, as timeless and transcendent? Or was there more to be said? More often than not great works of literature—or what once were considered great works of literature—end in the dustbin of history. Times change and so do our conceptions of what matters most. In nineteenth-century America, for example, the classics were generally Greek and Roman in origin. One hundred years later we have exiled these texts to the rough equivalent of academic Siberia. Now our ideas about what constitutes a classic are increasingly expansive and elastic: We aim to encompass a diverse range of peoples and cultures.

Thus the course (and the book) consists of classics as the word *classic* has come to be used today. First, every selection is about leadership, or is itself an act of leadership. Second, every selection has literary value, as literary value is currently conceived. Third, every selection is seminal: It changed how we think and what we do (or did). Finally, every selection is transcendent. That is, it transcends time and place. While some selections go back thousands of years, even the newest of the lot have already stood the test of time—they are at least a quarter century old. And they are from anywhere and everywhere, from America and Africa, Asia and Europe.

Of course, the great leadership literature is transcendent in still another way. It ignores conventional disciplinary boundaries as if they never even existed. The works that comprise this particular core curriculum emanate from history and politics, from psychology and sociology, from philosophy and fiction, from science and biography. Small wonder that they result in a panoply of big ideas, grand themes, and impossible dreams, that include but are not limited to the following:

1. *The importance of leadership instruction.* Confucius, Plato, Machiavelli, and W. E. B. du Bois, for example, all shared an interest in the question of how to teach how to lead.
2. *The importance of human nature.* What you think of leadership, and followership, depends on what you think of the human condition.
3. *The role of rage.* Some of the greatest leadership literature ever was fuelled by fury. The rage was at the status quo, and the purpose of the text was to incite change.
4. *The rise of the follower.* It is impossible to read the great leadership literature without being struck by the increasing importance of the powerless, and the decreasing importance of the powerful. Since the Enlightenment and the rise of democracy, the trend has been nearly everywhere in evidence, at least in the West.
5. *The power of the big idea.* The great leadership literature suggests the

most influential of all leaders are intellectual leaders—men and women willing and able first to conceive of, and then to convey, the right idea at the right time.

6. *The power of the pen.* Pens are potent. Words are weapons. Language matters.

Finally, a few lines on what was left out: What is the great leadership literature that I now omit from the course? And what is the great leadership literature that I cut, invariably reluctantly, from the book based on the course? To address the second question first: For reasons of space I cut from the book leadership literature that was imagined rather than real. (An excerpt from Tolstoy's *War and Peace* is the exception to the general rule.) Perhaps the most obvious example is Shakespeare, who is the supreme poet of power; an authority on authority, particularly authority associated with or derived from royalty; and an expert on influence, especially behind the scenes influence exerted by those who are weaker on those who are stronger. For reasons of taste I cut from the book leadership literature widely regarded as outrageously offensive—such as Adolph Hitler's *Mein Kampf.* (I do, however, continue to use Shakespeare in the classroom, and I do continue to assign sections of *Mein Kampf.*)

The content of the course is another matter. Rather than identify what I now omit from the list of required readings, let me say simply that the syllabus for Leadership Literacy is fungible, easily adaptable to different teachers and different students in different places. My own syllabus for the course is posted on my Harvard website. But it is not etched in stone. The material, while exalted, should not intimidate. The great leadership literature is so rich and variegated that any given syllabus should be considered a work in progress, easy to adapt as ideas form and the impulse arises. The point is to assemble classics of the genre: Exactly which classics should constitute the course is, and should be, left to the individual instructor to decide.

Content

Whatever the content of the course, the materials should be organized at the pleasure of the instructor. That said, there are, nevertheless, two obvious ways to arrange the materials. The first is chronologically, which is how I proceed, at least in the classroom. I trace the history of ideas as this history unfolded. The arc of history matters much in this case, if only, again, because it makes crystal clear that power and influence have devolved over time, away from leaders and toward followers.

A course based on Leadership Literacy can also be divided thematically. This is the way the book is organized. I divided the readings into three parts, each arranged chronologically. Part I is "About Leadership" and contains selections on dominance, deference, and governance; and power, authority, and influence. Examples include readings from Plato, Machiavelli, and Hannah Arendt. Part II is "Literature as Leadership" and offers selections that were intended to be, of themselves, acts of leadership. I include in this category works such as Thomas Paine's *Common Sense* and Betty Friedan's *The Feminine Mystique.* Finally, Part III—"Leaders in Action"—contains selections from leaders who communicated with their followers in so meaningful and memorable a way that their words will live forever. Examples include Abraham Lincoln's address at Gettysburg, Winston Churchill's speeches to the House of Commons (particularly in the years immediately preceding the Second World War), and Martin Luther King Jr.'s epistle to the American people from the cell of a Birmingham jail.

Incidentally, grouping the readings thematically (as I do in the book), as opposed to chronologically (as I do in the classroom), makes it apparent that the works are similar (and different) in ways that are—to understate it—surprising. For instance, though we never conceive of them as being in any way related, in fact both Plato (*Republic*) and Freud (*Moses and Monotheism*) were fascinated by tyrants. As a result, both wrote about them at some length, presumably with an eye to understanding how exactly they led, and why exactly we followed. Similarly, Elizabeth Cady Stanton (*Declaration of Sentiments*) and Rachel Carson (*Silent Spring*) were driven by the same strong desire to change the world, and so both wrote what turned out to be classics of the leadership literature. Both were, in other words, simultaneously writers and leaders.

No matter how the syllabus is organized, the content of the course leads to rich conversation about the human condition. The materials prompt questions such as these: Is it better for leaders to be loved or feared? What is the role of the great man (or, occasionally, woman) in history? How should leaders conduct themselves in democratic societies? What is effective leadership in large organizations? How do you make a revolution? Are leaders inevitable? Why do followers follow? How do the powerless become the powerful? Should violence ever play a part in the creation of change? When to turn to nonviolence? How to lead from the bottom up? What does it mean to lead wisely and well?

This leads to the question of how best to harness the conversation. How can we teach Leadership Legacy most effectively—beyond using the classics as grist for the mill?

As I conceive of it, the great leadership literature should be the heart of the course. It should be reveled in, read aloud, and constitute the core of the conversation. Why assign *The Communist Manifesto* only to leave the *Manifesto* behind? At the same time the instructor should situate each of these works in their larger context, in their time and place, and each of these works should be similarly accompanied by some sort of analysis or comment. My book offers suggestions for interpretation. In *LEADERSHIP: Essential Selections*, each excerpt is preceded by an introductory note, and each is succeeded by a critical comment. In addition to being learning aides, they are intended to be teaching aides.

It also helps to provide students with a brief handout at the start of each class that serves as an outline or guide for that particular class session. To allow additional time for reflection, these might be posted on the Web in advance. Here are some examples in shorthand only to show the way. The material that follows is organized chronologically. All the readings are in the book as well as in the syllabus, save Shakespeare and Hitler.

CONFUCIUS—ANALECTS

- Simon Leys: "No book in the entire history of the world has exerted, over a longer period of time, a greater influence on a larger number of people than this slim little volume."
- Confucius describes the good leader: self-aware, self-critical, and willing to self-correct
- Confucius asks—What is a good follower?

PLATO—THE REPUBLIC

- Plato as a teacher of leaders
- Plato as a romantic who imagines the leader as a philosopher-king
- Plato as a realist who fears the leader as a tyrant

MACHIAVELLI—THE PRINCE

- Personal history as prologue to political thought
- God and man in sixteenth-century Europe
- "A prince," Machiavelli wrote, "cannot afford to cultivate attributes for

which men are considered good." Does this apply to leadership in the twenty-first century? If yes, how so? If not, why not?

WILLIAM SHAKESPEARE—JULIUS CAESAR *(THE PLAY, THE FILM)*

- Who is the leading protagonist and why?
- Who are the most important followers and what part do they play in the proceedings?
- The use of language in the funeral scene, in which Brutus and Antony vie for the support of the crowd

QUEEN ELIZABETH I—SPEECH TO THE TROOPS AT TILBURY

- On being a woman leader in a man's world
- On using speech to incite for war, and prepare for death
- On dressing for the occasion; leadership as performance art

THOMAS PAINE—COMMON SENSE

- The impact of the Enlightenment on American revolutionists
- On overthrowing the old leadership cadre and installing a new one
- The writer as a leader

THOMAS CARLYLE—ON HEROES, HERO-WORSHIP, AND THE HEROIC IN HISTORY

- The hero in history
- The hero as prince, prophet, poet, and priest
- Carlyle's antagonists (including Tolstoy)—and the leader attribution error

KARL MARX AND FRIEDRICH ENGELS—THE COMMUNIST MANIFESTO

- The *Manifesto* as a work of literature
- The *Manifesto* as a revolutionary treatise
- The impact of the *Manifesto* on twentieth-century history—and the *Black Book of Communism*

ELIZABETH CADY STANTON—DECLARATION OF SENTIMENTS

- Women charge men with a long list of grievances
- They include, "He has endeavored, in every way that he could, to destroy her confidence in her own powers, to lessen her self-respect, and to make her willing to lead a dependent and abject life."
- From proselytizing for social change to leading a political movement

JOHN STUART MILL—ON LIBERTY

- Witness the decline of the leader
- Witness the rise of the follower
- Worry about tyranny of the majority

MAHATMA GANDHI—WHAT SATYAGRAHA IS (AND OTHERS)

- The powerless take on the powerful
- Differences among nonviolence, passive resistance, and civil disobedience
- Gandhi's legacy—especially as bequeathed to Martin Luther King Jr.

FREUD—MOSES AND MONOTHEISM *(AND OTHERS)*

- Freud as seminal psychologist—and as political philosopher
- The leader as father figure
- The followers and their "thirst for obedience"

ADOLPH HITLER—MEIN KAMPF *(MY STRUGGLE)*

- The power of propaganda
- The Jew as vermin
- National Socialism as Utopian dream

MARY PARKER FOLLETT—THE ESSENTIALS OF LEADERSHIP

- "Of the greatest importance" is the leader's "ability to grasp a total situation"
- On leading large organizations, corporations
- Followers should not "merely . . . follow." They should, with the encouragement and support of the leader, play an active part in the proceedings.

MARTIN LUTHER KING JR.—LETTER FROM BIRMINGHAM JAIL

- The rights revolutions of the 1960s and 1970s
- The leader as jailbird—with a golden pen
- The leader as conciliator—and freedom fighter

NELSON MANDELA—I AM PREPARED TO DIE

- Diehards: followers who lead, or the last shall be first
- On being nonviolent, and then turning violent
- The leader as martyr

STANLEY MILGRAM—OBEDIENCE TO AUTHORITY

- Obedience when obedience is a crime
- The significance, usually underestimated, of context
- On genocide

SAUL ALINSKY—RULES FOR RADICALS

- Power to the People
- The virtues of community organizing—but who organizes the organizers?
- Alinsky and . . . Obama

PETER SINGER—ANIMAL LIBERATION

- Giving voice to those who cannot speak for themselves
- Moral philosophy as political tool
- *Animal Liberation* as the "bible" of the animal rights movement

LARRY KRAMER—1,112 AND COUNTING

- Leading those who will not speak for themselves; gays in the early days of AIDS
- Language as an offensive weapon
- Crisis as a trigger for leading change

These pointers point to what happens in the classroom: learning *about* leadership, and learning *to* lead, by immersion in the leadership literature.

Conclusion

By now I've taught Leadership Literacy at the Harvard Kennedy School six or seven times, and each time the course has been highly rated by students who elected to take it. I've taught a similar course at Dartmouth to undergraduates. Does this mean that I accomplished what I set out to accomplish? Should any given course, in this case a leadership course, be judged by how well students *like* it or, for that matter, by how well they like the instructor?

The answer to the second of the two questions is, of course, no. However at the Harvard Kennedy School and, I suspect, at most other schools as well, as in most other leadership programs of whatever sort, leadership instruction, and instructors, are judged primarily by criteria that are other than rigorous, and that seem to me to be more about affect than about anything else. (How do I feel about the course? And how do I feel about the instructor?)

To be fair, that's not exactly what the current (2010) evaluation form asks for. Rather the two basic questions posed by the Kennedy School when a course comes to a close are: "How would you rate the course overall?" And "How would you rate the instructor overall?" In addition, students are asked to rank the course according to certain criteria, such as "academic rigor," whether or not the readings were "useful," the "discussions enhanced understanding of the subject material," and so on. Similarly, students are asked to rank instructors on their capacity to offer "insights and new ways of thinking about issues," on their willingness to provide "helpful feedback," and on their accessibility "to students outside of class." These kinds of questions are not unimportant—they say something about the students' learning experience. But how well queries like these assess what was learned or, more precisely, what was learned about how to lead is, at the least, an open question.

I would argue, in fact, that one of the primary problems associated with leader learning is precisely this: how to measure outcomes. Although I was asked by the editors of this book to do so, I cannot honestly say how any of my courses "affect" my students. Nor, in truth, are my "observations" sufficiently keen to determine if my "students think differently" after taking any of my courses than they did before. Maybe they do—they certainly seem to. But maybe after taking one of my courses students act in certain ways and say certain things simply because they want to gratify me, as they want to satisfy themselves. For various reasons they themselves prefer to believe that the learning experience was worthwhile, not a waste. Finally, I cannot comment with certainty on any "changes" students might experience "over the course of the semester," for how can I be sure that whatever the alteration, it is the result of what happened in the classroom, rather than what happened outside?

The bottom line is this. Any leadership course whose outcomes are impossible to quantify, and where students are not tracked years later by a longitudinal evaluation of some sort, is being judged by criteria best described as vague. This brings us back to the liberal arts, and why they in particular are under attack. It is impossible to measure with precision the benefits of a liberal arts education. This does not mean, obviously, that the benefits of such an education are few, or that they are inconsequential. It means only that they are difficult—if not impossible—to pinpoint and to prove.

Drew Faust addressed this very question at Harvard's 2010 Commencement. A liberal arts education, she declared, was "designed to prepare us for life without a script. . . . Since you cannot know what you need to be ready for, we have tried to get you ready for anything." This, I would argue, is *the* perfect description of the twenty-first-century leader: a man or woman who by definition is in a situation without a script, thus one of the virtues of a leadership course grounded in the tradition of the liberal arts, grounded in the great leadership literature that constitutes the leadership canon.

On the one hand, the course I titled Leadership Literacy is complex. How could it not be? After all, we are delving here into some of the greatest of all literatures penned by some of the greatest of all writers on some of the most vexing of all problems. But, on the other hand, the course provides the most basic, even rudimentary, of all learning experiences: reading and rereading timeless texts, here on dominance and deference and the human condition.

Bibliographical Note: As mentioned in the text, the course, Leadership Literacy, led to a book—*LEADERSHIP: Essential Selections on Power, Authority, and Influence* (McGraw-Hill, 2010)—which I edited and for which I provided the introduction and running commentary. In addition to the selections referenced above, the book includes writings of Lao Tsu, Plutarch, Machiavelli, Locke, Spencer, James, Weber, Burns, Milgram, Wollstonecraft, Truth, Lenin, and Havel. However, again, the great leadership literature is expansive. Individual instructors should freely adapt the ideas in this chapter to their particular template.

4

EDUCATING CONTEMPORARY PRINCES AND PRINCESSES FOR POWER

◆ José Luis Alvarez
ESADE Business School

Power, leadership's means of production, is a medium, a currency that exists only in action. If what separates leaders from academics is precisely an orientation to action, the quandary is this: How is a professor to teach a phenomenon so alien to his or her nature? This chapter addresses this question.

I begin by summarizing what classic political scientists have told us about power. I follow by arguing that the teaching of political dynamics should go beyond analytical methodologies, but stop short of experiential, or role-playing, methods; that it should retain a "knowing" approach. I will defend the case method as the best way to develop imagination for action, the faculty of the mind most needed by political actors. Afterwards I propose specific practices for the teaching of power and influence. Finally, I tackle the ethical legitimacy of teaching this topic because today's economic crisis finds its origins not only in financial institutions but also in the character of elites.

❖ ❖ ❖

The challenges of teaching the mustering of political capital and the exercise of influence to contemporary "princes" and "princesses"—found no longer in city states or kingdoms, but in corporations and, increasingly, in nonprofit organizations—are at the crux of the difficulties involved in the development of leaders. For while leadership cannot be reduced to power, power is its main resource and influencing people is its distinctive activity.

Power and influence are strange topics to teach. Power or political capital lacks ontological distinctiveness. Any resource can become political capital as long as it is valued by others. Power is abstract, a medium, a currency that exists only in action (Parsons, 1963b). But if Ortega y Gasset (2005 [1928]) was right when he said that what separates politicians (and executives and leaders, I could add) from intellectuals and professors is precisely the orientation to action, then the pedagogical quandary is the following: How is an academic to teach a phenomenon so alien to his or her nature? This question is the subject of this chapter.

After the next few pages, in which I state my main assumptions on the topic and justify the very existence of courses on power and influence in business schools, this chapter is organized as follows. First, since educating leaders for the mustering of political capital and the exercise of influence has occupied the minds of educators for centuries, I consider it worthwhile to summarize what the creators of political science, from the Renaissance to the Romantic era, have to tell us about the nature of power. Second, drawing on the conclusions of these authors, I argue that methodologies for the teaching of power and influence should go beyond purely cognitive or analytical approaches, but stop short of experiential methods. In other words, they should retain a "knowing" approach. I will argue in favor of the case method as the best pedagogical resource available to develop imagination for action, the faculty of the mind most needed by political actors. Third, although this is a confessedly instructor-dependent course, I make some specific proposals for the design, content, and teaching style of MBA courses on power and influence. I add in this section a few thoughts on the profile of the ideal course instructor.

Finally, I tackle the ethical dimension of teaching power and influence. In pre-Renaissance times, this likely would have been the first issue considered and we probably would have not been allowed to proceed further. Machiavelli liberated us from that precaution, however. In business education, J. Kotter did the same in 1982 with his MBA course "Power and Influence" and book of the same title, which found legitimacy and acclaim while detachedly analyzing the dynamics of political and power structures in organizations. But because today's economic crisis is not just one of finance, but also one of the character of elites, I must revisit this thorny issue and reflect on the appropriateness of the very existence of the course.

The Topic and the Justification for Teaching It to Managers

At the very least, scholars from different disciplines typically agree on the essential function of power. The American political scientist Mansfield (1989) and the Italian sociologist Crespi (1992) coincide in affirming that power arises from the impossibility of drawing action straightforwardly from a normative order. Power is the function that mediates between the general and the particular, between knowledge and action. For these authors power guarantees both the observance of laws and at the same time their modification or infringement, when they are inadequate in particular circumstances. Power is both guarantor and transgressor. This is why hypocrisy is an integral part of politics (Runciman, 2008). The eighteenth-century French essayists knew this so well that they posited the capacity for deception as the essential political skill.

White (2008), a sociologist intent on depicting the production of action in organizations, argues in a similar vein that the function of the leader is precisely to cut through the locked-in expectations created by rules. Power, to be effective in transformational efforts, has to transgress openly, à la Alinsky (1971). And to be effective in evolutionary change it has to operate in a more hidden manner, à la Lindblom (1959) or Wrapp (1984).

But this function of power has to be exercised under such idiosyncratic and unpredictable contingencies that facing *fortuna*, as Machiavelli called the uncertainty generated by the insecurity and confusion of political life, becomes power's phenomenology: the way it is subjectively and intensely experienced by social actors. It is, then, an ideal topic to observe the tension between nomothetic and idiographic research methodologies. The over-determination of politics was expressed by Tip O'Neill (1994) when he famously quipped that "all politics is local"; by Schattschneider (1975) when he acknowledged that the fogginess of politics is analogous to the famous fogginess of war; by Ortega y Gasset (2005 [1928]) when he observed that the more efficient politics in action, the more confusing in definition; and by Foucault (1982) when he said that it is "flat and empirical," a bricolage of *petit faits divers*. In fact, these characteristics apply well to the way senior managers discharge their duties.[1]

The overwhelming impact of politics on the subjectivity of social actors makes the effective exercise of power dependent on a psychological capability that is unevenly distributed across the population. Only a minority of people, the high self-monitors, are equipped with the kind of character that allows them to keep their cool under pressure and amid confusion, permitting them to efficiently influence others.

If, as Roethlisberger (1977) has expressed, human behavior is an "elusive phenomenon," influencing others is the most elusive of its manifestations. This is in part due to the intrinsic difficulties just mentioned and also because knowledge of power has mostly been, until the last century—and with the exceptions noted in the next section—an *arcana imperii*, a distinctive and secret resource of the powerful, a tool for the benefit of those who profit from the status quo. Kotter (1985) and Pfeffer (1992) started from precisely this assumption to justify the teaching of the topic: Let's teach real politics, the Machiavellian "world as it is," to those who do not have power, to the inexperienced, and to the low self-monitors in the hope that career opportunities will be more evenly spread out, organizations more efficient, the world more just.[2]

However, responsible instructors in power and influence have to walk a thin line between, on one side, helping those psychologically less endowed with the coolness and smoothness needed in power plays and, on the other side, infusing with a high purpose those who, in the same classroom, have characters better equipped for the exercise of influence. And this is a tall order because competencies and morality do not necessarily go together. As Yeats (1920) famously said, "the best lack all conviction while the worst / Are full of passionate intensity," while La Bruyère believed that the best and most sensible are always the first to concede, with the result that power is often held by the dogmatic and the crazy.

[1]Whitley (1989) characterizes managerial tasks as (1) highly interdependent, contextual and systemic; (2) relatively under-standardized; (3) changeable and developing; (4) combining both the maintenance of structures and their change; (5) rarely generating visible and separate outputs that can be directly connected to individual inputs.

[2]See in Geuss (2008) a passionate, philosophical defense of real politics.

But there is another ethical reason for teaching power and influence. Applying Alinsky's (1971) words to managers, we can say that the worst sin of executives is not trying to become more powerful—not acting, not daring to influence. And the responsibility of course instructors should be to promote and facilitate that moral courage.

There is one final rationale for teaching political dynamics in organizations: the current generalized suspicion of power, and of any power distance. This distrust may end up hampering the very capability of contemporary, developed societies to achieve great things, at the very moment when great transformations are called for.

LEARNING FROM THE CLASSICS: POWER AS WISDOM

The first purely political—that is, neither philosophical nor ethical—treatment of the concept of power appeared in the Italian Renaissance when political thinkers identified power as an alternative to legitimacy when explaining the turbulence of contemporary political life. But while legitimacy derived from moral principles, power emerged inductively. It implied from its beginning real politics. Greece and Rome had ceased to be the great models of truth, ethics, and beauty, and thinkers had to find their reference points in reality, as empirically defined as possible. Machiavelli in *The Prince*—less a how-to book than a reflection on the slim odds of survival for rulers not enjoying official legitimacy (Pocock, 1975)—used a selection of the main situations or contingencies that princes had to deal with to secure their survival.

After Machiavelli broke with the past by claiming the autonomy of the political realm, tactics of influence replaced ethics as the main concern of both practitioners and thinkers. Renaissance and later thinkers on power began with the realistic assumption that sources of power, like the societies they lived in, were immovable; that access to those sources was forbidden for most people, for whom the only option left was tactical skills, the give-and-take that so occupied Alinsky (1971) centuries later. But since the conditions under which tactics are implemented were, and still are, so contingent and often overwhelming, politicians then and businesspeople today desperately need help in navigating this terrain, where the truism that "in management there are no rules, only principles," is especially applicable. The focus on tactics of influence is what makes these modern classics so appealing across cultures and ages. Accordingly, tactics should be at the heart of any course on power and even in any course on implementation or getting things done: what do you do, to whom, and when, or, in Lenin's even curter phrase, "*Kto-Kogo*," "Who-Whom." Whether tactics are presented as a differentiated block in today's courses on power or not, a tactical mindset should pervade all education in power and in leadership.[3]

Significantly, the structural deficit in politicians' political capital, assumed by the classics, is the very point of departure for Kotter (1982), who began his pioneering book by exposing the myth of the all-powerful executive. Kotter argued that the executive's *formal* power was insufficient to be effective, and was in any case limited by the fact that, in modern firms, executives act on behalf of others. Leaders are structurally in a position of dependence if they want to accomplish relevant things. As the French moralists of the eighteenth century recognized, those who want to accomplish great things in society are slaves to the many. Independence comes with a price: irrelevance.

B. Gracián's *The Book of Worldly Wisdom*, dating from 1637, was one of the

[3]Pfeffer cleverly makes tactics the dominant perspective of his "Paths to Power" MBA course.

first and most influential books in the tradition of tactical advice.[4] Gracián based his counsel on the Machiavellian assumption that dependence—"necessity" in the parlance of the day—is a sounder basis for the prediction of human behavior than affection, which is much more capricious. A focus on dependence makes the "what" of tactics less mysterious and more easily calculable. Regarding the "how," or the style of tactics, the main recommendation for those wielding little power, the majority, was ambiguity—the best means of protection in a Hobbesian world (F. Mitterrand, a politician with the manners and self-awareness of a classic thinker, used to warn that one abandons ambiguity only at one's own peril). Gracián's and his contemporaries' tactics were then not conceived of for the accomplishment of great feats, but merely for survival. And this survival was always at stake because, as Gracián warned, politics is an endless series of action-reaction-counter-reaction. No one can ever relax. This perennial fear, even in the powerful, is uncannily captured in the distrustful eyes of Velázquez's *Innocent X* (c. 1650), so much so that when the pope saw his telling portrait, the infamous words *troppo vero* escaped him. Power-holders are conscious of the essential insecurity of their positions and need constant reassurance. This fact led French courtier La Rochefoucauld to counsel that flattery is the surest way to gain the favor of one's superiors.

The essential loneliness of being at the top, the impossibility of lasting trust, and the relentless, exhausting activity of politics were themes fully expressed in the memoirs of the Cardinal-cum-Chief Minister of Louis XIV, J. Mazarin. Mazarin is as dispassionate and realistic about human nature as only an Italian-born Cardinal in the French Court could be. For him, power is opaque, at least nebulous, and it needs to be that way in order for social actors to break the rules in the name of the legitimacy provided by those very norms. The manifestation of power is always a *trompe l'oeil*. This is why power games are so dangerous to young, naïve, eager MBA graduates. For the rationality of management is often just a façade put up by the powerful, and the sincere use of a technical rationality and language a manifestation of weakness, as Nietzsche told us. Power and rationality are inverse phenomena (Flybverg, 1998).

These reflections were shared by other French moralists such as La Bruyère, Montaigne, Pascal, and, in England, Shaftesbury.[5] In them we can find the nucleus of everything that is important about power and influence. They shared similar pessimistic assumptions on the contingencies of human nature—what was then not yet called psychology but anthropology. For example, Machiavelli recommended causing pain all at once but dosing out favors only slowly. He counseled arranging for damage to subordinates to be self-inflicted, since this creates less resentment than damage openly inflicted by the superior himself. And he argued that the surest way to create a long-lasting political relationship is, in modern language, asymmetrical dependence. The psychological foundations of Emerson's power dependence theory are already present in the classics.

The acquisition and use of power requires, then, the employment of all human beings' capacities, from their formal knowledge, to their savvy, to their psychology, to their moral character. This is why humanism—civic virtue—is only fully realized in politics, because no other activity demands so much of its practitioners (Pocock, 1975).

But the deep pessimism that characterizes all of these moralistic-cum-realistic thinkers and practitioners, whose influence waned in

[4]Centuries later the book made it to the *New York Times* bestseller list.

[5]A contemporary author, a politician, writing on politics, in this moralist tradition, in style, wit and wisdom, but with an optimistic outlook is Bullitt (1994).

impact with the coming of Romanticism and the return to Rome and Greece as true sources of classicism, limited the very impact of the political capital they sought to protect. For them, power does not serve leadership, understood as the accomplishment of great feats. Rather, it is merely an instrument for survival and, at most, independence, rendering it a sad endeavor. Power for leadership is a contemporary construction, very much a business school invention.

Using the Classics to Teach Power and Influence

If the virtuous exercise of politics—an activity more particular than universal and reproducible, more idiosyncratic than normative, more personal than abstract—requires civic virtue and this, in turn, requires wisdom beyond formal knowledge, what is the best pedagogical method to teach it? How can senior executives and leaders be provided with resources for action and not just models of action? How can we, instructors in the topic, create and disseminate wisdom for an activity so subject to innumerable and uncontrollable contingencies? Most important, how can we help practitioners imagine feasible courses of action in the midst of those necessities?

The authors I referred to, most of them either practitioners like Mazarin or political counselors like Machiavelli and Gracián, whose works were not unlike long memos intended to woo would-be patrons, used two basic pedagogical strategies.

The first was the gathering and distillation of collections of sayings, proverbs, witty remarks, and maxims encapsulating the essence of the wisdom these authors had accumulated through their experience. Examples are Gracián's *Art of Wordly Wisdom* (1637), Castiglione's *The Book of the Courtier* (2002[1528]), La Rochefoucauld's *Aphorisms* (2007 [1665]) or, in another culture, Sun Tzu's *Art of War* (1963 [c. 500 BCE]), and much later Mao's *Red Book* (1967 [1964]). These pieces of practical knowledge encapsulated the lessons on tactics that princes and princesses needed in order to survive in the over-determined world of politics, but that very over-determination prevented order or completeness in these writings. Not even Machiavelli in *The Prince* (1985 [1532]) or *The Discourses* (2003 [1531]) was able to deliver a systematic rendition of tactical counsel (Pocock, 1975). And even today it is not possible to establish a parsimonious set of contingencies for the design of corporate power (Alvarez & Svejenova, 2005).

The second pedagogical strategy, closer to contemporary business school teaching, was the pedagogical use *avant la lettre* of cases: a succession of stories with the most frequent or important contingencies that princes faced and the tactics they used to deal with them. As with the aphorisms, these collections of cases were never exhaustive or systematic.

Our classics prioritized for those cases the examples of heroes, successful (such as Gracián's *The Hero* [2003 (1637)] and *The Politician* [2003 (1640)], or fallen (Diderot's *Seneca* [1778]), or even, preferably from the pedagogical viewpoint, ambiguous ones such as Gracián's *The Discreet One* (2001 [1646]), or Machiavelli's all-time favorite, Cesare Borgia, the purest political entrepreneur, with no other source of power than his tactical savvy, with no other aim than complete power, who puts everything at risk for it (his slogan is the glorious *Aut Caesar aut nihil*), and who embodies one of the two most fundamental political tactics, the one favored by the Florentine: audacity. Among the practitioners in the Borgia tradition of audacity are H. Cortés, Mirabeau,[6] Napoleon, M. Thatcher, J. Welch, S. Jobs,

[6]A short but intense work on a morally ambiguous hero is Ortega y Gasset's *Mirabeau o el Político* (2005 [1928]), where the philosopher poses the French revolutionary as the archetype of politician, a Clintonesque figure.

and R. Branson. The alternative basic tactic, prudence or robust action, theorized centuries later by Neustadt, Padgett, Eccles, and Nohria,[7] has been practiced by the likes of F. D. Roosevelt, Eisenhower, and Mitterrand. It is more difficult to find good business examples of robustness, since, as Khurana (2002) has signaled, recent decades have favored a dramatic profile for senior executives, much more inclined to audacity.

The use of cases involving characters facing contingencies was based upon the pedagogy of the *specula*: In order to instill virtue in pupils—civil or moral—they have to be exposed to exemplars they will study, admire, and then strive to emulate. The use of negative examples would share the same pedagogy, but the other way around. These exemplars should be neither abstract prototypes nor purely personal models, but individuals who go beyond their own particular expression and embody collective values that inspire and move people to action. Analytical knowledge is not enough since, while descriptions may sometimes motivate, true energy for action comes from personal examples (as the classics liked to say *verba movent, exempla trahunt*). Emotion is *sine qua non*, since it comes before knowledge: As Scheler said, "the lover always precedes the connoisseur." These performative narrations, "sentimental pragmatics" as they were called, are of course well known to those who, as politicians, are concerned with the consequences of actions, such as the Catholic Church, as reflected in its use of the *imitatio Christi*.

But energy for action is not enough. The key question is Lenin's: What is to be done? What is the course of action? Political actors need plots for action, the capacity for imagining courses of advancement that navigate them through contingencies. Machiavelli called that indispensable action-oriented political imagination *fantasia*, which for him did not imply absurdity or foolishness but, on the contrary, the distinctive capability for imagining actionable futures.

In *Time and Narrative,* Ricoeur (1984–1988) explains that imagination has a fundamentally synthetic function, connecting the intellectual capacity with an intuition fed by characters, episodes, and changes of fortune—the experience of life. The imagination of the political actor, or of the top executive, like that of a narrative creator, performs the emplotment or configurational act—the composition of facts, the creation of a narration out of a mere succession of past and future events, and the intuitive presentation of what makes up the denouement. The configurational act is a reflective judgment where the political actor is capable of distancing himself from his own production, of splitting himself in two, of evaluating himself acting in an imagined plot with twists and turns, with action, reaction, and counter-reaction. High self-monitors are precisely those best equipped for politics, because they are the best at configurational acts, such as those taking place in fiction. Imagination is what allows for knowledge without experience.

From Aristotle's *Poetics* (1986 [c. 335 BCE]), Kant's *Critique of Judgment* (1952 [1790]), and Ricoeur's *Time and Narrative* (1984–1988), we know that imagination for action can only be developed by the pedagogical use of fiction, a concept that does not mean something untruthful, but something fabricated. Fiction is, according to Aristotle, poetical truth, one that looks for what may happen or may have happened, according to verisimilitude or necessity, the one needed by artists, politicians, and senior leaders. Its opposite, historical truth, refers to facts, to what has happened, and it is purely analytical, the domain of scholars.

The best-kept secret of the case method used in business schools, still dominant in the field of organizational behavior, is that it belongs to narrative fiction (Alvarez &

[7]See a summary of the robust action literature in Alvarez (2000).

Merchán, 1992). Cases are fabricated accounts of the truth and good cases are fictional materials with an open finale left to the reader's imagination that share the two basic conditions of possibility in narrative fiction. The first is the existence of a "narrative voice," usually called the "implied author," the result of the question: "Who is speaking here?" The second condition is the "point of view," which answers the question: "From where do we see what we see?" This is where the author of the case makes us direct our gaze in the same direction as the characters. A masterful use of the "narrative voice" and "point of view" narrative conditions is found in Jack Gabarro's "Erik Peterson" best-selling case series (1993–1994). In the Erik Peterson cases, a sequence of events is presented from the "point of view" of two different characters, with the students getting one point of view for most of the session and then at the end, in sharp and surprising contrast, the second subjectivity. Gabarro's "implied author" is not that of an all-knowing god but one with partial information who can only guess others' subjectivities, requiring the reader to make up for that incomplete knowledge with his or her imagination, as we all do in real life. Unfortunately, most business teaching cases, even in the field of organizational behavior, are only descriptive accounts of what happened, in which the author adopts the narrative voice of an all-knowing objective raconteur.[8]

Learning power is, then, the use of life experience—the accumulation of imitable examples in the life of a man or woman and the wisdom based on the similarity of life to those examples—to decide and act in future circumstances (Gomá, 2005). Cases based on characters are the closest pedagogical instrument to a real experience because of the imagination they elicit in their reading and discussion, an experience analogous to that of reading fiction (Alvarez & Merchán, 1992). The more action-oriented the cases discussed, the richer the life experience. In eliciting a classroom debate about the different readings of the subjectivities of the case's characters, participants clearly realize the difficulties of unilaterally assessing poorly structured situations—the scenario to which organizational politics is most prone—and the consequent need to realistically imagine the pressures and interests that persons or groups have, the need to get "under their skin."

Moreover, this fictional act of placing ourselves in others' shoes, viewing the world from that perspective and having a dialog about it in the classroom, reveals the connection between fiction and ethics. To act morally is to act in such a way that one is able to occupy the position of others, and as a consequence have the feeling of belonging to a community. To put it concisely: ethics' and politics' condition of possibility is one and the same, and this is the faculty of imagination.

In the teaching of organizational politics—and the same goes for leadership—using cases is not, then, purely analytical. It goes beyond conceptual knowing since it relies on the imagination. A purely analytical pedagogy of politics would be the case of a good lecture based on, for instance, Parsons (1963a, 1963b), probably the best succinct, abstract conceptualizations of influence and power. But, while more than analytical, the use of action-oriented cases as a means of educating imagination for action is less than experiential. Some behavioral methods in the teaching of power and influence run the risk of provoking perverse effects: When situations are de-contextualized, behavioral methods tend to reify targets of influence, given that politics is by nature over-determined (Zimbardo, 2007). So, out of restraint, educating for power of influence should generally remain less

[8]In fact, this is one of today's challenges in teaching power and influence, the scarcity of good action-oriented cases.

than behavioral. Of course, imagination-developing methods attempt to have an impact on the way managers exercise power, even ultimately on their identity. Yet this transformation would be a delayed one, that ultimately depends on how the pupils, once they leave the business school, continue using their political imagination for emplotments or configurations that profit from their life experience.

SOME TEACHING PRACTICES IN AN INSTRUCTOR-DEPENDENT COURSE

A course on wisdom for action, on getting things done, is instructor-dependent to a greater degree than other offerings, even in the leadership domain. The most important capacity for teaching a "power and influence" course is not a particular kind of knowledge or background, but style—the same way that the important thing in politics is not the "what" or the "content," but the "how" or the "process." I will begin this section by describing the ideal professor. Then I will follow up with some applied recommendations on some teaching practices that work well for me, though they might not necessarily be appropriate for all colleagues.

The profile and role of the instructor

There are several ideal characteristics for an instructor in power and politics. The first is that a "Falstaffian," expansive professor is better than, as the Bard would say, an analytical one with a lean and hungry look. With a topic such as this, the professor needs to feel comfortable with some of the theatrics needed for a "suspension of disbelief" aimed at conveying that power is a special type of wisdom, very rarely available, never a technique, that cannot be contained in articles, notes, slides, but needs to be captured through a kind of chemistry and understanding between the participants and the instructor. Instructors ought to be able to convey the hard truth that political wisdom will spare one from very costly experiences, even sometimes personal and professional misery. As with politicians, the more the instructor of power and influence is an actor, the better.

A second characteristic of an ideal teaching style in power and influence is a fast-paced and brisk rhythm. This is extremely important, since power is nothing in itself and, therefore, there is no substance to fall back on. If the rhythm of the session declines, the "suspension of disbelief," key for case-based teaching styles, implodes.

Third, the more years the instructor stays teaching the topic, the better. Jeffrey Pfeffer so greatly influences the teaching of the topic these days because he has been at it for many years and offers a continuous and abundant supply of new teaching materials and writings. Mastering its teaching requires familiarity with the cases (these, similarly, should not change much), to discover in them subtleties, deeper layers of meaning, to be prepared for more questions or insights from the participants, to find new anecdotes, new contingencies to bring in to the classroom and, very important, new ironies to point out to students.

A final requirement is a joyful and assertive approach to teaching the topic. In the same way that the more political capital people have, the more alive they are, as May (1989) expressed in his beautiful pages, the same thing happens with teaching power and influence. In no other subject is the instructor more free, that is, more alive, than in power and influence. The very fact that political capital is nothing in itself, and that tactics are so idiosyncratic, gives the instructor almost complete leeway to influence pupils in the classroom, since everything depends on her or his style, and this cannot be predetermined by any curriculum. The way—through many small things—the instructor develops rapport with the course participants is entirely the instructor's choice: ironic reactions to overly-analytical contributions, small pieces of wisdom delivered with seemingly nonchalance, the teasing of the overly enthusiastic, the chiding of the overly cynical, the use of all types of resources, from current social science to wisdom contained in ancient sources, etc. In teaching politics, style is content. And style is free.

Some teaching advice

The following practices have worked for me well in recent years and, hopefully, they will be helpful to interested colleagues. While they apply mostly to MBA programs, with some adaptation they could also be of help in executive education. The main difference between teaching the topic to MBAs and to seasoned executives is that the latter, thanks of course to their experience, have a much more realistic and nuanced imagination that allows for much more grounded tactical debates.

- Power and politics courses for MBAs should mostly focus on, but not be limited to, the predicaments that they face in their early and mid-career trajectories. Pfeffer adopts this approach in his Stanford MBA elective. Linda Hill also did that, years ago, at HBS, with even a perspective focused more on "career management."
- Executive Committees and Boards of Directors are the best settings for teaching materials on power and influence for use in executive education.
- The best way to teach how to acquire and exercise power is to have as many cases as possible where young managers actually lose power due to the sins of naiveté, ambition, enthusiasm, technocratic orientation, or carelessness. This should be a course on "political ironies," to use Pocock's fortunate expression in his masterpiece on Machiavelli (Pocock, 1975) or, more sociologically speaking, on the unexpected consequences of actions.
- I always mention in class, early in the course, the motto inscribed at the door of Dante's inferno: *lasciate ogni speranza voi ch'entrate*—Abandon all hope, ye who enter here. Participants should know that, although most of them will probably gain more power, sooner or later they will lose it as well. All power stories end up badly because contexts change more rapidly and substantially than human beings do.
- The overall conceptual framework I use to explain organizing political dynamics is based on a Teaching Note by McGinn and Lingo (2001), very useful as a conceptual organizer of the cases.
- However, the relative position of the different concepts or blocks in the overall theoretical framework (e.g., power bases, influence tactics, networks, etc.) should not determine the teaching sequence, which should follow not a theoretical but a "dramatic" order.
- The ideal sequencing of teaching materials is chronological or biographical, from the viewpoint of the age and wisdom of political actors or executives who are the main characters in the cases. So, junior characters ought to generally appear earlier in the course, while those older or in more senior positions of power should be placed in its second half.
- As a consequence, the course should grow to a crescendo: from power as technique to power as wisdom; from "shock and awe" before the realities of power, to comfort with them; from the exhilaration of gaining some tactical smarts to a final acceptance of the transient and ultimately uncontrollable nature of power.
- It is better to discuss cases in depth, and stay with the same characters or in

the same situation for more than one session, getting the students excited by the discovery of deeper layers of complexity in the same story, than to employ many different materials and only deal with them in a rush. Of course, the American presidency provides wonderful material, as does Shakespeare's Bolingbroke passages. Following in two or three sessions the history of firms such as Lehman or General Electric could be a fruitful exercise, and there are excellent materials on them. The goal of using *long durée* cases is that participants realize that there are some basic regularities in political dynamics, that history repeats itself.[9] This is precisely what allows us, as scholars, to say something on a topic so rife with contingencies.

- Staying with the same situation for a number of sessions features another advantage. The exercise of power in particular, or the flow of social action in general, cannot be only characterized as a series of discrete decisions or events. This view will limit teaching and power to what Lukes (1974) called the "first face of power," the most visible and easier to teach, but not necessarily the most influential. For power also deploys itself over continuous, covert, and ideological processes, not always evident even to the social actors most involved in them.
- When a case or other teaching material is very good but old or even very old, it should still be used shamelessly. As argued, this is not an information course, and does not cover the latest developments of a professional practice. This is a "classic" course—the professor should openly recognize this and welcome it, and not shy away from classic teaching materials.
- Clips from movies or documentaries should be used to illustrate examples or to accompany session wrap-ups, or even as material on which to base a full class discussion. We should help the students "see" power, to spot it in action. Power is more observable than most think.
- While cases where decisions are required should be the critical material input for learning, it is also important to equip participants with the capacity to grasp political dynamics from all types of sources: journalism (there are excellent pieces on Lehman); on influence tactics (e.g., movies such as *13 Days*); plays (Shakespeare's *Julius Cesar* [2010 (1599)] is an amazing story of coalition-making and how this is based on a deep knowledge of human nature, its generosity and frailties; the wooing by Henry Bolingbroke of the French princess at the end of *Henry V* [2010 (1599)] is a great example of a high self-monitor at the best of his game); classic authors on power (such as the aforementioned Machiavelli, Gracián, Alinksy); documentaries such as the one by the BBC on Margaret Thatcher that can be used as a companion to a great case on her by INSEAD's Ibarra (1996), etc. Obviously these materials are *post facto* accounts without a decision to make. However, the experienced professor can discuss Shakespeare's plays, even the well-known ones, by stopping the movie and asking "Now what?"
- Having one or two well-known classics is especially recommended, since this is a course on wisdom, for conveying the idea that we are dealing with eternal issues, not to be resolved technically once and for all. As mentioned, Shakespeare's *Henry V* and

[9]The *ritornello*, though, does not have necessarily the same tone. As Marx said, what is tragic the first time around can be comic the second.

Julius Cesar are great candidates for this, especially the former, because when it is accompanied by *Henry IV* (2007 [c. 1596–1599]) it is an oeuvre on the development of leadership in young people, and the message is precisely the preeminence of life experience over formal knowledge for that development. Moreover, *Henry V* is a play where the main character is a perfect exemplar of a high self-monitor, as attractive as he is ambiguous.

Teaching "Power and Influence" and Ethics

That this course should not be one on applied ethics does not mean that moral issues should not be considered in its design and teaching. The current economic crisis and its relationship with the unscrupulous behavior of some in power makes this question obligatory. But most importantly, and independent of the economic circumstances of the day, it is the very function that power plays as a social intermediary—between the norm and the action, the knowing and the doing, the general and abstract on the one hand and the concrete and idiosyncratic on the other—that makes the ethical question a key one. And because successful influence is necessarily exercised only after some reification of the target—a human being—the risk of manipulation is always there. This is a course where power should be taught in order to be put to the service of something non-instrumental. To paraphrase an expression from the HBS faculty teaching the course: The use of power should be personally non-destructive, organizationally effective, and socially responsible.

But one thing I never do, though, is to pretend in any way that amoral uses of power necessarily lead to failure, or that ethical uses of power lead to personal, organizational, or social success, as if a kind of perfect moral market operates whereby, in this world, good deeds are rewarded and bad ones are punished. À la Kant, people have to behave morally not because this leads to success, but because it is their universal a priori duty, regardless of consequences (Stevenson & Bhide, 1990).

I always finish my course by telling students that it is their moral obligation to be more powerful. First, because of an obligation to themselves, for if they are not powerful, they will be instruments of others, not active protagonists of their destiny (Crick, 1962). This was the main concern of our post Middle Ages classics. Second, because if they lack substantial political capital, they will not have the opportunity to go beyond their capacities—some honed through hard work and education, some gifts nature gave them—and put them at the service of others, of the organizations they belong to or the societies they live in. Leadership is a distinctively contemporary function, one that our aforementioned classics were not able to theorize, for which power—and lots of it—is essential.

When Kotter launched the "Power and Influence" course in 1982, as a standalone offering, not embedded in any other management topic, he marked a much-needed Machiavellian moment in business education, an organizational behavior-*verité* shift. But, thirty years later, is the teaching of power as a separate subject still needed? Since the time the course was launched, and in part thanks to it and to research on the topic, businesspeople have become much more educated in organizational power dynamics. Moreover, with the expansion of the business coverage by the media and the pressures in the last decade for corporate governance reform, we know much better what Machiavelli called the *verità effetuale* of organizational life. Adding to it, institutional politics have become much more transparent than decades ago, and the general public knows much more about politics as a process—perhaps too much, as there is an excessive focus on the spectacles of the electoral process and the rise and fall of leading business figures, to the detriment to substance. Moreover, today those MBA candidates—often in their late twenties and with five to seven years of working experience—who do not have, at least, a good notion of the essential political dynamics in organizations will probably never get them. And perhaps those who are already adept at those dynamics do not need much more political capacitation, lest they get too carried away by their own savvy. As the old saying recommends, "never give [or teach, we could say] power to those who want it."

Perhaps the Machiavellian moment in Organizational Behavior, a period of almost three decades already, has served its original purpose well and it is time for a new phase, embedding the teaching of political dynamics in courses where power can be applied to very specific business predicaments and managerial roles, such as courses on Strategy Implementation or General Management.[10] And, above all, it may be time to bring power and its dynamics into the inside of all leadership courses, which all too often run the risk of being excessively high on inspiration, too centered on the individual, and devoid of social context. When the teaching of power and influence is separated from leadership in the curricula, as differentiated courses, we risk ending up promoting the very cynicism and duplicity we ought to avoid: that there is, on the one hand, the preaching (norms and ideals) and there is, on the other, the reality of unspoken effective practices based on arcane wisdom. Perhaps it is time for those of us who believe in the importance of the topic of power and politics in organizations to influence the teaching of leadership not from the outside, as a separate course, but from within the leadership curriculum itself.

References

Alinsky, S. (1971). *Rules for radicals: A pragmatics primer for realistic radicals*. New York: Random House.

Alvarez, J. L. (2000). Theories of managerial action and their impact on the conceptualization of executive careers. In M. Peiperl & M. Arthur (Eds.), *Career frontiers: New conceptions of working lives* (127–137). Oxford: Oxford University Press.

Alvarez, J. L., & Merchán, C. (1992). Narrative fiction as a way of knowledge and its application to the development of imagination for action. *International Studies of Management and Organization, 22*(3), 27–46.

Alvarez, J. L., & Svejenova, S. (2005). *Sharing executive power: Roles and relationships at the top*. Cambridge, UK: Cambridge University Press.

Aristotle. (1986). *Poetics*. S. Halliwell (Trans.). London: Duckworth.

Bower, J. (1986). *Managing the resource allocation process*. Boston, MA: Harvard Business School Classics.

Bullitt, S. (1994). *To be a politician* (2nd ed.). Seattle, WA: Willows Press.

Castiglione, B. (2002). *The book of the courtier*. C. Singleton (Trans.). New York: Norton. Originally published 1528

Crespi, F. (1989). *Social action and power*. Oxford, UK: Blackwell.

Crick, B. (1962). *In defense of politics*. Chicago: University of Chicago Press.

[Diderot, D.] (1778). *Essai sur les regnes de Claude et de Néron, et sur les moeurs et les écrits de Séneque* (2 tom.). Bouillon, n.p.

Flybverg, B. (1998). *Rationality and power: Democracy in practice*. Chicago: University of Chicago Press.

[10]Bower (1986), on resource allocation, continues to be the best book on the workings of political dynamics at the top of complex organizations, and the best example of what I mean here.

Foucault, M. (1982). The subject and power. *Critical Inquiry, 8*, 777–795.

Gabarro, J. J. (1993a). Erik Peterson (A). HBS Case 494-005. Boston, MA: Harvard Business School Press.

Gabarro, J. J. (1993b). Erik Peterson (B). HBS Case 494-006. Boston, MA: Harvard Business School Press.

Gabarro, J. J. (1993c). Erik Peterson (C). HBS Case 494-007. Boston, MA: Harvard Business School Press.

Gabarro, J. J. (1993d). Erik Peterson (D). HBS Case 494-008. Boston, MA: Harvard Business School Press.

Gabarro, J. J. (1993e). Erik Peterson (E). HBS Case 494-009. Boston, MA: Harvard Business School Press.

Geuss, R. (2008). *Philosophy and real politics*. Princeton, N.J.: Princeton University Press.

Gomá, J. (2005). *Imitación y experiencia*. Barcelona: Crítica.

Gracián, B. (1892). *The book of worldly wisdom*. J. Jacobs (Trans.). London: Macmillan. Originally published 1637

Gracián, B. (2001 [1640]). *El discreto*. A. Egido (Ed.). Zaragoza: Institución Fernando el Católico.

Gracián, B. (2003 [1637]). *El heroe*. A. Bernat Vistalini & A. Madroñal (Eds.). Madrid: Castalia.

Gracián, B. (2003 [1640]). *El político Don Fernando el Católico*. V. Dini (Ed.). Napoli: Bibliopolis.

Green, R. (1998). *The forty-eight laws of power*. New York: Penguin.

Ibarra, H. (1996). Margaret Thatcher. HBS 497-018. Boston, MA: Harvard Business School Press.

Kant, I. (1952). *Critique of judgment*. J. C. Meredith (Trans.). Oxford: Oxford University Press. Originally published 1790

Kotter, J. (1982). *Power and influence: Beyond formal authority*. New York. Free Press.

La Rochefoucauld, F. de. (2007). *Collected maxims and other reflections*. Trans. E. H. and A. M. Blackmore and F. Giguère. Oxford University Press, Oxford. Originally published 1665

Lenin, V. I. (1961). "What is to be done?" In J. Fineberg & G. Hanna (Trans. & Eds.), *Lenin's collected works* (Vol. 5, pp. 347–530). Moscow: Foreign Languages Publishing House. Originally published 1902

Lindblom, C. E. (1959). The science of muddling through. *Public Administration Review, 19*, 79–86.

Lukes, S. (1974). *Power: A radical view*. London: Macmillan.

Machiavelli, N. (1985). *The prince*. H. Mansfield (Trans.). Chicago, IL: University of Chicago Press. Originally published 1532

Machiavelli, N. (2003). *The discourses*. L. J. Walker (Trans.). London: Penguin Books. Originally published 1531

Mansfield, H. (1989). *Taming the Prince: The ambivalence of executive power*. New York: Free Press.

Mao, T.-T. (1967). *Quotations from Chairman Mao Tse-Tung*. (S. R. Schram, Trans.). New York: Bantam. Originally published 1964

May, R. (1989). *Power and innocence*. New York: The Free Press.

McGinn, K., & Lingo, E. L. (2001). Power and influence: Achieving your objectives in organizations. Harvard Business School Note 801-425.

O'Neill, T. (1994). *All politics is local: And other rules of the game*. Holbrook, MA: Bob Adams Inc.

Ortega y Gasset, J. (2005). Mirabeau y el político. In *Obras Completas, Tomo IV:1926–1931*. Madrid: Taurus. Originally published 1928

Parsons, T. (1963a). On the concept of influence. *Public Opinion Quarterly, 27*(1), 37–62.

Parsons, T. (1963b). On the concept of political power. *Proceedings of the American Philosophical Society, 107*(3), 232–262.

Pfeffer, J. (1992). *Managing with power: Politics and influence in organizations*. Boston, MA: Harvard Business School Press.

Pocock, J. G. A. (1975). *The Machiavellian moment: Florentine political thought and the Atlantic republican tradition*. Princeton, NJ: Princeton University Press.

Ricoeur, P. (1984–1988). *Time and narrative* (vols. 1–3). Chicago: University of Chicago Press.

Roethlisberger, F. J. (1977). *The elusive phenomena: An autobiographical account of my work in the field of organizational behavior at the Harvard Business School.* G. F. F. Lombard (Ed.). Cambridge, MA: Harvard University Press.

Runciman, D. (2008). *Political hypocrisy: The mask of power, from Hobbes to Orwell and beyond.* Princeton, NJ: Princeton University Press.

Schattshneider, E. E. (1975). *The semisovereign people: A realistic view of democracy in America.* New York: Harcourt Brace Jovanovich.

Shakespeare, W. (2007). *Henry IV*, parts I and II. R.K. Levao (Ed.) New York: Pearson-Longman. Originally published c. 1596–1599

Shakespeare, W. (2010a). *Henry V.* J. Bate and E. Rasmussen (Eds.). New York: Modern Library. Originally published 1599

Shakespeare, W. (2010b). *Julius Caesar.* O. Arnold (Ed.). New York: Longman. Originally published 1599

Stevenson, H., & Bhide, A. (1990). Why be honest if honesty doesn't pay? *Harvard Business Review, 68*(5), 121–129.

Tzu, S. (1963). *The art of war.* S. B. Griffith (Trans.). Oxford University Press, Oxford. Originally published c. 500 BCE

Velázquez, D. (c. 1650). *Portrait of Pope Innocent X* [Painting]. Metropolitan Museum of Art, New York.

White, H. (2008). *Identity and control: How social formations emerge* (2nd ed.). Princeton, NJ: Princeton University Press.

Whitley, R. (1989). On the nature of managerial tasks and skills: Their distinguishing characteristics and organization. *Journal of Management Studies, 26*(3), 209–224.

Wrapp, H.E. (1984). Good managers don't make policy decisions. *Harvard Business Review, 62*(4), 8–15.

Zimbardo, P. (2007). *The Lucifer effect: Understanding how good people turn evil.* New York: Random House.

5

TEACHING GLOBAL LEADERSHIP

◆ Mansour Javidan
Thunderbird School of Global Management

This chapter defines global leadership as a process of influencing individuals, groups, and organizations whose cultural, political, and institutional backgrounds are different from the leader's. Surveys of executives with such responsibilities show that large numbers of respondents feel ill prepared for such a role. The chapter explains the concept of Global Mindset, a set of individual attributes that help facilitate effectiveness in global leadership positions. Global Mindset consists of three major dimensions of Intellectual Capital, Psychological Capital, and Social Capital. Intellectual Capital is the cognitive aspect and refers to the individual's knowledge of global issues and topics. Psychological capital is the affective side and refers to the individual's passion for diversity and willingness to try new things. Social Capital refers to the individual's ability to build trusting relationships with people who are different from him or her. Global Mindset Inventory (GMI) is an assessment tool designed to measure an individual's profile of Global Mindset. A program to teach global leadership should be able to provide an understanding of global leadership and Global Mindset, present ways of improving the elements of Global Mindset, and enhance the individual's self-efficacy as a global leader. The chapter presents a possible program consisting of pre- and post-assessment and a detailed curriculum focused on developing an individual's three capitals of Global Mindset. The proposed approach consists of case studies and a variety of educational and experiential activities anchored in our research on cross cultural and global leadership.

❖ ❖ ❖

"Today's global corporations are shifting their focus from products to production—from what things companies choose to make to how they choose to make them, from what services they offer to how they choose to deliver them. Simply put, the emerging globally integrated enterprise is a company that fashions its strategy, its management, and its operations in pursuit of a new goal: the integration of production and value delivery worldwide. State borders define less and less the boundaries of corporate thinking or practice." (Palmisano, 2006, p. 129)

The above description of the strategic imperative facing global corporations by the CEO of IBM is a succinct depiction of the opportunities and challenges facing global corporations. Globalization creates unique and unprecedented opportunities for corporations, but leveraging such opportunities is not easy. Corporations need a new and different breed of global leaders who can take decisions and actions that help develop and maintain the complex network of internal and external connections with individuals, teams, and organizations with diverse political, social, and cultural backgrounds. They require leaders who do not rely on traditional hierarchical approaches that tend to impede fluid and collaborative work relations and reduce trust and speed of decision making throughout the global network (Beechler & Javidan, 2007).

Despite the need for an increasing supply of global leaders, companies are having a difficult time filling these positions. For example, in the early 1990s Adler and Bartholomew (1992) in their study of international companies suggested that most companies are unable to implement their global strategies due to a lack of global leadership. In 2006, despite the increasing need for global leaders, the situation had not improved. A global survey by Mercer Delta of 223 senior executives from large corporations across seventeen industrial sectors in forty-four countries found that a majority of business executives believe their companies face leadership shortages in meeting the future global business risks that are threatening their corporate performance (Mercer Delta, 2006).

To further compound the problem, a recent survey of multinational leaders in global corporations (Howard & Wellins, 2008) shows rather disappointing sentiments about the state of affairs in developing global, multinational, leaders. Over 60 percent of respondents considered their own preparation as poor or fair. Almost 50 percent viewed the support from their own corporations as poor or fair. Only 12 percent considered their preparation very good and only 19 percent felt they received very good support from their companies. Executives in global leadership positions do not seem to benefit from the oversupply of advice, as evidenced by the fact that on January 14, 2011, Amazon.com was offering 1,120 books with the words "global leadership" in the title.

What Is Global Leadership?

Despite the plethora of advice and writing on global leadership, there is little effort to clearly define the concept. With few exceptions, much of the literature on global leadership tends to focus on lists of competencies and suggestions for improvement without offering a clear definition of global leadership (e.g., Black, Morrison & Gregersen, 1999; Brake, 1997; Mendenhall et al., 2001; Rhinesmith, 1996). We define global leadership as:

> The process of influencing individuals, groups, and organizations (inside and outside the boundaries of the global organization) representing diverse cultural/political/institutional systems to help achieve the global organization's goals. (Beechler & Javidan, 2007)

A few elements of the above definition need to be highlighted. First, we view global leadership as a process of influence, in line with the conventional literature on leadership where most definitions reflect the notion of intentional influence exerted by one person over other people (Yukl, 2006). Second, much of the extant literature is focused on how leaders can motivate their direct reports toward some common goals. While we agree with the importance of direct reports, we also explicitly acknowledge that the direct reports may be scattered around the world and may not neatly fit in a typical hierarchical structure.

Third, since a typical global organization is more of a network of supply chain partners, joint venture partners, or strategic alliance partners trying to execute integrated global strategies (Brake, 1997), the boundaries of the typical global organization are more permeable and fuzzy than the traditional organization (Ashkenas et al., 1995). Global leaders need to influence individuals, teams, and organizations from different parts of the world to help achieve their organizations' objectives. And they need to do this without relying on traditional lines of authority.

Fourth, much of the literature on global leadership tends to focus on leading across cultures (Adler, 1997; Dorfman, 2004; House, Hanges, Javidan, Dorfman, & Gupta, 2004; Javidan & Carl, 2004). While the difference in national cultures is indeed critical, it is not the only issue. The global leader's targets of influence may come from cultural backgrounds, institutional systems, legal frameworks, and social structures that are different from those in the global leader's home context (North, 1990). They may even have different views on the whole notion of the corporation and its role in the society (Hunt, 2000). In sum, global leadership is about influencing those who are different from the leader in many important ways. Global leaders need to navigate the differences across cultural, political, social, and institutional systems to be successful.

Global Mindset: The Key to Success in Global Leadership

In a recent presentation, Jeffery Immelt, the CEO of General Electric, referred to Global Mindset as the key to twenty-first-century leadership. We define Global Mindset as the set of individual attributes that help a global leader influence individuals, groups, and organizations from diverse cultural, political, and institutional backgrounds (Javidan, Teagarden, & Bowen, 2010). Global leaders who have a high level of Global Mindset tend to better understand the situations and individuals they are interacting with in a global environment. They are also better able to identify and enact the appropriate methods that would help effectively influence the stakeholders to work toward achieving the company's goals.

Identifying the attributes and elements of Global Mindset is an important step in teaching and developing global leadership because once we identify the requisite individual qualities, we can then design interventions that help a global leader take steps that would improve those attributes and enhance their effectiveness as a global leader.

The Global Mindset Project (GMP) started in late 2004 at Thunderbird School of Global Management. Eight professors reviewed the literature on global leadership, cross cultural leadership, and global mindset, conducted interviews with another twenty-six Thunderbird professors who are experts in various aspects of global business, and interviewed 217 global executives in the United States, Europe, and Asia. We also convened an invitation-only conference where more than forty academic experts known for their scholarly contributions to the global business field from around the world were asked to test, stretch, and refine our thinking—and so they did.

The above process helped us identify the scope and components of the concept of Global Mindset. We then worked with the Dunnette Group, a renowned instrument design firm, to empirically verify the construct of Global Mindset and to scientifically design an instrument that would measure an individual's profile of Global Mindset. We used an iterative process involving more than two hundred MBA students and more than seven hundred managers working for two Fortune 500 corporations in a series of surveys and pilot tests. The process resulted in an empirically verified construct of Global Mindset that consists of three major dimensions: Intellectual Capital (IC), Psychological Capital (PC), and Social Capital (SC). Figure 5.1 below shows the scientific structure of Global Mindset.

Intellectual Capital (IC) reflects the cognitive side of Global Mindset. As explained earlier, global leaders need to navigate differences on many fronts: cultures, political and economic systems, and institutional systems. Intellectual Capital (IC) refers to the leader's knowledge of his or her global surroundings, as well the ability to digest and leverage the additional level of complexity embedded in global environments. It consists of three key elements: global business savvy,

Figure 5.1 The Structure of Global Mindset

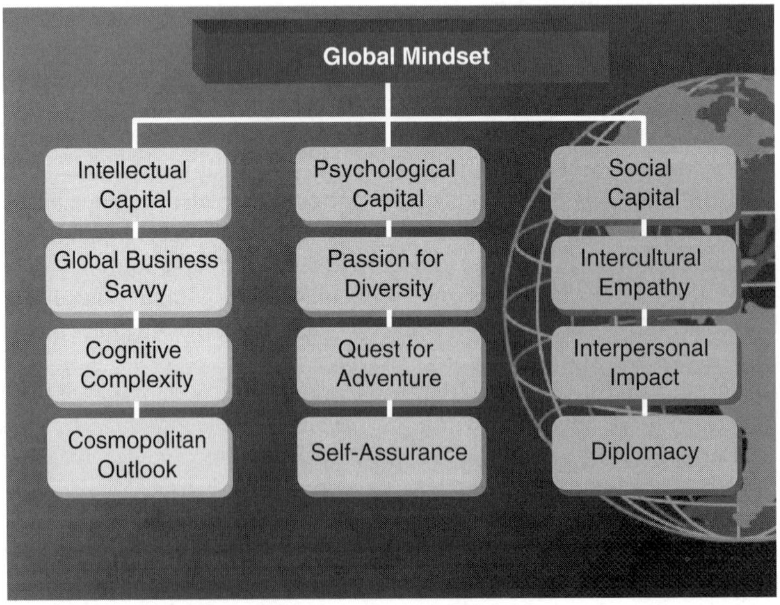

cognitive complexity, and cosmopolitan outlook. Below is a brief description of the three components.

GLOBAL BUSINESS SAVVY:

- Knowledge of global industry
- Knowledge of global competitive business and marketing strategies
- Knowledge of how to transact business and manage risk in other countries
- Knowledge of supplier options in other parts of the world

COSMOPOLITAN OUTLOOK:

- Knowledge of cultures in different parts of the world
- Knowledge of geography, history, and important persons of several countries
- Knowledge of economic and political issues, concerns, hot topics, etc. of major regions of the world
- Up-to-date knowledge of important world events

COGNITIVE COMPLEXITY:

- Ability to grasp complex concepts quickly
- Strong analytical and problem solving skills
- Ability to understand abstract ideas
- Ability to take complex issues and explain the main points simply and understandably

Psychological Capital (PC) reflects the affective aspect of Global Mindset. It refers to the psychological attributes that enable a leader to leverage his or her Intellectual Capital. Without a strong psychological platform, the leader's extensive knowledge of global industry and global environment is less likely to result in successful action. Psychological Capital consists of three elements: passion for diversity, quest for adventure, and self-assurance. Below is a brief description of the three components.

PASSION FOR DIVERSITY:

- Interest in exploring other parts of the world
- Interest in getting to know people from other parts of the world
- Interest in living in another country
- Interest in variety

QUEST FOR ADVENTURE:

- Interest in dealing with challenging situations
- Willingness to take risks
- Willingness to test one's abilities
- Interest in dealing with unpredictable situations

SELF-ASSURANCE:

- Energetic
- Self-confident
- Comfortable in uncomfortable situations
- Witty in tough situations

Social Capital (SC) refers to the behavioral aspect of Global Mindset. It reflects the individual's ability to act in a way that would help build trusting relationships with people from other parts of the world. Social Capital consists of three elements: intercultural empathy, interpersonal impact, and diplomacy. Below is a brief description of the three components.

INTERCULTURAL EMPATHY:

- Ability to work well with people from other parts of the world
- Ability to understand nonverbal expressions of people from other cultures

- Ability to emotionally connect to people from other cultures
- Ability to engage people from other parts of the world to work together

INTERPERSONAL IMPACT:

- Experience in negotiating contracts in other cultures
- Strong networks with people from other cultures and with influential people
- Reputation as a leader
- Credibility

DIPLOMACY:

- Ease of starting a conversation with a stranger
- Ability to integrate diverse perspectives
- Ability to listen to what others have to say
- Willingness to collaborate

The above structure of Global Mindset in terms of three capitals and nine elements has been consistently verified in a series of confirmatory analyses with large samples of executives and managers. We further show that a strong profile of Global Mindset is a predictor of success in global leadership positions (Javidan, Hough, & Bullough, 2010). In collaboration with the Dunnette group, we have designed a scientific Internet-based instrument called the Global Mindset Inventory (GMI), which contains 76 items and has strong psychometric properties (Javidan, Hough, & Bullough, 2010).

Teaching Global Leadership

An effective way to improve a global leader's effectiveness is by focusing on his or her Global Mindset profile and by improving its nine key elements. This section presents a possible endeavor to teach global leadership by focusing on Global Mindset. It is important to note that while there is strong evidence for the importance of international assignments and international experience (Aycan, 2001; Black et al., 1999; Evans et al., 2002; McCall & Hollenbeck, 2002), in this chapter we do not discuss such assignments. Instead, our focus is on various ways of teaching global leadership that can take place in or out of the classroom and in relatively short periods of time. Such an attempt consists of the following components:

OBJECTIVE

In teaching global leadership, we need to achieve four major objectives:

- To understand the concepts and elements of global leadership, Global Mindset, and their relevance and importance
- To present methods and ways of improving the nine elements of Global Mindset
- To achieve double-loop learning (Argyris, 1991)
- To enhance the participants' self-efficacy as a global leader (Bandura, 1989)

Most adults grow up in their societies learning about how to live and work with people who are like them. As a result of their childhood experiences, family and friends, schooling, and other activities, they develop a mental map (McCall Jr., 1998) that helps them build and sustain their relationships with people like them. The mental map contains an understanding of the cultural, political, and institutional systems operating in their society, as well as a set of values and beliefs about how things are done and should be done in that society (House, Hanges, Javidan, Dorfman, & Gupta, 2004). These values and beliefs in turn help develop deeply held implicit leadership theories that result in appropriate influence strategies employed by leaders in that society (Dorfman, Hanges, & Brodbeck, 2004).

Global Leaders, however, work for corporations that require them to work effectively with people who are different from them. And they are typically not trained for such a role. Their developmental experiences are unicultural but their role requirements are multicultural. Any attempt at teaching global leadership needs to find a way to help the manager go through a process of double-loop learning where they unlearn a few things, learn many new things, and are able to move from a unicultural mental map to a multicultural mental map that would enable them to identity the appropriate methods to influence people who are different from them (Javidan, Dorfman, Sully de Luque, House, 2006).

Teaching global leadership also means enhancing the participant's self-efficacy as a global leader (Bandura, 1989). Self-efficacy refers to an individual's belief about his capabilities to exercise control over events that affect him (Bandura, 1989, p.1175). Any attempt at teaching global leadership needs to focus on improving a manager's self-efficacy so that she is cognitively and affectively prepared for the higher level of complexity embedded in her role as a global leader (Rhinesmith, 2009). Global leaders face a high degree of diversity. A leader who lacks strong self-efficacy as a global leader is likely to fail regardless of his skill set or potential capabilities because he tends to find the diversity intimidating and frustrating rather than exciting and invigorating (Javidan & Teagarden, 2010, in press; Wood & Bandura, 1989). Self-efficacy is typically a product of performance mastery experiences, vicarious experiences, and verbal persuasion (Bandura, 1989). In teaching global leadership, we need to explain and clarify how and why it is complicated, but at the same time create opportunities for successful performance and feedback, as well as role modeling by other successful global executives.

ASSESSMENT

The Global Mindset Inventory (GMI) can be used to assess the manager's level of Global Mindset prior to the start of the teaching intervention. Pre-program assessment is helpful in creating a baseline for the manager, and for promoting self-understanding. It helps to identify each manager's areas of strength and areas in need of development. GMI is also a way of benchmarking and comparing a manager's profile with other global leaders. The GMI database currently holds more than ten thousand participants from many countries. They represent many organizational levels including more than four hundred CEOs in a large number of corporations in a variety of industries. Every year, all incoming Thunderbird MBA students are invited to complete the GMI prior to the start of their program. Eighteen other business schools use the GMI in a similar way.

Another important use of the GMI is at the post-assessment level, upon completion of the teaching intervention. In our work with Intel China, we have designed a multi-week global leadership program scattered over a one-year period. At the end of the one-year period, all participants complete the GMI again. Each individual receives his or her own pre-post results to examine their progress. The company's top leadership receives an aggregate report of the pre-post results to review the outcome of the program. This is an important and tangible way of examining the outcome of the teaching intervention. If the results show improvement, they also go a long way of improving each manager's self-efficacy. All Thunderbird MBA students are invited to complete the GMI six weeks prior to graduation.

MULTI-METHOD TEACHING

Due to the multidimensional nature of Global Mindset, teaching of global leadership requires diverse methods designed to cover diverse aspects of Global Mindset. As will be explained in detail later in the chapter, we will use a variety of lectures, individual feedback, individual reflection, case studies, videos, small group work, coaching, individual action planning, social media, and meetings (physical and virtual) with global executives and other relevant individuals and organizations.

The Curriculum

In this section, we present the sequence of learning experiences involved in a program to teach Global Mindset. This curriculum does not refer to one single course or workshop. It contains all the ingredients of what is an effective effort to teach Global Mindset. The effort could be a one-week executive education workshop, or an MBA course, or a full-fledged MBA program in global leadership. The length of the program depends on the availability of time and the relative importance attached to the nine elements of Global Mindset, and how much detail needs to be covered for each element.

Part 1. Consequences of a Low Global Mindset. The teaching of Global Mindset should start with an understanding of the consequences of a low Global Mindset. The concept of Global Mindset is intuitively appealing but needs clarity. It needs to be explained in tangible ways. We use several cases to discuss what happens when a manager with a low stock of Global Mindset is engaged in a global environment. Appendix 5.1 shows a brief Thunderbird case describing the situation facing an American executive who is appointed to lead the company's operations in China. He is struggling because his leadership style, which served him very well in the United States, is not producing the expected results in his new position. A thoughtful and practical discussion on the challenges a global leader faces and why and how a typical manager can fail or succeed serves to highlight the need for Global Mindset.

Part 2. Debrief on GMI Results. Early on in the course or program, managers need to receive feedback on their GMI results. A typical debrief session takes four to five hours to complete. Our Harvard Business Review article called "Making It Overseas" (Javidan, Teagarden, & Bowen, 2010) is a useful companion. The workshop consists of a presentation on the concept of Global Mindset and a debrief session on the individual results. It also includes a small group session in which small groups of managers work together to exchange ideas on what a low or a high score on any dimension means to them and how they can learn from each other. As the next step, managers are paired up in a fifteen-minute meeting. During this meeting, each manager acts as a coach to his or her partner to help identify ideas on how the partner can improve on a few elements of his or her Global Mindset. By the end of this workshop, managers will have a clear understanding of the concept and its relevance to them. They also learn the logic of the way the curriculum is designed. Thunderbird Global Mindset Institute offers a one-day certification program on how to facilitate a GMI debrief workshop.

Part 3. Managerial Application of Global Mindset. The purpose of this part is to help managers apply Global Mindset and its elements to a real-life managerial situation. One possible way is to use a case study or a panel of executives who share their experiences with the audience, using the framework of Global Mindset. By the end of this part, managers have a clear understanding of the elements of Global Mindset: what they mean, how they are measured, and why they are important.

Part 4. Teaching Intellectual Capital. Among the three capitals of Global Mindset, Intellectual Capital is probably the easiest to improve due to the fact that it is cognitively based. As shown earlier in Figure 5.1, Intellectual Capital (IC) refers to the three elements of global business savvy, cosmopolitan outlook, and cognitive complexity. Teaching Intellectual Capital can be done through reading various publications, taking traditional courses and workshops, case studies, and participating in group discussions.

A program designed for general audiences such as MBA students should be focused on teaching them to ask the right questions about global strategy as well as showing them examples of diverse global strategies and their rationale. Meetings (physical or virtual) with global executives can be a productive way to build their understanding.

When working with managers at one company, the focus is to help them understand their corporation's global strategy and its logic in comparison to major global competitors, as well as the company's global ambitions and their implications for the managers involved. This can typically be best achieved in one or more sessions with the company's senior executives.

Managers' cosmopolitan outlook can be enhanced by expanding their mental map to evolve from an ethnocentric unicultural map to a global map covering a wide range of cultural, political, and institutional systems. The GLOBE Project (House et al., 2004; Javidan, 2007; Hanges, 2010; Javidan & Dastmalchian, 2009; Javidan, Dorfman, Howell, Javidan, et al., 2006) offers a useful framework to study and understand the relevance of culture to global leaders. Our GLOBE study of more than 17,000 managers in sixty-two societies generated a template to compare national cultures across sixty-two societies in terms of nine dimensions. Table 5.1 below shows the list of the nine cultural dimensions. They offer a useful framework to compare the cultures of different countries.

Table 5.1 GLOBE Cultural Dimensions

Performance Orientation. The degree to which a collective encourages and rewards group members for performance improvement and excellence. In countries such as the United States and Singapore that score high on this attribute, businesses are likely to emphasize training and development; in countries that score low, such as Russia and Greece, family and background count for more.

Assertiveness. The degree to which individuals are assertive, confrontational, and aggressive in their relationship with others. People in highly assertive countries such as the United States and Austria tend to have can-do attitudes and enjoy competition in business; those in less assertive countries such as Sweden and New Zealand prefer harmony in relationships and emphasize loyalty and solidarity.

Future Orientation. The extent to which individuals engage in future-oriented behaviors such as delaying gratification, planning, and investing in the future. Organizations in high future oriented countries such as Singapore and Switzerland tend to have longer term horizons and more systematic planning processes, but they tend to be aversive to risk taking and opportunistic decision making. In contrast, corporations in the least future oriented countries such as Russia and Argentina tend to be less systematic and more opportunistic in their actions.

Humane Orientation. The degree to which a collective encourages and rewards individuals for being fair, altruistic, generous, caring, and kind to others. Countries such as Egypt and Malaysia rank very high on this dimension and countries such as France and Germany rank low.

(Continued)

Table 5.1 (Continued)

Institutional Collectivism. The degree to which organizational and societal institutional practices encourage and reward collective distribution of resources and collective action. Organizations in collectivistic countries such as Singapore and Sweden tend to emphasize group performance and rewards, whereas those in the more individualistic countries such as Greece and Brazil tend to emphasize individual achievement and rewards.
In-Group Collectivism. The degree to which individuals express pride, loyalty, and cohesiveness in their organizations or families. Societies such as Egypt and Russia take pride in their families and have fuzzy boundaries between business relations and personal relations.
Gender Egalitarianism. The degree to which a collective minimizes gender inequality. Not surprisingly, European countries generally were the most gender egalitarian. Egypt and South Korea were among the most male dominated societies in GLOBE. Organizations operating in gender egalitarian societies tend to encourage tolerance for diversity of ideas and individuals.
Power Distance. The degree to which members of a collective expect power to be distributed equally. (A high power distance score reflects unequal power distribution in a society.) Countries that scored high on this dimension are more stratified economically, socially, and politically; those in positions of authority expect, and receive, obedience. Firms in high power distance countries such as Thailand, Brazil, and France tend to have hierarchical decision making processes with limited one-way participation and communication.
Uncertainty Avoidance. The extent to which a society, organization, or group relies on social norms, rules, and procedures to alleviate unpredictability of future events. The greater the desire to avoid uncertainty, the more people seek orderliness, consistency, structure, formal procedures, and laws to cover situations in their daily lives. Organizations in high uncertainty avoidance countries such as Singapore and Switzerland tend to establish elaborate processes and procedures and prefer formal detailed strategies. In contrast, firms in low uncertainty avoidance countries such as Russia and Greece tend to prefer simple processes and broadly stated strategies. They are also opportunistic and tend to enjoy risk taking.

Source: Javidan, M., Dorfman, P., Sully de Luque, M., & House, R.J. (2006).

Our research has also identified an empirically based profile of the culturally endorsed implicit leadership theory (CLT) in each culture (Dorfman, Hanges, & Brodbeck, 2004). The CLT reflects a culture's expectations from its leaders. It is a set of criteria that members of a society commonly hold in assessing their leaders. For example, Figure 5.2 shows a comparison of the CLTs in the United States and France. It shows that, among other things, American managers expect their leaders to be much more compassionate and enthusiastic than do the French managers.

The purpose of the training in cross-cultural issues is to help the manager understand the concept of national culture and its impact on what global leaders do. Influencing people who are different from you is harder than influencing people who are like you, and culture has a lot to do with it.

Another aspect of cosmopolitan outlook is an understanding of diverse political, regulatory, and institutional systems. Global leaders need to influence a variety of stakeholders in the broader context of their business organization. They need to have a reasonable picture of how things are done in different societies. Our goal is not to turn the manager into a political scientist. Instead, it is to develop a mental framework

Figure 5.2

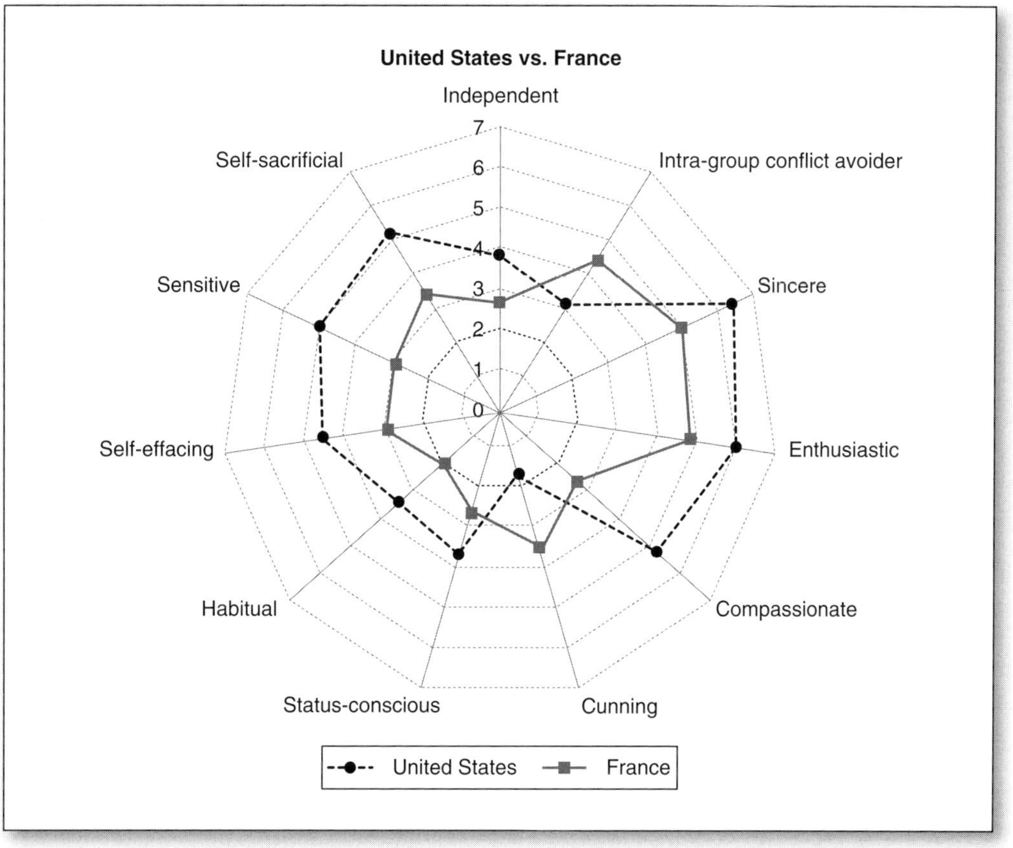

Source: Javidan, M., Dorfman, P., Sully de Luque, M., & House, R.J. (2006).

a manager can use to understand the macro political, regulatory, and institutional issues in other countries and to figure out what questions to ask when dealing with those from other parts of the world. We also need to help the manager determine how he can keep abreast of the major developments in the different parts of the world that are of interest to him.

Cognitive complexity is the third part of Intellectual Capital. An individual's cognitive framework helps drive attention toward some variables and away from others. It also impacts the process of sense making or how the information is interpreted, understood, and integrated with other sources and types of information (Daft & Weick, 1984; Levy, Beechler, Taylor, & Boyacigiller, 2007). Higher levels of cognitive complexity reflect the manager's ability to understand and pay attention to a wider range of issues and variables, and the ability to integrate a wider network of seemingly related or unrelated issues and variables together, under fuzzy and unclear conditions and weak signals (Kiesler & Sproull, 1982). As Hollingsworth described it:

> those with high cognitive complexity have the capacity to understand the world in more complex ways than those with less cognitive complexity . . . . High cognitive complexity is the capacity to observe and understand in novel ways the relationships among complex

> phenomena, the capacity to see relationships among disparate fields of knowledge. And it is that capacity which greatly increases the potential for making a major discovery. (Hollingsworth, 2007, p. 129)

There is much written about the increasing complexity of the world of global leaders. A major driver of complexity is the diversity of cultures, work forces, markets and customers, competitors, and regulatory and political systems (Rhinesmith, 2009). Another source is increased level of uncertainty driven by higher pace of change, and higher levels of risk (Bird & Osland, 2004; Levy et al., 2007; Rhinesmith, 2009). In other words, to manage the higher level of the complexity in the environment, global leaders need a higher level of cognitive complexity that would help them better understand the complex web of forces they are embedded in and make decisions that are anchored in a more integrated view of the vast number of variables to consider.

Teaching the other two elements of Intellectual Capital—namely, global business savvy and cosmopolitan outlook—will result in increased cognitive complexity in the sense that it will expand the web of variables and forces acting upon the leader and the organization. It will also help crystallize the reinforcing mechanisms among them. However, steps can be taken to further ingrain and internalize the manager's enhanced cognitive complexity.

In his study of scientists, Hollingsworth identified two processes that were particularly effective in enhancing their cognitive complexity: internalization of multiple cultures and having nonscientific activities and avocations (Hollingsworth, 2007). He showed that scientists who internalized multiple cultural identities through growing up and living in more than one society or ethnic group were better able to see the world in a more complex way. He further showed that scientists also enhanced their cognitive complexity by engaging in mentally intensive avocations: "Avocations enriched the complexity of their minds and . . . many of their scientific insights were derived by engaging in what often appeared to be nonscientific activities" (Hollingsworth, 2007, p. 141).

To enhance managers' cognitive complexity, they not only need to observe and learn at the cognitive level, but they also need to internalize the more complex picture of the world. This can be achieved through a variety of experiential and action learning activities. The key is to create an opportunity for them to experience (act), reflect, and receive feedback. The following options can achieve this in a varying degree:

- Two managers from two different parts of the world can be paired up to discuss relevant major business and leadership issues in their countries. For example, they can compare notes on what is trust and how it is created in their country, or how an effective team works in their countries. Then each manager reflects on the conversation and writes a learning log for himself or herself. Managers can then meet in small groups to discuss their logs.
- After a series of meetings with government officials from a different country, each manager creates a learning log of her understanding of how the regulatory/institutional/cultural regime in that country compares with her home country and what the implications are for her role as a global leader.
- Managers can be assigned to work on global teams or projects. They are then asked to prepare frequent learning logs on their experiences and how their work on a global team compares with their experience on a regular team. The team will then hold special meetings to compare notes on their experiences.
- Managers can be seconded to work for a short period in a foreign country. The purpose of the assignment is to go beyond just work and create a cultural immersion experience where, as much

as possible, they get to experience business and life the way the locals do. Managers will prepare learning logs and in specific intervals and upon return, will exchange notes on what they learned, and in what ways their worldview has been impacted by the experience.

As important as the above ideas are, they are all business-related. As explained earlier, it is critical to engage managers in non-business activities and environments to enhance their cognitive complexity. The object is to create an opportunity for the manager to move out of his comfort zone, namely, his business world and his normal environment. At Thunderbird, we offer a special program for Afghan women who want to start their own business. It is called the Artemis Project. We use this opportunity to get our students exposed to the participants so they can learn about life and its challenges under extreme conditions. Thunderbird has an office called Thunderbird for Good, which engages in a variety of social good activities. While its activities add clear value to its constituents, its major contribution in my mind is the opportunities it creates for our students to be exposed to non-business-related social issues. Another important program is the Thunderbird Emerging Markets Laboratory (TEM Lab), which engages our students in consulting projects in countries such as Albania, Peru, Vietnam, and Rwanda. While students get an opportunity to practice their business skills, they get to experience life and business practices in underdeveloped countries with very complex challenges. Corporations such as IBM, PricewaterhouseCoopers and UBS are now sending a select number of their managers to work on social projects like AIDS or economic development in several underdeveloped countries.

To sum up, in this section, we focused on what can be done to improve managers' Intellectual Capital, consisting of global business savvy, cosmopolitan outlook, and cognitive complexity.

Part 5. Teaching Psychological Capital. Psychological Capital refers to the three elements of passion for diversity, quest for adventure, and self-assurance. Psychological capital is probably the most difficult aspect of Global Mindset to develop in adults because much of it is shaped in childhood and youth (Gupta & Govindarajan, 2002) or rooted in the individual's psychology and personality (Howard & Howard, 2001). Nonetheless, corporations need global leaders with high levels of Psychological Capital (Black, Morrison, & Gregersen, 1999) and need to find ways of improving it. John Pepper, a former CEO at Proctor and Gamble, referred to appreciation for diversity as a critical leadership capability (Bingham, Felin, & Black, 2000).

Our own pre/post test comparison of MBA students who graduate from Thunderbird shows that of the three capitals, Intellectual Capital experiences the biggest improvement and Psychological Capital reflects the smallest improvement. But the improvement is still statistically significant and managerially relevant.

An effective program to teach Psychological Capital takes an integrative approach premised on the notion that the three elements of Psychological Capital are strongly related and can be enhanced together. Such an effort will consist of two critical components: individual or group coaching and experiential learning.

The ultimate goal in a program to develop Psychological Capital is increasing the manager's interest in learning, and curiosity in two areas: about people in another part of the world, and living and experiencing life outside of one's home base. The program should also increase the individual's willingness to take risks and to push oneself to do new and different things. A successful intervention helps a manager identify what questions to ask and how to engage with people who are different from them.

Coaching uses a process of personal discovery to build the manager's level of self-awareness, and it creates an environment for the manager to analyze, understand,

and integrate the new information and experiences. It helps the manager to better observe and relate to the challenges and forces they are dealing with. It promotes learning and change through action, practice, monitoring and feedback, and integration (Bacon & Spear, 2003; Handin & Steinwedel, 2006). Depending on the circumstances and resources, managers can be coached in individual sessions, or in groups. Regardless, the end point of coaching in this context is to help identify experiences that would enhance the manager's Psychological Capital and help him or her reflect on the experiences and their impact.

Role modeling can also play a big part in this regard. Those with lower profiles on Psychological Capital can learn from those who have higher scores. For example, pairing managers with high and low scores can be a useful exercise to help share experiences and ideas on various ways that one's profile can be improved. Managers can also learn through a conversation with other executives with much global experience who can share their excitement, experiences, successes and failures, and lessons learned. Technology can also help expand the manager's reach by making it possible to do the above suggestions virtually through the Internet and social media.

Another step is to engage in actual experiences that help improve the manager's profile. Examples would include joining multicultural teams, physical or virtual, at work or as a volunteer. In such cases, the manager needs to work closely with a coach to plan his or her actions, and to monitor progress and learning. Successful experience at this stage signals that the manager is probably ready to take on more substantive and higher risk challenges such as short expatriate assignments and travel to different parts of the world. In sum, a program to improve a manager's Psychological Capital consists of a series of progressive steps that enhance his or her profile gradually and incrementally, with the complexity and risk increasingly progressively. The learning from such experiences can be amplified and integrated into the manager's metal map with the support of a professional coach.

Part 6. Teaching Social Capital. Social Capital consists of the three elements of intercultural empathy, interpersonal impact, and diplomacy. Social Capital is the behavioral aspect of Global Mindset and refers to the propensity to build trusting relationships with people from other parts of the world. Executives with high levels of Social Capital are more effective in building sustainable relationships with individuals and groups from other regions.

In our work with executives, we have found that when two individuals trust each other, they can work effectively together regardless of where they are from. However, the definition of trust and how it comes about is different in different parts of the world. In other words, the drivers of trust seem to be culture specific but its consequences seem to be universal.

An effective program to teach Social Capital takes an integrative approach consisting of experiential opportunities and feedback. The manager needs to practice real life or simulated role play situations and receive feedback on the outcome and how to improve. Such a program can effectively focus on cross cultural communication, negotiation, and networking.

The manager needs to then engage in more substantive experiences such as meetings with individuals from other countries to discuss such topics as trust, communication styles, negotiation styles, and relationship building in diverse cultures. Another possibility is to work with a local university and accept an exchange student to live with the manager's family. As a next step, the manager can join his or her company's global teams or any of its international negotiation teams. Attending global industry or other related conferences can also help build one's networking capabilities, especially if it is done after taking a course on the techniques of networking.

In sum, through a series of experiential opportunities, a manager can enhance his or her understanding of trust and trust building across cultures and learn ways of improving their ability to build trusting relationships with people from other parts of the world.

Enhanced Self-Efficacy

This chapter provides a detailed account of the concept of Global Mindset and its components. It also presents a series of suggestions on how to enhance a manager's Intellectual Capital, Psychological Capital, and Social Capital. Following these suggestions will help the participants engage in double-loop learning (Argyris, 1991), develop a more robust mental map, and build the skills necessary to influence people from other cultures. The suggestions are also designed to enhance the manager's self-efficacy (Bandura, 1989). As Gist (1987) suggested, "Self-efficacy arises from the gradual acquisition of complex cognitive, social, linguistic, and/or physical skills through experience" (p. 472). And managers who demonstrate higher levels of self-efficacy tend to set higher goals, are more willing to take risks and try new things, and are more likely to select more challenging situations outside their comfort zone (Bandura, 2002).

AN MBA GRADUATE'S EXPERIENCE

As pointed out earlier, all incoming and outgoing students at Thunderbird are invited to complete the Global Mindset Inventory (GMI). They receive a report comparing their pre- and post-test results. Many graduating students are then invited to an interview to better understand their results. Below is an excerpt of an interview with such a student.

> I am from a small city in India. I came here with a pretty narrow view of international business. The courses and cases opened my eyes to the political and economic systems in many parts of the world. Country risk analysis techniques were so powerful. I was getting better and better in hard skills and technical knowledge. A huge set of tools to work with; so many cases about organizations in so many different countries. But it wasn't just about hard skills. I loved interacting with so many students from many other cultures. I learned not to make assumptions about others. I learned about the importance of collaboration with others from other cultures. I learned that what I'm saying and what I perceive from what you are saying is all different and I need to figure out how to do it right. It is about being sensitive to what people are saying not just verbally but in between the lines, reading their body language. I had a team member from Japan in my first project and had him again in my last project and I can see the improvement of how we interacted and how we interact now. A sea change. My self-confidence has drastically improved because of the tools, but more importantly because of my internships. I worked for a Canadian telecom company which wanted market entry in India. I worked in India but not for an Indian client but a Dutch company.

A word about proficiency in languages

Working with a database of 3,220 individuals who were born outside of Anglo countries, we showed that proficiency in English language is a predictor of the Global Mindset scores. Non-English speaking individuals with high levels of Global Mindset learn English because it facilitates their exploration of the world (Javidan, Hough, & Bullough, 2010). Furthermore, in a database of more than 6,200 individuals from many countries, we showed that familiarity with other languages is also correlated with Global Mindset. In short, there is strong evidence that proficiency in up to four languages is associated with higher levels of Global Mindset (Javidan, Hough, & Bullough, 2010). In this chapter, we do not discuss teaching languages due to space limitations, but our findings clearly show that proficiency in other languages is a powerful tool for global leaders. Therefore, a global leadership program needs to incorporate a realistic and simple way of addressing the participants' language requirements.

References

Adler, N. J. (1997). Global leadership: Women leaders. *Management International Review, 1,* 171–196.

Adler, N. J., & Bartholomew, S. (1992). Managing globally competent people. *Academy of Management Executive, 6*(3), 52–65.

Argyris, C. (1991). Teaching smart people how to learn. *Harvard Business Review, 69*(3), 99–101.

Ashkenas, R., Ulrich, D., Jick, T., & Kerr, S. (1995). *The boundaryless organization.* San Francisco, CA: Jossey-Bass.

Aycan, A. (2001). Expatriation: A critical step toward developing global leaders. In M. Mendenhall, T. M. Kuhlmann, & G. K. Stahl (Eds.), *Developing global business leaders: Policies, processes and innovations* (pp. 119–136). London: Quorum.

Bacon, T. R., & Spear, K. I. (2003). *Adaptive coaching: The art and practice of a client-centered approach to performance improvement.* Mountain View, CA: Davies-Black Publishing.

Bandura, A. (1989). Human agency in social cognitive theory. *American Psychologist, 44,* 1175–1184.

Bandura, A. (2002). Social cognitive theory in cultural context. *Applied Psychology: An International Review, 51,* 269–290.

Beechler, S., & Javidan, M. (2007). Leading with a global mindset. *Advances in International Management, 19,* 131–169.

Bingham, C. B., Felin, T., & Black, J. S. (2000). An interview with John Pepper: What it takes to be a global leader. *Human Resource Management, 39,* 287–292.

Bird, A., & Osland, S. J. (2004). Global competencies: An introduction. In H. W. Lane, M. L. Maznevski, M. E. Mendenhall, & J. McNett (Eds.), *The Blackwell handbook of global management: A guide to managing complexity* (pp. 57–81). Malden, MA: Blackwell Publishing.

Black, J. S., Morrison, A. J., & Gregersen, H. B. (1999). *Global explorers: The next generation of leaders.* New York: Routledge.

Brake, T. (1997). *The global leader: Critical factors for creating the world-class organization.* Chicago: Irwin Professional Publishing.

Daft, R. L., & Weick, K. E. (1984). Toward a model of organizations as interpretation systems. *Academy of Management Review, 9,* 284–295.

Dorfman, P. (2004). International and cross cultural leadership research. In B. J. Punnett & O. Shenkar (Eds.), *Handbook for International Management Research, 8*(4): 265–355. Ann Arbor, MI: University of Michigan Press.

Dorfman, P. W., Hanges, P. J., & Brodbeck, F. (2004). Cultural endorsed leadership. In R. J. House, P. J. Hanges, M. Javidan, P. W. Dorfman, & V. Gupta (Eds.), *Cultures, leadership, and organizations: The GLOBE study of sixty-two cultures* (pp. 669–720).

Evans, P., Pucik, V., & Barsoux, J-L. (2002). *The global challenge: Frameworks for international human resource management.* Boston, MA: McGraw-Hill Irwin.

Gist, M. E. (1987). Self-efficacy: Implications for organizational behavior and human resource management. *Academy of Management Review, 12,* 472–485.

Gupta, A. K., & Govindarajan, V. (2002). Cultivating a global mindset. *Academy of Management Executive, 16,* 116–126.

Handin, K., & Steinwedel, J. S. (2006). Developing global leaders: Executive coaching targets cross-cultural competencies. *Global Business and Organizational Excellence, 26*(1), 18–28.

Hollingsworth, J. R. (2007). High cognitive complexity and the making of major scientific discoveries. In A. Saules & M. Fournier (Eds.), *Knowledge, communication, and creativity*. Thousand Oaks, CA: Sage Publications.

House, R.J., Hanges, P.J., Javidan, M., Dorfman, P. W., & Gupta, V. (2004). *Culture, leadership, and organizations: The GLOBE study of sixty-two cultures*. Thousand Oaks, CA: Sage.

Howard, D.V., & Howard, J.H., Jr. (2001). When it *does* hurt to try: Adult age differences in implicit pattern learning. *Psychonomic Bulletin & Review, 8,* 798–805.

Howard, A., & Wellins, R.S. (2008). Overcoming the shortfalls in developing leaders. *Global Leadership Forecast 2008/2009 Executive Summary*. Pittsburg, PA: DDI.

Hunt, S. D. (2000). *A general theory of competition*. Thousand Oaks, CA: Sage.

Javidan, M. (2007). Forward-thinking cultures. *Harvard Business Review, 85*(7/8), 20.

Javidan, M., & Carl, D.E. (2004). East meets West: A cross-cultural comparison of charismatic leadership among Canadian and Iranian executives. *Journal of Management Studies, 41,* 665–691.

Javidan, M., & Dastmalchian, A. (2009). Managerial implications of the GLOBE project: A study of sixty-two societies. *Asia Pacific Journal of Human Resources, 47,* 41–58.

Javidan, M. Dorfman, P., Howell, J.P., & Hanges, P. (2010). Leadership and cultural context: A theoretical and empirical examination based on Project GLOBE. In N. Nohria & R. Khurana (Eds.), *Handbook of leadership theory and practice*. Boston, MA: Harvard Business Press.

Javidan, M., Dorfman, P., Sully de Luque, M., & House, R.J. (2006). In the eye of the beholder: Cross cultural lessons in leadership from project GLOBE. *Academy of Management Perspective, 20*(1): 67–90.

Javidan, M., Hough, L., & Bullough, A. (2010). *Conceptualizing and measuring global mindset: Development of the global mindset inventory*. Working paper, Thunderbird School of Global Management, Glendale, AZ.

Javidan, M., & Teagarden, M. (2010). Conceptualizing and measuring Global Mindset. In W.H., Mobley, & M. Lee, and Y. Wang, (Eds.), *Advances in global leadership*, Vol. 6.

Javidan, M., Teagarden, M., & Bowen, D. (2010). Making it overseas. *Harvard Business Review, 88*(4), 1–5.

Kiesler, S., & Sproull, L. (1982). Managerial response to changing environments: Perspectives on problem sensing from social cognition. *Administrative Science Quarterly, 27,* 548–570.

Levy, O., Beechler, S., Taylor, S., & Boyacigiller, N.A. (2007). What we talk about when we talk about "global mindset": Managerial cognition in multinational corporations. *Journal of International Business Studies*, 38, 231–258.

McCall, M.W., Jr. (1998). *High flyers: Developing the next generation of leaders*. Boston, MA: Harvard Business School Press.

McCall, M.W., & Hollenbeck, G.P. (2002). *Developing global executives*. Boston, MA: Harvard Business School Press.

Mendenhall, M.E., Kuhlmann, T.M., & Stahl, G.K. (2001). *Developing global business leaders: Policies, processes, and innovations*. Westport, CT: Quorum Books.

Mercer Delta. (2006). *Global study finds effective leadership development critical to corporate performance and competitive advantage*. Marsh & McLennan Companies, Press Release: 1–5.

North, D.C. (1990). *Institutions, institutional change and economic performance*. New York: Cambridge University Press.

Palmisano, S.J. (2006). The globally integrated enterprise. *Foreign Affairs, 85*(3), 127–136.

Rhinesmith, S.H. (1996). *A manager's guide to globalization: Six skills for success in a changing world* (2nd ed.). New York: McGraw-Hill.

Rhinesmith, S.H. (2009). Introduction to the leading in a global world section. In D.L. Dotlich, P.C. Cairo, S.H. Rhinesmith, & R. Meeks (Eds.), *The 2009 Pfeiffer annual leadership development*. San Francisco, CA: John Wiley & Sons, Inc.

Wood, R., & Bandura, A. (1989). Social cognitive theory of organizational management. *Academy of Management Review, 14,* 361–384.

Yukl, G. (2006). *Leadership in organizations* (6th ed.). Upper Saddle River, NJ: Prentice Hall.

Appendix 5.1

THE CURIOUS CASE OF DAVID AKEY

David Akey really did not know what to think, let alone what to do, next. He sat at his desk thinking about how things had gone in the past two months since his first meeting with his direct reports. As the new general manager for China in the consumer products division of his U.S. based employer, he had arrived in Beijing energized to expand business in what his bosses back home kept telling him was the fastest growing market in the world. It sounded so easy. All he had to do was to better integrate the different parts of the China operations to achieve the needed efficiencies.

When he arrived, David had been very hopeful because he recalled all he had heard about how "collectivistic" the Chinese were. But he had also been a little leery after hearing his returning U.S. predecessor say that the employees' "groupishness" was actually part of the problem in building a well-coordinated operation and that whenever he talked to them about it, they could not be more polite but rarely changed how they did things.

David recalled the first meeting he had with his Chinese team. He had emphasized the need for cross functional integration and even referred to the problems they were having because marketing and sales were making delivery promises to customers that operations and distribution could not meet. In the spirit of collectivism, he had established a cross functional team to address this problem, and others. Well, 60 days had passed, and coordination was no better. He had attended a couple of meetings and was struck by how things had evolved. Turf protection by function was more pronounced than anything he had ever seen in the States! The folks in each function were zealous about taking care of their own group, but indifferent to the other groups, even though they all spoke to one another in the nicest and most formal, polite and supportive of terms. Unfortunately, David was not seeing much improvement.

David was struggling to make sense of his cross cultural experience, a stretch assignment that was supposed to be so good and developmental for him! Instead, he was feeling very frustrated and having a hard time coming to grips with the whole experience, both inside and outside the workplace. He recalled a conversation with a colleague who had recently returned from her assignment in Brazil. Mary recounted some of the cross-cultural challenges and surprises she had encountered—and how she had been totally jazzed about what it had been like to work through them, how much she enjoyed mixing with locals outside of work and traveling, and her hope that she would get a new "foreign" assignment very soon.

David had anticipated that his brief preparations would have made the experience easier for him, but things were not as simple as he thought. He was also not a big fan of the local food. During the past two months, he had tried many Western restaurants in the city and had found a Western club where expatriates could get away from the local reality, a little piece of home away from home. He had begun to wonder if he was suited for global leadership assignments and, if not, why not? He felt less and less interested in the local culture and ways of doing things; and frustrated that he couldn't get things done with his Chinese team. He was wondering what kind of person really thrives on this cross cultural complexity? Is it a function of personality, life experience, what you know—or what? And if he doesn't have "it," can he get it? How?

6

THE SPIRIT OF LEADERSHIP

New Directions in Leadership Education

◆ Ken Starkey
Nottingham University Business School

◆ Carol Hall
University of Nottingham, School of Education

In this chapter we challenge the emphasis in business schools on an economic narrative of management that privileges a relatively narrow view of how leaders should think and act. As an alternative we propose a more varied, complex, social narrative of leadership grounded in a model of management education that encourages reflection upon the nature of identity, humanity, and "being together." We examine—with particular reference to the current financial crisis—what the economic narrative comprises and promises, why it is so powerful (for example, in promoting a particular MBA mind-set), and where it fails us because of its one-sided assumptions about individuals, business, and society.

We then develop an alternative narrative of management as a complicated balancing act and an identity project and describe how in our teaching we aim to promote a sense of a learning community, critical self-reflection, and intercultural awareness to challenge the lure of a narcissistic, self-preoccupied individualism that often goes with power and wealth. We then give a sense of what you would find if you joined us in the classroom. We foreground the virtues of compassion and empathy as a counterweight to the dominant discourse of rationality. We encourage our students to think and act in terms of dialogue, relationships, and intercultural learning, rather than just markets and a narrow bottom line. Our overarching goal is to facilitate the creation of richer, more inclusive narratives of self, of business, and of society.

❖❖❖

Introduction

In this chapter we discuss what we believe to be a very real challenge for leadership development: the emphasis in business schools on an economic narrative of management that privileges a relatively narrow view of how leaders should think and act. As an alternative we propose a more varied, complex, social narrative of leadership grounded in a model of management education that encourages reflection upon the nature of participants' views on identity, both personal and organizational.

The chapter is organized as follows. We use the current financial crisis as the basis for an analysis of an economic narrative that dominates business school thinking and argue that this gives a distorted view of the fundamentals of leadership. We suggest that business schools are implicated, at least in part, in the origins of the crisis and that they must play a pivotal role in ensuring that we do not repeat the same mistakes. We examine what the economic narrative comprises and promises, why it is so powerful (for example, in promoting a particular MBA mind-set) and why it fails us, not least because it is so one-sided in its assumptions about individuals, business, and society. We then set out our views of an alternative narrative of management as a complicated balancing act and an identity project.

We explain how we aim to develop an alternative management and leadership narrative from a mind-set that emphasizes humanity, plurality, and reflexivity. To do this, we aim in our teaching to promote an authentic learning community defined by critical self-reflection and intercultural learning to challenge the lure of a narcissistic, self-preoccupied individualism that often goes with power and wealth. We give a flavor of what you would find if you joined us in the classroom.

A Challenge

The economistic narrative of leadership narrowly focuses on economic return, which is largely defined in terms of material benefit to individuals, to corporations, and to shareholders, to the exclusion of other interest groups and broader societal needs. The economistic perspective is socially and culturally impoverished because, we argue, it is based upon a simplistic view of the way markets function. It assumes they are both rational and self-regulating and can be somehow trusted to operate toward the best possible outcomes. This perspective privileges individuals and markets at the expense of long-term relations. It also assumes a quasi-Darwinian view of competition in which business is an unremitting war of all against all in which only the fittest survive, and a view of evolution in which greed becomes a virtue not a vice. We contrast an economic orientation to business education with our approach, which aims to encourage the development of a richer narrative of leadership and of management enriched by a broader sense of personal identity, individual and collective possibility, and intercultural awareness.

In our teaching, we extend the view of leadership to include notions of complexity, and historically grounded knowledge rather than economic claims to empirical absolutes. We foreground the virtues of compassion and empathy as a counterweight to the dominant discourse of rationality. We encourage MBA students and clients to think and act in terms of dialogue, relationships, and intercultural learning, rather than just markets and contracts, emphasizing "being plural" rather than "being singular." Our overarching goal is to facilitate the creation of more humane, more inclusive narratives of self, business, and society.

Leading business schools across the world emphasize that their fundamental role and responsibility is to create outstanding leaders. Is it not ironic then that we are living through a financial crisis in which graduates of the world's top schools, particularly MBAs, have played leading roles in firms, such as Lehman Brothers in the United States and HBOS in the United Kingdom, who were themselves major contributors to the crisis itself? We have learned from experience that the leaders which business schools chose as exemplars or role models in their case studies (Enron springs to mind) too often prove to have clay feet. Key questions are: Where does the current crisis leave business schools? What should we be doing in response? What kind of leadership do we need for the future? And more fundamentally, is the business school a receptive or appropriate context for the task of recasting models of leadership that account for the cultural and social complexity of a global business environment?

We need to ask ourselves how our thinking about and our teaching of leadership has contributed to the crisis for which the MBA has been held partially accountable. First we suggest that one reason for the crisis is an excessively economistic focus on the tasks and responsibilities of management. A maladaptive belief in the primacy of economic causes or factors creates a dangerously limited perspective on the goals of business leadership. This focus has bred a damaging individualism, at odds with any sense of collective or transcendent purpose, and a preoccupation with a very narrowly defined "bottom line."

There is some evidence of discontent with and within business schools, expressed both in academic work (Khurana, 2007; Pfeffer & Fong, 2002; Starkey & Tiratsoo, 2007) and in the media (highly critical articles in, for example, *Wall Street Journal* and *The Economist)*. These titles give a flavor of the critique: "B-Schools Rethink Curricula Amid Crisis" in the *Wall Street Journal*, and "The Pedagogy of the Privileged" in *The Economist*. As a counterpoint, we have developed an intercultural perspective on and a teaching practice of leadership that combines insights from a range of the social sciences and humanities—particularly sociology, psychology, education, and philosophy—drawing on theory and practice both eastern and western. We argue that current financial economics, a key contributing factor in the financial crisis, focuses far too narrowly on the material world and on ethnocentric, individualistic models that are at best quasi-scientific and at worst have given us a distorted view of the way business and society intersect, or could intersect, in the making of a better world. We examine the implications of this critique for the teaching of leadership, and set out to develop an approach that does justice to its moral, social, emotional, and spiritual complexities and to the need for a more holistic, inclusive, and interdisciplinary perspective on the nature and responsibility of management and economy. We emphasize the spirit of leadership as its essential characteristic, remembering Max Weber's (1992) pioneering work on the spirit of capitalism, which emphasized the ethical aspect of modern organization while also warning that in the absence of spirit we run the danger that the organizations we create are prisons, "iron cages," rather than liberating. Weber (1992, p. 124) warns that at our stage of cultural development the danger is that those in positions of authority, "specialists without spirit, sensualists without heart," imagine that they have "attained a level of civilization never before achieved." We take this warning very seriously.

Business Schools, Economics, and Leadership: The Power of Narrative

Davis (2009, p. 42) argues that "[w]ithin the economic crisis is a unique opportunity for management scholarship to provide direction." Clearly, it is too early to comment definitively on the causes of the crisis but we would suggest that a precipitating factor was a particular narrative of business and of leadership. Narratives are a significant vehicle for human sense-making and meaning-making. They encapsulate the quintessential beliefs and assumptions we make about the nature of our reality, which in turn conditions the way we see the world and believe that it works. We frame our daily lives with stories. They embody and enact the world we want to live in and can provide predictability and reassurance by bringing meaning and a sense of order to complexity. We justify our actions with stories (Denning, 2007).

The intoxicating power of narratives is that they can capture and describe our sense of identity to ourselves and others so that we, and they, become predictable in an unpredictable world. Too often, though, these narratives, if habitual and unexamined, can be solipsistic, failing to do justice to how our stories and the stories of others (whether these "others" are in our own backyard or across the world) are inextricably intertwined, for better or for worse. One of our major concerns in facilitating leadership development is to engender an appreciation of the role and significance of narratives, personal and social, in shaping how we relate to others and to the immediate and wider world around us. The emphasis on critical reflection on personal, organizational, and cultural narratives, for example within an international MBA group, can be a powerful context for intercultural learning and dialogue. In our work we set out to develop an understanding of the way these often culturally determined narratives shape our perception and look at the intended and unintended consequences of this cultural myopia. In doing so, we challenge students to interrogate their own ontological and self-invested assumptions in order to co-create alternative narratives of business and leadership that are generative, transcultural, ethical, and sustainable. We argue that it is out of this critical reflection on personal narratives that genuine insights may emerge and personal and professional transformations occur.

Narratives can and are used ideologically to justify particular business practices. The financial crisis, as we have witnessed, was partially caused by a misplaced belief in a narrative of business and finance that came to be taken for granted and remained largely unquestioned. Built on economic theories, it became convenient for those powerful groups who benefited most from this narrative to adopt it whole-heartedly and in turn impose it on others. There was no alternative to the view that their representation of the world was the way the world is and must be. Our work with cohorts of international MBA students and clients consciously focuses on developing the psychological flexibility, intercultural competence, and creativity to generate alternative, less simplistic understandings of the way their worlds work, intersect, and diverge. Through authentic reflexivity, alternative, culturally more nuanced ways of perceiving the world and potential scenarios of the future become possible. For many of those centrally involved, the banking crisis was not only unthinkable but impossible, until it happened. Kotlikoff (2010, p. xvii) explains economists' failure to predict the financial crisis on the fact that they were obsessed with researching an "imaginary world in which people play by the rules." This simultaneous failure of theory, leadership imagination, and responsibility demonstrates the power of the narrative spell. Thus we consciously adopt and articulate the basic philosophical assumption that no one theory can serve as a definitive "mirror of nature" (Rorty, 1980).

Some narratives are more hegemonic than others in their claims and we suggest that economics possesses more of this characteristic than most. As a counterbalance we encourage a greater tolerance of a multiplicity of visions of the world, as well as a sense of the present, composed of a complex history and an uncertain future, "determined" by system-wide effects (Senge, 1990). Goodman (1978, pp. 2–4) argues this complexity cannot be appreciated or managed by the attitude of "the monopolistic materialist or physicalist who maintains that one system . . . is preeminent and all-inclusive, such that every other version must eventually be reduced to it or rejected as false or meaningless." An alternative explanation is to suggest that beneath the apparent objectivity and rationality of a scientific narrative, there lurks persuasion, rhetoric, seduction, and fantasy, even utopian dreams (Gibson, 1996) that, alas as we have seen, too often give rise to dystopian nightmares.

The narrative of leadership in business schools, in our view, has suffered in recent years, losing theoretical ground and moral authority to the narrative of economics. Ferraro et al. (2005, p. 10) examine what they see as the triumph of the economic in management discourse, arguing that economics has become the "reigning queen of the social sciences" and that there is "little doubt that economics has won the battle for theoretical hegemony in academia and society as a whole and that such dominance becomes stronger every year." Social science theories can become self-fulfilling by shaping institutional strategy and management practices, as well as social norms and expectations about behavior, thereby creating the very behavior they predict.

Behind this position was, as we have suggested, the rise of the economistic as the only true or real measure of value. This was supported by the whole theoretical edifice of modern financial economics. The efficient market hypothesis suggested that markets were magically self-correcting and knew far better than human actors about what was most efficient and effective. The emphasis on individual self-seeking, a position justified by several hundred years of political and economic philosophy, and by Darwinian biological metaphors such as survival of the fittest and nature red in tooth and claw, was lauded as the oxygen the market needed to survive and prosper. Adam Smith's metaphor of "the invisible hand," according to Greenspan (2007, p. 262), "captured the world's imagination—possibly because it seems to impute a godlike benevolence and omniscience to the market, whose workings are in reality as impersonal as natural selection." The market as a form of *deus ex machina* also relieves individuals from the burden of moral responsibility for their actions, the repercussions of which we are now experiencing.

Theories of commerce had their origins in theories of the relationship between trade, war, and economic growth (Hont, 2005). The business of business was business. A virtuous circle was imputed, in which the pursuit of individual self-interest led to the wealth of nations. Any other philosophy that detracted from this core role of business, such as corporate social responsibility, was to be resisted (Friedman, 1970). According to Miller (1999, p. 1053), it was the philosopher Thomas Hobbes in *Leviathan*, first published in 1651, who "enthroned self-interest as the cardinal human motive," and this has become a collectively shared cultural ideology, particularly hyperactive among students and practitioners of economics and business. Hobbes, Smith, Darwin, and Chicago economics collide to produce what Ross (1994) calls the "Chicago gangster theory of life"—or, more simply, "greed is good."

Davis (2009) describes the consequence of the ineluctable rise of finance as "the end of the society of organizations." An "overriding corporate focus on shareholder value as the ultimate measure of corporate and managerial employment" and the "orientation toward share price" led inexorably to a shift in perspective: the "old model of organization man was increasingly replaced by a model of the investor trading in various species of capital (financial, human, social)" (Davis, 2009, p. 28). Management education reinforced this, and probably to some extent still does. Khurana (2007, pp. 322–330) charts the inexorable rise of the economic narrative in business schools, "these ideas . . . transformed many business schools from training grounds for general managers to institutions that trained professional investors and financial engineers, especially in the areas of investment banking, private equity, and hedge fund."

Thus, economic theory—for example, agency theory—becomes taken for granted, "a type of shared cognition," excluding any sense of collective responsibility, positioning "managerial agents as distinct and dissociated from one another, defining an organization as simply a nexus of contracts among individual agents" (Khurana, 2007, pp. 324–325). Leadership was associated with unleashing individual entrepreneurial energies in highly driven workplaces where each competed with all for career advancement. Business is seen as a form of war, a war of all against all and the workplace the battlefield where compassion, empathy, and idealism are the fallen. MBA students (both men and women) enrolled on the leadership module regularly voice the fear that learning how to do what they called "the soft, fluffy stuff" and being "more human" in the workplace would make them appear weak and therefore become vulnerable targets for their more rapacious colleagues. The fear that becoming more human and respectful in the business environment will sound the death knell for career progression is a deep-seated one and has its roots in the narratives of leaders as aggressive, territorial, and driven. Inevitably, many said they chose to be an institutional predator rather than the predated. Top MBAs' career of choice was to join investment banks, private equity firms, or hedge funds (Delves Broughton, 2008). Hubbard (2006), himself a leading business school dean (at a more optimistic moment that now seems a long time ago), argued against critics of the business school and the MBA, that the key role of the business school was to develop leaders as champions of entrepreneurial capitalism, that their key weapon was new business models with finance as their core and valuation as the key skill. In these more "innocent" times, his central argument was that private equity was reshaping the world for the better.

Employment relationships are fractured and defined by individualism (Ghoshal, 2005; Ghoshal & Moran, 1996). Loyalty to the company or of the company to the employee is seen as old-fashioned, last-century thinking, and a culturally alien virtue. Individuals are encouraged to become independent and entrepreneurial, to capitalize on market opportunities irrespective of the outcomes. Traditional ideas of stewardship, service, and customer relationships were cast aside. Financial services became the prototype industry of the West, at least in the United States and United Kingdom. "The profits to be had from smart people making complicated bets overwhelmed anything that could be had from servicing customers, or allocating capital to productive enterprise" (Lewis, 2010, p. 258). Trading and dealing were the quintessential form of work, "beyond the bounds of rational constraint—or self-discipline" (Tett, 2009, p. 47).

Of course, what we now know is that the new financial instruments—the CDOs and their like—that proliferated in what was claimed by people such as Alan Greenspan to be a period of unprecedented financial innovation, were constructed on shifting sands. They were based on a lack of real wealth creation and bizarre accounting practices that permitted the reporting of profits before they were actually realized.

It was, as we now know to all our costs, a house of cards: "a memo had gone out on Wall Street, saying that if you wanted to keep on getting rich shuffling bits of paper around to no obvious social purpose, you had better camouflage your true nature" (Lewis, 2010, p. 63). Eventually even Greenspan admitted to a "flaw" in his economic ideology and the narrative he had been a key player in legitimizing. As he told a Congressional inquiry into the banking crisis, "I made a mistake in presuming that the self-interest of organizations, specifically banks and others, were such that they were best capable of protecting their own shareholders and the equity in the firms" (Greenspan, 2008). This insight unfortunately came too late. The gains of the market euphoria had been privatized while, in a perverse inversion of responsibility, its losses were socialized, with communities around the world picking up the bill for saving the banking industry.

In summary, the economistic narrative is based upon a particular philosophy of knowledge that assumes it has an accurate picture and theory of how the world works. The financial crisis calls this assumption into question. Economics defines the world into a narrowly pre-determined set of categories: a particular view of value, an emphasis upon management as trading for profit, individuals as rational and calculating profit-maximizers, a philosophy of individualism, and relationships as predominantly about competition and conflict. The economistic way of thinking accepts a particular way of viewing the world as the only way the world can work. This promotes a rigid sense of certainty based on the uncritical acceptance of a particular approach to finance and trust in its one-dimensional model of the world and particularly its approach to the management of risk. This strong belief system is exacerbated by the emphasis (the overemphasis, in our view) on economics and finance in the MBA curriculum in particular. It is reinforced by a simplistic Darwinian narrative of personal struggle for survival in a business environment where the winner takes all and individualism and fierce competition is emphasized at the expense of cooperation. It relies on a very narrow definition of the bottom line (Starkey & Tiratsoo, 2007). We find this way of thinking limiting, depressing, and dangerous. We also challenge is functionality in the light of the damage caused by the financial crisis in which MBAs from top business schools played key roles. We now go on to present our attempt in our teaching, grounded in our research activities, to develop an alternative narrative of leadership, management, and business that challenges the economic narrative with ideas of reflexivity, self-questioning, self-fashioning, identity, relationality, aspiration, and hope.

Teaching Leadership: Balancing Acts and Creating a Personal Leadership Identity

THE HUMAN DIMENSION: PLURALITY AND INTERCULTURALITY

Central to what we do is to emphasize that a key distinction between a leadership and management narrative and an economic narrative is the weight they attach to the human dimension, with all its social, cultural, political, and moral complexity. We use philosophy as our measure here, drawing upon, among others, the leading contemporary French philosopher, Jean-Luc Nancy (2000), who argues that developing ourselves as individuals, "being singular," is enriched only to the extent that we develop our capacity for "being plural." We contest a philosophy of individualism to argue that the essence of being human is interconnection and interdependence, which can be realized through authentic intercultural dialogue. We agree with Parekh's (2006, p. 338) view of "the cultural embeddedness of human beings, the inescapability and desirability of cultural diversity and intercultural dialogue, and the internal plurality of each culture." To be at one with others in this way puts a firm dividing line between the narrative we seek to co-produce with our MBA students and clients and the current emphasis on egoistic individualism, which the economic narrative demands of us all. This interconnection goes beyond the bounds of the local and familiar (being singular) to the transpersonal and spiritual (being plural). Authentic interconnectivity embraces similarity while celebrating difference; thus intercultural exchange becomes a vehicle for creating new learning spaces characterized by a respect and appreciation for difference and what it can teach us about ourselves.

Martin Buber, who was "considered by many to be the philosopher of dialogue par excellence" (Guilherme & Morgan, 2010, p. 1), provides rich insight and wisdom into how Nancy's ideas of plurality and interconnection can be realized in and through dialogic encounter. Buber's (1958) concept of I-Thou (as opposed to the I-It objectification of the Other, more suited to the scientific method) provides us with a model of relational exchange characterized by equality, being fully present in the moment, and mutuality. Out of this encounter emerges genuine dialogue, where each is heard and a new psychological space emerges that encompasses the field between the two. Buber's notion of a co-created, interdependent space links to current debates about the meaning of interculturality, defined by the Baring Foundation (2007) persuasively as "a dynamic process by which people from different cultures interact to learn about and question their own and each other's cultures. Over time this may lead to cultural change. It recognises the inequalities at work in society and the need to overcome these. It is a process which requires mutual respect and acknowledges human rights."

It is in this respect for the person, whatever their cultural background, where Buber's philosophical concept of I-Thou resonates most strongly with Carl Rogers' humanistic notion of the psychological "core conditions" that he argued needed to be present for facilitating effective human relationships and development: congruence, (universal) unconditional positive regard, and empathic understanding. For Rogers, like Buber, "the strongest force in our universe is not overriding power but love" (Rogers, 1980, p. 219).

We also draw on the work of Michel Foucault (1982), the world's leading public intellectual, who argues that a major, perhaps the major, political, ethical, social, and philosophical challenge is to promote new forms of intersubjectivity. Foucault encourages us to refuse the too easy seductions of the dominant business narrative, to enable us to reflect upon our history, where necessary contest it, and, if necessary, create a new, shared history. We situate our teaching of leadership and business and management in the context of key social debates as a counterpoint to a view that privileges market exchange and the calculating pursuit of individual self-interest.

The most significant intellectual challenge at present for management and leadership scholars is to counter an immature infatuation with seductive but ultimately dystopian pictures of the world that inform the view of business and management embodied in economic narrative and enacted, in its most extreme form, in the recent practices of the banking industry. The need is for a more human narrative that sets out an alternative to I-It or "purely calculative economic relations—asocial economic atomism— . . . individual, disembedded, rational, efficient, short-term, calculable, incontestable," the qualities associated with economic transactions mediated only by a market (Nancy, 2000, p. 83). We now need an alternative narrative rooted in the concept of a richer quality of human relationships that challenges an overly limited Eurocentric view of self-sufficiency and human behavior.

Managers as leaders, with the support of management scholars, can be challenged to design new institutions in which new narratives of self and of self and the other can be co-created. The implication is that we should encompass a concern for the other, both local and global, in our narratives as an alternative to management practices that are "successful" only at the expense of the other. We need to pay more attention to public value and develop a more intelligent appreciation of the "common good" (Moore, 1995) and we would add what that might mean in a global context. The challenge for the management research community is to create a narrative that fills the gap left by the eclipse of one version of the economic narrative by the financial crisis. The time is ripe for a new narrative of management grounded in notions of intercultural learning that expands our vision of the common interest.

Critical Realism and Reflexivity

In our teaching we do use a traditional business school technology, the case study, but we do so in a critical fashion, to deconstruct those case studies that have too short-term a notion of success, and to encourage a more "realistic" awareness of what success might mean in the longer term. For example, we draw on case studies of the present banking crisis and its precursor, Long Term Capital Management (Lowenstein, 2001), to encourage a realization of the importance of knowing and understanding history, not least to challenge Fukuyama's claim that history has ended and that there is no alternative to a particular form of social and economic organization. Our pedagogy is, in part, informed by a philosophy of critical realism (Bhaskar, 1978). This distinguishes between the "empirical" —what we observe—and the "real." The real is the actual driver of events and consists of the generative mechanisms, themselves a complex outcome of structure and agency, which produce the events in the world. "The real consists not of events but their causes: the generative mechanisms and structures, the potencies, so to say, of which events are but the effects" (Wilson & Dixon, 2006, p. 262).

We contest therefore a science that assumes that the empirical is an unproblematic mirror of the real. For example, what Hamel (2001) saw in his account of Enron might have had simple empirical validity in terms of his case methodology and his rather simplistic "great leadership" view of superior performance. However, it failed to do justice to a more critically nuanced explanation of the Enron phenomenon, its short-lived superior performance, and its spectacular fall. It presented Enron as a model company to be widely emulated. It gave no hint of the weaknesses that led to its ultimate fall. The same is true of many business school case studies with their infatuation with the present and with a success that is often stellar but short-lived.

Critical realism focuses upon trying to model and explain "why what happens actually happens" (Danermark et al., 2001, p. 52), which it does by challenging the assumption of a naïve empiricist positivism—that what we observe is what is important—and focusing on the generative mechanisms that are by definition unobservable. A prerequisite of the critical realist approach is the cultivation of reflexivity in the researcher. Hertz (1997, p. viii) argues that "to be reflexive is to have an ongoing conversation about experience while simultaneously living in the moment." We encourage reflexivity to develop the intellectual and emotional capacity to distinguish between the lasting and the merely fashionable and to develop the moral courage to point out if the emperor's new clothes are in fact illusory. The essence of reflexivity is the ability to challenge our own thoughts, feelings, values, attitudes, beliefs, and habits of mind. We are at once the subject and the object of our own study, which we might also call self-awareness. This moment by moment awareness—observing ourselves in process—enables us to reframe experience and abandon old negative or habitual modes of thinking and experiencing. However, reflexivity is not just a personal, affective process. It is also a cognitive process that challenges us to examine the personal, social, and political contexts from which theory, research, and practice derive, and to understand our relationship to them.

We see this approach as building a capacity for prescience rather than prediction. In this sense, social science is as much pre-science as a science in the narrowly positivist sense. The latter only applies in those clearly delineated areas where empiricism can legitimately deal with truly observable phenomena, though the evolution of science (for example, physics) teaches us that we can cling to what seems obvious at our peril. We need to learn to be more reflective, and to have the moral courage to challenge our mental models in a world that seems increasingly unpredictable. An awareness of the history of capitalism teaches us that it has developed and evolved as a complex interplay of social and economic factors, as an expression of deeply and sometimes contradictory human motives and values. What seems to have happened in the recent past is that a purely economic explanation has reduced the emphasis upon the social and cultural and centrifuged to the margins factors that are inconvenient for its mode of explanation.

Our approach is to redress the balance—"balance" is a key concept we continually emphasize—and to reinstate the human, relational element, complex motives, and competing values, and a sense of history to the fore of our thinking. For example, Lowenstein (2001) argues that one of the reasons why Long-Term Capital Management failed so spectacularly, almost bringing down the world's financial system, was that the human spirit was totally absent from its founders' (Nobel-prize-winning economists) understanding of how markets were supposed to work. What was also lacking, as the historian Niall Ferguson (2008) points out, was a sense of history. We also make this a philosophical touchstone of our teaching, agreeing with John Dewey (1939, pp. 316–318) that a major task for management is "remaking a profit system into a system conducted not just . . . in the interests of consumption, important as that is, but also in the interest of positive and enduring opportunity for productive and creative activity and all that that signifies for the development of the potentialities of human nature." We need a positive narrative, of hope and aspiration that privileges the human spirit as an alternative to the excess and irrational exuberance that is driven by "animal spirits" (Akerlof & Shiller, 2009).

Personal Leadership and Identity

The financial crisis, which began on Wall Street (the paragon career for many, if not the majority, of top MBAs), brings into sharp relief the need for a more holistic view of both management and management education. In the search for technical competence, business schools have championed expertise (often masquerading as science, particularly in economics and finance), which undoubtedly contributed to the financial crisis. However, it would be misplaced to attribute responsibility solely to the economists. Leadership and marketing scholars should also take responsibility for their part in the process. The current economic malaise, and resulting widespread social distress, poses both a legitimacy and identity crisis for business schools and a profound challenge to business school leaders. It appears that in the search for technical competence business schools have themselves lost their capacity for reflection and can no longer claim to be learning organizations (Senge, 1990). The MBA has rightly been criticized for focusing students too much on their own economic and social advantage at the expense of public purpose. The MBA curriculum design has also been criticized for being disproportionately focused on analytics, insufficiently integrative, and for failing to develop wisdom, intuition, and intra- and interpersonal awareness. It has even been suggested that the MBA "distorts" those subjected to it into "critters with lopsided brains, icy hearts, and shrunken souls" (Leavitt, 1996).

A key challenge that we address in our teaching is to promote reflexivity in an arena that has lost a large degree of its collective capacity for critical self-analysis, based upon inquiry rather than partisan advocacy, and for the creation of new educational spaces for experimentation in managing and leading. This requires integrative thinking, the nourishing of the mind with imaginative ideas, and creative alternative ways of seeing and being as well as attention to the needs of the heart, soul, and body. As the Chicago philosopher Martha Nussbaum (1997) neatly expresses it, the challenge we face as educators is to develop improvisers with creativity, passionate about their work and what can be achieved, and who can provide both personal and organizational leadership, rather than followers who need leading or technocrats motivated by self-interest. We need to challenge too rigid a sense of identity, too narrowly rooted in the economistic, to explore the possibility of the alternative and of the other (Cavell, 2005). To do this we need learning experiences that offer the opportunity of reflecting on our current ways of being and on authentic alternatives that nurture the spirit as well as promote reflection on the meaning and purpose of material success.

Academic studies of leadership have tended to over-simplify the multiplicity of ethical and psychological challenges leaders face, choosing to focus somewhat narrowly on case examples that offer an overly romanticized view of the leader as the "great man," an alpha-male who single-handedly drags a reluctant organization toward his vision of a great and glorious future. Successful organizations too often are seen as the reflection of this "great man" model of history. One of the problems with this kind of analysis is that it has tended to reproduce notions of outstanding leaders as heroic individuals. This characterization is both limited theoretically and problematic for leadership as well as organizational development. Primarily, it fails to acknowledge the unsung contributions that members of the wider organization make to any major growth or success. It can also have the unlooked-for effect of creating the phenomenon of pseudo-competence within the organizational hierarchy or what Clarkson (1994) calls "the Achilles syndrome." A culture of pretence emerges where individuals feel emotionally pressured to live up to the mythical standards of the heroic leader while feeling wholly inadequate to the task. Feeling like an imposter at work is not only corrosive of the self-esteem but is invariably demotivating and deskilling.

Recent history has taught us that the leader as superhero too often comes to be judged in the fullness of time to be far less impressive than was first claimed. Enron and its leadership for a number of years was the world's most admired corporation. Sir Fred Goodwin of Royal Bank of Scotland was widely perceived in the industry as a heroic, visionary leader. The banking crisis challenges much of our current thinking about what constitutes exemplary leadership and drives us to re-examine our taken for granted assumptions about the very nature of leadership. Lao Tzu's ancient maxim—"A leader is best when people barely know he exists, when his work is done, his aim fulfilled, they will say, we did it ourselves"—is a timely reminder of a very different and rather more humble vision of the task and responsibility of leadership. So we have argued that we need fresh and different ways of thinking about and practicing leadership. Our approach is to develop leadership programs that aim to re-examine and build the personal resources and attitudes of mind necessary for leading in turbulent times.

The MBA group itself becomes a medium for the development of a learning community and it is within the spirit and practice of authentic intercultural dialogue and enquiry that we aim to prepare them for the challenge of morally purposeful, values-driven leadership, safeguarding a sense of personal integrity while promoting the integrity of others. In this way individuals are enabled to take responsibility for the creation of a leadership identity that people are committed to and ultimately feel comfortable with because it resonates with their authentic values and beliefs. Throughout this process, we encourage learners to examine personal and work identities and the values they are rooted in and express, as well as develop supporting strategies to maximize interpersonal effectiveness in achieving morally complex organizational and societal goals.

As we said earlier, we emphasize the notion of balance and the ability to create harmony in relationship with the self and others. We see leadership as a challenging activity because it requires such a difficult balancing act, which is, by its very nature, intellectual, emotional, and spiritual. Leadership, we know to our cost, has a shadow side, thus we define leadership as a moral, ethical activity, best framed in terms of psychological and organizational integrity. We encourage students and clients to define their core aspirations in the leadership role and to examine how they can achieve these with the greatest sense of personal fulfillment. We examine the organizational context in which they lead and how they can reframe their thinking and actions to develop their own signature identity as leaders. We recognize that working at this level of relational and emotional depth is both demanding and rewarding but as Jersild (1955) reminds us, "to gain in knowledge of self, one must have the courage to seek it and the humility to accept what one may find."

We focus upon two concerns that are fundamentally intertwined: first, extending the capacity to think reflexively about the world and about how we think, feel, and experience it; while simultaneously elaborating and expanding an awareness of self and identity in relationship. Branden (1995, p. x1) argues that "it is a dangerous moment in history not to know who we are or not to trust ourselves"—but all too frequently management education sidesteps the responsibility of providing a safe space to develop social, emotional, and transpersonal awareness in favor of a less emotionally demanding technical education. To support this more intimate exploration, we work with our students and clients on understanding their personal and professional identities, and the role that cultures continue to play in (re)shaping that identity. The act of critical self-reflection and a desire to understand ourselves is not a narcissistic undertaking. The purpose of self-learning is a moral one. It serves to deepen our empathy for others and open our eyes to the inter-connectedness of humanity, making us more mindful of the consequences of our actions. The tension between, and the balancing of, the individual and the collective are major challenges that are addressed at the levels of philosophy, theory, and practice.

We see leadership as much an art as a science, and as much a communal as an individual act. We therefore provide a learning environment that enables participants to explore how to balance economic necessity with the challenge of professing our humanity in developing more humane and sustainable organizations. We do this by drawing on and integrating management and education best practice, eastern and western philosophy, psychology, the arts and humanities, systems thinking, action and narrative inquiry, story-telling, life histories, scenario planning, management learning, and personal development. We also mine the cultural diversity of the student community as a focus for rich intercultural learning and dialogue.

Importantly, we emphasize that leadership is about dealing with an inherently complex, sometimes chaotic, psychologically challenging, and always fast-moving world. Increasingly, a major task leaders must accomplish is to create some sense of order and meaning out of chaos, both for themselves and for those they lead without succumbing to the temptation of premature closure and rigid thinking as a defense against the anxiety of uncertainty. As Branden (1995, p. x1) reminds us, "The stability we cannot find in the world we must find within our own persons." We construe leadership as functioning optimally when it exhibits a capacity for prescience. We define prescience as a capacity to sense/know what is most important in the here and now to prepare for the future. In gestalt terms this means a willingness to be fully alert to and alive in the present moment, an attitude of mindfulness that promotes a deep intuitive appreciation of the patterns of experience in ourselves and others. This is a quality we find in the most inspirational leaders we work with. Prescience requires self-awareness and the capacity for deep, systematic reflection as well as openness to sensory experience and embodied learning. In this way, change, grounded in imagination, particularly moral imagination, becomes possible (Johnson, 1997).

Our pedagogical approach is primarily experiential (Kolb, 1984) but while active and participative in character is as much about being as doing. In supporting the development of social (Goleman, 2006), emotional (Mayer & Salovey, 1993), and spiritual intelligence (Zohar & Marshall, 2000) alongside and in balance with intellectual functioning, we give weight to the emotional component of the reflection cycle, using structured exercises to facilitate personal exploration of thoughts and feelings that have their roots in cultural narratives. Cooper and Sawaf (1998, p. xi) argue that "We have paid a drastic price—not only in our organizations but in our lives—for trying to disconnect emotions from intellect. It can't be done." The role of the tutor, or facilitator, in experiential work is to create an environment in which the learning community can flourish by first providing sufficient psychological safety to permit the learner to engage with difficult personal and professional emotions and issues. The facilitator needs the ability to hold or "contain" strongly felt or expressed emotion by members of the group and needs to be able to engender a sense of deep trust in learners. This requires a degree of emotional maturity and a commitment to one's own growth and self-care as well as that of learners.

If you were to peep into a leadership classroom what would you see and hear? The atmosphere would be relaxed yet alert, informal but disciplined. There would be series of paired, individual, and group work exercises and the culturally diverse student group would be encouraged to record their experiences and learning in a reflective journal. Students might be sitting around tables arranged around the edge of the room or in groups on the floor—whatever is appropriate to the task. At first glance it would be difficult to identify the tutor. We would work with the lived experience of the group and use guided imagery, metaphor, and visualization as a means of exploring narrative and to develop self-theories. We use learning sets to encourage collaborative learning and mutuality. There are protected spaces for reflection and goal setting and we encourage support systems such as "buddying" to encourage investment in each others' goals. In this way group affiliation and personal bonds are formed that endure well beyond the boundary of the course.

Our repertoire includes offering process-led exercises choreographed to enhance appreciation and understanding of individual and group dynamics. This experiential work promotes greater self-knowledge, for example, of personal and cultural blind spots, and an awareness of individual boundaries and the limits of personal risk-taking. In this way the interculturalism of the group itself becomes a supportive yet challenging vehicle for social and emotional learning because it provides a source of immediate, here-and-now interpersonal exploration. We foreground the importance of developing empathy for others, giving and receiving authentic feedback and mentoring and coaching as approaches to developing facilitative workplace relationships. The intercultural competencies of perception management, relationship management, and self-management are emphasized (Bird, Mendenhall, Stevens, & Oddou, 2010). The importance of handling and understanding the causes and effects of stress in the self and others is explored with a view to developing a capacity for mindfulness and compassion (Kabat-Zinn, 1990), while maintaining a healthy work-life balance through conscious, consistent self-care. Ultimately, we ask MBA students to inhabit their own personal authority and take responsibility for their lives and relationships, rather than projecting blame onto others or the "system" in defensive or unaware routines (Brown & Starkey, 2002).

From the perspective of rationality, we use cognitive techniques such as scenario planning to help participants imagine the future in more flexible ways, based on a range of different possible futures, which we capture through story-telling. To promote self-awareness, and a sense of inner rather than outer direction, using dialogue, we challenge participants to contest the dominant cultural models, their own and those of others, which are used to rationalize the darker side of leadership characterized by a lust for power, moral myopia, insatiability, envy, and greed. The aim here is once again to promote a more empathic, compassionate attitude to self and others and, thus, more sustainable forms of organization characterized by moral and ethical purpose. Here we would mention as an example the intensely moving narrative developed by a Nigerian MBA student to describe her own and her family's experience of living in Nigeria. Her powerful narrative linked generational and broader business and social developments, and, in particular, the devastation of the Niger Delta by oil exploration. What emerged out of the group discussion was a co-created, intercultural vision of the role of leadership as stewardship for the present and for future generations, grounded in feelings of care and compassion. We also use a series of case studies, written or chosen specifically to highlight the human repercussions of leadership decision-making. An case example is an analysis of a leadership disaster on Mount Everest (Ennew et al., 2006), which illustrates the darker side of leadership and the importance of recognizing limits, and how to balance risk-taking and self-interest with the greater good and safety of the group.

A key theme running through our work is collaborative inquiry based upon the process of listening in a more open-hearted, respectful manner to others and to the self, as well as the importance of both private and public value (Moore, 1995). In the yogic tradition the practice of listening to others in a community with humility and respect and an emphasis on creating harmony and balance through the quality of individual contributions is a spiritual practice known as "satsanga." We encourage this spirit of satsanga within the group so that members feel more able to talk about sensitive issues in their personal and professional histories.

Figure 6.1 presents a schematic representation of the architecture of our courses.

MBA courses and executive modules are run over intensive five-day blocks in order to maximize learning and capitalize on the group process. We also offer courses to executive education clients, with our preferred option a three-day course segmented in the following way: a two-day workshop typically comprising a balance of case study, experiential exercises, tutor input, and personal reflection; followed by an opportunity to apply what has been learned in the clients' own work environment. The course leaders provide on-going mentoring/coaching. Finally, we re-convene as a group

Figure 6.1 Leadership as Balancing Act

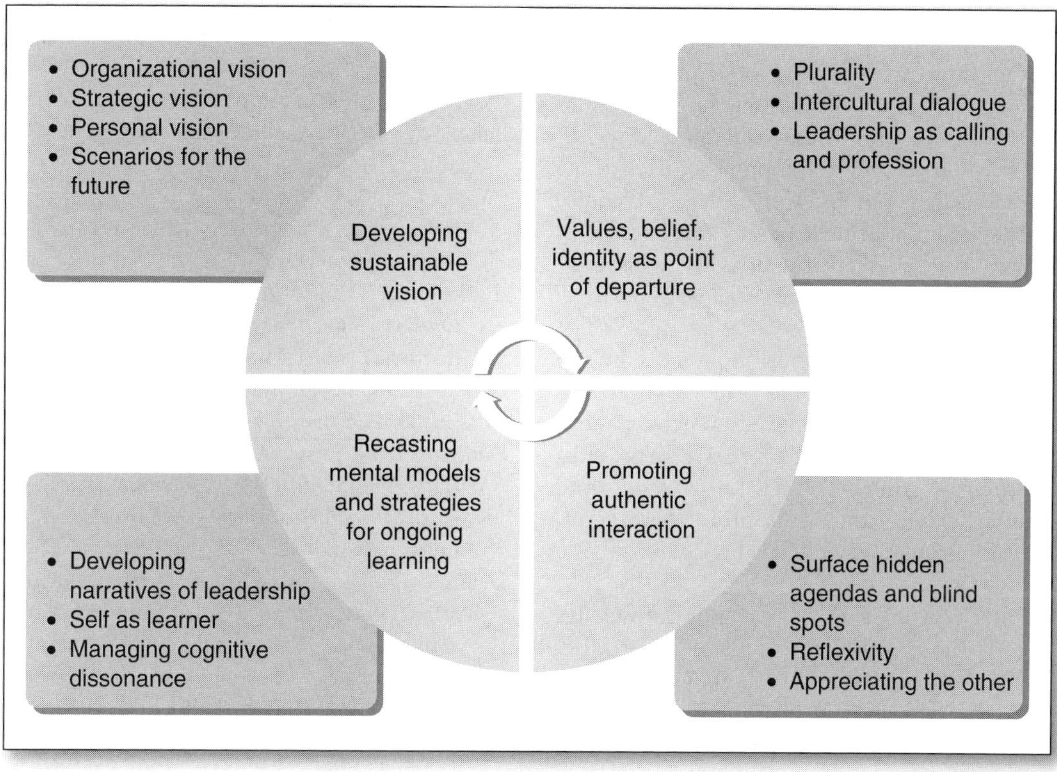

for a third day to focus on personal and organizational learning from the course and to think through next steps in developing a more balanced philosophy and practice of leadership for the future and what further work needs to be done individually and organizationally. However, we are client-led and tailor bespoke courses to meet the learning needs of the client.

Conclusion

We live in a challenging time for business and business schools. The financial crisis will throw a long shadow and it will require a rethinking of existing theories of business and management and of business and management education practices, if we are to avoid a damaging repeat that, were it to happen, would have even more damaging consequences. This challenge places a premium upon creative and critical thinking to help us in re-imagining a more effective and sustainable future (Datar et al., 2010). Leadership is the core of an organization. When it works well it has enormous consequences for the good of many: employees, customers, and society. When it works badly, which we have suggested happens when self-interest dominates without reference to the social consequences, it can be the source of great harm.

We have suggested an alternative model of teaching leadership grounded in an eclectic mix of social science, philosophy, and the humanities, combining organizational and personal development. By implication we would also argue that this is the direction in which business schools should move, broadening themselves to different forms of knowledge and experience to enable reflexivity and responsiveness in their own practices. There are significant barriers to such a change, not least the existing configuration of the *status quo*. Despite the financial crisis, there remains much inertia in the system and resistance to change. To counter this will demand imaginative ideas and a willingness to challenge entrenched opinion. Above all, it will require business school deans and other faculty as well as enlightened managers willing to exercise bold, imaginative leadership.

We finish with a cautionary tale, "The Announcement," a Sufi story told by the Mulla Nasrudin (Shah, 1968) that has something of importance to teach us about the folly of believing there are easy paths to easy solutions, self-knowledge, and insight. Nasrudin stood up in the marketplace and addressed the throng.

> "O people! Do you want knowledge without difficulties, truth without falsehood, attainment without effort, progress without sacrifice?"
>
> Very soon a large crowd gathered, everyone shouting; "Yes, yes!"
>
> "Excellent!" said the Mulla. "I only wanted to know. You may rely upon me to tell you all about it if I ever discover any such thing."

References

Akerlof, G.A., & Shiller, R.J. (2009). *Animal spirits: How human psychology drives the economy, and why it matters for global capitalism.* Princeton, NJ: Princeton University Press.

Baring Foundation. (2007). London: Annual Report.

Bhaskar, R. (1978). *A realist theory of science.* London: Verso.

Bird, A., Mendenhall, M., Stevens, M.J., & Oddou, G. (2010). Defining the content domain of intercultural competence for global leaders. *Journal of Managerial Psychology, 25*, 810–828.

Branden, N. (1995). *The six pillars of self-esteem.* New York: Bantam Books.

Brown, K., & Starkey, K. (2000). Organizational identity and learning: A psychodynamic perspective. *Academy of Management Review, 25*, 102–120.

Buber, M. (1958). *I and thou* (R.J. Smith, trans.). New York: Macmillan.

Cavell, S. (2005). *Philosophy the day after tomorrow.* Cambridge, MA: Harvard University Press.

Clarkson, P. (1994). *The Achilles syndrome: Overcoming the secret fear of failure.* London: Element Books.

Cooper, R., & Sawaf, A. (1998). *Executive EQ.* London: Orion Books.

Danermark, B., Ekström, M., Jakobsen, L., & Karlsson, J.C. (2001). *Explaining society: Critical realism in the social sciences.* London: Routledge.

Datar, S.M., Garvin, D.A., & Cullen, P.G. (2010). *Rethinking the MBA: Business education at the crossroads.* Boston, MA: Harvard Business School Press.

Delves Broughton, P. (2009). *What they teach you at Harvard Business School. My two years in the cauldron of capitalism.* New York: Penguin.

Denning, S. (2007). *The secret language of leadership: How leaders inspire action through narrative.* London: John Wiley & Sons.

Dewey, J. (1939). The economic basis of the new society. In *Later works of John Dewey* (vol. 13). Carbondale, IL: Southern Illinois University Press.

Ennew, C., Tempest, S., & Starkey, K. (2007). In the death zone: A study of limits in the 1996 Mount Everest disaster. *Human Relations, 60*, 1029–1064.

Ferguson, N. (2009). *The ascent of money: A financial history of the world.* London: Allen Lane.

Ferraro, F., Pfeffer, J., & Sutton, R.L. (2005). Economic language and assumptions can become self-fulfilling. *Academy of Management Review, 30*, 8–24.

Foucault, M. (1982). Afterword. In H. L. Dreyfus & P. Rabinow (Eds.). *Michel*

Foucault: Beyond structuralism and hermeneutics. London: Harvester Wheatsheaf.

Friedman, M. (1970, September 13). The social responsibility of business is to increase its profits. *The New York Times*.

Ghoshal, S. (2005). Bad management theories are destroying good management practices. *Academy of Management Learning & Education, 4*, 75–91.

Ghoshal, S., & Moran, P. (1996). Bad for practice: A critique of the transaction cost theory. *Academy of Management Review, 21*, 13–47.

Gibson, A. (1996). *Towards a postmodern theory of narrative*. Edinburgh: Edinburgh University Press.

Goleman, D. (2006). *Social intelligence: The new science of human relationships*. Suffolk: Random House.

Goodman N. (1978). *Ways of worldmaking*. Indianapolis, IN: Hackett Publishing Company.

Greenspan, A. (2007). *The age of turbulence: Adventures in a new world*. London: Allen Lane.

Greenspan, A. (2008). Testimony on "The financial crisis and the role of federal regulators," before the House of Representatives, Committee on Oversight and Government Reform. Washington, DC, 23 October, 768–772.

Guilherme, A., & Morgan, J. (2010). Martin Buber: Dialogue and the concept of the other. *The Pastoral Review*, September, 1–6.

Hamel, G. (2001). *Leading the revolution*. Boston, MA: Harvard Business School Press.

Hertz, R. (1997). *Reflexivity and voice*. Thousand Oaks, CA: Sage.

Hont, I. (2005). *Jealousy of trade: International competition and the nation-state in historical perspective*. Cambridge, MA: Harvard University Press.

Hubbard, G. (2006). Business, knowledge and global growth. *Capitalism & Society, 1*, 1–10.

Jersild, A.T. (1955). *When teachers face themselves*. New York: Teachers College, Columbia University.

Johnson, M. (1993). *Moral imagination: Implications of cognitive science for ethics*. Chicago: Chicago University Press.

Kabat-Zinn, J. (1990). *Full catastrophe living*. London: Piatkus.

Khurana, R. (2007). *From higher aims to hired hands. The social transformation of American business schools and the unfulfilled promise of management as a profession*. Princeton, NJ: Princeton University Press.

Kolb, D.A. (1984). *Experiential learning*. Englewood Cliffs, NJ: Prentice Hall.

Leavitt, H. (1996). The old dogs, hot groups, and managers' lib. *Administrative Science Quarterly, 41*, 288–300.

Lewis, M. (2010). *The big short: Inside the doomsday machine*. London: Allen Lane.

Lowenstein, R. (2001). *When genius failed: The rise and fall of Long-Term Capital Management*. London: Fourth Estate.

Mayer, J.D., & Salovey, P. (1993). The intelligence of emotional intelligence. *Intelligence, 17*, 433–442.

Miller, D.T. (1999). The norm of self-interest. *American Psychologist, 54*, 1053–1060.

Moore, M. H. (1995). *Public value: Strategic management in government*. Cambridge, MA: Harvard University Press.

Nancy, J.-L. (2000). *Being singular plural*. Palo Alto, CA: Stanford University Press.

Nussbaum, M. (1997). *Cultivating humanity: A classical defense of reform in liberal education*. Cambridge, MA: Harvard University Press.

Parekh, B. (2006). *Rethinking multiculturalism: Cultural diversity and political theory*. Basingstoke: Palgrave Macmillan.

Pfeffer, J., & Fong, C.T. (2002). The end of the business school? Less success than meets the eye. *Academy of Management Learning & Education, 1*, 78–95.

Rogers, C. (1980). *A way of being*. Boston, MA: Houghton Mifflin.

Rorty, R. (1980). *Philosophy and the mirror of nature*. Oxford: Blackwell.

Ross, A. (1994). *The Chicago gangster theory of life*. London: Verso.

Senge, P. (1990). *The fifth discipline: The art and practice of the learning organization.* New York: Doubleday.

Shah, I. (1968). *The pleasantries of the incredible Mullah Nasrudin.* London: Picador.

Starkey, K., & Tempest, S. (2009). The winter of our discontent: The design challenge for business schools. *Academy of Management Learning & Education,* 8, 576–586.

Starkey, K., & Tiratsoo, N. (2007). *The business school and the bottom line.* Cambridge, UK: Cambridge University Press.

Tett, G. (2009). *Fool's gold: How unrestrained greed corrupted a dream, shattered global markets and unleashed a catastrophe.* London: Little, Brown.

Weber, M. (1992). *The Protestant ethic and the spirit of capitalism.* London: Routledge.

Wilson, D., & Dixon, W. (2006). Das Adam Smith problem: A critical realist perspective. *Journal of Critical Realism, 5,* 252–272.

Zohar, D., & Marshall, I. (2000). *Spiritual intelligence: The ultimate intelligence.* London: Bloomsbury.

7

LEARNING TO LEAD AT HARVARD BUSINESS SCHOOL

◆ Thomas DeLong and Linda A. Hill
Harvard Business School

The Leadership and Organizational Behavior Course (LEAD) at the Harvard Business School was designed to address several fundamental aspects of managing and leading people. These include understanding and influencing group behavior and performance; working with and managing people on a one-on-one basis; and leading, motivating, and aligning people behind a common vision or direction. Finally, the course explicitly addresses some of the basic choices and strategic questions involved in learning to lead and managing one's career, especially in its early stages.

The LEAD course is aimed at providing the student with a number of critical concepts and competencies that will be useful in both the short term and long term. It will help them to make the transition from individual contributor to manager/leader and build over time a career that leverages their capabilities. The industry or country or specific function or size of organization matters much less than how our students make a difference within the organizational context.

❖❖❖

"Learning to Lead" is used in the title of this chapter because the Leadership and Organizational Behavior (LEAD) core course at Harvard Business School has used this phrase as the name of its concluding module for nearly twenty years. This final module in the course synthesizes learning on teams, interpersonal behavior, organizational alignment, leadership, and change and clearly draws together the components of the be-do-know paradigm. This chapter documents the theoretical basis for the development of the LEAD course and the chief learning objectives as well as the relevant concepts and topics the course is designed to address.

Most of this book is based on the assumption that individuals can be taught how to lead. At the very least, the goal should be to create the conditions where students develop an understanding of the myriad contexts in which they might find themselves performing as leaders and a capacity for self-awareness that will allow them to develop and deploy a repertoire of skills. At Harvard Business School (HBS), the prevailing belief is that leadership is about using oneself as an instrument. Students have to figure out how to match their intent with their impact. HBS faculty are not charged with the task of teaching students to lead; they are responsible for providing students with the tools and environments in which they can learn to teach themselves leadership skills.

The HBS curriculum is grounded in a learning theory that holds that leadership concepts and skills are learned most effectively when presented in context through a personal discovery process (e.g., heavy reliance on the case method and experiential exercises as opposed to lectures or more passive methods of instruction). In addition, the theory is grounded in the belief that we are all social learners and hence, the educational experience is based on a peer learning pedagogical model (i.e., the course topics are aligned with the students' evolving experiences of being part of year-long intact sections of eighty to ninety students from across the globe as well as members of smaller learning teams of six to ten students).

Organization of the Chapter

The foundation and theory of the course are described at the beginning of the chapter. The course has a rich intellectual history that cannot be emphasized enough. Outlining the evolution of the course begins with a description of the students, followed by an articulation of the course objectives, underlying goals, and themes of the course. The chapter concludes with a summary of the five modules that comprise the course.

Student Profile

Prior to attending business school most of the students' professional work experience is that of individual contributors in which their primary responsibilities lay in the performance of specific tasks in, for example, sales, engineering, financial analysis, or consulting. Their contribution to their organizations relies heavily on what many can draw upon from their individual expertise, experience, and actions. If future students are like most HBS graduates, they will be charged with significant management or leadership responsibility within three to five years of completing the MBA. Typically, this will involve leading a team or, for some, formally managing a subunit of an organization, a small organization, or, possibly, as an owner or part of an entrepreneurial venture.

The LEAD course is designed to address several fundamental aspects of managing and leading people. These include understanding and influencing group behavior and performance; working with and managing people on a one-on-one basis; and leading, motivating, and aligning people behind a common vision or direction. The course places particular emphasis on the importance of developing well-aligned, high-performance organizations and on the challenges of leading change in organizations. Finally, the course explicitly addresses some of the basic choices and strategic questions involved in learning to lead and managing one's career, especially in its early stages.

The LEAD course is aimed at providing the student with a number of critical concepts and competencies that will be useful in both the short term and long term. It will help them to make the transition from individual contributor to manager and build over time a career of increasing responsibility. The focus is on how individuals can make a difference *within* an organization. Although the impact of contextual factors (country, industry, function, size or life stage of the organization) on organizational dynamics is considered, they are background as opposed to foreground topics of the course.

High-achieving students often struggle with discomfiting evidence about their own talents and motivations as future leaders. With the case-method approach we can create a more psychologically safe way in which students can begin to face up to their developmental needs by encouraging them to step into the shoes of diverse case protagonists and learn vicariously from the experiences of those protagonists. With this information, we then provide reflection exercises to help students identify their personal developmental agendas.

The Process Begins

The process of learning to lead begins before students arrive on campus with the decision-making process to attend business school. The HBS application process is arduous enough that prospective students are compelled to comprehensively consider their motives, needs, and values. The application requires that they assess their abilities and past experiences and that they begin considering whether or not they want to be a "leader" and what that word means to them.

The word *leader* has different meanings for each applicant. However, articulating one's own philosophy and beliefs represents the early steps of the arduous process of self-discovery and awareness required for effective leadership. Likewise, students begin to interrogate what it means to be a leader and which qualities define a leader—considerations they will continue to engage throughout the course of their graduate school career.

Through this process of self-questioning, applicants begin to ask themselves different questions in new ways that allow them to change their frame of reference. While the process of learning to lead may have begun years ahead of an individual's decision to apply, the key fact is that it has now begun in earnest.

Historical and Intellectual Foundations of LEAD

Leadership is treated as a discipline at HBS. Given that, there are basic questions taken into consideration in the development of a curriculum:

- What exactly is leadership?
- Why does leadership matter?
- How do individuals learn to lead? What transformative experiences should be provided in order to make them willing and able to learn to lead?

These are questions that were asked by the forefathers of the Organizational Behavior program at HBS. From Elton Mayo and Fritz Rothlisberger to Paul Lawrence and Jay Lorsch to John Gabarro and John Kotter to Linda Hill, Nitin Nohria and current faculty, the commitment persists to update and refine our understanding of leadership and organizational behavior to prepare students for the growing demands to lead in ever-changing global economy. The course builds on the seminal work of Mayo, Rothlisberger, and George Homans on organizations as social systems and Lawrence and Lorsch on contingency theory. Moreover, their approach and insights provided us with a solid foundation for understanding and making the connection between good theory and practice in designing LEAD.

The collective thinking about what it takes to provide a transformative experience is guided in part by the work of our colleague and mentor, Paul Lawrence. Lawrence said in his paper entitled "Reflections on the History of Organizational Behavior":

> Organizational behavior is concerned with improving the performance of organizations in terms of the various criteria of different stakeholders. As a result, the practice of the field tends to focus on understanding the action alternatives available to decision makers inside organizations and predicting the consequences of their choices, on resolving conflicts about performance criteria and the distribution of outputs, and on the process of organizational change.

Until the early 1990s, the HBS curriculum focused on organizational behavior without an emphasis on leadership specifically. In 1992, data was collected from faculty, alumni, and employers through a major curricular review of the MBA program entitled "Leadership and Learning." These findings were instrumental in the design of a new course (see Figure 7.1). Later that year, the core organizational behavior course entitled "Leadership and Organizational Behavior" (LEAD) was created.

Course Objectives

The LEAD course design was conceived to satisfy the following parameters:

- To focus on the pragmatic, what students need to know to exercise effective leadership
- To focus on the basics of organizational behavior while including the lessons of the latest relevant theoretical and empirical work
- To have a bias toward early and mid-career dilemmas
- To place particular emphasis on action planning and skill building
- To bring into sharp relief and challenge students' implicit models and assumptions about human behavior in the context of organizational life

Based on the assumption that all management positions have leadership functions associated with them that need to be fulfilled throughout all levels of the organization, the distinctions between leadership and management were underemphasized. While providing training in fundamental concepts, a concerted effort was made to design a curriculum that accorded with the research areas of the teaching faculty. This allowed for a measure of flexibility in the course content and increased the likelihood of further case development and pedagogical supplements consistent with emerging leadership challenges and opportunities in the evolving global economy (see Figure 7.2).

The LEAD objectives were based on the following assumptions:

- Organizations are social systems.
- There is not one best way to lead or organize (contingency theory).
- Leadership development involves task and personal learning (learning identity theory).
- Enhancing interpersonal relations is central to building leadership skills (communication, power and influence, social exchange, social networking and diversity theories).
- There is not one best way to manage change (leadership, organizational change and organizational design theories).

Figure 7.1

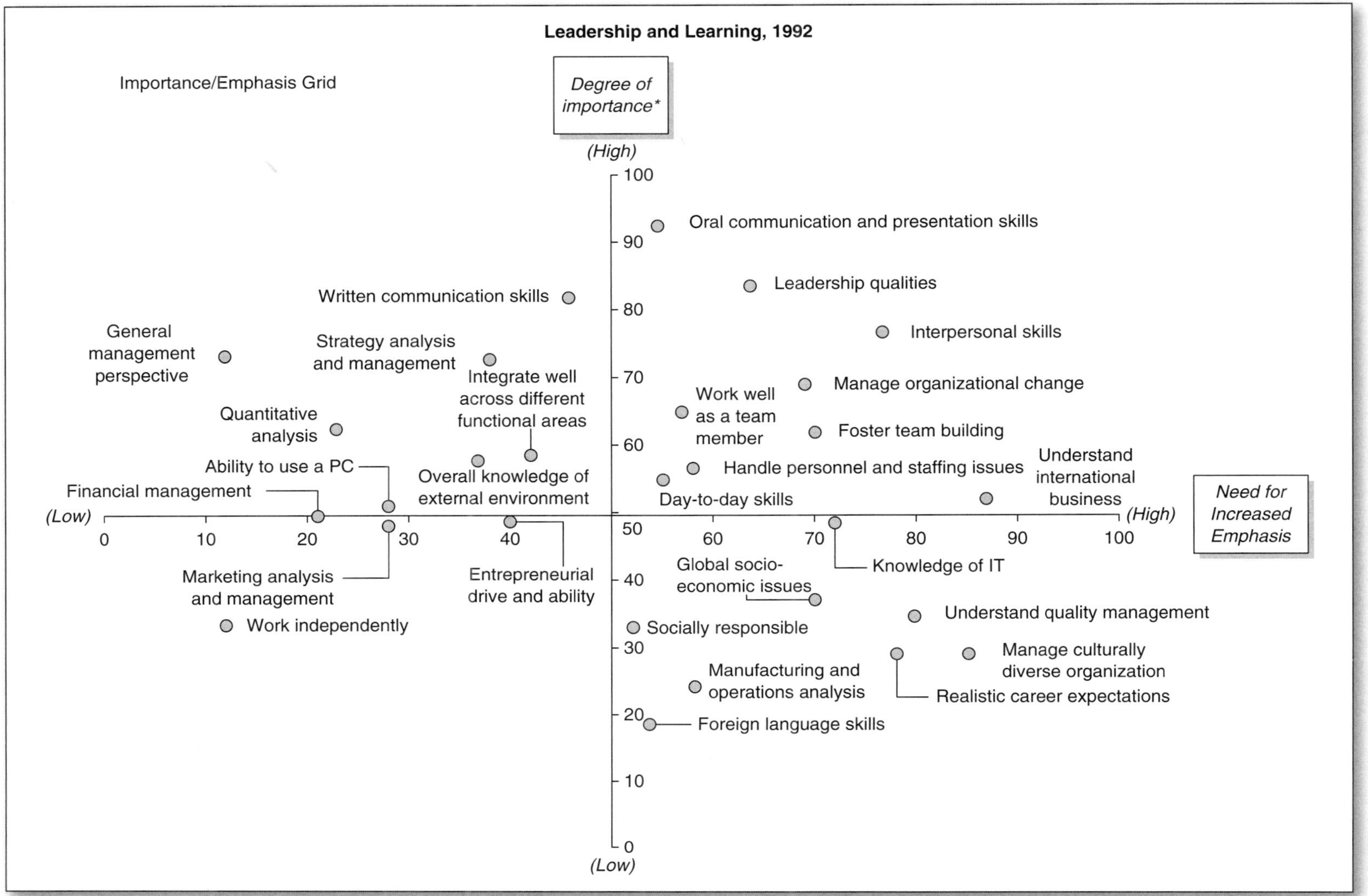

*Percent of respondents rating as 1 to 10 in priority either short or long term.

Figure 7.2 Research Interests in 1992

- The nature and functions of leaders and managers
- The careers and development of leaders and managers
- Managing diversity (race, gender, nationality) in organizations
- Interpersonal effectiveness
- Globalization and its leadership and organizational challenges
- Intra- and inter-group dynamics
- The structure and dynamics of teams
- The nature and structure of work and work life
- Organizational design, effectiveness, and change
- Organizational culture
- Innovation streams and organizational evolution
- Human resource management
- Corporate governance
- Intra- and inter-organizational networks

HARVARD | BUSINESS | SCHOOL

Underlying Goals and Themes of LEAD

The course is designed to engage several key challenges that managers encounter at various stages of their careers:

1. The course offers a realistic preview of what it means to manage. Most new managers' expectations of their jobs are incomplete and simplistic. Being a manager involves not merely assuming a position of authority, but becoming more interdependent with others, both inside the organization (seniors, juniors, peers) and outside it (suppliers, customers, competitors, investors, creditors). In fact, the higher your position in an organization, the more dependent you become on others to get things done. This is as true for entrepreneurs as it is for CEOs of large corporations.

2. The course helps students begin to transform their professional identity from individual contributor to manager. First-time managers are often surprised by how stark the transition from individual contributor to manager can be. Research shows that many of the attitudes and habits cultivated when people participate in an organization as individual contributors need to be unlearned. As individuals prepare for managerial roles, these attitudes must be replaced by thinking and behavior consistent with the leadership roles of having responsibility for a work unit or an entire enterprise. To use the analogy of an orchestra, people move from being violinists who concentrate on one part, to being conductors who must be intimately familiar with the entire score in order to coordinate the efforts of many musicians. First-time managers have to seek new ways of deriving satisfaction from their work and for measuring success—ways that often differ from those they experienced as individual contributors.

3. The course helps students confront both the task learning and personal learning involved in becoming a manager. Although most first-time managers anticipate the demands for task learning (the need to acquire new management skill competencies), they are often surprised by those associated with personal learning (the need to gain self-knowledge and cope with the stress and emotions of being a manager).

Effective managers are aware of their personal style and its impact, their strengths and weaknesses, and their motivations and values.

4. The course addresses the process of developing effective relationships with a diverse collection of individuals and groups. To be competitive in a global economy, companies are breaking down traditional boundaries to create lean, adaptive, and global organizations. Horizontal networks and inter-functional teams that cut across national boundaries are taking their place alongside, and sometimes replacing, functional, hierarchical organizational structures. Companies are forming strategic alliances with suppliers, customers, and even competitors—trends that have led to the erosion of formal authority as a source of power. Effective managers must consider the interests of various constituencies, and understand how to build relationships based on mutual trust and empowerment with a complex interdependent network of people.

5. The course helps the student develop an understanding of what it takes to be an effective leader. To compete in today's turbulent and demanding business environment, organizations must continually revitalize and transform themselves. As a consequence, the demand for effective leadership at all levels is growing. Leadership is about coping with change by developing a vision of the future for the organization, aligning the organization behind that vision, and motivating people to achieve the vision. Managers must be effective change agents who understand how to overcome resistance to change, deal with the inevitable stresses associated with change, and implement appropriate change strategies. Managers must also be able to design organizations to fit new competitive conditions.

6. The course helps students learn how to be proactive and entrepreneurial in developing their leadership talents over the course of their careers. Companies pressed to survive in today's hyper-competitive economy are reworking the psychological contract they have with their employees. Job security and vertical mobility have diminished in most societies today. To build a successful and satisfying leadership career, an understanding of how to make appropriate career choices and how to become a self-directed learner are essential. The ability to identify and capitalize on developmental opportunities is important to updating and broadening one's expertise. Learning to lead is a process of learning primarily from on-the-job experience—by doing, observing, and interacting with others. Effective managers know how to elicit feedback from others and engage in structured reflection so they can identify and consolidate the lessons of their experience. Effective managers also have a sense of excitement about the challenges lying before them.

Because research suggests that developing these skills requires teaching methods that best capture the realities of managerial work and encourage learning from experience, a combination of interactive methods including carefully selected cases, often supplemented with video material to capture the nonverbal dimensions of interactions, are integrated into the course. Students are able to learn from the opportunities and challenges faced by managers in a variety of settings. By analyzing common dilemmas managers encounter, students learn how to anticipate and avoid problems, and how to recognize opportunities. Throughout the course we engage in role-plays, simulations, and self-assessment exercises. These activities allow the student to see how they personally interpret and behave in different situations. Supplementing the classroom materials are readings that refine and integrate concepts and lessons that emerge in discussions.

The LEAD course provides students with tools to use throughout their managerial careers and to take charge of their own development. The frameworks presented are designed to help students make sense of on-the-job learning experiences and equip the students with basic diagnostic and action-planning skills that can be used on the job.

The structure of the course is modeled to align with the "psychological calendar" students encounter during their first semester at HBS (e.g., giving and receiving feedback is the key course topic during midterm season, and career development becomes front and center when recruiting begins). For this reason, the course begins with teams, moves on to interpersonal skills (power and influence, conflict, social exchange, and social networks), and then proceeds to change and alignment challenges followed by individual career development.

Course Content: Segment Objectives

The course is divided into five parts: (1) Leading Teams; (2) Enhancing Interpersonal Effectiveness; (3) Designing and Aligning Organizations; (4) Leading Change; and (5) Developing Your Path (see Figure 7.3).

Figure 7.3 Leadership and Organizational Behavior (LEAD)

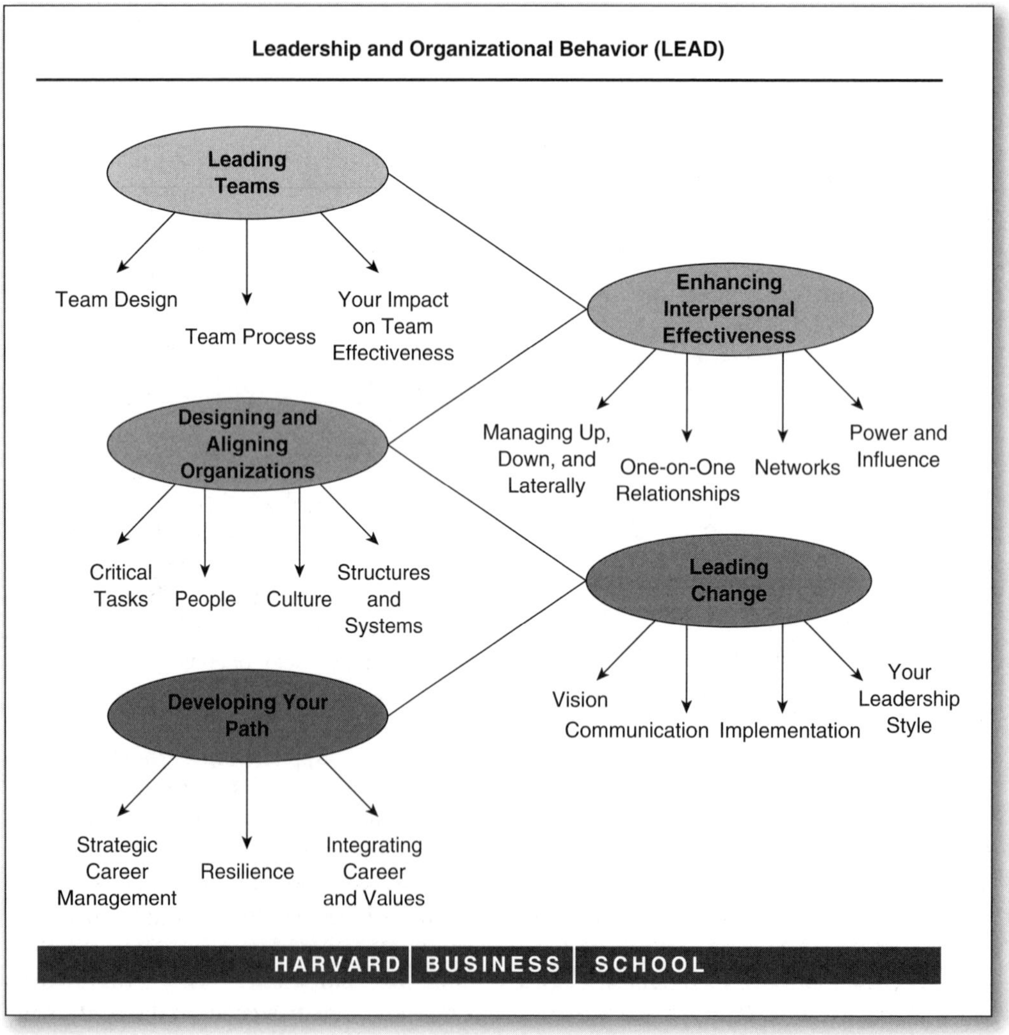

INTRODUCTION

The focus of this introductory module is threefold: First, it is to explore the realities of the expectations and pressures placed on managers and the challenges of making the transition from individual contributor to manager. What resources do new managers need to take charge and master their new assignments and how do they acquire them? Second, the problems and issues raised by the introductory cases provide a preview of the topics that the course will cover. Third, this section gives a hint of the career and life challenges that face new managers when entering an organization.

PART I: LEADING TEAMS

Because so much of the work in today's organizations is accomplished by teams, managers must be skilled at participating in and leading teams. This segment of the course explores the multiple factors that shape the development, dynamics, and effectiveness of groups. We look particularly at the determinants of group culture and performance and what happens when one attempts to change a group's culture. Building on this understanding, we then examine the manager's role in designing and building an effective team and the impact of the manager's style on the team's behavior and performance (see Figure 7.4).

The chief learning objectives in the Leading Teams section are:

- The key determinants of team culture and effectiveness with particular attention given to impact of leadership style on team culture and effectiveness
- The important and differential impact of structure and process on team decision-making and other dynamics
- The role of individual actors on the group dynamics and the ultimate outcomes of the team

Figure 7.4

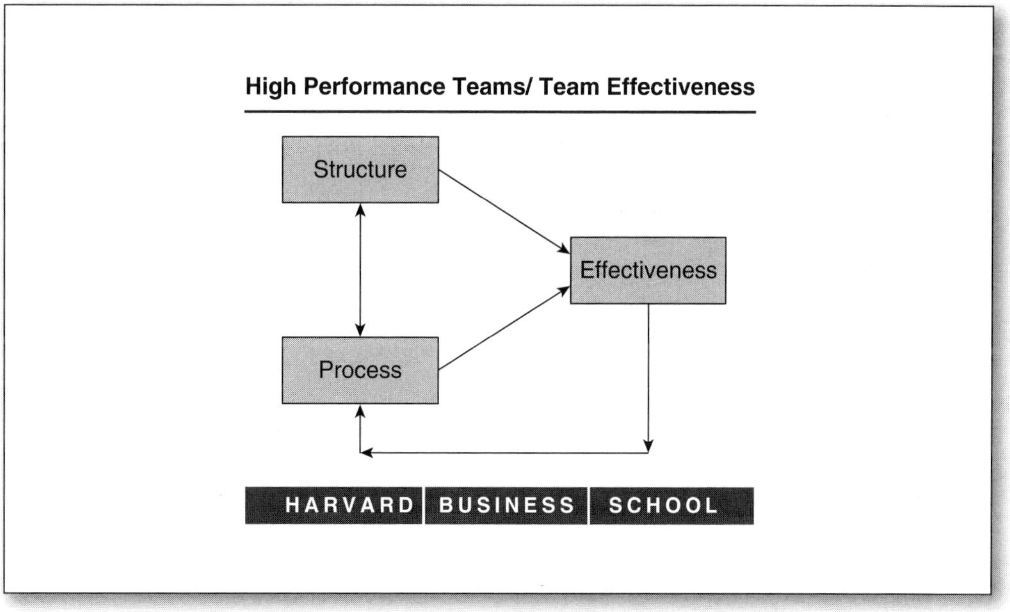

Particular emphasis is placed on the following key ideas:

- Organizations are social systems.
- Culture is an emergent phenomenon and a key determinant of team outcomes.
- The implicit psychological contract between individuals and teams is an emergent phenomenon and critical determinate of individual behavior and team outcomes.

PART II: ENHANCING INTERPERSONAL EFFECTIVENESS

Those in charge have always depended on others to get work done. This means building a network of effective work relationships. This segment begins by identifying the critical ingredients for building effective relationships with superiors, colleagues, and subordinates. The challenges of working with those with different demographic profiles (age, gender, and nationality) is given particular attention. The advantages and disadvantages of different communication and influence strategies, are investigated with the intention to enable students to successfully build effective work relationships with those on whom they are dependent to get their work done (consistent with the goals of the course, the focus is on individuals and groups within the organization as opposed to outside the organization such as customers or regulators) (see Fig. 7.5).

Students gain insight into the following:

- Managing individual performance
- Exercising power and influence
- Confronting issues of diversity and inclusion

During this module, we focus on:

- Determinates of human motivation
- Building effective interpersonal relationships
- Managing inclusion and diversity
- Advocacy and inquiry skills
- Conflict resolution through crucial conversations
- Exercising influence with those over whom you have no formal authority
- Analyzing and managing the political dynamics of organizations
- Cultivating effective social networks

PART III: ORGANIZATIONAL CONGRUENCE AND DESIGN

This segment of LEAD explores the qualities and strategies required for successful leadership. The experiences of leaders in different contexts with different backgrounds, talents, and styles are examined. The diversity is included to help students adopt a contingency perspective as they gain insight into the critical functions and personal qualities that contribute to effective leadership. This segment also examines what it takes to achieve "congruence" within an organization in terms of strategy, critical tasks, formal organization, people, and culture. To be effective, the critical elements of an organization need to be in alignment.

In this segment students learn:

- Diagnostic and design skills required to create organizational congruence given different organizational contexts and/or strategies
- How to develop action plans for leading change under different conditions (e.g., realignments versus turnarounds, from the position of a middle manager as opposed to the position of a CEO)

Figure 7.5

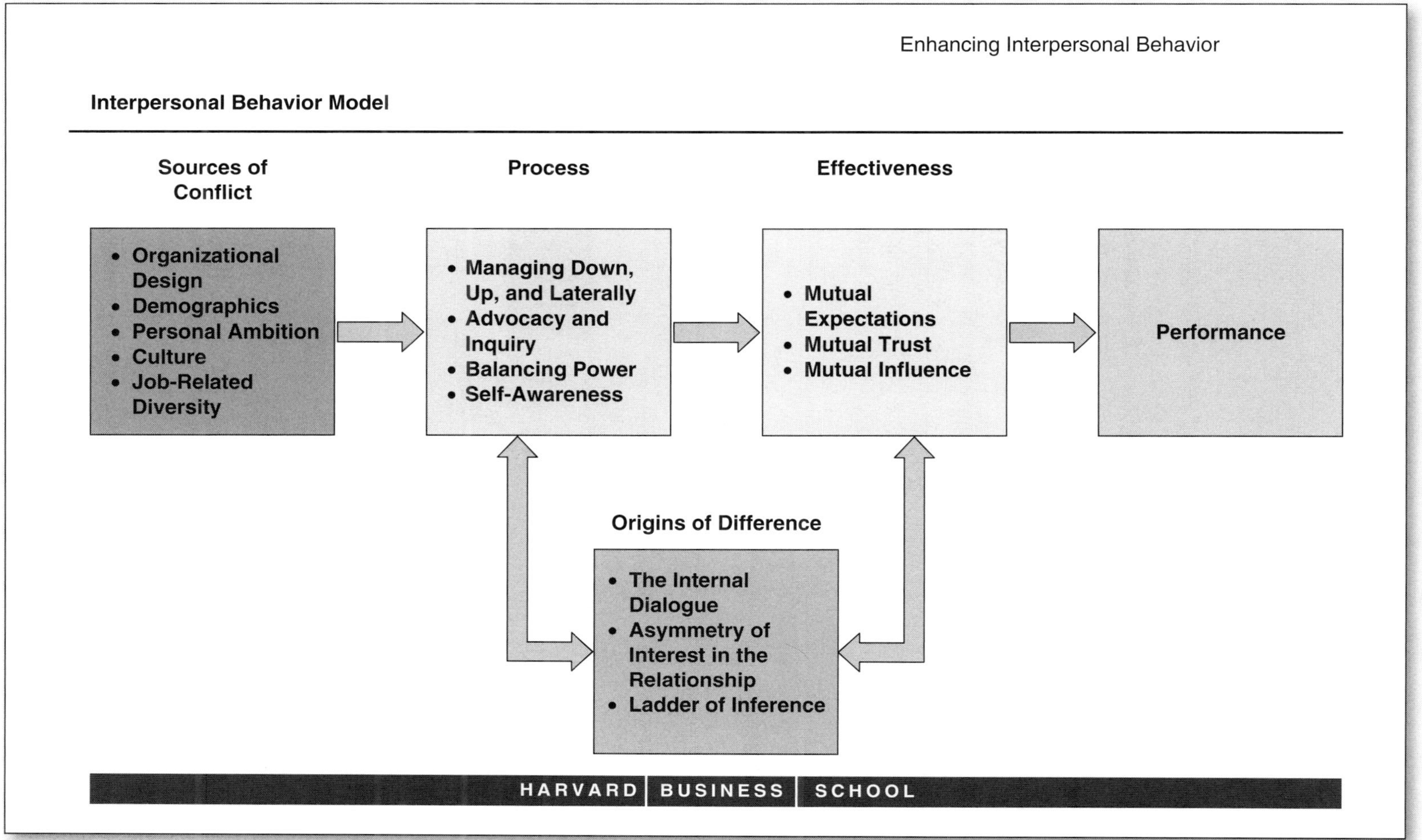

Enhancing Interpersonal Behavior
Interpersonal Behavior Model
Sources of Conflict
Process
Effectiveness
• Organizational Design
• Demographics
• Personal Ambition
• Culture
• Job-Related Diversity
• Managing Down, Up, and Laterally
• Advocacy and Inquiry
• Balancing Power
• Self-Awareness
• Mutual Expectations
• Mutual Trust
• Mutual Influence
Performance
Origins of Difference
• The Internal Dialogue
• Asymmetry of Interest in the Relationship
• Ladder of Inference
HARVARD BUSINESS SCHOOL

Particular emphasis is placed on the following:

- The critical role of leadership, as opposed to management, as a key function in times of change
- Organizational design in action (congruence and alignment)
- Again, organizations as social systems and what it takes to realign them during times of change
- The interplay of individual, organization, and contextual or environment factors
- Advantages and disadvantages of different change strategies as well as the basics of strategic human resource management

The congruence model below captures the critical factors and their interrelationships we explore in this module with students (see Figure 7.6).

Definitions of the different elements are provided below. These include:

1. Strategy: the strategic choices, objectives, and direction of the organization and its leaders
2. Critical tasks: the work flows, processes, and underlying critical tasks of the organization
3. Formal organization: the way the work is organized and the systems that reinforce that structure such as recruiting and promotion systems

Figure 7.6

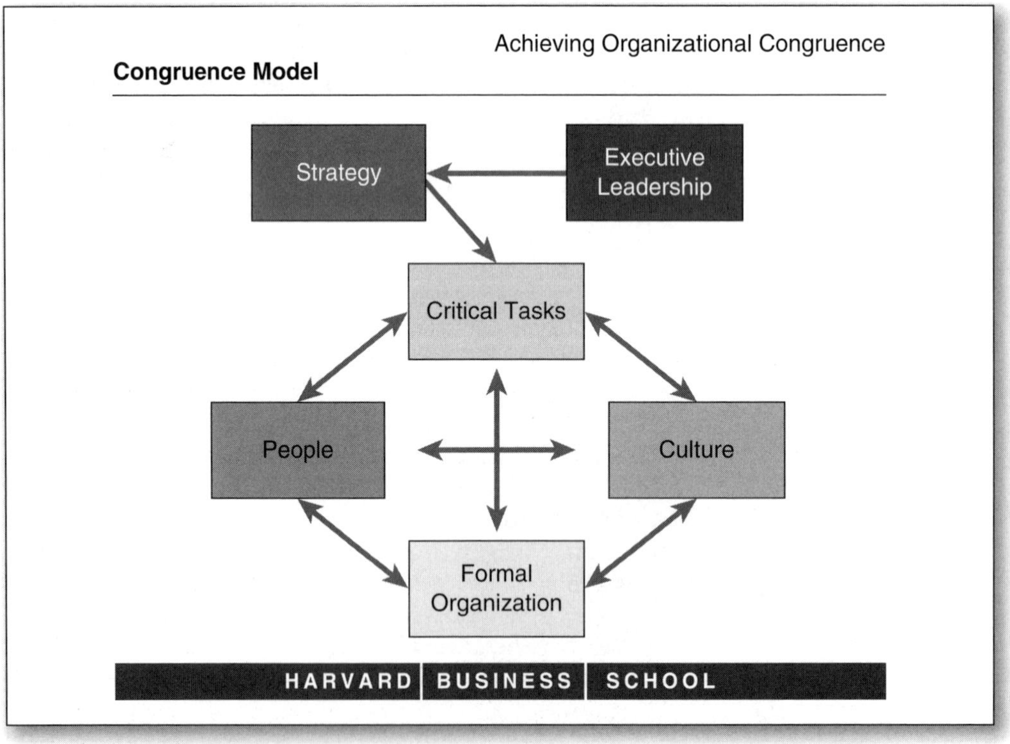

Source: Adapted from Tushman, M. C., & O'Reilly, C. A. (2002). *Winning Through Innovation: A Practical Guide to Leading Organizational Change and Renewal.* Boston: Harvard Business School Press, p. 59.

4. Culture: the values and norms as well as informal roles of the organization
5. People: staffing, skills, and human resources of the organization

PART IV: LEADING CHANGE

After organizational congruence and alignment are presented, the students are exposed to different theories of organizational change, including the work of Michael Beer, Michael Tushman, and John Kotter. John Kotter's model of leadership and change management provide the basic framing of this segment of the course (see Figure 7.7). These concepts of alignment and change are used to introduce basic macro-organizational behavior principles in action. By first understanding organizational alignment and then turning to the process of organizational change, the critical tasks a leader must address to successfully change an organization are explored.

The final module of the course pushes students to ask fundamental questions about their motivations, abilities, and willingness to be self-aware enough to begin the journey from student to leader (see Figure 7.7).

Figure 7.7

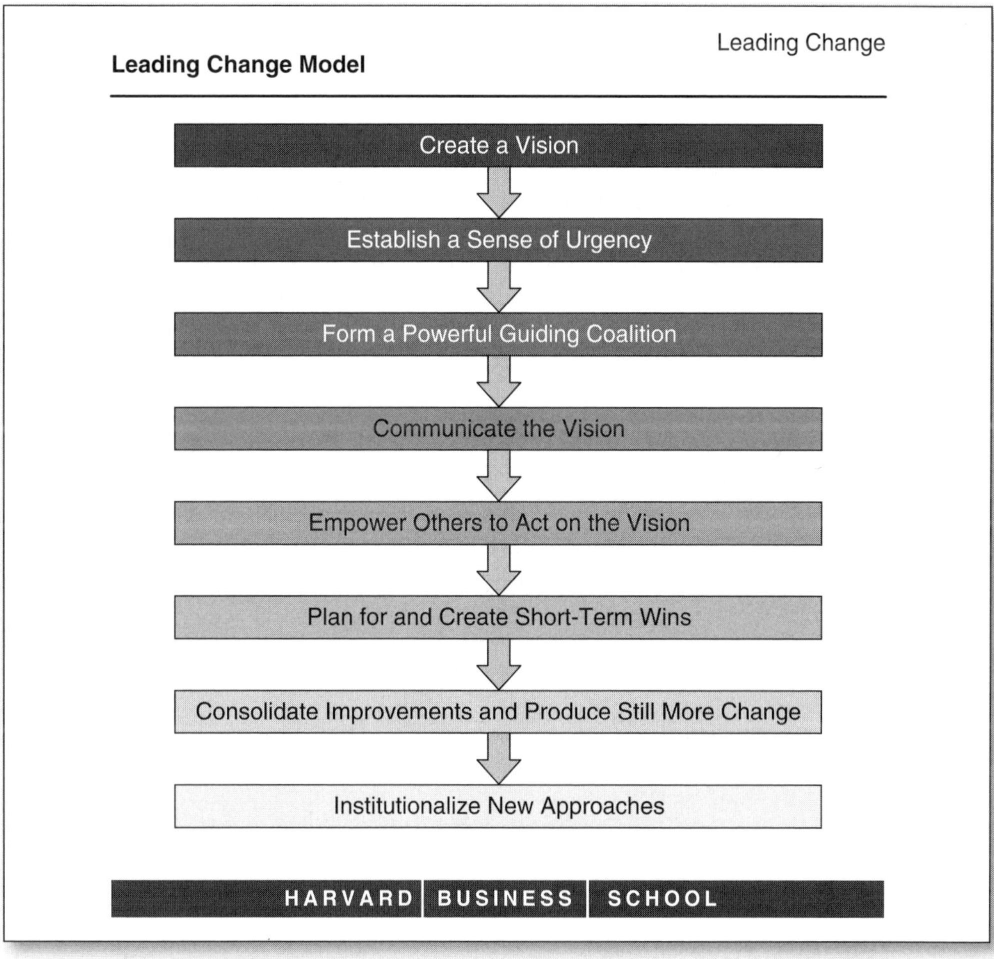

Source: Adapted from Kotter, J. & Cohen, D. S. (2002). *Heart of Change: Real-Life Stories of How People Change Their Organizations*. Boston: Harvard Business School Press, p. 7.

Leaders' attempts to renew or change their organizations often fail. This segment of the course compares and contrasts efforts to transform organizations in order to identify critical stages and activities in the change process. Different approaches for developing and communicating a vision and for motivating people to fulfill that vision are identified in this module. The following questions are addressed: What are the primary sources of resistance to change? What are the most appropriate ways of overcoming them? What change strategies are effective and under what conditions?

PART V: DEVELOPING YOUR PATH

In this final module, several strategic issues involved in building a dynamic career are examined with particular attention given to early- and mid-career choices and dilemmas. We consider the following topics: How do individuals learn to lead? What critical experiences and relationships are needed?

This final module emphasizes that each student must decide how leadership will play out in his or her own life. Students are compelled to examine their own willingness to become leaders and evaluate their skill set as leaders. They also are asked to assess the potential portability of their various skill sets over the course of their careers and hence, their likely career trajectory.

Within the context of in-class activities students have an opportunity to cultivate a capacity for meaningful conversations with peers about their past experiences, their evolving professional identity, and their career aspirations. Various learning and career theories serve as the basis for this segment of the course. Based on that work, we help students understand that leaders are made, not born.

- Leadership is about self-development.
- Leadership is learned from experience and relationships.
- Moral development is a priority.

In this segment we push student to ask fundamental questions about their motivations, talents, and style. With that self-awareness, they can begin to identify appropriate career opportunities and outline personal development plans (see Figure 7.8).

Figure 7.8

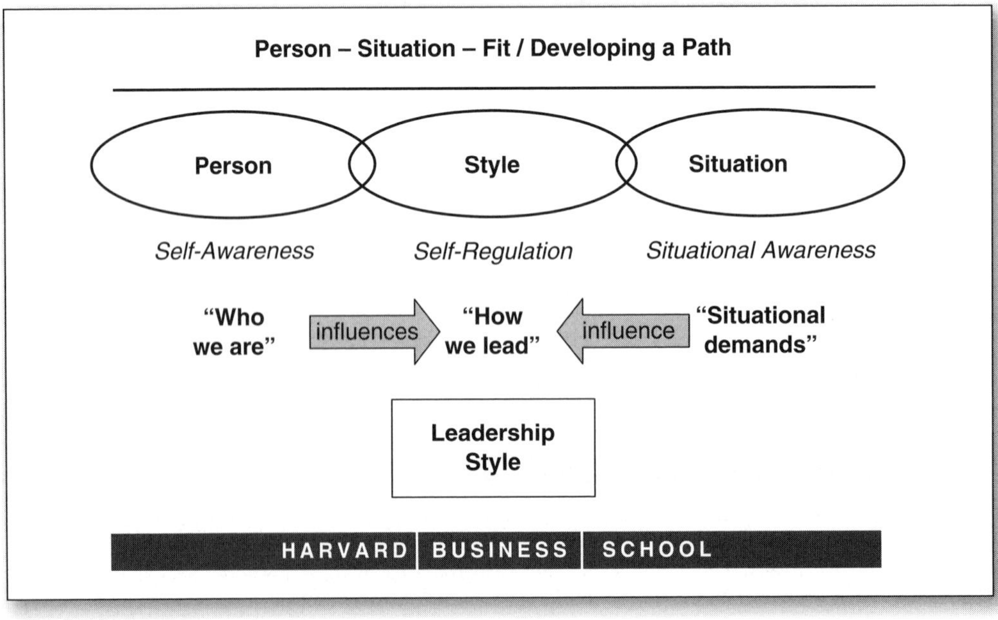

Summary

We know that there are myriad approaches to the study of leadership. Every MBA program takes a different tack in the pursuit of teaching students the critical elements of leadership and organizational behavior. Over the past approximately twenty years, the HBS course has evolved in a way that has advanced the knowledge for nearly 18,000 graduate students. The irony is that some students don't become believers in the importance of our course until after the fact. Often, it is the alumni of the school who communicate to us how they regret that they didn't take the course more seriously. It is the alumni who ask us to require more courses that focus on the human side of the enterprise. Part of the reason some students miss the importance of leadership courses is related to their own development and where they are on their path. They are more concerned in the short term with learning skills that will leverage their talents through their technical functionality. They feel like they must know finance and accounting now for survival. They do. They are right. Yet, we know from the reports of our alumni the fundamental principles that are introduced through our course will become ever more critical over the course of their careers. We see it as our responsibility to prepare the students for a life-long leadership development journey; to help them understand why leadership truly matters and what it will take for them to be prepared to live up to the rights and privileges as well as duties and obligations of leading others.

We continue to upgrade and refine what we teach to prepare students for the expectations of a growing number of organizational stakeholders. We have begun to rethink how we teach, because although we have made considerable progress in preparing students for the "knowing" dimension of leadership, we recognize we have much more to do in preparing them for the "doing" and "being" dimensions of leadership. Consequently, we are in the process of rethinking how we teach.

8

THE LEADERSHIP TEMPLATE

◆ Michael Useem
Wharton School, University of Pennsylvania

Leadership actions do not necessarily flow from leadership knowledge, and for overcoming this "knowing-doing gap," we believe that a pragmatic and compact approach is to create and instill a *leadership template*. Like a checklist for an aircraft pilot or general surgeon, the leadership template sets forward a set of essential principles that are generic enough to apply to many situations yet specific enough to provide tangible guidance for each. This chapter characterizes the key qualities of a leadership template, suggests ways for developing a template, and identifies methods for ensuring that it effectively informs managerial actions. For a leadership template to be useful, it should be (1) as simple as possible; (2) customized around evolving circumstances; (3) accompanied with warnings about its limitations; and (4) built on principles that are derived from witnessing leaders in action through a diverse set of sources, including informed observers, research-based conclusions, managers responsible for leadership development, and managers engaged in leadership programs. For instilling the leadership template, developmental initiatives usefully include (1) self-conscious self-directed study of others in leadership position, (2) mentoring and coaching, (3) experiencing stretch assignments, (4) learning from setbacks and crises, and (5) knowledge from after-action reviews. The leadership template provides a pragmatic device for suggesting and then triggering action from those in leadership positions.

❖ ❖ ❖

Identifying the leadership capacities that make a significant difference is challenging for any organization. What looks like it should make a difference often does not. Applying the capacities that do make a difference can be equally challenging. Though managers plan to apply them, they often do not.

The task of teaching leadership requires surmounting both challenges: first identifying what leadership capacities are essential, and then what it takes if managers are to be ready to apply what they know when their leadership is required. Though both are critical, we tend to focus more on the first than the second. Once we know, we often implicitly assume that we will also do, that leadership actions naturally flow from leadership knowledge. Yet this assumption is alas not always observed in practice.

By way of illustration, I still vividly recall when Enron chief executive Kenneth Lay described his guiding principles on the podium of the World Economic Forum in Davos, Switzerland, on February 3, 1997. Joining the Enron CEO on the podium were luminaries from the apex of European business: Percy Barnevik of the Swiss engineering firm ABB Asea Brown Boveri; Heinrich von Pierer of the German manufacturing firm Siemens; and Cor A. J. Herkstroter of the British-Dutch energy firm Shell.

The Enron CEO's account stood out for its compelling description of how he led the enterprise from a small pipeline company into a powerhouse energy provider. Yet some of Lay's professed leadership principles for doing so evidently failed to guide his actual behavior in the executive office or company boardroom. While publicly stressing executive character and insisting on compliance with the company ethics code, the CEO was soon pressing the Enron governing board to suspend its own code of ethics to permit formation of the special purpose entities that would help bring the company to bankruptcy in 2001 (McLean & Elkind, 2003; Swartz & Watkins, 2003; Useem, 2003).

Researchers Jeffrey Pfeffer and Robert Sutton have referenced this disconnect between principle and action as the "knowing-doing gap," where managers "say so many smart things about how to achieve performance" but "are trapped in firms that do so many things they know will undermine performance." People recurrently "knew what to do, but didn't do," Pfeffer and Sutton find, and that gulf between knowing and doing is "one of the most important and vexing barriers to organizational performance." Overcoming those barriers depends in part on ensuring that the knowing part is simple, tangible, and stirring (Heath & Heath, 2007; Pfeffer & Sutton, 2000, ix–x).

This gap may be especially pronounced in the field of leadership, where even modest differences between intentions and actions are often magnified and held against those who fail to close them. For overcoming the knowing-doing gap, as vital in leadership as almost anywhere in company management, we believe that a pragmatic and compact way for doing so is to build and instill a *leadership template*. Like a checklist for an aircraft pilot or general surgeon, the leadership template sets forward a minimum set of essential principles that are generic enough to apply to many situations yet specific enough to provide tangible guidance for each.

The purpose of this chapter is to characterize the key qualities of the leadership template, suggest ways for developing a leadership template, and identify methods for ensuring that the template effectively informs managerial actions. We draw on the work of others along with our own experience in leadership development. The latter has been undertaken in a variety of venues, from classrooms at my school to leadership programs in London, Sao Paulo, and Shanghai; and with a variety of groups, from Citigroup, Google, and Smithsonian to Brazil's Petrobras, China's Minsheng Bank, and India's ICICI. The concept of the leadership template proposed here reflects an iterative building on both academic research and personal experience, advancing, testing, and refining its formulation from one venue to the next.

The Value of a Leadership Template

In professions such as piloting and surgery where miscalculations can result in serious repercussions, one might think that well-selected, well-trained, and well-disciplined practitioners would rarely if ever overlook their procedure's mission-critical items. But accumulating evidence now indicates that the checklist can significantly reduce disastrous oversights by even the most prepared practitioner when working in even the most exacting of arenas.

One study, for instance, examined more than 7,000 hospital patients who were sixteen years of age or older undergoing non-cardiac surgery in eight countries, from Canada to Tanzania. After the study team introduced a "Surgical Safety Checklist" at the hospitals in 2007–08, the rate of inpatient complications dropped from 11.0 percent to 7.0 percent, and the rate of death declined from 1.5 percent to 0.8 percent (Birkmeyer, 2010; de Vries et al., 2010; Haynes et al., 2009).

For Atul Gawande, a general and endrocine surgeon and an advocate and developer of surgical checklists, one item on a pre-surgery checklist of his own became "the save" for him when he was operating on a 53-year-old company CEO and father of two. The procedure called for removal of a tumor next to the patient's vena cava, a primary vein carrying blood into the heart. Gawande accidentally tore the vein during the laparoscopic procedure, and in just sixty seconds the patient lost virtually all of his blood and entered cardiac arrest. Gawande had of course never expected that scale of loss, but fortunately the procedure's checklist had led a nurse in the operating room to set aside four units of blood, and their immediate availability saved the patient's life. "I have become grateful for what a checklist can do," Gawande wrote, "and I do not like to think about having to walk out to that family waiting area" to inform the patient's wife had his team not checked the checklist (Gawande, 2009, p. 193).

We believe that the same kind of value will be found in the consistent use of a leadership template. It can help ensure that a manager takes all the actions that are essential for successful leadership and forgets none whose absence can prove disastrous, helping assure the upsides of effective leadership and avoiding the downsides of flawed leadership.

Qualities of the Leadership Template

For a leadership template to be useful, in our experience, it requires four starting qualities. First, the template should be as simple as possible, though not simpler. Second, it should be customized around a leader's evolving circumstances. Third, it should come with warnings about what it cannot achieve and how it can even be misleading. And fourth, it should be built around principles that are derived from witnessing leaders in action through a diverse set of observational approaches.

SIMPLIFIED

A leadership template is intended to guide mastery of a complex reality by drawing attention to what is most imperative for succeeding in it—but nothing more. An effective leadership template follows a prescription by Albert Einstein (1934) that scientific theory should render the universe as uncomplicated as conceivable—though not more so. "The supreme goal of all theory," he wrote, "is to make the irreducible basic elements as simple and as few as possible." The leadership template should also be as simple as possible—but also not simpler.

The pre-flight checklist for the Cessna Citation 500, a twin-engine private jet, is designed for instance to identify all mission-critical actions but no more. Other actions are obviously important as well, which is why learning to fly the aircraft requires far more skill than reviewing a list. Still, the Citation pre-flight checklist contains the bare essentials, requiring pilots to confirm the fuel supply, check the oxygen reserves, and activate the anti-collision lights. For passengers and pilots alike, the pre-flight checklist is a reassuring measure for preventing pilot error before accelerating down the runway. Later pilot checklists help ensure a smooth flight and safe landing. Flying a Boeing 767 requires checking a host of items similar to those of the Citation, but it also includes its own distinctive elements, including a unique set of steps for extending and retracting the aircraft's wing flaps. While each aircraft brings its own blend of items, for all aircraft the list is a minimum compilation of what is indispensible (Atlas Aviation, 2010; Delta Air Lines, 2010).

One surgical checklist developed by the World Health Organization for hospitals worldwide, by parallel illustration, includes just nineteen items, such as awareness of whether the patient has an allergy, has received antibiotics an hour before the procedure, and has a pulse oximeter attached. Also listed is a readiness to respond if the patient loses half a liter of blood or more. On most such checklists, elements are grouped into several process phases, and this list is no exception. Its elements are clustered around three time points: The seven "Sign In" items that are reviewed before the application of anesthesia, the seven "Time Out" items just before the incision, and the five "Sign Out" items just before the patient leaves the operating room (World Alliance for Patient Safety, 2010).

In the case of a U.S. Army infantry company operating in Afghanistan in 2009–10, the commanding officer had developed a set of checklists for his unit's "tactical standard operating procedures." Tailored around the specific challenges his soldiers faced in a dangerous region, the checklists were simple but complete. For evacuating a wounded soldier, for instance, the list incorporated just ten items—but all the vital items—including whether the "patient" was in need of "urgent" medivac (within ninety minutes), "priority" (within four hours), or "routine" (within twenty-four hours); whether the injured was ambulatory or required a litter; whether the pickup zone would be marked by smoke, pyro, or other signs; and whether enemy forces were in the area (Linn, 2011).

The same search for simplicity should guide construction of the leadership template. Of necessity, it references only a fraction of a leader's capabilities, most of which have been acquired over many years of management experience. At the same time, it should include all the obligatory moves, those actions that a leader cannot do without any more than a pilot can go without a fuel check, a surgeon without a blood supply, or an army officer without a medivac plan.

CUSTOMIZED

The end state is not a timeless framework but rather a living template that requires updating and modification as new demands on the leader arise. It is also a framework that must be customized for time and place, just as the pilot's checklist for a Boeing 767 differs from that of the Citation 500, and the surgeon's checklist for removing a tumor differs from that of replacing a hip. The World Health Organization's surgical safety checklist comes with an important proviso: "additions and modifications to fit local practice are encouraged." The call for the checklist to "fit local practice" serves as apt guidance for a leadership template as well (World Alliance for Patient Safety, 2010, p. 3).

In a study of Indian business leadership, for instance, we found that many of the template principles that helped define effective leadership of American firms were also those that Indian executives readily embraced. Yet other principles were more unique to the Indian environment, including a holistic engagement with employees, an ability to improvise and adapt, a capacity to creatively serve demanding customers with extreme efficiency, and a commitment to board mission and social purpose (Cappelli et al., 2010).

Checklists for surgeons, pilots, and other professions are typically defined through an iterative process of specifying, testing, and revising the list by observing practitioners in action in a wide variety of circumstances. The defining principles of the leadership template—the contents—can be identified through much the same kind of process. It is a matter of witnessing leaders in action in a host of settings and then extracting what generally appears to be essential, followed by recurrent testing and further refinement of the emergent principles in a way that reflects a leader's distinctive context.

LIMITED

Leadership templates, however, bring several significant shortcomings unless the potential deficiencies are explicitly appreciated. The art of using a template is to recognize and resist the limitations in advance.

First, if the templates are viewed as complete guides to action, they can discourage thoughtful and creative measures that go well beyond the principles. Just as overly focusing on incentive compensation for company executives can discourage creative discretion, over-dependence on a template can deter inventive action. Treated mechanically, the template can be a prescription for perfunctory conduct.

Moreover, if leadership templates are viewed as complete guides for leadership behavior when in fact they are incomplete, that can also result in behavioral shortcomings. In our experience, for example, leadership templates should include a principle calling for an active "honoring of the room," the explicit expression of a leader's appreciation for the personal and professional qualities of the followers, a precept that Howard Gardner (1996) extracted from his study of how nine prominent twentieth-century figures built their followings. Think of South Africa's president Nelson Mandela who celebrated the country's nearly all white Springboks national rugby team at a time when the country was just emerging from its apartheid past. Many questioned Mandela's support, but by honoring the players he was indirectly honoring the multi-racial composition of the country, fostering unity at a time when racial divides ran deep (Carlin, 2008). But if an individual's template without this principle is nonetheless mistakenly viewed by its carrier as complete, use of the flawed template can prove sub-optimal in practice, as the leader fails to reference and respect the qualities of those he or she seeks to lead, a potentially serious misstep.

Finally, like the multiple checklists for the distinct time points such as "sign-in," "time-out," and "sign-out" for surgeons and such as "flight deck preparations," "starting engines," and "takeoff" for pilots, leadership templates need to incorporate subsets of elements for a variety of circumstances, ranging from a major merger or division divestiture to an investor briefing or strategy meeting. A single leadership template will not suffice, as distinct templates are required for such specific moments as restructuring a firm, weathering a crisis, or launching a product.

Leadership templates should thus be seen as coming with attached warnings about potential misuse or incompleteness. Their application should be seen as one discrete step in the exercise of leadership and not as a substitute for the full and creative exercise of leadership. Their principles should not only be simple but also complete. And separate templates should be created for the distinctive challenges faced by a leader.

PRINCIPLED

At the core of a leadership template is a defining set of essential principles. And constructing those principles is an inductive process, a matter of first specifying, then testing, and then continuously refining the items that are required. The process depends much upon the careful and extended observations of leaders in action.

For building those principles we have found that four distinct ways of witnessing leaders in action have proven especially and cumulatively fruitful for identifying what is most vital for those facing a wide array of leadership moments. None is fully sufficient, in our experience, but all provide a useful foundation in combination with one another.

A first way for identifying the template's essential principles is to draw upon the holistic conclusions of those who have been especially well informed observers of leadership. A second is to utilize research-based conclusions of academic investigators. A third is to depend upon the conclusions of leadership-development managers who have appraised their own organization's leadership demands. And a fourth is to build the principles by engaging with experienced managers in leadership programs.

For teaching leadership, we have found that the first three ways have proven useful prologues for a final testing and consolidation via the fourth way of the classroom. By extracting ideas from others' experience and then testing them with our own experience, the template's principles can be more fully sharpened and compellingly appreciated than through other approaches.

Informed Observers

A first way for identifying the defining principles of a leadership template is the oft-travelled path of drawing upon what informed observers have extracted from their close and extended study of leaders. Experienced witnesses typically set forward a small but distinct handful of primary principles.

Briefly consider the conclusions of six such observers:

- Psychologist Howard Gardner (1996) concluded from study of nine prominent 20th-century leaders that their leadership template included repeated public expression of (1) a vision of a better future, (2) a strategy for getting there, and (3) an honoring of the followers and the past.
- Drawing on a host of academic studies and a range of consulting engagements, psychologist Daniel Goleman (1998) placed emotional intelligence at the center of his leadership template, singling out the importance of (1) self-awareness, (2) self-regulation, (3) motivation, (4) empathy, and (5) social skills.
- Leadership observer Warren Bennis (1999, 2003) found from a lifetime of studying and consulting with organizational leaders, and even serving as one himself, that the leadership template should include (1) a strong determination to reach a goal, (2) an ability to generate and sustain trust, (3) a capacity to communicate hope and optimism, (4) a bias for action, and (5) a readiness to act with incomplete data.
- Researchers and consultants David Nadler and Michael Tushman (1990), drawing on both academic research and their consulting experience in helping to change organizations, identified three personal qualities—envisioning, energizing, and enabling—and three organizational qualities—structuring, controlling, and rewarding—for leading organizational change.
- Management professor and former General Electric leadership developer Noel Tichy (1997) concluded from his

work at GE and other large firms that the defining principles should comprise (1) a clear-eyed view of reality, (2) an ability to change an organization to meet that reality, and (3) a readiness to create leaders throughout the organization.

- Independent observer Jim Collins (2001) draws upon a depth study of eleven companies that had risen from "good to great"—and a comparison group that did not—and he found that the template of those who led the great firms included (1) a commitment to build a team with the right people, (2) an unwavering drive to achieve the organization's goals, and (3) an abiding belief that the leader's personal interests come last.

These and insights by other well-informed observers on the defining principles of the leadership template are not completely consistent with one another. Their sets of principles may also not be complete, and some principles may point to what is required under certain conditions but not others. Still, since their defining principles are grounded in extensive observations and experience with leaders in action, they offer valuable indicators of what should go into a leadership template.

Academic Researchers

University researchers have been on the trail of the leadership template for decades, using analytic framing, field studies, and even laboratory experiments to identify what should define the template. Again, their conclusions vary considerably with context, though the recurrent emergence of specific themes would suggest certain leitmotifs across many contexts (see, for instance, Nohria & Khurana, 2010).

Consider a comprehensive project that gathered survey data from 17,000 middle managers of 825 companies in sixty-two countries, ranging from Albania to Zimbabwe, in three industries: financial services, food processing, and telecommunications. The study found both common threads across all countries and distinctive strands that differed from country to country.

The researchers asked company managers to evaluate which personal capacities enhanced or impeded outstanding management of their firm. In response, the investigators found that middle managers almost universally favored company leaders who were dynamic, decisive, honest, and motivating, and who brought a negotiating style and focus on performance. At the same time, managers in all countries disfavored company leaders who were autocratic, egocentric, and irritable.

Yet the investigators also reported that certain leadership capacities were favored in some cultures though not others, including the display of individual ambition, personal formality, status-consciousness, risk-taking, and self-effacement. They found a high value placed on more participative leadership styles, for instance, in countries such as the United States that exhibit a tolerance for uncertainty, downplay status differences, and stress personal assertiveness.

Given the cross-national and product diversity in the study, the common elements found in all countries would point toward a set of template principles of near universal applicability. At the same time, the country-specific principles also point toward the importance of customizing the template around the culture of a given context (House et al., 2004; Javidan et al., 2006).

Leadership Developers

Many large firms house a leadership development function, typically reporting to the senior manager for human resources. Those directing such offices have often identified a set of leadership principles based on the informed guidance of senior managers in the company, and they use those principles to design their leadership development programs.

One assessment of more than five hundred companies worldwide in 2009 that had applied for recognition of their leadership development initiatives had asked the companies to rate themselves on the following question: "How well defined and explicit are the desired and/or required leadership behaviors in your organization?" The assessment found a mean rating of 3.98 on a 1-to-5 scale with a standard deviation of 1.16, implying that many companies had indeed identified the key principles for a leadership template at their firm (Hewitt Associates, 2009; Useem & Gandossy, 2011).

In working with dozens of large companies in the United States and abroad on leadership development, we have found that most have set forward a prescribed set of leadership behaviors that in effect constitute a leadership template as defined here. Their development often begins with interviews of the company's senior managers, asking them to reflect on what is most critical for leadership at their firm. Then, the emergent precepts are refined through internal dialogue and field testing. Given the inductive process by which they are built, such templates are exceptionally sensitive to the culture and market of the initiating firm. While they may not work well in other companies, they can be particularly effective within the firm that gave rise to them. A sample of items we have drawn from four large companies appears in Figure 8.1.

The value of creating a leadership template in this fashion—but also one of the pitfalls of the process—can be seen in a leadership initiative of a major division of a large American financial services company. With a workforce of 4,000, the bank division's performance depended much upon the leadership of a small cadre of managers at the top. To identify the leadership capacities that seemed to make greatest difference among them, a human-resource manager conducted hour-long interviews with nearly all of the division's leaders, and from systematic coding of the interviews he identified some two hundred distinctive leadership behaviors that the division leaders believed made significant difference. The two hundred principles were far too many for an effective template, but they provided a grounded start for what should be included.

With some consolidation of that list, the human-resource manager returned to the division's top executives, asking them to rank the two hundred leadership behaviors, and the manager used this to further reduce the principles to thirty-nine that the executives consistently ranked most highly. Then, he grouped the thirty-nine principles into seven overarching categories, including building effective teams, coaching individuals, and promoting integrity and trust. On their face, all of these thirty-nine qualities appeared to be essential to those who led the division. Still, the manager questioned

Figure 8.1 Leadership Template Principles From Four Large Companies

Company 1: Foster teamwork, build relations, and draw on diversity.

Company 2: Engage others in decisions that affect them to ensure optimal choices and ownership of outcomes.

Company 3: Build inter-dependence and emphasize relationships across product areas and divisions.

Company 4: Reinforce values by frequently reminding others of the company's culture and mission.

whether they were all vital, and to test their value he opted to examine whether they actually predicted desired behavioral outcomes among their followers. For the outcomes, he collected data on the leaders' impact on the subordinates' operating performance, measured as the annual net growth in income that the subordinates generated for the division leaders. Analysis revealed that most of the thirty-nine principles had little or no significant impact on that measure of performance—but also that nine did display significant impact. The nine are shown in Figure 8.2.

In the wake of this analysis, the bank division concentrated its leadership development program on the subset of nine capacities rather than the full set of principles that many bankers had thought would make a difference but in fact did not. With 360-degree feedback information on their leadership capacities, division leaders could now more precisely pinpoint where they individually needed to improve their own leadership in a way that would most improve division results. Not surprisingly, this evidence-based approach to defining the leadership template attracted widespread attention in the bank.

Prior to the development of a data-tested leadership template, the bank division had employed an uneven process for evaluating its leaders. Some bank managers received rigorous annual appraisals, others virtually none at all, and the criteria varied considerably from leader to leader. But in the wake of this process, rather than relying upon their own theories of which leadership capacities made a difference, division leaders focused on the evidence-defined capacities. Other divisions within the firm subsequently embraced this method for template development since it promised to enhance the financial performance of their managers as well.

The bank division had first created its evidence-based leadership template in 2001, but on the premise that evolving market conditions might call for a different blend of principles, the division retested the template in 2004 and again in 2007. The division found that a changed environment resulted in a partially different set of leadership capacities having greatest impact

Figure 8.2 Refined Leadership Template Principles of a Large Financial Institution

1. Develop proactive sales strategies that capitalize on regional trends or changes in the local market.
2. Support [division] goals by growing investment product sales while maintaining superiority in core services.
3. Help each banker sell, and add value to the banker's sales process.
4. Remove roadblocks and administrative obstacles that impede the sales team's performance.
5. Establish ways to pilot test new sales initiatives.
6. Maintain frequent contact with the entire sales team and provide actionable feedback.
7. Organize people, tasks, and activities to expedite the workflow and maximize team effectiveness.
8. Motivate individual team members to continually acquire both product and sales acumen.
9. Pinpoint development needs and coach individuals in progressing to the next level.

on revenue growth among their subordinates in later years. The eighth and ninth capacities of the refined template in Figure 8.2, for instance, remained important across all three time points, but the evidence in 2004 and 2007 pointed toward the importance of focusing more on business strategy and planning, capacities that had not figured prominently in the earlier years. Accordingly, the division altered its leadership template for guiding development of its bankers in the latter part of the decade, adding emergent principles and dropping those that had faded in salience (Useem et al., 2011).

This evidence-based leadership template development process is of special value for customizing the template and then evolving it over time in response to changing company and market conditions. And since the leadership capacities so identified are tied to delivering tangible results, the process is also of particular value for persuading managers to both appreciate and apply the template capacities, essential steps for closing the knowing-doing gap.

Leadership Program Participants

A fourth avenue for identifying the principles for the leadership template is to turn to leadership development program participants themselves, whether high school students, university undergraduates, MBA students, mid-career managers, or top-level executives. We have frequently worked with all five groups, and while engagement with each yields a distinctive blend of defining principles for the template, fewer than a dozen principles tend to recurrently emerge from all.

In pursuing this fourth way, it is helpful to initially create a suggestive foundation by drawing upon the first three sources of leadership template principles. But that is only a starting point, and the art of drawing upon program participants themselves is to build inductively from their own insights and experiences. In doing so, this way brings the advantage of helping to make the emergent principles indelible, actionable, and customized.

One fruitful method within this fourth way is to take participants into a moment when they can directly observe and experience a leadership challenge and then collectively extract what seems to have made or should have made greatest difference to the leader at that moment—and thus should end up on the leader's template. By way of personal classroom example, we often recreate a moment when IBM chief executive Louis Gerstner faced a major leadership challenge. On June 11, 1995, IBM had announced that it was acquiring Lotus Development Corporation for $3.5 billion, a purchase first resisted and then finally embraced by Lotus Chairman Jim P. Manzi. Preeminent computer maker IBM, famous for its big-company and tradition-bound mindset, will be incorporating a software startup known for its free-wheeling culture. Lotus meanwhile intended to proceed with a pre-announced program of cost-cutting and downsizing. Lotus outside director Richard Braddock had been working part-time to supervise a 15 percent reduction in the managerial ranks and a $50-million reduction in the company budget.

Now, on the day after the acquisition, IBM CEO Gerstner, with Lotus CEO Jim Manzi at his side, is about to address 2,200 Lotus employees, nearly half the workforce, who had been gathered in Boston's downtown Wang Center. As the IBM chief executive walked on stage to face the anxious employees whom he now owns, he will need to quell any rebellion in the newly acquired ranks, work to retain the talented software force, and identify how the two companies working together will help Lotus reverse its losses. He will make a brief speech and then take questions from the disgruntled workforce filling the cavernous hall.

We ask program participants to imagine they were Louis Gerstner: to write their speech in collaboration with several other participants, and then to anticipate the kinds of questions that they are likely to be asked on stage. I encourage the participants to draw upon but not be constrained by the template principles already introduced from the first three ways. Then, we request one of the participants to nominate a neighbor to actually deliver the speech in the classroom. Soon we have a volunteered volunteer at the front of the room, and we note that participants are now exceptionally focused on what they are about to hear, in part because they are relieved to have avoided being volunteered themselves. With their attention so concentrated, participants are more likely to both identify what is vital for Gerstner's template and later remember what they had identified to guide their own behavior if they had been in his shoes, another knowing-doing closer.

The volunteer's speech is typically very brief, like Gerstner's itself. In the actual address, later provided to the participants, Gerstner issued a call to arms for historic battle with their competitors, above all Microsoft, and he bid for the commitment of all Lotus employees: "My expectations for Lotus are very simple," he declared. "I want you to win in the marketplace. I want you to beat our competitors. I want you to grow fast. I want you to execute a set of strategies brilliantly to deliver what we all want, which is leadership for our customers." The cause is just: Our standards are "what the customer deserves." We are joined together to support one another: IBM and Lotus must "find ways to work as a team." The days ahead are critical: "Over the next couple years, a huge battle will be waged for where this industry is going to go." Cutbacks are not the future: "We want all parts of Lotus to grow fast." We will assure autonomy: IBM will work "without in any way destroying what's important to you as a group of people and as a culture." And we need you: "You represent the leading edge of fundamental change in this industry" (the full text can be found in Useem, 1998, p. 144; see also Gerstner, 2003).

The classroom volunteer's presentation usually touches on most of these elements, and many are reiterated in the dialogue that follows as the Gerstner avatar takes questions from the concerned workforce. Then, drawing on what program participants have just witnessed, we ask them to identify the leadership qualities that they would want to see displayed that day if they as Lotus employees were to remain with IBM and work harder in the months ahead—precisely what Gerstner was seeking today by coming to address them. This inductive process typically leads to a relatively small set of template principles that most groups of students or managers tend to extract, regardless of venue, company, or country, as displayed in Figure 8.3.

Figure 8.3 Leadership Template Principles From a Classroom Leadership Moment

1. *Articulate a vision:* Formulate a clear and persuasive vision and communicate it to all members of the enterprise.
2. *Specify a strategy:* Set forth a pragmatic strategy for achieving that vision and ensure that it is widely understood.
3. *Honor the room:* Frequently express your confidence in and support for those who work with and for you.
4. *Identify personal implications:* Help everybody appreciate the implications of the vision and strategy for their own work and future with the firm.

(Continued)

Figure 8.3 (Continued)

5. *Think strategically:* Look to the long-run, consider all the players, and anticipate reactions and resistance before they are manifest.
6. *Convey strategic intent:* Make it clear what is expected of those who work with and for you, and then—assuming that they are well trained and prepared to do what is expected—avoid micro-managing.
7. *Motivate the troops:* Appreciate the distinctive motives that people bring, and then build on those diverse motives to draw the best from each.
8. *Convey your character:* Through gesture, commentary, and accounts, ensure that others appreciate that you are a person of integrity.
9. *Say it so it sticks:* Communicate all the above in ways that people will not forget; simplicity and clarity of expression help, as do elements ranging from personal gestures to grand events.
10. *Decide decisively:* Make good and timely decisions, and ensure they are executed.

The exact definition and weighting of the leadership template principles depends to some extent on the group in the room, but these ten principles tend to recurrently emerge. The modest variation from setting to setting, however, is a good reminder of the fact that the leadership template can be treated as both universal and particular at the same time. Some principles such as articulating a vision emerge everywhere, but the emphasis on other principles depends much about the unique blend of challenges and opportunities in the participants' own work setting. This method thus has the advantage of identifying a template customized to the circumstances that the program participants are personally facing.

Mastering the Leadership Template

Whatever the particular blend of the principles on a leadership template, what then becomes important is to incorporate the principles into developmental experiences that strengthen their retention and readiness for application. The challenge is to ensure that the template principles remain top of mind, actively serving leadership actions the way such principles were evidently not in the case of Enron's Kenneth Lay.

Standard leadership development initiatives, adopted by many organizations, can be used to strengthen a manager's ability to draw on a template. They include (1) encouraging self-conscious self-study of leadership and building a personal template through witnessing others, reading history, and taking programs; (2) mentoring and coaching by others that fosters template principles; and (3) seizing or receiving opportunities to take on assignments and challenges outside one's comfort zone that put the principles of the template to test. Described by Kouzes and Posner (2008), these three methods are widely used by company leadership development programs (Betof, 2009; Conger & Riggio, 2006; Hewitt, 2009; McCall, 2004).

Three other avenues are useful as well, we have found, including what might be labeled touching the void, reviewing past action, and learning experientially. All can serve to strengthen an individual's readiness to apply the template, especially if they complement a prior application of the first three modes of mastery.

Touching the void: Nobody seeks to suffer a setback. But by concentrating attention, a crisis experience can help strengthen a sense for what is critical for the template and how important it is to apply what is on the template.

By way of brief example, General Electric's Jack Welch had asked Cisco Systems' chief executive John Chambers if he had ever come close to a near-death experience, implying that he had not really mastered a leadership template until experiencing such a moment. Yes, Chambers affirmed, he faced such a time when the Internet bubble burst in 2000–01. Cisco flipped from a growth rate of 70 percent to a decline rate of 45 percent. Its share price plummeted by more than 80 percent. The crisis forced Chambers and other executives into more active listening for innovative ideas, customer preferences, and disruptive technologies. Cisco returned to life in part because of that near-death experience, and Chambers reported that his own leadership had been enduringly strengthened by it (Useem, 2009).

After-action review: By looking back on immediately past experience and explicitly asking what went right, what went wrong, and how forthcoming actions can be improved by past actions, an "after-action review" helps identify what should be added to a template and how it can be applied. Performed frequently, the after-action review is a disciplined avenue for immediately moving the essence of daily actions into informed judgment for future actions.

An example comes from Liu Chuanzhi, chairman of China's computer maker Lenovo. He had been an engineer without management experience working for a state-owned research enterprise when he founded the company with one other employee in 1991. Liu reported that the personal development path for getting from there to leading the world's fourth largest personal computer maker less than two decades later was his own executive debrief every Friday afternoon. At first with a single worker, later with managers who themselves presided over thousands, he looked back on his weekly successes and errors to build his own leadership template through a weekly after-action review (Useem, 2006, pp. 213–214).

Experiential learning: Taking a leadership template into a setting where the concepts can also be put to a personal test can constitute an indelible way to drive home the value of the template, placing its principles in active memory, not just deep storage. With the experience of putting a template to personal test, its contents are more readily moved in the future from generic abstraction to tangible application.

We place an emphasis in our MBA program on making good and timely leadership decisions, for example, and we develop a set of guiding principles for doing so that come to constitute a decision-making template. We then arrange for 180 of our students to take a deep dive into an intense learning experience hosted by the Officer Candidates School of the U.S. Marine Corps at its base at Quantico, Virginia.

The Marine instructors form our students into five-person "fire teams" to face a set of decision-laden tasks, such as moving a heavy steel-drum from one side of a high vertical barrier to another within ten minutes but without stepping on areas that are painted red to signify explosive devices. The fire teams strategize, then act, but after the first station, where they often fail, they receive critical feedback from the Marine instructors on how their leadership decisions could have been much better.

The Marines explain that the fire team was slow to draw upon the suggestions of its individual members for solving the problem, and then slow to turn the personal suggestions into collective actions. With this feedback, the fire team approaches the next physical challenge, such as moving across a water barrier with several ropes and boards, all of which are less than the width of the pool. Knowing the decision-making template but stung by the criticism of failing to apply it in practice, the fire teams are typically far more self-conscious about integrating ideas, building a strategy, and executing collectively as they approach the next challenge. As they subsequently delve into one challenge after another, their active use of the leadership decision-making template becomes strikingly more evident.

The experiential learning helps drive home the value of the precepts for making good and timely leadership decisions, and that formulation is further reinforced by exposure to the Marine template for making decisions. Students learn, for instance, that officers in training are expected to appreciate the "70-percent"solution: When a fire team has acquired 70 percent of the required information, has built 70 percent agreement among its members, and is 70 percent prepared to move, it should not wait for still better data, more consensus, or greater preparedness. Instead, act now. By implication, the MBA students when later in business will need to balance the need to think and the need to act, a point they knew beforehand but one that has now been driven home by their early failure and later mastery of the Marine Corps leadership way (Freedman, 2000; Useem, 2010; Useem et al., 2005).

Even without direct personal experience, deep immersion in understanding what happened when others failed to lead because of a flawed application of a leadership template, or succeeded in leading because of the effective application of a template, can also help close the knowing-doing gap. This can often be achieved through a detailed focus on the events around a leadership moment of somebody who would have benefitted from application of a template.

Consider a mountain guide who had been leading his clients to the summit of Mount Everest on May 10, 1996. During their climb to a high camp, the guide repeatedly instructed the clients to turn back from the summit attempt if they had not reached the top by 2 p.m., an important template principle for leading a group up the world's highest mountain that is subject to stormy weather in the late afternoon and whose safe descent requires that climbers have returned to a high camp by nightfall. Yet in fact the guide himself proceeded to strive for the summit well after 2 p.m., and a violent storm would later strand him and several clients who had also not abided by the turn-around principle on the template (Krakauer, 1999).

On the affirmative side, recall that Atul Gawande's surgical team had checked on the requisite blood supply before operating on the patient with a tumor next to his vena cava, as stipulated by their checklist. Heeding the team's surgical template would prove very providential for the patient (Gawande, 2009).

No single development technique can be relied upon to build and instill a leadership template. But taken together the six developmental approaches can help ensure that managers have at the ready not only a framework for knowing what they should do but also a readiness to do what they know they ought to do.

Conclusion

The leadership template can be seen as a management device, a method by which the key principles for leading people and organizations are first specified and then activated. Like pilots and surgeons with a checklist, leaders with a template are more likely to apply the principles that help define effective leadership behavior. When fully applied, the right template should not only help a leader prevent blunders but also make better strategic decisions, create more motivated employees, and generate greater financial returns. The template thus offers an actionable framework for both preventing mistakes and creating value.

What is critical for building an effective template is first to identify a dozen or fewer key principles that should be uppermost—keep it simple and make it complete would be a guideline—and then to customize the template around the challenges facing the leader. The tops of most templates, regardless of context, are likely to include such enduring and transcendent principles as thinking strategically, communicating persuasively, and deciding decisively. Yet each individual is also likely to require a distinctive mix of principles of their own unique blend, crafted around their personal history and working environment.

Informed observers and academic researchers provide a useful first step for identifying the principles that should define the leadership template. Engaging leadership developers and program participants themselves in the selection and refinement of their own principles is an essential next step for ensuring that the templates fit the leaders' contexts. Equally vital is for the template principles to be field tested, evidence based, and ever evolving as work contexts change.

Even then, with the template principles clearly delineated, the operating value of the template is only as good as extent to which it resides in the leader's active memory, ready to drive decisions and shape actions. Otherwise the knowing-doing gap can remain large, and we believe that closing it requires a combination of self-directed study of leadership and its principles; mentoring and coaching around the principles; work assignments outside one's comfort zone where the principles are put to the test; and learning from touching the void, after-action reviews, and direct experience. None are adequate alone, just as no single template principle is sufficient, and the best leadership development programs around the template are likely, in our experience, to be those that rely upon a combination of all.

By encouraging leaders to focus on key principles, a template may inadvertently focus attention away from creative measures not so identified, and if the template is viewed by the carrier as complete but is not so in fact, the incomplete checklist can inadvertently constrain a leader's actions. Both errors are correctable if a template has been fully developed and warnings about its misuse are understood. But with no template at all such adjustments cannot be made as a manager accumulates experience, and then leadership runs the risk of being an undisciplined product of past experience and untutored intuition.

One might wish that leadership were so straight-forward that it would come naturally to all without a knowing-doing gap for any. But we have concluded from our observations and experience that leadership requires far more than that, and the leadership template provides one powerful and pragmatic device for appreciating what should be done and then being reminded to do it.

References

Atlas Aviation. (2010). Cessna Citation 500 Eagle normal checklist. Retrieved from http://www.atlasaviation.com/checklists/cessna-citation/C500Eproc.pdf

Bennis, W. (1999). Lead time. *World Link, 12*(1), 49–52.

Bennis, W. (2003). *On becoming a leader.* New York: Perseus.

Betof, E. (2009). *Leaders as teachers: Unlock the teaching potential of your company's best and brightest.* Alexandria, VA: ASTD Press.

Birkmeyer, J.D. (2010). Strategies for improving surgical quality—checklists and beyond. *New England Journal of Medicine, 363,* 1963–1965.

Cappelli, P., Singh, H., Singh, J., & Useem, M. (2010). *The India way: How India's top business leaders are revolutionizing management.* Boston, MA: Harvard Business Press.

Carlin, J. (2008). *Playing the enemy: Nelson Mandela and the game that made a nation.* New York: Penguin.

Collins, J. (2001). *Good to great: Why some companies make the leap . . . and others don't.* New York: Harper Business.

Conger, J.A., & Riggio, R.E. (2006). *The practice of leadership: Developing the next generation of leaders.* San Francisco, CA: Jossey-Bass.

Delta Air Lines (2010). Company-Checklist Boeing 767. Retrieved from http://www.justflying.ch/download/Normal%20Procedures%20Checklist%20B767.pdf

de Vries, E.N., Prins H.A., Crolla, R.M.P.H., den Outer, A.J., van Andel, G., van Helden, S.H., Schlack, W.S., van Putten, M.A., Gouma, D.J., Dijkgraaf M.G.W., Smorenburg S.M., Boermeester M.A., for the SURPASS Collaborative Group. (2010). Effect of a comprehensive surgical safety system on patient outcomes. *New England Journal of Medicine, 363,* 1928–1937.

Einstein, A. (1934). On the method of theoretical physics. *Philosophy of Science, 1,* 163–169.

Freedman, D.F. (1996). *Corps business: The thirty management principles of the U.S. Marines.* New York: Harper Business.

Gardner, H. (1996). *Leading minds: An anatomy of leadership.* New York: Basic Books.

Gawande, A. (2009). *The checklist manifesto: How to get things right.* New York: Holt.

Gerstner, L.V., Jr. (2003). *Who says elephants can't dance? How I turned around IBM.* New York: Harper Collins.

Goleman, D. (1998). What makes a leader? *Harvard Business Review, 76*(6), 93–102.

Haynes, A.B., Weiser, T.G., Berry, W.R., Lipsitz, S.R., Breizat, A.-H.S., Dellinger, E.P., Herbosa, T., Joseph, S., Kibatala, P.L., Lapitan, M.C.M., Merry, A.F., Moorthy, K., Reznick, R.K., Taylor, N., Gawande, A.A., for the Safe Surgery Saves Lives Study Group. (2009). A surgical safety checklist to reduce morbidity and mortality in a global population. *New England Journal of Medicine, 360,* 491–499.

Heath, C., & Heath, D. (2007). *Made to stick: Why some ideas survive and others die.* New York: Random House.

Hewitt Associates. (2009). *Top companies for leaders 2009.* Lincolnshire, IL.: Hewitt Associates.

House R.J., Hanges, P.J., Javidan, M., Dorfman, P., & Gupta, V. (Eds.). (2004). *Culture, leadership, and organizations: The GLOBE study of sixty-two societies.* Thousand Oaks, CA: Sage.

Javidan, M., Dorfman, P.W., Sully de Luque, M., & House, R.J. (2006). In the eye of the beholder: Cross-cultural lessons in leadership from Project GLOBE. *Academy of Management Perspectives, 20,* 67–90.

Kouzes, J.M., & Posner, B.Z. (2008). *The leadership challenge* (4th ed.). San Francisco, CA: Jossey-Bass.

Krakauer, J. (1999). *Into thin air: A personal account of the Mt. Everest disaster.* New York: Anchor.

Linn, S. (2011). Alpha Company, 52nd Infantry Regiment (AT), 5/2 Stryker Brigade Combat Team, U.S. Army, Kandahar, Afghanistan, 2009–2010, personal communication, February 8–9.

McCall, M.M. (2004). *High flyers: Developing the next generation of leaders.* Boston, MA: Harvard Business Press.

McLean, B., & Elkind, P. (2003). *The smartest guys in the room: The amazing rise and scandalous fall of Enron.* New York: Portfolio.

Nadler, D.A., & Tushman, M.L. (1990). Beyond the charismatic leader: Leadership and organizational change. *California Management Review, 32*(2), 77–97.

Nohria, N., & Khurana, R. (2010). *Handbook of leadership theory and practice.* Boston, MA: Harvard Business Press.

Pfeffer, J., & Sutton, R.I. (2000). *The knowing-doing gap: How smart companies turn knowledge into action.* Boston, MA: Harvard Business School Press.

Swartz, M., & Watkins, S. (2004). *Power failure: The inside story of the collapse of Enron.* New York: Crown Business.

Tichy, N. (1997). *The leadership engine: How winning companies build leaders at every level.* New York: HarperCollins.

Useem, M. (1998). *The leadership moment: Nine true stories of triumph and disaster and their lessons for us all.* New York: Random House.

Useem, M. (2003). Corporate governance is directors making decisions: Reforming the outward foundations for inside decision making. *Journal of Management and Governance, 7,* 241–253.

Useem, M. (2006). *The go point: When it is time to decide.* New York: Random House.

Useem, M. (2009, November). John Chambers, CEO: Whether up or down, always innovating. *U.S. News and World Report*, 54.

Useem, M. (2010). Four lessons on adaptable leadership from the military. *Harvard Business Review, 88*(11), 86–90.

Useem, M., Barriere, M., & Ryan, J. (2011). *Looking south to see north: Upward appraisal of tangible leadership*. Philadelphia: Wharton Center for Leadership and Change, University of Pennsylvania.

Useem, M., Davidson, M., & Wittenberg, E. (2005). Leadership development beyond the classroom: The power of leadership ventures to drive home the essence of decision making. *International Journal of Leadership Education, 1,* 159–178.

Useem, M., & Gandossy, R. (2010). *Corporate governance and leadership development: A strategic partnership model for director engagement in leadership development in China, India, and United States.* Philadelphia: Wharton Center for Leadership and Change, University of Pennsylvania.

World Alliance for Patient Safety. (2010). WHO surgical safety checklist and implementation manual. World Health Organization. Retrieved from http://www.who.int/patientsafety/safesurgery/ss_checklist/en/index.html

SECTION II

DOING

9

MASTERING THE ART OF LEADERSHIP

An Experiential Approach From the Performing Arts

◆ Belle Linda Halpern and Richard Richards
The Ariel Group

This chapter addresses two questions: What specific elements of an actor's training are useful in teaching leadership—and leadership presence in particular? How can the metaphor of theater create a robust environment where transformative learning can occur and extend beyond the classroom? In addition to many task-related competencies—including strategic planning, negotiation, crisis management, and media or community relations—leaders also need to be able to inspire, mobilize, and align individuals behind a goal. In other words, they need leadership presence: the ability to authentically connect with the thoughts and feelings of others in order to motivate and inspire them toward a desired outcome.

Experiential learning through theater provides a valuable metaphor for developing leadership presence by allowing for an expansive experience of self and other (physical, emotional, rational, relational, and sometimes spiritual) and allows individuals to learn about themselves and their capacity to connect through interactive/introspective exercises actors have used to develop roles and characters. It also provides an opportunity for the application of that newfound awareness to the very real challenges they face day-to-day. This chapter discusses the PRES—Presence, Reaching out, Expressiveness, and Self-knowledge—model of leadership presence that the authors have developed for use in theater-based leadership seminars and concludes that preliminary efforts to assess the impact of their techniques are promising.

❖ ❖ ❖

In twelve short years, John Kavanagh rose from the rank of regional petrochemical sales representative to Managing Director of Phillips Petroleum Europe-Africa, a $700 million division of the American oil giant with rigs in the North Sea, refineries in Belgium, factories in South Africa, and thousands of employees across the region. How did this Liverpool-born, non-college-educated son of Irish immigrants rise to such prominence and power in such a short period of time?

He was certainly smart and hard working, but that is only part of the story. Early in his career he was a lab technician by day and a stage performer at night. He and his partner formed "Kavanagh and Dunne," a sort of British Abbot and Costello, delivering comedy and song at theaters and clubs across the north of England in the 1950s.

In part, it was this experience in theater that helped him develop his ability to lead a multi-million-dollar company. The stage presence needed to captivate audiences in major theaters and working class pubs is a cousin of the leadership presence needed to persuade the Spanish Interior Minister to build a new refinery or inspire the workers at the refinery to full engagement.

John Kavanagh mastered these skills. It wasn't just an innate gift. John Kavanagh was a living example of the fact that great leaders—effective, inspiring, relationship-building leaders—need *presence*, in addition to technical skills and discipline.

Connection Matters

Of course, there are many dimensions of leadership beyond presence: decision-making, strategic planning, financial acumen, operational excellence, negotiation, crisis management, media and community relations, etc. Conventional leadership theory tells us that a leader needs to be versed in all these components (and others) or have advisors who can close the gap where they find themselves not as able. Conventional wisdom also tells us that one cross-cutting capacity that leaders seem unable to skimp on is the ability—in fact the need—to inspire, mobilize, and align individuals behind a goal.

Call this key leadership competency *presence*: the ability to authentically connect with the thoughts and feelings of others in order to motivate and inspire them toward a desired outcome.

Leadership Development Is in the Doing

Learning to lead with presence is no different from learning to walk. Think of the child learning to walk, holding onto the furniture as it rounds the room—falling down, getting up. Mastery comes from the repetition and adjustment of the baby's approach to walking over time. Mastery does not come from sitting on the blanket and watching others walk. And so it's no surprise that learning theory tells us that adults learn best by doing. Thus leaders need to be put into the very challenge they are trying to master in order, ironically, to master it.

Theater-Based "Doing"

The question, then, of how best to teach leadership rests in part on how best to create an experience of "being there" for the leader so that they can experiment, try on new behaviors, fall down, get up, and eventually round the room without touching the furniture. Experiential learning through theater provides a valuable metaphor for leadership development. In particular, actor training is a context that allows for an expansive experience of self and other (physical, emotional, rational, relational, and sometimes spiritual). Experiential leadership development through the performing arts, thus, allows individuals to learn about themselves and their capacity to connect through interactive and introspective exercises actors have used to be credible and engaging in each role they play. It also provides an opportunity for the application of that newfound awareness to the very real challenges leaders face day-to-day.

In this chapter, we want to answer two questions: What specific elements of the actors' training are useful in teaching leadership? How can the metaphor of theater create a robust environment where transformative learning can occur?

Presence: The Ability to Authentically Connect

At this point you may be wondering what "serious" business leaders or teachers or politicians or government managers can hope to learn from actors. Sure, they can learn how to speak better, to project their voices, to stand up straight. But actors "act" for a living. They pretend to be other people. What could they know about the "real" world that a lawyer or a Fortune 500 CEO doesn't?

Think about the last time you were really moved by an actor in a live theatrical performance, a movie, or even a television program. We mean really moved to feel something deeply, to understand something more completely, to think about something from a new perspective, or even, perhaps, to change your mind about something. Now think about the last time you were truly moved in the same way by a presentation made by a leader in your organization. We're not saying moved to tears but moved to understand a different point of view, be excited about a new possibility, or be motivated to adapt and grow with changing times.

The goal of the actor or the leader in these instances is the same: to connect with an audience in some fundamental way. Unfortunately, most people will say that this experience is much rarer at the office than it is at the movies.

This is exactly our point. The skills that actors use to move, convince, inspire, or entertain have direct and powerful applications in the worlds of business, politics, education, and organizations in general. They are not only useful for leadership, they are essential. That leaders and actors share some skills and characteristics should come as no surprise. Actors and leaders face a common challenge. They must form connections, communicate effectively, and work with others as a team. They must be prepared to play different roles, as the situation requires. They must be prepared to influence and move people every day.

This all leads us to a paradox: How can leaders learn to be more authentic from people who act or pretend professionally? There are two answers to that question. Just as actors play a variety of roles, leaders play roles: captain, visionary, coach, and facilitator, to name a few. Do they behave differently in each role? Yes. Are they therefore faking it? No. Beneath all those roles is the same person. The same can be said of actors (Halpern & Lubar, 2004).

The second answer is found in the approach to theater pioneered by Russian Konstantin Stanislavsky, which emphasizes emotional authenticity. In the United States, Stanislavsky's work became known as "Method Acting" training. It is a paradox of "Method Acting" that, in order to pretend, the actor must be real. That need requires the actor to delve inside himself, because the only way an emotion can be authentic is if it comes from within the actor. Actors, consequently, are probably more aware of authenticity than anyone else, because they've studied it, and themselves, so carefully (Halpern & Lubar, 2004).

KEY DRIVERS OF LEADERSHIP PRESENCE

If we accept that the competency within leadership that acting training can best address is "authentically connecting with the hearts and minds of others," one way to structure leadership training using theater is to develop a model of the very skills and behaviors that both actors and leaders need in order to authentically connect—or to have leadership presence.

Present: The ability to be centered and aware in each moment of communication, to be agile and flexible in the face of change and the unexpected

Reaching Out: The ability to build and sustain an authentic relationship

Expressive: The ability to communicate dynamically and congruently with voice, body, mind, and emotion

Self-Knowing: The ability to reflect upon and leverage one's unique identity as a person and a professional

PRESENT

Keith Johnstone, a master of improvisational acting training, understood the need for being one hundred percent present as he talked about the agility and flexibility required to "receive and build on" other actors' contributions—even those that may seem unrealistic, with the goal of creating a cohesive story (Johnstone, 1999). Leadership is no different in that it requires the leader to synthesize, analyze, and correct in midcourse, while staying centered and aware of the larger, overall goals.

REACHING OUT

An actor needs the fundamental skill of empathy in order to get inside the skin of another character. A leader needs empathy in order to build relationship with stakeholders. The fundamental building block of getting work done in an organization is people and people do not operate in vacuums. They operate in relationship. Reaching Out describes leaders who have a particular way of connecting with their stakeholders—an empathetic one.

Leaders with presence listen from the outside in, not focused on what they are saying, but rather on how others are receiving what they are saying. Leaders with presence realize that their words have impact not only substantively, but emotionally and relationally.

EXPRESSIVENESS

Stanislavsky's major technology for achieving congruent, realistic, and expressive acting was establishing an "objective" or a "passionate purpose" behind every line of text and every action on stage. Leaders need to be congruent to align intention, word, and action. We all know what it feels like to be "handled." You hear the words coming out of the mouth. You look at the facial expressions. You watch the body language, and something just doesn't seem right. Trust is harder to come by when a person is saying "yes" but nodding "no." Leaders with presence send a single message. They pay attention to eye contact, body language, voice variability, pacing, silence, the use of space to express a uniform message. Concerned? They pause. Excited? They speak faster. Eager? They lean forward. They use language and story to reach the hearts and minds of their audiences—to make sure their message lands. You know good acting when you see it because you believe what you see and that transports you into the story. You know good leadership for the same reasons.

SELF-KNOWING

In her book *Respect for Acting* (1973), Uta Hagen, a leading "method acting" educator, explains why actors desperately need to be self-knowing. "Your own identity and self-knowledge are the main sources for any character you play . . . . Once we are on the track of self-discovery in terms of an enlargement of our sense of identity . . . we now try to apply this knowledge to an identification with the character in the play" (pp. 29, 34).

Leaders need self-knowledge for different reasons. They need to know and manage themselves in order to be seen as trustworthy and authentic. Leaders with presence work to identify and describe their sense of purpose, their values, their personal dedication, and reason for being. They see their career ups and downs as the markers of self-discovery as much as the milestones of progression. Thus, the strongest leaders are life-long learners. Leaders with presence take every bump in the road as a moment for reflection, an opportunity to evaluate, and the chance for adjustment and growth. And this self-knowing guides them as they do the key work of leadership: developing the next leader. A wise leader once told her protégé who was lamenting how hard the job of leader was, "You wouldn't be doing enough if you weren't making mistakes."

Finally, experiential exercises developed from actor training can offer an unexpected boon to leadership development. Senior leaders who naturally have strong left-brained critical instincts can be willing to abandon some of their left-brain critique and become like sponges soaking up learning because they do not expect themselves to be experts in acting training; they can find the "Zen mind beginner's mind" that is a critical mindset for taking on new behaviors and skills.

Experiential Learning the Theater Arts Way

Since the metaphor of theater is at the heart of how we teach, the structure of our workshops reflects the arc of a well-written and well-performed play.

Think about the last time you went to the theater. The experience often starts the moment you enter the theater, where you are seated in an environment that is disconnected intentionally from the hustle and bustle of your usual day. Distractions are shut out so that you can fully experience the show you have come to watch. As you sit in your seat, you read through the program: the list of characters, the structure of the play (how many acts and intermissions), and some background information provided by the program—just enough to set you up but not too much to spoil the experience or give away the surprises. The lights dim, the audience becomes hushed, and the curtain rises on a set that transports us to a new place—a set of new possibilities—regardless of whether a painted set or a minimalist black box.

In the opening scenes, we are gently introduced to the actors: their characters, relationships, dreams, fears, and desires. We are being warmed up for the story ahead. Before the end of Act I, the playwright and actors have introduced the conflict, central to the play. The lights come up on the intermission and we are hooked—there's a new buzz in the hallways, around the bar, where people congregate to explore together what they saw, what they experienced, what they are learning about the people, place, and situation told in the story on stage.

Fifteen minutes later, the lights blink, the bell rings, and the audience members return to their seats refreshed and ready to dive in to Act II. The fifteen-minute break has given them an opportunity to reflect on what they saw and experienced, talk about it with a friend, and return prepared to be transported on the rest of the playwright's journey.

As the curtain rises on Act II, we are dropped straight into the action—no need for introductions. We know the characters and we have bought into the reality created by the actors, the lighting and scene designers, the director, and playwright. In Act II, the conflict becomes heightened, the action more frenzied, and we are taken on a roller-coaster experience during which (at least in good theater) our emotions are engaged, our beliefs challenged, and our impressions of people, the world, and what we know about it are all presented in a different light. We are certainly out of our comfort zone, but because the playwright and actors have carefully prepared us for this, we don't walk out—we stay engaged, fascinated to see where this all leads.

As the conflict moves beyond its frenetic peak, we sense that things are beginning to resolve themselves. We haven't returned to the original status quo, but there is a sense of integration in a new world order. The characters are complete and the situation is stable but something has changed: in the characters, in us, in what we believed when we walked in, in the way we think about things now. We have a new lens through which to consider the subject matter of what we saw—we are not quite the same.

The lights go up on stage, the actors enter, and we applaud, appreciative of what they have shared of themselves and their story. The lights go up on the audience and we leave, walking out into the cooler night air, clearly changed, if only for a few moments, as the mantel of a new experience wraps us in a new understanding of our selves, of others, and of a sense of an experience shared with others.

So, in practical terms, how can we translate this metaphor into the art of leadership development strategy at the organizational level, and into the art of leadership learning at the programmatic level?

No question, theater is best enjoyed when the audience member is excited to attend and has an interest in the play's theme and subject matter. So, in the same way that an audience member must be prepared for a play ahead of the show (via advertising, reviews, invitation to attend, word-of-mouth recommendation), a leader needs to be prepared for a development experience. "Advertising" for an experiential leadership development initiative comes in the form of connecting the initiative to relevant business strategy. In the same way that the audience sits down and prepares by reading a playbill, experiential learning is enhanced by providing the leader with context—what's the business problem this is going to help me solve and how will it change how I work, what I produce, and how I improve my personal, team, and organizational results? Program notes in the theater become preparation for learning where enthusiasm, energy, and commitment are built.

Curtain Up: The Play Begins. The Experience Continues

As with a play in the theater, an experiential program begins by placing people in an unusual setting. No tables and laptops here! A circle of rolling chairs, six to eight participants, and a facilitator in a large room is the scene. Creating the sense of an empty stage into which the participants enter is the goal. Learning via experience, dialogue, reflection, and coaching is the method.

Like many good plays, there is a gentle entry into the program. Participants enter the room—still in thinking mode—looking for an intellectual outline of the day with business-like goals they can wrap their analytical minds around. This is their comfort zone. The introductory module and the check-in that follows help to prepare the participants and create a safe space for the experiencing that will follow soon enough and take them out of their comfort zone.

As with the best stories, a playwright takes us on a journey, introducing people, places, and events in an order that allows us to follow along. The plot gets increasingly complex as we get to know the characters and their situation. In the same way, an experiential learning program begins with short, simple, and low-risk exercises that become longer, more complex, and "riskier" as the workshop progresses, gradually moving people out of their comfort zone into significant and powerful experiences. As social scientist Shoshana Zuboff (1988) put it, "Ordinary experience has to be made extraordinary in order to become accessible to reflection" (p. 13). Below are some responses from participants in Ariel's two-day experiential learning program based in the performing arts.

> "One of the most unique courses ever attended. The course provided a non-threatening environment to test new techniques and receive immediate feedback."

> "Extremely helpful. Gets you out of your comfort zone. By the end of the day your comfort zone increased and you're very happy to do the things that you hated a few hours earlier—loved it."

> "This was the most impactful experience I've been through. It stretched me, for sure. We don't typically go here in the corporate world and we need to! This is the first class that has invested in me as a person rather than try to fill my head with information."

Generally, the flow is one where leaders are put into an experience without much preparation or guidance about desired outcomes or learning objectives. Placing them in the very challenge we are trying to help them master, leaders work through an exercise; they have an opportunity to reflect on that experience and make sense of it in their own context. Then, and only then, is that experience rooted back into a cognitive framework or model. Cognitive understanding comes second and serves mostly to underscore the "felt experience." This sequence of experience followed by analysis is the hallmark of experiential learning.

> "It was structured in a very unorthodox way that allowed us to open up and leverage the contents of the course effectively."

> "The whole program was a hands-on approach and gives you the opportunity to work on expanding the skill and not merely the identification of it."

Do. Reflect. Do. Have the experience. Reflect on your own. Get some feedback. Try again.

For a richer description of what it might feel like inside a leadership development program using an experiential approach based on the actors' training, let us examine how a leader might experience parts of the program.

Mary Ann is VP of marketing for a mid-size pharmaceutical firm. She is very quick-thinking, analytical, no-nonsense with a sense of humor. She has received feedback that she can be "formidable" from direct reports and "hard to form relationships with" from peers. She thinks of herself as approachable and open to ideas and is surprised by the feedback. Her boss suggested a program in Leadership Presence as a way of understanding how she is seen and helping her work on aligning intention and impact.

After the opening module, where Mary Ann has seen a cognitive model and a very big-picture road map of the two-day program, we ask Mary Ann and the rest of the participants to jump into the first exercise—an actor's warm up—where they simply pass a sound around the circle in an ordered and then random way. We first ask them to take a leap of faith and try on the exercise without much preamble about purpose—we promise we will debrief and place it in context after

(Continued)

(Continued)

the experience! DO! Mary Ann complies and afterward is asked "what was that like?" REFLECT! "How do you feel now compared to before the exercise?" She notices and speaks about increased energy, concentration, and a feeling of camaraderie. We then ask "what skills were we working on?" She and others come up with voice, energy, congruence, and the ability to stay present. We then debrief in the leader's day-to-day context. "What would it be like if your meetings had everyone be present the way we just were in that exercise?" A lively discussion begins about ways the leaders in the room have tried to get themselves and others to be present, fully there (not thinking about the last meeting or the next email), and the rich rewards that can ensue: making people feel seen, heard, and valued—and therefore more productive. Mary Ann has her first "aha" revelation about how task-focused she is and how that could be perceived as not being present and therefore not valuing her team when they need her undivided attention.

Next we build on the same exercise, but add the task of remembering names. The exercise is designed so that people have to fail . . . and then recover and change their habitual thinking around making a mistake. They have to say "how fascinating!" when they make a mistake with a name and the whole group then bows to them which makes everyone laugh. Again, a lively dialogue occurs about how we habitually talk to ourselves with anger when we make mistakes and are imperfect, and we explore how else we might talk to ourselves. Mary Ann has the "aha" that there is a voice inside her head—the inner critic—but it is not her, it's only one of a committee of voices she can listen to.

Built into the design of each exercise is the possibility for a participant to take a risk, succeed, and experience a breakthrough: *If I can do this here, I can surely do this outside these walls, back in the office.* Just as the actor, directed, is given "notes" on their "take" and then asked to integrate those ideas into their performance, so the leader in an experiential classroom is asked to iterate through a process of being/doing it, reflecting/talking about it, and then being/doing it again, yet differently. That is the essential rhythm of experiential learning.

A third experience for Mary Ann is an improvisational exercise in which she is encouraged to spontaneously talk about a topic from many different points of view. She works in a pair with a peer coach and then in front of the room with a purposefully over-empathetic audience. She receives her first feedback and coaching from us. We agree with her peer coach that she has lots of energy and ideas, verbal agility, and add that she is not breathing or pausing so that the audience can take her in. We ask her to do the exercise again but this time to pause after each idea and actually say the words "I really care that you get this" while making eye contact with one person. The group immediately notices feeling kinesthetically more connected with her. We talk about the power of pausing to let people take you and your ideas in—to let your audience feel you as more than a talking head. Mary Ann talks about how "unnatural" and long the pauses felt and we begin to distinguish between "unnatural" and "unhabitual." Mary Ann tries again and, with sideline in-the-moment coaching from us, is able to pause and breathe while thinking on her feet. In the final debrief she is excited about the group response to her new way of being (breathing, pausing, slowing down) and surprised about the impact her small behavior changes had on the way she was perceived.

Central to any experiential learning program that uses theater as a metaphor are role-plays specific to the reality of a leader's daily challenges. Consider these role-plays "dress rehearsal" for opening night. When coaching learners in a role-play exercise observed by others, the metaphor of audience and actors continues. Ideally, new options for behavior are integrated into the leader's repertoire. Sometimes this occurs because the audience suggests different actions in an attempt to change the outcome of what they were seeing. Sometimes it occurs in a structure whereby the group discusses and agrees to give different people roles in the scene. The protagonist may even become a "director" exploring different ways of resolving the interaction using the skills learned so far, and sharing how the scene resonated for them personally.

Coaching for Transformation

The performance arts training world almost always includes small group or individual coaching—offering actors the ability to take in feedback and immediately try again to incorporate it behaviorally. This is profoundly useful and different from other feedback-rich environments. Often leadership training involves getting feedback on your style from various sources, but does not include the element of trying on behavior change and integrating in real time.

Because receiving individual coaching in theater exercises is so unusual for leaders, and the personal insights can be profound, "aha" or transformative moments can occur. These are opportunities for people to step into a bigger and deeper sense of who they are and who they could be—experiences that transcend the everyday. Julian Olf envisions the experience as being "yanked free of the everyday reality" (O'Carroll, 2003); Zander and Zander (2000) talk about "stepping into a universe of possibilities" (p. 17).

Experiential leadership development through the performing arts focuses leaders' attention on their main instrument of communication (themselves) and ultimately holds up a mirror to leaders' impact on relationships in their organization. Receiving that feedback, in the context of a classroom, allows the leader to integrate it and, as a result, hone their ability to communicate, to inspire, and to lead.

Let's peek into Mary Ann's world again. It's the morning of the second day of the program. We are set up theater-style to listen to each other tell personal stories, and this will be another opportunity for us to coach Mary Ann.

We have been working on threading together the P, R, E, and S elements of the PRES model in this culminating exercise. Practicing the craft of telling a personal story authentically and in a compelling way allows Mary Ann to practice being Present, Reaching out to connect, and being Expressive. Accessing the stories that make her who she is allows her to develop Self-knowing. Mary Ann has been asked to think of a turning point moment story, a "crucible moment" in Bennis and Thomas' terms (p. 161), or a story where a value was clarified. She has also been actively rehearsing her story with a peer coach: focusing on the three Cs of narrative (Conflict, Climax, Change) in crafting her story; then focusing on playing characters (narrator, self, others), in the story; and finally focusing on voice, body, and being viscerally in the story as she tells it. As a leader, what she is working on here is both the ability to access the moments in her life that have made her the woman and leader she is, and also to speak them in such a way that she shares core values with others and enables them to know her, trust her, and want to follow her.

(Continued)

(Continued)

She is standing in front of the group taking a moment to center and breathe, then she launches in. She tells of a time in her early adolescence when her mother got very sick and needed caretaking of body, heart, and soul. She talks about how her father was not up to the task, so it fell to her at age thirteen. She ends by talking about learning resourcefulness at that early age, that she could do things she never thought she could do.

The group comments on her high energy, her memorable use of sensory detail, also on how hard the experience must have been. We say, "Mary Ann, your vitality and energy are remarkable. We all sit up and listen when you speak. You also have such an ease with words. You create a world and bring us in. That's a gift. Our question for you is about what you chose to emphasize in your story. In your audience today, we were inspired by your courage and resourcefulness and it sounds like that's where a big strength of yours is as a leader–leading by inspiring example of going above and beyond the call of duty. But, it feels like there is another theme in this story that you left out. You talked about resourcefulness–what about more vulnerable feelings? Did the thirteen-year-old in you feel scared of losing your mom or scared of taking on all that responsibility?"

Suddenly, Mary Ann puts together what we are saying with some of the 360 feedback she got before the program. She says, "You mean letting people know I was afraid would help people connect with me?" The whole group nods yes. Mary Ann tells the story again incorporating our coaching.

This time, she shares how scared she was when her mother was taken to the hospital and how unnerving and overwhelming it was for her at thirteen that her father seemed unable to cope. She breathes and even lets herself re-experience some of these feelings. The whole room is breathing with her. Many in the group viscerally experience her fear and pain and have tears in their eyes. When she finishes, there is silence for a moment and then vigorous applause. The group acknowledges how moved they were and how they feel a greater connection to Mary Ann.

Because the risks of being a non-actor coached in acting exercises feel very big, it's critical that the facilitator creates a very safe space for risk and recovery and that every participant experiences a "win"—to acknowledge an inherent strength. In asking leaders to surrender to a foreign world of acting training, they can begin to discover unique gifts and contributions, the untapped and sometimes hidden qualities that everyone has within them. The goal is to unlock these qualities and mobilize them in service of the individual and the world. We go so far as to set our mission—"The Ariel Group envisions a world where people authentically engage with others and unlock their most generous selves"—at the root of everything we do in the classroom.

> "This course was effective in challenging me to improve on areas while building on the core of who I am."

After hearing Mary Ann's second telling of her story, we move into integrating her learning back in her day-to-day context. During group dialogue about how much vulnerability is appropriate Mary Ann captures her learning as "strategic vulnerability is required in leadership." Mary Ann takes away ideas of how she might share herself more with her team, even strategically share that she is not always so sure of herself or share some of her developmental goals.

She also recognizes that her modus operandi of a confident, resourceful, no-nonsense persona can make her seem unreachable and that people assume she is judging them. To counteract that assumption, she commits to acknowledging strengths in peers and direct reports as a regular part of her communication. The group underlines what a difference they feel it will make in Mary Ann's impact as leader.

In talking with Mary Ann in a phone coaching session after the program, she says, "I am definitely seeing results—my team is sharing more with me about how things are going so I can help and peers are more willing to collaborate. I think my mindset has shifted around vulnerability as a strength instead of a weakness. That has helped me the most, plus I am breathing more!"

How Do We Know It Works?

> *"The class allowed me to take an extremely difficult business situation and creatively work through how I can handle it. The class has made me really aware of the emotional content in the business environment and how it can be leveraged."*
>
> *"Feedback from customers was exceptional . . . [they] observed that the team seemed to be some of the most genuine representatives they had encountered and that their stories and perceived genuineness allowed them to connect on a personal level, opening them up to the rest of the conversation."*
>
> —From the leader of a sales team who enrolled his group in a custom storytelling program

As effective as the experiential approach to teaching leadership presence is, the critical question is: Does it really stick, and how can you tell? We can state unequivocally (and level one evaluations attest) that theater-based, experiential learning gets rated very highly. But, how do we assess the long-term impact? The question of assessment has been a thorny one. Skeptics will tell you that a "rising tide lifts all boats," and that there is very little available that can isolate, identify, and quantify the effect of specific development efforts on the progress, and more importantly, the impact of formal leadership development initiatives. Developing leaders without developing methods for capturing data about how those leaders are shaping the environment, output, and morale of their organizations may seem, at best, irresponsible. However, assessment is possible, albeit complex and not yet particularly widespread.

The Ariel Group has developed leaders in more than twenty-five countries with a unique approach to Leadership Presence that is derived from our roots in the performing arts. Our participants are largely senior executives, consultants, and emerging leaders within corporations, non-profits, and executive education programs. An Ariel program typically lasts two days and includes one facilitator and six to eight participants.

Let us share two examples of recent assessment initiatives we employed around the delivery of our experiential learning programs on Presence: one from the non-profit world and one from the corporate sector. The first helps to show how assessment can track and connect development needs with learning. The second one addresses how to then connect learning with specific results.

ASSESSMENT TRACKS AND CONNECTS NEEDS WITH LEARNING

Teach For America is a national non-profit dedicated to building a movement to eliminate educational inequity. The organization recruits and trains outstanding recent college graduates who commit to teach for two years in low-income urban and rural communities and become lifelong leaders in the effort to expand education opportunity.

The methodology we employed with one group of eight Teach For America alumni on the pathway to school leadership included a front-end (pre-training) baseline assessment of participants current level of "leadership presence" as measured by how well they interacted with, communicated with, and influenced others. This front-end "look" included self-disclosure of a personal leadership challenge and the learner's specific career aspirations. Facilitators then tailored the two-day workshop, follow-up one-on-one coaching sessions (in person and over the phone), and a one-day mastery workshop to provide targeted, specific learning experiences relevant to the individual learners' development needs and goals. Post-training assessments were conducted after the coaching sessions (i.e., sixty days after the two-day workshop) and at the end of the learning sequence (i.e., sixty days after the one-day mastery workshop).

The self-assessment protocol in each case invited the participants to consider how successful they were in applying seventeen key principles (drivers) from the PRES model, framed as four competency areas that were critical for their success as leaders: influencing others; connecting and communicating; being yourself; and building authentic relationships. They were asked to describe their challenges in each of these competency areas as well as to identify their focus area for personal development and a specific situation that they would bring to the workshop to role-play and get feedback.

Given the opportunity to self-evaluate themselves in these seventeen dimensions prior to the workshop, we found that participants were thoughtful and frank about their challenges in leadership presence. We had familiarized them with the concepts of the PRES model by asking them to read the first chapter of the book *Leadership Presence*, so they knew the language to describe their challenges. However, although they knew what was not working for them, they were often surprised in the workshop by how this showed up for others. For example, one participant was aware of needing improvement in "being yourself," but was not aware of what his own behaviors looked like to others: poor eye contact, stiff arms, or nervous pacing. In addition, he was not aware of how frequently these behaviors showed up.

With background information from the baseline assessment, the facilitator was able to corroborate the learning needs of each participant on meeting and observing them for the first time, and then target the coaching and feedback, making bolder choices to challenge their learning experience early in the workshop. It also allowed him to adjust the focus of the workshop and individual learning modules, working with common themes and learning needs of the group as a whole.

In the first post-training assessment, sixty days after the two-day workshop, participants were asked to comment on the skills they applied and the outcomes they experienced in using the skills. They indicated an overall 4–10 percent improvement in the four competency areas. Despite the small sampling size, this was a significant improvement over sixty days when compared to training programs with a similar focus.

Additionally, built into the assessment protocol is the evaluation of success stories that involve the application of the leadership skills—i.e., demonstrating transference of the learning to the workplace. During the baseline assessment prior to the workshop, participants were asked to identify an upcoming situation—a communication challenge—that they could use to role play during the final session of the workshop as a way to practice the skills: delivering a presentation; facilitating a discussion or meeting; managing a one-on-one conversation. Having practiced the skills in the workshop, participants would then complete the interaction in real life and report back in the first post-training assessment. Participants were asked to "tell the story" about the situation, who was involved, what skills from the course did they apply, what were the outcomes, and what was the impact of the skills learned in the workshop.

Although 50 percent of participants chose to role play a situation during the workshop that was different from the one they had identified in the baseline pre-workshop assessment, due to new insights created by the learning, most participants followed through on their workshop role play after the workshop, completed the interaction, and reported back. In every case, the skills they learned positively impacted the interaction by anything between 50 percent ("made some difference") and 100 percent ("made all the difference").

> "I wish I had taken this class five years ago when I was a first-year school leader . . . it might have been the single greatest act I could have done to increase my effectiveness as a leader. I would recommend this to anyone who wants to increase their impact!! Outstanding."

ASSESSMENT TRACKS AND CONNECTS LEARNING WITH RESULTS

Assessment can also be used to track and connect learning with results at the back end of a leadership development experience. American Express looked at the impact of leadership development efforts on leaders' behavior and the results created due to their changed behavior. A back-end (post-training) assessment measured how often, how well, and to what effect participants were using the skills and behaviors introduced. In particular, the question of what role a supportive manager (aka the leaders' leader) played in maximizing application and the subsequent increased likelihood of improvement and impact over time was asked and answered.

Eighty-seven percent of leaders in this study and 83 percent of their managers (leaders' leaders) reported an observable improvement in the Leadership Presence of learners as defined by their ability to build and leverage relationships; communicate effectively; and demonstrate personal excellence in their role. Additionally, the data indicated that those leaders who had their manager's support showed greater improvement than those who did not, underscoring the role the leaders' leader plays in maximizing leadership development potential and return (American Express & The Ariel Group, 2006).

So, though the assessment technology of tracking need to learning to results may be new to some in the field, leadership development can be measured, and some might argue must be, so that we ascertain that those competencies, abilities, and skills that are introduced serve not only the individual leader on their path, but also the organization to which they are accountable, the market they "play in," and the future generation of leaders they themselves are nurturing.

INITIAL RESISTANCE TO THEATER-BASED EXPERIENTIAL LEARNING

In the sales process, Chief Learning Officers are often concerned that analytical, cognitive learners will find it hard to follow the classic experiential approach described in this chapter. This approach is inverse to how an analytical learner might approach the absorption and adoption of new ideas where they would normally begin with a model. Similarly, there is concern that introverted learners may find the focus on talking about an experience, "processing it out loud," runs counter to their default method of reflection which may be quiet thinking without sharing.

Paradoxically, more than 50 percent of Ariel's clients come from the worlds of IT, management consulting, and quantitative finance where these kinds of learners predominate. Given their specific learning styles, they need more time to "warm up" and trust the facilitator and the process in the classroom. But, there is evidence, based on repeat programs with these kinds of learners, that experiential theater-based programs can jumpstart learning effectively for those who need to influence others and come to the program with an analytical/cognitive or introverted learning style.

Additionally, at the start of programs, there is often a general bias against "actor skills"—the perception that to use the skills of the actor "make believe" or faking it. Within the first morning, participants understand that, ironically, upon closer inspection, the skills of the actor are all about authenticity and "digging deep" to find the true self of the role, which in the end is at the heart of good leadership as well.

> "I would never have thought that the theatrical world would translate to leadership skills."

> "Very relevant—I was a little skeptical at first about what I could learn that was new, but with the design of the course I got a lot out of it."

Conclusion

In conclusion, the theatrical metaphor serves leadership development in both content and context. In terms of content, exercises inspired by acting training can build skill and awareness in the ability to be present, reach out, be expressive and self-knowing—all of which lead to the crucial leadership competency of being able to authentically connect with the hearts and minds of others, in order to inspire them to do great things. Borrowing from actor training allows for an expansive experience of self and other (physical, emotional, rational, relational, and sometimes spiritual) which can be leveraged to move from introspection toward application to everyday leadership challenges.

In terms of context, the theater metaphor is tremendously useful in designing the arc of a complex, multi-modal, and engaging leadership program that offers a robust environment for learning. Elements of coaching style from the performing arts serve to deepen the possibilities for transformative experiences. Being immersed in the unfamiliar world of actor training also allows leaders to drop into a mindset for being able to receive new and important insights about themselves and their own possible growth.

> " . . . a fantastic journey of introspection and empowerment . . . "

Finally, in our ever more virtual and digital age, where there is a push for e-learning to replace in-person classroom learning, it can seem anachronistic to ask leaders to participate in an artistic learning environment consisting of face-to-face small groups with tremendous opportunity for connection to self and other. Perhaps, though, as we are "connecting" to thousands of "friends" on Facebook, we, as human beings, are ever more lonely. Perhaps as we move into an ever more fragmented age, leaders counter-intuitively need the ability to authentically connect more than ever—to move their teams, organizations and society at large toward the possibility of a better world. As E.M. Forster articulated in *Howards End* (2000):

> Only connect! That was the whole of her sermon.
> Only connect the prose and the passion, and both will be exalted,
> And human love will be seen at its height.
> Live in fragments no longer.
> Only connect . . . (p. 159).

Acknowledgements

For inspiring and guiding these words, we would like to thank:

Joel Gluck, Madeleine Homan, Steven Holt, Ariel CEO Sean Kavanagh, Ariel Founding partner Kathy Lubar, Mark Rittenberg, Gabriella Salvatore, our partners at BeyondROI, and the late Martha Schlamme.

References

American Express & The Ariel Group. (2006). *Maximizing ROI: How American Express creates an effective leadership development climate.* New York & Arlington, MA: Leone, P., Marino, M., & Richards, R.

Bennis, W.G., & Thomas, R.J. (2002). *Geeks & geezers: How era, values and defining moments shape leaders.* Boston, MA: Harvard Business School Publishing.

Forster, E.M. (2000). *Howards End.* New York: Penguin Classics. (Original work published 1910)

Hagen, U., & Frankel, H. (1973). *Respect for acting.* New York: MacMillan.

Halpern, B.L., & Lubar, K. (2004). *Leadership presence: Dramatic techniques to reach out, motivate, and inspire.* New York: Penguin.

Johnstone, K. (1999). *Impro for storytellers: Theatresports and the art of making things happen.* New York: Routledge/Theatre Arts Books.

O'Carroll, C. (2003). *It's the "aha" experience: Julian Olf's vision of the performing arts.* UMASS Magazine Online, Winter 2003 Issue. Retrieved from http://www.umass-mag.com/winter_2003/It_s_the__Aha__experience_399.html

Zander, R.S., & Zander, B. (2000). *The art of possibility: Transforming professional and personal life.* Boston, MA: Harvard Business School Press.

Zuboff, S. (1988). *In the age of the smart machine: The future of work and power.* New York: Basic Books.

10

TEACHING EXECUTIVES TO BE THEMSELVES—MORE—WITH SKILL

A Sociological Perspective on a Personal Question

◆ Rob Goffee and Gareth Jones
London Business School

Our approach to teaching leadership is shaped by our sociological background and several decades working with executives in business schools. It is shaped by three conceptual axioms. Leadership is situational, relational, and non-hierarchical. The first explains the difficulties in establishing universals for good leadership—and the profound significance of situation sensing skills. The second reminds us that it is not possible to be a leader without followers—and that, with the flattening of hierarchies, the management of social distance becomes a vital skill. The third warns of the danger of assuming those in senior organizational positions will inevitably act as leaders—an assumption that has undermined the understanding and teaching of leadership. Our argument is that it is the skillful use of distinctive personal attributes that define leadership rather than attributes of position.

Our recommendation to executives is "Be yourself—more—with skill." This reminds them that leadership is about knowing and selectively showing their true selves and skillful deployment of attributes in particular situations. Balancing authenticity with skill is teachable and can help executives provide purpose and excitement as leaders.

❖ ❖ ❖

Introduction

Before we begin to set out our approach to the teaching of leadership we need to say a little about ourselves and how we came to be interested in both the study and practice of leadership. We are European sociologists educated in the early 1970s, obsessed with classical social theory as it manifests itself in the nineteenth and early twentieth centuries. Our research focus has always been the sociology of work and organizations and it was this that eventually beached us on the shores of departments of organizational behavior in some of the world's leading business schools.

In some respects it was initially a profoundly alienating experience. We found ourselves predominantly surrounded by psychologists who seemed to us largely intent on the measurement of individual differences—and puzzled by our interests in relationships, communities, and social origins. Nonetheless, we were asked to teach leadership to groups of earnest MBA students and to often tired executives glad of a break from the corporate rat race (Goffee & Scase, 1989).

To equip ourselves we attempted to master the modern behavioral science literature on leaders. We were struck by how inconclusive it was—and therefore, pragmatically, how difficult it was to teach in any way that helped people to become more effective leaders! It began with trait theory—the attempt to find the common characteristics that effective leaders share. To this end leaders were weighed, measured, and subjected to a battery of psychological tests. The rather unsatisfactory outcome was a body of research characterized by weak correlations where the causal connections were indeterminate.

It was succeeded by style theory, which began to become predominant in the late 1930s in the United States. It argued that effective leaders shared a common behavioral style—and the style recommended was socially close, democratic, and inclusive. It was a recipe that precisely fitted the zeitgeist—for this was America of FDR and the New Deal. However, by the time we reach McCarthyism and the cold war the spirit of the age had changed again. Now it appeared that leaders needed to act like cold war warriors.

So while style theory correctly argued that effective leaders identify and exemplify prevailing values and mores it hardly provides a firm basis for pedagogic practice. The logical outcome of the need to adapt to context is contingency theory. This raised interesting questions for executives. Who are you trying to lead? What is the nature of the task? Which aspects of the external situation can you turn to your advantage? We have used these questions to help aspiring leaders focus their efforts on critical success factors. However, it comes close to saying, "Leadership—it all depends!" We found this a hard sell to beleaguered executives and ambitious MBAs who preferred something a little more practical.

So what was the central problem with this large research tradition? In our view it had produced a considerable (although inconclusive) body of evidence about *leaders*. But of course what the executives we were attempting to teach were effectively interested in was *leadership*—a relationship between the leaders and the led. If it is a relationship then the study of leadership should be as much informed by sociological concepts as it is by psychological ones. Our subsequent work has been the attempt to provide just such a framework (Goffee & Jones, 2003, 2006). It has come as a welcome surprise to us that those who aspire to leadership find just such a framework both illuminating and practical.

Or to put this in epistemological terms, *praxis* proved a good test.

Conceptual Framework

Our work has been informed by three conceptual axioms. These, in turn, have profoundly shaped the approaches and issues we have attempted to deal with in our leadership teaching.

LEADERSHIP IS SITUATIONAL

What is required of the leader will always be influenced by the situation. This is commonsensical, but true.

History is full of examples of individuals who found their time and place—but whose characteristics lost their appeal when things moved on. Churchill, for example, was an inspirational war-time leader but his bulldog style proved ill-suited to the reconstruction agenda of post-war Britain. Similarly, George Bush Sr. had a very large opinion poll lead in the immediate aftermath of the first Iraq war and yet in the following year he lost to Bill Clinton. By contrast, Nelson Mandela's ability to show leadership across widely differing contexts exemplifies situational adjustment from a prison cell on Robben Island to the graceful lawns of Union House in Pretoria.

There are many parallels in organizational life. For example, hard-edged, cost-cutting turnaround managers are often unable to provide leadership when there is a need to build and grow. But their more flexible colleagues may adjust to shifting agendas—and so carry their teams with them.

The ability to observe and comprehend existing situations, *situation sensing,* is vital to leadership. It involves a mix of sensory and cognitive abilities. Effective leaders pick up important situational signals. They tune into the organizational frequency and penetrate beneath the surface. This is both a micro and a macro skill—visible in daily routine encounters (meetings, walking the corridors, elevator conversations) as well as in high-level, strategic decisions (Does this acquisition feel right? Are these people we can work with?). Effective leaders are able to adjust appropriately, self-consciously deploying their personal capabilities. But in so doing, they are able to impact—and therefore reshape—the situations within which they lead. Through their interactions, they build *alternative contexts* to those that they initially inherited. They use their personal leadership assets to reconfigure for the benefit of followers. This last point is important. It is not sufficient to reframe a situation to personal advantage; true leadership requires reframing to the benefit of those who are led. That is the basis on which the relationship is established.

Our starting assumption is a simple, undeniable observation: Human actions—whether involving leadership or not—do not take place in a vacuum. They are conditioned by the social context in which individuals act. These social realities can be no more wished away than can gravity. Effective leadership involves recognizing the limitations of context as well as the potential opportunities. Skillful leaders are realists. They have a well-developed idea about what can be changed—and what cannot. They understand the real conditions in which they must operate and work within those constraints (Durkheim, 1984). When teaching leadership it bring us to the difficult idea that leadership implies a necessary degree of conformity. Individuals who fail to master this are like engines whirring with no connection to the drive shaft. They never achieve organizational traction. Those who conform too much never get to express those things that might excite others to exceptional performance.

The notion that leadership is dependent on context is not new. The sociologist

George Homans (1951) captured it perfectly many years ago:

> There are no rules for human behavior that apply in every situation without limit or change. Humanity yearns for certainty; it has looked for such rules for thousands of years but has not found them. For every principle it has discovered, it has also discovered a conflict of principles. In recent years men of practical affairs—industrial executives, for instance—have often come to psychologists and sociologists begging for a plan or set of rules that the executives can apply "across the board"—that is, in all circumstances—in dealing with their employees. There are no such rules, and if there were, they would be dangerous. They might work well for a time; then changing circumstances would make them inappropriate, and the leader would have to deal with a new situation while his mind was clogged with old rules. The maxims of leadership we shall state are, therefore, not to be taken as absolutes but only as convenient guides for the behavior of a leader. They apply only within limits determined by the situation that faces him, and there are situations where the maxims will conflict with one another. What a leader needs to have is not a set of rules but a good method of analyzing the situation in which he must act. If the analysis is adequate, a way of dealing with the situation will suggest itself. And if, as a working guide, the leader does have some simple rules in mind, analysis will show him where their limits lie. (p. 424)

There are three separate but related components to effective situation-sensing. The first is made up of observational and cognitive skills. Leaders see and sense what's going on in their organizations—and then use their cognitive skills to interpret these observations. They pick up and interpret soft data, sometimes without any verbal explanation. They "know" when team morale is shaky or when complacency needs challenging. They collect information, seemingly through osmosis, and use it to understand the context in which they are aspiring to lead.

The process is often very subtle, so that it is not always easy to "see" it. But there are some key moments where you may often observe this skill—or its absence—in workplace interactions. Consider meetings, for example, when a colleague joins late and then acts very clumsily. This kind of disruption typically reflects "negative" situation-sensing. Others seem to be able to join a meeting and immediately tune in, effortlessly picking up on atmosphere or ambience.

The skill will also be seen when deals are being done. There inevitably comes a point during merger negotiations, for instance, when all the numbers have been run, but the vital determining factor will be a sense of whether it "feels right" to proceed. Those who make the right call have good situation-sensing capabilities.

Highly task-oriented executives very often neglect this basic observational work. They are inclined to charge into action before fully understanding the situation—sometimes with very negative consequences. As we show later, there are useful observational frameworks that can help individuals to develop awareness of this skill and start to practice it.

The second element of situation-sensing is made up of behavioral and adaptive skills. Having observed and understood the situation, effective leaders adjust their behaviors. They adapt without ever losing their sense of self. Elsewhere we have called these leaders *authentic chameleons* (Goffee & Jones, 2005). They adapt dramatically to environment or context without ever ceasing to be a chameleon. For leaders, this behavioral element of situation-sensing involves the deliberate use of social skills to maximize their impact in a particular context. As we discuss below, these individuals are able to use a wide range of behaviors:

they can create both closeness and distance; leverage their strengths but reveal their human weaknesses; move fast but seem to be in control of time.

The final element of effective situation sensing is that leaders use their own behavior to change the situation. They exemplify an alternative context. When Greg Dyke arrived at the BBC, he was shocked by the number of unhappy people he encountered. His response was to model a more positive, energized vision for the organization. Similarly, at Europe's largest airline Ryanair the pugnacious Chief Executive, Michael O'Leary, frequently and aggressively asserts opportunities in the face of adversity. Recently, for example, he proclaimed that the harsh economic environment for airlines simply provided more opportunities for growth at Ryanair.

The lesson is that leaders are not passive recipients of the context. On the contrary, they work with others to socially construct a shared alternative reality (Berger & Luckman, 1966). This capacity is what differentiates those who merely react to situations from those who have the capacity to transform them.

Leaders know that situation-sensing is important. They also know that it becomes more critical as you move up organizational hierarchies. Elevation brings with it increasingly sanitized information—filtered through the eyes and ears of others who may have a view about what the leader should know. As you get nearer to the top, you receive more information, but it can become less reliable. As one CEO explained to us, "If you are successful, you are held more and more in awe, and, as a result you get less and less honest information." Effective authentic leaders know this and take steps to ensure they remain connected to the action, sensitive to the ever-changing context.

The question now becomes: Can situation-sensing be learned? Although it may often appear "intuitive" or "natural," our view is that there are clearly skills that can be developed. As is the case for many leadership skills, first-hand experience is vital. As others have shown, there are few substitutes for early, diverse, rich experiences. But learning through these "crucibles of experience" can be painful, risky, and slow (Bennis & Thomas, 2002).

The teaching environment can offer safer options—with more scope for reflection. All the world's leading business schools, for example, have developed courses in "interpersonal skills training." Central to any improvement in this area is improved situation sensing. One technique is to videotape executives in specific situations—setting targets, giving feedback, communicating vision—and then review them working through what may have been missed or misinterpreted. Such courses effectively highlight the common neglect of observational skills. Many driven executives will not give themselves the time to simply watch what is going on around them. Their desire to get things done leads them to neglect even the most basic observational tasks. And of course, skilled observation is not easy. Think about how we experience a visit to an art gallery: If you can use the audio guide, you simply see more things. We take executives to art galleries and ask them to spend time looking at five exhibits without the audio guide. They then repeat the exercise with the head phones. The results are startling. Their perceptions are transformed. Leaders need that guide playing all the time.

In our own work we regularly use a couple of simple techniques to help executives sharpen their situation-sensing capabilities. First, we suggest that they keep a brief diary of their observations whenever they start a new assignment, work with a new team, or change location. We recommend no more than fifteen minutes a day for this task. Even busy executives can find this time. We urge them to write down, in as unmediated a way as possible, their observations: Who spoke first at the meeting? Who didn't speak? Did people come on time? How did they relate to each other? To begin with, the observations may appear unrelated and chaotic but over time they start to reveal patterns that map the organizational reality. Our experience suggests that if executives are prepared to give this exercise concerted effort it has a marked impact on their ability to read situations.

Second, we ask people to draw a network diagram (not a hierarchy) that places themselves at the center and maps the people who have the biggest impact on their performance. Then they are asked to populate the network diagram with answers to the following questions: How are these individuals motivated? What are their greatest strengths? What are their allowable weaknesses? Which roles in teams do they play best? What are their fatal flaws? Of course, to begin with there are gaps on the diagram and individuals are encouraged to collect observational data that will allow them to fill in the gaps. We suggest that this exercise is continued for about six months—after this time for many executives they no longer need the diagram because they are doing the situation-sensing as a leadership habit.

Teaching the adaptive and transformational aspects of situation sensing is more difficult. We invite participants on our programs to consider a variety of scenarios and to discuss with their colleagues what actions leaders can take to reframe context. For example, the photograph of Nelson Mandela awarding the Rugby Union World Cup to Francoise Pienaar not long after his release from prison usually provokes a rich discussion. We then ask executives to think of how they can apply techniques of redefining the context to their own situations—this of course produces less dramatic examples than Nelson Mandela but nonetheless it helps people to grasp and practice the key leadership ability to both read and redefine context. They are often pleasantly surprised by the opportunities that they have around them to make things different. As we often say to those we work with, small (but symbolically rich) shifts in behavior can have a big impact.

LEADERSHIP IS RELATIONAL

Our second conceptual axiom is that leadership is relational. Put simply, you cannot be a leader without followers.

Much of early trait theory seemed to ignore this. By trying to distill the characteristics of leaders it often underplayed the fact that leadership is a relationship built actively by both parties. In reality, leadership is always a social construct that is re-created by the relationships between leaders and those they aspire to lead. Effective leaders are not simply amalgams of desirable traits; they are actively and reciprocally engaged in a complex series of relationships that require cultivation and nurture. Like all social creations, it is fragile and requires constant re-creation.

This is confirmed every time you talk to a successful CEO, a sports coach, or a team leader. All will tell you that much of their leadership effort is devoted to the maintenance of particular kinds of relationships with their followers. This insistence on the relational nature of leadership does not mean that these relationships are necessarily harmonious—they may well be edgy—but they are about leaders knowing how to excite followers to become great performers.

In effect, they can empathize with those they lead, step into their shoes, get close to them. Yet, at the right moment, they also seem able to communicate a sense of edge, to remind people of the job at hand and the over-arching purpose of the collective endeavor. In doing so, they move skillfully from closeness to distance and back again. They are able to get close to their followers yet, paradoxically, keep their distance.

The concept of social distance derives originally from another founding figure of sociology, Georg Simmel (1950 [1908]).

Writing in the early twentieth century, Simmel conceived of social distance as a complex interpretation of sociability, as forms of distance in both a geometric and metaphoric sense. In modern social science it is increasingly regarded as a measure of intimacy between groups and individuals. In turn, the degree of intimacy directly affects the degree of influence that one individual may have over another.

There are good reasons for believing that the management of social distance may be an even more important skill for contemporary leaders. Hierarchies, for example, have been flattened, partly for cost-control reasons but mainly to increase speed of response to customer desires and market changes. But hierarchies have always been much more than structural devices; they have also been sources of meaning (Sennett, 1998). Moving through stable hierarchies gave some illusion of becoming more of a leader. Indeed, the "lazy" senior executive relied on the crutch of hierarchy to establish social distance, jealously guarding their status privileges as a way of establishing their difference.

Those days are gone. Leaders need alternatives for establishing separation and perspective—to see the big things that may shape the future of the organization without jeopardizing the closeness necessary to know what is really going on inside their business. They cannot rely on hierarchy to supply the former.

This movement between closeness and distance is rather like a dance, with leaders basing their movement and timing on refined situation-sensing skills. It is just one of the adjustments they must constantly make and remake at the core of the leadership relationship. The balance is forever changing and it explains why style theory was unable to identify the *one best* leadership style.

So what are the benefits of closeness? First, it enables the leader to know and understand their followers—a vital prerequisite for effectiveness. But beyond this, closeness enables followers to know more of the leader. By being close leaders show who they are. Closeness offers a context for intimacy and disclosure—of personal weakness as well as strength. As we discuss below it is a mechanism for revealing the *person* in the position.

Our observations suggest that effective leaders take this opportunity for disclosure but remain in other ways interestingly enigmatic. They disclose personal differences and human fallibility—but never entirely. In this context, the popularity of emotional intelligence is sometimes worrying. The important point to realize is that being intelligent with our emotions may require them to be hidden. Good leadership often involves *withholding* rather than displaying emotions, and maintaining distance.

Distance confers different advantages. Primary here is that distance signals to the followers that the leader has an over-arching purpose. Leadership is not an end in itself. To be legitimate, a leader always has a larger, superordinate purpose. Establishing distance enables the leader to build solidarity with followers based on a shared view of this over-arching goal. When great leaders do this skillfully, they do it in pursuit of a goal—making money, building beautiful buildings, eradicating human illness, making great movies.

The practical question again becomes, can those who aspire to leadership learn the practice of social distance? Again, our experience is that there are teachable skills. We use a number of techniques that can help. The start point is to ask individuals to identify their "default mode"—that is, to say, do they habitually slip into closeness or is their preference for the maintenance of social distance? Then they are asked to practice the opposite of their default mode. We use role-playing practice based on conversations derived from the workplace—these could be to do with giving feedback on performance, both positive and negative, or handling confrontational interactions. For some, for example, those who seek to avoid difficult conversations, this can be a painful process but it is almost universally useful. Indeed for leaders it is a useful habit to practice those social situations that they normally find difficult. The process of practice sharpens their ability to both understand and exhibit appropriate behavioral cues that communicate either closeness or distance. For example, they learn that distance works best in a more formal context where symbols, like dress code and physical space, can be used to signal appropriately. Finally, individuals learn that using social distance involves understanding the concept of "bandwidth." That is to say that the range between closeness and distance can be neither too big nor traveled too abruptly. For if it is, the leader is in danger of behavioral shifts that are disconcerting to others, or more worrying, which lead them to perceived as inauthentic. Important clues about perceived inconsistencies in leader behavior often emerge from careful consideration of 360 feedback from colleagues. We also use role-playing practice where participants are coached to act "inappropriately. " It soon becomes clear to them, often in quite humorous ways, that the impact of their behaviors generates almost the opposite effect from the one they intend. Judgments about range and timing inevitably take us back to many of the situation-sensing skills which we discussed earlier.

LEADERSHIP IS NON-HIERARCHICAL

Our final axiomatic assumption is that leadership is *non-hierarchical.* Much of the leadership literature (and arguably, much of what is taught in business schools) is overly concerned with those who reach the top of organizations. The persistent misconception that people who occupy senior organizational positions are leaders has damaged our capacity to understand and teach leadership. It has blinded us to the true nature of leadership.

While we recognize that there is a relationship between hierarchy and leadership (they may fulfill a similar function, for example, by investing authority), we view the relationship as contingent. A particular organizational title—team leader, section head, and vice president—may confer some hierarchical authority but it certainly does not make you a leader. Hierarchy alone is neither a necessary nor sufficient condition for the exercise of leadership.

Indeed, it can be argued that the qualities that take individuals to the top of large-scale—and often highly political—organizations are not obviously the ones associated with leadership. People who make it to the top may have done so for a whole variety of reasons—including political acumen, personal ambition, time-serving, even nepotism—rather than real leadership quality.

Our interviews and experience inside organizations confirms that leadership is not the sole preserve of the chosen few. Great organizations have leaders at all levels. Some of our early work on leadership involved examining military organizations. Our assumption was that their hierarchical nature would make leadership development difficult. Nothing could be further from the truth. The best military organizations understand that when they move into action they simply cannot rely on hierarchy. It may be obliterated when the first mortar lands. It is imperative that they develop leadership capability throughout. The best do.

It is not just the military that has reached this realization. Successful organizations—be they hospitals, charities, or commercial enterprises—seek to build leadership capability widely and to give people the opportunity to exercise it.

So if job title does not confer leadership, what does? If leadership is non-hierarchical, the question "Why should anyone be led by you?" can only be answered by reference to personal qualities that are authentically yours (not attributes of position). Effective leaders seem to know their differences and use them to their own—and crucially their followers'—advantage. They are also aware of their weaknesses and do not seek to hide them all. They avoid the fatal error of pretending that they are perfect.

Consider the following examples. Richard Branson uses his air of casualness to indicate that Virgin is a different kind of organization—informal, fun, and innovative. Bill Gates at Microsoft looks a little like the "geeks" who have made Microsoft one of the most powerful organizations in the world. This leads us not to the trait type list of personal qualities, but rather to a deep consideration of what we think of as personal idiosyncrasies. We regularly ask executives to consider the following: What is special about you that might excite others to exceptional performance? And which of your weaknesses invites others to help you? Our questions are driven by the simple assumption that potential followers have a basic need: They want to be led by a person, **not by a slick role player or corporate apparatchik.** Leaders are unlikely to inspire, arouse, excite, or motivate others unless they can show others who they are, what they stand for, and what they can and *cannot* do.

So how can individuals be encouraged—or even taught—to do this? Knowing, and expressing, your real self is easier said than done. Workplaces often make it difficult for individuals to easily express themselves, without fear of ridicule or failure. The result? Individuals spend much of their waking hours in organizations that inhibit their authentic selves. They save their "real" selves—and much of the energy that goes with it—for their families, friends, private lives, and communities.

Although it is rarely discussed in these terms, this inability to be ourselves at work is an important element in the work/life balance debate. Our workplace cultures mean we are unable to reconcile our working selves with our private selves. Work/life balance means much more than spending time at home. It means transforming workplaces into arenas for the display of authenticity. And, even where self-expression is encouraged, individuals may not be equipped to respond. Their experiences may have already damaged their capacity to both know and show themselves.

To show people who you are requires a degree of self-knowledge (or at least self-awareness) *as well as* self-disclosure. One without the other is hopeless. We have observed individuals who know themselves well but fail to communicate this to others. Since their colleagues are not mind readers these individuals often remain frustratingly enigmatic. Equally, there are others whose efforts at self-disclosure are fatally undermined by their lack of self-knowledge. They communicate—but the image they project of themselves appears false. Colleagues often perceive them as phoneys.

So to *be* yourself you must *know* yourself and *show* yourself—enough. Put another way, you must be sufficiently self-aware and also prepared to self-declare. This judgment is particularly acute when it comes to the revelation of personal weaknesses.

A number of issues are involved here. First, leaders do not—and should not—reveal all their weaknesses. Not only is this impractical (we are unlikely to know all our weaknesses) but it is also asking too much. After all, if you are aware of every flaw in another person this is likely to destroy rather than enhance their leadership credibility. In effect, their weaknesses will drown out their strengths.

So, good leaders focus dissatisfaction. As with the personal differences they transform into leadership assets, so the weaknesses they reveal are *real* and *perceived.* But in addition, these weaknesses are *not fatal flaws*; they *show how others may help*; and, above all, they are *humanity-confirming*. Let's take each of these qualities in turn.

First, authentic leaders emphatically do not invent mock weaknesses to distract attention from the real ones. This lack of authenticity is swiftly spotted by others. If you have ever interviewed someone, asked them to report their weaknesses, and heard them piously reply "I am a little too ambitious" or "I expect too much of others," then you will have witnessed first hand the doomed attempt to serve up (yet another) strength as a so-called weakness.

Nor does it wash if individuals try to cover underlying weaknesses with a fake alternative. Think, for example, of how you might react to someone who pleads absent-mindedness to cover inconsistency or lies.

So for weaknesses to "work" they must be real. But if a real weakness is central to task performance then this will most likely be a fatal flaw. The new head of the accounting department is unlikely to gain much credit if she announces that she never did quite understand discounted cash flow; equally, the sales director who hates customers is unlikely to build leadership credibility. We return again, to situation sensing. We have to be careful about the contexts within which it might be possible to display leadership—some places simply won't work for us.

This makes generalization difficult. A famous, and extremely successful, English soccer coach, Brian Clough, very skillfully used one of his weaknesses (arrogance) by standing back and making fun of it. Equally, the entrepreneur Anita Roddick was forgiven her irrascibility, just as Bob Geldof is forgiven his short temper—largely, it seems, because we can see these qualities are an inevitable by-product of the higher purpose that each of these individuals passionately pursued. It is not difficult to imagine other individuals and other contexts where these particular weaknesses might prove fatal.

How can we help people to discover more about themselves in ways that enable them to maximize their leadership assets? This is not a question that has a simple answer. As with much leadership learning, experience and feedback are vital—but so too is time for reflection. Our experience is that no matter how rich the classroom discussions, there is no substitute for skillfully delivered 360-degree feedback and time for guided reflection. We routinely build this into much of our leadership teaching. Indeed, this time for reflection away from work is one of the ways in which business schools can help with leadership development. Too often, however, business school programs are driven by an imperative to squeeze in as much as possible and push executives from one case analysis to the next. This may be beneficial for many kinds of *executive* development but not necessarily *leadership* development.

But there is a bigger and more pressing organizational development challenge—to build organizations where individuals can both uncover and express their authentic selves. To do this we need to examine yet more social rather than individual variables—culture, structure, relationships, communities (Goffee & Jones, 2009). This is an extremely hard ask in the lecture theater—but clearly there are opportunities to encourage executives to confront these shared challenges, particularly in the context of custom-designed programs where colleagues share the same classroom.

Assessment and Conclusions

The whole issue of how to assess the effectiveness of leadership teaching is, of course, complex. However, it helps if you are at least clear about your original objectives. We end attempts to develop leadership using the framework we discuss here by urging people to remember the last paragraph of our *Harvard Business Review* article "Why Should Anyone Be Led by You?" (Goffee & Jones, 2000). The injunction is clear: If you wish to be a more effective leader you should, **Be Yourself—More—With Skill.**

It is a beguilingly simple message that of course involves more than seems the case. We are really concerned with measuring two variables: authenticity—the extent to which individuals both know and selectively show their true self; and skill—the extent to which individuals deploy themselves in situationally appropriate ways. These variables are represented in the simple matrix reproduced below (Figure 10.1). We ask people to consider three questions: Where are you in the matrix now? Where do you want to get to? And what do you need to work on in order to get there? In box B, individuals combine skill and authenticity to produce effective leadership. Perhaps their only challenge is to avoid complacency. In box A, individuals have a profound sense of who they are, what made them, and what values they stand for. Entrepreneurs are often successful in this way—able to be themselves in "their" business. However, they may lack the skills to make adequate use of their leadership assets in other contexts. They become "one-hit wonders." They fail to adapt to other contexts, to communicate differently, and to adjust social distance appropriately with other followers. In box C, we find individuals who exhibit considerable interpersonal skills but who lack a strong sense of self. Their followers may feel that they are being manipulated. These individuals can be helped by coaching that facilitates self-discovery and some forms of experiential learning that jolt them from their comfort zones. In box D, we find the clumsy individuals so successfully satirized in television's *The Office*. Although this may represent the most challenging start-point, we are continually surprised at the extent to which individuals can achieve improvements in the way their leadership is perceived by others—so long as they can convince them that they are trying!

The matrix helps—but it also conceals some significant differences between the two variables. Measuring improvements in leadership skills is easier. We use repeated 360-degree feedback to give us a sense of how people's leadership skills are developing. In general, the results are encouraging. Individuals can learn relational skills, situational skills, and communication skills that improve their leadership impact.

The power of this technique rests upon the notion that you can't be a leader without followers. Their perceptions matter. If the feedback says that you're not a great team leader—then you aren't. We are operating in an area where, insofar as things are defined as "real," then they are "real" in their consequences.

The other variable—authenticity—is much harder to measure. How can we know whether individuals have really come to know and show themselves? Do we sometimes confuse effective leadership with skillful role-playing?

There are no easy answers to these difficult questions. We stress that leadership development is not an event but a process, arguably lifelong, and we are reminded of General De Gaulle's poignant observations of those who aspire to leadership "the price they have to pay for leadership is unceasing self-discipline, the constant taking of risks, and perpetual inner struggle . . . whence that vague sense of melancholy which hangs about the skirts of majesty"(Adair, 2002).

However, this is too gloomy an ending. We are constantly and pleasantly surprised by the ways in which leaders in a wide variety of context bring meaning and performance to organizations. They provide purpose and excitement. They balance authenticity with skill—and they can make a big difference. The thrill for teachers is that they can really help with this noble task. We shall never forget bumping into an old student in the headquarters of a major European multinational. We first met him when he was a beleaguered middle manager faced with the threat of redundancy and we had tried to teach him some leadership skills. Now he was the Chief Executive of a major product division. He told us that we had given him the courage to be a leader and had changed his life. We still feel a wonderful warm glow from this encounter.

Figure 10.1 Balancing Authenticity and Skill

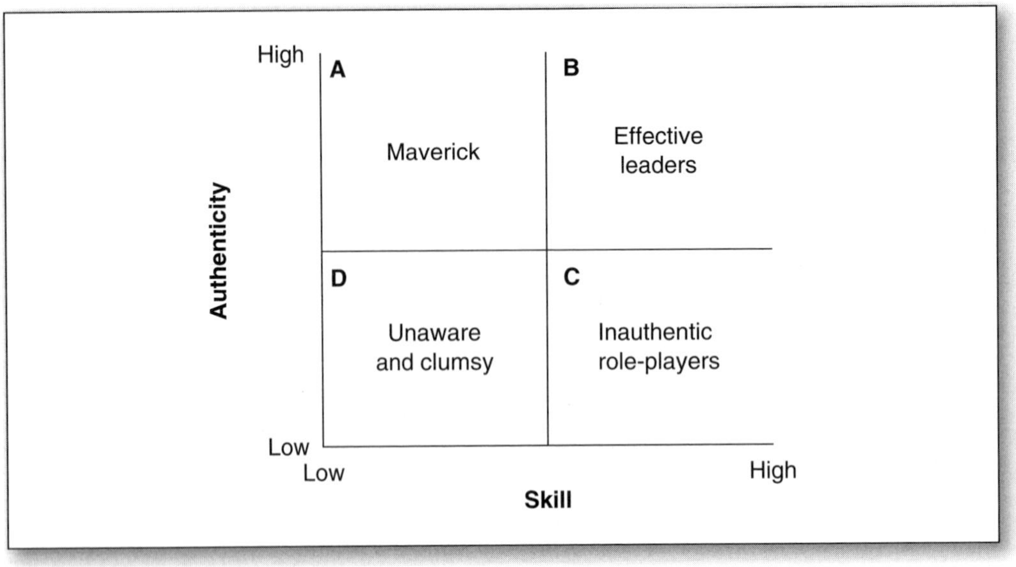

Source: Reprinted with permission © Creative Management Associates.

References

Adair, J. (2002). *Inspiring leadership*. London: Thorogood.

Bennis, W., & Thomas, R.J. (2002). *Geeks and geezers*. Boston, MA: Harvard Business School Press.

Berger, P.L., & Luckman, T. (1966). *The social construction of reality*. New York: Anchor Books.

Durkheim, E. (1984). *The division of labor in society*. W. D. Hall (Trans.). New York: Free Press, 1984. Originally published 1892

Goffee, R., & Jones, G. (2000). Why should anyone be led by you? *Harvard Business Review*, *78*(5), 62–70.

Goffee, R., & Jones, G. (2003). *The character of a corporation* (2nd ed.). London: Profile Books.

Goffee, R., & Jones, G. (2005). Managing authenticity: The paradox of great leadership. *Harvard Business Review*, *83*(12), 86–94.

Goffee, R., & Jones, G. (2006). *Why should anyone be led by you?* Boston, MA: Harvard Business School Press.

Goffee, R., & Jones, G. (2009). *Clever*. Boston, MA: Harvard Business Press.

Goffee, R., & Scase, R. (1989). *Reluctant mangers: Their work and lifestyles*. London: Unwin Hyman.

Homans, G.C. (1951). *The human group*. London: Routledge and Kegan Paul.

Sennett, R. (1998). *The corrosion of character*. New York: W. W. Norton.

Simmel, G. (1950). *The sociology of Georg Simmel*, K.H. Wolff (Trans. & Ed.). New York: Free Press.

11

HIGH PERFORMANCE LEADERSHIP

◆ Andrew Meikle
($\Sigma lkiem)^2$ ©

High performance leadership is not passive, and so the approach to teaching high performance leadership described in this chapter is active, not passive, by design. The Elkiem High Performance Masterclass applies twenty years of research into some of the world's greatest performance environments, such as the Juilliard School of Music, elite academic institutions and Military Special Forces, to a group of executive leaders who are accountable for the performance of their respective businesses. The Masterclass asks those who participate to take action, to maintain momentum, and to extract high standards of execution from those they lead. To participants, the Masterclass feels more like a series of executive board meetings with their leader, focused on current business execution and results, than a leadership development program.

The program is founded on three pre-suppositions: (1) People change when their circumstances change; (2) certain changes in circumstances will stimulate an improvement in performance from the humans impacted by those circumstances; (3) it is the leader's role to create these changes in circumstances. We therefore focus exclusively on teaching leaders how to create the circumstances that stimulate higher performance in their populations.

❖ ❖ ❖

I am a researcher. For the last twenty years I have, through my research, sought to gain a deeper understanding of the dynamics behind humans at their best. My business—*Elkiem*—is founded on my personal research into Human High Performance, and Elkiem's leadership development program—the *High Performance Masterclass*—is focused exclusively on educating leaders in how to extract the best possible performance from the people they lead. The High Performance Masterclass is unashamedly action-oriented, and this is predicated on the simple truth that if something is going to happen—if real improvements are going to be seen—then sooner or later the leader must take action. We educate leaders to take the right action and to take it sooner rather than later.

Also integral to Human High Performance is momentum. The longer a population produces 5 percent growth the harder it will be for those within that population to believe that 10 percent is possible. Stimulating and maintaining momentum is therefore an essential ingredient of High Performance leadership. A high standard of execution is also vital. Bright people are everywhere so strategic capability may not be the differentiator. More important is the leader's ability to extract high standards of execution from the population he or she leads. Elkiem's High Performance Masterclass has therefore been designed to stimulate those who participate to take action, to maintain momentum, and to extract high standards of execution from those he or she leads.

Research Background

The research—which comprises mainly one-on-one interviews with subjects—has two main areas of focus: high-performing individuals and high-performance environments.

HIGH-PERFORMING INDIVIDUALS

This was where my research began and my primary focus for the first twelve years, during which time I was fortunate enough to have the chance to pick the brains of high performers from all walks of life, from Nelson Mandela and Sir Edmund Hillary to Carl Lewis and Sir Richard Dawkins; from business leaders, mathematicians, and scientists to samurai masters, Inuit hunters, and military generals; from elite athletes and other sporting achievers to artists and dancers and singers. I have always kept a wide definition of human high performance in order to ensure our research covers a lot of ground and that we are able to look at performance from as many different angles as possible.

HIGH-PERFORMANCE ENVIRONMENTS

Over the last eight years my focus has shifted from high-performing individuals to high-performance environments, i.e., those places where the environmental dynamics are such that humans perform at their very best within them. This area of my research has taken me to the Juilliard School, The Royal College of Music in London, and to many elite military, sporting, and academic environments around the world.

Each year the research continues and my understanding deepens, and it is this that provides the backbone to Elkiem's leadership development work.

Approach

Elkiem's approach to leadership development is driven by two key factors: who we teach and what we teach.

WHO WE TEACH

Our clients are exclusively corporate leaders—the majority of those who participate in our *High Performance Masterclass (HPM)* lead either a whole business or a significant-sized division within a large business. One of the most obvious implications of this is that HPM participants are very busy people. One of our observations is that these corporate leaders often feel that they are too busy to be a part of any leadership development program and, of those who do make the time, few return to their business and fully apply what they have learned. Another implication is that corporate leaders are generally pretty confident in what they know and most feel that they have more than a modicum of expertise in the area of leadership development—this can make them horrible students.

WHAT WE TEACH

We believe that the dynamics of any leadership development program should replicate as closely as possible the content being taught. In order to explain our approach to leadership development it is therefore important to provide an overview of what we aim to teach participants in our HPM.

Elkiem's High Performance Masterclass is our most advanced leadership development program and while it is relatively new—only three years old—it captures all the key learnings from our sixteen years' experience in leadership development and our research into high-performance environments. The program is founded on three presuppositions:

1. People change when their circumstances change.
2. Certain changes in circumstances will stimulate an improvement in performance from the humans impacted by those circumstances.
3. It is the leader's role is to create these changes in circumstances. *We therefore focus exclusively on teaching leaders how to create the circumstances that stimulate higher performance in their population.*

The model we use as a basis for our education is shown in Figure 11.1: We call this the High-Performance Environmental Structure (HPES™). For ease of understanding an overview providing further definition for each of the components has also been included (see Figure 11.2). The High-Performance Environmental Structure is the culmination of all of our research into High-Performance Environments. It describes the circumstances required to stimulate a population to perform and it exists in all environments that require high performance whether it be military special forces, the Juilliard School of Music, the Olympic Games, elite academic institutions, or a corporate executive team. The principle behind the HPES™ model is that for an environment to stimulate the population within it to significantly improve its performance some or all of the following dynamics or components need to be present within that environment:

Achievement

- There must be clear, meaningful, objectives.
- The population must perceive these objectives to be challenging but within their control.

Significant emotional pleasure

- There must be meaningful, proportional rewards for the achievement of these objectives.
- The greatest share of the rewards must be distributed to the highest performers.
- The population must have significant pleasure associated with the rewards.

Approach

- The dominant philosophy should be performance-related.

- If adopted, the philosophy should enhance human performance and balance out *win at all costs* risks. The military would use the language "code," others "charter" or "values."
- The approach must be practical and inspirational.

Failure

- There must be clear definitions of what would represent sub-standard performance.
- The population needs to know what is *not good enough*.

Significant emotional discomfort

- The consequences for sub-standard performance must be proportional.
- The population need to perceive that sub-standard performance cannot be sustained.

Exposure

- There must be clear and fair methods of exposing and giving honest feedback on the team's current performance.
- These exposure systems must be seen to be credible by the population.

Figure 11.1 High-Performance Environmental Structure Model

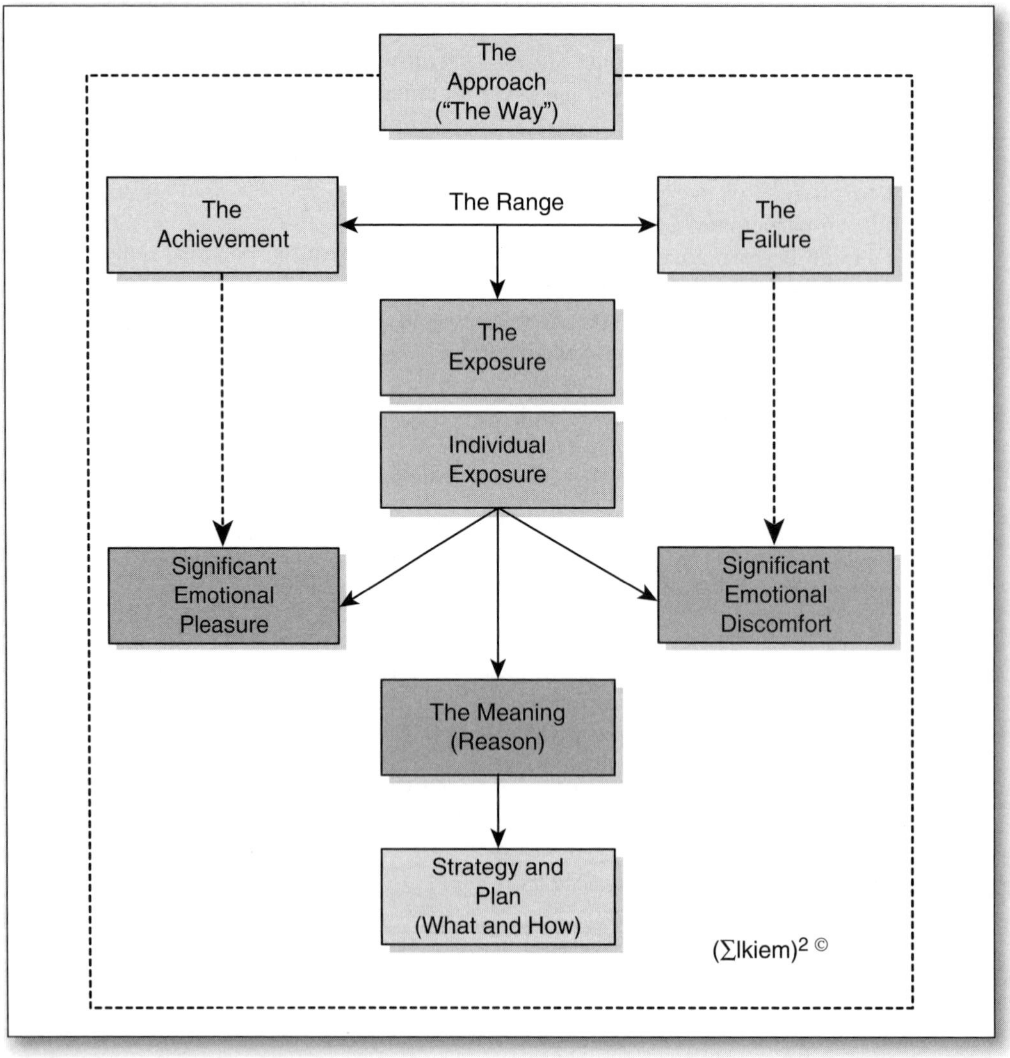

Source: Reprinted with permission © Elkiem.

Figure 11.2 HPES™ Definitions and Functions

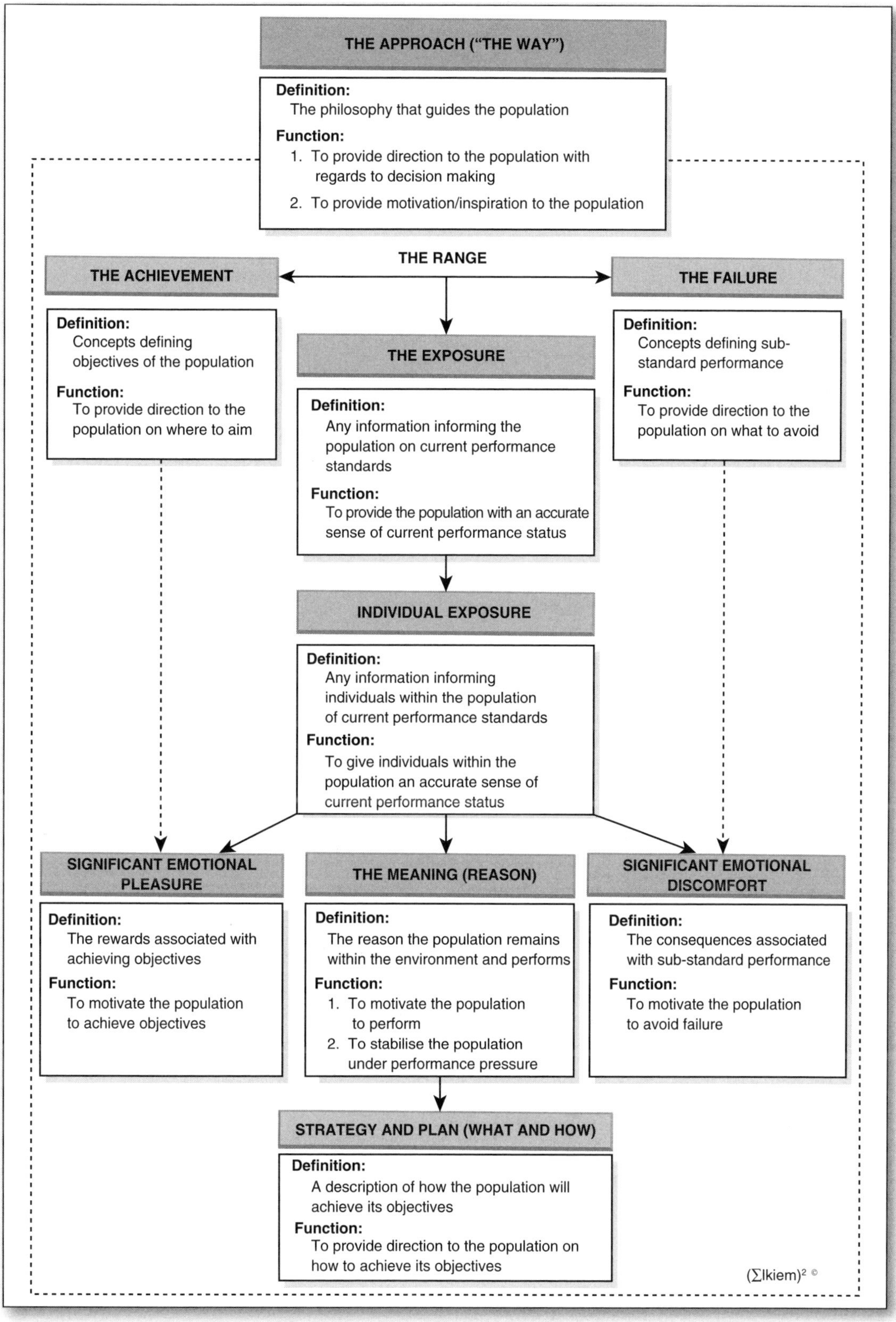

Source: Reprinted with permission © Elkiem.

Individual exposure

- There must be clear and fair methods of exposing and giving feedback on the truth of each individual's current performance.
- Individual exposure systems must be seen to be credible by the population.

Meaning/reason

- The environment must provide strong reasons for the population to stay and to perform.

Strategy/plan

- The strategy must be perceived as clear and effective. The population must feel that the quality of their strategy or plan is equal to challenge of their objectives.

The range

- The range is the distance between Achievement and Failure; within a team it is the gap between the highest and lowest performer.
- As the range widens, performance pressure releases.
- As the range narrows, performance pressure increases.

As mentioned previously our curriculum has a couple of implications for our High Performance Masterclass. First, it is action-oriented: if the circumstances within a leader's control are going to change the leader will have to do something, i.e., take some kind of action: our education is worthless as an intellectual exercise. Secondly, we believe that to be effective, any education or development program needs to, as much as possible, replicate that which it is aiming to teach or develop. Our High Performance Masterclass must therefore replicate the realities of a true High-Performance Environment. To this end our program involves the following (I will expand on how we create these dynamics later in a discussion of structure).

PERFORMANCE PRESSURE

Without apology we create an environment where there is a significant level of performance pressure. We also make adjustments to the level of pressure during the program so that the leaders can feel the change and understand what caused it.

Performance measurement that makes it virtually impossible to hide

Given that we teach how performance is measured and accountability created in environments such as the Juilliard School, a military special force, or an Olympic team, we use those same methods to measure performance and create accountability for the leaders in our program.

Winners and losers, rewards and consequences

We do not shy away from the fact that in a High-Performance Environment not everybody wins. We are also very concerned with demonstrating that the greater rewards should be distributed to the higher performers and that there should be consequences for low performance.

Clear, accurate, ongoing performance feedback

We have created several systems that aim to ensure leaders are left in no doubt regarding their own performance, both good and bad.

Accountability for financial performance

Financial performance matters in every corporate environment. Any time spent on the improvement of the performance of the population should show a financial return. We have created ways of ensuring this reality is ever-present.

BALANCING THE WIN AT ALL COSTS RISK

Any time performance pressure dynamics are created there is the risk of rule/ethics/approach breaches. Our program creates the risk and replicates systems to minimize it.

The ever-present nature of these two factors (action orientation and replication) also means that our program has to be structured in such a way as to provide a solid answer to the following questions: Given the competition for their attention, how do we get and hold their focus? Given the demands on their time, how do we stimulate them to act on what they learn? How do we replicate a High-Performance Environment in the training so that participants *feel* it rather than intellectualize it? How do we make the actions stimulated by the program show a financial return within the timeframe of the program itself?

In this chapter I will endeavor to explain how we have gone about answering these questions in the design of our High Performance Masterclass. This explanation is broadly divided into three areas: structure, content, and style. I will also touch on some of the results of the program as well as some of the key learnings since the program was launched.

Program Structure

THE BASICS

Our program is one year in duration with a total of only six and a half contact days. Contact days are broken into three two-day blocks with an additional half-day to complete the program. We try very hard to get what we want to get done quickly and in some cases the two-day sessions can be reduced by half a day. The leaders we work with need to be on the ground in their businesses, so it does not serve to extract them for extended periods. Our time together is taken very seriously.

There are ten participants in each program, normally from the same corporation. We have found ten to be the right number for several reasons: You cannot hide in a group of ten. Everyone sits around a boardroom table for the contact days and therefore, if someone is not contributing, the others will notice: If someone disengages the others will see it. As the style of teaching draws conversation from everyone at the table, adding more people would add more time to the duration of each session. Fewer than ten would reduce the feeling of exposure when making a contribution at the table.

THE DIAGNOSTIC

Prior to starting the program a diagnostic is completed for each participant's business or business unit. Elkiem's diagnostic, which comprises fifty-eight questions, has been specifically developed to measure the quality of the current High-Performance Environmental Structure within a business or business unit by assigning a numerical score (out of one hundred) to each of the components within it (see Figure 11.3). It also provides more detailed information on the factors contributing to these component scores, for example, whether or not the current measures of performance are stimulating individual accountability or whether the performance rewards are leading to increased performance. Once this diagnostic is completed a comprehensive report is generated, which gives us a clear picture of the state of the current HPES™ for each business or business unit.

Figure 11.3 HPES™ Diagnostic Results—Model A

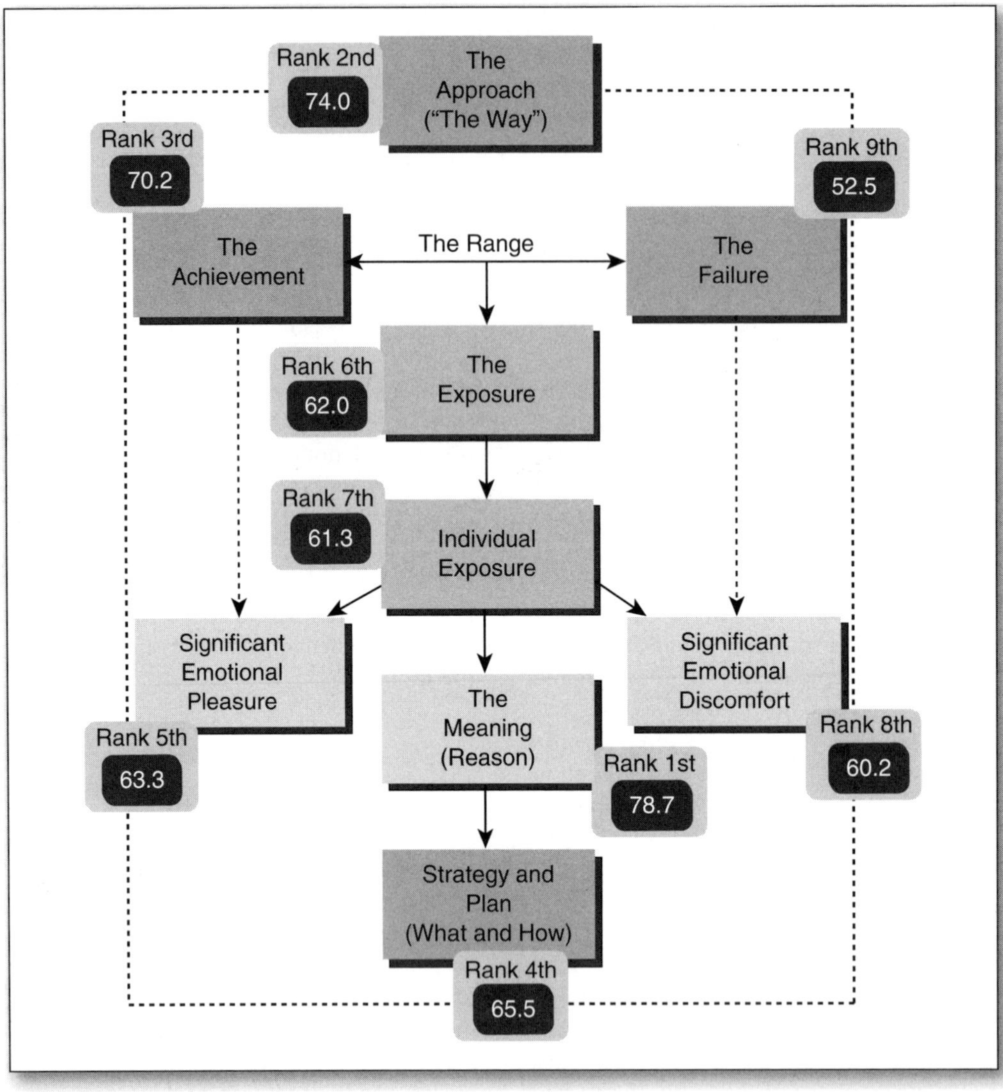

Source: Reprinted with permission © Elkiem.

A high score indicates that a component is having a strong positive effect on the performance of the population. For example, a high score for the Achievement component indicates that the objectives/goals are meeting certain criteria that we have identified in our HPES™ research. Specifically, if the Achievement component score is high then the population perceives their objectives to be clear, meaningful, challenging, within their control, and measurable. If any of these criteria is compromised the component score will reduce according to a mathematical weighting system. There is a set of effectiveness criteria for each of the nine components in the HPES™; our diagnostic measures each of these criteria and identifies the strengths and weaknesses in the structure.

The diagnostic also measures the level of performance pressure *felt* by the population (Figure 11.4) and this level of pressure is then compared with other important performance dynamics such as *meaning* and

Figure 11.4 HPES™ Diagnostic Results—Model B

PERFORMANCE PRESSURE COMPARISONS

PRESSURE MEANING COMPARISON

This compares the performance pressure within the environment with the Meaning (Reason) component of the HPES™. It is advisable to keep the Meaning (Reason) component stronger than the Pressure Indicator.

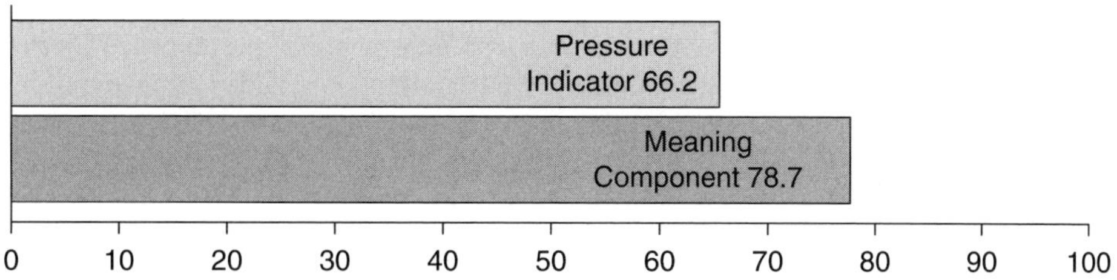

PRESSURE CLARITY COMPARISON

This compares the level of performance pressure in the environment with the level of clarity regarding the HPES™ components. It is the aim of a high performance environment to have both reasonable pressure and high clarity (refer to Environmental Clarity Indicator). If an individual is unclear on what they are to do and how they are to do it, adding pressure can reduce performance. It is therefore advisable to keep the Clarity Indicator stronger than the Pressure Indicator.

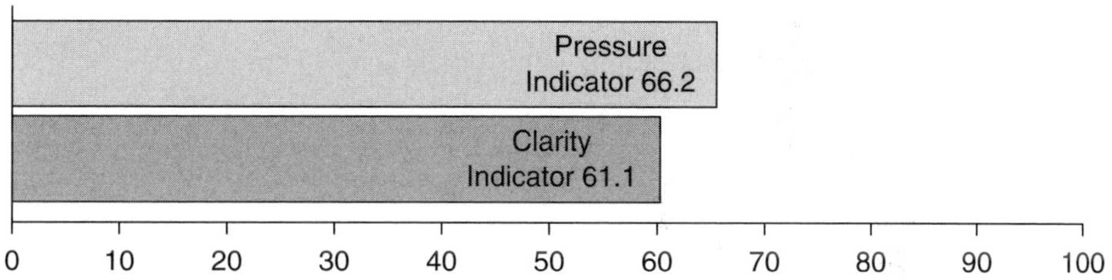

PRESSURE MEASUREMENT COMPARISON

This compares the perceived level of pressure in the environment with the perceived quality of measurement within the environment. This comparison can assist in understanding some negative effects that may happen within some performance environments. For example, if pressure is high and the measurement systems are low, negative effects such as frustration/confusion, excuses for non-performance, and blame may eventuate. It is advisable to keep the quality of measurement higher than the level of pressure.

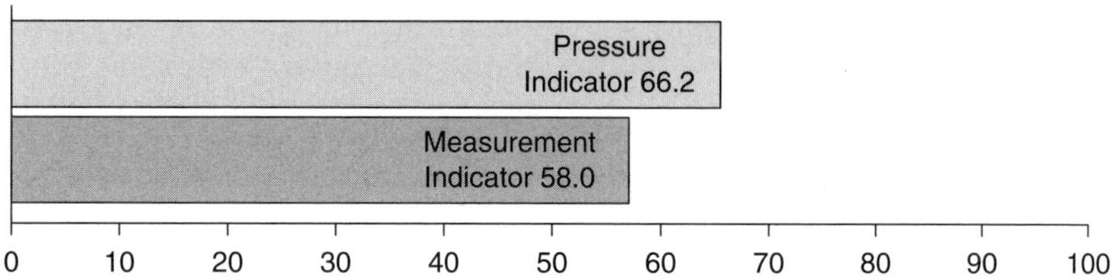

Source: Reprinted with permission © Elkiem.

clarity. The *Pressure Meaning Comparison* compares the level of pressure with the strength of the *reason*, i.e., the reason they have for staying in the environment. This comparison provides insight on whether increasing the level of performance pressure might lead to people exiting the environment. The *Pressure Clarity Comparison* measures the level of pressure against the levels of clarity—clarity being comprised of elements such as clear goals, clear strategy, clear measurement systems, etc. If pressure exceeds clarity then people tend to become disorganized. If pressure exceeds trust in performance measures it generally means that any additional pressure will escape the structure—we refer to this as *pressure leakage*.

Our diagnostic is designed to identify the two main opportunities for performance improvement. We call these two opportunities *The Next Two Moves*.

Using the diagnostic as part of our leadership development approach serves several purposes: First, it allows us to be efficient in the design of the educational content: we design the contact days around the needs identified in the combined diagnostics and leave all other content out of the program. Secondly, it gives the leader a clear picture of the current situation within their business or unit and this will obviously assist in their decision making throughout the program. Most importantly it provides a measurement of their performance during the program. Two months after the completion of the final two-day contact session but before the final half-day, we run the diagnostic on their business again. If they have made progress it will be exposed and if they have not made progress it will be exposed. This dynamic helps focus their attention.

THE PEER EXPOSURE SYSTEM

The two-day blocks in the program run to a specific formula. Each leader is briefed to prepare a short presentation to be given at the start of the session on actions taken since the last session. (Obviously this does not happen in the first of the three sessions. The first session gets straight into content.) The others are briefed to probe and question the leader to understand precisely what has been done, why, and the results. This takes approximately three hours. We then spend the next day and a bit on new content. At lunch on day two we break and each of the participants is given two hours to prepare a short presentation outlining what actions they will now instigate based on the new content. These presentations fill the rest of the afternoon. Again those listening are briefed to probe and question as to why each participant has chosen a particular course of action and the expected results. We call this approach the *Peer Exposure System*. There are a couple of benefits to such a system.

Cross-pollination of thinking and learnings

Each participant starts to form a view as to which actions are likely to be the most or least effective. At the end of the program most participants will say that they learned most from the other students. The participants feel a pressure to put some rigor around their thinking. People of this caliber are very good at assessing who is fabricating what they have done and will probe accordingly: Everyone knows this and it is therefore very unlikely that a participant would risk turning up for one of the two-day sessions without having done what they committed to do at the last session.

The Peer Exposure system is also formalized via voting forms distributed to participants at the end of each two-day session (i.e., at the end of the program each participant will have voted three times). The voting form asks participants to vote on who they think will make the most progress with their diagnostic when measured later in the year and who will make the least progress. Votes are collected and used as the backbone for performance feedback in the days following each session.

When participants complete their voting form they are also required to vote on who they believe have been the top three students for the two-day session. We take time to explain our definition of a *good student* at the start of the program. We pinpoint two characteristics: curiosity and contribution. Put simply, a good student for Elkiem is one who shows the capacity to learn and makes a worthwhile contribution to the discussion. The votes on best student become important later in the program.

Most importantly the Peer Exposure System is designed to serve two key purposes. First, it focuses participants' minds in each of the sessions. To be effective in our leadership program participants need to quickly translate the education into logical action plans that will have relevance in their business. Secondly, the Peer Exposure System demonstrates to participants the mechanics and potential benefits of peer exposure systems so that participants are then equipped to implement similar systems within their own team or business. We find that at the end of the program many are using these peer-based systems to stimulate increased individual accountability in their teams.

Note that a peer exposure system is one where individual accountability is stimulated by peer observation and expectation. Formal and informal systems of this type are prevalent in sporting teams and elite military units, among others.

WINNERS, LOSERS, AND CONSEQUENCES

There are winners and losers in our program and we rank individuals based on their results—although, other than the winner (and sometimes the loser—see later) we do not publicize the final results of the ranking. The winner receives a Global Research Tour for the following year. Elkiem tailor-makes a ten-day tour for the winner of each High-Performance Masterclass during which he or she has the chance to interview individual high performers and leaders of High-Performance Environments. The reward includes two airfares so the winner can take his or her partner if desired.

The winner is determined according to two criteria: First, he or she must make the most progress on the diagnostic during the year. Our diagnostic lends itself well to the task of establishing who has made the most progress as all results are represented in 0 to 100 scores. Secondly, he or she must be ranked in the top five as voted by the other participants. We have had a case where the person who made most progress on the diagnostic did not make the top five in the student ranking. We add the student ranking criteria to show them how to create what we call *balancing systems*. A balancing system moderates the *win-at-all-costs* possibility that occurs when performance pressure is high. If a person in our program decides to put his or her head down and compete to win by not sharing ideas and actions he or she will not receive the student vote and therefore lose the prize.

We articulate at the start of the program that the loser will be the person who makes the least progress on the diagnostic during the program period. We also make it clear that if the person who makes the least progress on the diagnostic is also the person that has been voted by his or her peers as the one most likely to make the least progress then he or she will be publicly named. In support of this consequence we do make it clear that if a participant has been receiving negative feedback during the year that he or she is off track and still doesn't move to fix it, then he or she deserves the consequences. This of course replicates a real High-Performance Environment.

We include the winner/loser element in our leadership development program for several reasons: For one thing, it focuses participants' minds and stimulates action. It means there is nowhere to hide—the results of their actions will be exposed. It also allows participants to *feel* what we call the *Worth-It Principle.* This principle states that performance pressure will be tolerated by the population so long as it passes the *worth it* test. This is the reason why we introduce the Global Research Tour as a reward late in the program. By the time participants are made aware of the potential reward the pressure of the other systems is starting to show. We want them to *feel* the change when they perceive a reward worth pursuing.

We want to replicate the findings of our research into High Performance in our program.

THE LEADER

We insist on the CEO or Chair of the corporation being present for the duration of all six-and-a-half contact days. This makes a total of twelve people in all—the ten participants, their CEO or Chair, and me. We find that having their leader present serves to increase their focus. It also means important decisions can be made on the spot and many excuses for inaction are removed before they are made. The CEO or Chair needs to be well briefed on five simple principles:

- To play the role of coach to the ten
- To ensure the action plans developed and presented by the participants are relevant to the current needs of the whole corporation
- To be willing to give accurate feedback
- Where possible, to remove obstacles that may inhibit the momentum of the leaders in the program
- To adopt a minimalist approach, i.e., do not dominate proceedings

Obviously the style of each CEO or Chair can have a huge effect on the program. We only offer this program to organizations where we believe the style of the CEO or Chair is a good match.

THE FINAL PRESENTATION—HALF-DAY SESSION

The Board or Executive Team of the corporation is present for the final half-day of the program. This generally means that there will be approximately twenty people in the final session: the ten program participants, the Board, the CEO, and me. Each participant has been asked to prepare a ten-minute presentation and to expect five minutes of questions from the board. The participants are briefed to focus their presentations on three areas:

What action have you taken and why? Participants are instructed to include only actions or plans stimulated by the program.

What are the measurable results of what you have done? The board members are briefed to analyze the financial benefits directly attributable to the program and much of the questioning is focused in this area. We communicate the board's intent on day one of the program.

How has the High Performance Masterclass made you a better leader?

It is our observation that leaving these presentations until the final day keeps participants focused for the entire program. From the beginning it is made clear to all participants that they must keep their actions and plans closely aligned to tangible business results. We like this dynamic as the leadership program then becomes highly relevant throughout the year as opposed to some sort of distraction. In addition, the CEO and others who are largely responsible for giving the okay to leadership development programs of this type are more comfortable doing so when the program is so closely aligned to the very real short-term need for action and execution, and so focused on stimulating measurable business results.

STYLE

My teaching style has evolved as the result of a combination of factors. First, our participants are generally in their forties, fifties, or sixties and so have as much to learn from each other as they do from me. The leaders in our programs also have a low tolerance for lectures. One can feel the engagement in the room decrease when any monologue extends beyond a few minutes. The same happens when the conversation focuses on theory without a direct line back to relevant business challenges. Interestingly, most in the room are *meeting fit*: in other words, they are able to remain focused for long meetings, but are not *classroom fit*. This is perhaps because they are so used to *directing proceedings* in meetings and can therefore tend to fatigue quickly when the control dynamic is not resting with them. When this factor is added to their general fatigue—most of our participants work extremely hard over long hours and are generally tired—it takes very little for the energy in the room to plummet.

Contact days are more like board meetings than classroom lessons. This is represented not only in the environment—it is a boardroom, after all—but also in my teaching methodology. Most of the time I am following a simple formula: principle—questions—action.

THE PRINCIPLE PHASE

First, I pitch up a principle, for example: *Great measures of performance come from an intelligent definition of performance.* Then we clarify exactly what is meant by this principle, using examples from research case studies, for example: *In military special forces, if they define performance as "Elite soldiers who make good decisions under pressure," what are their primary performance measurement systems?*

The process of clarification takes the form of a conversation among the group. A conversation starts with a *cold call* from me to someone at the table and runs its course. I will then pitch up another principle, for example, *Too many measures can reduce individual accountability. How?* Another conversation is then started and runs its course. The pace is fast and rarely do we stay in one place for a long period. At the end of the principle phase I have covered all the important content of how to measure human performance.

THE QUESTION PHASE

During this phase I ask questions of the group with the objective of uncovering how each of the Performance Principles applies to their current business environment(s), for example, *If we were to research your environment, where could we find hiding places—places where performance is not measured?* Each leader will then be given a few minutes to gather his or her thoughts before broadcasting an answer back to the group, effectively starting another conversation. Then I ask another question and start another conversation and so on. This phase will end with a final question, which might be something like, *So what is the biggest opportunity you have to stimulate performance improvement through improved performance measurement?* Again, all get airtime and must answer the question.

THE ACTION PHASE

This phase is designed to identify the specific actions that could be taken to create improvements in the topic being discussed. Importantly, leaders are not asked to make decisions at this stage in the process; final decisions regarding what they decide to action are not made until late on day two when all topics have been discussed. (Up to four topics will be discussed during a two-day session.)

What we call the *tight/loose approach* is introduced during the early stages of our program. A tight/loose approach means that the education will be very *tight* around the topic of high performance but *loose* on prescribing the action that each participant should take in his or her business. It is the responsibility of each participant to develop his or her own idea of *what to do* with the education.

As I mentioned earlier in the chapter, each participant has to present his or her action plan to the group in the final hours of day two. The others, the CEO and I, are briefed to give accurate feedback on the quality of the action plan. Whether the plan is good or poor the participants will receive accurate feedback.

My teaching style follows a set of clear guidelines.

- Make it risky for them to disengage.
- Make it relevant to their business.
- Let them learn from each other.
- Stimulate thinking but translate it quickly to action.

THE RESULTS

There are both objective and subjective measures of the progress made by the leaders in our HPM program. The objective measures are two-fold: progress made against original HPES™ diagnostic and financial results.

PROGRESS MADE AGAINST ORIGINAL HPES™ DIAGNOSTIC

Figures 11.5–11.7 are three *before and after* diagnostics from leaders in the program. Note that the timeframe between before and after is ten months.

For the purposes of this chapter it is quite difficult to demonstrate what these diagnostic results mean in a practical sense. In the simplest terms, if the number on the Individual Exposure component increases it means that the population measured by the diagnostic perceive that the systems are creating stronger levels of individual accountability. If the number on the Significant Emotional Discomfort component increases it is perceived by the population that there are greater consequences for underperformance.

We measure improvement on the diagnostic using a percentage of available upside equation. For example, if the diagnostic started at a score of 60 on every component and increased to 80 over the period, we would say they have achieved 50 percent of the potential upside. We use this methodology because the higher the scores, the harder it is to gain ground. Most participants in our program achieve a score of between 10 percent and 50 percent of the potential upside in their HPES™ diagnostic.

FINANCIAL RESULTS

The final presentations to the board are focused on this measure. Roughly 70 percent of HPM program participants are able to demonstrate solid financial results as a result of their efforts; about 20 percent claim the timeframe is too short but successfully convince the board that the result will come. One in ten is unable to demonstrate progress.

In terms of more subjective measures, we have observed three major developments in the leaders who go through our High Performance Masterclass. First, they learn what will or won't lead to performance improvement in their population. The participants learn the effect that the prevailing circumstances are having on the performance of their people and the

Figure 11.5 The Results—1. (Before/after)

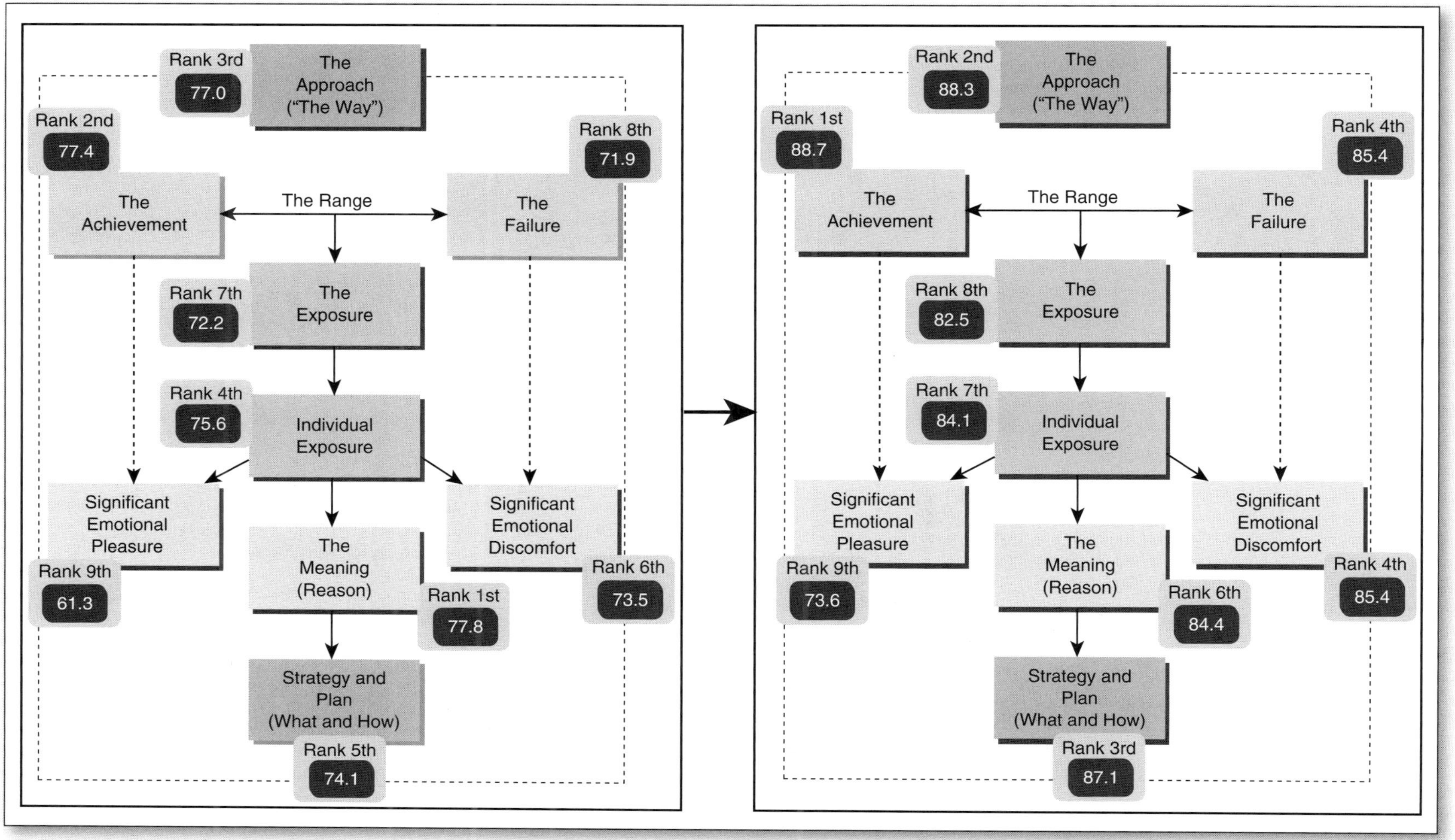

Source: Reprinted with permission © Elkiem.

Figure 11.6 The Results—2. (Before/after)

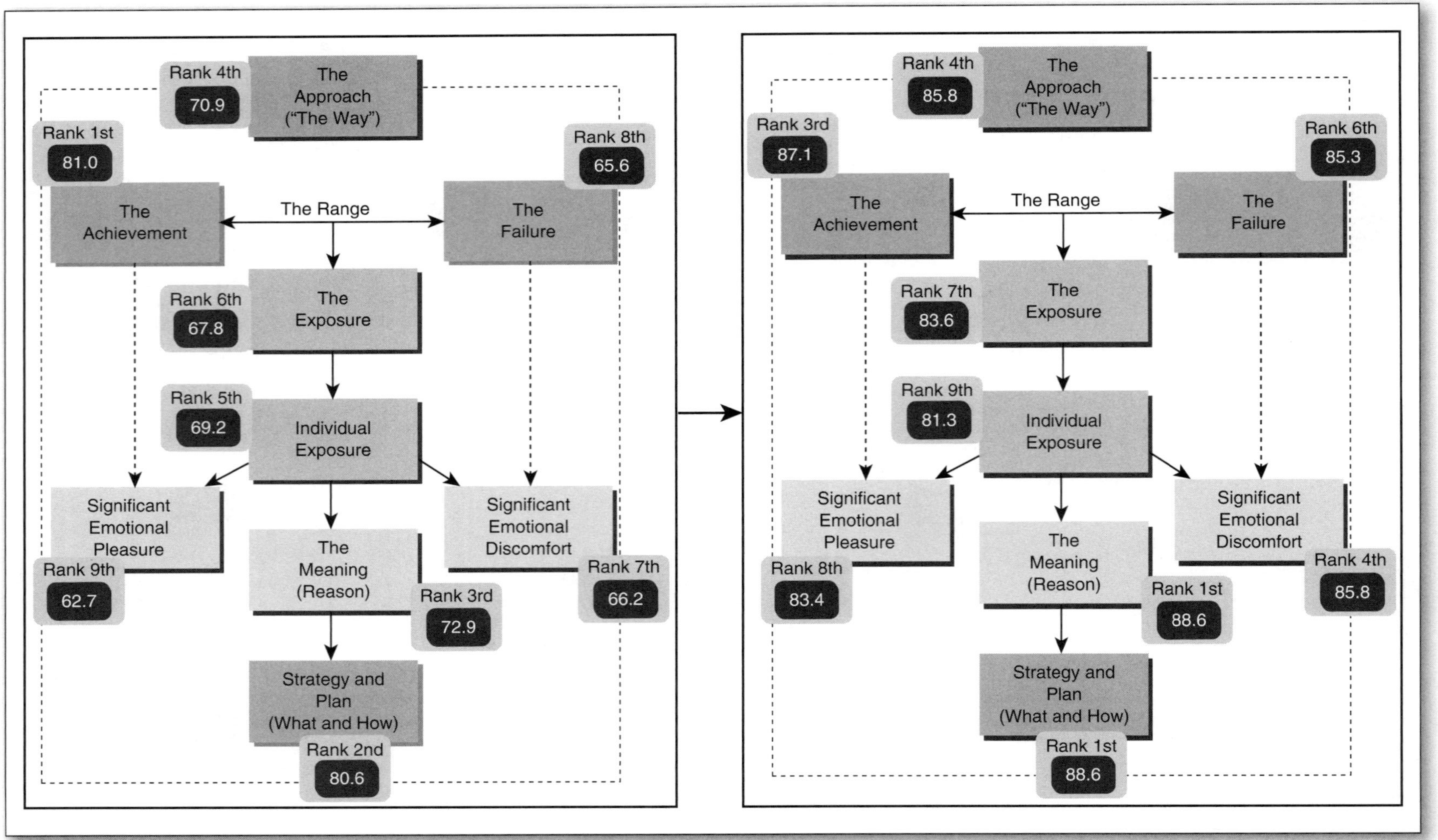

Source: Reprinted with permission © Elkiem.

Figure 11.7 The Results—3. (Before/after)

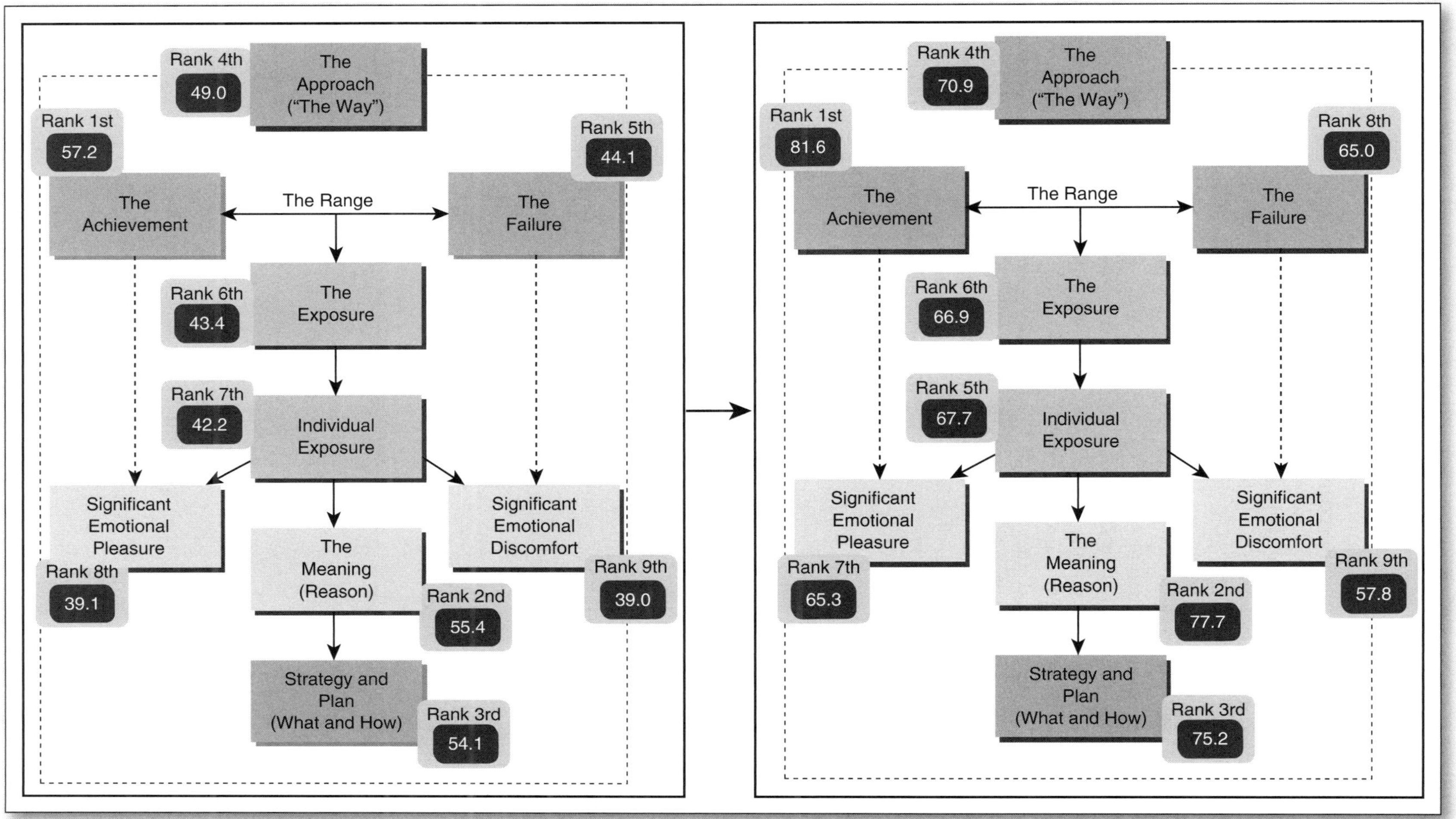

Source: Reprinted with permission © Elkiem.

effect of carrying low performers, of poor quality performance measurement systems, or an impotent performance philosophy. Most importantly, they learn what levers within environmental circumstances they need to pull to create the desired performance effect.

Secondly, they learn how to modify performance pressure by making modifications to the dominant systems in the environment. Primarily they learn this by *feeling* it. The HPM program itself is a high-pressure environment. I alter or add systems throughout the program to ensure participants understand how the changes in systems effect the pressure they are experiencing.

Finally, the vast majority of those who complete the program will say the program has taught them to be more definitive about what action to take and stimulated them to reduce the timeframe between thinking and taking action.

Our leadership development approach is centered on teaching how to stimulate high performance. We aim to do the same with our participants—to stimulate High Performance. Although the objective measures of our program are an important measure of its impact, I personally assess the quality of the HPM program on whether it has jolted the leader to higher levels of action. It would horrify me to learn that a person could go through our program hypothesizing. High-performance leadership is not passive. The educational content will serve them in the years to come but if they have not learned to act, to execute "real time," then the program has failed in its primary objective. It is my hope that this chapter has been successful in communicating this intent.

12

LEADERSHIP EFFECTIVENESS AND DEVELOPMENT

Building Self-Awareness and Insight Skills[1]

◆ Jeffrey Anderson and Stacey R. Kole
University of Chicago Booth School of Business

For more than twenty years, the full-time MBA program at the University of Chicago Booth School of Business has had only one mandatory class. Leadership Effectiveness and Development (LEAD) focuses on building self-awareness and teaches students how to extract the "right" lessons from experience. Utilizing second-year MBA "teachers" in a unique facilitator role, every first-year MBA student is able to enhance his or her existing talents through a combination of classroom instruction, experiential learning, and observation-rich, one-on-one coaching. A successful LEAD experience is encapsulated by the student who has developed an accurate view of strengths and development needs and who has learned how to gain actionable insight from experience in an unbiased and replicable way. In this chapter, the authors explore the research foundation for

[1]We thank Selwyn Becker, Chris Collins, Harry Davis, Linda Ginzel, and Alice Obermiller for their feedback; their insights sharpened our thinking and this piece.

the course, its specific content that bridges the knowing and doing aspects of leadership education, and offers representative experiences of participants in the course. Some challenges presented by the course are discussed.

❖❖❖

Introduction

At the University of Chicago Booth School of Business, our focus in the required leadership curriculum is to enhance self-awareness and to teach students how to learn the "right" lessons from experience. This approach is based on experience in laboratory classes that reveals the importance of, and difficulty with, translating knowledge into the appropriate leadership actions as well as a substantial body of literature in psychology on self-assessment and its systematic biases. Students' self-interest (manifest in the desire for personal and professional success) ensures a high level of engagement in skill development that helps establish a routine for learning from experience.

Now in its third decade as the only mandatory course in the MBA curriculum, the Leadership Effectiveness and Development (LEAD) course deploys second-year MBA students to "teach" in a unique facilitator role combining course design and delivery through instruction, experiential learning, and one-on-one coaching. Positioned at the start of the MBA experience, first-year MBA students are guided through a series of modules and events that culminate in customized development plans that highlight opportunities for skill development during the two-year MBA experience and beyond. A successful LEAD experience is encapsulated by the student who has developed an accurate view of his or her strengths and development needs and who has learned how to gain actionable insight from experience in an unbiased and replicable way.

Foundations of LEAD

RESEARCH ON SELF-AWARENESS

Decades of psychological research documents that self-assessments can be flawed, and that misperceptions of self adversely affect decision making and individual effectiveness. Dunning, Heath, and Taylor (2004) summarize the evidence of the literature in the fields of health, education, and the workplace and find that "[p]eople's self-views hold only a tenuous to modest relationship to their actual behavior and performance." In fact, the potential impact of these misperceptions is so significant that organizations have created extensive processes to correct for the expected distortions. Dunning and colleagues highlight the fact that at senior levels of organizations, where key decisions on strategic direction are being made by individuals for whom candid, independent feedback is rare, the risk of missteps due to distorted perceptions of one's abilities is particularly severe. These findings underscore the importance of developing an accurate self view early in one's career and maintaining it over time by engraining learning habits that are not dependent on the formal processes of an organization.

UNDERPINNING OF EXPERIENTIAL LEARNING AT CHICAGO

Recognizing that business schools can play a role in shaping self-awareness, faculty members Harry Davis and Robin

Hogarth posed two questions of business educators in their 1992 working paper entitled "Rethinking Management Education: A View From Chicago." First, Davis and Hogarth asked, "how can we enable students to achieve exceptionally high levels of performance on a consistent basis?" and second, "how can we add value to students in a way that endures throughout their careers?" To answer these questions, Davis and Hogarth describe a means of systematically developing students' ability to learn and grow from experience in a way that allows for insights that enable action.

Figure 12.1 reproduces a schematic that Davis and Hogarth used to illustrate their "Chicago approach" to leadership development. The hashed box encompasses an individual's conceptual expertise and domain knowledge on which decisions are made. Collectively, these areas of expertise connote the content knowledge and organizational understanding embodied in a decision-maker. These resources are critical to sound decision-making but without the ability to articulate the connection between actions and outcomes through goal-setting, persuasion, and collaborative skills, an individual's ability to successfully drive results to achieve a stated outcome are lessened. In this way, though necessary, conceptual and domain knowledge alone are not sufficient for effective leadership.

In graduate business education, students bring domain knowledge from their work experience and from the research on industries and companies. Conceptual knowledge is developed through the MBA curriculum: At Chicago, a discipline-based approach to management education teaches a deep understanding of economics, psychology, sociology, statistics, and accounting that

Figure 12.1 Translating Knowledge and Action to Desired Outcomes

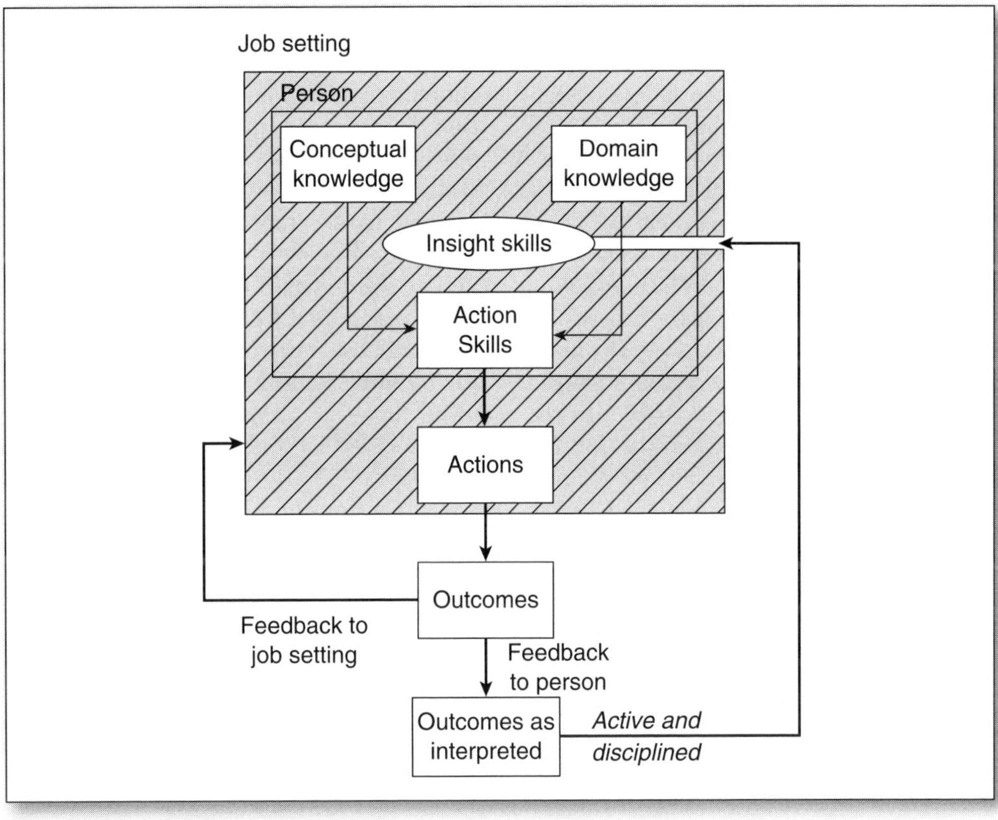

enables students to see the fundamental elements of, and develop solutions for, complex business problems. Davis and Hogarth stressed the importance of creating opportunities in MBA education to learn about the process of translating these two components of knowledge into action. These translational skills involve both the ability to perform in different settings (action skills) and the awareness to select the appropriate behaviors and strategies in a given setting (insight skills). From a curricular perspective, this requires that students be open to feedback and willing to participate in an engaged way, and it requires of the learning environment frequent, specific, and actionable feedback as well as a rehearsal and performance space where students can do, receive constructive feedback, and do again.

Just as seeing the right solution is not the same as implementing that solution, the acquisition of insight is far from automatic. It depends on our ability to learn generalizable lessons from experience. In an employer-employee relationship, for a host of reasons (see Dunning et al., 2004, p. 91) much of the feedback offered can convey the wrong lessons or reinforce inaccurate beliefs of personal effectiveness. For this reason, Davis and Hogarth suggested that business schools go beyond their traditional role in teaching conceptual knowledge to help students develop this critical, career-long skill.

Their notion of business schools as a laboratory "in which students experiment and practice action and insight skills without downside risks to their careers" spurred curricular innovation across areas.[2] At the core of the laboratory experience was the requirement that "fellow students, faculty, and staff provide frequent feedback, untainted by the personal or political factors within an organization."

Leadership Effectiveness and Development (LEAD) Program

The LEAD Program was created in 1989 as an outgrowth of Davis's and Hogarth's thinking. Today, the LEAD Program bridges the *knowing* and *doing* dimensions of the leadership framework outlined in the introduction to this volume by engaging students in a variety of hands-on exercises designed to provide them with an accurate view of their strengths and developmental needs, and guiding them to accurately process feedback from various sources. The program raises a figurative mirror for students (using tools including 360 appraisals, videotaped interactions, and standardized assessment instruments) to enable them to see and hear what others observe; this mirror reveals clues regarding their impact on, and effectiveness with, those with whom they interact. LEAD also challenges students to reflect on what they are learning and to set a personalized plan for continued professional development. While at Booth, these plans may guide the choices students make about course selection, co-curricular involvement, and other optional activities. Ultimately, however, the responsibility to become more insightful and to develop in critical areas rests with each student.

The next section details the current components of LEAD. It is important to note that the structure and governance of LEAD intentionally embeds experimentation, tinkering, and fresh looks at the course's content and delivery. Elements of today's LEAD are rooted in earlier ideas and executions and it is this institutionalized fluidity that guarantees that the course will change form while holding

[2]This model spurred the creation of a variety of laboratory courses at Chicago Booth. In the mid-1990s, Selwyn Becker (1994), Professor of Psychology and Quality at Chicago Booth, wrote about his efforts to create one such course on Total Quality. His thinking was influenced by the transition he had made in a course on Small Group Dynamics—from a traditional lecture format to one that was almost entirely experiential. In designing the new course, Selwyn said "if we talked about and discussed culture change we would teach students how to talk about culture and culture change, but not how to do anything about it."

fast to the underpinning Davis and Hogarth set for LEAD.

PROGRAM COMPONENTS

The LEAD program is the only required class in the Chicago Booth curriculum and the only cohort-based course in the full-time MBA program.[3] Unlike the typical course at Chicago Booth that fits within the University's quarter system of eleven-week sessions, LEAD begins with summer assignments and runs through the first half of students' first quarter on campus.

Summer pre-work

In preparation for the course, students complete a series of assignments (detailed below) that carry forward prior experiences and insights from professional settings into LEAD. These assignments are designed to initiate a process of reflection wherein students explore their leadership style, motivations, and actions. Assignments are completed roughly three weeks prior to the start of Orientation (a two-week-long period held before the academic year begins) thus enabling the LEAD coaches and student instructors to familiarize themselves with the students and provide a more customized learning experience.

The following three areas are covered in summer pre-work for LEAD:

> A 360-degree evaluation that collects confidential feedback from an average of ten to fifteen people who know the student well, and who the student feels will provide candid input. The evaluators offer feedback on critical leadership competencies: relationship building, communication, personal integrity, teamwork, problem solving, interpersonal style, and strategic thinking. Students are encouraged to select raters who have had the opportunity to observe the student over time, preferably in multiple roles or on different types of projects. In addition, the assignment directs students to build a diverse pool of evaluators consisting of subordinates, superiors, peers, and external constituents (such as customers or suppliers).
>
> A survey designed to collect the students' thoughts about leadership—e.g., the attributes that they admire in a leader. The results are aggregated for the entire class and, during the introductory session of LEAD, common themes in student responses are discussed as well as how the results vary based on industry experience, gender, and cultural background. The central tendencies of the MBA student responses are also compared to research results for non-MBA populations. This discussion begins a process in which students are asked to "step outside" themselves (and their beliefs and biases) to see leadership through the eyes of those they wish to lead.
>
> Personality characteristics are measured using standardized instruments including the Myers-Briggs Type Indicator and the Thomas Kilmann Conflict Style Indicator. Information from these metrics is used as a benchmark for beginning conversations with students about their personal style and how they interact with others.

Immersion retreat

The class begins with a three day, two night retreat called the Leadership Outdoor Experience, or LOE, at a resort about one hundred miles from Chicago. From the perspective of students, this outing is seen as part of Orientation. The event intentionally removes students from the familiar

[3]For an overview of the structure and philosophy of the curriculum and MBA experience at Chicago Booth, see Datar and Garvin (2008).

and places them all in a new setting with minimal outside distraction. The change of scenery signals a new beginning in a setting surrounded by colleagues and second-year MBA students who act as leaders of the multi-day event. Over time, we have found that the setting has a meaningful impact on the ability of students to get to know their new colleagues and begin their guided self-discovery process in a fun and interactive manner.

While at LOE, the students participate in relationship-building activities, improvisation exercises designed to get students comfortable with a highly-participatory learning environment, ropes courses intended to offer personal challenge and an opportunity for group cohesion, and social events that encourage learning about one another. To facilitate the administration of the program and to build trust and familiarity that is critical for giving and receiving feedback, the student body is divided into ten cohorts of fifty-five to sixty students and, within each cohort, into squads of seven to eight students. Students first meet their cohortmates at LOE and for the majority of their "work" time in LEAD, students are either with their squad or cohort exclusively.

LEAD coursework

In the six weeks following LOE, students participate in seven three-hour class sessions. LEAD coursework is complete by the end of the fourth week of Autumn Quarter.

Foundations of Leadership. This session is an introductory discussion about leadership, first impressions, and career derailment risks. During the module, students receive a synthesis of their 360 evaluations as well as an initial impression description completed by their squad mates at the conclusion of the Immersion Retreat. To draw out the most important lessons from these sources of feedback, students work within their squads and discuss the following types of questions:

What was the biggest surprise in your feedback?

Where is your self-evaluation most out of sync with the feedback from your raters?

How does the feedback from people who have worked with you for an extended period of time differ from those who just met you?

Are you projecting the type of initial image you desire?

What derailment risks does the feedback identify for you (i.e., what skills/behaviors are likely to hold you back or cause your career to plateau)?

What were your five highest and five lowest average scores?

What does this profile say about you?

Personality and Work Style. Using the Myers Briggs Type Indicator, this module helps students understand how they gather information, make decisions, and interact with others. The focus is on how to use the information contained in this indicator in a business setting to enhance communications and deliver improved outcomes. For example, each squad is asked to construct and deliver a short sales presentation to persons with differing personalities. The module also explores how personality preferences affect the type of behaviors students value in others and underscores the importance of developing a variety of interpersonal approaches.

Group Process. During this activity, teams of students are given a challenging task and are videotaped as they work on the assignment. The group then reviews the recording and students are asked to tally the number of times they speak and the nature of their contributions (initiating, challenging, supporting, and facilitating). This data allow each student to "see," in an objective manner, the role that they play in group settings. By aggregating the data for the entire group, the concept of the group's dynamics—for example, did a few people dominate the discussion? how did the group make decisions? who emerged as the leader and why?—unfolds. At the conclusion of the module, each student has a one-on-one session with a facilitator who offers an assessment of the student's effectiveness in the group setting and strategies for enhancing individual effectiveness where appropriate.

Interpersonal Communications. This session allows students to assess their communications skills and "executive presence" —posture, eye contact, vocal quality and variety, gestures, listening, etc. Through a variety of exercises, students have a chance to practice each element and receive feedback from the facilitators and their classmates. During this module, students are also asked to deliver feedback to one of their squad mates (based on their observations in the preceding classroom sessions). The use of "real" input allows students to hone their ability to offer actionable feedback (and to receive feedback on their effectiveness at offering feedback).

Conflict Management. This module examines conflict through the lens of the Thomas-Kilmann Instrument (TKI) with the goals of enabling students to understand their preference in dealing with conflict and its impact, as well as how to recognize and work with other styles to resolve conflict more effectively. Specifically, students record how they perceive that they would react to a series of professional conflict scenarios, and then discuss their approaches in small groups. The facilitators use the following types of questions to help students better understand how their default style manifests itself in real situations as well as the advantages and limitations:

> What influences you to react in the way that you do?
>
> When have you tried other approaches? What happened?
>
> What would it take for you to approach the situation differently?
>
> Are you overusing a particular conflict resolution style? What are the implications?

Audience Captivation Training. This session applies the communication skills introduced in Interpersonal Communications to more formal, public speaking settings. Each student is given three opportunities to deliver a speech on a topic of his or her choice, to view the performance, and to receive feedback from facilitators and a group of peers on perceived effectiveness. This process (perform, review and critique, then try again) allows students to quickly incorporate feedback and evaluate its impact. Specifically, students are able to see how modifying their behavior impacts their effectiveness as a speaker.[4]

Decisions and Integrity. Through surveys and discussion of cases, this module helps student gain an understanding of how they think about sensitive and ethically complicated business issues (and how others approach the same issue). The focus is on identifying potential biases and tendencies in decision making.

At the conclusion of each classroom session, students are asked to answer three to four questions to draw out lessons learned about themselves—their strengths and key developmental needs. Reflection of this type has two purposes. First, it captures the students' thoughts when they are fresh and it challenges them to translate experience into specific and actionable insights. It also provides data for students who prefer to process the experience in private. Different formats for reflection—small group discussions,

---

[4]Anecdotally, it is common to hear during mid-summer discussions with rising second-year MBA students that they use this process in preparing for culminating presentations at their summer internships. Specifically, ad hoc groups form regionally with classmates independent of industry or internship function. So it is fair to assume that for some participants, this module establishes a routine for translating insight into action.

class-wide recaps, and individual, written exercises—are used throughout the course and enables students to identify which, if any, format they prefer.

At the end of the program, all of the written observations are consolidated and serve as a reference for students as they prepare a draft Personal Development Plan. With the help of facilitators and staff coaches, these drafts are reviewed and refocused to prioritize areas of developmental opportunity for each student.

Cohort events

LEAD concludes with two events that engage a subset of the first-year class from each of the ten cohorts:

LEADership Challenge. One hundred students (ten from each cohort) are selected by their peers to compete in a day-long case challenge judged by dozens of Chicago Booth alumni who hold senior leadership positions in their firms. When making their selections, we ask students to evaluate their classmates on:

- The leadership and interpersonal skills that they have displayed throughout the program
- Their openness to an intense and challenging experience that involves candid feedback from distinguished business leaders
- Their ability to work within a team and with a partner in an unpredictable setting

Each cohort team rotates through five different cases designed to test the leadership and interpersonal skills discussed during the classroom sessions (e.g., dealing with an unhappy client, bringing together a management team in conflict, bridging cultural differences to advance a corporate priority, etc.). The event serves to underscore the routine of learning from experience by simulating real-world leadership challenges and boss-like evaluators in a feedback-rich environment.

In 2010, the event was expanded to include a business crisis simulation. In this scenario, teams of students work together over several hours to navigate issues that arise in an intense, fast moving crisis (regulatory and legal issues, media relations, customer management, continuity of operations, etc.). The goal of the business crisis simulation is to test students' teamwork, communication, and decision making skills in an unfamiliar and dynamic setting.[5]

Golden Gargoyles. The capstone experience within LEAD, Golden Gargoyles is the awards ceremony that recognizes the creative output of the cohorts. Early in the series of LEAD modules, the cohorts are tasked with producing a short film highlighting some aspect of life at Chicago Booth as well as a thirty-second commercial promoting a product for the sponsoring organization. The films are shown at a school-wide awards ceremony and the winners are recognized in categories such as Best Use of the Entire Cohort, Best Incorporation of Faculty and Staff, and Best Overall Film. In addition to providing an enjoyable, high-energy end to the LEAD experience, this event showcases the creativity and teamwork skills of each of the cohorts, and helps to reinforce the unique culture and community at Chicago Booth.

FACILITATING FEEDBACK

When creating LEAD, the faculty at Chicago Booth decided to tap students first as co-creators, and then as co-instructors, of a course that was intended to make the acquisition of insight skills both contemporary and meaningful for students. Rather

[5]The business crisis simulation is a perfect illustration of the fluidity of the content of LEAD discussed above.

than rely exclusively on faculty as the experts who design and deliver the course, the vision for LEAD was one that recognized that students could play a central role in the development of learning routines that would more closely match how graduates develop post-MBA. In this way, LEAD is unique at Chicago Booth: Second-year students, elders in the MBA setting, are tapped as observers, content designers, presenters, facilitators of in-class discussions, and personal coaches.

Each year, the LEAD program is evaluated and redesigned anew, then delivered by forty second-year MBA students (referred to formally as LEAD Facilitators, less formally as Facils).[6] Selected shortly after the LEAD class ends, Facilitators enroll in a class during the Spring Quarter of their first year that prepares them to step into their multi-faceted role. The course requires students to research the content in the LEAD class to create rich and robust classroom experiences. Specifically, teams of Facilitators working closely with staff coaches reexamine each module, revise the content and experiential learning activities based upon student feedback and their own research and experiences, and customize the presentations with personal stories and experiences. In this way, the content and discussions are grounded in ways that make them immediately relevant to the students.

Since Facilitators are introduced to incoming MBA students at a time when, due to scheduling, there are few student-elders available, Facilitators play a key role with the initial assimilation of first-year students into the Booth community. Each Facilitator is assigned fourteen to sixteen students to "mentor" through the program. They work closely with their assigned student-mentees during classroom activities and actively engage them through private, one-on-one meetings. This structure ensures that all students have an elder vested in their learning and development.

The intentional use of peers to deliver the program plays an important role in skill assessment and content delivery. Facilitators enable the School to:

- Leverage the knowledge and experience of a small number of professional coaches to manage the peak-load challenge of interacting with and coaching more than 560 students simultaneously. More specifically, it engages the entire first-year class at the very beginning of their MBA experience—a critical inflection point in their professional lives—with specific and actionable feedback.
- Foster a feedback-rich environment. Facilitators help to create a safe environment that encourages personal disclosure, experimentation, and shared learning.
- Take a fresh, critical look at all aspects of the course—schedule, content, activities, etc.—each year. Their "ownership" of the course is consistent with Chicago Booth's value to challenge established wisdom and helps ensure that the topics and approach of LEAD remain relevant.
- Observe each student in a variety of situations. These observations become the data on which actionable feedback is based and on which insight skills are built. The most powerful insights have been gained when students receive consistent feedback across settings about their behavior and its impact.

THE STUDENT EXPERIENCE

At Chicago Booth, we use a variety of approaches to gauge the effectiveness of the LEAD programming and to better understand the experience of students. All students offer written feedback at the close

[6]The selection process for LEAD facilitators is among the most competitive selection processes for a leadership position within the full-time MBA program.

of each LEAD session; this feedback is shared with the Facilitators and staff coaches and is summarized for the next generation of Facilitators. First-year students also complete the School's standard course evaluation form at the completion of the course. Completion rates for the class session and end-of-course surveys are near 100 percent. These evaluations address the effectiveness of the instructors as well as the perceived usefulness of the content delivered. Over the last three academic years, the course evaluations of the LEAD class outperform the average Chicago Booth course.

The School also gathers student input on a wide range of topics (including LEAD and other leadership development programming) as a part of comprehensive year-end surveys administered by the Deputy Dean for the Full-time MBA Program at the end of students' first and second year of study (80–85 percent of students completing these surveys). Feedback in these surveys comes both in the form of quantitative assessments of different aspects of student life and in the form of qualitative comments, which students offer in response to open-ended questions that elicit the best aspects of their year and the areas where the School has the greatest opportunity for improvement.

Finally, to assess whether students incorporate their learning from LEAD when they return to the work setting, roundtable conversations with rising second-year students (with approximately 40 percent of the class participating) at the mid-point of their summer experience and conversations with dozens of company representatives add texture to the School's understanding of the value generated by LEAD and other academic coursework. Although less systematic, this anecdotal evidence affirms that students draw on their LEAD coursework during their summers and express appreciation for having had the opportunity to practice their skills in a low-stakes environment.

The LEAD facilitator experience

Each year, more than 100 students enter the selection process to become a LEAD Facilitator. The decision to apply is jointly a statement about the student's desire to contribute to the evolution of LEAD and to continue his or her development as a leader. All applicants go through an intense, multi-step screening process designed to assess their skills including:

- The ability to form effective working relationships
- Openness to challenging feedback
- Commitment in a fast paced and ambiguous environment
- The ability to model the types of skills discussed throughout LEAD
- Effective facilitation skills

At its core, the Facilitator program is a classic action learning model that spans two academic quarters across the first and second year of the MBA. The 40 students selected are divided into squads of eight and are given overall responsibility for managing the classroom experience for two cohorts (approximately 110–120 students). Each facilitator serves on four to five different teams, each responsible for designing and delivering a classroom session or major event. While each team has a coach to serve as an observer and advisor, the teams are given considerable autonomy. They elect a leader, set the agenda, decide how they will operate, and are allowed to struggle—the experience of having to work with and influence peers with widely varying personalities is one of the most powerful parts of the experience. It is intentionally designed to mimic the matrix environment used by global business organizations.

The Facilitator experience contains a number of structural elements designed to drive and enrich the learning experience:

- Each Facilitator is assigned a coach to work with throughout the experience. The coach meets regularly with their mentees to discuss their development objectives, to provide independent feedback and real-time coaching on team and individual effectiveness issues.
- Team members provide formal written feedback to each other twice during the two-quarter experience.
- The entire group of forty comes together twice per week in the Spring Quarter to handle administrative matters and to receive training on topics like facilitation skills, classroom management, and team dynamics.
- After the first quarter, each Facilitator submits an insight paper outlining what he or she learned about himself or herself, identifying areas for additional work in the second quarter.
- Facilitators play an active role in recruiting and evaluating the succeeding group of facilitators. This helps with the transmission of informal knowledge.
- The Facilitator experience ends with each facilitator submitting a legacy letter containing insights and advice for the succeeding group.

The learning from experience generated in the sequence of courses taken by the Facilitators delivers transferable skills to all participants. Specifically, Facilitators learn to establish rapport with, and deliver value to, individuals with varied backgrounds and motivation. In addition, the Facilitator experience creates a deep connection among the forty in this cohort, broadening students' collegial network in ways that might not otherwise occur.

The nature of the Facilitator experience also has a highly individualized aspect that is hard to categorize. To provide a flavor for the more idiosyncratic benefits realized by Facilitators, here are a few passages from recent legacy letters:

"I developed the ability to lead a 'conversation' with sixty participants, and became comfortable with the unpredictable nature of such discussions. Over time, my communication style evolved to become more relaxed and nimble."

"I have at times struggled to gain credibility as a woman in a male-dominated work environment. The Facilitator experience enabled me to explore this concern—first by articulating it (something I had never done) and then by working with my coach to experiment with subtle changes in my communication style to hone my effectiveness as an influential leader regardless of the gender of the audience."

"As the most reserved member of the entire Facilitator group, I thought it was crazy when I was chosen to lead my extroverted, vocal peers. Over time, however, I realized that my unflappable, inclusive style was highly effective with this group. This insight, and our group's great successes this year, did wonders for my confidence as a leader."

"By necessity, a Facilitator offers feedback day-in and day-out. Some of the feedback I offered was positive but much of it highlighted areas for development. This experience wasn't easy and I often struggled to share observations in a way that was constructive while not losing the importance of the message. I will use this critical leadership skill every day for the rest of life."

"Working as closely with my Facilitator peers as we did, with so much to deliver, I learned to let go of control and trust my teammates. I can't imagine a more important leadership attribute."

First-year students who participate in the LEADership Challenge

The annual LEADership Challenge competition enables selected first-year MBA students to showcase their leadership and interpersonal skills in front of distinguished alumni judges. This is both a humbling and energizing experience and is quite different from the typical case challenge that involves analyzing a business problem. In LEADership challenge cases, students analyze a situation and then enact their preferred solution in a realistic role play.

Logistically, each participant operates within a team of ten. While each team member participates in only one challenge, the team helps to prepare and support individual performers. Each participant works with at least one partner during the actual role play. Invariably, the students must quickly decide how to react to situations such as when a partner is struggling or whose approach is failing, when a partner decides to dominate the conversation or deviate from a previously agreed-upon strategy, or when the situation moves in an unanticipated direction. The students grapple with questions such as the following: How do you intervene in a way that is positive and helpful? How do you assert your views and get an opportunity to showcase your skills? How do you coordinate actions with someone you may have never worked with before?

Finally, the cases are designed to replicate the competing forces that tug at leaders every day. In one case, a student assumes the role of the newly designated CEO of a struggling company owned by a private equity firm. The company has been experiencing extreme performance and liquidity challenges. In the first meeting with her new leadership team, the student knows that the banks and sponsors are expecting the meeting to deliver a realistic and achievable budget. While all of the attention seems to be on gaining agreement on the budget, the judges assess how well the students balance the need to complete this specific task with the objective of getting to know their new team members and setting the proper tone for working together prospectively.

First-year students

For the majority of students, LEAD ends with a series of adjournment meetings after the final learning module. Looking at this group, their experiences do not fall into neat, easily differentiated categories. For illustrative purposes, we highlight a few examples of insights gained through LEAD:

SCENARIO 1: A young woman enters LEAD convinced (despite what she had written in her admissions essays) that she was not a leader. In her mind, a leader has the answer and is an extroverted, assertive member of a group. What became obvious to her through the team-based activities in LEAD was that she had the ability to draw out all of the members of her team and to provide structure that kept the group moving without stifling creativity. She had a positive, engaging style that allowed her to manage some tough, outspoken team members and to influence them positively in a subtle manner. She knew when (and how) to offer her ideas and when to let others dictate the direction. Still, she was surprised when her peers and the student facilitators told her that she was the "glue of the team," and that they looked to her to provide leadership and direction. Over time, she better understood, and learned to leverage, the unique skills that she had always possessed. The experience changed not only how she viewed herself but also how she thought about her future.

SCENARIO 2: Imagine a bright, driven, and extremely detail-oriented young man who came to Chicago Booth from a role where all of his colleagues had similar backgrounds and styles. Based on his professional experiences, he placed a high value on a narrow set of attributes and adopted a bias that undervalued differing styles. During the sessions on personality preferences and conflict management, his beliefs about the characteristics of successful individuals were challenged. This realization stayed with him throughout his first year and he found himself thinking about diversity as he formed study groups and led student group initiatives. Over time, he found himself seeking out complementary styles and consciously incorporating them into his teams. Interestingly, he also discovered that he could access previously underused aspects of his personality that allowed him to connect effectively with almost anyone. These insights enabled him to develop into a universally respected and highly effective student leader.

SCENARIO 3: Consider a young woman regarded in her personal interactions as intelligent, generous, and caring but whose professional reputation was as an overly serious and at times "mean" colleague. She was devastated when, at the end of the Immersion Retreat, she received feedback from her new classmates that she was distant and difficult to engage. Almost immediately, she sought the help of one of the program's coaches to work on her "presence." She made a commitment to smile and consciously project a positive, optimistic air. These relatively simple actions quickly changed how others reacted to her. In addition, her focus on how others received her altered in a positive way both her outlook and resiliency.

Each year yields new and different examples. The point is that the variety and flexibility of the LEAD experience gives all students the freedom to find the place, the content, or the relationships that are the most valuable for them. One of the major strengths of LEAD is that it does not prescribe or advocate a single path or approach. Instead, LEAD challenges each student to chart a course and to take ownership for his or her development experience.

Challenges for LEAD and Chicago Booth

CONTINUING THE LESSONS OF LEAD BEYOND THE CLASS

Learning from experience takes on various forms for students once they leave LEAD. Many courses offer students the opportunity to refine their team skills and communication skills both inside and outside of the classroom. However, with very few exceptions, after LEAD the non-evaluative feedback offered by Facilitators and team mates is replaced by evaluative (e.g., performance-related) feedback. This creates a challenge for students seeking to extend the safe, feedback-rich environment of LEAD.

At the time LEAD was created, Chicago Booth had more than ten years of experience with its New Product Laboratories. These courses brought real-time projects into the classroom where teams of students worked for two quarters to define, research, and analyze a given problem for an external client. As its title suggests, many of these courses related to the challenge of taking an existing product into a new geographic market or launching a new product. The teams would conduct market research and make recommendations to the client on market entry.

In designing LEAD, the constructive feedback offered to students by faculty, peers, and the external client within the New Product Lab was emulated. Today, there are ample courses with *laboratory* in their title but few that have the focus on intense process coaching offered in LEAD.[7] Students can register for experiential classes focused on nascent business, the venture capital arena, in private equity, in social

[7]One exception is Management Lab, a quarter long course for which students receive two (rather than one) course credits and for which there are both content and process coaches working with teams of eight to ten students; typically about forty to fifty MBA students participate in Management Lab annually.

entrepreneurship, and in the more traditional marketing area for immersion experiences in these types of organizations.

FACILITATOR ENGAGEMENT

The success of LEAD is tied closely to the degree of engagement in and professionalism among the Facilitator team for two academic quarters. In recent years the group has adopted performance standards and mutual monitoring practices to ensure high performance. That said, exogenous factors as well as interpersonal conflict can undermine Facilitator engagement.

When students serve as Facilitators they are also students themselves. Stepping into the Facilitator role is a powerful learning experience for these students and it requires great focus to remain committed to the learning of others throughout the experience. This was evident most recently with the downturn in the global economy in the 2008–09 academic year. In "normal" times, Facilitators resolved their internship search well before their Spring commitments to LEAD course began. Most Facilitators would return from their summer internship with a post-graduation offer. However, the Facilitators from the Class of 2010 faced a fundamentally different experience and had to manage the tension of their own job search at a time when the demands on Facilitators were greatest.

Interpersonal dynamics can also create challenges within the Facilitator group. Over the more than two decades of LEAD, there have been a small number of incidents where conflict among a squad of Facilitators reduced the trust and teamwork to such an extent that it compromised the delivery of the LEAD course. From a programmatic perspective, these experiences pointed to the need for modifications in the selection process, clearer expectation setting of the Facilitator role by a wider group of professionals involved in the full-time MBA program (including the Dean of Students and representatives of the Dean's Office), and more coaching of the Facilitators by the staff.

Finally, there is always pressure on Facilitators to be a "normal" member of the student community—to let down their guard and interact socially with first-year students or to find time to spend with their second-year colleagues who are not LEAD Facilitators. A loss of focus can comprise these students' effectiveness as extensions of the faculty.

DELIVERING VALUE TO EACH AND EVERY STUDENT

Since its inception, faculty and LEAD's professional staff have experimented with the format, tone, and focus of the course. At different points in its more than twenty-year history, LEAD has produced varying distributions of students who are passionate about wanting more of, and those insistent that there be less of, LEAD.

The existence of lovers and haters can present unique challenges for the management of this course.

A key learning over the last decade that has maximized the set of LEAD lovers is to resist attempts to standardize the LEAD experience. While uniformity of experience can reduce the likelihood of bad outcomes, we have found that this type of coursework is especially difficult to standardize and tends to deliver the least benefits to those with the strongest baseline skill set when standardization is achieved. In addition, the degree to which first-year students hone their skills in LEAD depends on their individual engagement and in the ability of facilitators to "connect" with their cohorts. Attempting to mute idiosyncrasies across facilitators proved counterproductive in building rapport.

IMPLICATION FOR OTHER SUPPORT TEAMS AT CHICAGO BOOTH

Each student leaves the LEAD course with a customized plan for continued development (the PDP). With clear direction on areas of continued developmental growth in hand, the philosophy at Chicago Booth is to offer students opportunity but to allow each student to "own" his or her experience. In the context of the PDP, students can access hundreds of different curricular offerings, participate in and/or lead one of more than seventy-five student career-related and social groups, and participate in dozens of school-led programs as a means to continue to develop their insight and action skills.

In practice, the LEAD course ends just as students' interactions with prospective employers around summer employment begins. This in effect passes professional development to the staff dedicated to career services with the same challenges of peak-load demand experienced in LEAD. Through a series of class sessions and events designed to expand students' knowledge about alternate career paths (career exploration) and to prepare students for interviewing, students receive feedback on their presence and persuasive abilities in one-on-one and group settings. Over time, the role of second-year Career Advisors—a core of forty to forty-five second-year students selected to represent knowledgeable peers who serve as peer leaders on the career "communities"—has evolved. These students are supplemented by no fewer than another hundred second-year students who are called into service in periods of high demand such as the five-day window just prior to the launch of on-campus interviewing when thousands of mock interviews occur, complete with actionable debriefs.

In addition, it is common for a student to present a PDP to his or her academic adviser and career coach to solicit continued professional guidance on development. This practice challenges the School to better prepare these professionals to assist students in their development as self-aware leaders.

Conclusions

The LEAD course is a highly interactive leadership development course that offers students a method for self-assessment that is transferable beyond their academic experience. Built on Davis and Hogarth's structure for developing insight and action skills, the course extends the faculty by training second-year MBA students who play a central, multi-faceted role in the course of instructor-mentor-coach. The experience is transformative for this select group of forty Facilitators and offers each Chicago Booth MBA a rich portfolio of interactions and feedback on which a personalized development plan is built.

References

Becker, S. W. (1994). The laboratory class in quality management. University of Chicago Graduate School of Business Working Paper.

Datar, S.M., & Garvin, D.A. (2008). The University of Chicago Graduate School of Business. Harvard Business School Case N9-308-059.

Davis, H.L., & Hogarth, R.M. (1992). Rethinking management education: A view from Chicago. The University of Chicago Graduate School of Business, Selected Paper No. 72.

13

DEVELOPING NATURALLY

From Management to Organization to Society to Selves

◆ Henry Mintzberg

Desautels Faculty of Management, McGill University

By considering organizations as communities of human beings rather than collections of human resources, appropriately guided by engaged managers rather than heroic leaders, we have created a family of programs to transform how their managers are developed. We began with a master's degree for practicing managers in business, which has carried management education into management development by encouraging managers to reflect their own experience and share it with each other. We built a shorter program on this, to bring management development to organization development, as teams of managers from different companies engage each other in "friendly consulting" on key issues in their enterprises. Next came another master's degree, for practicing managers in health care, which has brought in social development, as the managers reached out to major concerns in their communities and brought these into the classroom for friendly consulting. And the latest program has carried all of this into the workplace for self-development, as small teams of managers meet periodically on their own, without faculty or facilitators, to develop themselves and their organizations. We are now in the process of combining these programs in ways that point to a new generation in management and organization development.

❖❖❖

For the past fifteen years, and especially since I published *Managers not MBAs* in 2004, we have been on a journey: to renew organizations by transforming how their managers are developed. We have come a long way, through our own development of a family of programs that suggest some novel ways by which organizations can be renewed. This has been based on three assumptions.

First, organizations are communities of human beings, not collections of human resources. As human beings, we engage with our communities. Indeed, we cherish the very sense of community, since it is the social glue that bonds us together for the social good, and so allows us to function energetically. Organizations thus work best when they too are communities, of committed people who work in cooperative relationships, under conditions of trust and respect. Destroy this, and the whole institution of business and other organizations collapses.

Consider the organizations you most admire: is that because of their measures, their rhetoric, their downsizing, and their outsourcing? Or do they rate highly in your mind because of their devotion to mission, their culture, the enthusiasm of their people—ultimately their sense of community?

Second, communityship is built through an engaged management that cares, not a heroic leadership that cures. It may be fashionable to distinguish leaders from managers, but would you like to work for a manager who does not lead? That can be pretty discouraging. How about a leader who doesn't manage? That can be awfully disengaging: How is he or she supposed to know what is going on? We have had more than enough of detached, heroic leadership: It is time for more engaged management, embedded in "communityship."

Third, instead of programs to create tomorrow's leaders, we need initiatives that commit today's managers. No manager, let alone leader, has ever been created in a classroom. In other words, it is my belief that we don't *teach* leadership, the title of this handbook notwithstanding. Management/leadership is a practice, rooted in experience, not a science or profession, rooted in analysis. What a classroom can do is take people with that experience and the demonstrated skills of leadership, and leverage that alongside their natural inclination to drive necessary change. It has been said about bacon and eggs that while the chicken is involved, the pig is committed. Development is about commitment: to the job, for sure, but also to the organization, and beyond that, to society in a responsible way.

Our Own Development

This brings me to the efforts that we, as a community of colleagues—academics, consultants, developers, and managers—have been engaged in and committed to since the mid-1990s.

We began in our own place, with "management" education in the business school. But our journey has taken us well beyond that, out to society where management has its impact, and into the workplace where it is practiced.

Unhappy with the business schools' flagship program, the MBA, years ago I began to question it. This led to an embarrassing question that should never be asked of an academic: "What are you doing about it?" I thought academics were not supposed to *do* anything about anything.

As the question kept coming up, a group of us decided to act: to rethink business education as management education combined with management development, in a master's degree program for practicing managers committed to their companies. The intention was not for them to *get* a better job, but to *do* a better job.

As our journey progressed, one program led to another. Next, we were drawn into organization development: how much more powerful it could be to have the managers developing their organizations while they were developing themselves. The consequence was a shorter program, for teams of managers sent by the companies, to work on key issues in a process we came to call "friendly consulting."

The subsequent step took us to social development. We created a program like the first, but for practicing managers in health care. Here we found them inclined to reach out to the broader issues of their external communities, and to bring these into the classroom from some of that friendly consulting.

And the final, unexpected step has taken us to the most natural place of all: self-development, as managers take collective responsibility for their own development and that of their organizations.

All of these activities can be called *natural development*. Together they constitute a family of endeavors that changes how management is practiced—as engaging—and how organizations are renewed—as communities. Each program is discussed in turn, for the insights it offers, before considering the four of them together in conclusion.

Carrying Management Education Into Management Development: Grounded Reflection for Insight

The conventional MBA is just that: It is about *business* administration. It does a fine job of teaching the business functions—finance, accounting, marketing, etc.—but little to teach management and leadership. In fact, giving young people without management experience the impression that they have been trained to manage as well as to lead all too often promotes hubris instead.

Much of this education relies on learning from other people's experience, either indirectly, in the form of theory—the distillation of experience—or directly, through cases. For years the Wharton School has boasted on its website that its EMBA students, people with considerable work experience, receive "the same" "innovative curriculum" as in the "full-time MBA program" (downloaded February 2011). How extraordinary: being proud of not doing any more for experienced managers than for people who have never managed!

There is nothing wrong with learning from other people's experience. We all do it. But there is something far more powerful about learning from our own experience. T. S. Eliot wrote in one of his poems that "We had the experience but missed the meaning." Management education should be about getting the meaning. In fact, in his book *Rules for Radicals*, Saul Alinsky claimed that "Most people go through life undergoing a series of happenings, which pass through their system undigested. Happenings become experience . . . when they are reflected on, related to general patterns and synthesized" (1971, pp. 68–69).

MBA OR MPM?

Reflecting on one's own experience, and sharing that with other managers, is thus key to management learning. This has been *our* learning, which began in 1996 when we set out to rethink the education of managers, bringing management development into management education under the label of our International Masters in Practicing Management (www.IMPM.org).

The IMPM, which has been running since then, takes managers around the world in five ten-day modules over sixteen months, each based on a different managerial mindset: the reflective mindset (managing self), the analytic mindset (managing organizations), the worldly mindset (managing context), the collaborative mindset (managing relationships), and the action mindset (managing change—see Mintzberg & Gosling, 2001).

Most of the participating managers in the IMPM, who average over forty years of age, are sent by their companies, which strengthens the bond between the two—that is, enhances commitment, both ways. In fact, a number of companies—Panasonic, Fujitsu, Lufthansa, LG, Alcan (now Rio Tinto)—have been sending groups of managers to most or all of our IMPM classes since 1996.

USING WORK, NOT MAKING WORK

Managers these days are busy people. The last thing they need, when taking time off for development, is more work back at work. The logical solution is to *use* work more than *make* work, in other words, to build as much of the learning as possible into the classroom itself, drawing on the natural experiences of the participating managers.

One key way to facilitate this, we have learned, is by having the managers sit at round tables in a flat room so that they needn't "break out" to share their experience. (See the box on "The Architecture of Engagement.") Ideas that come up—from the managers or the faculty—can be turned into instant workshops for the managers to consider in light of their experience, and to pursue their implications. In fact, a 50:50 rule in our IMPM classrooms calls for half of the classroom time to be turned over to the managers—*on their agendas.* The other half drops in more conventional inputs to stimulate these discussions, via faculty presentations, exercises, sometimes case studies, etc.[1]

Beyond the classroom, we try to blend the other components of the program with the managers' natural needs and schedules as much as possible. For example, *reflection papers* are written after each module, to link what the managers learned to themselves, their jobs, and their organizations. And between the second and third modules, the managers pair up and do a *managerial exchange*, spending the better part of a week visiting and hosting at each others' workplace. This is a hugely popular part of the program—getting into the shoes of a colleague and offering comments on his or her activities and concerns.

"THE BEST MANAGEMENT BOOK I EVER READ"

The learning philosophy of the IMPM manifests itself most clearly in what we call "Morning Reflections." (See Figure 13.1 on page 209.)

All the managers in the IMPM get an "Insight Book." It has their name on the cover but is otherwise blank. First thing each morning, everyone writes quietly in this book: reflections about themselves and their work, issues that came up the day before and overnight, etc. After five to ten minutes, the managers engage each other around their table to share these reflections. And after about fifteen minutes of this, a plenary discussion, sometimes in one big circle without any faculty, draws out the most interesting of the insights.

[1]Faculty are obviously prepared for this other half. As for the reflective half, we have been surprised how easily seasoned professors with a general knowledge of business and organizations have adapted to it, at least those who have no need to be in perpetual control of the class. As soon as they appreciate how much of a learning experience this can be for themselves too, which happens rather quickly, they become very enthusiastic.

These morning reflections have become the integrative glue that bonds together the learning across the entire program—in fact, in all our programs.[2] As a senior vice president at the Royal Bank of Canada, sitting in on one of these discussions in a class that included some of the Bank's people, told a reporter from Fast Company: "That was the most fascinating conversation in an academic setting that I have ever seen. We zoomed around the room discussing everything from political to economic issues, and then got into ethics and business" (in Reingold, 2000, p. 286).

Lufthansa holds a meeting each year to welcome its new participants to the IMPM. One year a graduate held up her insight book and declared: "This is the best management book I ever read!" If we are serious about engagement, about managers taking responsibility for their own development and that of their organizations, shouldn't every manager's best management book be the one they have written for themselves?

IMPACT TEAMS

Most managers come home from developmental programs alone, even if they have been their with colleagues from their own company. There has been no easy way to anchor and extend their learning into the organization, for impact.

Since the outset, we have been concerned about this. To what degree have the managers in the IMPM been carrying their learning back to the workplace, for *coaching impact* (the learner in the classroom becoming the teacher on the job) and *action impact* (carrying the learning into activities to change the organization). We have encouraged these in all sorts of ways, and much has happened: For example, some managers have replicated parts of the modules with their staff while others have made changes in their organizations based on what they learned. But this had to go further.

In 2009, after an IMPM module, a group of faculty met with representatives from two of the companies that had long been involved in the program, Lufthansa and Rio Tinto, to brainstorm about impact. There the suggestion arose to establish a team back at work behind each of the managers participating in the program: a kind of virtual team to do the program too, by proxy. This would leverage the learning from the classroom into the workplace and spread the costs: send one manager, develop five more.

Whereas a team in the classroom is rarely a team back in the organization, a team around the manager at work is a natural team—and a potential community of learning and development, since it is made up of people who work together on a regular basis.

As I described in an earlier article entitled "Rebuilding Companies as Communities" (Mintzberg, 2009), small teams at middle management levels may be more effective at changing an organization than driven efforts from the "top." Such managers are often remarkably committed to the enterprise, and sometimes ideally connected as well: close enough to the operations, where ideas often begin (and get lost), yet able to appreciate the big picture.

Thus was born IM*pact*, a pact between the manager in a learning program and the team he or she designates back at work—of reports, peers, associates, whoever makes the most sense—for management development carried into organization

[2]The three photos of Figure 13.1 show these three stages. A faculty member used to lead the third stage while the participants stayed at the tables. But then someone had the idea to push back the tables and get everyone in a big circle. The third photo shows this, but with a faculty member still up there leading. We have whited this person out, to reflect how the process works now, with any faculty members present being seated in the circle like everyone else.

development. It has now been successfully applied in the IMPM.

Connecting Management Development to Organization Development: Friendly Consulting for Company Change

Of course, not all managers can take a full degree program. So to extend our efforts, we next gave consideration to a shorter program for management and organization development.

AMP, OR ALP?

Most popular have been the Advanced Management Programs (AMPs), generally offered by business schools. But how advanced are they?

Many are, in fact, shorter replicas of the conventional MBA: They use many of the same cases and much of the same theory; are built around the same business functions; seat the managers in the same linear rows; and so on. Do managers who are just coming into general management need to be pushed back into the functional silos? Do people with a great deal of personal experience need the second-handedness of the MBA? If a management development program is to develop insight and innovation, shouldn't its own design be insightful and innovative?

Some of these programs promise boot camp, to keep the managers busy. Most managers these days live boot camp all the time. What they desperately need is to pause, step back, and reflect thoughtfully on their own experience.

Accordingly, we took a hard look at these AMPs and developed what we call an ALP, an Advanced Leadership Program (www.alp-impm.com). It comprises three modules of five days each spread over six months, making use of the ideas of the IMPM: the engaged seating, the morning reflections, the managerial mindsets, etc. But the ALP has taken an additional step, by combining organization development with management development.

ADDRESSING COMPANY ISSUES THROUGH FRIENDLY CONSULTING

Most programs offer chairs. We decided to offer tables, asking companies to send teams of six managers who could work at the round tables. Each team is asked to bring to the ALP a significant issue from the company, and together the different teams work on each other's issues in a process we call *friendly consulting*. It has proved to be a powerful addition: The managers love it—better than a busman's holiday.

As practicing managers, these people bring their expertise and experience to these issues: They understand them because they have all lived them in one way or another. Just consider a couple of these issues: "How do we enhance and sustain a culture of customer service?" and "How do we motivate our first-line employees?" As a result, the managers can contribute to each other's problem solving as well as learning—consulting with no axe to grind. This creates an environment rich in inquiry, dialogue, and sense of community. Accordingly, the managers learn as much being friendly consultants as they do receiving the advice of their consulting colleagues—sometimes much more, as we shall see.

Organizations have two common ways to deal with a difficult issue: strike an internal task force, or bring in outside consultants. Either can be helpful, although one can suffer from insularity, the other from detachment. So imagine the two together. That is what friendly consulting is all about. More than half of the class time is devoted to the company teams working on their own and each others' issues: framing the issue; receiving feedback from the others and then reframing it; undergoing field visits to each other's companies to probe into their issue; and getting deeper into what needs changing and how to go about doing it.

MOTIVATE WHOM?

Let's go back to that issue of motivating the first line employees, because it illustrates what can be done with this approach. The company was VIA Rail, Canada's passenger railway (which cleared for publication what is described below). The friendly consultants spent a day in the company, to probe into this issue with managers at all levels as well as within the operations, to experience the basic services and to speak with those first-line employees. They returned to announce to the company team: "You don't need to motivate your first-line employees; they are plenty motivated. You should use them to further motivate your managers." This was obviously an insight for the VIA team, but it proved equally so for the friendly consultants. "Do you think the same thing is happening in your company?" I asked one of them. "Exactly!" she answered. They just never did a comparable field study in their own company.

This example makes clear something else: A specific issue may be assigned, but ultimately the company is the issue. What really brings the ALP to organization development is that the team members begin to see more deeply into their own organization, and especially into its culture. As one manager of another VIA team commented after a field visit: "Our discussions, exercises, and reflections made us realize that we were a product of our organization's culture. . . ." From this they "learned how to work as a cross-functional team and how to leverage their individual contributions" (Patwell & Seashore, 2007).

Back home, the team organized a two-day retreat that "re-energized the organization, created a shift in mindset, and aligned people from across [the company] around a common goal and action plan. . . . Three years later . . . the ALP team continues to meet regularly and has become the think tank of [the company's] customer focus initiatives. The customer is talked about every day at every level of the company." Another of the team members commented that "I am amazed at the impact that a group of individuals [in middle management] can have on an organization." After years of engaging in this kind of development, we were not amazed!

ENOUGH ANALYSIS: TIME FOR COFFEE AND DONUTS

The first thing that many of these ALP teams want to do is analyze: hire marketing researchers, do a business plan, and so on. "Enough analysis," we say. "You have decades of experience among yourselves about the company. Use it right here, now!"

We hadn't planned on field visits in one running of the program: The company sites were too widely dispersed around the world. But when we told the story about the first-line employees, the class decided, spontaneously, to self-organize for field trips between the first and second ALP modules.

A manager of one of the teams, from Motorola, who was based in Singapore, visited Hanson, the building materials company, in one of its Australian facilities. Its issue concerned customer service. Back in class, he told the Hanson team that while he was riding in a truck delivering aggregate to a building site, the driver stopped for coffee and donuts. "Why don't you give them coffee and donuts while the truck is being loaded?" the friendly consultant suggested. This wasn't exactly a momentous recommendation—he had others of greater consequence—but it provided an opening for the faculty: "Here you have it. Customer service is not about marketing research reports in some distant office; it's about coffee and donuts on the ground!" That's how to change the practice of management.

Extending Management and Organization Development to Social Development: Outreach to Surrounding Communities

Our programs, as noted, are about community building: the classroom itself becomes a community, as does each of the teams within it, plus all of this is designed to enhance the sense of communityship back in the organization. But the world of organizations also extends into the social communities that surround the organization.

In 2006, we created a third initiative, the International Masters for Health Leadership (www.imhl.info) modeled after the IMPM, also using the innovations of the ALP, for managers from all aspects of health care worldwide.[3] The managers sit at the same kinds of tables and engage in similar reflections, in five modules based on similar mindsets. Plus they bring in their issues, and act as friendly consultants to each other on them. The content is different—health care is not a business, even if it is significantly supplied by businesses—even though the architecture of the classroom and the processes within it have proved applicable.

But we wanted to take another step, bump up this organization development to social development, by having teams in the class address the big issues in health care. For example, one physician, head of a large family practice clinic, defined his issue as engaging the clients in the practice. So why not see this as an issue that cuts across so much of health care?

That was easy enough to encourage. For many of its people, in the operations and administration alike, health care is a calling. They are there to contribute to the greater good.

OUTREACH

But something else happened that took us by surprise. Groups in the first class began to reach out in various ways, using the class to address specific health care issues in their communities.

For example, two physician managers from Uganda, one with the World Health Organization, the other in the Ugandan health ministry, organized a conference in Kampala to carry this philosophy of natural learning into African health care. It was attended by sixty health care managers from seven African countries. Despite some initial reservations about whether the approach would work in this setting, the conference turned out to be a great success. The morning reflections, for example, were every bit as animated as what we have come to expect in our own classrooms.

Imagine creating IMHL-type programs in Africa, using IM*pact* teams for all the participating managers, to help build the management infrastructure so needed in African health care today.

When the government of Quebec announced the formation of a major commission to address concerns about health care financing and administration, the Quebec members of the IMHL class felt they had to convey to it some of their learning about the management of health care, especially concerning the engagement of clinicians in the administration. So these people approached the commission and were granted two hours to present their message. That went so well that the commissioners asked how they could get more deeply into these recommendations. They were thus invited to join the class for some friendly consulting.

The three commissioners accepted immediately, and a few weeks later, each joined

[3]Two other initiatives are the EMBA Roundtables, where students from different EMBA programs around the world get together for one week of an IMPM experience (www.EMBAroundtables.org), and the McGill-HEC EMBA (www.emba/mcgillhec.ca), run by these two schools in Montreal, which is much like the IMPM, except that the modules are shorter and more frequent, the students work on business as well as management issues, and there is more functional content.

one of three round tables to discuss: How do we enhance local autonomy (namely loosen up central controls)? How do we promote collaboration (on the ground and between clinical operations and administration)? And how do we change the culture to take on more responsibility at the local level? The head of the commission called after their report was issued to say that this experience had a major impact on their recommendations.

Such an experience was certainly unusual for a commission of this kind, and perhaps for the field of management development as well. Yet in a classroom of engagement, commitment, and community, it was perfectly natural. Think of what can be accomplished by bringing key social issues into thoughtful forums of informed and engaged managers.

Combining All the Above in Self Development: Coaching Ourselves

Imagine taking all of this beyond the classroom, into the managers' workplaces. That is what has happened in the fourth initiative, except that it came from neither faculty nor facilitator. A manager with a need came up with this.

PHIL CALLED

Phil LeNir, my stepson and director of engineering in the Montreal branch of a high technology company at the time, called one day. His engineers had become managers, he said, because their programming was outsourced to Eastern Europe, and they were struggling. "What should I do?" he asked. "And, by the way, I have no budget!"

You can guess my response. Get them around a table periodically, I suggested, in a quiet atmosphere where that they can at least pause, share their concerns, and reflect on their experiences in dealing with them.

Phil took this up with a vengeance. He and his managers met every second week or so for about seventy-five minutes at lunch. It had to be fun, he said, or they wouldn't keep coming. They did, for two years. Soon Phil established another group, of peer managers on site, then a third, spread across three countries of the company's operations, that met on conference calls. Members of these groups also started their own groups, one eventually commenting that "I've been doing it for three years—first as a member of the pilot group, then leading my own group. It's never old because it's always about what you are doing day-to-day."

When I showed Phil the material we were using in our programs, available in loose-leaf binders by module, he went through that. Phil has no MBA, had hardly attended management courses at all, but he learned quickly. (Later he did the IMPM.) Eventually he developed all kinds of topics to stimulate the group discussions, ranging from negotiating skills to figuring out the balance sheet. Phil introduced the equivalent of morning reflections too—experiences to be shared at the start of every session. He even used field studies: In one session on culture, they all went into the hall to interview whoever they found about the company's culture, and reported back. The key for him was to take their discussion into organizational development, by having the groups consider the implication of their learning for changing their jobs and the company.

The balance sheet topic was particularly telling. "Financial Management for Non-Financial Executives" is likely the most popular short course for managers. Phil reversed it. He brought in copies of the company's annual report as well as a list of definitions of the terms in the balance sheet. "We have seventy-five minutes to figure this out," he told his group of engineering managers without finance experience. They did, and had a great time, especially when they began to understand the footnotes!

COACHINGOURSELVES.COM

All of this went so well that we incorporated the whole exercise under the label of CoachingOurselves.com, to enable other managers to take responsibility for their own development.

Groups of five to seven managers form, or are formed, inside their own organizations—sometimes comprising peers, sometimes a manager with his or her reports, sometimes across two parts of the organization that need bonding (such as managers from the two sides of a merger). They subscribe to the Coaching Ourselves catalog of topics (for example, "Dialoguing," "Dealing With the Pressures of Managing," "Developing Our Organization as a Community," "High Performance Teams," most authored by prominent management writers), and discuss them in an informal setting, say over lunch, for about ninety minutes, once every two weeks or so. There is no faculty, no facilitator, no formal coach—just the managers learning from each other and coming up with ways to improve their practice and their organization.

Organizations around the world are now using CoachingOurselves with multiple groups. The topics number over seventy and are available in eight languages. Most interesting is how the companies are using CoachingOurselves for organizational development—"consulting-for-ourselves," if you like. One major Japanese firm has applied CoachingOurselves to effect turnaround in some of its divisions. A Canadian bank was concerned about communication across its silos. When a senior executive heard that we have a topic called "Silos and Slabs in Organizations" (slabs being horizontal barriers between different levels of management), she decided to use it in a meeting of her own managers. They split into two groups, each of which used the topic to consider how to facilitate better communication, and then they met together to compare their conclusions and decide what actions to take.

Combining the Initiatives

As these initiatives progress, we begin to see how all of them end up in the same place: managers at all levels becoming increasingly engaged in developing themselves while developing their communities, internal and external.

As we have seen, each new program has built on the existing ones. Now they are feeding back to each other, in interesting combinations that suggests their full potential. For example, Coaching Ourselves topics are being used in classroom programs, to cover certain subjects and provide a change of pace. They are also being given to the IMPM managers to take back home for use with their IMpact teams—to expose their colleagues to materials discussed in the classroom.[4] Meanwhile, the IMPM has begun to use friendly consulting on issues of concern to its class members.

A most interesting initiative is for companies to use the ALP together with CoachingOurselves to rebuild community. In the ALP, a group of senior managers can define the main concerns in the company and establish CoachingOurselves groups of middle managers to address them. Later the ALP group can bring these groups together in a major in-house forum to consolidate the learning and advance the drive toward communityship.

[4]The IMHL has recently joined forces with a group of senior Kenyans in health care to submit a proposal to one of the major foundations. It proposes combining IMHL participants with IM*pact* teams as a way to build up the health care management infrastructure in Africa.

As this continues, all of these initiatives can be seen to bond into a single family of programs that offers all sorts of opportunities for the development of managers, their organizations, and their broader communities.

Managing Naturally for Communityship

As noted, our intention from the outset has been to change how management is practiced. But not until recently did it become clear that we were also developing organizations as communities. And not until the CoachingOurselves initiative did we realize that all of this happens most naturally when managers take significant responsibility for developing themselves. We can show the way in the classroom, and provide materials, but this becomes much more powerful when teams at work run with it on their own terms. Indeed, what could be more compatible with the philosophy of truly engaged management embedded in communityship? For years, all kinds of organizations have been sending their managers to development programs, as selves in silos, sitting there to get "developed." Imagine development where the managers participate as representatives of their organization, connected to it to make it a better place.

To repeat, management is not going to be *taught* to anyone—not by any professor or human resource expert or even by the manager's own manager. Managers have to learn primarily through their own efforts. We have seen that this can be helped in a classroom. But we have also learned how potent it can be when it happens spontaneously, as managers reflect on their experience, learn from each other, and together drive improvements in their organization and society. The message of our own experience is that there is nothing so powerful, or so natural, as engaged managers committed to developing themselves and their communities.

THE ARCHITECTURE OF ENGAGEMENT

When we were designing our first program, Nancy Badore, who created a distinguished program of executive development at Ford, was giving us advice. "Henry, how do you plan to seat them?" she asked me at one point. "I don't know; I guess we'll use one of those U-shaped classrooms," I replied. "Not those obstetric stirrups!" Nancy shot back.

That did get us thinking! It brought us to the seating at round tables in a flat classroom, to facilitate discussion, particularly in applying the learning without having to "break out." The key for us has been to use this seating to leverage the experience of the managers. Even just asking for "table questions"—that is, "Take five minutes to come up with a question together"—can enhance the thoughtfulness of a discussion.

These tables become little communities unto themselves, which ensures that the whole classroom is owned by the participating managers, not just the formal "instructors." This seating has worked so well that it has become an intrinsic part of all our programs. And sometimes beyond: A manager who attended one of our programs emailed back with a picture of the round table he installed on the floor of his factory in Mexico City, which "we use . . . very often." (See Figure 13.2 on page 210.)

Of course, some other programs use this seating too. But thanks especially to our colleague Jonathan Gosling at Exeter University in England; we have developed all kinds of related seating configurations for special purposes, as follows. (See Figure 13.3 on page 211.)

Big Circle

Sometimes everyone sits in a big circle, to share insights—for example, in the plenary stage of morning reflections. We have even done so on the floor, for example when Bonner Richie,

(Continued)

(Continued)

storyteller par excellence from Brigham Young University, has worked with our class. Sitting this way reinforces the sense of community in the classroom.

Eavesdropping

Particularly interesting is what we call eavesdropping, where some managers sit with their backs to discussions taking place around the tables. In the ALP, for example, after a company team has introduced its issue to the class, its members spread out to the tables around the room, and sit backward while the managers from the other companies discuss what they have heard, as friendly consultants. Once finished, the company team members reconvene at the front to share in the class what they picked up at the tables, and to consider how they might use this to reframe their issue.

Clamshell

Sometimes we get one set of managers facing another in a kind of clamshell arrangement, while the rest of the class looks on. For example, the managers who have been on a field study to a company in the ALP face the managers of that company, to tell them what they found (such as "You don't need to motivate your first-line employees . . ."), and elicit their reactions. In another adoption of this by a colleague, after eavesdropping discussions at all of the tables of a meeting of four hundred municipality managers, a clamshell was formed at the front, with some of the eavesdroppers facing discussants of some of the tables, to tell them what they heard and then respond to their questions. The result: "It was a great way to turn a large meeting into a series of meaningful conversations."

Fishbowl

Here a small group of managers discuss some issue or topic, sitting in a circle in the middle, while everyone else sits around listening in. One time we had visiting executives from a company, who attended for their teams' final ALP presentation, sit in such a fishbowl and respond to what they heard.

Roll In, Roll Out

A particularly intriguing variation of this last arrangement is when, after awhile, anyone can roll forward his or her chair, tap someone in the fishbowl on the shoulder, and replace that person in the discussion. This can make for much deeper probing. On one occasion, the managers from one ALP team were discussing their company when several other managers in the room, bothered by what they were hearing, rolled forward and replaced them all. They then proceeded to tell them, in a determined yet friendly way, just what they thought about their conclusions!

The Neutral Zone

Recently, at the end of morning reflections in one of our master's programs, someone asked why we could not use eavesdropping during the morning reflections: have one member of each table eavesdrop and these would be the participants reporting out in the plenary.

We noted the idea and went on to the topic of the day: managing retrenchment. Abhirup Chakrabarti of McGill, who was running the session, had polled the class on their experience about this: positive, negative, none. He had decided to create a big clamshell, of the positives facing the negatives, with those of no experience in retrenchment in the middle. But a clamshell of thirty-six people proved unwieldy, so we asked them just to sit at the round tables in those groups and discuss their experience. But what were the ones with no experience to discuss? So we sent to them to the other tables, to eavesdrop.

Each of them did this very seriously, taking profuse notes. And then, instead of putting them at the front, to report out, we sat them in a circle in the middle, in fishbowl fashion, to discuss what they heard.

The class was elated with the experience. One member of what came to be called "The Neutral Zone" reported that, despite their lack of experience on the subject, she and her colleagues probably learned more about retrenchment than anyone else. A manager in the other group said that this was one of the best reporting-out plenaries ever because those doing the talking had no axe to grind, no brilliant experience of their own to boast about.

These are all simple seating ideas that make for interesting learning. They also help to enhance the sense of community, certainly in the classroom, but beyond it too, into their organizations.

Figure 13.1

Figure 13.2

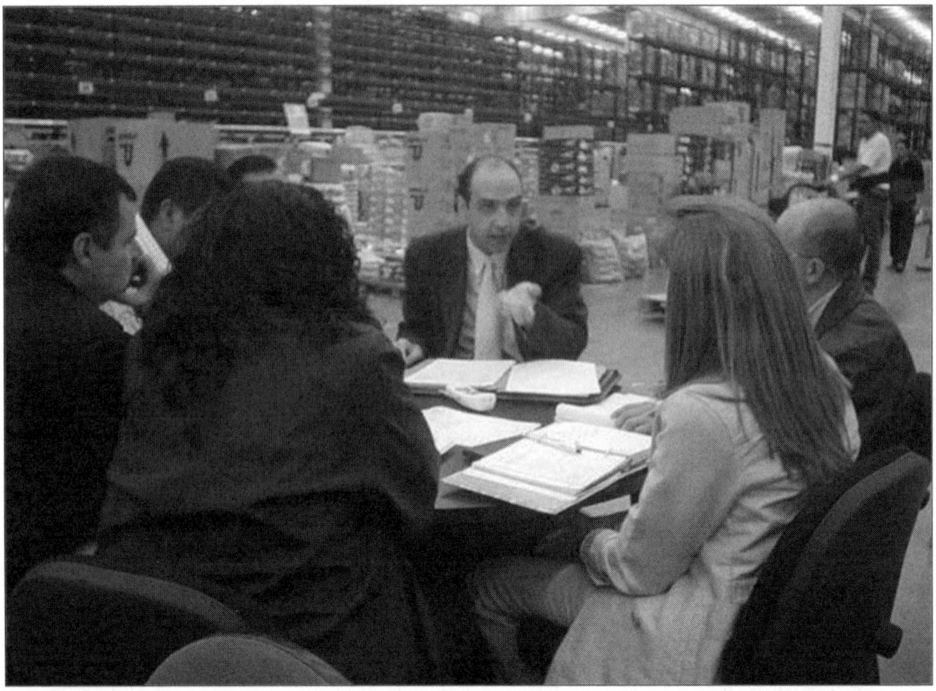

Figure 13.3

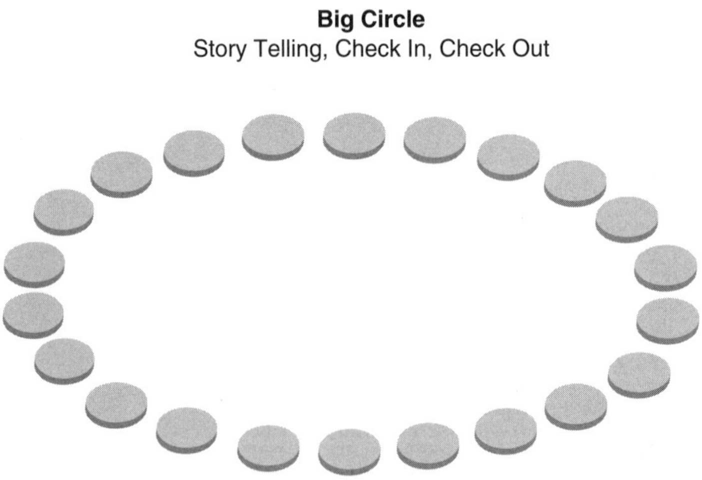

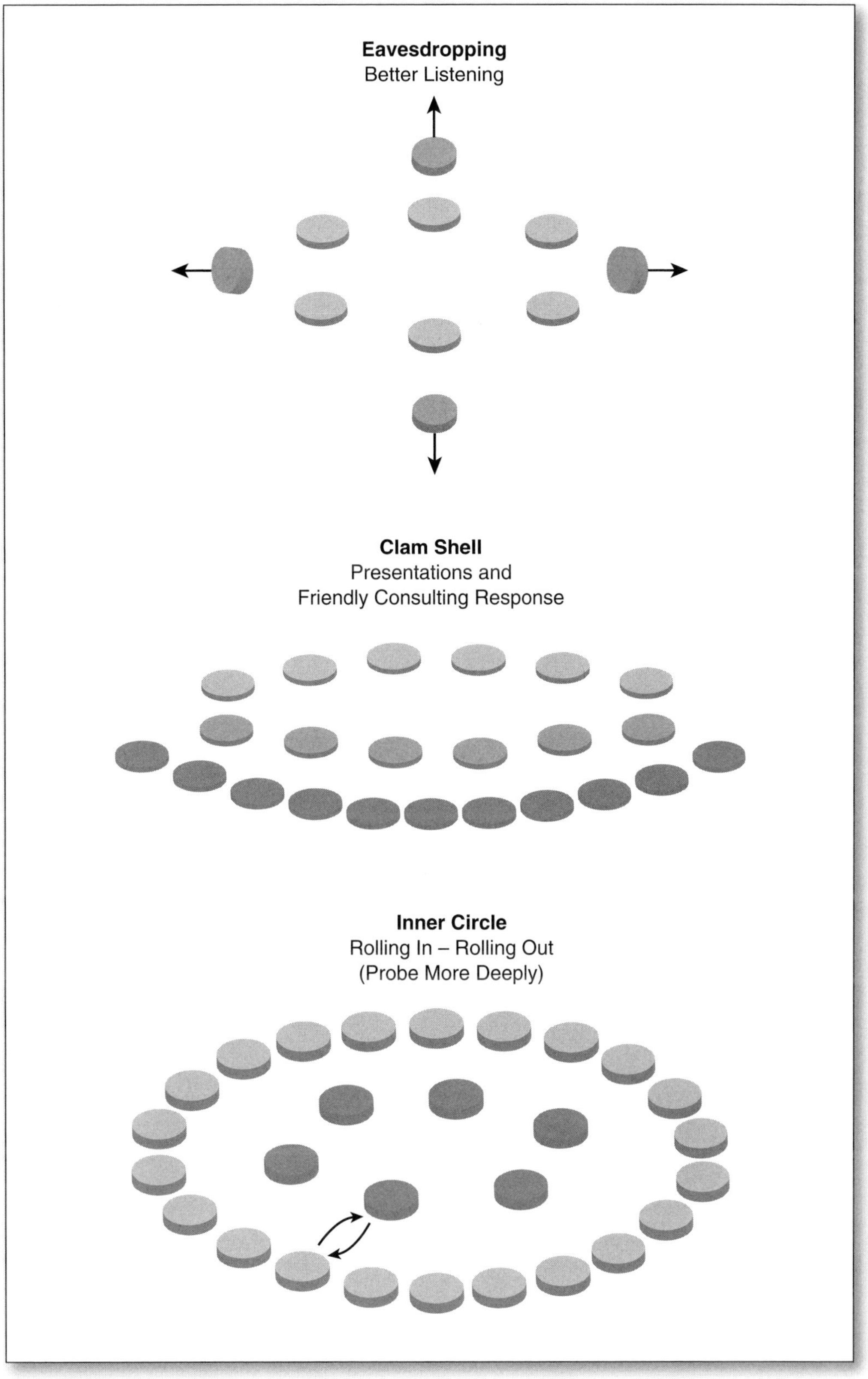
Eavesdropping
Better Listening
Clam Shell
Presentations and
Friendly Consulting Response
Inner Circle
Rolling In – Rolling Out
(Probe More Deeply)

References

Alinsky, S. D. (1971). *Rules for radicals.* New York: Random House.

Mintzberg, H. (2009). Rebuilding companies as communities. *Harvard Business Review, 87* (7/8), 140–143.

Patwell, B., & Seashore, E. (2007). *Triple impact coaching: Use of self in the coaching process.* Victoria, B.C.: Patwell Consulting.

Reingold, J. (2000). You can't create a leader in a classroom. *Fast Company, 40,* 286–294.

14

BEING A LEADER

Mental Strength for Leadership

◆ Louis S. Csoka
Apex Performance, Inc.

As companies face the challenges of global competition, their leadership capabilities have become paramount for success. With leadership high on organizational priorities and companies short on leaders, the selection and development of leaders have become top priorities. This chapter introduces an overlooked approach to business leader development and enhanced leadership effectiveness. Business leader development programs continue to focus on traditional succession planning, education, and on-the-job training of leaders, with an emphasis on traditional functional and management skills. Training is not development, however. Development requires commitment to a long-term process involving allocation of effort and resources. But most of all, leader development needs to focus on the development of the individual leader's capabilities for exceptional leadership under extreme conditions. The world has changed. The old tried and true methods no longer carry the day.

In a highly volatile, uncertain, and ambiguous environment, leaders must arm themselves with certain deep-rooted mental skills that will prepare them to not just survive but thrive in such an environment. Drawing on extensive work and research training elite athletes and soldiers who must reach their peak performance to succeed, I apply these critical lessons to the business domain.Yet the mental skills introduced in this chapter—goal setting, adaptive thinking, stress and energy management, attention control, and imagery—eventually develop into more than just skills. They evolve into deep-seated capabilities that become a part of who an individual is. In other words, mastery of these root skills makes them a permanent part of the full capacity and capability of the leader.

Introduction

Peak performance is about performing at your very best when it matters the most—and it matters the most in critical situations where one action changes everything! In sports we call that momentum. Knowing what that action is and when to do it automatically are keys to exceptional leadership in extreme conditions. As in sports, achieving such heights in leader performance can be learned. Unfortunately, leader development as often taught and practiced today places too much emphasis on knowledge and leader behavior while overlooking a particular suite of mental skills that are critical for attaining peak performance. A key aspect of *being* a leader is developing these mental skills, which I refer to as "root skills," not only to enhance leader performance and effectiveness but also to acquire and apply them as life skills, i.e., they become a part of you. This process will be better understood after the discussion in the section that presents new brain science breakthroughs that are changing how we view who we are.

Leadership education and training today use approaches that seem to be little more than re-naming, re-framing, and re-packaging techniques that are outdated in a rapidly changing world, characterized by increased volatility, uncertainty, complexity, and ambiguity (VUCA). While many of these approaches are essential for learning how to function as an effective leader, they only provide short-term leader effectiveness. Being an exceptional leader comes from within. It comes from confidence and the ability to adapt to rapidly changing circumstances. It derives from thinking effectively under pressure and from having clear focus on the essentials of a task. It is demonstrated to others by clear and effective communications. "Leading from within" is more than knowing and doing things; it requires *being* a leader.

By developing leaders to think more effectively and to control the emotional and physiological responses that can limit cognitive resources available for a task, leaders can bring to bear all the knowledge and professional skills they have acquired. The suite of mental skills and the technology used to assist in their development comprise a methodology developed over 20 years ago at West Point and integrated since then into leader development programs in business, government, military, and sports organizations. West Point decided to invest in a first-of-its-kind Performance Enhancement Center (PEC) and to develop a program that taught and trained future officers a host of mental abilities to enhance their performance and develop their leadership effectiveness. First offered to the Academy's intercollegiate athletes, the program was eventually expanded to include all aspects of cadet performance: academic, military, and leadership. This chapter will develop the theory and methodology behind planting these root skills, but first, a story.

A TALE OF TWO MOMENTS: THE LOCKER ROOM AND THE BOARD ROOM

Army-Navy, 1992. As a West Point football player, this is your ultimate game. It's life or death! It's the fourth quarter with two minutes and 30 seconds remaining. You are the field goal kicker for Army. In the last eight minutes of the game, Army has just delivered a remarkable comeback bringing the score back to within two points from a 14-point deficit, bringing the score to 22-24. The crowd is absolutely wild! Army has the ball, is driving down the field but gets stalled on the 27-yard line with 40 seconds remaining. It is fourth down. A field goal is the only chance to win the game. It is up to you. You have kicked a 44-yarder only once in your entire football career. The ball is snapped, you slowly but assuredly step into the kick. The ball's in the air and it's good! The stadium erupts in wild celebration. Your teammates rush onto the field. You have beaten Navy in the most important moment of your life as a West Point athlete. But wait! There is a flag. Delay of game by Army and a five-yard penalty. Kick it again. But now it is a 49-yarder. You have never even attempted that distance before, let alone make it. The ball is snapped. One more chance. You kick, it is in the air and travels dead center through the uprights, with yards to spare. Army wins 25-24!

Now, imagine yourself as the CEO of a $3 billion company. The company strategy has been to grow through acquisitions. Your M&A team had been working the first big deal for over 10 months to acquire a promising new firm. After long and difficult negotiations, agreement has finally been reached. Now it's just a matter of taking care of the formalities and an important acquisition under your watch can become reality. But wait! There is a call from the other company. Their CEO wants to have a telephone conversation with you, and only you, tomorrow morning, eight o'clock sharp! All of a sudden, the entire deal is in jeopardy and comes down to a telephone call where the outcome is dependent entirely on *your* personal performance in that call. You make the call and you're at your best. The deal is sealed!

Two very different situations; two identical explanations. Both are real. These individuals enhanced their ability to perform at their absolute best under tremendous pressure by engaging in a systematic training program that developed critical mental skills needed for this kind of performance. Such training and preparation for peak performance is readily accepted today in the locker room, but rarely in the boardroom. The preparation and execution described by peak performers are much the same regardless of their profession. The key ingredients are a powerful goal, confidence, calm and composure, razor-sharp focus, and imagination. The performance context does not really matter. As long as the desired outcome is exceptional performance under extreme conditions, the mental strength required is the same.

Theoretical Framework

Much of the mental preparation and training described above comes from the field of sports psychology. It is here that a key set of mental skills has evolved as essential ingredients for achieving exceptional performance at the elite athlete level. The link between mental skills and athletic performance is much easier to measure and thus has a very solid evidence-based history. Its efficacy outside of sport is just now beginning to be documented. For example, a recent study demonstrates the relationship between sport-related psychological skills and soldier physical fitness (Hammermeister, Pickering, McGraw, & Ohlson, 2009).

Knowing who we are as leaders is as important as, if not more important than, whom we lead. Can we really lead others before we have learned to *lead ourselves*? *Leading ourselves* at the most basic level is mastery over what we think, say, and do. After all, these are really the only things a leader can **directly** control. Leaders especially feel the need to exercise control over a myriad of activities, events, and people.

However, in truth, controlling people is a myth. People are free to choose even if the choice is harmful. Witness the countless historical examples of attempts to control people who resisted even to their death. That is not to say that leaders do not exercise influence, but influence and control are distinct. The ultimate goal of leadership is to *influence* people to do to the best of their abilities what is needed; but what is first needed is self-control to enable leaders to be at their best.

A leader development approach overlooked in the literature and in practice focuses on the development of a suite of mental skills that are essential for developing greater self-control and self-regulation, so critical for exceptional performance in extreme conditions. The theoretical framework for such an approach is based on a number of disciplines such as sport and performance psychology, cognitive psychology, kinesiology, counseling psychology, and more recently, neuroscience. These disciplines have generally been combined under the heading of performance enhancement. The model in Figure 14.1 depicts a systematic and integrated approach that was developed for the West Point program and that still serves as the general performance enhancement framework for developing elite performers.

The Problem: Unrelenting Challenges and Impossible Expectations

Each and every day, business leaders face seemingly endless challenges brought on by external forces and events. Unlike athletes, business leaders are "in the game" all the time. There is no clearly defined time frame, no practice period, no off-season. To be successful, both individually and organizationally, they must be at their best each and every day. Consider the following

Figure 14.1 APEX Performance Model

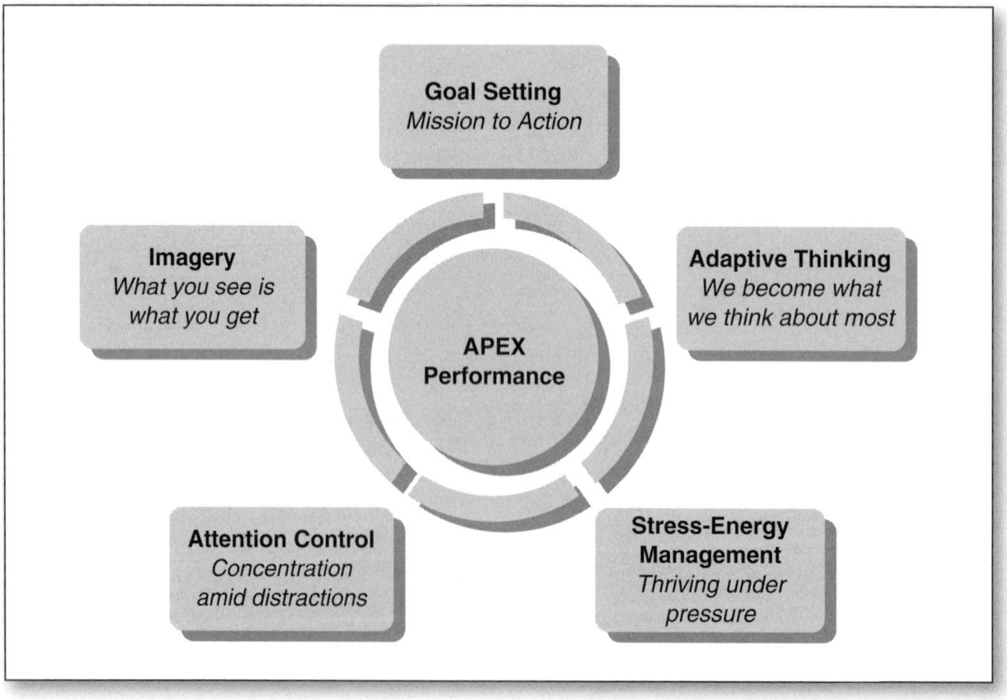

summary of everyday business challenges for today's executive:

Relentless Pressure to Deliver. This intense pressure has become especially challenging with the emphasis on cost cutting and downsizing. Inevitably, these lead to fewer people doing more and often with less. No matter how hard you try, at some point there just is not enough time in the day or the resources to get it done. Over time, this can lead to overload and a sense of feeling overwhelmed.

Rapidly Changing Skill Requirements and Job Assignments. After a company downsizes, survivors typically are asked to engage in many tasks with which they are unfamiliar and for which they have not been trained or prepared. Thrust into such situations, the chances for failure are very high. The learning curve for acquiring skills and tasks that are very different is very sharp. Over time this can lead to a loss of confidence.

Empowerment and Emphasis on Teams. Companies have come to widely adopt the use of teams as a means for increasing efficiency and productivity. However, using teams can lead to unintended consequences. Many people are very comfortable and highly productive as individual contributors, but not so when placed on teams. They find themselves very uncomfortable with the added requirement of being accountable to and responsible for teammates. For the discomforted, the sense of responsibility for the team and the added accountability for others' performance can be a source of stress.

Transformation of Work Through Technology. Technology has transformed the way we live, work, and play. We marvel at what technology has done to enhance our lives. However, with the good have come the bad and the ugly—the emails, the voicemails, the Blackberries, the laptops, the PDAs, etc. In other words, what was supposed to be anywhere, anytime has become everywhere, all the time! Technology has intruded into every aspect of our lives. Given a finite amount of time in the day, we allow the demands on our time from work to creep into our family time, and if our family life is important to us, we push that demand further into our personal time. Eventually we notice that there is little or no personal time. We can lose a sense of our own individuality. Ultimately, this overreliance on technology has contributed significantly to a work-life imbalance.

Discontinuous Change. Change is the constant. It is an overused phrase but nonetheless true. In order to adapt to the world around us and to the daily changes that come about as we grow and develop, we come to expect change and for the most part handle it fairly well. Of course, there are differences in how well we do adapt. In any case, this kind of change, which we call continuous, follows a linear path and is easier to predict and accommodate. There is another kind of change, however, that can disturb and upset the predictability we all seek in life. This is called discontinuous change. It is sudden, unexpected, and unanticipated and catches us by surprise. On a national level, it is the 9/11 attacks and the Katrina storm. In our personal lives, it is the sudden death of a loved one or the unexpected loss of a job. Discontinuous change can create an extended period of loss of direction and purpose, a blurred vision of tomorrow.

The cumulative effect of all of the above can be enormous stress and anxiety. The problem is that these challenges are not going away. In fact, they will continue and become even more pervasive in our lives. When confronted with unmitigated stress driven by such things as productivity demands, work-life imbalance, uncertainty about purpose and direction, etc., we realistically have only three courses of action: (1) we can always opt out of the situation and sometimes we do, (2) we can attempt to eliminate the causes of the stress that most of the time is out of our control or not possible, or (3) we can significantly improve our ability to respond cognitively, emotionally, and physiologically to highly stressful situations. Learning to directly control these responses will significantly impact the level of our performance and eventually our success.

By the way, motivation is not the problem, at least for leaders. An all-too-common practice is to seek out motivational speakers to inspire and fire up the troops. Or employees are provided an assortment of books on motivation. Be wary of books that teach how to motivate people. You can't. Real motivation comes from within. It is something that individuals must develop for themselves. They themselves must find the passion and inspiration for what they do. Highly effective leaders are very good at influencing the likelihood that their followers will find inspiration, drive, and passion to excel. It is certainly part of a leader's job to help them. But ultimately it must come from within. This is why self-awareness, self-control, and self-regulation are so essential in achieving exceptional performance. The suite of mental skills described herein is at the heart of developing that self-awareness, self-control, and self-regulation to help us manage these unrelenting challenges and impossible expectations.

The Solution: Building Leader Capacity

Most business leaders do work hard to learn to adapt and adjust to achieve effectiveness under trying and changing conditions. But in these times of unparalleled global competition, the question has to be asked, "Is being effective good enough?" Without competition, it is. But competition changes everything. Everyone has to perform to the best of their ability. Being effective just won't carry the day for the long haul anymore. Psychologists continually remind us that the human spirit is such that people want to excel. Have you ever met a person who wants to be just ordinary?

As in any training and development process, quality and accurate feedback are essential for learning. Since peak performance mental skills are internal, learning to master them is best achieved with advanced biofeedback and neurofeedback technologies that measure covert activities such as heart rate variability, respiration, blood pressure, brain activity, etc. Once the domain of clinicians and biofeedback therapists, these technologies are now used to provide accurate and measurable feedback as individuals learn to master control over their mental, physiological, and emotional responses to events. Research in performance psychology continues to validate the importance and effectiveness of the mental capabilities depicted in Figure 14.1 above and discussed in more detail below.

GOAL SETTING: EYES ON THE PRIZE

Oliver Wendell Holmes once said, "The greatest thing in this world is not so much where we are, but in what direction we are moving." A journey starts with knowing where you want to end up and then determining how you are going to get there. Identifying a goal is usually not that difficult. Making it happen is. An effective goal setting process becomes a clear and systematic goal **plan** when completed. A key part of any lasting goal setting process is having a "dream," shooting for something that is worth your time and effort, that fuels your passion, makes you jump out of bed in the morning eager to start the day. Much has been written about goal setting techniques, but setting the target and working toward it is not only about having a systematic process but also creating a strong mind set for what one really wants to accomplish.

A highly successful process is a cascading one (see Figure 14.2) wherein an

Figure 14.2 A Systematic Goal Setting Process

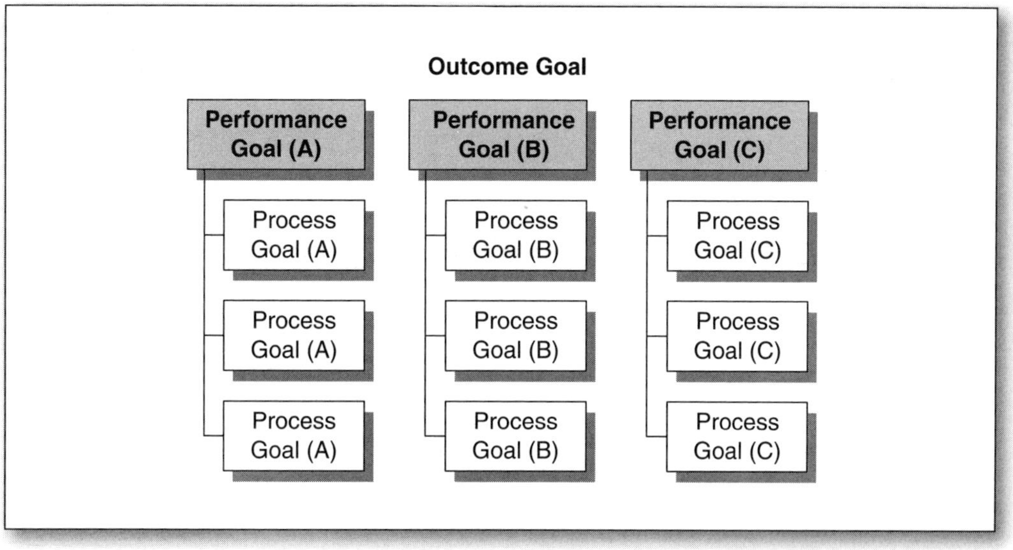

outcome goal is identified, followed by key **performance goals** that are essential for achieving the outcome goal. The performance goals must be actions that are directly in your control. Under each performance goal are listed key **process goals,** which are really enablers. These become your daily "to do list" that keeps you on track with the most important actions that move you toward your performance goals. Think of a ladder. To get to the top, you must step on each rung in succession. Consider the rungs your performance and process goals. The achievement of the goals at each level ensures that the next level will also be achieved. To enable this progression most effectively, you have to choose your performance and process goals wisely.

There is one more step that few, if any, goal-setting processes consider. We need to activate the energy needed to see the goals through to completion. They must be deliberately connected to our daily thoughts and inner conversations. Transforming the process goals, which in their simplest form are actions, into affirmations (positive self-talk statements) connects what we are doing with what we are thinking. By recording these affirmations on a CD and having people listen to them regularly, we mimic the way very young children learn language at home—hearing it repeatedly, creating new neural connections. In other words, we use what we know about the brain's processes for language.

As an example, let us take a business leader who sets as one of her Outcome Goals "to be a highly inspirational leader." In order to accomplish this broad goal, she must set some very specific Performance Goals. She probably can think of a number of them, but it is important to pick the most important ones, those that most directly move her toward her outcome goal. As the saying goes, "if everything is important, nothing is important!" She might choose, for example:

- to develop a clear and compelling vision
- to fully develop my capabilities as a powerful communicator
- to build a highly cohesive and effective team

Let us take one of the above Performance Goals, say "to develop a clear and compelling vision," and develop some Process Goals that would serve as enablers. Process goals might look like the following. (Remember, process goals are stated as affirmations.)

- Using imagery, I develop a clear and vivid picture in my mind of the desired outcome
- I communicate this same picture to my team by telling powerful stories

There will be some others. The same procedure is then followed for the remaining performance goals. It is best to limit both performance and process goals to three or four but certainly no more than five. If you have too many, it will be difficult to stay focused.

Commenting on the goal-setting process he experienced, a CEO of a $3 billion health care company had this to say: "I have done goal setting exercises before. We in business do this all the time. But taking it to the next levels is something I had not done before. The added impact of listening to the goal process I developed brings in another whole dimension. It's like constantly feeding your brain with what you want to accomplish and how you are going to get there. The power of this process is truly remarkable."

ADAPTIVE THINKING: WE BECOME WHAT WE THINK ABOUT MOST

Confidence is a key determinant of success. We see and hear this all the time in sports, but when it comes to business leaders, the traditional view is that confidence is not an issue. Yet our experience in working with business leaders has shown us that confidence can very much be an issue. Confidence comes from within. No one can give it to you. It reflects how you view yourself and your preparation for future challenges.

People carry around images of themselves—of who they are and how they perform. These "pictures" start to form in childhood and are continually created throughout the life cycle, capturing all of our experiences. These experiences reflect both the successes and failures and the manner in which they are interpreted and stored. Much of this self-image is driven by our thoughts (positive and negative) and maintained and reinforced by our self-talk. Cognitive psychologists estimate that we have anywhere from 12,000 to 50,000 thoughts a day and 80 percent of them are negative (Miller, 2003)! Given the basic negativism surrounding our lives, being positive and optimistic and having trust and confidence in one's ability is really hard work.

Martin Seligman, in his 1998 book *Learned Optimism*, writes about the power of optimism over pessimism. He explains how we all develop an explanatory style as a way to explain the cause of events to ourselves (a form of self-talk). Our styles say much about how we will react cognitively and emotionally to an event. The development of our styles comes directly from **how** we think and **what** we think, cemented by the repetition of these patterns of thought over time. Seligman has identified implications of his work and offers practical tools for developing a more positive and optimistic outlook.

Individuals can be trained to shift from negative to positive patterns of thinking and to control self-talk that produces those patterns. Recognizing that people need to take responsibility for their cognitions, systematic training is available that helps them achieve that control. Thought-stopping, cognitive restructuring, and self-regulated positive self-talk are similar techniques used for achieving the desired control over negative, performance-inhibiting thoughts (see Figure 14.3).

The technique is a simple process—concentrating on, stopping, and replacing negative with positive self-talk. Doing is it is harder. It requires becoming very much aware of our daily thoughts and replacing

Figure 14.3 Changing Your Self-Talk

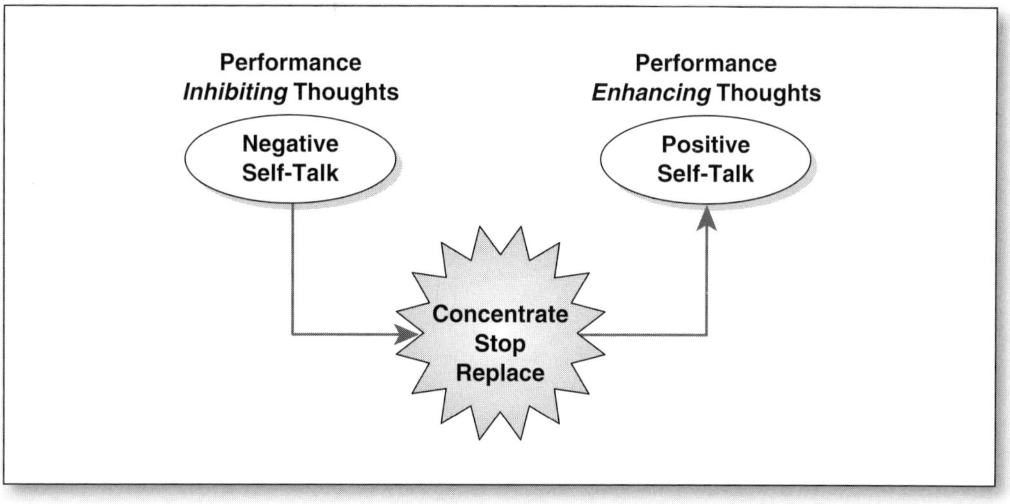

negative ones with positive self-talk affirmations. The key is repetition. The brain learns through repetition, repetition, repetition. Based on recent scientific research on language learning, positive-effective thinking can be systematically developed by creating affirmations (self-talk statements) and then recording them on an individualized CD for repetitive listening. It is an effective tool for transforming negative thoughts to positive ones and moving from a pessimistic to an optimistic mindset. Mastery of this technique can transform a person into a highly effective and adaptive thinker.

STRESS AND ENERGY MANAGEMENT: THRIVING UNDER PRESSURE

Stress and energy go together because the underlying physiological mechanism is arousal. High levels of stress equate to high levels of arousal. Anyone can perform well when everything is going just right. But what about when conditions are unfavorable, when things are going against you, when the pressure is on, when things are not going according to plan? When you become overly aroused and activated mentally, emotionally and physiologically? Who really delivers then? There are performers who actually thrive under these conditions. They welcome the pressure. It drives them. It gives them energy and desire coupled with the ultimate satisfaction of having overcome all odds while doing something exceptional. These are your peak performers. The debilitating effects of stress in business organizations reveal themselves as diminished performance, low morale, and increased health care costs.

As mentioned earlier, one of the major stressors in business is relentless pressure to deliver results through higher and higher levels of performance and ever increasing productivity. Many companies offer stress management seminars in hopes of raising awareness about the effects of stress and providing simple coping mechanisms. However, research on high performance in sports and the military has shown that the ability to handle oneself in high pressure, high arousal situations is less about the stressors and more about the individual's response to them.

The culprit behind these debilitating effects is the well known *fight-or-flight* response. In response to a threat, the autonomic nervous system triggers a flood of adrenaline, epinephrine, and cortisol in order to prepare a human to fight or flee from danger. In pre-historic times, this response was a highly useful survival tool in an era when nearly everything outside the cave was a physical threat. Unfortunately, this same mechanism still exists and is triggered by threats beyond physical ones, as when we worry that the boss is going to fire us because of a mistake we made. When this stress is unrelenting and high arousal continuous, serious consequences arise in the form of health and wellness issues and decreased performance. Learning techniques that counter this mechanism is the primary purpose of any stress and energy management program. The ultimate purpose is to attain the ability to calm and compose oneself in stressful situations, to lower arousal levels.

The solution lies in a more systematic and integrated approach to providing the necessary tools for actually thriving, not just surviving, under pressure. It must combine controlling our thoughts and emotions and learning relaxation techniques that can bring us back to "neutral" in terms of our physiological response to stress. Traditional relaxation exercises help to counter the automatic stress response and bring arousal back to equilibrium. Most common relaxation techniques include:

- The Progressive Muscle Technique. This exercise instructs you to tighten and relax various muscle groups in sequence. By learning the sensation of the muscles tightening, which is one of the elements of the stress response, you learn to recognize and adjust the muscle tension in the moment.
- The Autogenic Technique. Learning to let go is a very powerful tool for regaining control over one's response to stressful situations. This technique directs you to focus on different areas of your body and letting them become "loose and heavy," triggering an overall feeling of relaxation and calm.
- Imagery Techniques. Imagine yourself lying on a sunny beach with the sun warming your body as the ocean waves break with a soothing sound. Or, in your mind, place yourself in a time and place where you felt total calm and peace. Your body will respond accordingly to the imagery. (We will discuss imagery in more detail in a later section.)

To gain the most powerful effects of any learned relaxation techniques, traditional stress management techniques must be integrated with innovative use of biofeedback to develop the ability to control the underlying physiological responses such as heart rate, respiration, blood pressure, muscle tension, and so on. Understanding how stress works from a neurophysiological perspective, having means at your disposal for altering its effects, and receiving quality hi-tech feedback on how you are doing are all powerful tools for learning to not only thrive in pressure situations but also to live your life. The ultimate goal of this kind of training is to reduce overly high levels of arousal, and to be able to remain calm and composed under pressure. You accomplish this goal by having relaxation and control tools at your disposal when you need them the most.

The primary reason for developing techniques that can bring stress responses under control is not to be relaxed but to use that capability to achieve a state of calm and composure that allows you to perform at your best in extreme conditions. Figure 14.4 depicts the relationship between arousal and performance. Reaching peak levels of performance is about achieving an optimal level of arousal and activation (the middle of the curve). Having the tools to move from either end to the middle is what stress and energy management are all about.

For example, if a leader finds herself in a situation where her people are at the lower end of the performance curve, she must find ways to energize, to motivate, to actually increase arousal levels. Athletes

Figure 14.4 The Arousal-Performance Curve (Adapted From Yerkes & Dodson, 1908)

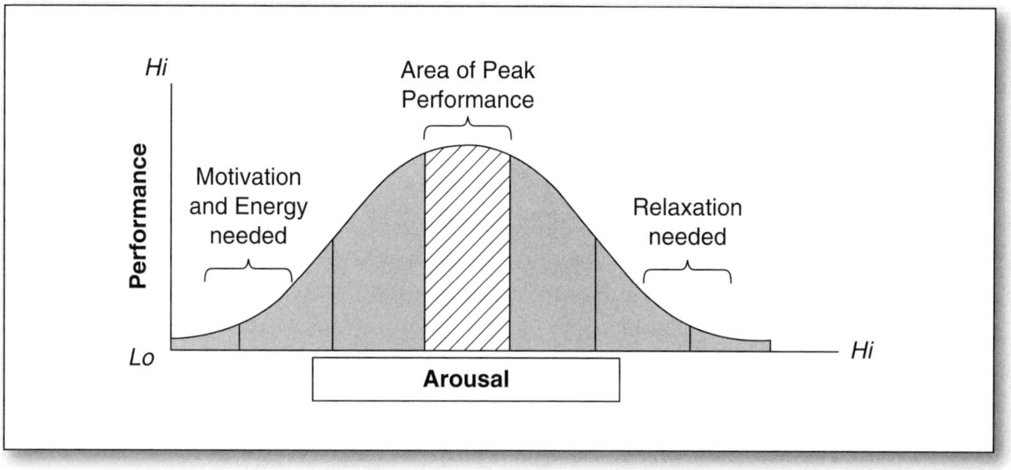

call it "getting pumped up." On the other hand, if another leader finds himself in a situation at the other end of the curve, what is needed is the ability to help his people to become calm and composed, to lower their arousal levels, through various relaxation and self-regulation techniques. The target for highest performance is the middle, the area that is characterized by an optimal level of arousal and energy needed for a given task. What that optimal level is varies from situation to situation. Using a basketball example, the arousal and energy needed for making a free throw is going to be different from that required to come down the court and make a powerful layup. For a leader, the right amount of energy and arousal for a delicate cognitive task will differ from that required in a difficult labor negotiation. Regardless of the performance situation, the task is always to find your way to the middle. Control your arousal and you control your performance.

ATTENTION CONTROL: CONCENTRATION AMID DISTRACTIONS

In their insightful book, *The Attention Economy*, Thomas Davenport and John Beck (2001) discuss how in today's attention economy "the new scarcest resource isn't ideas or talent, but attention itself." The demand for our attention in modern society is unparalleled in both scope and intensity. Yet the way in which we attend to these demands has not significantly changed over time. We still primarily learn to attend to the right things at the right time through trial-and-error and, if fortunate, through good coaching by parents, teachers, coaches, etc. Through this method, we learn what is useful for our attention and what is not as we encounter new situations.

However, given today's stimulus-rich environment, with multiple demands competing for our attention, the traditional ways of learning to attend to them are no longer sufficient. The resultant attention deficit threatens to seriously cripple the workplace. In fact, Davenport and Beck (2001) have coined a new phrase, "Organizational ADD," a condition wherein there is "an increased likelihood for missing key information when making decisions, diminished time for reflection . . . difficulty holding others' attention . . . and decreased ability to focus when necessary" (p. 7).

Business leaders can now take advantage of innovative and scientific approaches to addressing the attention challenge. Attention control training can provide a simple but robust framework for understanding how attention works and a means for navigating that framework. Since attention occurs in the brain, new brain wave (EEG) technology can provide accurate feedback regarding attention, enabling improvement in **how** we pay attention—the key to permanent change in how we focus and concentrate. In a world characterized by volatility, uncertainty, and ambiguity, the **what** of attention becomes very difficult to define. The solution lies in improving our ability to control and direct the attention mechanisms.

One method for providing some sense of control over a given situation is a model that conceptualizes attention as an intersection between two dimensions, width and direction. This produces four quadrants that are labeled: broad-external, broad-internal, narrow-external, narrow-internal (see Figure 14.5). One aspect of attention control training then involves understanding each of the quadrants and learning how to navigate around the model. Answering three questions provides a mechanism for identifying where we should be with respect to our attention—where am I, where should I be, and when and to where do I shift?

Let us take an example of how one might navigate this model to achieve better control of our attention functioning. Imagine yourself going through a decision-making process wherein you have to decide a course of action for developing a new product line. Where do I start? To what do I pay attention? With all the information available and overwhelming you, it is easy to become overwhelmed and confused. This model provides an answer. By controlling your attention, you control your decision. You most likely will start with the **Broad-External** quadrant, attending in the widest possible way to all of the external variables: market, competitors, technology advances, etc. Having completed the assessment, you switch your attention to the **Broad-Internal** quadrant, turning inward and focusing on digesting and analyzing all the information you have gathered in order to select viable courses of action.

The next quadrant is critical but often overlooked by decision makers. **Narrow-Internal** focus requires you to assess your own readiness to act on a selected course of action. Here you might ask yourself questions like "Am I ready to do this?", "Why am I so anxious about what I must do?", or

Figure 14.5 An Attention Model (Adapted From Nideffer & Sharpe, 1978)

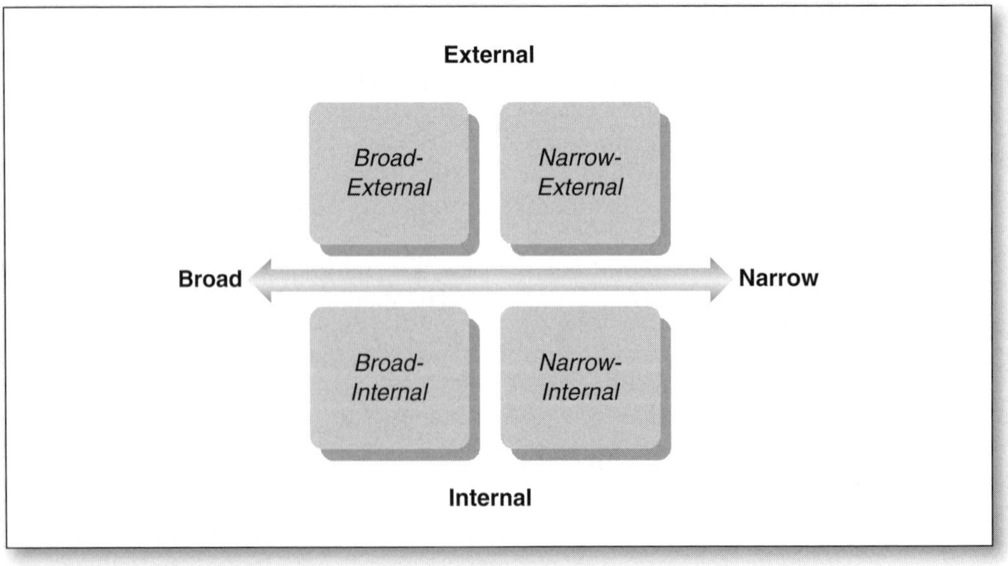

"Am I too biased to see the right course of action?" Once you are satisfied with your own readiness, you move to the last quadrant, **Narrow-External**. In this quadrant all of your attention is focused on the task, the course of action you have selected to take. Nothing else matters at this point. A razor-sharp focus with no distractions is essential for carrying out any worthy action.

As you approach any situation, there will always be one place (quadrant) to start, one place to direct your attention. Remember to ask the three questions with relation to the four quadrants to ensure your attention is at the right place at the right time—where am I, where should I be, and when and to where do I shift?

IMAGERY: WHAT YOU SEE IS WHAT YOU GET

Achieving a challenging goal is to see it already accomplished. Imagery, commonly referred to as visualization, is a powerful tool for doing exactly that. It involves using all the senses to create or re-create an experience in the mind. We all use imagery in one form or another all the time. We differ, however, in our sophistication and effectiveness. Some visualize very effectively with no formal training while others do so only after systematic training and practice. The neurological wiring, however, is in everyone. How well we visualize is a function of our developmental experiences. The early and consistent use of imagination in play and work helps build the brain "muscles" for imaging. Imagery maximizes potential for performance by helping to develop greater confidence, energy, concentration, and feelings of success. The power of imagery comes from the fact that the brain does not differentiate between real and imagined experience. It treats both as if they were real and thus evokes the same emotional and physical responses.

In the 5-Point Apex Performance Model (see Figure 14.1 on page 216), imagery is developed as a specific peak performance mental skill. Starting with simple imagery scripts, the individual mentally pictures the desired performance with all five senses. With sufficient repetitions, the performance is wired into our brain, and we are ready to act out what was wired in. The first step in any mental training program, of course, is to determine how developed an individual's imagery skill really is. We have discovered through biofeedback and neurofeedback instrumentation that high-quality imagery is characterized by a deep physiological and mental coherence coupled with an optimal level of alertness and concentration. The power of imagery comes from the confidence gained by "experiencing" successful performance in the mind before it actually happens. The common description of this experience is "I have been here before."

Imagery has been widely used by elite athletes for many years now. Our soldiers are increasingly using this skill in preparation for action. Business leaders need to follow suit. Let us take, for example, a CEO who is about to meet with his Board to propose a dramatic strategic shift, one he knows will be controversial among Board members. What can he do to prepare, beyond rehearsing the content of his message? He can mentally and emotionally prepare himself by creating an "imagery script," which he will then use to mentally go through the meeting in vivid detail. This script is a written document detailing, in all five senses, what he will do, say, feel, etc., from beginning to end. In his mind he can create alternative possibilities of the meeting's progress and outcome. It is said in the performance psychology field that the only place you can practice perfectly is in the mind. Done correctly, imagery is a powerful tool for enhancing performance.

Conclusion: Extraordinary Leadership Through Mental Skills Development

Achieving sustained high performance in today's competitive and pressure-filled business environment, influenced heavily by organizational and workplace structures, policies, and processes, can be a very daunting task. Traditional emphases on organizational and workplace solutions for meeting the challenges have not produced the desired results in performance improvement and productivity increases. These methods have typically focused on the more peripheral issues and have not addressed the heart of the challenge, which is how to fundamentally change the manner by which people approach their own performance and tap into their full potential. Non-business organizations have experienced significant success in applying performance enhancement techniques to achieve exceptional performance.

The military especially has demonstrated the effectiveness of such programs via the US Military Academy's Center for Enhanced Performance (CEP) and the more recent Army Centers for Enhanced Performance (ACEP). Elite athletes, of course, have demonstrated for decades the relationship between their performance and their mental training and preparation.

It is time for business leaders to recognize that these same mental skills that athletes use to develop themselves in order to reach their full potential are the very same skills that leaders need to develop their full potential as exceptional leaders. In an ever-changing, highly competitive, and uncertain business environment, leaders must sharpen and develop their mental strength and readiness.

Mental strength and readiness are built with the essential mental skills discussed in this chapter. The time has come for business organizations to make leader self-development an imperative for assuming leadership roles within the organization. Leaders must think and act as peak performers in order to be exceptional leaders. Sustaining such high performance levels requires deliberate and systematic training in peak performance mental skills that most directly impact what we think, say, and do. It requires the honesty to admit that growth and development are a continuous process with a willingness to learn and change. If we do what we have always done, we will get what we have always gotten!

Performing at our best when it matters the most requires mental skills that help define a goal and the path to reach it, build confidence and optimism in the face of great challenges, calm the beast within us when under pressure and stress, provide razor-sharp focus amid distractions, and envision success before it happens. Nowhere is this more important than in leadership.

References

Davenport, T. H., & Beck, J. C. (2001). *The attention economy: Understanding the new currency of business.* Boston, MA: Harvard Business School Press.

Hammermeister, J., Pickering, M. A., McGraw, L., & Ohlson, C. (2009). Relationship between sport related psychological skill profiles and soldier physical fitness performance. *Military Psychology, 22,* 399–411.

Nideffer, R. M., & Sharpe, R. (1978). *A.C.T.: Attention control training,* New York: Wyden Books.

Seligman, M. E. P. (1998). *Learned optimism: How to change your mind and your life.* New York: Pocket Books, Simon & Schuster, Inc.

Yerkes, R. M., & Dodson, J. D. (1908). The relation of strength of stimulus to rapidity of habit-formation. *Journal of Comparative Neurology and Psychology, 18,* 459–482.

15

DEVELOPING LEADERS OF CONSEQUENCE[1]

◆ Joseph LeBoeuf, James Emery, Sanyin Siang, and Sim B. Sitkin

Fuqua School of Business

Business education programs have long focused on educating competent business managers, but have only in recent years fully recognized the important role of business schools in preparing MBA students to lead responsibly as well. This chapter describes the approach used by Duke University's Fuqua School of Business to build a behaviorally based, programmatic, "end-to-end" leader development process that integrates all aspects of the students' educational journey. The program is built around three key design principles: a research-based leadership model with 360 feedback processes, an end-to-end perspective built around personal and leader development experiences, and a focused emphasis on integration across all student activities. Through these design principles, Fuqua is distinctively leveraging students' graduate experiences to build a specific leadership identity at the individual and collective level, one we have characterized as "being a leader of consequence."

[1]We would like to thank Claire Preisser and the COLE Leadership Fellows for their help in preparing this chapter.

Leadership is based in behavior. We recognize great leaders not because they know a lot about leadership, or on account of the depth of their character (although both are important), but principally because they *act* in ways that influence others. So, in the teaching of leadership, we believe it is essential to create the conditions for our students to be able to *practice* and, in so doing, develop behaviors essential to effectively lead.

But as any athletic coach will tell you, all practices are not created equal. They must be carefully designed. Three principles, explored in depth in this article, guide the design of the "practice" experiences we craft for students at Duke, as well as our leadership development writ large:

1. Grounding in a research-based leadership model (the "Six Domains" model developed at Duke—see Sitkin, Lind, & Siang, 2006) that gives students a deep theoretical understanding of leadership and, more important, steers them toward building a set of leadership behaviors that can be practiced and learned
2. An "end-to-end" perspective that encourages students to view their MBA training as an integrative leadership development process, and to view their various experiences at Duke as part of that process
3. An emphasis on integration that uses 360 data and other feedback collected by students to drive a shift in identity, both at the individual level, and, in time, at the collective level

These design principles interact and feed into one another, as illustrated in Figure 15.1.

Figure 15.1 Design Principles for Developing Leaders of Consequence

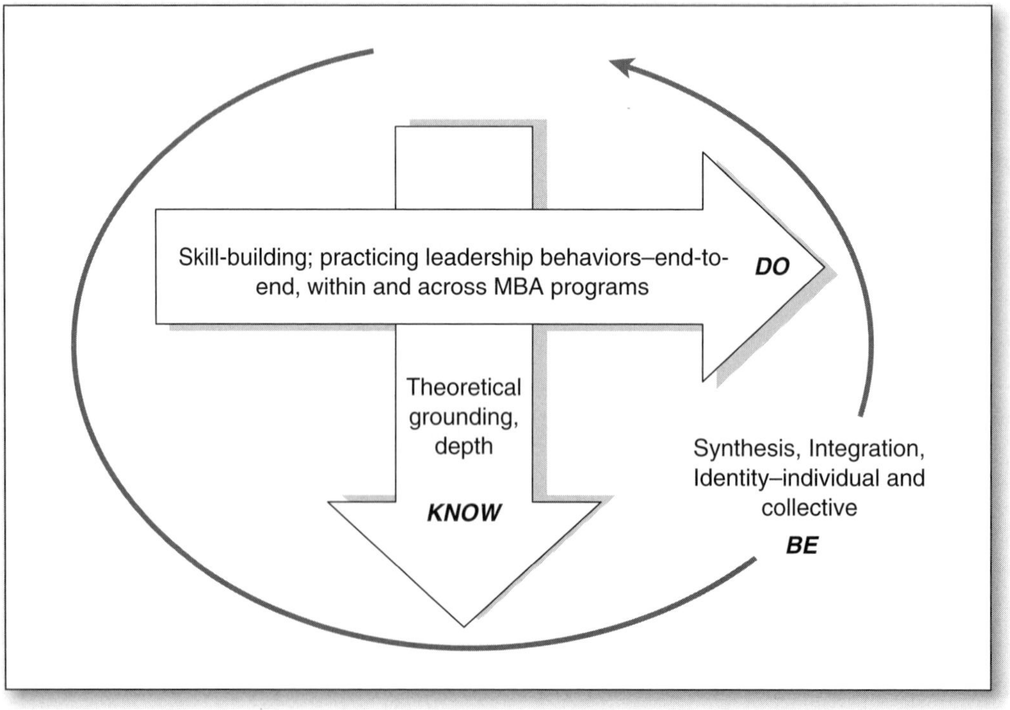

By way of introduction, it might be useful to locate these principles within the two frameworks that help organize this volume: the Be-Know-Do[2] and the Readiness-Experience-Reflection continuum.[3]

At Duke University's Fuqua School of Business, students are exposed to the Six Domains Leadership model (the downward arrow in Figure 15.1) through its Fuqua/Coach K Center on Leadership and Ethics (COLE) that grounds them in leadership theory—*know*—and identifies specific behaviors that comprise effective leadership. The student's time at Duke becomes an intensive developmental process, organized around a set of experiences—*do*—that build these leadership behaviors. These experiences (the horizontal arrow in Figure 15.1) are sequential and progressive and unfold across a student's time at Duke. As students learn more about leadership and themselves, and practice behaviors that support effective leadership, they become—*be*—what we call at Fuqua "leaders of consequence." Further, as students begin to identify individually as leaders, the collective identity of the school begins to shift (the circular arrow in Figure 15.1).

Put another way, theoretical depth, or the downward arrow in Figure 15.1, builds *readiness*. Because the Six Domains model is behaviorally based, it presents students with a way of thinking, systematically and concretely, about leadership, their own development, and the impacts of effective leadership on organizations and society. This theoretical grounding allows students to truly leverage their *experiences*, shown in the horizontal arrow in Figure 15.1. It focuses their attention on building behaviors that most directly contribute to attaining desirable leadership outcomes, such as credibility, trust, and a sense of community. Through peer coaching and 360 feedback exercises, the student's time at Fuqua is also marked by deep *reflection* on one's identity as a leader and the attendant responsibilities. According to JP Hill,[4] "before coming to Fuqua, I simply saw teams in transactional terms; as a means to get work done. But, after experiencing Team Fuqua, initially in ILE I,[5] I have realized the value of teams in promoting a more personal and collective transformational experience." This leader development, on an individual level, also drives a collective, team-based development, which is shifting the culture of the school—building a learning community around leadership, as represented by the circular arrow in Figure 15.1.

Taken together, these principles are recasting our Daytime MBA program, as well as our other offerings, from a process focused on career outcomes that are transactional in nature (What job will I be able to land at graduation? What will my salary be?) to a process focused on development and transformation (Who will I be at

---

[2]The Be-Know-Do framework has been developed by the US Army through the work of LTC Mac Harris, and first appeared in 1983 in FM 22-100, *Military Leadership*, the Army's statement of its leadership doctrine. It has been the organizing framework of the Army's leader and leadership development program for nearly thirty years.

[3]This continuum emerged from the research associated with the Center for Creative Leadership in Greensboro, North Carolina, and is the framework that guided the development and publication of their *Handbook of Leadership Development* (2004). This framework was further leveraged in the re-crafting of the Cadet Leadership development system at the United States Military Academy. This work was led by COL [R] Scott Snook, one of the authors and editors of this book, while he worked for the Superintendant, USMA in the office of strategic plans and policy.

[4]Second-year MBA student leaders, with experience in our program, were asked to comment on the issues discussed in this chapter. Unless otherwise attributed, all quotations cited here were drawn from their individual and focus-group responses. Those quoted had occupied various leadership roles in the school and in student groups.

[5]ILE refers to Integrated Leadership Experience—embedded leader development opportunities in Fuqua's core program.

graduation? What new competencies will I have?), with attention to consequential impact (What difference will I be able to make?). In a recent student focus group, Matt Lehigh remarked that "Fuqua has created a powerful enabling environment which facilitates a more 'mindful' approach to our graduate experience, particularly around our development as leaders of consequence." Since 2008, we've redesigned curriculum throughout our offerings to better provide a supportive programmatic underpinning for students to experience leadership as distinct from management, experience the impact of leadership as being about influence rather than status or formal authority, and use leadership as a lens on the world and one's self.

We can do all of this at Duke, in part, because we have a clear and compelling goal that serves as the anchor for our efforts. We're driven by the notion of developing "Leaders of Consequence," who are "entrepreneurial leaders of exceptional character, ethically grounded and possessed of a global mindset. These leaders will inspire their followers to meet and exceed an organization's goals through actions that are, at one and the same time, highly productive and highly ethical, while continuously serving the best interests of all the organization's stakeholders."[6] Fuqua Dean Blair Sheppard emphasizes that these leaders can manage what appear to be dilemmas. Two of these dilemmas are 1) being an effective team member *and* a leader, and 2) being really, really smart *and* real; understanding what it means to be human in its complete form.[7] We address these dilemmas, particularly through the challenge prescribed by our Integrated Leadership Experiences (ILEs), under the rubric of "Getting Along and Getting It Right." We aim to equip students with the self-knowledge, willingness, and ability to both build strong relationships and, at the same time, hold each other to the highest standards of behavior.

This chapter describes our efforts to produce these consequential leaders and focuses on changes we've implemented since 2008, driven by the three principles above—a theoretical grounding, an end-to-end perspective, and an emphasis on integration. We look principally in this chapter at our Daytime MBA program—but also touch on Duke's Executive MBA programs and even undergraduate offerings.

We believe that the culture has been shifting at Fuqua, and that this shift is in itself a powerful learning experience for students. Fuqua has for many years prided itself on its team-based culture. According to Management Professor Rick Larrick, "we're moving toward a culture that is still based in the team-based character of the school but makes clear the role that leaders play in succeeding through collaboration and taking responsibility for the larger community." Paige Elisha observed that "Fuqua has allowed me to understand the connection between being a leader on a team and being a good team member. Leading for me is no longer only about what I can help others to accomplish as a manager, but it is connected to how I can contribute as a team member." Indeed, there is an element of co-creation in our efforts at Fuqua. As students increasingly conceive of the MBA program as a leadership development opportunity, they are suggesting more and more curricular and infrastructure changes that can stabilize a shift in the school's culture toward one that supports leader and leadership development. We hope, in the

[6]This definition was revised by COLE Leadership Board Member Keith Reinhard (Business for Diplomatic Action and Chairman Emeritus, DBB Worldwide) during an April 2010 visit to the Fuqua School of Business. It has become the current representation of our conception of what it means to BE a leader of consequence.

[7]Source: Summer 2008 interview.

process, that students are not only learning how to thrive in a culture that supports leadership development and learning, but also how to shape and build such an organization. According to Caleb Varner, "Fuqua has created a partnership in that student's feel compelled to contribute to and co-create this powerful learning community." While we have much yet to do in our journey, we hope to usefully share our progress to date with the larger community committed to the development of consequential leaders.

Motivations and Experiments

Designing effective leadership development programs can sometimes feel uncomfortably familiar to Donald Campbell's characterization of designing public policy. In his milestone paper, "Reforms as Experiments," Campbell (1969) observes: "It is one of the most characteristic aspects of the present situation that specific reforms are advocated as though they were certain to be successful" (p. 410). In this paper and later work, he goes on to champion pursuing multiple reform options so as to experiment among them and discover which ones work best.

Of course, at the heart of any experimental design is variation. At Duke, we are fortunate to have four MBA programs. Students in each—the Daytime MBA, the Cross-Continent MBA (CCMBA), the Weekend Executive MBA (WEMBA), and the Global Executive MBA (GEMBA)—are at different points in their careers, in different contexts, and thus have markedly different leadership development needs. We have pursued the opportunity inherent in the challenge of meeting these different groups of students where they are and constructing distinctive approaches for moving them to where they need to be as consequential leaders. An upside to this challenge is that we can use these different programs as venues for different pilots, offering variations from group to group, while still holding true to our intent to produce leaders of consequence.

As we find solutions that work for one group, we can then transfer and translate them for another group, sometimes with modifications. Indeed, there has been a high degree of cross-fertilization in the last three years, in a variety of directions. Deputy Dean and Professor of Marketing Bill Boulding notes that it is important to recognize that

> Students in each of our MBA programs wrestle with different leadership issues depending on the context of their career stages, cultures, and format of the program. As a response, while personal coaching is one of the prescriptions for addressing leadership needs that is seen in both the Daytime MBA and Global Executive MBA programs, how this translates to application in the programs themselves are quite different. In the Daytime MBA program, where we see students in the earlier stages of their career, the coaching focuses on the school team environment (e.g., leading peers, handling team conflict) during the first year of the program and utilizes second-year MBA peer coaches who have received specialized training. In the GEMBA program, where students are already senior executives, the coaches are executive coaches and focus on the current workplace challenges faced by students who are leading entire divisions and are also wrestling with work-life balance issues.

Even as we take different approaches for our full-time and executive MBA audiences, the different leadership development offerings within each are united in important ways.

First, across audiences, we seek to respond to the leadership development needs of today's organizations and societies. One has to read no deeper than the news headlines to see that much of business culture has run off the rails, driven by a relentless pursuit of short-term share price maximization. Public trust and confidence in business as an institution is depressingly low. (Business has ranked near the bottom of most of the Gallup surveys of trust in organizations over the last ten years.) Today's graduating students will set the tone in business and the non-profits and governmental organizations they join. The need for responsible and effective consequential leadership is pressing.

Second, in each program, leadership and management are presented as part and parcel of one another. A long-standing debate within and outside the academy considers the fundamental purpose of business education within the always-changing context of global business. An important thread of this debate weighs the merits of training in management versus training in leadership (Kotter, 2008). Yet, at a practical level, it is widely recognized that the ability to lead, without an attendant ability to manage, can risk diffuse efforts—and even excellent management, without leadership, will inherently be limited in scope. "Leadership, Ethics, and Organizations" (LEO), a required leadership course in our Daytime MBA and two of our Executive MBA programs, explores leadership and management as distinct challenges. Differentiating the two, in the structure of the class and classroom discussions, allows us to treat each as a critically important activity.

Third, and in a similar way, an important aspect of our framing of leadership is to focus on a set of behaviors that are relevant and effective whether or not one is the formal leader of a team. Leadership, as we seek to teach it at Duke, allows one to thrive as a team member *and* a team leader. In team-based projects in the MBA course "Management Communications," students rotate through positions of team member and team leader. In both cases, students must exercise leadership without formal authority. Students then receive structured feedback from their teammates on their performance in each role through several feedback mechanisms created in the course. All this occurs under the careful supervision of Fuqua faculty and the COLE Leadership Fellows (CLFs).

Finally, our leadership development efforts rest on an assumption that our students are also developing two critical competencies: technical excellence and global awareness, both important attributes of effective, consequential leadership. Leaders do what they do in a complex, rapidly changing, and multi-dimensional world. This point of view has resulted in several systematic changes in our Executive MBA programs, designed to enhance our students' personal and contextual leader-development experience. In both our Cross-Continent and Global Executive MBA programs, students take two core courses that span multiple terms and are focused on the role of global markets and institutions, and the important nuances of leading within and across cultures and civilizations. In these courses, which are held mainly outside the United States many assignments take the student out of the class and directly into the cultural context for meaningful developmental experiences, focused on increasing their personal leadership through enhanced self-awareness and to better demonstrate how context, region-specific institutions, markets, cultures, and civilizations shape the manner of business discourse and international commerce, and shape the demands placed upon leaders and managers of consequence.

Three Design Principles

As an educational institution, we have abundant opportunities to help our students develop—in class (with traditional case studies, video case studies, small group projects) and out of class (with extracurricular offerings). Students have a breadth and depth of experiences. But do we know how students make sense of these experiences? Who will help them do this? How many students have a given experience, yet miss the meaning? How much of a student's time at Fuqua is focused on completing requirements and moving on to the next one, without making sense of what one is learning, particularly as a consequential leader?

We attempt to answer these questions in light of the three themes that run throughout our leadership development efforts (theoretical grounding, end-to-end development, and an emphasis on integration).

GROUNDING IN A BEHAVIORALLY BASED MODEL

The Be-Know-Do framework is inherently iterative and all of our leadership and personal development is (happily) a lifelong process. Still, we must both "start somewhere" and "keep going," preferably in a somewhat structured process. In our leadership development offerings at Fuqua, we start with our Six Domains framework.

As the very existence of this volume makes clear, the field of leadership does not suffer from a lack of theory or compelling ideas. But given its nascence, students of leadership are sometimes susceptible to a "pick your own guru" phenomenon that can limit their view of leadership and their efforts to learn how to be more influential.

The Six Domains framework integrates extant theory and, because it is behaviorally based, reveals a path to students seeking to become better leaders. The framework was developed by reviewing the social science research literature published in organizational behavior, as well as psychology, sociology, and political science, and centered on topics such as trust, fairness, and control—even more than on leadership itself. From this research effort, six distinct clusters of leadership behaviors emerged, each with its own distinct effect on followers (Sitkin, Lind, & Siang, 2006).

These six domains—personal leadership, relational leadership, contextual leadership, inspirational leadership, supportive leadership, and responsible leadership—together create a comprehensive and dynamic model of leadership activities, as illustrated in Figure 15.2. In the "knowing" sense, the model helps students understand how leadership works and builds awareness of how they can grow as leaders, through the practice of specific behaviors—the "doing" sense.

The model promotes "readiness" in students by incorporating not only the intellectual aspects of leadership but also the emotional and reflective aspects that shape individual leaders, their relationship with others, and their ties to a larger community. This allows the model to guide students and professionals across multiple levels. On an individual level, students explore their own leadership potential. On a team level, they reflect on interpersonal relationships among team members and team leaders (for example, their skill in developing emotional connections with others and their willingness to both support and challenge others as needed). On an organizational level, students come to see a leader's responsibilities for conveying a coherent sense of the situation, clarifying personal and collective goals, and forging a shared sense of community.

The Six Domains model supports "readiness" in another way: it does not challenge students to discard how they think about leaders and leadership—though it certainly challenges students to think about them more systematically, expansively, and deeply. Because the model integrates a variety of theories and research traditions, most people recognize their own favored theory of leadership within the model and also can put it into a broader context. Students can build on what they already understand about leadership and what they already know about

Figure 15.2 The Six Domains of Leadership Model

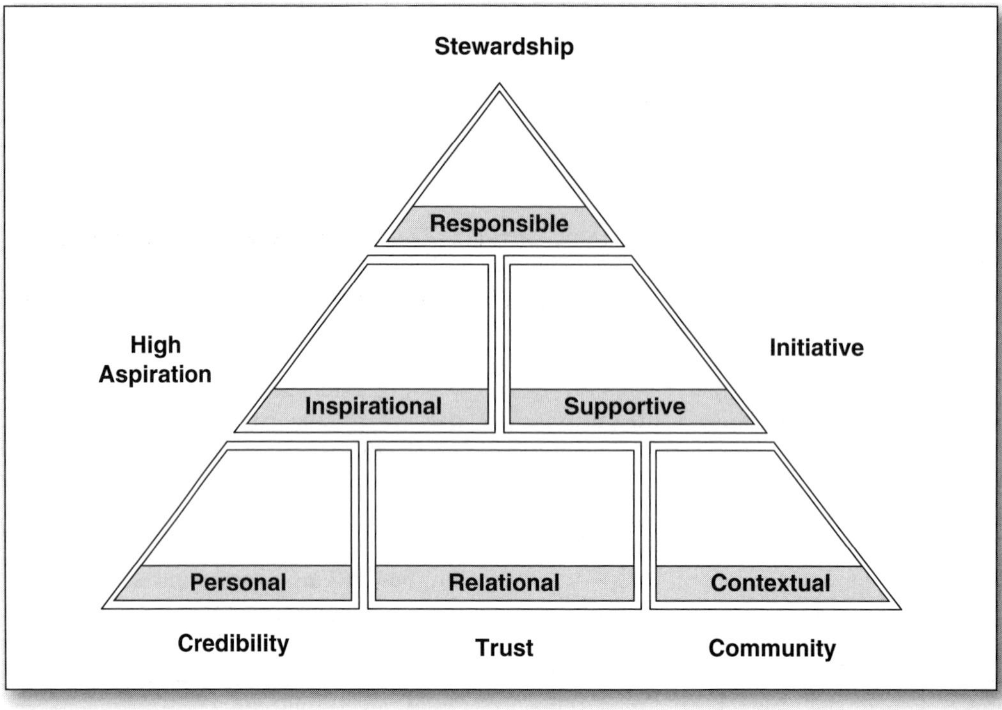

themselves as leaders. And because the model is grounded in the actual behavior of leaders, it motivates students and gives them an "on-ramp" for practicing these behaviors.

We "read" the Six Domains model, in a sense, from left to right and bottom to top (see Figure 15.2). And so the first domain is what we call *personal* leadership. This domain translates into behaviors that give followers a deep sense that the leader is personally capable of leading, is authentic, and is dedicated to the team. As with each domain in the model, this domain flows naturally to the next, *relational* leadership, which is comprised of behaviors that build trust and shows the followers they are understood, respected, and cared about. Next, good *contextual* leaders provide a sensemaking function that enables coherence and coordination, fosters a sense of identity at both the individual and collective levels, and helps harness this sense of identity for the good of the team and its goals.

Inspirational leadership is not about charisma or charm—rather, it is about behaviors that help create raised aspirations in others by providing a motivating vision and communicating optimism about the ability to achieve it. The neighbor of inspirational leadership in the model is *supportive* leadership, which concerns a leader's role in providing the necessary support (e.g., resources, funds, protection, and critical feedback) for effective action by followers. *Responsible* leaders balance needs in the long and short term and across constituencies, "leading by example" as they consider and balance corporate profits with what is good for the team, organization, and larger society.

In leadership development, in academic or practitioner-oriented settings, a question inevitably comes to us: Can leadership really be taught? Put another way, and in an MBA context, how does the concept of "readiness" relate to recruiting for our MBA classes? We believe that leaders can be made and whatever inherent leadership qualities exist can be maximized effectively through learning and practice. Hence, the Six Domains model is not only a theoretically grounded framework, but it is also oriented toward learning. It ties each domain to a specific set of learnable behaviors and thus gives direction to students who wish to build leadership capacity. We make each leadership behavior concrete through videos, 360 feedback/coaching, exercises, and tools—such as implementation checklists, card decks that focus on specific behaviors, and diagnostic action guides. These all help translate key leadership concepts into easily enacted and concrete behaviors.

Let's use the domain of personal leadership as an exemplar. Personal leadership is about projecting to followers who the leader is as a person and as capable of assuming the leadership role. What this means is that the leader must be perceived as having relevant competencies such as the **vision** to lead, and must be viewed by others as **authentic** and **dedicated** to the team. Each bolded concept is associated with specific and learnable leader behaviors. To project vision, for example, a leader must demonstrate mindfulness, curiosity, and confidence. Here, we use clips of Martin Luther King Jr.'s 1963 "I Have a Dream" speech as a basis for small group exercises in which the students identify the relevant leader actions and the resulting outcomes, and then reflect on examples from their own experiences that illustrate the application of these behaviors in their own leadership or that of others.

As we'll see in the next section, the Six Domains model also serves to organize a series of reflective practices for students that help tie together their practice of leadership behavior, inside and outside the classroom, across their time at Duke.

END-TO-END PERSPECTIVE AND EXPERIENCES

We challenge our students through experiences that encourage them to develop a new, enriched sense of the world. We leverage the recognition that "experiences that generate tension, disequilibrium, and even pain set the conditions for growth because they force us out of our comfort zone" (LeBoeuf, 2006, p. 42; Sitkin, 1992). Once unfrozen, students are motivated to experiment with new ways of being.

We've probably all had experiences that were incredibly powerful in the moment, yet faded when we were faced with, for example, our email inbox. And so at Fuqua, we're trying to build a developmental "highway" through the MBA curriculum—a series of sequential, progressive, and powerful developmental experiences intentionally linked one to the next. The highway is designed to guide students toward a sense of intention, ownership, and some measure of accountability with respect to their development as leaders while at Duke, a "nudge" (Thaler & Sunstein, 2008) that helps them move toward enhanced leadership. When students are intentional and feel ownership for their own development, their time with us takes on a different character: It is more of a trajectory, and less of a series of boxes to check. They experience what is happening as something they do for themselves, and not something imposed upon them. Brian Alvo suggested, "the introduction of the PDP[8], and embedding the COLE Fellows in first year team development in a core course experience, has created a journey of development and reflection that has inspired in the program an increased motivation for personal growth and enhanced self-awareness."

In this section, we will illustrate the end-to-end perspective by looking at our Daytime MBA program and our COLE

[8] PDP refers to Personal Develop Plan.

Fellowship program, which is an exemplar and incubator for our leadership development innovations.[9]

If the end-to-end perspective is a highway, our Daytime MBA students are required to stop at important markers. The most visible are two Integrated Leadership Experiences sessions (ILE I & II and a proposed ILE III) that are for-credit leadership immersions that last three or four days at the beginning of an MBA's first and second years. These immersions are designed to push students outside their comfort zones—whether by getting through a ropes course, taking on an unfamiliar role in a team (rotating leadership roles is again required), or practicing what we call courageous communication with a teammate.

Some elements of the ILEs stand out. In ILE I, which occurs at the beginning of the first year experience, students participate in several core activities that initiate their leadership development journey, particularly in a team context. In their First-Year Teams, students spend a day with Triangle Training, an experiential education camp, participating in a high ropes team building experience. They follow this experience with a Habitat for Humanity opportunity to further their team building process, but in the context of contributing to the local community. Finally, during ILE I, the first-year students experience a three-hour Improvisational Leadership session, getting outside their comfort zones as leaders, learning a "YES . . . AND" methodology designed to facilitate the Getting Along and Getting It Right theme associated with the developmental experience here at Fuqua. In other words, they learn that building a strong team culture and a commitment to task excellence are both critical parts of effective leadership.

In ILE II, students participate in "Leader's Court," a mock court case, where the MBA class as a whole is "tried" on three counts[10]. These counts are based on research we do with the class and can vary by class. The following counts were associated with ILE II, 2010:

- **Count One:** Creating an environment in Fuqua that champions courage (e.g., difficult conversations, dealing with conflict, providing feedback, enforcing the honor code) and candor, and facilitates the development of individual leadership, and the building of an effective community of learners and leaders.
- **Count Two:** Courageously integrating and leveraging the multi-national nature and rich diversity of the Fuqua community to fully enhance the individual and collective learning and leadership developmental experience, creating a culture of ethics and development.
- **Count Three:** Courageously applying "Team Fuqua" (both in and outside of Fuqua) to create teams and a learning environment that hold each other to high standards and accountability for both individual development and team performance, as opposed to just getting along, avoiding conflict and disagreement, getting good grades, and just getting by.

After the trial, in which students act as jury and render judgment on themselves, students create a "Marketplace of Ideas," where they put forth recommendations to improve their class performance in respect to the "charges." Sample recommendations have included (1) a public commitment to the school's honor code through an oath ceremony, and a signed, publicly

[9]We operationalize the End-to-End perspective differently in our Executive MBA programs, where we take more of a "bookends" approach, with opening and closing required courses on leadership. The same faculty member teaches both the opening and closing courses, allowing for continuity.

[10]The counts we used are framed in positive terms, although the "prosecution" side has to defend the negative while traditional court "counts" are framed negatively, we have found students respond more reflectively to positively-framed counts, so we have continued to use this format.

displayed document to make the honor code more visible and central to the student experience and (2) a "brand check" mechanism—where students can "call" each other on behaviors that they feel are counter to the mission to develop leaders of consequence (e.g., being late to class or checking a Blackberry during a team presentation). All recommendations that emerge from the "Marketplace of Ideas" are formally presented to Fuqua's Dean for review and discussion at the end of the ILE II experience. The student leadership then accepts responsibility for the planning and implementation of the recommendations.

As introduced above, another important theme of ILE II, "Getting Along and Getting It Right," examines tensions that are built into Fuqua's conception of leadership, creating the dilemmas mentioned earlier: how to be a leader *and* a member of a team, and how to be humble *and* ambitious. The first has particular currency at Fuqua, a school that prides itself on being team-oriented. With a team orientation so deeply embedded in the school's culture, "leadership" was initially viewed with a degree of suspicion and counter to Fuqua's core value of teamwork. Historically, for Fuqua students, being a good team member meant placing a priority on being "nice" and working to maintain team harmony rather than stepping up and leading. In ILE II (and other places), we give students an understanding of the interdependence associated with teaming and practice in supporting one another while also giving difficult feedback and holding each other accountable for team-based outcomes. This has taken hold and Fuqua students now view leading and teaming through an "and" lens rather than an "either/or" lens. ILE II sets the stage for the student's second year experience, encouraging them to leverage this year for transformation, both to improve their own leadership development but also to improve Fuqua and the developmental culture we are trying to construct.

If ILE I and II are markers on the leadership development highway, the Six Domains Leadership Survey (SDLS)[11] is a student's dashboard, and the Personal Development Plan (PDP) is their navigation system. As a COLE Fellow responsible for helping implement the PDP process for the school, Jen Bosl enthusiastically commented that "one of the most powerful leadership development experiences associated with the PDP was the ability to get 360 feedback that forced me to deliberately think about my leadership skill set." The SDLS, which is required for first-year students in ILE I (and has been both required and optional for second-year students in ILE II) is a starting point for students in thinking about their own leadership development goals. The SDLS is based in the Six Domains Leadership Model, and gives a 360 snapshot of how others—peers/colleagues, subordinates, and supervisors—rate a student's behavior in each area. In the required "Management Communication" class, SDLS results are an important input as students develop their own plan for their development during their time at Duke. Because the SDLS is grounded in both the research framework and the behaviors used in other parts of the program, these assessments help to tie together all the elements of the MBA program in a way that is simultaneously comprehensive and also very easy to remember and use.

Peter Drucker, in his classic essay "Managing Oneself," throws down a gauntlet: that today's "knowledge workers must, effectively, be their own chief executive officers" (Drucker, 2005, p. 100), charting their own career trajectory and learning to develop themselves (Hill & Wetlauf, 1998). It is in this spirit that our PDP process unfolds at Fuqua. In a robust

[11]Delta Leadership, Inc., a company built around the Six Domain Framework, has been instrumental in making the SDLS 360 feedback tool available to all Fuqua students, both in our Day program and Executive programs, as an important input into their personal developmental planning process, and as on-going feedback for their developmental progress.

process, students first explore their values and beliefs, then examine strengths and weaknesses, especially in light of the 360 data they've collected, and then create a set of challenging, measurable personal development goals to guide their Fuqua journey in an intentional manner.

The PDP process helps reframe graduate school: from something done to a student to an intentional, self-driven experience. According to Management Professor Rick Larrick, "we've seen a shift in recent surveys of Fuqua students towards a belief that most fellow students act on the basis of intrinsic rather than extrinsic motives." In the PDP process, we explicitly talk about graduate school as a twenty-one-month gift that the students give themselves. The PDP, which students complete for credit at the outset of their first year and revise at the outset of their second, is a structured way of thinking about how they will use this gift. It is the map for the student's know-do-be journey at Fuqua, taking them from what they *know* about themselves and about leadership, giving them a concrete way to think about what activities they will *do* and what behaviors they want to practice while at Fuqua, and providing a structure for reflection on who they want to *be* when they leave. Jen Bosl continued her commentary about the value of the PDP by observing that "the PDP is a great example of effective signage on the highway of intentional leadership development. It is structured to 'nudge' us to think about short and long term goals along a number of very consequential dimensions with regular check-ins and a process for structured feedback. For some, the PDP was a great way to stay on track and intentionally grow with high-impact. Others, who saw the PDP as just another requirement, did not get as much out of the process."

And so, the end-to-end perspective in our Daytime MBA connects coursework such as LEO and Management Communications with intensive leadership development experiences such as ILE I and ILE II. The reflective processes, the PDP, SDLS, and many opportunities for peer coaching, are designed to move students, in some intentional and integrated way, toward becoming a leader of consequence. Taken together, the coursework, ILEs, PDP, and SDLS create a baseline leader development experience for all our students, the minimum essential components for moving toward Fuqua's brand enabled destination—Leaders of Consequence. In addition, Fuqua has created opportunities for students who want to go beyond the baseline and engage in more advanced leadership development (e.g., leadership roles in the student government, the MBA Association, and in the many clubs that the school supports).

One advanced leadership development experience is the COLE Fellowship, which is an exemplar of our leadership development approach. Each year, about one-quarter of the Daytime MBA class of about 440 will apply to become COLE Leadership Fellows (CLFs); thirty-six will be accepted. The Fellowship is an intensive leadership development experience. In addition to taking part in the baseline leadership development that has been described thus far, Fellows have extra opportunities: they coach and mentor first-year teams, they interact in dedicated sessions with local and alumni leaders, and they participate in a powerful two-day team-building experience, which includes a day-long leadership challenge, focused on enabling the Fellows to effectively come to get together as a team and learn about effective team development.

The COLE Fellowship is not only the apex of our leadership development work—it is also an incubator where we can pilot new coursework or exercises for students. We've very intentionally used the experience of the COLE Fellows as a wedge to shift the experience for all students at Fuqua. For example, before committing to the large scale application of the SDLS and the PDP with the student body as a whole, these processes were tested in the Fellowship during the summer internship experiences. Any issues with the process were corrected, and then these activities have now become embedded developmental experiences for all Fuqua Daytime MBA students.

A current example of such piloting is a reflection component around a student's summer internship. As we're writing this chapter, we are planning to more intentionally link the summer internship and the PDP process. This year, for the first time, students will revise their PDPs at the end of their first year, to better leverage their summer developmental experience. They will also incorporate a summer reflection into their PDP revision in the fall of their second year. The COLE Fellows have taken this route and have reported it to be very effective in framing their internship as a developmental experience, instead of (solely) a job search opportunity. This past summer, COLE Fellows also served as peer mentors to one another throughout the summer. This is another practice that will be incorporated into the Fuqua experience for all students.

AN EMPHASIS ON INTEGRATION

But what does this all add up to? How do students make sense of what they learn (know) about leadership and the experiences that they have (do) during the MBA? In other words, who do they become (be), and how does development at the individual level spur and feed the creation of a culture of development?

While answering these questions is difficult at best, there are several things we do that we know have a positive impact on identity development at the individual (student) level. The PDP process, for example, requires that students take an intentional approach to their development. Graduate school is a hard, consuming experience that can easily overwhelm even the most organized students. The PDP process asks students to articulate, among other things, who they want to be at graduation. Raising the question of identity, at the very outset of the MBA process, helps frame the discrete experiences that make up MBA life—coursework, ILEs, team-based projects, extra-curricular activities, and summer internships—as experiences that will contribute to a shift in identity. Liz Liedel observed that "the PDP has created a community of personal development at Fuqua, and has facilitated the generation of accountability and making development a more fundamental aspect of a journey to becoming a leader of consequence, the Fuqua student identity."

Coaching and mentoring are another critical support to a real shift of identity at the individual level. Although the SDLS and PDP are in a real sense intensely personal and individual, much of these processes unfold in a team-based environment. Leadership, after all, is inherently a team-based experience. In our Daytime MBA, first-year students are organized into teams of five or six, with attention to diversity of professional and personal backgrounds, and complete many team-based projects as part of their coursework. A COLE Fellow is matched to each team and is responsible for helping the team develop a charter, facilitating the team-building process, helping resolve conflict, leading after-action reviews, and orchestrating the team's requirements to provide feedback to each other as part of the PDP process.

This coaching and mentoring is important in another way: Working with the first-year teams and with individual team members, COLE Fellows are provided a very challenging and developmental experience as facilitators and coaches. They learn how to effectively diagnose team dynamics, engage in building the conditions for high performance, develop skills in conflict resolution and having difficult conversations, and learn to coach and mentor individual first-years in maximizing their experience for personal and professional development. This particular aspect of the COLE Fellows' responsibilities has become the signature element of the Fellowship and is the most personally developmental opportunity they experience in their year-long journey as Fellows. Meleata Pinto reflected on this experience by noting that "the PDP creates a process of self-awareness and development that forces us out of an operating mode, just getting 'stuff' done, into an improving mode focused on the real work of becoming a better person, and a better leader."

In our Global Executive MBA leadership course, meanwhile, our students receive individual executive coaching support to help them make sense of their SDLS 360 feedback, their course experiences, and to help in the development and implementation of their Personal Development Plan. Much like the intent behind the PDP processing in the day program, but tailored to meet the needs of these more senior executives, who are in a different place in their developmental needs.

But just as the data obtained from the SDLS supports individual development, so too can it support our evolution as an institution. We've already seen, in our discussion of ILE II and the "Marketplace of Ideas," how students shape their experience at Fuqua through their recommendations for educational, developmental, and institutional changes. These recommendations have contributed to a change in the culture of the school, particularly as one characterized by leadership development. According to Paige Elisha, "Fuqua is a student-driven community. The culture and the institution promote and demand student leadership in every avenue. From club leadership to initiative creation, to welcoming and integrating the next year's class, students take the lead in planning and execution. This becomes a virtuous cycle: as first years see the hard work and dedication put forth by the second year class, they become more invested in leading and giving back, and they follow that example."

RESEARCH ON IMPACT

In keeping with our approach in leveraging experiments to grow our leadership development efforts, we are conducting a longitudinal study, based in 360 feedback data, that will help us get at questions important for our future offerings at Duke—and perhaps help other educators shed light on their own leadership development efforts. Among these are (a) Which experiences, curricular and extra-curricular, contribute to development? (b) How do individual differences in students affect skill development? and (c) What factors (e.g., campus culture) play an important role?

At the MBA level, upwards of 90 percent of students give us permission to use their SDLS for research purposes and to help us answer important questions such as: What are patterns in feedback and how do they relate to program design? With data, we can better determine whether a given activity, topic, or exercise moves our students toward becoming leaders of consequence. These answers then contribute to helping us make modifications to our experiments in all our programs, and our effort to continuously be moving forward in our developmental mindset.

And much more is possible. At our undergraduate level, we've piloted a modified version of the SDLS survey (adapted for undergraduate students, who do not have the degree of workplace experience that is embedded in some questions). We're now planning to use this research instrument in a larger, longer longitudinal study that pairs the modified SDLS with surveys looking at educational experiences and the campus climate. Taken together, data from these surveys can help us, over time, assess, understand, and ultimately influence five factors that predict leadership skill development, as illustrated in Figure 15.3.

Figure 15.3 Model of Leadership Skill Development

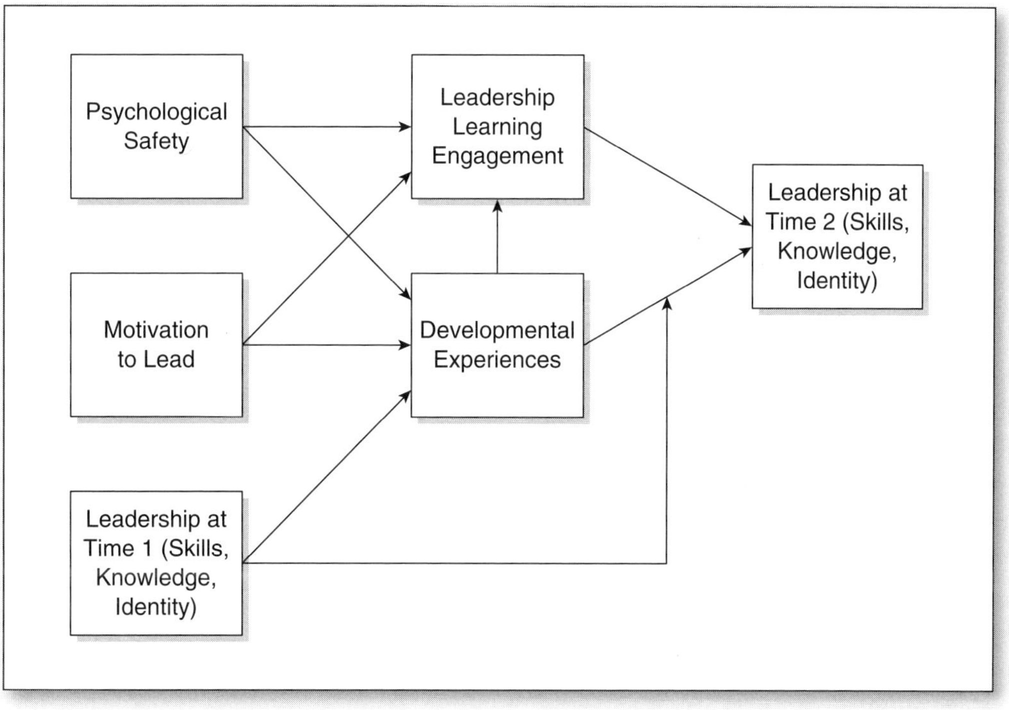

Conclusions

In a real sense, we've attempted in this chapter to answer just one question: What is it that we do at Duke's Fuqua School of Business that is distinctive and attempts to create the conditions that enable the "product" of Leaders of Consequence? In the United States, surveys examining the quality of leadership across sectors, paralleling those on trust in institutions, show "a startling 80 percent of the American people believe there is a leadership crisis in this country" (Gergen & Zelleke, 2008, p. 1). The need for leaders of character, courage, and integrity is striking.

At Fuqua, we've attempted since 2004 to put an infrastructure in place in our MBA programs that combines a deep theoretical grounding in leadership knowledge with an emphasis on the MBA experience as a venue for practicing leadership behaviors. We've tried to tie together discrete leadership development experiences that students may have across their time with us, through the use of a common leadership framework and a combination of sequentially structured, integrative processes. Finally, we've attempted to create conditions such that these sequential experiences are not only connected but add up to something: that the MBA experience, as a whole, helps students conceive of themselves as leaders of consequence and of their MBA experience as both educational and developmental. As this last piece falls more and more into place, students themselves then begin to shift the culture of the school.

We have anecdotal evidence that Fuqua is beginning to attract students on the basis of its emphasis on leadership. Abbey Blume described her process. "While the reasons people choose to go to business school vary, I fell into the camp of people who make the choice to attend graduate school to become a better self and leader. During my search for the right school, I visited many great programs, but Fuqua stood out because of the amazing leadership development opportunities available as embedded programs in the design of the curriculum. I knew that Duke was a place where I could feel comfortable exploring my capabilities while at the same time challenging myself to grow as a leader." While we have a long way to go to fully realize our ambitious goals, a change in the type of student Fuqua is attracting suggests we have made good progress along that path. As Liz Riley-Hargrove, Fuqua's Associate Dean for Admissions, suggests "that we are seeing an increase among applicants who are not only interested in honing their team skills, but in developing and refining their leadership ability. Fuqua's emphasis on both dimensions resonates with prospective students who want more than just the credential and a better employment opportunity."

In an educational environment, all these infrastructure changes raise a very standard issue of push versus pull. As educators, we are accustomed to and comfortable with a model where we deliver what we know (push). And yet, perhaps especially in the realm of leadership, this model may only be partially adequate. Students, in the optimal scenario, will begin to practice leadership in their own classrooms and institutions, voicing the need for new or different content in coursework or experiences at the institutional level (pull). Perhaps in the realm of leadership, we sometimes need to trust that they can co-create the consequences we are striving for, thus allowing both the educators and students to simultaneously lead each other in an inspiring and developmental partnership.

References

Campbell, D. T. (1969). Reforms as experiments. *American Psychologist, 24,* 409–429.

Drucker, P. (2005). Managing oneself. *Harvard Business Review,* January, 100–109.

Gergen, D., & Zelleke, A. (2008, October 22). America's other deficit: Leadership. *Christian Science Monitor*, 1–2.

Hill, L., & Wetlaufer, S. (1998). Leadership when there is no one to ask: An interview with Eni's Franco Bernabe. *Harvard Business Review, 76*(4), 81–94.

Kotter, J. (2008). What leaders really do. In J. Gallos (Ed.), *Business leadership* (pp. 5–15). San Francisco, CA: John Wiley & Sons.

LeBoeuf, J. (1999). The building blocks of leadership development. In F. Hesselbein & P. Cohen (Eds.), *Leader to leader: Enduring insights on leadership from the Drucker Foundation's award-winning journal* (pp. 40–46). San Francisco, CA: Jossey-Bass.

McCauley, C., & Van Velsor, E. (Eds.) (2004). *Handbook of leadership development* (2nd ed.). San Francisco, CA: Jossey-Bass.

Sitkin, S., Lind, A., & Siang, S. (2006). The six domains of leadership. *Leader to Leader* (pp. 27–33). San Francisco, CA: Jossey-Bass.

Sitkin, S. B. (1992). The strategy of small losses: Learning from failure. *Research in Organizational Behavior, 14,* 231–266.

Thaler, R. H., & Sunstein, C. R. (2008). *Nudge: Improving decisions about health, wealth, and happiness.* New Haven, CT: Yale University Press.

US Army, FM 22-100, *Military leadership.* US Government Printing Office, October 1983.

SECTION III

BEING

16

CREATING LEADERS

An Ontological/Phenomenological Model[*]

◆ Werner H. Erhard
Independent

◆ Michael C. Jensen
Harvard Business School

◆ Kari L. Granger
Sunergos LLC and
Center for Character and Leadership Development,
United States Air Force Academy

[*]Because this research project is ongoing, further developments will be contained in updated versions of this paper downloadable at http://ssrn.com/abstract=1681682.

Acknowledgments: We thank Professors Ron Heifetz and Warren Bennis for their generosity in sharing not only their time with us, but their leadership insights and wisdom as well. Steve Zaffron, CEO of Vanto Group, is a co-author of our leadership program. Some of the material in this program is derived from the programs of Landmark Education, LLC. We also thank Miriam Diesendruck, Sandra Carr, Michael E. Zimmerman, Chip Souba, Jeri Echeverria, Joe DiMaggio, Gonneke Spits, and Matthew Granger for their support in this effort. We thank the Harvard Business School Division of Research for financial support for Jensen. The authors are responsible for all errors or incompletions in this work.

The sole objective of our ontological approach to creating leaders is to leave students actually being leaders and exercising leadership effectively as their *natural self-expression*. By "natural self-expression," we mean a way of being and acting in any leadership situation that is a spontaneous and intuitive effective response to what one is dealing with.

In creating leaders we employ the *ontological* discipline ("science of being"; see Heidegger [1927]). The ontological model of leader and leadership opens up and reveals the *actual nature* of being when one is being a leader and opens up and reveals the *source* of one's actions when exercising leadership. And ontology's associated phenomenological methodology (explained in the next paragraph) provides *actionable access* to what has been opened up.

The *being* of being a leader and the *actions* of the effective exercise of leadership can be accessed, researched, and taught either (1) as being and action are observed and commented on "from the stands," specifically as these are *observed by someone, and then described, interpreted, and explained* (third-person theory of) or (2) as being and action are actually experienced "on the court," specifically as these are *actually lived* (real-time first-person experience of). As a formal discipline, the "on the court" method of accessing *being* and *action* (that is, as being and action are actually lived) is named *phenomenology*. In short, an epistemological mastery of a subject leaves one *knowing*. An ontological mastery of a subject leaves one *being*.

Of course students do not need to study ontology or phenomenology; they only require the *access* to *being* and the *source* of *action* (provided by ontology), and the *actionable pathway* to *being a leader* and the *actions of effective leadership* as these are lived (provided by the phenomenological methodology).

❖❖❖

Introduction

Because this chapter is about *creating* leaders rather than teaching *about* leadership, the approach and language will be unfamiliar to and in fact challenging for many readers. In the eight years that we used our classroom as a laboratory for developing a course that would actually create leaders, we found that *creating* leaders requires the use of models, methodologies, and techniques that are different from those generally employed in business schools to teach business and management.

It is inescapable that, if one is successful at creating leaders, one has left students actually *being* leaders. We found the discipline of ontology (the study and science of *being*) to be the appropriate discipline for accomplishing this task. And, the *effective exercise of leadership* is the inescapable result of actually being a leader.

However, when a person is "on-the-court" engaged real-time in the exercise of leadership, it is for that person a first-person experience, an "as lived" phenomenon. We found the discipline of phenomenology, the methodology for *accessing* first-person, as-lived, real-time phenomena, to be uniquely powerful in providing actionable access to the effective exercise of leadership as it exists on the court. We believe that this unique approach—the ontological model with its methodology of phenomenology—will create a new science of leadership by enabling scholars to access, study, research, and teach the phenomena of being a leader and the effective exercise of leadership as these are actually lived and experienced (as first-person phenomena).

We started this project with nothing more than a commitment for students to leave the course we would create actually being leaders. As experienced educators, our backgrounds variously include expertise and practice in economics, finance, management, applied philosophy, entrepreneurship, management consulting, behavioral science and organizational psychology, military officer training and on the ground battlefield leadership experience, along with being avid students of neuroscience. Nevertheless, we did our best to put aside everything we thought we knew about what leader and leadership* are or how they should be taught. We started with empty minds, simply committed to standing in *wonder* in the face of the challenge of actually creating leaders.[1] We used our classroom as our laboratory to experiment with what it takes to create leaders.

Being a Leader and the Effective Exercise of Leadership as One's Natural Self-Expression

The sole objective of this ontological approach to creating leaders is to leave students who complete a course designed to create leaders actually being leaders and exercising leadership effectively as their *natural self-expression*. In other words, the exercise of creating a leader is complete when being a leader and exercising leadership effectively has become that student's natural self-expression. By "natural self-expression" as used in the previous sentences, we mean a way of being and acting in any leadership situation that is a spontaneous and intuitive effective response to what one is dealing with.

The Ontological Model

We employ the ontological model (from the Latin *ontologia* "science of being"[2]) in creating leaders because of its unique power to reveal (open up) the *nature* of being when one is being a leader and to reveal (open up) the *source* of one's actions when exercising leadership.[3]

While ontology as a general subject is concerned with the nature and function of *being* of anything, here we are concerned with the ontology of human beings—the nature and function of *being* for human beings. Specifically we are concerned with the ontology of leader and leadership (the nature and function of *being* when being a leader and the source of *action* in the exercise of leadership). Who one is *being* in a leadership situation shapes and colors one's perceptions, emotions, creative imagination, thinking, planning, and one's actions in the exercise of leadership.

The Access Provided by the Phenomenological Method

Leader and leadership can be taught employing either of two possible methods for providing students with *access* to what it is to be a leader and what it is to exercise leadership effectively. The *being* of being a leader and the *actions* of the effective exercise of leadership can be accessed and taught either (1) "as being and action are lived and experienced *on the court*" or (2) "as being and action are observed and commented on *from the stands*." Specifically, "from the stands" is to access, research, and teach what it is to be a leader and what it is to exercise leadership effectively as these are *observed by someone, and then described, interpreted,* and *explained* (third-person theory of). By contrast, "on the court" is to access, research, and teach what it is to be a leader and what it is to exercise leadership effectively as these are *actually lived* (first-person experience of).

As a formal discipline, the "as lived" (as experienced) method of accessing *being* and *action* is named *phenomenology*.[4]

*When we use the phrase "leader and leadership," "leader" should be understood as "being a leader," and "leadership" should be understood as "the exercise of leadership."

> The discipline of phenomenology may be defined initially as the study of structures of experience, or consciousness. Literally, phenomenology is the study of 'phenomena': appearances of things, or things as they appear in our experience, or the ways we experience things, thus the meanings things have in our experience. (Smith 2009)

In short, phenomenology is a discipline that provides *actionable access* to being and action as an "as lived" first-person experience. As Martin Heidegger (1927) said regarding accessing *being*, "Ontology is possible only as phenomenology" (p. 33).

In summary, the ontological model of leader and leadership opens up and reveals the actual *nature of being* when one is being a leader and the *source of one's actions* in the exercise of leadership, and the phenomenological methodology provides *actionable access* to what has been opened up. The ontological model with its methodology of phenomenology provides scholars with the opportunity to access, study, research, and teach the phenomena of being a leader and the effective exercise of leadership as first-person phenomena—that is, as these are actually lived and experienced.

Of course the students themselves do not need to study ontology; they only require the access to *being* and the access to *action* that is provided by the ontological perspective. And, they don't need to study phenomenology; they only need to be provided with the *actionable pathway* to the being of being a leader and the actions of effective leadership made available by the phenomenological methodology.

Two Approaches to Accessing, Researching, and Teaching Leader and Leadership

Eight years ago, starting with nothing more than a commitment to *leave students being leaders and exercising leadership effectively as their natural self-expression*, we began to design and teach an annual course, which course served as our experimental laboratory to discover an approach that would fulfill that commitment. The course, taught for the first five years at the University of Rochester, Simon School of Business, each year included 70 to 115 undergraduates, graduate students, faculty, administrators, alumni, and business executives and consultants.[5] We found the course to be effective with each of these categories of participants. We have also taught the course to a group of more than 200 consultants from more than 60 firms who now offer the course to their clients; and in 2008 and 2009, Kari Granger successfully taught the course to military service members at the United States Air Force Academy where it continues to be taught by other faculty members.

In our laboratory classrooms, faced with designing a course that would actually create leaders, we experimented with both the theoretical (from the stands) and the phenomenological (on the court) approaches. Drawing on our team's experience and our experiments with methods of providing an actionable pathway to actually being a leader, we concluded that studying leaders (characteristics, styles, cognitive processing, and values, etc.) and their exercise of leadership (general principles, rules or algorithms for action, and situational awareness, etc.) leaves students knowing *about* what it is to be a leader and what it is to exercise leadership effectively. Yet, students being able to speak cogently about leader and leadership, and even with the ability to explain the style or characteristic, the principles and actions, and so forth that made or would have made this or that leader effective in this or that case, does not reliably leave students being leaders as their natural self-expression.

Given that when a person is actually being a leader and actually engaged in the exercise of leadership it is for that person a first-person experience, an "as lived" real-time phenomenon, we found the phenomenological methodology (the "on the court" perspective) uniquely powerful in providing an actionable pathway to being a leader and exercising leadership effectively *as one's natural self-expression.*

In short, an epistemological mastery of a subject leaves one *knowing*. An ontological mastery of a subject leaves one *being*. (Of course when one *is* a leader, then "knowledge is power.")

As an illustration of just how radical this course approach is, consider the following: If one were satisfied only when students are actually left being leaders and exercising leadership effectively, and if in a course on leadership nothing were said about leader and leadership (while this would probably be impossible), but students completed the course actually being leaders and exercising leadership effectively as their natural self-expression, that would fulfill the *raison d'être* of such a course.

One's Way of Being and Acting Are in-a-Dance-With (Mutually Arising With) the "Occurring"

For a simple everyday example of the difference in access provided by the theoretical-epistemological methodology (from the stands) and the ontological-phenomenological methodology (on the court): When we hammer a nail (an example Heidegger also used) we don't do it from some *theory* about hammering, where a hammer is composed of a lever and mallet, and the lever functions to multiply the force at the mallet head and so forth. The *theory* of hammering a nail, which can be reduced to a mathematical formula, is nowhere present for one in the *act* of hammering. Rather we hammer the nail *as lived*. That is, in the presence of our intention to have the nail go into the wood, our *actions* in hammering are "in-a-dance-with" the way the hammer and nail *occurs* for us. (Note that our coined phrase "in-a-dance-with" is used as a verb [as in "dancing"], and we mean by it, "is naturally, necessarily closely connected with, mutually arising": a specific kind of correlation.[6]) Or said rigorously, hammering as it is actually lived happens as: *the way the hammer and nail occurs for us in order to make the nail go into the wood* in-a-dance-with (correlated with) *the action appropriate to that occurring*—all as a unity for us.

In fact, any theory or knowledge about hammering or even trying to recall what someone showed you about hammering, if present in the act of hammering, will get in the way of the act of hammering. Think about trying to drive your car safely in traffic while trying to remember and then apply what someone showed you, or thinking about how much you need to turn the steering wheel or when to put your foot on the brake.

In Any Leadership Situation One's Way of Being and Acting Is in-a-Dance-With (a Correlate of, Mutually Arising With) the Way in Which That Situation Occurs for One

As with the example of hammering, regarding leader and leadership the *theoretical* methodology provides an *understanding* of the constitutive elements and an *explanation* of the way they work with respect to one's being a leader and one's actions in the exercise of leadership; whereas the *phenomenological* methodology provides *actionable access* to the being of being a leader and to the actions of the effective exercise of leadership *as these are actually lived.*

In other words, a person's *way of being and acting* in response to any leadership situation is analogous to the example of hammering. That is, if one examines from the as-it-is-lived perspective a person's way of being and acting in any leadership situation, one finds that that person's way of being and acting is in-a-dance-with (correlated with) the way in which that situation occurs (shows up) for that person.[7] While perhaps obvious in the matter of hammering, this is likely to be somewhat difficult to accept in the matter of a person's way of being and acting in a leadership situation.

The proposition that a person's way of being (mental and emotional state, bodily sensations, and thoughts and thought processes) *does not cause* a person's actions, but rather that a person's actions are *in-a-dance-with* (a correlate of) the way in which what they are dealing with occurs for them (their perception of it), may at first seem counter-intuitive. It seems counter-intuitive because a person's *actions* have traditionally been explained as being *caused* by some combination of the person's mental/emotional state (including memory), personality traits, body sensations, and their thoughts and thought processes (or as we have termed it, their "way of being").

However, neuroscience has established that neural patterns of perception (phenomenologically speaking, the way something occurs to a person) and the neural patterns that give rise to a person's way of being and acting are virtually always, as neuroscientists term it, "networked" together in the brain. Specifically, the neural patterns that give rise to a person's *way of being* are networked together with neural patterns of perception (including stored neural perception patterns—memory); and likewise the neural patterns that give rise to *action* are also networked with those neural patterns of perception.

As Clancey (1993) concludes, "Perceiving, thinking, and moving always occur together as coherent coordinations of activity" (p. 5), and Hawkins and Blakeslee (2004) conclude in their book *On Intelligence,* "perception and behavior are almost one in the same" (p. 157). And in contrast to the idea that thoughts are the cause of action, Libet (1993), in his book *Neurophysiology of Consciousness*, summarizes his and others' research findings as follows: "the brain 'decides' to initiate or, at least, to prepare to initiate the acts before there is any reportable subjective awareness that such a decision has taken place" (p. 276).

Saying the foregoing from an ontological/phenomenological perspective, one's way of being and acting arise *as one system*, and they do so as an *in-a-dance-with* correlate of (from a neuroscience perspective, networked together with) the way in which what one is dealing with occurs for one. That one's *way of being and acting,* and the way in which what one is dealing with *occurs* for one, are actually "lived as" (experienced as) a unity is critical to accessing the power of the ontological/phenomenological perspective on leader and leadership.

The Way in Which a Leadership Situation Occurs for a Person (the "Occurring") Is the Access to Being a Leader and Exercising Leadership Effectively as One's Natural Self-Expression

For purposes of the following discussion, a "leadership situation" could be defined simply as a situation in which the current circumstances, and the possible futures (outcomes) that can be realized in the prevailing context for those circumstances, are unacceptable or non-optimal.

As we said above, a person's *way of being and acting* in any leadership situation is in-a-dance-with (correlated with, networked with, mutually arising with) the way in which the situation they are dealing with *occurs* for them. Therefore, for a person to be a leader and to exercise leadership effectively, the situation they are dealing with must *occur* for them (show up for them) such that their naturally *correlated* way of being and acting is that of actually being a leader and exercising leadership effectively. Given that in any leadership situation a person's way of being and acting is a correlate of the way the situation occurs for them, *the way in which the situation occurs for them* is the actionable access to the being of being a leader and the actions of the effective exercise of leadership *as their natural self-expression.*

And put simply, the actionable access to the way in which a leadership situation occurs for a person is the *context* that person brings to or creates for leadership situations.

The Context Is Decisive

In general, the context a person has for what they are dealing with shapes and colors the way in which what they are dealing with occurs for them. Specifically, the way in which a leadership situation *occurs* for a person (with which their way of being and acting in that situation is correlated) is shaped and colored by their *context for what it is to be a leader and what it is to exercise leadership effectively.*

A person's context for what it is to be a leader and what it is to exercise leadership effectively is made up of their worldview as it relates to leader and leadership, and more directly their specific frames of reference for leader and leadership. It is as though the context for leader and leadership that a person brings to a leadership situation creates a kind of "clearing" in which that situation shows up for them, and that clearing shapes and colors the way in which that situation *occurs* for that person. Specifically, that clearing determines the way in which the circumstances they are confronted with occur or show up for them, and what they can see of possible futures (outcomes) that can be realized in those circumstances. And that person's way of being and acting in that situation will be naturally correlated with that occurring.

Given that one's context for leader and leadership determines the way in which a leadership situation occurs for a person and as a result their correlated way of being and acting, we utilize what Jack Mezirow (2000) terms "transformational learning" to provide students first with an opportunity to examine and eliminate the grip of their everyday common-sense worldview and their existing frames of reference (received ideas, beliefs, and taken-for-granted assumptions) relative to leader and leadership. We then provide students with an opportunity to create for themselves a context for leader and leadership that shapes and colors any leadership situation they deal with, such that their natural self-expression (their naturally correlated way of being and acting) in dealing with that situation *is* one of being a leader and exercising leadership effectively.

The Content of This Course Creates a Context for Leader and Leadership

Employing the insights provided by the ontological model and the phenomenological methodology, the *content* of the course for creating leaders (covered in the following section) creates a *context* for leader and leadership that once mastered shapes and colors any leadership situation such that the students' naturally correlated way of being and acting (their natural self-expression) is reliably that of being leaders and exercising leadership effectively.

What follows in the next section is an outline/description of the three-part underlying theory of the course we created from the ontological/phenomenological discipline. We employ this perspective because of its power to provide students with an as-lived, first-person experience that leaves students "being used by" the context for leader and leadership that is created in the course. The outline also illustrates how the course unfolds for students. We have adapted this section directly from the pre-course reading assignments used for the Texas A&M University, Mays School of Business course taught in June 2010.

Every participant is required to complete extensive pre-course reading assignments before arriving at the first session of the course. We have edited the material somewhat to fit our use here; however, we have left it in the language used with the students so the reader can get an unfiltered impression of how the course is communicated to the students (who, in the case of the Mays School of Business course, included 110 undergraduate and graduate students, faculty and administrators, military service members, CEOs, and consultants). The pre-course reading assignments for the most recently delivered course and the links to download them are given in Appendix 16.1. The rest of the materials for the course are downloadable from SSRN (740+ pages) at http://ssrn.com/abstract=1263835.

Course Outline/Description Excerpted From the Pre-Course Reading

THE FUNDAMENTAL THEORY UNDERLYING THIS COURSE: BEING A LEADER AND THE EFFECTIVE EXERCISE OF LEADERSHIP

This course is designed to give you access to creating for yourself a *context* for leader and leadership that once mastered has the power to leave you in any leadership situation being a leader and exercising leadership effectively as your natural self-expression. As has been said: "The context is decisive." We call the kind of context that has the power to leave you with the *being* and *actions* of effective leadership *as your natural self-expression* "a context that *uses* you."

When a context uses you, there is nothing to remember and no rules to apply. Rather, when "what it is to be a leader and what it is to exercise leadership effectively" exists as *a context that uses you*, that context shapes and colors any leadership situation such that your naturally correlated way of being and acting is that of being a leader and exercising leadership effectively—that is, it is your natural self-expression. When you have learned something, that is, when you have an epistemological grasp of it, appropriately you remember what you learned and apply it. However, there can be a point where what you have been trying to learn actually becomes a part of you—or saying this in another way, *instead of you using what you have learned, it has become for you "second nature," it so to speak uses you*—this is mastery. For example, great martial artists, skateboarders, and dancers all experience this, not to mention great physicists and great teachers. While what it means for a context to use you may not be entirely clear for you at this point, the methodology we will employ in the work we do together during the course will provide an opportunity for you to create for yourself what it is to be a leader and what it is to exercise leadership effectively as a context that uses you.

You will create this new kind of context for yourself by mastering (1) the three Foundational Factors of leader and leadership and (2) the four distinct aspects of the Contextual Framework for being a leader and for the exercise of leadership—and you will do so as they are actually lived (first-person experience of). When (1) the Foundation and (2) the Contextual Framework come together as a whole for you, they create a context that has the power in any leadership situation to shape and color the way the circumstances you are dealing with occur for you such that your naturally correlated way of *being* and *acting* is that of being a leader and exercising leadership effectively.

THE UNDERLYING THEORY OF THIS COURSE: PART I

The Three Foundational Factors on Which Being a Leader and the Effective Exercise of Leadership Are Built

1. Integrity:
    - Without being a man or woman of integrity you can forget about being a leader. And, being a person of integrity is a never-ending endeavor. Being a person of

integrity is a mountain with no top—you have to learn to love the climb.

- Integrity leaves you whole and complete as a person. It is achieved by "honoring" your word when you will not be keeping your word (as we define "honoring" your word). Integrity creates workability and develops trust.

For details of this positive theory of integrity see the two pre-course readings on the subject at http://ssrn.com/abstract=1511274 and http://ssrn.com/abstract=1542759.

2. Authenticity:
   - Without authenticity you can forget about being a leader.
   - Authenticity is *being* and *acting* consistent with who you hold yourself out to be for others, and who you hold yourself to be for yourself. When leading, being authentic leaves you grounded, and able to be straight with yourself and straight with others without using force.
   - The only actionable access to authenticity is being authentic about your inauthenticities. To achieve this you must find in yourself that "self" that leaves you free to be publicly authentic about your inauthenticities. That self, the one required to be authentic about your inauthenticities, is who you authentically are.
   - In the first of the pre-course readings on "Authentic Leadership," Bill George (2003) (former Medtronic CEO and now Harvard Business School Professor of Leadership) was able to be completely straight about his weaknesses and failures. To be a leader you must be big enough to be authentic about your inauthenticities. While counter-intuitive, in fact this kind of bigness is a sign of power and is so interpreted by others.
   - As with integrity, being authentic is a never-ending endeavor.
3. Being Committed to Something Bigger Than Oneself:
   - Being committed to something bigger than yourself is the source of power in leading and in exercising leadership effectively. Being committed to something bigger than yourself creates for a leader the kind of power that replaces the need for force.
   - Being committed to something bigger than yourself is the source of the serene passion (charisma) required to lead and to develop others as leaders, and the source of persistence (joy in the labor of) when the path gets tough.
   - In a certain sense, all leaders are heroes. Heroes are ordinary people who are given being and action by something bigger than themselves.
   - What we mean by "committed to something bigger than oneself" is being committed in a way that shapes one's being and actions so that they are in the service of realizing something beyond one's personal concerns for oneself—beyond a direct personal payoff. As they are acted on, such commitments create something to which others can also be committed and have the sense that *their* lives are also about something bigger than themselves. This is leadership!
   - Each of us must make the personal choice to be a hero or not, to be committed to something bigger than ourselves or not, to go beyond the way we "wound up being"

and have the purpose of our lives and our careers or schooling be about something that makes a difference or not, in other words, to be a leader or not.

- Not everyone will choose this path, that is not everyone will choose to be a leader, and that is certainly OK.
- The following is a quotation from George Bernard Shaw (1903) from his play "Man and Superman" that captures this idea of being committed to something bigger than oneself:

"This is the true joy in life, the being used for a purpose recognized by yourself as a mighty one; the being a force of nature instead of a feverish selfish little clod of ailments and grievances complaining that the world will not devote itself to making you happy.

"I am of the opinion that my life belongs to the whole community and as long as I live it is my privilege to do for it whatever I can.

"I want to be thoroughly used up when I die, for the harder I work the more I live. I rejoice in life for its own sake. Life is no "brief candle" to me. It is a sort of splendid torch which I have got hold of for the moment, and I want to make it burn as brightly as possible before handing it on to future generations."

4. Integrity, Authenticity, and Committed to Something Bigger Than Oneself as a Context That Uses You

Of course, merely *knowing* that integrity, authenticity, and being committed to something bigger than oneself is the foundation required to be a leader and exercise leadership effectively, and clearly *understanding* what each of these is, and even being *resolute* about being each of these, will not leave you being a man or woman of integrity, authenticity, and committed to something

Figure 16.1

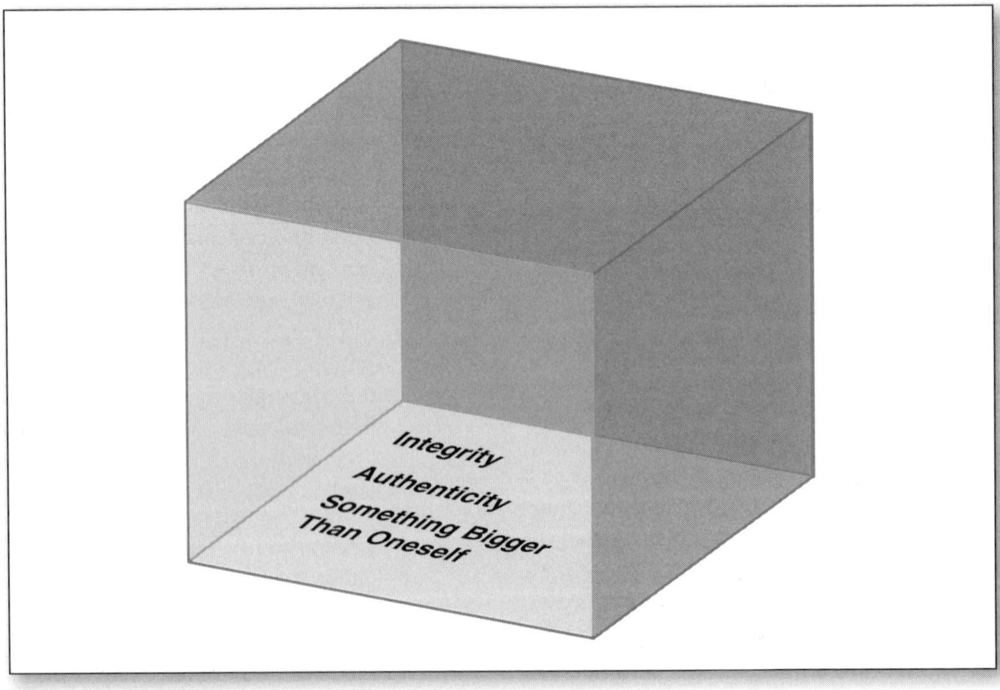

bigger than yourself *as your natural self-expression*. In the course, we will employ a methodology to deal with integrity, authenticity, and being committed to something bigger than oneself *as they are lived*, and such that you have the opportunity to create them for yourself as a context that uses you.

These three Foundational Factors of leadership form the base of the context that once mastered becomes the context that leaves one being a leader and exercising leadership effectively as one's natural self expression.

THE UNDERLYING THEORY OF THIS COURSE: PART II

With the three Foundational Factors for being a leader and exercising leadership effectively in place as a part of the context that uses you, the context that uses you is completed by mastering the Contextual Framework that distinguishes what it is to be a leader and what it is to exercise leadership effectively as these are lived.[8]

1. The Four Aspects of the Contextual Framework for Leader and Leadership

In short, Leader and Leadership, each as:

- ***Linguistic Abstractions*** (leader and leadership as "realms of possibility")
- ***Phenomena*** (being a leader and exercising leadership as they are actually experienced, that is, as they are lived; or conversely the experience of being led)
- ***Concepts*** (the temporal domain in which leader and leadership function)
- ***Terms*** (leader and leadership as definitions)

As an illustration, the space contained by the four surfaces of the cube over its foundational base of integrity, authenticity, and committed to something bigger than oneself represents the context for leader and leadership that is created by all five sides of the cube.

Figure 16.2

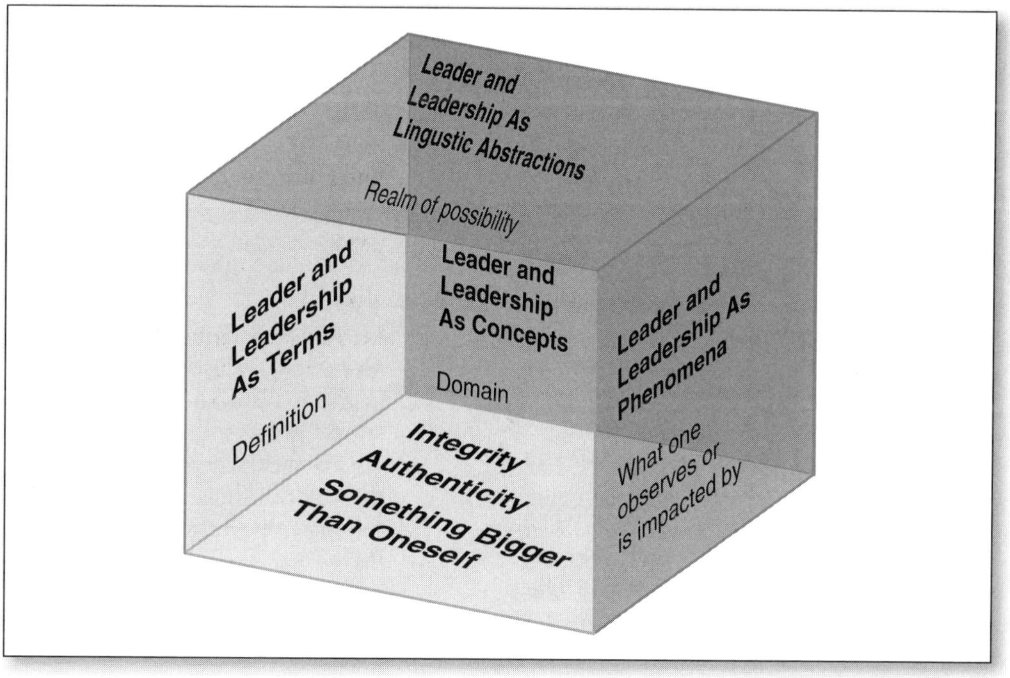

The following more fully explicates the four aspects of the *contextual framework* for leader and leadership:

- As ***linguistic abstractions***,
    - leader and leadership create leader and leadership as *realms of possibility*
    - in which when you are being a leader all possible ways of *being* are available to you,
    - and when you are exercising leadership all possible *actions* are available to you.

The point is: Mastering leader and leadership as realms of possibility leaves you free to be and free to act, rather than being constrained by common notions about what it is to be a leader and what it is to exercise leadership effectively. Instead of one's attention being on acting in a particular way or style, one is unconstrained—that is, one has all ways of being and acting available, and such freedom is often required to "get something done." This is the beginning of mastering leader and leadership as a context that uses you.

- As *phenomena*,
    - leader and leadership exist in the *sphere of language*,
    - whether that be literally speaking, or speaking in the form of writing, or
    - speaking and listening to yourself, that is, thinking,
    - or the speaking of your actions, as in "actions speak louder than words," or
    - in providing what we distinguish as "authentic listening."

The point is: If you look for yourself you will find that when you see someone being a leader or exercising leadership, or when you have experienced being led, you see someone functioning in the sphere of language. And, more pointedly when you are being a leader and exercising leadership you will be functioning in the sphere of language. (Remember that sometimes actions speak louder than words.)

- As ***concepts***,
    - leader and leadership exist in the domain of *a created future*,
    - a future that fulfills the concerns of the relevant parties,
    - that the leader and those being led come to live into,
    - which future gives them being and action in the present consistent with realizing that future.

The point is: Being a leader and the exercise of leadership are all about realizing a future that wasn't going to happen anyway.

- As a ***term***,
    - being a leader is defined as,
    - *committed* to realizing a future that fulfills the concerns of the relevant parties, but that wasn't going to happen anyway, and
    - with the availability of an unlimited opportunity set for being and action,
    - *being the kind of clearing* for leader and leadership that shapes the way the circumstances you are dealing with occur for you
    - such that your naturally correlated way of being and acting is one of being a leader and exercising leadership effectively.

- As a ***term***,
    - leadership is defined as
    - an exercise in language that results in the realization of a future that wasn't going to happen anyway,
    - which future fulfills (or contributes to fulfilling) the concerns of the relevant parties,
    - including critically those who granted the leadership (those who lead you, and those you lead).

The point is: Leader and leadership as *terms* are based on the previous three aspects of leader and leadership. Of course, each of these four aspects that constitute the Contextual Framework for leader and leadership will require full explication during the course. And after that full explication, if this Contextual Framework is valid, what you will see when you see someone actually being a leader and exercising leadership effectively will be as defined.

2. The Contextual Framework for Being a Leader and Exercising Leadership Effectively as a Context That Uses You

As was the case with the three Foundational Factors, in the course we will employ a methodology to deal with the four aspects of the Contextual Framework *as they are lived*, and such that you have the opportunity to create them for yourself as a context that uses you.

The foregoing is the fundamental theory on which this ontological/phenomenological perspective on being a leader and the effective exercise of leadership is founded. Having created a context that uses you by mastering the three Foundational Factors and the four aspects of the Contextual Framework for leader and leadership and with complete freedom to be and act, then specific knowledge regarding the situation in which one is leading has an empowering and enabling impact. But without this empowering context and freedom to be and act, and without a transformed frame of reference for leader and leadership that creates being a leader and effectively exercising leadership as one's natural self-expression, specific knowledge regarding the situation in which one is leading is little more than a "good idea," like trying to drive your car while having to remember how to do it.

3. An Example of Our Employment of the Phenomenological Methodology in the Course

In order to transform the context for leader and leadership presented in the class from something understood and adopted as a theory by the students to a context that has the power to use them, we utilize an application of the phenomenological methodology in the in-class and the out-of-class exercises and assignments. Each exercise and assignment is specifically designed for students to experience for themselves *as an actual experience* the various elements of the context for leader and leadership presented in the course. For the students, this transforms what is presented in the course from received ideas to phenomena (something realized in the senses, i.e., something actually experienced). Based on their own experience, the students are then able to generate for themselves the context for leader and leadership presented in the course. They take what is so for them as an actual experience, and confirm for themselves that it is rigorously captured by the articulation of the context for leader and leadership presented in the course. When they do, they have mastered the context by making it their own—the context belongs to them and they belong to the context; it uses them. This process works because locating in one's experience the actual phenomenon that is present as an experience when being a leader and effectively exercising leadership, and then working out a rigorous articulation that captures that experience as a phenomenon is also the process that we instructors went through in developing the context that we present in the course.

THE UNDERLYING THEORY OF THIS COURSE: PART III

1. Ontological Perceptual and Functional Constraints:

• Having mastered the context that leaves one being a leader and exercising leadership effectively as one's natural self-expression, what remains is to remove what interferes with or limits one's natural self-expression. Some of these obstacles are inherent in and shared by all people—a consequence, without an intervention, of the way our brains work. And some of these obstacles are specific to each individual—the result of individual history and experience. In the course we will provide you with exercises that allow you to become aware of and remove, or at least sufficiently relax, these obstacles to your natural self-expression. We term these obstacles to the freedom to be and act "Ontological Constraints."

• Ontological Perceptual Constraints: The source of our ontological perceptual constraints is our network of unexamined ideas, beliefs, biases, prejudices, social and cultural embeddedness, and taken-for-granted assumptions about the world, others, and ourselves. These ontological perceptual constraints limit and shape what we perceive of what is actually there in the situations with which we are dealing. As a consequence, if we do not remove these perceptual constraints, then in any leadership situation we are left dealing with some distortion of the situation we are actually dealing with.

• Ontological Functional Constraints: In everyday language the behavior generated by an ontological functional constraint is sometimes referred to as a "knee-jerk reaction." Psychologists sometimes refer to this behavior as "automatic stimulus/response behavior"—where, in the presence of certain stimuli (triggers), the inevitable response is an automatic set way of being and acting. From a neuroscience perspective, many ontological functional constraints could be termed "amygdala hijacks." When triggered in a leadership situation, one's ontological functional constraints fixate one's way of being and acting. Saying the same thing in another way, these ontological functional constraints limit and shape our opportunity set for being and action. As a consequence, the appropriate way of being and appropriate actions may be, and in fact often are, unavailable to us.

Promise of the Course

In conclusion, the combination of Parts I, II, and III of the underlying theory of the course allows us to make the following promise to our students:

- You will leave this course being who you need to be to be a leader.
- You will leave this course with what it takes to exercise leadership effectively.

While you will not necessarily have all of the experience and knowledge you need to be a truly extraordinary leader, you will have experienced whatever personal transformation is required for you to leave the course being who you need to be to be a leader, and with what it takes to exercise leadership effectively.

Realizing the Promise of the Course: Outcome Measurements

In response to the following course evaluation question, "This is one of the three most important courses I have taken in my life," 53 out of 57 cadet and faculty participants (21 faculty members completed a special faculty-focused course) at the US Air Force Academy gave this question a 6 out of 6. In the Erasmus course 75 of the 101 participants that answered this question, and in the Mays School of Business at Texas A&M University course 68 of the 100 participants that answered this question, gave this question a 5 out of 5 with overall averages of 4.5 and 4.29, respectively.

In response to the question, "I will be able to use the teachings of the course in my personal and professional development," 87 of the 103 Erasmus participants that answered this question and 85 of the 104 participants that answered this question at the Mays School of Business gave this question a 5 out of 5.

In response to the question, "This course delivered on its promise: 'You will have experienced whatever personal transformation is required for you to leave the course being who you need to be to be a leader, and with what it takes to exercise leadership effectively. In other words, you will be a leader,'" 97 out of the 104 Erasmus Academie participants who answered this question, and 91 of the 103 Mays School participants who answered this question gave it a 4 or 5 out of 5.

Because the US Air Force Academy course was unique in that the semester-long course spanned four months, we were able to ask whether or not the course had had an impact on their actual leadership performance. In response to the following course evaluation question, "I have witnessed my leadership shift to a new level in my personal and professional life here at USAFA in this term as a direct result of my participation in the course," 54 out of 57 cadet and faculty participants gave this question a 5 or 6 out of 6 (with a large preponderance of 6's).

Complete course evaluation summaries for the USAFA courses, the Texas A&M course, and the Erasmus Course are provided in Appendices II, III, and IV respectively in the online version of this chapter, downloadable at http://ssrn.com/abstract=1681682. As we continue to provide this course in different venues, the evaluation findings will be available in the online version of this chapter.

Our assessment of the results and our experience as faculty members gives us a strong belief that teaching the course over a semester (as was done at the Air Force Academy) is much more effective than teaching it over 5 or 6 days as we have done in our experimental courses. The "soak" time that is available for the students to put the course to work in their day-to-day lives over a semester course plus the ability to more effectively work on a personal leadership project are, we believe, strong reasons for this increased effectiveness.

Part of what makes measurement a difficult issue is that most evaluative efforts on leadership development rely on psychological constructs to show an indirect and implied leadership ability. While we experimented with these evaluative techniques and achieved a statistically significant increase ($p < 0.05$) in both the Authentic Leadership Questionnaire and the Psychological Capital Questionnaires in a pre-/post- self-report, we were left wanting a more direct line to actual results in the lives of the leaders.*

In following up with many of the participants from each of the courses, they express the different ways in which they are being a leader and exercising leadership. For example, in addition to securing high-level positions, cadets at the Air Force Academy have gone on to lead significant efforts in diverse areas such as combating domestic violence, leading the Air Force Academy to more sustainable "green" programs, starting an African American male mentorship program in inner cities, and reducing recidivism amongst juvenile delinquents, as well as other leadership initiatives in education, generational poverty, supporting our deployed troops, health and well-being, and many more.

We believe further research efforts will require a scholarship appropriate to the ontological model of leader and leadership with its methodology of phenomenology that acknowledges that being a leader and the effective exercise of leadership is a first-person as lived experience.

*Avolio, Bruce J., Gardner, William L., and Walumbwa, Fred O. 2007. Authentic Leadership Questionnaire (ALQ). Mind Garden, Inc. www.mindgarden.com. Luthans, Fred, Avolio, Bruce J., and Avey, James B. 2007. Psychological Capital (PsyCap) Questionnaire (PCQ). Mind Garden, Inc. www.mindgarden.com.

Summary and Conclusion

While both are useful in their own right, teaching about leadership is distinct from creating leaders. The exercise of creating a leader is complete when being a leader and exercising leadership effectively has become a student's natural self-expression. Given that being a leader and exercising leadership "on the court" is an as-lived phenomenon, we draw on the ontological/phenomenological methodology to provide actionable access to the source of a person's way of being and acting in any leadership situation. From that perspective we find that a person's way of being and acting are a natural correlate of the way in which a leadership situation occurs for a person. Based on that, we provide our students with the opportunity to create for themselves a context for leader and leadership that shapes and colors any leadership situation such that their naturally correlated ways of being and acting are those of being a leader and exercising leadership effectively.

Appendix 16.1

DIRECTORY OF LINKS FOR THE PRE-COURSE READINGS

What follows are links to the four PDF files that contain the 6 Pre-Course readings for our leadership course "Being a Leader and the Effective Exercise of Leadership: An Ontological Model" taught in June 2010 at the Texas A&M University, Mays School of Business in College Station, Texas.

PRE-COURSE READINGS 1–3 AVAILABLE AT http://ssrn.com/abstract=1513400

This document (compiled by Erhard, Jensen, and Granger) is the first, second, and third of six pre-course reading assignments for our full semester leadership course. The PDF file contains the following three documents:

"The Transformational Experiences That Leave Ordinary People Being Leaders"

(primarily contains quotes selected from Warren Bennis & Robert Thomas, "Crucibles of Leadership" [2002], and most of Chapter 2 from Bill George, "Authentic Leadership" [2003], regarding "crucibles," reprinted with permission and with commentary by us).

"Access to a Context That Uses You"

(primarily contains quotes selected from Carol Dweck, "Mindset: The New Psychology of Success" [2006] regarding the contrast between "fixed and growth mindsets," with commentary by us).

"Education as Stretching the Mind" by Jamshed Bharucha (2008).

http://www.edge.org/q2008/q08_16.html#bharucha

PRE-COURSE READING 4:

Integrity: Without It Nothing Works (Interview of Jensen by Karen Christensen).

http://papers.ssrn.com/abstract=1511274

PRE-COURSE READING 5:

Integrity: A Positive Model That Incorporates the Normative Phenomena of Morality, Ethics, and Legality—Abridged (by Erhard, Jensen, and Zaffron).

http://ssrn.com/abstract=15427594

PRE-COURSE READING 6:

Introductory Reading for Being a Leader and the Effective Exercise of Leadership: An Ontological Model (by Erhard, Jensen, Zaffron, and Granger).

http://ssrn.com/abstract=1585976

Notes

1. Wonder is an aspect of the phenomenological methodology. It requires that we bracket (put aside) the attitude of taken-for-grantedness and aim to awaken a profound sense of wonder about the phenomenon about which one is interested. The methodology implies an approach that can shatter the appearances of the taken-for-grantedness of our everyday reality. The "way" to wisdom, knowledge, and understanding, to paraphrase Socrates, "begins in wonder" (drawn from Phenomenology Online, http://www.phenomenologyonline.com/).

2. Originally from the Greek, the earliest occurrence of *ontologia* dates back to the 1606, *Ogdoas Scholastica* by Jacob Lohardus. Wikipedia "History of Ontology," http://en.wikipedia.org/wiki/Ontology#History_of_ontology accessed 12/20/2010.

3. Ontology as we use the term is meant as it is explicated by Martin Heidegger (1927) in *Being and Time*, his groundbreaking book on ontology and its methodology of phenomenology. As we use the term and as Heidegger makes clear, this is not ontology in its medieval metaphysical sense—what some have termed ontotheology—e.g., in an a priori argument for the existence of God, or in the Platonic sense of an a priori existence of ideal forms or archetypes, and also not as a synonym for "noumenon."

4. We are indebted to Heidegger, and to those other thinkers who drew on Heidegger's ideas in their own work in the field, for having developed ontology and phenomenology as rigorous disciplines that we were able to draw on to develop an actionable pathway to being a leader and exercising leadership effectively as one's natural self-expression.

5. We also taught this developmental course with our co-author of the course Steve Zaffron in 2009 at Erasmus Academie, Rotterdam, in 2010 at Texas A&M University, Mays School of Business, and we also taught the course in November 2010 in India under the auspices of the IC Centre for Governance and MW Corp. The course is also currently taught as part of the academic curriculum to cadets and faculty at the US Air Force Academy (since 2008), a version of it is taught at the Erasmus University Law School (since 2009) and the Texas A&M Health Science Center and Mays Business School as an inter-professional directed study course (since 2010). The course will be taught as part of the academic curriculum at the Dartmouth Medical School in 2012. We taught a program at the US Air Force Academy to train 41 scholars in 2010 (from various academic institutions in Europe and North America) in delivering the course (all of whom had previously taken the course) under the sponsorship of the Kauffman Foundation, the Gruter Institute, and the Air Force Academy. We are indebted to Dean Mark Zupan (Simon School of Business), Professor Richard DeMulder and Ad Hofstede (Erasmus University and Academie), Associate Dean Marty Loudder, Dean Jerry Strawser, and Assistant Professor Katalin Haynes (Mays School of Business), and Col. Gary Packard and Col. Joseph Sanders (US Air Force Academy), for their support in providing us with the laboratories we needed to develop the course. We also thank our colleague Allan Scherr for his contributions to the development of early versions of the course.

6. Note that this correlation is not a mere statistical correlation.

7. For an extensive discussion of the relation between action and the way what one is dealing with occurs for one, see Erhard, Jensen, and Barbados Group (2010), "A New Paradigm of Individual, Group, and Organizational Performance," http://ssrn.com/abstract=1437027.

8. Simply defining leader and leadership, no matter how accurate and complete the definition may be, cannot provide actionable access to what it is to be a leader and exercise leadership effectively.

References

Avolio, B. J., Gardner, W. L., & Walumbwa, F. O. (2007). Authentic Leadership Questionnaire (ALQ). Mind Garden, Inc. www.mindgarden.com.

Barucha, J. (2008). Education as stretching the mind. http://www.edge.org/q2008/q08_16.html#bharucha (accessed 21 December 2010).

Bennis, W., & Thomas, R. J. (2002). Crucibles of leadership. *Harvard Business Review, 80,* 39–45.

Clancey, W. J. (1993). Situated action: A neurophysiological response to Vera and Simon. *Cognitive Science, 17,* 87–116.

Dweck, C. S. (2006). *Mindset: The new psychology of success.* New York: Random House.

Erhard, W., Jensen, M. C., & Group, Barbados. (2010). A new paradigm of individual, group and organizational performance. *Harvard Business School NOM Unit Working Paper* No. 11–006; *Barbados Group Working Paper* No. 09–02. Available at SSRN: http://ssrn.com/abstract=1437027.

Erhard, W., Jensen, M. C., & Zaffron, S. (2008). Integrity: A positive model that incorporates the normative phenomena of morality, ethics and legality. *Harvard Business School NOM Working Paper* No. 06-11; *Barbados Group Working Paper* No. 06-03; *Simon School Working Paper* No. FR 08–05. Available at SSRN: http://ssrn.com/abstract=920625.

Erhard, W., Jensen, M. C., Zaffron, S., & Granger, K. L. (2010). Introductory reading for being a leader and the effective exercise of leadership: An ontological model. *Harvard Business School NOM Working Paper* No. 10-091; Barbados Group Working Paper No. 08-01; *Simon School Working Paper* No. 08-02; Available at SSRN: http://ssrn.com/abstract=1585976.

George, B. (2003). *Authentic leadership: Rediscovering the secrets to creating lasting value.* San Francisco,CA: Jossey-Bass.

Hawkins, J., & Blakeslee, S. (2004). On intelligence. New York: Henry Holt LLC.

Heidegger, M. (1996 [1927]). *Being and time.* (Joan Stambaugh, Trans.). Albany, NY: State University of New York Press.

Mezirow, J. (2000). *Learning as transformation: Critical perspectives on a theory in progress.* San Francisco, CA: Jossey-Bass.

Libet, B. (1993). *Neurophysiology of consciousness: Selected papers and new essays.* Boston, MA: Birkhauser.

Luthans, F., Avolio, B. J., & Avey, J. B. (2007). Psychological Capital (PsyCap) Questionnaire (PCQ). Mind Garden, Inc. www.mindgarden.com.

Phenomenology Online. http://www.phenomenologyonline.com/inquiry/11.html (accessed 21 December 2010).

Shaw, G. B. (1903). Man and superman, epistle dedicatory to Arthur Bingham Walkley. http://www.gutenberg.org/files/3328/3328-h/3328-h.htm#2H_4_0001.

Smith, D. W. (2009). Phenomenology. Stanford Encyclopedia of Philosophy. http://plato.stanford.edu/archives/sum2009/entries/phenomenology/ (accessed 29 June 2010).

17

TRANSFORMATIONAL LEADERSHIP DEVELOPMENT PROGRAMS

Creating Long-Term Sustainable Change

◆ Manfred F. R. Kets de Vries
INSEAD and ESMT

◆ Konstantin Korotov
ESMT

This chapter describes the principles of creating transformational leadership development programs that lead to long-term change in the mindsets and behaviors of executives. Transformational programs are viewed as transitional spaces where executives can get free of the constrains of their daily environments and engage in self-learning, reflection, and playfulness. The pedagogy on transformational programs is based on the clinical paradigm that underscores the illusion of rationality, the challenge of seeing what's happening beyond the level of consciousness, the impact of the past on current behaviors and thinking, the importance of transference and countertransference, the role of emotions, and the motivational need systems important for human functioning. The chapter further elaborates on elements of transformational programs based on the clinical paradigm and touches upon the requirements for faculty engaged in design and delivery of such programs. The challenges of evaluation of the outcomes of such programs, as well as ways to interpret occasional participants' decision to leave their companies after such a program, are discussed. The chapter provides examples of applying the principles discussed in an open-enrollment executive education program and in an Executive MBA.

❖ ❖ ❖

Once upon a time, in a land far away, there lived a wise king, who had among his subjects a village chief named Gabriel. The village chief had three sons, of whom the eldest, Roland, was the most talented. Given his son's abilities, Gabriel was ambitious for Roland to become an advisor to the king, so he sent him away to study political sciences at one of the greatest academies of learning in the land.

When he had mastered all that the academy had to offer, Roland was taken by his father into the presence of the king. "Great King," said Gabriel, "I have this youth, my eldest and most talented son, specially trained in the political sciences, so that he might obtain a worthy position at your Majesty's court, knowing how much you appreciate learning."

The King didn't even bother to look up, but only said, "Come back in one year."

Somewhat disappointed but still with high hopes, Gabriel sent Roland abroad to a famous center of learning, so that the time before returning to the king was not wasted. When, a year later, he arrived once more at court with his son, he said, "Great King, my son has just returned from a long and perilous journey to further educate himself. Please examine him, and see if he is worthy to be at your court."

Without hesitation, the King said, "Let him come back in another year."

Very upset, but not showing it, Gabriel had his son cross the oceans to Greece and Italy, to study the foundations of Western civilization, and continue onward to China and India to become familiar with their ancient cultures and religions. Once more, when he returned to the court, Gabriel explained to the King all the wonderful things his son had done. But the King simply looked at him and said, "Maybe he should come back after another year."

Roland was sent by his father to the Americas, travelling from the North to the South, visiting all the centers of learning on the way. But when his father took him once more to see the King, he was told, "Now find a teacher, if anyone is willing to have you, and come back in a year."

But when that year had passed and Gabriel wanted to take his son to the court, Roland was no longer interested. He preferred to meet with his teacher and discuss philosophy and the sciences. Whatever his father did to have him visit the court was in vain. Finally, Gabriel gave up: "I am the unluckiest of fathers in the land. I have wasted all this time and money to try to get my son a position at court, and now he is no longer interested. Woe to him who has failed the tests of the King!"

Some time later, the King said to his counselors, "Let us prepare for a visit to our main center of learning, for there is someone there I need to see."

As the King and his courtiers, in all their splendor, approached the center of learning, Roland's teacher led him to the gate where they stood and waited. "Great King," said the teacher, "here is the young man who was a nobody while he was a visitor of kings, but who is now himself visited by kings. Take him to be your counselor, he is ready."

Beyond the Quick Fix

As this parable illustrates, leadership development is not a quick fix. Although many people (including those entering leadership development programs) are impatient for results to materialize, quick-fix solutions put unrealistic expectations on everyone. Gimmicky programs promising supposedly instant results are not what leadership development is all about. In our experience, such programs rarely produce lasting results. Like it or not, developing leaders takes time—it can't be done overnight.

Ironically, although leadership problems may take time to emerge, when it comes to finding solutions many people in the talent development business lose patience. They prefer instant answers and want instant change. But knowing what we know about human development, we should understand that people need time to evolve. Educating leaders is not something that can be achieved by a single event. It is a process.

Leadership development is a serious business. Investing in educational opportunities is what differentiates great businesses from the simply mediocre. Organizations that fail to heed this message do so at their peril. Senior leadership has a responsibility to recognize their people's developmental needs, to help them cultivate new skills, and to provide opportunities for their professional and personal growth. Retaining talent is like pushing a wheelbarrow full of frogs; if not taken care of, they can jump out at any time.

Members of senior management need to align the objectives of the organization with those of their people. They have the ultimate responsibility for talent management initiatives. Above all they must monitor the leadership pipeline in order to create a sustainable organization. They must make an effort to bring out the best in people, create high-performance teams and high-performance organizations. How to go about this, however, is another matter. We have learned from experience that leadership development means different things to different people.

In running executive education programs at leading business schools and in corporate settings, we have discovered that a fairly common agenda is the participants' desire to make a real change in their professional and personal lives. Many executives enter the program with the aim of taking a significant next step on their career trajectory, hoping to acquire the necessary skills to make such a step successfully. Other applicants have come to the realization that they have been functioning on "automatic pilot"; although reluctant to admit it openly, they are bored with what they are doing and hope that the program will get them out of the rut and push them to reinvent themselves. Whatever they are doing—and successful as it may seem at first glance—has lost its meaning. For others also seeking that elusive commodity—meaning—they are looking for profit with purpose; they want to leave some kind of legacy. There are some instances where enrollment in a leadership development program is a reward for services rendered, recognition that the company appreciates the executive's efforts. In others, the reasons for participating may be much simpler: a quest for specific skills and competences that will make them more effective. In such cases, executives want to work on their emotional intelligence, their visioning ability, team-building capacity, or it could be they have been told that they need to adapt their style to changing circumstances.

As our experience has shown, a busy executive entering a leadership development program, particularly an open-enrollment program (where the application process is self-initiated rather than imposed by the HR department), will be seeking support and help in making some kind of personal transformation. Similar motives can be ascribed to executives who enroll in an Executive MBA (EMBA). Unlike the other parts of the program, the leadership-related modules of an EMBA are viewed as a critical part of the curriculum (as we have learned from comments made during admission interviews and post-program evaluations). According to feedback received from executives, learning more about themselves, taking stock of their lives, and being able to "improve" or "reinvent" themselves are among the primary drivers (Kets de Vries, Guillen-Ramo, Korotov, & Florent-Treacy, 2010; Kets de Vries & Korotov, 2007; Kets de Vries, Korotov, & Florent-Treacy, 2007; Long, 2004; Petriglrieli & Petriglrieli, 2010). In other words, they are seeking a transformational learning experience, a term frequently used to describe the types of programs that help executives deal with the concerns mentioned above.

We define transformational leadership development programs as learning experiences that use specific methodologies to create a transitional, intermediate space for experiencing inner and outer worlds that enables executives to "play" fantasy games. These transitional phenomena belong to the realm of illusion, which is at the basis of the initiation of experience (Winnicott, 1951). Such make-believe games give them the freedom to identify and practice the desired behavioral changes—they are powerful activities that create tipping points (Kets de Vries & Korotov, 2007). To set such a transformational process in motion, however, the pedagogy used must conform to the expectations of executives: The aim is to increase self-awareness, to overcome personal blockages, and to acquire a more sophisticated repertoire of behaviors.

It is a truism among students of leadership that to succeed in a leadership role requires the leader's capacity to reflect on his or her behavior, to understand the effect that such behavior has on followers, and to find congruence between observable behavior and the deeply held beliefs, drives, motivators, and other elements of their "inner theater." But the ability to use oneself as an instrument, the capacity to reflect and (when necessary) to go deep into oneself and explore the effect of our inner world on our behavior and that of others, is not something that comes automatically. Indeed, the capacity for reflection-in-action runs contrary to the currently popular view of the contemporary leader as solely interested in action. For the leaders of today, action clearly takes precedence over reflection; to think deeply about our own leadership style and its connection to the success of the organization within the context of our personal satisfaction and happiness is regarded as an unaffordable luxury.

Despite the prevailing culture of action, ways need to be found to help busy executives reflect on their leadership styles. If the setting is right, an open-enrollment leadership development program will be perceived as a precious opportunity, to deal with the knotty issues that have been piling up over the years (in the form of hopes, fantasies, fears, anxieties, opportunities, and dangers), but have not had a fair chance of being processed. To make time for reflection and create a discipline of reflection can have a transformational effect on the executive concerned. It may become part and parcel of the overall change executives want to make for themselves in order to function at their best.

In responding to these needs, we aim to design activities of a transformational nature. We go to great lengths to create a space where executives will be encouraged to engage in reflection, exploration, and experimentation. This process—fueled by various forms of personal feedback—increases the likelihood that participants will embrace personal change. As a result of such personal change efforts, we expect them to become more effective in leading others, in leading organizational change efforts, and in creating high-performance teams and organizations. We also hope their subjective well-being or happiness will improve, and that they may attain a better work-life balance.

Our leadership development programs tend to attract individuals who possess considerable organizational leadership experience. Although it is stimulating to work with experienced executives, it can be both a blessing and a curse. On the one hand, there is no need to "preach to the converted" about the importance of leadership in organizations, leaders as role models, or the effects leaders can have on their subordinates; on the other hand, to do things differently—to have a real impact on these individuals—can be quite a challenge.

After presenting an overview of what could be categorized as more traditional leadership teaching (definitions, models, and theories)—much of which our participants are already familiar with—in our programs, we move on to what could be described as more serious psychological work, exposing them to such themes as resistance to change, the leader's "shadow side," social defenses, group dynamics, the consequences of transference, interpersonal conflicts, authenticity in leadership, social responsibility, and the quest for meaning. To make these themes comprehensible and alive, they are introduced in non-traditional ways. We put participants in front of a metaphorical mirror to make them realize that there is more to organizational life that meets the eye, and that their current way of doing things may no longer be effective.

To have them look into this mirror is not always easy. They may not like what they see, nor take the information lying down. While they acknowledge that something is not working, many are convinced that they are doing the right things, or that nothing better or different can be done. But while in business the client is always right, in the case of leadership development programs the client is often wrong—because the client doesn't want to see. We have to make participants understand that whatever has worked in the past may no longer be an adequate response to the leadership challenges of the present and the future. This is no easy task. As the philosopher Seneca once said, "The mind is slow in unlearning what it has been long in learning."

The Clinical Paradigm

To deal with the challenge of helping experienced and (seemingly) successful but somewhat "stuck" leaders, our interventions and program design are based on the clinical paradigm (Kets de Vries, 2006a, 2006b, 2011). The latter derives from the following premises:

- Rationality is an illusion.

Irrationality is grounded in rationality. "Irrational" behavior is a common pattern in our lives, although in fact there will always be a "rationale," or meaning to it. Nothing we do is random. Elements of psychic determinism are a fact of life. To understand this rationale will be critical in making sense of our own and other people's inner theater—the core themes that affect personality and leadership style.

- What you see isn't necessarily what you get.

Much of what happens to us is beyond our conscious awareness. Most of our behavior tends to be unconscious. To gain a better understanding of unconscious patterns, we need to explore our own and other people's inner desires, wishes, and fantasies; we need to pay attention to the repetitive themes and patterns in our lives, and the lives of others.

- The past is the lens through which we can understand the present and shape the future.

All of us are products of our past. Like it or not, there's a continuity between past and present. We are inclined to view the present through the microscope of past experiences. As the saying goes, "The hand that rocks the cradle rules the world." Our personality is formed by the developmental outcome of our early environment, modified by our genetic endowment. To make sense of our behavior, we must explore our interpersonal "history," including our original attachment relationships.

- We must understand the significance of transference and counter-transference relationships.

Because of the heavy imprinting that takes place in the early stages of life, we tend to adopt certain behavior patterns. To make sense of what makes us behave the way we do, we need to explore our interpersonal relationships. Adaptive and nonadaptive aspects of our operational mode will be affected by how our original attachments have evolved—the relationships with our first caregivers. Just as there are repetitive themes in our own past, such themes will be activated in the relationships we have with the people we deal with in the present. To understand our and others' behavior, we need to identify these recurrent themes and patterns. Problematic relationship patterns (which are technically described as transference and counter-transference reactions) provide a great opportunity to explore and work through difficult issues in the here-and-now. To explore the relationships between past and present can be illuminating as it enables us to be liberated from stereotypical, ingrained behavior.

- Nothing is more central to who we are than the way we express and regulate our emotions.

Intellectual insight is not the same as emotional insight, which touches us at a much deeper level. Emotions play a vital role in shaping who we are and what we do. In understanding ourselves and other people, we need to heed our emotions first and to explore the full range of emotions experienced. Emotions determine many of our actions and emotional intelligence plays a vital role in who we are and what we do.

- We all have blind spots.

There are many things we don't want to know about ourselves. We all have our shadow side. We use our defensive mechanisms and resistances to avoid aspects of experience that are problematic. Many people derail due to blind spots in their personality. But exploring this avoidance of distressing thoughts and feelings provides another snapshot of our own personality and that of others. We need to realize that this resistance comes to the fore due to conflicts within ourselves, and to accept that inner dissonance is part of the human condition. We also need to recognize that most psychological difficulties were, at one point in time, adaptive solutions to the problems of existence.

- Motivational need systems determine our personality.

The motivational need systems that represent the interface between nature and nurture create the tightly interlocked triangle of our mental life (the three points being cognition, affect, and behavior). There are five basic motivational need systems. Three of these impact the workplace only indirectly. The first encompasses a person's physiological requirements, such as food, drink, elimination of waste, sleep, and breathing; the second encompasses a person's need for sensual enjoyment and (later) sexual excitement; and the third encompasses a person's need to respond aversively to certain situations through antagonism and withdrawal. Two systems impact the workplace directly and powerfully: the need for attachment/affiliation and the need for exploration/assertion. Humankind's essential humanity lies in its need for attachment/affiliation—in seeking relationships with other people, in striving to be part of something larger. The *need for attachment* drives the process of engagement with another human being; it is the universal experience of wanting to be close to another, to have the pleasure of sharing and affirmation. When this need for intimate engagement is extrapolated to groups, the desire for intimacy can be described as a *need for affiliation.* Both attachment and affiliation serve an emotional balancing role by confirming the individual's self-worth and contributing to his or her sense of self-esteem. The other motivational need system that is crucial for the workplace—the need for exploration/assertion—involves the ability to play, think, learn, and work. Like the need for attachment/affiliation, these needs begin early in life. Playful exploration and manipulation of the environment in response to exploratory-assertive motivation produces a sense of effectiveness, competency, autonomy, initiative, and industry.

By applying the clinical paradigm, we aim to help executives in our programs to revisit past experiences and expand their freedom of choice to explore new challenges in life, and to become more aware of their choices in the here-and-now. It is essential for healthy functioning that we do not remain strangers to ourselves. We need to free ourselves from the bonds of past experience to be able to explore new challenges in life. The clinical paradigm offers participants in a transformational program a lens through which they can explore the script of their behavior—the "play" that can be found in their inner theater (McDougal, 1985). The key actors on the stage are the people and relationships that have played an important role in the executive's past, and that, through unconscious associations, continue to influence the person's emotions, behavior, and style and, through the latter, even the type of organizational culture they perpetrate (Kets de Vries & Miller, 1984). We believe that with the help of the clinical paradigm, executives, if they really want to, can achieve transformational change, take the next step in their development as leaders, overcome the internal barriers to effectiveness and happiness, and construct more productive relationships with key constituencies in their organizations.

Bringing this paradigm into our leadership education efforts means that we as educators have to create, on the one hand, a hunger for psychological inquisitiveness among participants, and, on the other, foster courage and trust to engage participants as both the subject and object of research and investigation. We have noticed, however, that the executives who enter our programs are themselves often initiators of change or change agents in their organizations, i.e., they are trying to *change others*. Our challenge is to help them *change themselves*, so that they eventually become more effective in helping others change (Korotov & Kets de Vries, 2010).

The "Life" Case Study

To set the process of transformation in motion, from the start of the program we encourage participants to use their own work and life as major sources of analysis and learning. For these often somewhat narcissistic executives this is an attractive proposition. Although we do use case studies and stories about other people (the standard set of activities in leadership education), the main focus of our work is the life case study approach. Nothing has a more powerful effect than giving our participants the opportunity to talk about themselves, their hopes, fears, and the challenges they have to deal with.

In line with the tenets of the clinical paradigm, we create experiences that help participants discover the power of the unconscious, their shadow side, the irrational aspects of organizational life, the interlocking system of cognitions, emotions and behaviors, and, last but certainly not least, the role of the past in affecting today's behavior. This observation becomes an important issue in our transformational work: Time and time again we go to great lengths to show participants that what was once an appropriate response at one point in their life's journey may be inappropriate in their present situation.

PRE-SEMINAR MENTAL WORK

We believe that for the kind of audience we have in mind—executives looking for transformational opportunities—the learning process needs to start before they even set foot in our classrooms. An important part of the learning process for us and for participants is the application process and personal interviews with the candidates. Before they are accepted into the program, we ask them to engage in reflective essay writing. In addition, we interview them in person or over the phone. Doing so helps us to learn more about the participants and gives us the opportunity to assess the fit between the individual and the program. The main idea is to give them a sense of the type of educational and psychological work they will be expected to engage in once admitted. These initial activities serve to set their expectations, increase their curiosity, and start the learning process—or so participants have reported at a later stage in the learning cycle. Thus, when they first come to the classroom, the program has already been underway for quite some time (Korotov, 2005, 2006).

We like to reiterate (as the opening parable shows) our belief in multi-modular designs for executive education, or leadership development via longer programs with certification, rather than in short-term, one-off events. The multi-modular design allows participants to take some of their learning points from the classroom back to real life, practice what they have learned, obtain feedback, and then bring these experiences back into the safety of the classroom for further reflection and analysis. The multi-modular format is also more conducive to the evaluation of the changes that take place within the individual. By reporting to the whole class, within small working groups, to the coaches, or to the faculty, we are better able to evaluate the progress made, as seen by themselves, fellow participants, and by the program staff. We have learned from experience that change is unlikely to occur after a single event.

THE FEEDBACK PROCESS

Effective leadership development programs start with feedback. To see ourselves as others see us is a great driver of change. This is the reason that multi-modular programs are so much more effective; longer-term programs allow for the use of reflective methods—instruments designed to help executives see where they stand, and how they are viewed by others. We offer participants a number of 360-degree assessments. The repertoire of tools we work with includes the Global Executive Leadership Inventory (GELI), the Personality Audit (PA), the Leadership Archetype Questionnaire (LAQ), the Internal Theatre Inventory (ITI), and the Organizational Culture Audit (OCA) developed at the INSEAD Global Leadership Center (Kets de Vries, 2005; Kets de Vries, Vrignaud, & Florent-Treacy, 2004; Kets de Vries, Vrignaud, Korotov, & Florent-Treacy, 2006).

As a caveat, we should add that before admission many participants have been exposed (perhaps even overexposed) to various 360-degree assessments as part of an organizational educational effort implemented by HR or related departments. That's fine, but what concerns us is that an increasing number of companies have adopted multi-party assessment techniques without taking the debriefing process seriously—with considerable negative consequences. To avoid falling into the trap of using these instruments in a ritualistic manner, we pay special attention to how these instruments are introduced, and how they are linked to the overall objectives of the program. We also go to great lengths to present participants with the best possible data (which, in our opinion, should include rich verbal commentary rather than be limited to numerical answers) from their various respondents (Korotov, 2008a, 2010b).

Processing the feedback from one or more of the named instruments involves an effort by the faculty and the participating leadership coaches to help executives make sense of the reported findings. To thoroughly deconstruct the material, we subject the participants to individual and clinical group coaching interventions (Kets de Vries, 2011). We have found that the most effective form of debriefing is the group coaching method, which allows the members of a group to practice peer coaching. It is designed in such a way that each participant of the group (usually five to six people) will have a stake in the action plans of all the other members (Kets de Vries et al., 2010; Kets de Vries et al., 2007; Korotov, 2010a).

In our leadership developmental work on feedback tools and the debriefing process we also stress that participants should go back to their respondents and debrief their feedback with them (especially with their superior). By encouraging participants to respond to the feedback in such a way, we hope to cement their commitment to change even further. To enlist others in helping them set the change process in motion is essential, particularly if these people are encountered on a regular basis.

One of the outcomes of the above-mentioned coaching intervention is the formulation of an action plan in which participants distill two or three areas where they would like to make a change. We encourage the participants to share their action plan with a peer coach—another program participant whose task is to stay in touch with the coachee between the program modules and/or after the program. The peer coach plays the role of a monitor, sounding board, and sparring partner. Peer coaches will remind the executive about the commitments he or she has made during the program (Kets de Vries, 2006a; Korotov, 2008b). The coaching, action planning, and subsequent follow-up with a peer coach ensure that participants continue the learning process and do not fall back into previous behavior patterns. Interpersonal learning, support, self-revelation, and insight play a critical role to create the desired transformational experiences. Given the multi-modular nature of our programs, there will be ample opportunities for participants to practice new behaviors in their daily life, and then come back to the program and report to the group, the peer coach, and to the faculty their experiences in a context of mutual reflection. Thus a virtuous cycle of action and reflection is created and practiced.

THE NARRATIVE

As mentioned, in our programs the life case study takes a central position. All participants are invited to engage in "story telling." One after the other, participants take the so-called hot seat—volunteering to tell their stories to the rest of the class, engage the class in a free-flowing attention and association mood, and then listen to the fantasies, feelings, associations, metaphors, and resonance reactions from the audience. The idea is to provide each participant with the opportunity to use narrative as a learning tool (McAdams, 1993; McLeod, 1997; Rennie, 1994; Spence, 1982). Not only can the telling of one's own story provide much insight and be cathartic, listening to other people's stories can enable vicarious learning, using projection, transference, and identification as tools for better understanding themselves (Balint, 1957; Balint, Ornstein, & Balint, 1972; Etchegoyen, 1991; Kets de Vries, 2007).

EXAMPLES OF TRANSFORMATIONAL PROGRAMS

In Appendix 17.1 we describe "The Challenge of Leadership," an INSEAD Global Leadership Center program that is based on clinical/systemic paradigm principles and is positioned as a transformational opportunity for senior executives. This program (which has over a 20-year history) has been (semi-jokingly) referred to by the participants and faculty as the "CEO recycling seminar." Many aspects of its structure, process, and content have been transferred to other leadership transformational programs aimed at helping executives have a significant emotional experience. (For an example of how the principles and methods developed through "The Challenge of Leadership Program" have been transferred to the leadership development component of an Executive MBA program at the

European School of Management and Technology, see Appendix 17.2.)

Program Effectiveness

A question that frequently comes up in discussion about transformational programs is how to assess whether a leadership development program has had a significant effect on the participants. Like all designers of leadership programs, we face methodological challenges in so doing (Yorks, Beechler, & Ciproen, 2007). If we had the luxury of a laboratory setting, we could add a control group of almost identical executives who are facing similar types of issues, but who are not attending this specific transformational program. Moreover, for reasons of consistency, we should use the same instruments for whatever measures of leadership we want to use, have the same observers, and take account of all possible biases that may interfere with such a process. Also, from a methodological point of view we would need to isolate the effects of the program from all other possible influencing factors.

While such a design sounds good in theory, to make it happen in practice is another matter altogether. Researchers should not forget that people may (and do) learn, change, and grow outside business schools and without specific leadership interventions. Creating controlled conditions is made more complicated by the fact that we need to be able to take longitudinal measures in order to see whether programs truly have a long-term effect. Such a research design is far from realistic or possible when it comes to *real* leaders in *real* organizations, due to natural design constraints. To constitute a control group to measure personal transformation among a group of senior executives with the types of the issues worked on can be a real nightmare.

Hence, to make some kind of assessment of change, we have chosen an approach that is both pragmatic in design and educational for the participants: an ongoing evaluation of personal progress made over the course of the program (as opposed to an end-of-program evaluation), in combination with continuous feedback from fellow participants, faculty, and coaches. We are not dealing with a simple process of input-transformation-output, but rather an iterative process whereby the participants not only begin to view the world they work in, and themselves, differently, but also internalize ways of continuing this developmental journey (Florent-Treacy, 2009; Korotov, 2005, 2006; Kets de Vries & Korotov, 2007; Kets de Vries et al., 2007). In other words, the evaluation of the progress made is part of the transformation process that participants go through as part of their program work.

In response to the need to evaluate the longer-term effectiveness of our programs, we conducted an exploratory study with graduates of the 2005 Challenge of Leadership Program at INSEAD (Kets de Vries, Hellwig, Guillen-Ramo, Florent-Treacy, & Korotov, 2009), which was designed to see whether participants had changed, and whether these changes could be viewed as an outcome of the program. About half of the class graduates (N = 11) agreed to participate in our research. While we realize that the sample was very small, given the senior positions of the participants, we considered it a success that so many agreed to participate. The study combined quantitative data from the 360-degree feedback taken and retaken by the program graduates and qualitative data from their semi-structured post-program interviews.

Prior to the retake of the Global Executive Leadership Inventory by the graduates of 2005, the two faculty members that ran the program were asked to make predictions about the magnitude of transformation concerning each of these executives. They based their predictions on the notes taken at the admittance interview, the results of the various questionnaires, and the interface with the participants during the program. The participants that volunteered were interviewed before they received the results of their retake of the 360-degree feedback. The analysis of the interview transcripts found the following repeated regularities in the participant's accounts of what had actually changed in them as a result of the program:

- An increase in self-awareness due to in-depth self-analysis, contributing to the discovery of the forces hindering their personal development; obtaining a clearer understanding of what made them tick; and gaining a clearer view of their desires and goals in their career and life in general
- A change in behavior patterns, contributing to better listening skills, team-building skills, performance management, feedback giving, and other people-oriented behaviors

When asked what contributed to these changes in behavior and leadership style, the participants attributed the changes to the following elements of the program:

- Group coaching appeared to be a major vehicle to increase self-awareness and building commitment among the members of the group to execute their self-development goals.
- Action plans helped provide focus on what needed to be done and served as a commitment-enhancement mechanism.
- Experimentation with new behaviors between the modules was seen as an important way to continue to learn and use feedback for self-improvement.
- Staying in contact with the learning community (made up of the members of the program) was viewed as a foundation for current and possible future personal transformations.

These more structured findings validated what we had observed in the leadership development programs. Clearly, the multimodular format was helpful in monitoring change among the participants and following their development through the program. Important when monitoring their progress was the "hot seat" experience and the content of the reflection papers. These papers, written up after each module, served as a proxy for the developmental efforts taking place (Florent-Treacy, 2009). Other progress measures included regular conference calls and post-program interviews with the participants (Korotov, 2005, 2006), as well as discussions with the coaches and faculty as part of the program analysis and feedback work (as described in Appendix 2).

The Change Trajectory

Obviously, change doesn't happen merely in the classroom. Much of the transformation work is done outside. Given the immersion that takes place inside and outside our programs, they nurture elements of what have been called "therapeutic communities"—miniature societies whereby fellow participants, coaches, and faculty all fulfill the role of helping each participant change (DeLeon, 2001). In such a community, confronted by others about possible dysfunctional behavior patterns, it is hard for participants to resist the need for change. Pushed by others, each participant begins to see a connection between what needs to be stopped or started, and what would be a desirable future state. Through this process, they are able to identify possible ways of starting a process of change. They learn to watch out for barriers to change and, no less importantly, identify who needs to be involved in their transformational efforts (boss, subordinates, colleagues, professional community, family members, therapist, coach, etc.). Given the design of the program, parallels with making (then breaking) New Year's resolutions cannot be drawn. Encouraged by their colleagues, group coaches, and faculty, the process of change becomes a reality. During the leadership development program they have acquired a number of "tools" to monitor their progress and get feedback and support along the way. And what further accelerates the process is that they have internalized a way of looking at things—they have acquired a new lens—that will be helpful for processing current and future changes. For example, they will be able to use the self as a reflective tool, they will have fostered their emotional intelligence, and they will have become insightful as a "psychological detective."

During these transformational journeys a number of variables come into play:

- Crystallization of the need for change: seeing the connection between the need for change and the individual's desirable "after-change" state
- Ability to make a connection between the past and the present and future states: identifying entrenched behaviors, based on past experiences that require change
- Accepting personal responsibility for the current status and the expected outcome of the change effort: developing self-efficacy in relationship to the change effort
- Drawing up an action plan that includes a timeline and various forms of behavioral experimentations outside and inside the classroom
- Ability to reflect on their own experimentation: reaching out for feedback about their progress, and engaging with critical social support mechanisms to create experiments for long-lasting change
- Learning how to engage other people in the personal change process: for example, working with a coach, engaging in peer coaching activities, using feedback productively
- Accepting that personal change is not a one-off event but rather a continuously evolving process

The fact that our programs are not Band-Aids gives us great satisfaction. To help people develop for the better touches the altruistic motive inside us. To continue helping them on their life journey, we make an effort to stay in touch with our former participants—and alumni events also help in monitoring their progress. Personal development doesn't end with the termination of the program.

We acknowledge that some participants are not always 100 percent successful in whatever change efforts they undertake. We accept that our programs can have side effects. As a result of the intense, personal journey the participants undertake, they may come to the realization that there is some kind of mismatch between the way they see themselves and the expectations of the organizations they work for. Such cognitive dissonance may lead to their departure.

Naturally, the fact that at times participants in what we call transformational leadership development programs ask themselves if they should stay in the organization that has supported them through the program may cause concerns and nervousness among sponsoring executives and HR professionals. People, however, don't leave companies only due to attendance of a leadership program. The course is usually a place for exploration of questions that have been brewing for some time. The mere fact of facing an issue that may be important for the individual, but that can't be productively discussed in traditional organizational environment, can cause stress and anxiety. Providing participants with a non-threatening opportunity to explore their issues, including fit with their current employer or career trajectory, is often experienced as a valuable part of the executive's journey. The stress of exploring whether one is on the right track often prevents people from doing a serious analysis of the issue. The environment and the tools and support structures provided by a transformational executive program take some of that stress away by giving legitimacy to the question.

While some participants may end up being more motivated to use their insights and transformational experiments for progressing in their current organizations (and we actually hear reports of reduced stress, higher clarity of goals, and higher self-efficacy from the program alumni), other may choose to move on. We understand that this may be frustrating news to a sponsoring executive or an HR person, who may have expected that the individual would return concerned to boost the sales numbers after the program, and who now says that they want to do something completely different. We still think that people have the right to realize that they may be stuck in a wrong job. It could very well be that as a result of the program they have a clearer view of what in the past seemed to be an uncomfortable gut feeling. For example, they may see that their psychological mindset and the culture of the company don't match. In such instances, both parties are in fact better when each goes their own way. The alternative scenario is that they realize they are riding a dead horse, and that it is high time that they dismount. To do the same thing over and over again and expect a different outcome is the definition of insanity. Due to the transformational journey participants are on, they may discover other ways to arrive at their full potential.

Not for the Faint of Heart

Designing, marketing, and delivering transformational leadership programs is not for the faint-hearted. Creating transformational programs founded on the clinical paradigm requires knowledge, skills, and attitudes that are not typically found in a traditional business school academic. Faculty members wishing to help individuals change need to be well-versed in the principles of human functioning, group dynamics, short-term dynamic psychotherapy, techniques such as motivational interviewing and paradoxical intervention, and other methodologies (Kets de Vries, 2011). They also need a deep understanding of what management is all about.

In such programs, educators are seen not just as repositories of knowledge about particular subjects but rather as sparring partners, guides, confidants, and even transferential "father/mother figures"—a role that is not for everyone (Kets de Vries & Korotov, 2007; Korotov, 2005, 2006). Faculty will inevitably spend an enormous amount of emotional energy engaging with participants and challenging them, while simultaneously showing empathy and care. The time commitment required from faculty is much greater than for more traditional programs. Undoubtedly, this "Socratic" role goes far beyond the traditional demands made of faculty involved in executive education.

Furthermore, and ideally, faculty and program directors involved in clinically oriented leadership development programs should themselves undertake a process of personal self-exploration, experimentation, and change before they try to help others. They may need regular supervision to be able to recognize irrational behaviors in themselves that may lead to negative reactions from the people around them (Levinson, 2007).

But the clinical approach to leadership development can generate remarkable progress in helping program participants bring the learning from the classroom to their organizations, their careers, and their personal lives. Obviously, incorporating such an approach into program design is quite different from, say, selecting a case study or a set of PowerPoint slides. The rewards, however, of working in a clinically oriented program can be very high, particularly when program participants show signs of liberation, enthusiasm, and self-efficacy at the end of such a program, and especially when participants get in touch with faculty members months or years after the program.

Running such programs is a tough experience that requires the faculty to constantly look at themselves, their own inner scripts, and the way they react to participants and their challenges. They may even find the program transformational in the sense that they realize they need to transform something in themselves in order to help others in their transformational efforts. To quote Plato, "We can easily forgive a child who is afraid of the dark. The real tragedy of life is when men are afraid of the light."

Appendix 17.1

THE CHALLENGE OF LEADERSHIP AT INSEAD: AN EXAMPLE OF A TRANSFORMATIONAL LEADERSHIP PROGRAM

Once a year the INSEAD Global Leadership Center runs *The Challenge of Leadership*, an open-enrollment leadership development program that is aimed at the creation of reflective leaders who are capable of reinventing themselves and their organizations. About twenty very senior executives are selected to participate from a large number of applicants from all over the world. The underlying guiding motivation for the applications from apparently successful executives is often seemingly insoluble dilemmas. At times it is centered around negative feelings about the self, or on perceptions of the world and others that make fulfillment of personal aspirations seem impossible. Usually, however, this central challenge is not clearly articulated in the application or even in the applicant's mind when he or she applies to the program.

The program consists of three 5-day workshops held at two month intervals, plus a final 4-day module six months later. The program helps participants learn more about themselves during each on-site week. It is also expected that on the basis of that knowledge, participants will agree on a "contract" of personal transformation that determines what they should work on at work and at home during their time away from the workshop. Because small group leadership coaching and subsequent peer coaching is part of the design of the program, "homework" assignments are monitored among the participants. Although the basic material of the workshop is the life case study of each participant, the first week also contains a number of interactive sessions on high-performance organizations, organizational culture, the impact of mergers and acquisitions, effective and dysfunctional leadership, the career life cycle, cross-cultural management, and organizational stress.

With that foundation, participants can then move on to the workshop's central model of psychological activity and organization: the personal case history (McAdams, 1993; McLeod, 1997; Rennie, 1994; Spence, 1982). Each participant in the workshop takes a turn to sit in the "hot seat" once during the program, offering his or her case for reflection and analysis by the group and self. This experience constitutes a positive step toward self-discovery in that experience and actions become sequentially organized as a person tells his or her story. It also serves an educational purpose for the other group members, who gain an additional understanding of their own opportunities and challenges as they hear about the parallel issues or problems of others. They realize that most issues are universal; they are not alone in their confusion. During each case presentation the other participants are asked to listen carefully with a "free-flowing attention span," and not to interrupt. When a presenter is finished, clarifying questions can be asked for the purpose of understanding the narrative better. Once the narrative has been clarified, it is the turn of the presenter to be silent and listen to the associations, interpretations, and recommendations of the other members of the group. A considerable amount of time is devoted to the associations (fantasies, feelings, and thoughts) that the presentation arouses in its listeners. Participants are taught about the use of transference and counter-transference observations as an essential tool to understand the salient themes in the presenter's life (Balint, 1957; Balint et al., 1972; Etchegoyen, 1991; Kets de Vries, 2007). A special effort is made to prevent quick recommendations and premature closure. Once the feedback from the class is over, the presenter is given the last word, commenting on the various observations and airing any additional thoughts. The executive in the "hot seat" concludes by presenting a proposed "contract for change," outlining the things that he or she will work on in the interim period.

During the second workshop, some time is devoted to the processing of a number of the feedback instruments mentioned in this chapter. The coaching sessions use this information as the basis for a more refined action plan in the time period between the second and third modules of the course. The main focus of the third workshop is the consolidation of acquired insights and the internalization of change. The "hot-seat" presentations continue and become increasingly multilayered and rich as the workshop progresses. The last workshop session, held at a six-month interval, furthers the internalization process and allows for some kind of a conclusion with regard to the effectiveness of the transformation effort.

In addition to the plenary sessions, participants spend a lot of time in small groups in and outside the class. The interactions within these groups helps to consolidate newly acquired attitudes and behavior patterns. Whether in subgroups or in the plenary, the twenty participants form an intense learning community—an identity laboratory (Korotov, 2005). Whenever a group member backslides into a behavior pattern that he or she is trying to unlearn, the other participants offer constructive feedback. By the third week, many participants say that they feel they know each other better than members of their own family. With that increasing intimacy, the interchange in the plenary sessions becomes extremely free-flowing. The group, exhibiting considerably more emotional intelligence with each new session, turns into a self-analyzing community, so that much less intervention is needed by faculty. The follow-up session after six months is there to see how well the action plans have been dealt with. In many instances, follow-up sessions (or smaller ones) at participants' initiative are held year after year—offering participants and faculty alike an opportunity to assess the degree to which certain new behavior patterns have become truly internalized.

The start-of-program get-together for drinks has the artificial quality common to similar occasions. There is the usual nervous laughter, the noise of glasses. People mill around, making an effort to meet others, trying to initiate conversation. Quite a few of the people present seem ill at ease. There is a certain charge in the air. What to talk about? How to relate to each other? The topics range from recent political events, to travel, to cross-cultural anecdotes. Is this just another random encounter of a group of executives? Not really. In spite of appearances, the cocktail party is carefully choreographed. There is a purpose behind the ritual. It is an awkward but necessary step to get the leadership workshop underway.

Participants have come here from all over the globe. Now they are trying to feel their way around. Specialists in group behavior would say that this way of acting is part of the "being polite" group phase. The members of the group struggle with questions of inclusion and exclusion. The participants are trying to find out about the other members. Who has been selected into the program? What are the other participants like? What countries do they come from? Their behavior demonstrates excitement mixed with a certain degree of anxiety. A spectator from Mars, however, would be amused to see this gathering where so many captains of industry look like fish out of water. For once, they aren't in control. For once, they don't really know what to expect. For once, they aren't masters of the universe; other people seem to be pulling the strings. There is nobody to push around. Instead, they are anxiously putting out feelers. They introduce themselves to each other. They engage in small talk. Some feel awkward and don't quite know how to position themselves. Consequently, some of them talk too much, their way of coping with an uncomfortable situation. Others try to numb their anxiety by drinking too much. At a subliminal level, however, they are aware that, in contrast to the role they play in the office, it will be harder to keep their mask on. They are caught up in a totally unknown situation with its specific fantasies and defensive reactions. Many thoughts race through their mind: Why didn't I stay at the office? Why did I leave familiar ground? There must be a better way to spend my time. What am I going to get out of all this? Isn't this all a waste of time? What am I doing here? What am I doing to myself?

Although, over the years, word-of-mouth has been the most powerful driver for applications to the program, for a number of executives the process starts when their vice president of human resources or another colleague gives them the brochure about the program. It sounds quite interesting. The design arouses their curiosity and stimulates their fantasy. Some see the workshop as an opportunity to do something different to take a break from the routine of office life and do something for themselves. It looks as though the program might provide answers to some of the questions they have been asking themselves. Lately, life has lost much of its novelty. Work doesn't feel the same any more. The original sense of excitement is gone and work has become too much of a routine. They are stuck in a rut and are doing nothing new. What has happened to their original sense of discovery? Their creativity? When was the last time they experienced that feeling of total involvement? They are no longer losing themselves in their activities. Instead, all they seem to be doing is more of the same. The original rush of having reached the top of the pyramid has faded away.

Completing the complex admission form, however, is a total drag. The form asks too many personal questions and it is a real pain having to respond to them all. Such forms are OK for MBA students, but at their level? Some of the questions still puzzle them—they weren't the sort of questions they usually got from journalists or investment analysts. Who wants to write about the things they aren't good at? How do you respond when asked about the risky things you've done in your life? Whatever irritation they had, the type of questions asked on the admissions form indicates that this is not going to be a traditional executive program. But then, they didn't really want another traditional executive program. They had tried them all—been there, done that.

Then there is the telephone interview. Out of the blue, there is this person—apparently one of the seminar leaders—at the other end of the line asking bizarre questions. Why should he give you a place in the program? What would you contribute? What complaints does your spouse make about you? What kinds of thing make you angry? Why does he want to know about your wild fantasies? What has all this got to do with becoming more effective as a leader? Strangely enough, when asked—at the end of the interview—if they still want a place in the program, they had all said yes. Of course, without their realizing it, the workshop had already begun.

A short introduction follows the first get-together, describing the daily workshop schedule, followed by a tour of the campus and dinner. That takes care of the initial formalities. There is a last chance for polite dinner conversation, but by now they know that was the calm before the storm.

The next day the seminar starts in earnest. At the opening session anxiety seems high; people appear apprehensive and look expectantly at the workshop leader, who gives a short lecture on emotional intelligence, effective and dysfunctional leadership, and irrational behavior in organizations. Subsequently, he reiterates the basic premise of the workshop—the "life" case study. Case presentations will be the main learning tool. Each life case study presents a unique situation that will contribute to the learning process. He explaines that there could be "no interpretation without association": Participants wil get as much out of the workshop as they put into it. The workshop leader makes it clear that he has spoken to all participants, that all have accepted the ground rules to work on a number of significant problems—professional or private—that needed resolution.

From then on the workshop is on its way. How the various participants will handle the emerging anxiety depends on their personality structure, their historic defense mechanisms, and the specific dynamics that evolve within the group. The immediate behavioral data that will emerge in the group will be used as data to explore conscious and unconscious material, and defensive operations. And with that, the first life case study has begun.

Appendix 17.2

INDIVIDUAL LEADERSHIP DEVELOPMENT ITINERARY IN THE ESMT EMBA PROGRAM: AN EXAMPLE OF ON-GOING PROCESS OF EVALUATION OF PERSONAL TRANSFORMATIONAL EFFORTS

The ESMT Executive MBA program includes a leadership development component called the Individual Leadership Development Itinerary (ILDI). This is a structured element of the EMBA curriculum spanning the overall 21-month course. The idea behind this leadership component of the program is to help participants identify areas of personal change that they would like to work on during the program, provide them with the supporting mechanisms for such a transformation, and encourage active exchange with fellow participants. The ILDI is introduced to the participants during the very first module of the program. Participants get acquainted with the approach, learn about the 360-degree process and the instruments used for it (e.g., the Global Executive Leadership Inventory mentioned above), and get an initial introduction to the topics of personal development. There is also a day of team building spent in the forest. In one of the subsequent modules, participants get the results of their 360-degree feedback and participate in a full day of small group coaching. An action plan is developed at the end of the group coaching process, and participants form peer-coaching dyads. Peer coaches get familiarized with the action plans of their colleagues and agree on a periodic follow-up.

In the modules that follow, the program dedicates a special session to the peer-coaching meetings (Korotov, 2008b). During those meetings participants discuss with their peer coach the progress toward the established goal, barriers and difficulties encountered, and possible alterations in their course of action. Peer coaches support one another and offer a sounding board for testing ideas and assumptions. There is a structural element in the process: a peer coaching written summary of the progress made by their peer coachee. Each participant is expected to summarize the main points of the discussion with their fellow participant and provide the latter with a copy of it. Such a document helps the participants see how their progress is viewed by a colleague, and enhances responsibility for their own success. It also helps the participants acting as peer coaches pay attention to the content of their peer coaching discussions and feel responsibility for helping the coachee in his or her progress. Support from faculty and in-house coaches is provided on demand.

Approximately one year after the first 360-degree assessment, the participants go through another round of the Global Executive Leadership Inventory and meet again for one day with the same coaching group, the discussion being facilitated by the same professional coach who did it twelve months earlier. This session is dedicated to the evaluation of the progress made and to discussion of the necessary changes, given the results of the experimentation or the current reality of the participants, and of the learning outcomes of the process of personal transformation.

The ILDI activities also include skills-building workshops on negotiation, leadership style, management of necessary evils, dealing with resistance to change, etc. The ILDI curriculum is coordinated with a number of required courses such as Organizational Behavior, Managing People, and Consulting for Change, as well as various electives. The latter include a number of reflective activities that often end up being related to the personal change agenda of the participants. For example, as part of the post-course assignment in the Managing People course, participants have to complete a "Personal Career Workout for Executives" (Korotov, 2009)—a structured exercise involving reflection on one's career and planned career progression, as well as discussions with superiors, colleagues, subordinates, and family members about the meaning of career success, current performance, and expected changes, if the individual want to progress further. Participants receive written commentaries from the faculty and are offered an opportunity of an individual consultation that brings together their personal change efforts and the career issues.

About two months before the end of the program, participants take part in an international field seminar (for example, in Russia, Turkey, Brazil, Argentina, Chile, etc.) where special attention is paid to the leadership styles and practices in the visited countries. In addition, during the field seminar (despite a very heavy schedule), the participants are provided with one more coaching opportunity—this time individual—with a leadership faculty member trained in the clinical-paradigm oriented coaching methodology (Kets de Vries, Guillen-Ramo, Korotov, & Florent-Treacy, 2010) to discuss the results of their learning during the program and planned post-graduation development work.

The last two sessions of the EMBA program are dedicated to the issues of continuous growth and development for leaders. These sessions are open not only to the participants but also their family members who get engaged in a discussion of the costs of leading and learning to lead.

References

Balint, M. (1957). *The doctor, the patient and the illness*. New York: International Universities Press.

Balint, M., Ornstein, P. H., & Balint, E. (1972). *Focal psychotherapy*. London, UK: Tavistock.

DeLeon, G. (2001). *The therapeutic community: Theory, model and method*. New York: Springer Publishing Company.

Etchegoyen, R. H. (1991). *The fundamentals of psychoanalytic technique*. London, UK: Karnac Books.

Florent-Treacy, E. (2009). Behind the scenes in the identity laboratory: Participants' narratives of identity transition through group coaching in a leadership development program. *International Coaching Psychology Review, 4*(1), 71–86.

Kets de Vries, M. F. R. (2005). Leadership archetypes: An exposition. *INSEAD Working Paper* 2005/75/ENT.

Kets de Vries, M. F. R. (2006a). *The leader on the couch*. London, UK: Wiley.

Kets de Vries, M. F. R. (2006b). *The leadership mystique*. London, UK: FT Prentice Hall.

Kets de Vries, M. F. R. (2007). Are you feeling mad, bad, sad or glad? *INSEAD Working Paper*. Fontainebleau & Singapore: Nr. 2007/09/EFE.

Kets de Vries, M. F. R. (2011). *The Zen of group coaching: Caring for Schopenhauer's hedgehogs*. London, UK: Wiley.

Kets de Vries, M., Guillen-Ramo, L., Korotov, K., & Florent-Treacy, E. (2010). *The coaching kaleidoscope: Insights from the inside*. Houndmills, UK: Palgrave.

Kets de Vries, M., Hellwig, T., Vrignaud, P., Guillen-Ramo, L., Florent-Treacy, E., & Korotov, K. (2009). Sustainable effectiveness of a transformational leadership development program: An exploratory study. *INSEAD Working Paper* 2009/34/EFE/IGLC.

Kets de Vries, M., & Korotov, K. (2007). Creating transformational executive education programs. *Academy of Management Learning & Education, 6*(3), 375–387.

Kets de Vries, M., Korotov, K., & Florent-Treacy, E. (2007). *Coach and couch: The psychology of making better leaders*. Houndmills, UK: Palgrave.

Kets de Vries, M. F. R., & Miller, D. (1984). *The neurotic organization*. San Francisco, CA: Jossey-Bass.

Kets de Vries, M., Vrignaud P., & Florent-Treacy, E. (2004). The Global Leadership Life Inventory: Development and psychometric properties of a 360-degree feedback instrument. *International Journal of Human Resource Management, 15*(3), 475–492.

Kets de Vries, M., Vrignaud, P., Korotov, K., & Florent-Treacy, E. (2006). The development of the personality audit: A psychodynamic multiple feedback assessment instrument. *International Journal of Human Resource Management, 17*(5), 898–917.

Korotov, K. (2005). Identity laboratories. *INSEAD PhD Dissertation*.

Korotov, K. (2006). Identity laboratory: The process of going through an executive program. In M. Weaver (Ed.), *2006 Academy of Management Annual Meeting Best Paper Proceedings*, August 11–16, in Atlanta, Georgia. ISSN 1543-8643.

Korotov, K. (2008a). Preparation for 360-degree feedback in leadership development programs and executive coaching. In S. Reddy (Ed.), *Leadership development: Perspectives and cases* (pp. 87–98). Hyderabad: The ICFAI University Press.

Korotov, K. (2008b). Peer coaching in executive-education programmes. *Training and Management Development Methods, 22*(2), 3.15–13.24.

Korotov, K. (2009). Personal career workout for executives. *ESMT Courseware ESMT 409-0092-1*. Available via ECCH.

Korotov, K. (2010a). Executive coaches in organizations: Insiders from outside. In V. Vaiman (Ed.), *Talent management of knowledge workers: Embracing the non-traditional workforce* (pp. 180–196). Houndmills, UK, and New York: Palgrave.

Korotov, K. (2010b). Bringing the clinical paradigm into executive education programs: Fantasies, anxieties, and hopes. In M. Kets de Vries, L. Guillen-Ramo, K. Korotov, & E. Florent-Treacy (Eds.), *The coaching kaleidoscope: Insights from the inside* (pp. 20–36). Houndmills, UK: Palgrave.

Korotov, K., & Kets de Vries, M. (2010). Fast times, fast development? Coping with the challenges of accelerated leadership development. In D. Dotlich, P. Cairo, S. Rhinesmith, & R. Meeks (Eds.), *2010 Pfeiffer annual: Leadership development* (pp. 107–118). Pfeiffer: An Imprint of Wiley.

Levinson, H. (2007). Executive coaching. In R. Kilburg & R. Diedrich (Eds.), *The wisdom of coaching: Essential papers in consulting psychology for a world of change* (pp. 95–102). Washington, DC: American Psychological Association.

Long, S. (2004). Really . . . Why do executives attend executive education programs? *Journal of Management Development, 23*(8), 701–715.

McAdams, D. P. (1993). *Stories we live by: Personal myths and the making of the self*. New York: William Morrow and Company.

McDougal, J. (1985). *Theaters of the mind: Illusion and truth on the psychoanalytic stage*. New York: Basic Books.

McLeod, J. (1997). *Narrative and psychotherapy*. London, UK: Sage.

Petriglrieli J. P., & Petriglrieli J. (2010). Identity workspaces: The case of business schools. *Academy of Management Learning & Education, 9*(1), 44–60.

Rennie, D. L. (1994). Storytelling in psychotherapy: The client's subjective experience. *Psychotherapy, 31*, 234–243.

Spence, D. P. (1982). *Narrative truth and historical truth*. New York: Norton.

Winnicott, D. W. (1951). *Transitional objects and transitional phenomena. Collected papers: Through paediatrics to psycho-analysis*. London, UK: Tavistock Publications.

Yorks, L., Beechler, S., & Ciproen, R. (2007). Enhancing the impact of an open-enrollment executive program through assessment. *Academy of Management Learning & Education, 6*(3), 310–320.

18

MY APPROACH TO TEACHING LEADERSHIP (AND HOW I STUMBLED ONTO IT)

◆ James O'Toole
University of Denver, Daniels College of Business

This is a personal account of what and how the author teaches about leadership. Using the Socratic method, he attempts to help executives and MBA students discover for themselves what leaders *do* to create followers and to construct conditions under which those followers can achieve the ends they seek. In the classroom, the author plays the role of a Platonic "midwife" by "educing" from the students their own implicit theories of leadership. The goal is to encourage them to surface—and then rigorously test—that which they "already know" about leadership, and then to clarify, modify, and refine that knowledge.

In this process, the author does not pretend to be neutral or relativistic with regard to the ethical aspects of leadership. While students can and will effectively lead in countless different ways, the author encourages students continually to assess the moral or ethical components of whatever approaches they may choose. Yet the classroom focus is always on the practical aspects of leadership, particularly on helping students to become more effective leaders themselves. It is the author's hope that, in the end, students will find their own ways to lead that are equally effective *and* ethical (he calls such a fusion of practicality and morality "values-based leadership"). While class discussions are informed by such diverse disciplines as philosophy, economics, history, political science, and social anthropology, the focus is on the behavior of actual leaders, ranging from biographies of Mohandas Gandhi and the presidents on Mount Rushmore, to current HBS cases dealing with business executives. In all, the author creates conditions under which the students test their own theories—and the theories of scholars—against the actual behavior of such successful leaders, and then capture what they have learned by creating their own personal "handbooks for leading change."

Introduction

We are all, to one degree or another, prisoners of our disciplines. I was trained as a social anthropologist, a now largely moribund field whose intrepid, pith-helmeted practitioners once embedded themselves, often uninvited, in foreign cultures where they attempted to understand the exotic behaviors of "others." The greats of that discipline—Margaret Mead, Bronislaw Malinowski, et al.—produced a body of work that today is deemed either unscientific or politically incorrect (and, frequently, both). At any rate, by the time I was putting the finishing touches on my doctoral thesis in 1969, social anthropologists had pretty well run out of "primitive tribes" to discover and "pristine, alien cultures" to limn.

Nonetheless, the primary legacy of the field remains pervasive and important, albeit not widely acknowledged: As early as the 1880s, social anthropologists were employing what we now call "systems theory" in their research. They attempted to understand culture as "that complex whole which includes knowledge, belief, art, morals, law, custom and any other habits acquired by man as a member of society" (Tylor, 1976 [1871], p. 1). What they learned from their study of small-scale communities was that all social institutions—legal, political, familial, economic, and religious—were *complexly interrelated* and, when well-integrated, allowed those cultures to function smoothly and effectively. Although anthropologists recognized that the interactions among such institutions were too complex and numerous to scientifically model or quantify (even in the extremely small and "simple" societies they studied), by immersing themselves in those cultures they nevertheless began better to understand why some practiced such hard-to-fathom behaviors as "mother-in-law-avoidance," witchcraft, and dramatic displays of wealth destruction (see, for example, Evans-Pritchard, 1976 [1937]).

Given that background, I suppose it was natural for me to apply this way of thinking to the study of business organizations when, on receiving my doctorate in 1970, I failed to find employment as an anthropology professor (thank heavens b-schools were hiring!). Shortly thereafter, I met Warren Bennis at a seminar in Aspen and our career-long collaboration began almost immediately when we drafted a survey instrument designed to capture the essence of "that complex whole" we dubbed "corporate culture."[1] Given the academic direction in which Warren and I then headed over the next four decades, it is more than a touch ironic that a major element missing from our "whole" was leadership. And that oversight was largely a consequence of my anthropological background. As I now think about my graduate education, I don't recall ever having read the word "leadership" in any anthropological text. And there is a reason for that omission: Before coming into contact with European civilization, small-scale societies around the world tended to be rather static (or, as noted above, "smoothly functioning"). In those societies, the role of a "tribal leader," "chief," or "headman" (as so named by the first Western visitors) was typically that of an enforcer of the existing norms of social behavior. Those who fulfilled these roles were thus more akin to judges, or wise elders, than they were to the "take charge" instigators of change we call leaders in the modern world.

In light of that, it is perhaps paradoxical that the second lasting legacy of social anthropology is the study of "social change"—which originally was defined as interpreting why and how institutions in traditional societies disintegrated on contact with Western culture. Indeed, it took me nearly a decade to overcome my trained incapacity to appreciate the necessary roles corporate leaders play as *creators* of corporate culture and shapers of positive change. Yet, even as Warren gradually convinced me of the importance of leadership in modern business organizations, I never abandoned my concomitant focus on the *cultural context* in which such leadership occurs. To this day, I believe leadership is best understood as part of "that complex whole" of corporate culture. Hence, I have never been much interested in research that purports to identify the personality traits and characteristics of "the leader," *per se* and *ab situ*, even as the body and acceptance of that approach has grown.

Today, the academic field of leadership has been largely captured by the discipline of psychology and, thus, most business school leadership courses are taught by psychologists or organizational behavioralists who draw almost exclusively on the research findings and methods of psychology. Hence, most of my colleagues who teach leadership administer diagnostic tools to pinpoint the personality types of their students, and use psychological tests to measure how well they interact in small groups and how they are perceived by others. In general, I am uneasy about subjecting students to such methods of self and peer assessment, for several (admittedly debatable) reasons:

- They often lead to stereotyping or, at least, pigeon-holing students into assuming they are fixed "types" instead of each being a multi-faceted—and developing—individual.
- There is little evidence that people change positively as the result of such assessments, certainly there is nothing to indicate they become better leaders.
- Most of the diagnostics and assessment tools used—even when scientifically validated—have been designed to fit some preconceived psychological theory and, thus, are self-fulfilling (which is why astute individuals can "game" them, and become any "type" they choose to be).
- Even when these methods are valid in studying personality, they have little or nothing to do with leadership.

The ultimate test of any idea is common sense: *Does it square with the reality of the world we see?* And when I take hard look at the behavior of leaders in the business world, I find it impossible to conclude the observed complexities can be explained solely by a study of their personalities (any more than it can be explained solely in terms of profit-maximizing behavior, as some business professors attempt to do). Nor do I find the currently fashionable short-gun marriage of psychology-cum-economics adequate to capture the complexity of the world of corporate leadership. To build a broad and useful model of effective—and might I add, *ethical*—corporate leadership would require an almost limitless concatenation of considerations, including a leader's technical knowledge, strategic capabilities, interpersonal competence, financial acumen, knowledge of the market, ability to create followers, moral philosophy, values, luck, timing, and all those within shifting and situational social, organizational, political, competitive, and economic contexts. Even reducing all the above to an absolute minimum that still reflects reality, leadership is the most complex of all social roles because it entails not only the behavior of the leader but that of followers as well, and that interrelationship occurs in a changing environment.

Since I have no idea how one would scientifically study or model such complexity, or how any academic discipline by and of itself could be useful in teaching would-be leaders, I sometimes fear that, like Gertrude Stein's Oakland, "there is no there" with regard to knowledge about leadership and, hence, *it can't be taught*. But then I am reminded by examples of effective leaders that *it can be learned*: After all, biographies of leaders typically chronicle a process of personal development and growth from leadership failure to success. That being the case, I began my own teaching with neither a model of leadership nor from a disciplinary perspective but, instead, from the needs of the learners: What kind of leaders do they want to become? What do they want to learn about leadership in order to realize those aspirations? What do they need to do to develop as leaders?

My (decidedly unscientific) laboratory in this enquiry was some seventy, two-day to two-week seminars I moderated for business and other leaders under the aegis of the Aspen Institute, and another thirty or so I conducted for various corporations and organizations in the United States, Europe, Asia, and South Africa, all over a twenty-year (1985–2005) period. Among the participants in those seminars were ten or more CEOs of Fortune 100 companies, dozens of CEOs of smaller companies, hundreds of division heads, entrepreneurs, and partners from top-management consulting firms, along with a smattering of elected and appointed government officials. This non-random "sample" amounted to between 1,500 and 2,000 practicing, and would-be, leaders.

I began by asking them all "who comes to mind when you hear the word leadership?" As one might imagine, the question elicited a wide variety of responses yet, also not surprising, a few names were mentioned with greater frequency than others. Curiously, the names of business executives seldom were cited by my seminarians who, overwhelmingly, were business people themselves. From the realm of religion, Moses, Siddhartha Gautama ("the Buddha"), Jesus of Nazareth, and the prophet Mohammed were cited. In the secular realm, such non-Western leaders as Mustafa Kemal Ataturk, Indira Gandhi, Deng Xiaoping, Jomo Kenyatta, and Julius Nyerere were mentioned. From the United States Lincoln, Washington, Jefferson, Kennedy, the two Presidents Roosevelt, and Eleanor Roosevelt were the most-cited politicians, along with Winston Churchill, Charles De Gaulle, Jean Monnet, Margaret Thatcher, Vaclav Havel, and Golda Meier from other Western democracies. What has been most remarkable—given that my seminar participants were overwhelmingly white businessmen—is that the most-cited individuals were three "radicals" of color: Martin Luther King Jr., Nelson Mandela, and, the most frequently mentioned of all, Mohandas Gandhi.

As seminar participants nominated such leaders, I would record their names on a flip chart. Then, I would ask participants why they cited each of them. No matter the participant's race, religion, gender, political leanings, occupational status, or nationality, the reasons cited almost always had two dimensions, one having to do with the manifest effectiveness of the leader, the second with the morality (or "goodness") of his or her cause. As a follow-up, I asked the participants what personal lessons about leadership they might draw from a study of their model leaders. Here they would almost invariably cite something the leaders *did*—some actions they took, policies they introduced, ways they behaved toward followers—that the seminarians felt had relevance or applicability to their own leadership challenges. Building on insights gained from those responses, I stumbled on the theory of leadership and approach to teaching I describe below.

Values-Based Leadership

In 1989, I put a name on the approach to leadership that, or so it seemed to me, was the "implicit theory" held by so many of my Aspen seminarians: I called it "values-based leadership," and my thinking about it has been evolving ever since (O'Toole, 2008). Demonstrably, something like the practice of values-based leadership had existed for centuries—actually millennia—before I "discovered" it (with a big assist from my students), but whether or not others before me had identified, or named, it is of little importance. What matters is that the approach seems particularly suited to the needs of a modern society characterized by extreme individualism and diversity: simply put, people today have remarkably differing and divergent ideas, goals, and aspirations. I think it is safe to assert that a major source of the disagreement, conflict, and misdirection rife in today's world is the result of the fact that people differ on what they hold dear, that is, on their *values*. That is why modern leadership is often compared to "herding cats." Indeed, if everybody wanted the same thing—desired the same ends—there would be no need for leadership. In that condition, everyone would march off happily in the same direction. But because reasonable people disagree on both ends and means, I conclude the role of a modern leader is to create conditions in which those with differing agendas can unite behind a common purpose. This act has a moral basis when leaders motivate followers by holding out the promise of helping them to realize the things *they* hold most dear, that which they *value*. And such leadership seems so rare today precisely because we value different things.

So how does one herd cats in a fashion that is both effective and moral? On this score, I have noted that my executive seminarians have been particularly impressed by reading what America's founders had to say on the subject of leadership. In *The Federalist*, James Madison (1787–1788) wrote that the nation's leaders need to listen intently to the expressed desires of the public, but should not be prisoners to the public's literal demands. Instead, he said leaders in a democracy should "discern the true interests" and common needs of the people, and then "refine the public view" in a way that transcends the surface noise of pettiness, contradiction, and self-interest.

Theodore Roosevelt's (1910) "New Nationalism" speech offers some insight into what Madison's words mean in practice. In that speech, delivered in a Kansas cornfield, Roosevelt addressed the specific and legitimate interests and needs of industrialists, farmers, financiers, laborers, small business owners, and conservationists, showing equal respect for each of their competing values and claims. But he didn't stop there. Roosevelt then elevated the discussion by offering a transcendent vision of a good society that encompassed those conflicting values in a way that each group, acting alone, had been unable to articulate from their narrower perspectives. He thus showed the nation the way forward by identifying overarching values that the disparate, often-warring special interests had in common and, in the process, he created a compelling vision of a better future than could be achieved by continuing conflict.

Significantly, Roosevelt did not spell out the particulars of how that would be done; instead, he outlined the basic conditions under which it *could* be done. He realized the key to implementation was the involvement and participation of all the relevant constituencies. In discussing this speech, my Aspen seminarians often noted that the role of leaders is to help followers to focus on attaining ends that are good for them all. Ultimately, leaders must act, and that requires them to translate the cacophony of competing interests into a simple harmonious vision of a good end all can collectively seek. For leaders to effectively cut through the complexity of diverse interests, they must create transcendent, or overarching, visions that followers can recognize as morally superior to their own narrow interests, while at the same time effectively encompassing those interests. Leaders thus create followers by allowing them to take the leader's dream as their own, because, in fact, it is their own (O'Toole, 1995). Seminar participants noted that this approach to leadership is particularly appropriate when followers are deeply divided by ideology, religion, and ethnic backgrounds. Significantly, corporate leaders at the seminar have noted that this approach is also effective for business organizations in turbulent environments.

The basic insight that emerged from the seminars is this: People today only follow leaders who manifest the ability and willingness to take them where *they* want to go. Hence, the seminarians concluded that effective leaders must set aside the culturally conditioned "natural" instinct to lead by push—particularly when times are tough—and always adopt the "unnatural" behavior of leading by the inspiring pull of common values.

Seminarians also observed that only a small set of leaders always do, or did, that—among them, Lincoln, King Jr., Mandela, Havel, Mother Teresa, Eleanor Roosevelt, Monnet, and, of course, Gandhi. It was noted that these leaders had a few common characteristics: They were not driven by the desire for wealth or power. Their leadership was not about *them:* not about realizing their personal needs for status, fame, or ego satisfaction. Instead, their actions were based on helping followers realize *their* true needs. These leaders consistently acted on behalf of their followers, seeking to provide the conditions and resources their constituencies couldn't provide on their own. The importance of this quality of "servant-leadership" has been observed by many, but what is most unusual about these leaders was the *consistency* of that behavior. And they each displayed a high degree of *selflessness.* That does not mean they were without ambition, but rather their ambition was of an unusual sort: They found personal satisfaction and fulfillment through providing the opportunity for others to realize *their* goals and potential.

Most singularly, these leaders stand out in terms of the clarity of their values. Gandhi never spoke without reference to the dignity of all men and women, and he made it clear that non-violence was his highest value, higher even than his practical goal of Indian independence. Gandhi would negotiate and compromise with the British—for example, he stood by them during World War I—but when engaging in such necessary, practical transactions he made certain those acts were consistent with, and in service of, his highest values. Similarly, Jean Monnet spent years negotiating quotas and prices for steel and coal while founding the European Common Market, but he never lost sight of the ultimate purpose of such acts: the creation of a lasting peace in Europe (Monnet, 1978).

Of course, the danger of defining values-based leadership in terms of the characteristics of such rare individuals is that the vast majority of leaders, and potential leaders, may feel excluded. If we are honest with ourselves, most of us recognize we lack the unique integrity of a Gandhi, the clear and steady vision of a Lincoln, and the selfless virtue of a Mother Teresa. So why should we aspire to the heights if we know we only are going to end up disappointing ourselves and our followers? In fact, a reading of the biographies of such exemplary leaders reveals that each had numerous flaws and common human frailties. They were all, in fact, *imperfect*—just like the rest of us. Indeed, each had to learn to lead, learn to overcome (or compensate for) their weaknesses, and, especially, to learn to discipline themselves to serve others. As their biographies show, and as Warren Bennis reminds us, values-oriented leaders learn to lead by reflecting honestly on their experiences—in particular, on their failures. I believe the lesson to draw from a study of great leaders is not that they are perfect humans but, instead, that almost all people are capable of becoming effective values-based leader *if* they choose to be, and *if* they choose to do the hard work entailed in becoming one. Clearly, few leaders will become as great as the exemplars cited above but, in reality, very few leaders face circumstances where they need to be among the greatest to succeed.

It is a long way from the grand stages on which Gandhi, Lincoln, and Mandela led to the quotidian concerns and common platforms of business leadership. Yet my seminarians tended to conclude that, in the practical world of commerce, it is possible—with a little effort at translation and a large commitment of dedication—to practice values-based leadership.

Elsewhere, I have identified four retired business executives who I would put on my Mt. Rushmore of corporate values-based leaders: Max DePree, Robert Galvin, James Houghton, and Jan Carlzon (O'Toole, 1995). There are also more-contemporary CEOs who I believe may make the grade after they are retired for long enough and enough information about them is available to make definitive assessments of their performance. In fact, it is a lot easier to be a corporate values-based leader than it is to be one at the national level: There is less divergence in a company than in a country with respect to values. And while the overarching and unifying values that business leaders cite—product quality, customer service, organizational excellence—may not be as lofty as the political values of liberty and equality, they can be every bit as important to the lives of followers. Selfless corporate leaders who put respect for their followers ahead of their own needs for fame, power, and wealth can be as virtuous in their own small domains as values-based political leaders are on grander stages. Hence, the difference is in degree, not in kind, between the business leader who creates the conditions under which all of her employees can develop their potential, and the political leader who uses public policy to do the same for all citizens.

In sum, unique among the various forms of leadership, values-based leaders create followers by enabling them to see clearly—and to achieve effectively—that which *they* hold dear. Absent a stricter definition, the role, task, and responsibility of values-based leaders is thus to help followers realize the most important ends they cannot obtain by themselves. I believe firmly in such leadership, but I also believe there are other effective ways to lead, and those beliefs contribute to how and what I teach.

What, and How, I Teach About Leadership

GANDHI AS THE EXEMPLAR

First, I began by showing my executive seminar (or MBA class) the 1982 film *Gandhi*. I do this for a half-dozen reasons: (1) Mohandas Gandhi tends to be the most universally admired, hence least-controversial, leader with whom to begin a discussion of leadership; (2) the film usefully and clearly focuses on what Gandhi did as a leader, and how he did it; (3) his challenge was so enormous, and his resources so few, that it disarms those who feel their own corporate leadership task is a "mission impossible"; (4) the film is a historically accurate account of what Gandhi actually did and said; (5) among all great statesmen, Gandhi left the most-detailed record of what he did, why he did it, how he dealt with set-backs, and how he developed as a leader; and (6) Gandhi engaged in almost all the admirable behaviors that seminar participants cite their favorite leaders as doing.

I then spend two to three hours in dialogue with the participants, getting *them* to identify Gandhi's leadership activities and behaviors. Below is a summary of what they typically mention:

Gandhi's Actions (What he did as a leader)

- Developed a philosophy grounded in universal moral precepts
- Clearly articulated and prioritized his values
- Identified an over-arching ethical principle to guide his actions
- Changed his own behavior in order to later change others
- Gained sufficient book knowledge
- Set a clear goal
- Created a strategy in which practicality and morality were complementary
- Defined and focused on his own leadership task
- Clarified his primary role and distinguished it from the roles other leaders would play in the campaign
- Demonstrated his effectiveness
- Set realistic expectations
- Created conditions under which followers could achieve their desired ends
- Practiced servant-leadership
- Gave followers reason to hope
- Empowered and energized followers
- Practiced widespread involvement and participation
- Delegated and decentralized all authority for strategy implementation
- Practiced transparency and candor
- Admitted errors
- Made use of universal symbols
- Consistently communicated and reinforced his message
- Created disciples

Gandhi's Leadership Behaviors (His character traits)

- Practiced humility, selflessness, patience, and persistence
- Reflected on experience/learned from his failures and mistakes
- Engaged in honest introspection, critical self-examination, and self-discipline
- Displayed moral courage
- Behaved consistently
- Acted with integrity, and always as servant to his followers
- Displayed the requisite ambition and willingness to step forward and lead

In light of these two generic lists, I then ask my students/seminarians to consider several questions: Are there any items listed that would be *inappropriate* in any setting—business, government, or other modern organization? Would any of these be *ineffective* at any time, or in any place? Is there any leadership action or behavior listed that would be *impractical* in any context today? Are there any essential leadership actions or behaviors not on the list that should be? And, finally, how and to what extent can they, the students, translate what Gandhi did into a corporate setting, and apply it themselves?

In my experience, most students admire Gandhi's actions as leader of the Indian independence movement, yet many (if not most) harbor doubts about the applicability of those actions to the world of business, and almost all are unsure how they personally could apply the lessons derived from the discussion. Thus, the remaining agenda of the course (or seminar) is designed to deal with those two issues in such depth that each student becomes able to clarify and articulate his or her own philosophy or approach to leadership, whether that is consistently Gandhian or not.

USE OF BUSINESS CASES

In order for the participants to answer the questions above—that is, to test for themselves the practicality and usefulness of the leadership behaviors they have identified—I then ask them to turn to an analysis of six to a dozen business cases (depending on the time available) that document efforts by corporate executives efforts to lead organizational transformations. I do this for several reasons: (1) because the students/seminarians are not ascetic pacifists leading struggles against the world's mightiest empire, they need to see how and to what extent Gandhi's practices can be successfully applied in business organizations; (2) leadership needs to be studied in an organizational context (see my comments above regarding systems theory); and (3) modern leadership is always about a process of change (those whose task is to preserve the status quo we call "administrators" or "managers," and not leaders).

Here I draw heavily on Harvard Business School cases, specifically ones authored by, or prepared under the supervision of, Richard Walton, Michael Beer, Nitin Nohria, Christopher Bartlett, and their colleagues. These cases—for example, those relating to the Corning, ABB, and Asda corporations—are uniquely rich in providing detail about what leaders do and how to bring about change in large organizations. In essence, these cases allow students to analyze the process of leading change *in a context*: the cases provide relevant information about both the leader's actions and the organization's challenges and culture. I supplement these cases with shorter, informal ones I prepare concerning change at such companies as General Electric, W.T. Gore, and Whole Foods.

Time permitting, I also assign books (or excerpts from them) by executives who describe their own efforts to lead change. Among the ones I have used successfully are Jan Carlzon's (1989) *Moments of Truth,* Louis Gerstner's (2003) *Who Says Elephants Can't Dance?*, and Gordon Bethune and Scott Huler's (1999) *From Worst to First,* each a first-hand, thoughtful account of not only how these CEOs brought about change but also an assessment of the setbacks and the mistakes they made in the process.

I conduct the class discussion of these cases and books Socratically, much as they would be at Harvard: I start by asking the students to describe the business situation, to clarify the issues the company is facing, and then to identify what its leaders are doing and why, and then to assess if and why they are successful and what other options they might have had (*What else might they have done?*). Then, in light of what they have learned from these business examples, I ask the students to go back to their Gandhian lists and to modify them—adding, subtracting, restating items as they see fit.

USE OF THEORY

In this iterative process at least a few participants will want access to some leadership theory to provide an intellectual framework for their own evolving thoughts. When so pressed, I review the ten major theories of leadership enumerated below (along with brief descriptions and parenthetic reference to the names—or disciplines—of scholars associated with advancing, or describing, each perspective):

- Biological. "The leader has the most testosterone" (bio-sociologists, primate behavioralists)
- Power. "Might makes Right" (Thucydides, Hobbes)
- Paternalism. "Rule by the brightest and most virtuous" (Plato)
- Contingency/Situational. "It all depends: leaders do whatever it takes" (Machiavelli, Spencer, Gary Wills [see Wills, 1994], business school social scientists)

- Great Man. "The hero as leader; it's about personality and charisma" (Carlyle, Weber)
- Transactional. "Followers act in their self-interest" (economists, political scientists)
- Cognitive. "Leaders lead by ideas" (Marx, John Gardner [see Gardner, 1989])
- Transformational. "Leaders are moral agents and enablers of followers" (James MacGregor Burns [see Burns, 1978], Ronald Heifetz [see Heifetz, 1994])
- Shared. "Leadership is a team sport" (Center for Effective Organizations [see O'Toole, Galbraith, & Lawler, 2002])
- Servant-Leadership. "Leaders help followers achieve their goals" (Max De Pree [see De Pree, 1989])

I often assign writings by some of the authors mentioned above, most notably Max De Pree, Ronald Heifetz, and James MacGregor Burns whose theories are particularly cogent and relevant to business executives and students. I also use classic texts, such as Machiavelli's *The Prince* and Plato's *Republic.* Although my colleague Warren Bennis's name doesn't appear on the list above (because he is an eclectic intellectual "hedgehog" and not a "fox" with a narrow theory), I often assign his *On Becoming a Leader* to highlight the importance of the issue of development (learning from experience) to the process of becoming a leader (Bennis, 1989). And I occasionally will have them look at Robert Townsend's (1984) *Further Up the Organization* to see how smart executives translate good theory into their own language, and then practice it effectively. In all, my main purpose in using theory is to help students to surface their own, personal implicit (and often unconscious) theories of leadership—and then to rigorously test those against what they know and are learning in the class.

PERSONAL EXPERIENCES

At this point, I ask the students to create their own cases, based either on their personal experiences as leaders or what they have observed as followers in organizations where those above them have attempted to lead change. I ask them to discuss their experiences in small groups and, then, to present them to the entire class in exactly in the way they have analyzed the Harvard cases. Obviously, the success and usefulness of this exercise depends on the depth of experience of the participants. It works beautifully with older students in executive seminars, and less well with younger MBA candidates who have had little or no work experience. (I can't imagine it working with undergraduates.) While not all students can do so, the best of them have prepared deep, insightful, and instructive cases, more than a few concluding that *based on what I have now learned, my effort was flawed for the following reasons, and here's what I would do now instead.* This is often a key step in helping them to clarify and refine their personal (now conscious) theories of leadership.

At the end of the course, I ask each of the students/seminarians to prepare his or her own "Leading Change Guide Book." In whatever form or format they choose, this is their personal "takeaway" from the course, a brief handbook to keep on their desks or in the top drawers to remind them of what they each have concluded are the few essential things leaders must do to bring about change. At the final class session, each student presents his or her guide to the class. This exercise always works. No two of the hundreds of guides my students have prepared have ever been the same, and I am continually overwhelmed by the creativity demonstrated in the choice and design of formats, and surprised by the diversity of lessons students draw from discussing the very same theories and books. Significantly, no student has ever stayed with the original list of Gandhian behaviors identified in the first class session. (My biggest surprise came when the CEO of a *Fortune 500* company offered an impassioned, and *not altogether* unreasonable, guide based on Biological reasoning, stressing why high levels of testosterone were essential to lead change!)

THE MODERATOR'S ROLE

My own role in this process is *maieutic*. Like Plato's "midwife," I see my primary role as educing from the students what is already in them. My goal is to help them to make conscious and to clarify what they already implicitly know about leadership (and perhaps to reinforce positive behaviors they may fear to try). Since changing the personality or "style" of others is nearly impossible (and I think it is presumptuous on the part of a teacher to try to do so), my goal is more modest: to leave students better informed about the diverse and multifold whys, ways, and hows of leadership—theirs and others—and perhaps to equip them with a few things they might do themselves to become more effective leaders.

That does not mean I am (or anyone could be) without my own thoughts and beliefs about leadership. Indeed, I blatantly stack the deck in favor of values-based leadership by starting the course with a discussion of Gandhi; for example, if I were to start with Jack Welch (who gets his due in the second or third session) everything that followed might turn our quite differently! While I attempt to be objective about, and not critical of, any of the ten theories advanced above (each, in fact, has merit), if pressed I say my values-based views are closest to the last four theories listed. Indeed, I admit that is why I am attracted to Gandhi's leadership—even though I don't share his religious perspective or his philosophical views relating to personal conduct (such as veganism and celibacy).

I am not ethically neutral. Near the end of the course, I say I believe it would be better if all leaders practiced values-based leadership because that approach has both an effectiveness *and* a moral dimension (I am, after all, an ethics professor). But I also add that many leaders succeed by ignoring the latter dimension (or, as is most often the case, they set ethical considerations aside when those are perceived to be in conflict with effectiveness). In the final analysis, I conclude leaders can succeed either by taking the moral high road or the amoral low one, and it is up to them to choose which they follow. It would be prettier if the evidence showed that the high road led more frequently to greater effectiveness, but the world is not organized that way. So, the course comes down to a matter of choice: The students are free to choose, and I encourage them to make the choice *consciously*.

Assessment

There is much concern in business schools today with assessment, and I offer some general observations about that topic elsewhere (O'Toole, 2009). But the reader of this chapter may well want to see evidence that the approach outlined above "works." In short, to what extent have my courses and seminars helped people to become better leaders? I fear I can't provide any hard data in that regard. I have the usual course and seminar evaluations (which basically measure immediate joys and satisfactions) along with anecdotal cards, letters, and emails from students I have long forgotten but who claim not to have forgotten the course. I take particular heart from the latter because I believe the true measure of success of my enterprise is the extent to which my courses *years later* affect the behavior of my students when they become leaders. But, in fact, do I know that anything they learned from my class later influenced what they did on the job? Truly, I have no idea. So I recently turned to my colleague Warren Bennis who, at age 85, has an impressive number of former students now actively leading business organizations. I asked him what data he had about the degree to which his teaching had contributed to their growth. I think it is useful to end this chapter with the gist of his response (as stated in my words).

Warren said that issues of development are today front and center in the social science disciplines: economic, political, and human. Yet we know very little about the process of development in any of those fields: Why do some nations develop economically, while others do not? Why do some nations develop robust, democratic institutions, while others do not? Why do some individuals develop their talents, while others do not? When it comes to leadership, we lack the sophisticated, longitudinal data that would allow us to understand how leaders develop over a lifetime. We don't even know when—at what age, or under what circumstances—people are open to the experiences that cause them to grow as leaders. Until we better understand that essential process called development, we are left with the casual observation that people seem to learn and to grow in different ways, at different times, and based on different kinds of experiences.

So does my approach to teaching values-based leadership work? I trust that it does—at least for some former students, at some times, and under some circumstances!

Note

1. Warren and I think that Robert Blake and Jane Moulton may have coined the term "corporate culture" in their *The Managerial Grid* (Blake & Moulton, 1962). We first published our little instrument, using "culture" in the anthropological sense, in James O'Toole (1981), *Making America Work*.

References

Bennis, W. (1989). *On becoming a leader*. Reading, MA: Perseus Books.

Bethune, G., & Huler, S. (1999). *From worst to first: Behind the scenes of Continental's remarkable comeback*. London, UK: John Wiley & Sons.

Blake, R. R., & Moulton, J. S. (1962). The managerial grid. *Advanced Management Office Executive, 1*(9).

Burns, J. M. (1978). *Leadership*. New York: Harper & Row, Publishers, Inc.

Carlzon, J. (1989). *Moments of truth*. Cambridge, MA: Ballinger.

De Pree, M. (1989). *Leadership is an art*. New York: Doubleday.

Evans-Pritchard, E. E. (1976 [1937]). *Witchcraft, oracles and magic among the Azande*. Oxford: Oxford University Press.

Gardner, J. (1989). *On leadership*. New York: Free Press

Gerstner, L. (2003). *Who says elephants can't dance? Leading a great enterprise through dramatic change*. New York: HarperCollins.

Heifetz, R. A. (1994). *Leadership without easy answers*. Cambridge, MA: Belknap Press.

Madison, J. (1787–1788). Federalist Paper No. 10.

Monnet, J. (1978). *Memoirs*. London, UK: Collins.

O'Toole, J. (1981). *Making America work: Productivity and responsibility*. New York: Continuum Publishing.

O'Toole, J. (1995). *Leading change*. San Francisco, CA: Jossey-Bass.

O'Toole, J. (2008). Notes toward a definition of values-based leadership. *Journal of Values-Based Leadership, 12*, 84–92.

O'Toole, J. (2009). The pluralistic future of management education. In S. Armstrong & C. Fukami (Eds.), *The SAGE handbook of management learning, education and development* (pp. 547–558). Thousand Oaks, CA: Sage.

O'Toole, J., Galbraith, J., & Lawler, E. E. (2002). When two (or more) heads are better than one: The promise and pitfalls of shared leadership. *California Management Review, 44*(4), 65–83.

Roosevelt, T. (1910, August). The new nationalism. Speech presented at Osawatomie, KS.

Townsend, R. (1984). *Further up the organization*. New York: Knopf.

Tylor, E. B. (1976 [1871]). *Primitive culture: Researches into the development of mythology, philosophy, religion, language, art, and custom*. New York: Gordon Press.

Wills, G. (1994). *Certain trumpets: The nature of leadership*. New York: Simon & Schuster.

19

IDENTITY WORKSPACES FOR LEADERSHIP DEVELOPMENT

◆ Gianpiero Petriglieri
INSEAD

Profound changes in individuals' relationship with their employers and expectations for their work lives have generated an increasing demand for leadership development, while at the same time exposing the limitations of traditional leadership programs focused on the acquisition of conceptual knowledge and requisite skills. This chapter explores how conceptualizing leadership programs as "identity workspaces" helps to meet the demand for leadership in ways that benefit individuals, organizations, and society. Alongside the acquisition of knowledge and skills, identity workspaces facilitate the revision and consolidation of individual and collective identities. They personalize and contextualize participants' learning, inviting them to wrestle with the questions "What does leading mean to us?" and "Who am I as a leader?" Attention to both activity and identity deepens and accelerates the development of individual leaders and strengthens leadership communities within and across organizations.

Acknowledgments: I am deeply grateful to Jennifer L. Petriglieri and Jack D. Wood. Their influence on the ideas and approach presented here goes far beyond our joint work researching and practicing leadership development. Declan Fitzsimons, Robin Fryer, Aideen Lucey, and Mark Roberts offered valuable feedback on this chapter and contributed much to the development of the approach it describes.

I describe the conceptual foundations, learning processes, design principles, and professional competences that enable leadership programs to function as identity workspaces. Designing such programs, however, takes more than adopting the methods described here. It calls for revisiting the role of leadership developers as professionals and demands of us the same mindfulness, curiosity, courage, integrity, and social responsibility that we invite leaders to demonstrate.

❖❖❖

We live and work in times of unprecedented change, or so we are told. Globalization has increased the uncertainty, complexity, diversity, and amount of information we face daily (Kanter, 2010). Hardly a month goes by without a new crisis in the economic, political, or environmental domain. In organizations, multilayered hierarchies have given way to flatter team-based structures in the pursuit of efficiency and flexibility. Gone is the traditional bond between corporation and employees, wherein the latter offered long-term commitment in exchange for security and career ladders (Rousseau, 1990). No longer expecting, or expected, to offer life-long loyalty, the commitment of talented employees often lasts only as long as an organization provides valued opportunities to exercise and develop their skills (Capelli, 2008). Itinerant careers that unfold across organizations, sectors, and countries are held in high regard (Arthur, 2008; Sennett, 2006). Such careers are viewed as a prerequisite for developing the perspective and skills necessary to operate effectively in a globalized world, as well as a status symbol—the mark of being among those valuable few for whose services companies engage in global "wars for talent." As the head of research at a major investment bank once told me, gesturing toward the expanse of desks that hosted some of the world's most respected analysts, "I can't preach loyalty to these people. I would be laughed at. All I can say is—if you work here you have more learning opportunities than elsewhere."

I am sure you have heard this story. The world is flatter, faster, and less predictable than ever before—and so are organizations. A diverse pool of talented individuals hops freely across them in pursuit of experience, opportunity, and meaning. We might ask whether this picture reflects the lives of most people or whether it is more a product of media hype and management gurus preoccupied with the whereabouts of a small elite. The answer matters little. The popularity of the story is undeniable, as is the uncertainty it generates. Either as a new social context, a dominant narrative, or both, this background affects the meaning and exercise of leadership and requires revisiting the way leadership is developed.

The Essence of Leadership: Activity and Identity

Calls for more and better leadership are ubiquitous—in business, in politics, in the professions—and appear as contemporary as the turbulent, globalized, and hyperconnected contexts in which leaders are meant to operate. The allure of leadership and the concern with developing it, however, are not new. Since the dawn of time, the survival and success of any community has hinged on its ability to develop leaders who are able to hold it together, help it address current challenges, and articulate its possible future. Who is entrusted with leading a tribe, a military operation, an academic department, a multinational company, or an insurrection—and how they are expected to lead—may be very different. The essence of leadership, however, never changes.

Regardless of time and place, leadership serves two purposes—one symbolic and the other functional—that respond to fundamental human needs. The first is the need for living examples of what we believe is right, good, and worth pursuing. The second is the need to stick together and get things done. The *identities* of leaders we admire and follow reflect the values, customs, and desires of a community at a point in time. But whether an individual or a group, one thing remains the same: Leaders are symbols of possibility. They define the chasm between who we are and who we hope to be. The *activities* we regard as effective ways of leading also change depending on how we expect to be treated. But whether autocratic or empowering, resolute or open-minded, ruthless or gentle, leaders are always a means to an end. They mobilize performance to accomplish a task.

Much has been said about how leaders must act to mobilize performance in this day and age. First, leaders cannot rely solely on the authority formally vested in their position. They need to influence and inspire, understand the web of networks within and across organizations, and cultivate them. Second, leaders need to recognize and value the unique styles of their people in order to retain, motivate, and develop them. This requires awareness and empathy as well as facility with giving and receiving candid feedback. Third, leaders need to be comfortable with initiating or dealing with change. This involves the capacities to provide direction, mobilize others, and control progress—as well as the sensitivity to offer reassurance, hope, and containment for the inevitable tensions that change entails. Fourth, leaders need to check their ego at the door. The scope and complexity of today's challenges demand that leadership be shared with one's team, if not even more broadly. Leadership is not the preserve of senior executives. It is exercised at all levels, regardless of someone's job title. Organizations do not need lonely heroes at the top. They need all the leadership they can get.

Whether these leadership activities (or disillusionment with leadership mores of past generations) are truly new or not, it would be imprudent to discount the importance of acquiring such a leadership tool kit alongside one's technical competence and strategic insight. Honing skills of informal influence, networking, emotional intelligence, change management, teamwork, and so forth, however, is not enough. Consider the development of a musician. Just because you have a musical ear and practice relentlessly to refine your skills, it does not mean that you will become a successful concert pianist. We speak of a masterful interpretation when a musician gives personal expression to the score and makes us feel like we are hearing it for the first time. Albeit grounded in years of practice and infused with the musician's personal identity, an interpretation is only masterful when it resonates with listeners. The audience may be silent, but it is not passive. The sensitivity of their ears is as important in making an interpretation moving as is the pianist's touch. Magic occurs when the pianist's enactment of "who I am as a musician" vibrates in accord with the audience's sense of "what this music means to us." One moves the other, and vice versa.

Leadership is much like that. Talent and skills are necessary but not sufficient. Followers ultimately bestow leadership. Leaders are most inspiring and effective when their message is deeply personal and yet touches shared concerns—when what they do is intertwined with who they are and resonates with what followers are ready to hear and able to appreciate. (This is also when leaders can be most dangerous and are most vulnerable.) Leaders' actions are most effective and meaningful when their enactment of "who I am as a leader" ("who we are . . . " if a group) is in accord with followers' sense of "what leading means to us."

Here lies a pressing challenge for the exercise and development of leadership. In a world of thick boundaries, homogeneous groups, and long-term employment, leaders had much in common with those they led: the same culture, broadly similar upbringings, comparable lifestyles, perhaps a long shared history in the organization. None of this can be taken for granted today. In a world of porous boundaries, increased mobility and diversity, and reduced organizational identification, questions such as "Who am I as a leader?" and "What does leading mean to us?" are harder to answer. Leaders, like musicians, are expected to move audiences whose members have varied views of what music means and who hold no season ticket. More than ever, leaders need to grasp the interplay between activity and identity. Unfortunately, much of what goes under the banner of "leadership development" remains limited to the former, focusing on abstract knowledge and behavioral competencies and offering little insight into the ways leaders are made, or broken, in the space between their personal history and aspirations, and the dynamics of groups and social systems in which they live. This raises two questions: *How* can this latter insight can be fostered? And *where*?

Identity Workspaces and the Demand for Leadership

In the past, employers were central to individuals' professional and personal identity and hosted its unfolding over time. This is less likely today. Given the fluidity of work environments and the loosening of the relationship between individuals and organizations, many people no longer deem it wise or desirable to entrust their development to their employers. As a result, as Jennifer Petriglieri and I have argued, employing organizations are less likely to be experienced as "identity workspaces" (Petriglieri & Petriglieri, 2010).

An identity workspace is a holding environment for identity work—an institution entrusted to facilitate the process of consolidating existing identities or crafting new ones. Institutions are entrusted as identity workspaces when they offer a combination of three features: conceptual frameworks and routines that help members make sense of themselves and their environment, as well as feel comfortable and act competently in it; communities they identify with and that provide a mixture of belonging, support, and challenge; and rites of passage that facilitate and integrate identity development and role transitions. It is our hypothesis that the growing psychological distance between organizations and their employees has led the function of providing identity workspaces to be invested in business schools in general, and leadership courses in particular (Petriglieri & Petriglieri, 2010).

Requests for support in crafting identities seldom lie far below the surface of organizations' or individuals' interest in leadership programs. In sponsoring such programs, corporate representatives usually seek assurance that the course will develop a community of leaders whose aspirations, worldview, and behavior are closely aligned with the company's strategic intent, desired culture, and competency models—which are, from an identity perspective, local attempts to answer the question "What does leading mean?" On entering a program, however, most participants are less concerned with the way it is tailored to be consistent with organizational models than with how it fits with their concerns and aspirations. They want to know to what extent it will help answer the question "Who am I as a leader?" as well as enhance their effectiveness and future potential within and beyond the organization. In this dual intent lies a struggle for control: of employees' hearts and minds, on the one hand, and of career trajectories and work environments, on the other. While the agendas of organizations and individuals can be aligned, this does not always happen. Furthermore, another agenda needs consideration: Since leaders and their organizations influence and are influenced by society at large, a social agenda is at play, whether we are mindful of it or not.

Leadership programs realize their full potential as identity workspaces when they add value to all three constituencies, that is, when they deepen and accelerate individuals' development as leaders, strengthen a leadership community mindful of (not subservient to) their organization's culture and aims, and define leadership to encompass responsible citizenship in society at large. Leadership programs underdeliver as identity workspaces when they serve one agenda only, for example, when they are thinly veiled attempts at indoctrination and demand that individuals fit academic, organizational, or cultural templates without offering opportunities to inquire what these molds mean to individuals. Or when they are too focused on individual participants, helping them understand the origins of personal idiosyncrasies and the impact of habitual behaviors with little opportunity to examine how one's experience is constantly shaped by the social context. Such one-dimensional programs fuel illusions of control: for example, the illusion that a program can yield a motivated and aligned workforce, a pool of leaders in name only who follow corporate directions as if they were their own; or the illusion that the right mix of soul-searching, feedback, and skill may allow one to stay true to oneself, influence others, and shape organizations without having to wrestle with the power struggles, emotional tensions, and moral questions that are part and parcel of leading.

This is the main obstacle to maximizing the potential of a leadership program to serve as an identity workspace: a widespread desire—on the part of organizations, participants, and faculty—to control the learning process and over-determine up front what will be learned. Everyone wants leaders who are better equipped to deal with uncertainty and surprise. We just do not want either in leadership programs. (Perhaps there is too much of both everywhere else.) As a result, many such programs are designed, more or less consciously, to foster compliance rather than open possibilities—the very opposite of what we say leaders must do. This does not mean that sponsoring organizations and faculty should not identify desired outcomes for their leadership programs. Rather, it means that the pursuit of prescribed outcomes must be balanced with the provision of spaces in which participants can pursue, discover, and question their learning agendas, both individually and collectively.

Working With Experience, Identity, Emotion, and "the Unconscious"

The conceptualization of leadership development programs as identity workspaces—and my approach to designing, staffing, and working within programs that can function as such—rests on three streams of research. The first highlights the primacy of experience in leaders' development, the second links identity to leaders' development, and the third concerns the role of emotions and unconscious factors in the exercise and development of leadership.

Experience. Researchers agree that the primary means through which leaders develop are experiences of leading and following (DeRue & Wellman, 2009; Kolb, 1984; McCall, 1998). Experiences, however, do not automatically turn into learning. Learning from experience is an active process, and scholars have suggested that a major question in leadership studies is not "what should be taught in leadership courses, but *how can leaders be helped to learn?*" (Hackman & Wageman, 2007, p. 46, italics in original). This involves helping leaders maintain an attitude of personal responsibility toward their development (McCall, 2010) and enhancing their motivation and ability to learn from ongoing experiences (DeRue & Ashford, 2010a).

It also involves exposing the psychological and social underpinnings of the ways we learn and addressing potential limitations in both areas.

At the psychological level, becoming better learners requires examining how the "images, assumptions, and stories that we carry in our minds of ourselves and others" (Raelin, 2007, p. 509) influence the ways we approach, understand, and draw conclusions from experiences (Snook, 2007). At the social level, it requires grasping how the communities we come from and those in which we live—our families, schools, organizations, and cultures—enable, channel, and constrict our capacity to learn (Reynolds & Vince, 2004). Learning about how our inner and social worlds affect the ways we make sense of and act on our daily experiences inevitably requires engaging with experience and reflecting upon those engagements—personally and with others (Raelin, 2007). It cannot be done by just thinking about past experience or discussing others' experience (Hackman & Wageman, 2007). Such learning is best accomplished when we are removed enough from the rush and familiarity of our daily routines and contexts. The distance allows us to reflect on experience more than we usually do and to experiment with conclusions we draw and actions we take (Day, 2010; Ibarra, 2003; Petriglieri, Wood, & Petriglieri, 2011).

Identity. A growing body of research has examined the role of identity in the emergence and effectiveness of leaders. This work suggests that the acceptance by others and the effectiveness of leaders hinge on their internalization and enactment of identities that are congruent with their life story (Shamir & Eilam, 2005) and symbolize what is good and unique about their social groups and organizations (Haslam, Reicher, & Platow, 2011; Van Knippenberg & Hogg, 2003). Building on these insights, a literature on the importance of identity development in the process of leaders' development is emerging (Day, 2001; Day & Harrison, 2007; DeRue & Ashford, 2010b; Ibarra, Snook, & Guillen Ramo, 2010; Lord & Hall, 2005).

Complementing traditional concerns with the acquisition of knowledge, skills, and abilities, this research suggests that developing leaders entails deep personal work (Lord & Hall, 2005; Mumford & Manley, 2003; Petriglieri & Stein, 2010; Shamir & Eilam, 2005). Such personal work involves examining and revising the ways leaders make meaning of, respond emotionally to, and act on situations, encounters, experiences, goals, and aspirations (Petriglieri et al., 2011). Central to the process is reflecting on how one's life story orients one's understanding of and actions in the world (Kegan, 1982). Leaders who through this process integrate their life story and leader identity are said to be "authentic," that is, they "have made [their] values and conviction highly personal through their lived experiences, experienced emotions, and an active process of reflection on these experiences and emotions" (Shamir & Eilam, 2005, p. 397). Assisting this kind of personal work requires professionals with the appropriate training and expertise (Berglas, 2002; Hart, Blattner, & Leipsic, 2001; Kilburg, 2004; Sherman & Freas, 2004; Wood & Petriglieri, 2005a).

Emotions and "the Unconscious." While corporate and academic competency models put much emphasis on observable characteristics and behaviors, managers are keenly aware of "the emotional and moral labor of creating choices and meanings for themselves and others" (Bolden & Gosling, 2006, p. 159). Leading well often requires moving toward anxiety-provoking situations in order to learn more rather than attempting to reduce anxiety quickly. It also requires the abilities to manage one's (and others') emotional arousal, resist acting on impulse, and sometimes temporarily to raise anxiety in the service of fostering learning and change (Hackman & Wageman, 2007). This emotional labor is most pronounced when organizations face "adaptive challenges"—major crises, shifts in their environment, and/or radical organizational changes. Such challenges call for leaders to ignite and contain strong feelings—ranging from hope and excitement to fear and loss—as organizational members revise deeply held values, beliefs, and habits (Heifetz, 1994).

Emotions, in leadership as elsewhere, are not always conscious. A recent review of research in this area concluded that "the notion that much of what we do is influenced by processes outside our conscious awareness is no longer a theoretical claim or the province of clinical observation" (Barsade, Ramarajan, & Westin, 2009, p. 145). Learning to lead, therefore, involves "learning about the way emotions irrationalize supposedly rational processes and make them what they are" (Fineman, 1997, p. 21). Clinical approaches that invite the exploration and integration of the emotional forces that impinge on the exercise of leadership are best suited to foster such learning (Kets de Vries, 2005; Petriglieri & Wood, 2005a). Central to these approaches is the idea of "the unconscious," a term best intended as shorthand for the assortment of covert psychological and social forces that elude human rationality.

Whereas some clinical perspectives portray the unconscious as a repository of demons left behind by early trauma—much as Freud did a century ago—the approach that informs my work builds on a characterization of it as a surprising but well meaning and often enriching element of human nature (Petriglieri & Wood, 2005a). This approach views the psyche as not only bound by the past in endless repetition of infantile experiences and early identifications but also as pulling the individual toward the achievement of a fulfilled life and purposeful work (Petriglieri et al., 2011). In addition, it pays much attention to systems psychodynamics (Gould, Stapley, & Stein, 2001; Jaques, 1955; Menzies, 1960; Miller & Rice, 1967), that is, to the ways in which the emotional needs of individuals and groups shape structures, processes, and cultures in a social system and to how these structures, processes, and cultures, in turn, shape the experiences of those individuals and groups.

Learning Process: Contextualization and Personalization

Drawing on the research outlined above, I consider leadership programs well suited to serve as identity workspaces when they include a significant experiential component, involve learning about the activities and identities associated to leading, reveal the interplay between individual functioning and group dynamics, integrate the acquisition of knowledge and skills with opportunities for personal reflection and experimentation, and expose the emotional and often unconscious dynamics at play within individuals, groups, and organizations. These programs must be connected to, yet removed from, participants' organizational context, everyday experience, and familiar mores. Each needs to be present but not dominate the program so that it can be examined and experimented with. Getting the balance right makes it possible to contextualize and personalize the learning process.

Contextualizing the learning means embedding it in the language and culture of participants' organizations and social contexts. The purpose of doing so is not uncritical indoctrination. It is to use those languages and cultures as templates that orient individual and community development, to reflect upon and examine them, and to take ownership of their existence, maintenance, and change if necessary—rather than viewing them as external to one's practice. When all participants work in the same organization, that organization's culture is often enacted and easiest to examine in program interactions. When participants come from different organizations, the cultural enactments often reveal, and make it possible to examine, widespread assumptions and practices that pervade many organizations' cultures.

Personalizing the learning means linking it to participants' historical and current experiences (Petriglieri et al., 2011). The purpose is to help individuals examine and integrate the ways their history and aspirations interact with social pressures to affect the way they think, feel, and act. The main vehicle for this process is the program's experiential component, which magnifies participants' habitual patterns of cognition, emotional response, and behavior, and makes them available for exploration. This, in turn, sustains experimentation with both interpretations of further events and behavior within those events.

Providers of leadership programs often put much emphasis on learning contextualization, usually referred to as "program customization." Learning personalization is equally important. Contextualization assures that a program is relevant, personalization that it is meaningful. Their combination deepens leaders' development by linking what they do to their history and context; accelerates it by helping them learn more from their experience; and strengthens leadership communities by increasing their openness and shared ownership of the organization's culture. The integration between contextualization and personalization has long been a feature of rites of passage, which are a central component of identity workspaces.

Design Principles: The Leadership Journey

Traditional rites of passage—such as initiation rituals—facilitate the transition from one social status and life stage to another. They transmit current knowledge, values, and cultural norms; impart moral principles; and instill a sense of belonging to a community while providing a container for personal transitions (Campbell, 1972; Trice & Beyer, 1984). Through them initiates do not just learn the narratives of the group they are entering; they become part of those narratives. While the content of rites of passage is tied to local cultures, their unfolding is universal (Eliade, 1995; Van Gennep, 1960). They involve a separation from one's familiar context; a period of "liminality" that includes reflection, instruction, and experimentation; and, finally, reintegration into society with a new identity and the perspective and behavior associated with it. This cycle is portrayed in countless narratives of mythical journeys (Campbell, 1994), which offer both an apt metaphor and useful principles for the design of leadership programs as identity workspaces.

The metaphor of a journey is fitting for leadership programs that aim to involve development of practical skills, acquisition of relevant knowledge, inspiration to pursue long-term development, and strengthening of a community and shared culture. A journey is an experience that can transform our view of the world and of ourselves. The metaphor suggests that these programs engage participants cognitively, emotionally, and practically, and that the learning may result from the pursuit of desired aims as well as from the surprises encountered along the way. Such journeys are deeply personal, and yet they cannot be taken alone.

A focus on groups is the first design principle. Participants are divided in study groups of 6–7 members. Leadership cannot be exercised or developed in isolation, and these learning units provide both the material and context to investigate the ways in which individuals influence groups, and vice versa. Groups discuss cases and readings and, most importantly, engage in a series of activities during which the focus of the group's "study" is its own experience. These sessions allow participants to explore and experiment with their interpretations and behavior, give and receive candid feedback, and examine how their group develops or reflects a culture and how it interacts with other groups.

A progression through four stages is the second design principle. Building on the developmental process portrayed in mythical journeys, Jack Wood and I have suggested that meaningful experiential leadership development unfolds in four stages—preparation, orientation, experimentation, and integration (Wood & Petriglieri, 2005b).

Preparation occurs before the program convenes. Participants read cases and articles that will be discussed in the first part of the program and give some thought to their learning objectives in consultation with colleagues and significant others. The main activity of this stage is drafting a "Personal and Professional Identity Narrative" (PPIN), a confidential autobiographical document that will serve as a basis for individual coaching and inform their development plans. The PPIN kick starts the process of exploring participants' history, communities, and aspirations, and invites them to bring their whole self to the program. Sometimes, a 360-degree feedback instrument brings the views of participants' managers, colleagues, subordinates, and clients into the program as well.

Orientation occurs in the first portion of the program. The leadership concepts and ideas outlined earlier are introduced using traditional case discussions, minilectures, and role plays. These sessions touch upon the functional and symbolic aspects of leadership; the reciprocal influence between leaders and groups; and the centrality of unconscious dynamics and emotional factors to the experience of leading. Early on, the central idea is introduced that anyone can lead and learn. However, who leads and what they learn has much to do with their identity and those of their followers. Besides introducing these concepts, the sessions problematize leadership and leading as personal and social phenomena rather than abstract entities. In suggesting that personal history and social processes affect the meanings we associate with "leadership" and the ways we exercise it, they provide the conceptual backbone for the experiential portion of the program and invite participants to engage fully in it.

Experimentation occupies the central part of the program, which features an experiential "leadership in action" workshop. At the outset, groups are introduced to their "leadership consultants" and invited to articulate their learning aims and concerns. This contracting session marks the transition into a part of the program in which learning derives from examining and experimenting with the experience of leading and following. Experience in and between groups, in the present, provides the primary data for individual and collective exploration. Accounts of past experiences (such as those in participants' PPINs) or others' observations (such as those in 360 feedback reports) are not shared in groups but, rather, provide secondary data to support participants' further reflection on their experience. Participants are free to explore as much, and as fast, as they decide—and they are invited to take responsibility for their learning and that of classmates. Much as one cannot lead without taking responsibility, one must be free and responsible for learning to lead. After the contracting session, groups go through a series of activities over a day or two, each followed by a debriefing during which the group explores its experience with the assistance of their consultant.

Some activities are indoors, other outdoors. Some privilege creativity, others execution. Some involve other groups, others do not. The activities are not intended as simulations, team building exercises, or role plays. Their purpose is not to push participants into physical or emotional discomfort in order to generate feelings of confidence and connection on their accomplishment. Instead, they are meant to generate data for reflection, provide opportunities for giving and receiving feedback, and offer a context for experimentation (Petriglieri & Wood, 2005b). The experiential workshop provides a space in which it is possible to be curious about, play with, and endeavor to make sense of both the overt, conscious, and rational aspects of individual and group behavior and the covert, unconscious, and emotional ones. Learning derived from this portion of the program is usually what participants remember most vividly.

I recently met a manager who had attended a program featuring this experiential workshop seven years earlier. He recognized me as his group's leadership consultant and came over to say hello. "I remember as if it was yesterday," he told me. "You stopped us in the middle of much activity, about 45 minutes into a one-hour project, and said, 'If you believe the structure you are so busy building will actually work, please raise your hand.' We looked sheepishly at each other. Everyone's hand was down. No one had any faith that we were going to succeed." The group was persevering on a course of action to which no one was committed. Individuals felt it inappropriate, as well as rude to the member who had first proposed it, to express their doubts. Keeping busy had helped them avoid giving much thought to, and expressing, their misgivings and concerns. "Every time I have been in a group since, and everyone is quietly busy," he continued, "I always ask myself, 'Is the purpose of all this activity succeeding? Or is it to stop ourselves from thinking and saying what we think?' I learned in that moment that you can't expect dissent unless you actively encourage it." This story suggests that insights gained from experience are most memorable and also exemplifies the nature of that learning. It is about doing something differently, such as encouraging constructive dissent, and about being attentive to one's own and others' experience without taking it at face value.

All activities are filmed, and participants have an opportunity to review and discuss the videotapes of their group in action. The video review is followed by a plenary session during which each group prepares a short presentation on their learning and dilemmas up to that point and engage in a dialogue with other groups. This gives participants, who have so far explored experiences primarily within their groups, a chance to share and further each other's learning across groups. A debriefing follows the session to explore the intergroup dynamics that may emerge in the dialogue. An interpersonal feedback exercise—in which group members have a chance to give each other systematic feedback—ends this part of the program. If a 360 instrument is used, the report is distributed at this point so that participants can compare the feedback received in the program with that collected back home.

Integration is the focus of the last portion of the program. This phase aims to help participants deepen the connection between the program learning and their everyday context, and to encourage their ongoing development back home. It begins with a structured exercise that helps participants identify the deeply held assumptions that may limit progress in achieving personal changes they intend to accomplish (Kegan & Lahey, 2009). An individual coaching session with the leadership consultant further helps participants connect the dots between the learning in the program and their experience and development back home. It also invites them to explore potential links between their life story and their experience in current roles. Sessions on leading across differences in culture, personality, and career orientations conclude this portion of the program, which ends with a mini-lecture on reentry and a transition ceremony. Follow-up telephone coaching and peer coaching reinforce integration by inviting participants to articulate learning that has emerged after the program, and by supporting their efforts to apply and continue their learning.

Confidentiality is the third design principle. The purpose of these programs is development, not assessment. To maximize the possibility of experimentation and learning, all events occurring within the program are held in full confidentiality. No information pertaining to individual participants, or to their organization, is retained on file or divulged by the program faculty and staff under any circumstance. For the same reason, observers are not allowed in these programs, as their presence inevitably affects the dynamics in the room, regardless of the observers' integrity and intentions. I usually invite those that express a desire to observe to join the program as a participant.

Layers of Learning

The learning in such programs does not derive from dissecting the deeds of "great leaders"—prime ministers, CEOs, mavericks who succeeded against all odds—to gain inspiration and abstract lessons that can be practiced in one's daily work. It entails more than clarifying one's preferences through psychometric instruments, or receiving feedback on how one's behavior lives up to others' expectations and devising plans to close current gaps. Rather than putting the spotlight on how participants should and shouldn't lead, these programs put it on how they do lead every day—and why. The program functions like a microscope on the experience of individuals in social systems. Issues that participants face every day inevitably come to the fore, especially in the experiential portion. The difference between the program and everyday life is that within the program these issues can be discussed and reflected on more deeply because the community's primary task is to learn from its experience rather than getting on with any other job. Let me offer one example.

During the experiential workshop in a recent program, one group of international executives was faced with the challenge of crossing a (fictitious) piranha-infested river with the help of some planks, crates, and poles. Rather than trying to assemble a bridge using their allotted equipment, the group started splintering. The appointed leader kept being sent back to review the instructions in search of "the phrase that hints to the solution." Two members disappeared briefly into the woods nearby, returning with large stones which they started throwing "to kill the piranhas." Another was busy attempting to open a box—which had been inadvertently left in the "river" but was not part of the equipment—using a long pole. Two more members observed in silence. As the end of the exercise approached, frustration kept mounting. I commented that the group had devised the most creative ways to avoid working with the equipment they had been offered, and with each other. "It is not fair," the member holding the pole responded. "We are trying to think out of the box." I noted that, on the contrary, she seemed rather too preoccupied with what may be inside the box. My attempt at humor did not ease the tension, and the time fizzled out without much progress.

While one may describe such a group as having lost its mind, it is more accurate to say that its mind was exposed. As we debriefed this memorable debacle, the discussion slowly shifted from what could have been done differently (listen better, build a prototype, brainstorm, and so on) and all the ways in which a bridge could be built with the material provided, to a more generative question: Why did a group of intelligent and skillful people behave in such a seemingly irrational manner? They worked in a company that glorified employees who devised creative solutions to poorly defined problems. The company attracted individuals who prided themselves, above all, on their technical ability and commitment to innovation—and they were the cream of that crop. Their interpretation of the exercise and behavior within it was coherent with what, more or less consciously, leading meant to them—being able to devise a clever solution to an intractable problem and getting others to "buy into" it. In the absence of an idea that all could line up behind, they were looking for inspiration everywhere but in the equipment they had, and in each other. "Doing something simple and easy just would not feel right," one member candidly remarked.

The learning from that experience continued to ripen as the program progressed. Reviewing the videotape of the activity changed one group member's interpretation of what had happened: "I thought that there had been no leadership in the group and we were not truly committed to succeeding, but the video showed something different." Individuals had been committed to finding a way for the group to get across. There were plenty of moments in which various members offered the spark of a viable solution. Their leadership, however, was not taken up and the fire of collaboration never got going. As the group began reflecting on why they had kept working in parallel, it emerged that some competition for being the most creative (hence for being "the" leader) may have been at play. But it was not the whole story.

They admired each other's skills and wanted to live up to the high standards they held themselves up to. Group members intended to, and did, help each other, but help always came in the form of advice. Asking questions without offering an alternative felt disrespectful. Clever ideas were the valued currency in relationships. Everything else classed as showing incompetence and wasting time. Everyone was eager to offer help, but few seemed comfortable asking for it. Their difficulty in working collaboratively was not due to lack of ability. It did not fit what leadership meant to them—a view moulded by the contexts they had spent most of their lives in. As this group shared these reflections with other groups in the program, it became clear that the issue had manifested itself elsewhere, in many forms.

Another group described how they had realized that they were prisoners of a related individualistic assumption, that putting the "right people" in the right positions was all that it took to succeed. The realization had matured while examining their difficulty to get across a low-intensity rope course—easy to complete for groups that work together but practically impossible for an individual. They had chosen the member who seemed fittest and sent him across, while others overwhelmed him with encouragement, cheers, and advice. When he fell a few meters from the start, the group "generously" gave him several opportunities to "try again," with even more raucous encouragement and copious advice. After a few attempts, doubts had begun to linger, and someone suggested trying another member, who met a similar fate. This is not uncommon. I have seen groups replace every single member, unconsciously giving everyone the same humiliating experience of failure, and then concluding that the exercise is "impossible." In fact, it isn't. It can easily be completed when team members—literally—give each other a hand. That is very hard to imagine and do, if leading to you means either showing the way from the front or directing from the sidelines.

These reflections showed in stark relief how participants unconsciously enacted, again and again, what leading meant to them personally and in their context. It also highlighted that their behavior was not fated. Revisiting those meanings would make different choices possible. The learning did not stop there. "I am sorry for snapping at you. I realize you were trying to get us thinking," said the participant who had spent part of that fateful hour trying to open the empty box, as we sat down for the coaching session that concludes the experiential workshop. I reassured her that no apology was needed, and we set out to discuss what had happened. She had been really irritated with me then. As she saw it,

I had given them unclear instructions, stood watching while they floundered, and (as if that wasn't enough) I had criticized her best efforts to come up with an idea. That evening, while reviewing the videos, a group-mate had surprised her by not sharing her frustration. "It's just like at work. We take on projects where the brief is unclear," he had told her. "We put a brave face on and we find someone to blame when we can't get our act together." This remark had jolted her, and she had begun mulling over why she reacted so strongly, and in a way that felt familiar.

As I learned in the hour that followed, her history had been punctuated by subtle but painful betrayals by authority figures. These experiences had moulded the fierce independence on which her success rested. It had also left her with a constant feeling of mistrust about the intentions of people in authority. She could take up a challenging task and over-deliver but seldom let her guard down. She gravitated toward being the devil's advocate in groups and had several difficult relationships with past bosses. These conflicts were, in some way, a safe way to relate. They prevented the possibility of disappointment. They were also exhausting and often unnecessary, left her feeling unsupported, and deprived her of connections she may have enjoyed and benefited from. That was, to use her word, unfair. I noted that in sharing her irritation and reflections, she was showing great trust and in fact breaking that familiar pattern. She admitted that it was not as difficult as she thought it may be, and we ended our discussion strategizing potential ways to break that pattern, and take the risk to trust.

Revisiting what leading means in the communities we live in, and exploring the connections between our life story and our experiences in work roles, are not philosophical endeavors. They are steps that enable us to think differently, act differently, and relate differently. Long lasting change hinges on understanding and challenging both our assumptions and habits, and the social arrangements that reinforce them. Follow-up conversations after the program often reveal similar themes. "I left the program with as many open questions as new insights," participants often report. (I regard such mix as a sign of these programs' success.) Once back home, however, they find themselves looking at everyday situations—a management team meeting, a performance review, a conversation with their spouse—from a different angle, more able to draw links between their personal experience and the dynamics of those interactions, and more inclined to act upon those insights.

Another learning participants commonly report is the realization that they are deeply implicated in shaping the culture and atmosphere of their groups and organizations. Every choice they make can reinforce those cultures or challenge them. The learning reported most often, however, goes beyond increased individual mindfulness, ability, and sense of responsibility. It has to do with changes in relationships with fellow participants, and with people back home. "I had worked with Lily for years," one executive once told me after a program, "and we had never been so direct with each other. The program was a landmark moment in the development of our relationship." I hear such remarks frequently and often made with a tone of surprise, as they contradict a concern harbored by many at the beginning of such a program—that opening up may compromise their relationships with other participants.

The layers of learning that I have described above touch on and connect the organizational, group, and personal levels. They are not, of course, a function of the program activities. The same river crossing debacle may have yielded more superficial learning had it been framed as a "game" and followed only by a short discussion focused on how the group could "improve" and what its members "should do differently." Participants would have behaved differently in the next exercise, and reverted to type a few days later. The deeper, potentially transformative layers of learning would have remained hidden in plain view. Making those layers available requires giving time to the reflection process; allowing space for reflecting in large and small groups, in dyads, and individually; and focusing the reflection not on what should have happened but on why events unfolded the way they did. It requires participants who have the willingness to put judgment aside, the curiosity to give their experience a fresh look, and the courage to challenge each other's views. Finally, it requires professionals with the sensitivity and competence to facilitate personalized and contextualized learning.

Masters of Delivery and Facilitators of Development

Discussions among practitioners and within academic communities give little consideration to the individual and collective professionalism of leadership developers. Prospective clients, journalists, and even colleagues are often more interested in what pedagogies and designs I use, on the assumption that those drive the effectiveness of my programs—which they do in part. Design matters a good deal. The most common request I get, and always politely refuse, is to deliver a shortened version of the experiential workshop with fewer of the reflective sessions. The conceptual framing and flow of activities just described are necessary for a program to unveil the layers of learning and function well as an identity workspace. But they are not sufficient. Some learning will always occur with a good design, much like something will sprout in spring from a fertile, well-located field, regardless of how well it is farmed. Farmers who know the field and tend it with care, however, make a significant difference.

When I visit organizations that are interested in this approach to leadership development, after describing its general principles I refrain from showing a sample program design as is the norm in these meetings. I flick a slide, instead, with a picture of the group of professionals I collaborate with in delivering such programs. The point I am making is simple: Making good use of the design described here requires professionals who have the competence, sensitivity, and integrity to facilitate participants' inquiry into their experience—and to help integrate the learning back in their everyday life. Facilitating personalized and contextualized learning requires the ability to work with, and make links between, dynamics at different levels of analysis: the individual, the group, the organization, and the broader culture. This is why I favor the term "leadership consultant" rather than "coach." It requires different skills than those involved in teaching, coaching, or psychotherapy (Wood & Petriglieri, 2005a).

When I flick that slide, I talk about my colleagues' professional backgrounds and attitude as well as our way of working together. The former encompass training in the fields of adult development, group dynamics, and organizational behavior; the willingness to enter each program as a new venture; the ability to follow participants' pace and learning agendas; and the curiosity to learn from experiences. The latter rests on a professional commitment to be as reflective and engaged in our development, individually and collectively, as we ask participants to be. During each program, the consulting staff engages in extensive clinical meetings in order to reflect on its own experience and to share leadership and responsibility for the atmosphere and learning of the whole community. Between programs, everyone pursues ongoing personal development, participates regularly in experiential learning events from different traditions, and is engaged in examining and refining our practices.

Who Will Benefit From This Approach? (And How Can We Tell?)

I have been involved in the application of this approach in organization-specific programs, in open-enrollment executive programs and MBAs, for cohorts identified as "junior managers" or "senior executives" in the private and public sector, and as a stand-alone offer or in the context of a multi-module design. The aim of developing individual leaders and leadership communities remains constant across settings, as does the effort to foster personalized and contextualized learning and the centrality of learning from experience. Specific design elements change depending on the program context. Since the agendas, concerns, and cultures participants import into the program are central to the learning process, however, leadership programs of the kind described here have only one thing in common: Each is unique.

Depending on their intent for the program, there are several ways in which companies and individuals assess these programs' value and effectiveness. These metrics include, for corporations, internal surveys that probe employees' morale, well-being, organizational identification, actual turnover and intention to quit, external surveys assessing the company's appeal as a workplace, or bosses' and direct reports' subjective assessment of participants' ability as leaders, and of the changes in the organization's culture. For the individual, such measures often include access to coveted jobs, increases in salary and opportunities, or subjective experiences of clarity, ability, and meaning. Both organizations and individuals often value repeated 360-degree evaluations data, respectively as a measure of increased fit with a desired behavioral profile, or increased leadership ability as perceived by one's key counterparts. There is often much talk about leadership programs' "return on investment." However, it may be more relevant to assess these programs' *return on experience*, that is, the extent to which they enhance the ability of individuals and organizations to attend to, make sense of, and learn from a broader range of events and encounters. While this may be harder to quantify and measure, it may be the domain where such a leadership program delivers most value. Assessing it will involve qualitative inquiries into how participants make meaning within and among themselves before, during, and after a program.

Conclusion

The more fluid and turbulent the business world becomes, the more leadership development programs are asked to provide identity workspaces that harbor the development of individual leaders and leadership communities. Leadership courses concerned only with the acquisition of conceptual knowledge and the practice of behaviors prescribed by "leadership models" are of limited use in fulfilling this mandate. Doing so requires approaches that foster the personalization and contextualization of participants' learning and pay equal attention to what leaders do, who they are, and where they lead. The approach I espouse in my work, and have described here, helps participants examine and revise the ways they think, feel, and act as leaders (and followers) and recognize how these are constantly shaped by their history and aspirations, as well as by the dynamics of groups, organizations, and societies to which they belong. It invites them to examine their experience, encourages them to take personal responsibility for their development and joint ownership for the state of the systems they operate in, and enables them to work with the covert emotional currents that influence visible behaviors. Ultimately, it invites leaders to see themselves as instruments, rather than masters, of their purpose and community—and to rely on both for direction and support.

Conceptualizing leadership development as a potential identity workspace takes more than advocating suitable pedagogical methods and program designs. It involves revisiting the role of institutions and individuals who cater to the demand for leadership. To fulfill this function, we cannot just see our role in terms of creating and disseminating knowledge that allows better understanding of leadership and more efficient and effective leading. We must embrace a broader mandate that involves hosting individuals' identity development and shaping the meaning and exercise of leadership in organizations and society. This entails developing new skills alongside those required to conduct rigorous research and dazzle muted classrooms with articulate displays of knowledge and expertise. In addition, if leadership programs are important identity workspaces for current and future leaders, those who host them carry significant authority and responsibility toward individual participants, their organizations, and society at large. This calls for being mindful of all three when selling, conducting, and assessing our work—and not assuming that their interests are aligned. It also requires the courage to choose for whom we aim to serve as identity workspaces—what kind of leaders and organizations we are willing to help develop. There is no such a thing as a value-free identity workspace. Trying to be one only exposes us to the risk of becoming an identity workspace for leaders without concern for values.

References

Arthur, M. B. (2008). Examining itinerant careers: A call for interdisciplinary inquiry. *Human Relations*, *61*, 163–186.

Barsade, S. G., Ramarajan, L., & Westen, D. (2009). Implicit affect in organizations. *Research in Organizational Behavior*, *29*, 125–162.

Berglas, S. (2002). The very real dangers of executive coaching. *Harvard Business Review, 80*(6), 86–92.

Bolden, R., & Gosling, J. (2006). Leadership competencies: Time to change the tune? *Leadership, 2*, 147–163.

Campbell, J. (1972). The importance of rites. In *Myths to live by* (pp. 44–60). London, UK: Penguin.

Campbell, J. (1994 [1949]). *The hero with a thousand faces*. London, UK: Fontana

Capelli, P. (2008). *Talent on demand*. Cambridge, MA: Harvard Business Press.

Day, D.V. (2001). Leadership development: A review in context. *Leadership Quarterly, 11*, 581–613.

Day, D. V. (2010). The difficulties of learning from experience and the need for deliberate practice. *Industrial and Organizational Psychology, 3*, 41–44.

Day, D. V., & Harrison, M. M. (2007). A multilevel, identity-based approach to leadership development. *Human Resource Management Review, 17*, 360–373.

DeRue, D. S., & Ashford, S. (2010a). Power to the people. Where has personal agency gone in leadership development? *Industrial and Organizational Psychology, 3*, 24–27.

DeRue, D. S., & Ashford, S. (2010b). Who will lead and who will follow? A social process of leadership identity construction in organizations. *Academy of Management Review, 35*, 627–647.

DeRue, D. S., & Wellman, N. (2009). Developing leaders via experience: The role of developmental challenge, learning orientation, and feedback availability. *Journal of Applied Psychology, 94*, 859–875.

Eliade, M. (1995 [1958]). *Rites and symbols of initiation*. Woodstock, CT: Spring Publications.

Fineman, S. (1997). Emotion and management learning. *Management Learning, 28*,13–25.

Gould, L. J., Stapley, L. F., & Stein, M. (Eds.). (2001). *The systems psychodynamics of organizations: Integrating the group relations approach, psychoanalytic and open systems perspectives*. London, UK: Karnac.

Hackman, J. R., & Wageman, R. (2007). Asking the right questions about leadership. Discussion and conclusion. *American Psychologist, 62*, 43–47.

Hart, V., Blattner, J., & Leipsic, S. (2001). Coaching versus therapy: A perspective.

Consulting Psychology Journal: Practice and Research, 53, 229–237.

Haslam, S. A., Reicher, S. D., & Platow, M. J. (2011). *The new psychology of leadership: Identity, influence and power.* New York: Psychology Press.

Heifetz, R. (1994). *Leadership without easy answers.* Cambridge, MA: Belknap/Harvard University Press.

Ibarra, H. (2003). *Working identity. Unconventional strategies for reinventing your career.* Cambridge, MA: Harvard Business School Press.

Ibarra, H., Snook, S., & Guillen Ramo, L. (2010). Identity-based leader development. In R. Khurana & N. Noria (Eds.), *Leadership: Advancing an intellectual discipline* (pp. 657–678). Cambridge, MA: Harvard Business School Press.

Jaques, E. (1955). Social systems as a defence against persecutory and depressive anxiety. In M. Klein (Ed.), *New directions in psychoanalysis* (pp. 478–498). London, UK: Tavistock.

Kanter, R. (2010). Leadership in a globalizing world. In R. Khurana & N. Noria (Eds.), *Leadership: Advancing an intellectual discipline* (pp. 569–610). Cambridge, MA: Harvard Business School Press.

Kegan, R. (1982). *The evolving self: Problem and process in human development.* Cambridge, MA: Harvard University Press.

Kegan, R., & Lahey, L.L. (2009). *Immunity to change: How to overcome it and unlock the potential in yourself and your organization.* Cambridge, MA: Harvard Business School Press.

Kets de Vries, M. F. R. (2005). Organizations on the couch: A clinical perspective on organizational dynamics. *European Management Journal,* *22*(2), 183–200.

Kilburg, R. R. (2004). When shadows fall: Using psychodynamic approaches in executive coaching. *Consulting Psychology Journal: Practice and Research, 56,* 246–268.

Kolb, D. A. (1984). *Experiential learning: Experience as the source of learning and development.* Englewood Cliffs, NJ: Prentice-Hall.

Lord R. G., & Hall, R. J. (2005). Identity, deep structure and the development of leadership skills. *The Leadership Quarterly, 16,* 591–615.

McCall, M. W. (1998). *High flyers: Developing the next generation of leaders.* Cambridge, MA: Harvard Business School Press.

McCall, M. W. (2010). Recasting leadership development. *Industrial and Organizational Psychology, 3,* 3–19.

Menzies, I. E. P. (1960). A case-study in the functioning of social systems as a defence against anxiety. *Human Relations, 13,* 95–121.

Miller, E. J., & Rice, A. K. (1967). *Systems of organization.* London, UK: Tavistock.

Mumford, M. D., & Manley, G. G. (2003). Putting the development in leadership development: Implications for theory and practice. In S. E. Murphy & R. E. Riggio (Eds.), *The future of leadership development* (pp. 237–261). Mahwah, NJ: Lawrence Erlbaum Associates.

Petriglieri, G., & Petriglieri, J. L. (2010). Identity workspaces: The case of business schools. *Academy of Management Learning & Education, 9,* 44–60.

Petriglieri, G., & Stein, M. (2010). The unwanted self: Projective identification in leaders' identity work. *INSEAD Working Paper* N. (2010)/107/OB.

Petriglieri, G., & Wood J. D. (2005a). Learning for leadership: The "engineering" and "clinical" approaches. In P. Strebel & T. Keys (Eds.), *Mastering executive education: How to combine content with context and emotion* (pp. 140–154). London, UK: Financial Times-Prentice Hall.

Petriglieri, G., & Wood, J. D. (2005b). Beyond "fun and games": Outdoor activities for meaningful leadership development. In P. Strebel & T. Keys (Eds.), *Mastering executive education: How to combine content with context and emotion* (pp. 252–266). London, UK: Financial Times-Prentice Hall.

Petriglieri, G., Wood, J. D., & Petriglieri J. L. (2011). Up close and personal: Building foundations for leaders' development through the personalization of management learning. *Academy of Management Learning & Education, 10,* forthcoming.

Raelin, J. A. (2007). Towards an epistemology of practice. *Academy of Management Learning & Education, 6,* 495–519.

Reynolds, M., & Vince, R. (2004). Organizing reflection: An introduction. In M. Reynolds & R. Vince (Eds.), *Organizing reflection* (pp. 1–14). Aldershot, UK: Ashgate.

Rousseau, D. M. (1990). New hire perceptions of their own and their employer's obligations: A study of psychological contracts. *Journal of Organizational Behavior, 11,* 389–400.

Sennett, R. (2006). *The culture of the new capitalism.* New Haven, CT: Yale University Press.

Shamir, B., & Eilam, G. (2005). "What's your story?" A life-stories approach to authentic leadership development. *Leadership Quarterly, 16,* 395–417.

Sherman, S., & Freas, A. (2004). The Wild West of executive coaching. *Harvard Business Review, 83*(3), 82–90.

Snook, S. (2007). Leader(ship) development. *Harvard Business School Note* N. 408–064.

Trice, H. M., & Beyer, J. M. (1984). Studying organizational cultures through rites and ceremonials. *Academy of Management Review, 9,* 653–669.

Van Gennep, A. (1960 [1905]). *The rites of passage.* Chicago, IL: The University of Chicago Press.

Van Knippenberg, D., & Hogg, M. A. (2003). A social identity model of leadership effectiveness in organizations. *Research in Organizational Behavior, 25,* 243–295.

Wood, J. D., & Petriglieri, G. (2005a). On coaches, counsellors, facilitators and behavioural consultants. In P. Strebel & T. Keys (Eds.), *Mastering executive education: How to combine content with context and emotion* (pp. 155–169). London, UK: Financial Times-Prentice Hall.

Wood, J. D., & Petriglieri, G. (2005b). Fundamental for a world class leadership programme. In P. Strebel & T. Keys (Eds.), *Mastering executive education: How to combine content with context and emotion* (pp. 364–380). London, UK: Financial Times-Prentice Hall.

20

AUTHENTIC LEADERSHIP DEVELOPMENT

◆ Bill George
Harvard Business School

This chapter focuses on Harvard Business School's "Authentic Leadership Development" (ALD) course—based on developing leaders from within—as well as my unique history with the program.

Authentic leadership results from knowing yourself—your strengths and weaknesses—by understanding your unique life story and the crucibles you have experienced. ALD's overarching premise is that leaders are most effective when they follow their True North—their beliefs, values, and principles. Following their True North requires them to be sufficiently grounded to withstand the pressures of leadership without compromising their principles.

Each of the course's twelve weeks has three elements: (1) readings from *True North* and introspective exercises drawn from *Finding Your True North: A Personal Guide*; (2) small group discussions with six-person Leadership Development Groups (LDGs); and (3) classroom case discussions of various leaders' life stories. The LDGs provide a confidential environment characterized by trust, intimacy, and candor in which to discuss course content and individuals' life histories.

The initial portion of ALD is devoted entirely to leaders' life stories and their greatest crucibles. The second part examines the five key elements critical to leadership development: (1) self-awareness, (2) values, (3) motivated capabilities, (4) support teams, and (5) integrated life. The final section addresses the purpose of leadership, empowering others, and leadership effectiveness. By examining their crucibles and framing their life stories, participants gain self-awareness, self-compassion, and self-acceptance.

The course format is designed to facilitate participants being reflective about themselves and the origins of their leadership. Through ALD they learn their best leadership results from being authentic and empowering others to lead.

❖❖❖

Introduction

Throughout my life I have taken on leadership roles and been fascinated by ways leaders develop. As I concluded my business career after thirty-three years of working for three major corporations, I decided to spend the next decade trying to help develop the leaders of the future by teaching leadership and mentoring leaders at all stages of their development.

However, my life in leadership did not start well. Urged on by my father to lead a major company, I was never selected to lead anything in school, not even student council or my tennis team. Frustrated, I put my name in the hat for president of my senior class, but lost by a margin of two to one.

After graduating from high school, I went to Georgia Tech, 800 miles from my home in Michigan, where I didn't know anyone. I was eager for a fresh start in leadership—too eager as it turned out. At this stage I hadn't learned Jon Kabat-Zinn's warning, "Wherever you go, there you are." I ran for office six more times and lost all six. Not exactly a sterling start to a leadership career!

Then a group of university seniors took me aside and told me, "Bill, you're so ambitious and eager to get ahead that no one is ever going to want to work with you. You need to spend more time with other people being interested in their concerns, not your own." Their advice was like a blow to the solar plexus, but it spurred me to undertake my personalized version of leadership development. Gradually it worked, as I was selected to hold many leadership roles at Georgia Tech and later at Harvard Business School.

During my corporate career, which spanned thirty-three years with Litton Industries, Honeywell International, and Medtronic, I was disappointed to see how few high-quality leadership development programs existed. Most of them seemed rather superficial and prepared by people who had never led themselves. These programs focused more on acculturation to the corporate culture and its norms than to the developmental needs of the individual. They also seemed to have a bias for leaders to be "nice" people, but were rather insensitive to the challenges leaders face in performing under enormous pressure.

After completing ten years as CEO of Medtronic and an additional year as board chair, I went to Switzerland to teach leadership at two Swiss institutions, IMD International and École Polytechnique Fédérale de Lausanne (EPFL). During my year in Switzerland, I watched as Enron, WorldCom, Qwest, and many other companies imploded and their leaders went to jail. My greater concerns about these corporate fiascos were the leaders of more than one hundred companies that had to restate prior-year financial statements. These admissions of improper accounting were not just accounting errors but the result of flawed leaders chasing short-term gains at the expense of long-term sustainability. What had happened to my generation of leaders? In 2003 this question stimulated me to write my first book, *Authentic Leadership*

(George, 2003), based on leadership ideas I developed during my career.

In January 2004, I joined the Harvard Business School faculty as professor of management practice to teach the new required MBA course, "Leadership and Corporate Accountability" (LCA). LCA examines leadership primarily from a process and systems viewpoint, but does not focus on the development of individual leaders. I felt MBA students needed a leadership development course based on inner-directed leadership, not just learning how to master external forces and their demands.

Creating Authentic Leadership Development (ALD)

Before developing this course, I made an informal survey of leading business schools to see what leadership development courses existed. It revealed numerous ethics courses but didn't turn up anything significant on leadership development, with the exception of the Center for Creative Leadership in North Carolina. In discussions with faculty at several institutions, I learned that many academics were hesitant to offer courses focusing on the personal side of leadership due to lack of an established framework for leadership substantiated by research.

For this reason I invited six MBA students from three different schools—Harvard, Stanford, and Duke—to a weekend retreat in Colorado in the summer of 2004 to get their input on how they would like to see leadership development taught. All six held top leadership development responsibilities in their respective MBA programs. The Stanford students, in turn, developed a leadership development elective, receiving faculty support. Based on their input, I decided to create a second-year elective course at HBS on personal leadership development, which I called "Authentic Leadership Development" (ALD). Intended to fill the gap identified in business school curricula, ALD was built around my beliefs about what leaders need to do to develop themselves.

The following spring I initiated a field research study to ascertain how leaders developed. Our four-person research team consisted of Peter Sims, who worked with me in writing *True North* (George & Sims, 2007), Diana Mayer, who currently teaches ALD at New York University, and Andrew McLean, my HBS research assistant. One of my senior colleagues at HBS suggested the hope that our research would finally determine the traits, characteristics, and styles of successful leaders. A survey of the literature identified more than one thousand studies that had been conducted for this purpose, none of which had proven definitive or replicable through additional research.

In our study we interviewed 125 leaders, ages 23 to 93. The research objective was to find out how they developed as authentic leaders, based on in-depth first-person interviews. They were extremely honest and forthcoming about their mistakes, the difficult times they faced, and what enabled them to succeed while retaining their authenticity. In parallel, I launched a pilot version of the course in the spring of 2005. In this way the course and the research informed each other, as the course was developed through a series of successive iterations. The course structure was somewhat controversial at HBS because over half of class time is devoted to six-person Leadership Development Groups, not to be confused with study groups or learning teams. Since this structure impacted several HBS norms, it required special approval from the dean's office, which was subsequently granted for full course credit.

In spite of its limited content, the pilot version was very well received. Consequently, I created a formal elective for second-year students in the fall of 2005, focusing on the inner side of leadership. Meanwhile, the field research continued through the spring of 2006. In reading the 3,000 pages of transcripts generated by these interviews, it became clear that the success of these leaders was *not* due to any common set of traits, characteristics, or leadership styles, nor their leadership development programs.

What became clear from the interviews was the importance of their life stories and the crucibles they faced at key points in their lives. Through first-hand retelling of these often-painful stories, these leaders learned who they were and what was important to them. They spoke in compelling ways about how their unique life stories had empowered them to succeed. By testing themselves through real-world experiences and reframing their life stories, these leaders were able to unleash their passions and discover the purpose of their leadership. But they also struggled to cope with the pressures of leadership and avoid its seductions while staying on course of their inner compass—their True North.

The research led to the publication of *True North* in early 2007, written with the support of Peter Sims (George & Sims, 2007). Its thesis was that leaders develop by embracing their life stories and their crucibles, enabling them to become self-aware and make sound values-based decisions. A year later Andrew McLean, consultant Nick Craig, and I published a companion book, *Finding Your True North: A Personal Guide* (George, McLean, & Craig, 2008), containing 65 exercises for leaders and small groups to complete in parallel with reading *True North*.

ALD Course Structure

The initial portion of ALD is devoted entirely to leaders' life stories and their greatest crucibles. The second part examines the five key elements these leaders identified as critical to their development. The final section addresses the purpose of their leadership. The course does not address more traditional elements of leadership development such as leadership style and use of power until the very end. As the research demonstrated, these external elements of leadership are far less important to the development of leaders than their inner journeys.

The course format is designed to facilitate the intensely personal nature of leadership, requiring students to be reflective and have personal curiosity about themselves and the origins of their leadership. Students need to be open personally and willing to share in the leadership development groups (LDGs) and in class discussions.

Each of the twelve weeks examines a crucial element of leaders' development. The week begins with the introspective portion that includes readings from *True North* and other relevant readings to the week's topic. Then the individual students complete a set of introspective exercises from *Finding Your True North: A Personal Guide.*

In the second part of the week, students meet with five other students in their Leadership Development Group (LDG) to discuss their introspective exercises and what they learned from them. The norms of the small group must provide the safety of trust and confidentiality so students feel comfortable sharing personal experiences and viewpoints they would be unlikely to express in the classroom. These sessions last for 110 minutes, led by rotating peer-facilitators. Students consistently rate these groups as the most valuable part of the course.

Following their LDG meetings, students study cases of leaders facing dilemmas similar to those they discussed with their LDGs. The cases enable them to compare their approach to these challenging issues to those used by case protagonists. The class discussion that follows includes processing the LDG discussions, sharing personal stories, and discussing the case. Often the leaders are present to offer personal reflections of the dilemmas they faced.

In searching for effective cases to illustrate how leaders develop, I found existing leadership cases focus on instant decisions of leaders facing dilemmas. I decided we needed a different kind of case that examines the leaders' entire life profile, in order to understand better how they think about these decisions. This meant writing twenty new cases for the course, many of which were drawn from expanded versions of interviews from the *True North* research project.

The leaders chosen as case protagonists were *not* intended to be role models of authentic leadership; rather, they reflect the challenges leaders confront when faced with extreme difficulties in maintaining their authenticity and staying on course of their True North. Classroom discussions probe how leaders maintain their authenticity, address their shortcomings, and learn from their crucibles.

The classes raise personal issues that cause students to probe their most fundamental beliefs—about themselves, other leaders, how organizations work, how careers are built, and how leaders are developed—and enable them to develop their own leadership philosophy and plan for their development. Because these issues are so personal, the classroom must represent a safe, confidential environment as well. This means students can share both their experiences and points of view without being judged by fellow students or the professor. In contrast to traditional case discussions in which students analyze and evaluate protagonists, ALD students are asked to "walk in the shoes of the protagonist," trying to place themselves in the situation and determining what they would do.

Some of the cases selected for the class discussions were chosen to illustrate protagonists facing difficult challenges. Examples include Anne Mulcahy at Xerox, Wendy Kopp at Teach For America, Richard Grasso at the New York Stock Exchange, Martin Luther King Jr., Oprah Winfrey, Tad Piper of Piper Jaffrey, Martha Goldberg Aronson at Medtronic, and Philip McCrea of Vitesse Learning.

Other case studies take a different approach. Instead of a specific challenge, they offer a lifelong profile of how the protagonists were influenced by the entire arc of their life stories and how they drew upon these experiences in facing greater challenges as their responsibilities grew. These cases include Howard Schultz of Starbucks, Jeff Immelt at GE, Narayana Murthy of Infosys, Kevin Sharer at Amgen, Andrea Jung of Avon Products, and John Whitehead at the Lower Manhattan Redevelopment Commission.

The latter type of case is more difficult to teach, because it requires a deeper level of probing and integration of the protagonists' lives and philosophies of leadership. These cases convey a powerful message that, in addressing specific challenges, leaders must call upon all they have learned about their leadership to deal with the situation at hand. The message that comes through is that leaders who don't learn from past experiences and acknowledge difficult times in their lives rather than suppress them are likely to repeat their mistakes.

ALD's Conceptual Basis

ALD's overarching premise is that leaders are most effective when they follow their True North—their beliefs, values, and principles. This requires them to be sufficiently grounded to withstand the pressures of leadership challenges without compromising their principles or being seduced by external rewards such as money, recognition, and power.

In my experience I have never seen leaders fail for lack of raw intelligence, or IQ, but have observed hundreds of leaders fail due to lack of emotional intelligence (EQ). ALD enables emerging leaders to build their EQ by increasing their self-awareness, self-compassion, and self-regulation. It also enables them to develop an approach to leading that is authentic to who they are and congruent with their life stories. They learn how to enhance their EQ through the building of authentic relationships with peers and empower other people rather than exerting power over them.

Three things are required to enable people to become effective and authentic leaders who can sustain their leadership: (1) experience in leading others; (2) processing experiences through introspection and reflection; and (3) sharing experiences openly with peers and gaining their feedback.

While ALD does not contain an element of direct experience, it draws upon the full range of life experiences participants have had, as well as the processing the experiences of other leaders through case studies. The exercises cause participants to be introspective. The Leadership Development Groups provide a safe place to share in a trusting, confidential environment and seek feedback. As the culmination of the course, students create a Personal Leadership Development Plan as a living document they can update throughout their careers.

In the opening class I ask students, "When will you go from seeking the world's esteem to fulfilling your own intrinsic desires?" MBA students typically have worked extremely hard and have been successful as individual contributors in school and initial career assignments. As a result, they feel they are constantly being judged and guided by others, especially their parents. In this sense ALD represents an important juncture in figuring out what they want to do with their lives.

The small group process often unlocks hidden issues, such as conflicts between the desire to meet others' expectations and students' inner motivations. To capture the importance of defining their own leadership direction, I share a fragment from Chilean poet Pablo Neruda's first poem:

> *Something ignited in my soul,*
> *fever or unremembered wings,*
>
> *And I went my own way, deciphering that burning fire.*

For most students the discussion of their greatest crucibles is the pivotal point of the course. In writing about their crucibles, sharing them with their LDGs, and reframing them in the context of their life journeys, they frequently share deep emotions and painful experiences not previously discussed with others. These crucibles range from the impact of divorce, discrimination, rejection by friends and family members, sexual abuse, chemical dependency, sexual identity, and death of family members to failures in school and at work.

As they progress through the course and look at their passions and motivations, many students align their leadership aspirations with their intrinsic desires rather than extrinsic motivations such as money, prestige, and recognition. They learn that leaders who understand themselves well, have high levels of self-awareness, and consciously develop their leadership abilities throughout their lifetimes will be more effective and successful leaders, and ultimately have more satisfying and fulfilling lives.

ALD Objectives

The objectives of ALD are:

- To enable students to understand their leadership journeys and their crucibles through framing their life stories and experiences to date
- To understand why leaders get off track and lose their way
- To develop the emotional intelligence (EQ) and self-awareness required to stay grounded and avoid derailment
- To gain clarity about their values, leadership principles, and ethical boundaries, and to recognize how they will respond under pressure when severely challenged
- To understand what is motivating them, both extrinsically and intrinsically, and to find leadership paths that will enable them to utilize their motivated capabilities
- To learn how to build support teams
- To lead an integrated life that balances responsibilities to oneself, one's family, organizations, and communities

- To discern the purpose of their leadership and how it evolves over time
- To become empowering leaders who motivate others to achieve exceptional results
- To optimize their leadership effectiveness through skillful use of style, power, and influence
- To create a Personal Leadership Development Plan that they can use to guide them throughout their careers

Course Content

ALD students are required to read *True North* in its entirety and complete the exercises in *Finding Your True North*. The twelve-week course is divided into three parts:

Part I. Examine Your Leadership Journey (4 weeks)

Part II. Discover Your Authentic Leadership (5 weeks)

Part III. Put Your Authentic Leadership Into Action(3 weeks)

In Part I students examine their life stories and the impact they have on their leadership. After examining their life stories, students study how leaders often lose their way and attempt to apply these lessons to themselves. In the final week of Part I, they examine and frame the greatest crucible of their lives. In understanding their crucible experiences, they learn to recognize that in order to become authentic leaders they must make the transformation from "I" to "We," or from the hero's journey to the leader's journey.

Part II concentrates on the five areas of personal development essential to developing as authentic leaders. The five areas include (1) self-awareness; (2) values, leadership principles, and ethical boundaries; (3) motivated capabilities; (4) support teams; and (5) integrated leadership.

Having examined the required areas for leadership development, Part III focuses on putting authentic leadership into action. It begins with a module on the purpose of one's leadership, followed by empowering others to lead. It concludes with optimizing leadership through effective use of style, power, and influence.

Students prepare three papers in the course. First, they complete an introductory one-page paper before the course on "Why I want to take this course." After six weeks, they submit mid-term papers of approximately 1,500 words on "The greatest crucible of my life." This paper comes at a critical time in the syllabus and is one of the course's most important aspects. Their final papers include 2,500-word essays on "The purpose of my leadership," and their Personal Leadership Development Plans. Each week after the conclusion of their LDG discussion, students send to the professor their confidential reflections on what they learned from that week.

The diagram in Exhibit 20.1 describes the overall course flow.

Leadership Development Groups (LDGs)

The Leadership Development Groups (LDGs) are central to ALD. They provide a vital link between the individual assignments and the classroom discussions, providing students a small group with whom they can share intimate details of their lives in a safe, secure environment, and receive reinforcement and feedback from group members. Without the LDG experience, students are unlikely to delve into their individual assignments as deeply, nor will they do the deeper level of introspective work that enables them to understand their experiences fully. Describing personal aspects of themselves to people they trust is a cathartic and enriching experience.

What stands out consistently in the student evaluations—and hasn't varied since the first pilot course—is the value students place on the LDGs. They provide a level of trust, intimacy, and candor in a confidential environment that most have not found elsewhere in their lives, often not even in their families. The LDGs bond very quickly and tend to stay together long after the course is over. During the course, many LDGs get together for additional sessions, such as dinner meetings, in addition to scheduled meeting times.

The professor should assign class members to their respective LDGs prior to the start of the course, rather than permitting students to pick their own groups. In order to ensure diversity, groups should be balanced for gender, national origin, work experiences, race, religion, and sexual identity. It is important to avoid prior friendships influencing the openness of the group or equality of group members. Past experience has shown students are more open with group members they do not know than with longtime friends, where there may be an implicit understanding *not* to probe certain aspects of the person's life story.

Attendance at LDGs must be mandatory and enforced, just like regular classes. Having only four or five people present, or permitting students to come late or leave early, can destroy the intimacy of the group. The facilitator's report contains a section for noting anyone who missed the class or was late in arriving or early in leaving. There should be no excused absences from LDGs, other than illness, as there is no way to make up sessions. It is not a good practice to permit groups to change the time or place for LDG meetings.

To establish agreed-upon ground rules at the outset, LDGs develop written contracts in their first session regarding their group's norms (see Exhibit 20.2). All group members should sign these contracts and send them to the professor as an indication of their commitment to these norms. This step is essential to reinforce the importance of openness, trust, and confidentiality.

LDGs utilize peer facilitators rather than professionals. Facilitator responsibilities are rotated each week among group members, based on assignments made by the professor at the start. Peer facilitators are preferred over professional facilitators for the following reasons: (1) with a professional facilitator, group members tend to look to the expert for guidance, rather than working things out among themselves or learning new ideas by sharing experiences; (2) it is more difficult to establish trust with a professional facilitator, as group members may worry that the facilitator serves as a conduit to faculty members; (3) it is important for MBAs to learn how to facilitate small groups; and (4) the peer facilitator model is infinitely expandable and has no costs or logistical challenges.

Post-course surveys indicate 80 percent of students have strong preference for using peer facilitators. Many observe they are more open without a professional facilitator in the room and feel greater responsibility for the group's success. As one student says, "Bringing in an outside person would disrupt the chemistry." Another notes, "Having everyone on the same level makes it more comfortable to open up. Having one student facilitate each week means you're all on an even-level playing field, all the time. Introducing a professional or outsider wouldn't work well from a confidentiality perspective."

To ensure effectiveness of the LDGs, professors should meet with facilitators in advance of the LDG meeting to review how the groups are working, problems they may be encountering, and how to approach the week's assignments, as well as answering questions facilitators have.

Following LDG meetings, the facilitators should email the professor a written report (Exhibit 20.3), describing how the group went, any process difficulties encountered, general questions remaining, and attendance of individual group members. The questions can be used in preparing for class discussions.

It is not necessary, or even desirable, for faculty to participate in LDGs, as their presence may inhibit the free flow of the group's discussion. The success of the LDGs derives from the trust and openness that develop among the six peers. Should the professor receive oral or written feedback that the group is having difficulties, then it is quite appropriate—in fact, necessary—for the professor to meet with the group to discuss the difficulties and help resolve them.

In the only case of an LDG splitting due to one person's refusal to be open with other members of his group, the contract became extremely important. When the group went around the circle with five people sharing openly, he always elected to pass. Two of the women got frustrated, feeling he was acting like a voyeur. They eventually left the group and decided to meet on their own. When I learned what was happening, I invited all six students to my office. After the women described the situation, the man said people rarely share openly in his home country. I noted he had signed the member's contract committing to be open and also observed that several other students from his country had no trouble in sharing. He agreed to give it another try. The group resumed meeting weekly with much greater success after talking through their differences as he finally opened up.

The comments that follow represent a cross-section of student comments about the value of their LDGs. Some of them are drawn from an ALD student field research project conducted in the spring of 2008:

- "The groups are the most valuable vehicle for introspection I've ever encountered. I was more open with them than I've ever been with anyone in my life. The group's confidentiality, structure, and syllabus combine to create a meaningful and critically important experience."

- "LDGs were the best experience I've had at HBS. We're under a lot of stress and pressure, and a specific time to meet with a small group and talk about personal issues each week goes a long way toward personal well-being, not just professional development. This works so well because of the explicit assumption of trust and confidentiality within our LDGs and in the classroom."

- "This group provided support, encouraged introspection, and consisted of the best and most intellectual discussions. It gave me an opportunity to reflect on my life and share in an open and supportive environment. As a result, I faced things about myself I always knew were there, but tried to hide."

- "LDG groups are far and away the most effective and important part of the course. We got to a level of knowledge and intimacy that is unusual anywhere, especially at HBS. It was trial-by-fire, as the first few weeks were tough, but effective at building instant bonds, openness, and intimacy necessary for real conversation to happen."

- "The leadership discussion groups were a highly effective way to reflect on experiences, relationships, and leadership skills. They provided valuable structure for synthesizing course content with life experience, and for thinking about how to understand and adapt behaviors. HBS's standard class structure is often quite limiting in that it rewards a certain type of intelligence and communication style, and is not conducive to discussions about some of the most important issues of business management."

- "Much of our future success will be determined not by our mastery of content, which is what traditional courses emphasize, but our ability to identify our talents, understand others, and shape optimal working environments. The six-person groups helped move me toward a new understanding of my ability to lead."

Teaching ALD

Early in my teaching I was asked by a student, "Bill, are you going to teach us leadership and values?" I explained, "I cannot teach you leadership or values, but I hope that we can create an environment where you can learn about your leadership and explore your values in a non-threatening environment."

With every group of new students, I start off suggesting that the ALD classroom is a place of *knowledge exchange*, not *knowledge transfer*. As faculty members teaching ALD, it is not our job to act as the expert and transfer wisdom to students. Our role is to encourage them to share their wisdom with their peers.

That said, I believe it is essential for anyone teaching ALD to be open with their students in sharing their personal experiences and reflecting honestly and candidly about them. There will also be many opportunities in the classroom for faculty to share pertinent vignettes from their experience that can be useful to students.

While many faculty members feel they should not provide students with their opinions for fear of suppressing student views, ALD is quite different. This course should not be "values neutral." Students have a right to know where faculty members stand on important issues, especially those concerning values and ethics. Students should be encouraged to challenge faculty members about their opinions. I set aside the last five to ten minutes of the class to offer my insights and opinions about the issues discussed. We owe our students at least that much.

Since 2005, ALD has been taught at Harvard Business School to a total of 900 MBAs by six different faculty members. It has expanded from a single section of 60 students to four sections. Even with this increase, the course only takes one-third of the students who request it. This high level of demand far exceeds any expectations I had at the outset. Back then, I envisioned the course would only appeal to a highly selective group of students interested in exploring who they are.

In addition to HBS, ALD is currently being offered at New York University, Georgia Tech, and other institutions. The course is also being used in a shortened version for executive education courses at Harvard and Wharton business schools. Variations of the course are being used by major corporations, government organizations, and the Young Global Leaders of the World Economic Forum.

Thanks to colleagues who teach ALD, it is clear that this course can be taught by many faculty members, provided they are prepared to share their experiences with students. The initiatives they have brought to ALD have made it much better. For example, my Harvard colleagues Robert Kaplan, Joshua Margolis, and Scott Snook have restructured the weekly flow to place case discussions *before* LDG meetings.

To open up classroom discussions and engage students personally, they developed a series of exercises that cause students to engage at a personal level. For example, in the class on life stories, students are asked consider the "dueling narratives" of their stories, the positive version of who they are and the negative version, something that all of us wrestle with, even in our dreams. Nitin Nohria, now dean of HBS, initially proposed this idea when he taught the course.

Assessing ALD's Value

The best assessment of ALD's value comes from the students themselves. Across a variety of instructors, students have consistently rated the course highly, and demand for gaining entrance continues to be exceptionally strong. Here is a cross-section of comments from their evaluations:

- "This course was one of the best gifts I have ever received. The carefully laid out weekly readings and the enforcement of those readings within the Leadership Development Group (LDG) were incredibly helpful in providing me with tools to figure out who I am and what I want from my personal and professional life."

- "I am still shocked by how much I learned about myself and others in this class. Because of this class and the feedback I received from my LDG, I have a totally different outlook on my personal life and my career search."

- "I have never had a class that made you examine yourself as 'close-up' as this class forced you to. It really made you confront yourself and never let you off the hook with the easy answer. My professor was the very definition of authentic—unbelievably committed to teaching and getting the most out of his students."

The course engenders on-going relationships between faculty members and their students. I continue to receive emails and personal contacts from former students, some of whom graduated six years ago, about how important the ALD experience has been in their leadership roles and how it influences their decisions and career choices. Many of them still get together with their LDGs or arrange for telephone meetings.

During the 2011–12 academic year we plan to launch a formal study of ALD graduates to get feedback on their retrospective assessment of the course's importance to their lives and their leadership, as well as their suggestions for improvement.

Conclusion

The changing nature of leadership in the 21st century is having a strong influence on the development of ALD. Today's leaders at all levels are eschewing hierarchy, bureaucracy, and command-and-control structures. Rather than running their organizations just with systems and processes, they are focusing on the importance of aligning people around mission and values. They recognize that true leadership is not exerting power over other people, but empowering them to step up and lead.

Corporate leaders are shifting away from solely serving shareholders—which has often devolved into short-term profit maximization—to serving customers and employees, and ultimately society. Finally, they are recognizing that leadership effectiveness comes not from driving individuals to perform, but rather getting people to collaborate across organizational lines and creating teams of empowered people.

All of these principles underpin Authentic Leadership Development and are discussed throughout the course. While many students begin the course believing that leadership results from exercising power and developing a certain leadership style, they learn through ALD that their best leadership results from being authentic and genuine in empowering and inspiring others to lead.

Most importantly, the intimate peer relationships built through the LDGs and the classroom enable students to feel accepted for who they are, regardless of the difficulties they have encountered in life. By examining their crucibles and framing their life stories, they are able to gain self-awareness, self-compassion, and self-acceptance. As our leadership studies have demonstrated, these qualities will be essential for them throughout their lives, regardless of the leadership challenges they ultimately face.

In understanding how they coped with difficult problems and unrelenting pressures, they learn how they can withstand even the greatest pressures they will encounter in leadership roles. In following their intrinsic desires instead of being driven by the expectations of others, they can avoid being seduced by money, power, and fame. In these ways they learn to follow their True North, becoming more effective leaders and leading more fulfilling lives.

As one student wrote, "This is the most effective and insightful course I have ever seen at any level of my education."

Exhibit 20.1 Structure of Authentic Leadership Development

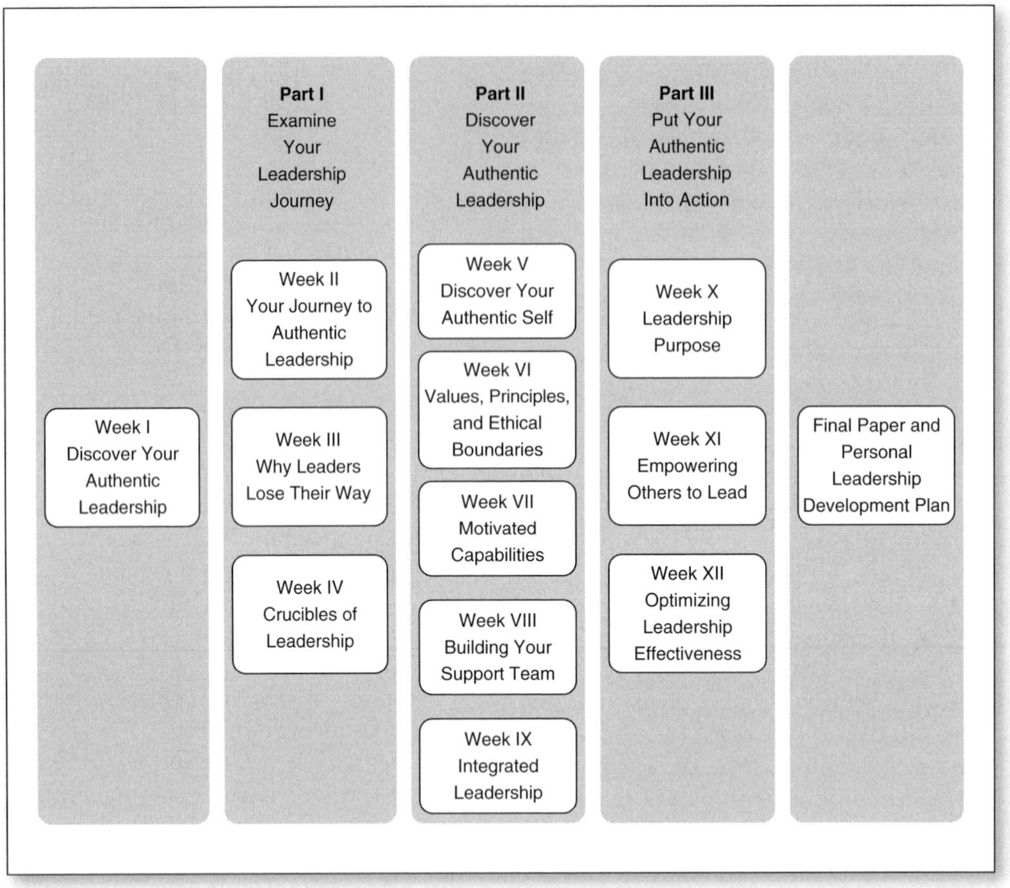

Source: Reprinted with permission © Bill George.

Exhibit 20.2

Leadership Development Group Contract (Group __)

Following are a set of norms that should be discussed by each group and incorporated in whole or in part into the signed LDG Contract:

1. Openness
To be effective, open sharing with group members is essential to learning. If individuals are not sharing openly with the group, it is the responsibility of group members to raise this with them for discussion within the group. However, it is important that group members not push individuals beyond their comfort zone on personally sensitive matters.

2. Trust
For the LDGs to be effective, it is essential that group members trust each member of the group and the group as a whole. Trust is built through honest, open communications and the sense that individuals care about the other members of their group and sincerely would like to help them in growing into effective leaders.

3. Confidentiality
A firm agreement should be reached that nothing said within the group is discussed with others outside the group.

4. Differences
The group should allow for individual differences and make accommodations for what each member would like to get out of the group experience.

5. Tolerance
There are no "right" answers when priorities/values are discussed, nor should group members make judgments about others in the group.

6. Feedback
Group members offer and receive constructive feedback from each other on their ideas, leadership traits, and communication styles. There will be two opportunities to receive formal feedback during the course: the first of them will come during LDG #6 and the final feedback during LDG #12 at the conclusion of the course.

7. Challenges
Challenges by other group members are considered to be healthy, if expressed in a respectful manner in which individuals do not engage in personal attacks. If managed well, respectful challenges can contribute to meaningful learning for all.

Signed by (name and date):

__________________ __________________ __________________

__________________ __________________ __________________

Source: Reprinted with permission © Bill George.

Exhibit 20.3

LDG Facilitators Feedback Form

LDG: ______________________ **Facilitator:** ______________________

Members Absent: ______________________

Members Arriving Late: ______________________

Summary of Group Discussion:

____

____

____

____

Process Issues Within the Group:

____

____

____

____

Questions Left Open After Group Discussion:

____

____

____

Note: This facilitator's report must be sent electronically to your professor no later than midnight of the LDG meeting.

Source: Reprinted with permission © Bill George.

References

George, B. (2003). *Authentic leadership: Rediscovering the secrets to creating lasting value.* San Francisco, CA: Jossey-Bass.

George, B., McLean, A. N., & Craig, N. (2008). *Finding your true north: A personal guide.* San Francisco, CA: Jossey-Bass.

George, B., & Sims, P. (2007). *True north: Discover your authentic leadership.* San Francisco, CA: Jossey-Bass.

21

FORGING CONSCIOUSNESS AND (OCCASIONALLY) CONSCIENCE

A Model-Based Approach to Leadership Development

◆ Mihnea Moldoveanu

Rotman School of Management, University of Toronto

I introduce an approach to leadership development based on self-understanding and self-transformation and drawing on the tradition of analytic philosophy and psychoanalysis. The new approach uses structured, logically consistent models of a person's modes of being as tools that the trainee uses to understand his or her own behaviors—including mental behaviors, aka "thoughts"—and to effect purposive and lasting changes in these behaviors, aka "transformations." I guide the reader through several detailed case studies of transformation-oriented interventions that are guided by precise, specific, and detailed models of the behavioral pattern that a trainee is attempting to modify and highlight the relevance of this approach for the broader field of leadership development.

The mind and the world together make up the mind and the world.

Hilary Putnam

For Warren Bennis

If it is the case, as Warren Bennis once pointed out, that we "know a lot" about leadership—for some meaningful interpretation of the word "know"—but barely anything about leadership development, and if it is also true that we have been engaged, as a field, in "leadership development" for the better part of the last fifty years—then we are in a curious situation, provided that we manage to behold this tension before the mind's eye without flinching. On one hand, we have been doing something that we do not understand. On the other hand, our justification for persisting in the quest to develop leaders has to lie precisely in our *understanding* something about leadership development, something that goes beyond "just doing it"; for otherwise, our advice to a budding leadership trainee could only be: "Go out and observe some leaders as they lead!" I suggest that the key to—and a possible way out of—this sticky situation is to focus closely on what we mean by words such as *know* and *understand* and to attempt to reconstruct a program of leadership development that is informed by the best "knowing" and "understanding" that humans as a bunch have been able to produce through centuries and millennia and, undaunted by Bennis's brutally honest and painfully valid remark, to embark on a massive reconstructive process by which we can pursue leadership development as a practice, a craft, an art, and even, sometimes, a science. This chapter reports on one path to such a project.

Nuts, Bolts, and Screws

> *Man is the self-interpreting Being.*
>
> Martin Heidegger

The model-based approach to leadership development has two important components. The first is to get the trainee to *understand* himself or herself and in particular the behavior that he or she would like to change through the lens of a structured, coherent model. He can, for instance, understand his behavior as the outcome of a choice, his choice as the result of a decision and the decision as a result of an algorithmic process that weights his beliefs by his desires and calculates a preferred course of action. Implicit in this understanding are two steps. The first is *self-interpretation*: Behavior is understood as a choice. The second is *self-analysis*: The apparatus of decision theory is brought to bear on the original interpretation in order to make it more precise, more intelligible, and more actionable. The second major component is that of *self-transformation*. Having interpreted himself as a chooser and analyzed his choice through the prism of decision theory, the trainee proceeds to *manipulate* his own behaviors by changing, in a purposive fashion, the value of some variable in his self-model, which might require him to *tinker* with his self-model and to engage in the requisite amount of *self-experimentation,* which will lead to a new and causally efficacious self-understanding.

For instance: Are you paralyzed by decisions among a very large number of options? Then, restrict the number of options under consideration at any one time, by making some of the options inaccessible. Are you paralyzed by very *small* menus of options? Then, postpone deciding until you will have created a sufficiently rich option set. Of course, not all self-manipulation efforts succeed the first time around, and hence it is critical for the trainee to acquire an inclination toward *self-experimentation*—toward searching for the best (most effective and efficient) ways by which a behavior can be brought under the willful control of the subject. Having successfully *manipulated* his own behavior through the use of a model, the trainee proceeds to *re-engineer* her own behavior, by *practicing* the successful manipulation until it fades away from the stark light of consciousness and becomes one of those very useful semi-conscious behaviors we refer to as habits. By the end of the process, a *better decision maker* is made, and it (he, she) is *made* via a process of consciously *selecting* a model by which one *makes sense* of one's life and world, *using* that model to manipulate one's own behaviors, and *incorporating* the resulting—and more productive—set of behaviors into one's behavioral blueprint, or way-of-being. The cognitive becomes the behavioral, "categories" become ontologies, word becomes deed, image becomes reality, and what used to be reality is understood as a possible manifestation of being, not as a precondition for it, or a fact.

The "menu of modeling and self-modeling options" at the disposal of a human creature inhabiting this early part of the 21st century is dazzling and (possibly) dizzying. A forty-six-year-old CEO of a public company (one of the subjects of the model-based self-transformation interventions of the type I shall describe below), presenting with the "phenomenology" (or, is it "symptomatology"?) of "being perceived as being manipulative, which often forces me to *actually* be manipulative in order to cut through the emotional dynamics that the perception generates," can amply benefit from a deep-dive into the modeling toolkit of modern behavioral science. His "everyday" problems—those that keep him up at night and take up the lion's share of his mental behavior when "doing nothing," and which take the grammatical form *How do I get person X to take action Y?*, can be "parsed" using models of humans as embodied minds capable of reasoning and ratiocination or models of humans as brains attached to neurons attached to muscles attached to bones and viscera that produce complex responses in response to complex stimuli (Figure 21.2).

The different (implicit) models of "what a human is" entail very different views about what manipulative behavior is and is not. The question *How to get X to do Y?* becomes, in the "embodied mind" model-of-man, *How to persuade X to do Y?*, and, in the "biological machine" model-of-man, *How to get X's brain to send the right signals to X's motor neurons, muscles, and viscera?*, with immediate attending implications for what "leading X" actually means. Faced with these opposing and vastly divergent models, and with the apparent incommensurability between these different ways of seeing a human, our CEO realizes that *his own* implicit "model of man" (or, woman)—the model that he *reveals* through

Figure 21.1 Model-Based Leadership Development: A Synoptic View of the Intervention

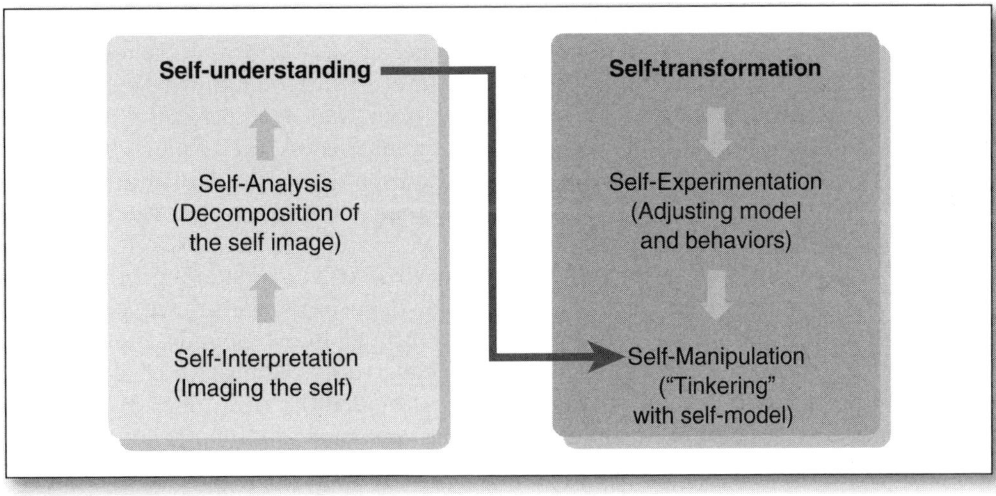

Figure 21.2 Self-Modeling Exercise

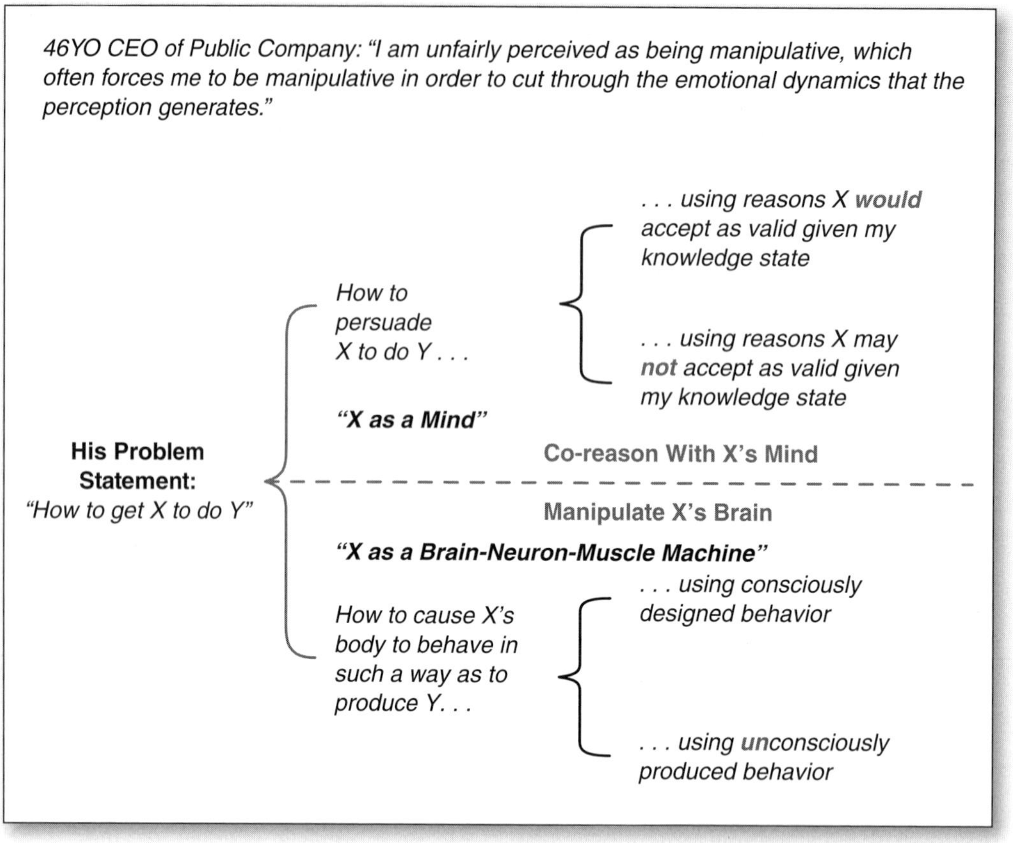

his actions—is a mixture or superposition of these different models: He "sometimes" manipulates and "sometimes" persuades, and quite often he must manipulate (one) in order to persuade (another); and he understands that "manipulating" is not at all an all-or-nothing concept, which is intrinsically "bad" or "good," but rather, that it can be understood as leading to a very precise form of the question *How to get X to do Y?*

Armed with these models, he attempts to make sense of himself as a leader who uses the "embodied mind" and "biological machine" models in order to frame "situations and predicaments" and bring about better outcomes for his team and organization as a whole, and becomes (thereby) a more sophisticated and conscious user of these models and of the moves and maneuvers that each model enables. He comes to understand his own role as an agent in choosing the model through which he sees other humans, and their roles as agents in choosing the model through which they see his own actions. He becomes at once less "manipulative" in the everyday common-parlance sense of the term and less defensive about his manipulativeness, even though he realizes that this, too, is a choice that he has made, one that is not in any way "determined" by either of the models. Through the renewed self-understanding that these polar-opposite models have given him, and through his newfound sense of agency engendered by the need to choose among these models in real time, he develops embryonic forms of both consciousness and conscience about his everyday actions.

It is thus that the "model-based approach to leadership development" works not only as a tool for increasing the productiveness and effectiveness of leadership behavior, but also for doing so through the development of a heightened awareness of one's self, and of the predicament of that self as a being-in-the-world.

Grounds, Roots, Branches (and Leaves)

> *. . . and of whatever we cannot speak, that we must pass over in silence.*
>
> Ludwig Wittgenstein

I shall propose, outline, and defend herein a *model-based* approach to leadership development and will exemplify it with several "live" cases whereby leadership trainees have engaged in supervised projects to understand and transform themselves using this approach. This project is not "rootless" and there is no sense in which it is improvised on an *ad hoc* basis; indeed, its roots run very deep in the Western intellectual tradition, alongside Hindu, Taoist, Buddhist, and Islamic traditions. I will limit my discussion to the Western tradition, for the purpose of devoting space and time to the precise description of the discipline of self-modeling itself.

The self-modeling approach to leadership development relies on a "move" in the Western tradition that is usually associated with Martin Heidegger's work, *Sein und Zeit* (Heidegger, 1927 [1963]). The move is one that questions and undermines the Cartesian schism between mind and world, alongside the Cartesian distinction between representation and reality. Representations, in Heidegger's thinking—including images, metaphors, logical models, theories, and even narratives—are closely and intimately related to their beholder's ways of being. No longer, after Heidegger, are "behaving" and "representing," or "modeling" cleaved and isolated. They go hand in hand; thinking of oneself as a decision maker evaluating costs and benefits when choosing among potential life mates or lovers is not either *natural* or *easy*; and that because mind and mood conspire together to produce behavior, thought and deed must go hand in hand, and *mood* is what binds thought and deed together. Man, according to Heidegger, is the *de-distancing being*—the being that wants to annul distance and get closer; it is for this reason that humans are known to speak of plants, animals, and inanimate objects as having intentions, feelings, and desires: it makes them feel "closer" to the object of their talk if some human-like trait can be *ascribed* to the entity in question.

Model-based leadership development closely heeds this *ascriptive* faculty of humans, focuses on it closely, and makes it the subject of the conscious attention of the trainer. If Heidegger is right and man is characteristically and "naturally" a de-distancing being, then, *modeling* is a distancing maneuver: It is a move by which the trainee distances herself from her own behaviors (Moldoveanu, 2010). This distancing maneuver itself pre-dates Heidegger's thought by almost half a century. It dates back to Friedrich Nietzsche's analysis of the Overman (Nietzsche, 1891) as the person who can hold himself or herself out as an object of objective inquiry. Sigmund Freud (1931) echoed Nietzsche (without proper attribution) and made it one of the aims of psychoanalysis (of the kind he was himself practicing) to produce an ability and propensity in the analys and to hold herself out before her own eyes as the object of "scientific" inquiry; and even though "scientific" had a naively positivistic resonance in Freud's time, the aim of model-based leadership development *remains* that of producing an ability of the trainee to achieve *distance from her own self*, which is precisely what precise, tight, crisp *modeling* purports to do.

But it was Wittgenstein (in both early [Wittgenstein, 1923] and later [Wittgenstein, 1953] embodiments) that provides one of the most important *practical* tools for model-based self-transformation. Wittgenstein-the-earlier recognized that "the limits of my language are the limits of my world"—way before a plethora of neurologists and psychologists started to realize that most human creatures will only "see it when they believe it." Accordingly, model-based approaches to self-transformation *stress models*, for it is these models that stretch and expand the range of variables and values of those variables that the trainee will *heed*. Wittgenstein-the-later—rebelling to some extent against Wittgenstein-the-earlier—proposed that words may not *represent* at all: There is nothing five-like about the Arabic number "5"—nor anything five-like about its Roman counterpart "V"; and, indeed, the search for five-like-ness among visual, oral, and aural representations of "five" is a fool's errand. "Meaning"—if such a word can be used intelligibly—is only loosely connected to the picture that represents the object to which the word is supposed to refer, and is rather conferred upon words by the intentions of the speaker, the accepted practices of the community to which speaker and hearer belong, and the set of rules by which these practices are supposed to apply (or, not) to the meaning of the words as they are used in sentences. This is not an easy insight to either behold or apply, but the model-based leadership development practitioner finds it useful: The humans who have developed models of decisions and choices, of degrees of belief and degrees of desire, of impulsiveness and self-control, of inference and ratiocination have been able to do so in part because they have grown up in the cloistered enclaves of places like Cambridge, Oxford, and Chicago, have evolved stable sets of *norms and rules* for gauging whether or not a sentence is meaningful or otherwise, and have learned to submit their individual wills and caprices to these rules in times of visceral or emotional discomfort and temptation; and this *discipline* is worth appropriating, for it is part and parcel of a person's increased ability to detach himself or herself from his or her own moods, perceptions, and immediate desires.

Finally, a stray root—or, perhaps it is a branch; in any case, it is not to be taken lightly. It comes from Jean Paul Sartre's (in)famous discussion of "bad faith" (*mauvaise foi:* for once English and French agree in both connotation and denotation) in *L'Etre et le neant* (Sartre, 1945 [1996]). Bad faith, according to Sartre, is a condition that besets most beings who are fated to be free (aka humans). It has two components. The first is a choice to reject that freedom, and to adopt various "necessitarian" poses and stances toward the world and one's place in that world ("I have no choice," "there can be no choice," "it is not *my* choice," etc.). The second is a choice to forget that one has made the choice to reject that freedom, and to go about "business as usual" in way one lives one's life. Combine move #1 and move #2 together and you have a close-enough picture of incorrigibility in human affairs: for how, without at least the inkling or suspicion that a choice is possible (even if it poses all kinds of problems to some who know just enough neurophysiology to be dangerous) can the project of self-transformation even get off the ground? *Transformation*—perhaps, yes; but *self*-transformation, emphatically, no. And, it is the *self*-transformation "market" that leadership development "industry" aims at—unlike the psycho-pharmaceutics industry, which may well be content with transformation *tout court*. Now, why is this particular root *essential* to our project, i.e., why do I even speak of it as a "root"? Well, because the would-be leader needs to at least *feel* capable of choosing the model by which he will represent his life and his world—otherwise, the self-transformation interventions I am about to describe will be (vaguely remembered) as either a bizarre form of info-tainment

Figure 21.3A

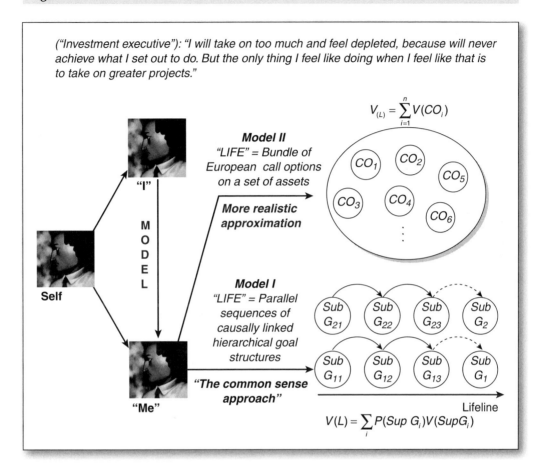

("Investment executive"): "I will take on too much and feel depleted, because will never achieve what I set out to do. But the only thing I feel like doing when I feel like that is to take on greater projects."

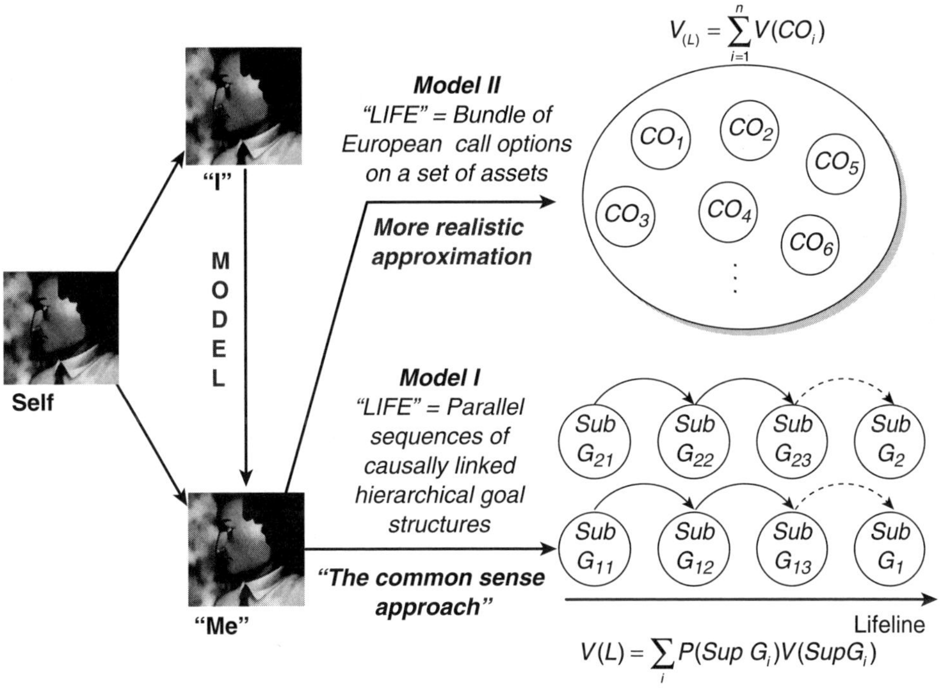

or as a superficial exposure to some "interesting ideas" peddled by leadership wanna-bes—dimly recollected as they will likely turn out to be.

The Heart of the Matter: How Model-Based Leadership Development Works

The model-based approach to leadership development takes the form of a targeted self-transformation project, which closely follows the map of Figure 21.1 on page 331: the trainee chooses a behavior that he or she would like to transform, learns to use—sometimes by trial and error—a structured model that functions as a map to that behavior, uses the model to analyze the behavior by mapping sense experiences into observable, controllable, unobservable, and uncontrollable variables in the model, along with a set of logical relationships among these variables (self-interpretation and self-analysis, which, together with self-interpretation, corresponds to a new self-understanding), tinkers with the controllable set of variables of the model to the end of producing the desired modification of his or her target behavior (self-manipulation and self-experimentation) and proceeds to practice new behaviors, which correspond to the optimal combination of the controllable variables to achieve self-transformation. Because the process that takes on from self-interpretation to self-transformation is effortful and occasionally painful (in psychological and even physiological terms), it is essential for the trainee to be *able and willing to choose the behavior that he or she would like to address*. Likewise, the trainer must have a well-developed and adaptive "library of models" that could function as useful transformational blueprints—as he or she does not know, in advance, what behavior or class of behaviors the trainee will focus on. The rate-limiting step of the process is often not either self-experimentation or self-manipulation (which "sound" hard to conceive and carry out). Rather, the rate-limiting step is that by which the trainee engages with both the behaviors he or she would like to change and the models of that behavior in a way that is *intellectually honest* (and not just honest) and *authentic*—and not just sincere.

The success of the intervention relies critically on the ability of the trainee to be precise and unflinching in apprehending and addressing a particular behavior, and to distance himself or herself or from that behavior sufficiently to be able to analyze and parse it in detail. This is *precisely* where the use of a detailed analytical model of the trainee's behavior is helpful, and perhaps even critical. A precise model that pictures everyday quantities (thoughts, wishes) in terms of a structured representation (rational choice and rational belief, for instance) simultaneously enables the trainee to practice *behavioral microscopy* and *emotional distoscopy* (Moldoveanu, 2010). Let me demonstrate: Jim (the trainee) is an executive who is "perceived as being driven by envy in his decision-making," whereas he perceives himself as being "a competitive, fair-minded, self-motivated self-starter." He is intrigued by a quick exposition of Sartre's idea of *mauvaise foi*, which leads him to consider the possibility that he is, in fact, envious in his evaluation of outcomes and that he masks this envy via a self-concept that prominently features competitiveness as one of its sub-headings; and is therefore interested in (a) exploring his behaviors and others' perceptions of them in greater detail, and (b) intervening to change these behaviors if, in fact, "envy" is the most plausible inference that a fair-minded observer can make about them. (It helps the case of the trainer that Jim considers himself to be "a fair-minded person.")

The trainer introduces a model that "dissects" Jim's utility or value function and helps Jim make more precise distinctions among the ways in which he values that which he values. The model posits that Jim's value depends on the ratio between two quantities. The first quantity is itself a ratio between the level of effort that Jim perceives he has invested in a project or activity and his own payoff. The second quantity is also a ratio, between the level of effort Jim perceives his peer or subordinate has invested in the same project and that co-worker's payoff. Now the difference between "ambitious competitiveness" and "envious destructiveness" can be made more precise, as follows: Jim can increase his own value function by two broad sets of maneuvers. The first is the "competitive" set: Jim expends more effort to the end of securing a greater reward than the person he is "competing" with, and tries hard to avoid "falling behind" his competitor by working harder. In this case, the competitor's payoff functions as an anchor for Jim's aspiration level. The second is the "envious" set: Jim attempts to increase his own value by decreasing or destroying part of the competitor's payoff, by subjectively inflating his own perception of his own level of effort and subjectively and often falsely down-grading the level of effort he perceives his competitor to be investing for the payoff the latter achieves—and broadcasting his estimate of his peer's level of effort to whomever wants to listen.

Now, Jim has a "map" of sufficient resolution and precision to "watch himself" and "track himself." The map is detailed enough to map a set of "sense data" (Jim's and his observers', which he will force himself to heed, in order to live up to his "fair-minded" self-portrait) onto a set of variables in Jim's self-model. He can observe and attempt to measure and control variables whose causal connections are specified by his self-model. He can go out into the wilds of his organizational life and try to *measure* (rather than "eyeball," or "estimate") his own and others' level of effort invested for a particular contested payoff. Because he knows he is prone to biases that might arise from his own *mauvaise foi*, and because he understands that fair-mindedness requires him to seek to be impartial, he attempts to make these measurements as precise and inter-subjectively agreeable (i.e., "objective") as possible; and he does the same with his perceived competitor. Now, *les jeux sont faits*—as Sartre might have put it. Equipped with a causal self-model and a map between his own sense perceptions and the variables of the model, Jim makes a prediction about how he will feel in various states of the world—corresponding to different payoffs for himself and his peer, and about what he will do, conditional upon how he will feel. The model has become much more than a pretty picture: It has become Jim's user's guide to his self, and is on its way to becoming a self-transformation tool. Jim then watches as payoffs materialize and his feelings and perceptions (do or do not) change as a function of who-did-how. He watches his own behavioral dispositions toward his peer change (or otherwise) in the event that he did worse than he had or hoped or predicted; he records his own actions leading up to the moment when he finds out how he and his peer did, and in the moments just after the momentous event. He registers these changes and, if his gaze continues to be unflinching, he may glimpse, perhaps for the first time, the inner work that he now has to do. For Jim, this simple little model—general enough to say something precise about how any human might value what he or she values as a function of the payoffs of his own self and of other selves—has become a guide to observing and potentially transforming his own perception and action. It at once *magnifies* a particular set of behavioral dispositions or proclivities that Jim might have (hence: "behavioral microscope") and *distances* Jim from his own behavior sufficiently so that he can take it in, analyze it, and attempt to re-engineer it "from first principles" (hence: "emotional distoscope").

The example highlights not only the architecture of an intervention aimed at model-based leadership training, but also the nature of the intervention itself. Like the case studies in psychoanalysis which Freud originally introduced as a "research tool"—the currency, to this very day, of published findings in psychoanalytic psychotherapy—model-based leadership training proceeds on a case-by-case basis. However, *unlike* Freud's case studies—justly criticized by Karl Popper (see, Popper, 1983, for instance) as being suspiciously successful in every single application, to the point where psychoanalysis itself came to be suspected of being a pseudo-science because it can explain "too much"—the model-based approach to leadership development rests on a method and a discipline that transcends the particular case at hand. It uses *structured* models of choosing, deciding, feeling, inferring, perceiving, and acting in each case, to give the trainee a causally or logically connected map of his or her behavioral, affective, visceral, cognitive, or perceptual dispositions, and co-opts the trainee to use the model not only as a "way of thinking about the self and its behaviors," but also as a guide to *intervening* upon the self and its behaviors. The model-based leadership developer has learned from Chris Argyris (2006) that a useful sign of *understanding* a behavior is the ability to *produce it* and not just to *talk about it*; and she has learned from Karl Popper the fact that testability is not an ethereal phenomenon that publishers of papers in the *Journal of Irrelevant Research* invoke to get past sleepy reviewers; but, rather, that it is a here-and-now tool for building better models for the purpose of solving real problems, of which behavioral transformation is clearly one.

Notice that the models used by the trainer—though structured—need not be based on any presumption of rationality or reasonableness on the part of the trainee. It is true that rational choice and rational belief-based models are considered to be a "standard" of structured modeling in the social sciences, and that they critically rely on the ascription of rationality by the modeler to the modelee—and, implicitly, by the trainer to the trainee. But, a great many models—such as neurophysiological models of brain function and psychoanalytic and psychodynamic models of the self-narratives and self-identities of trainees—make no such assumptions. Rigor in modeling and intervention need not rely on the imputation of rationality by the modeler to the modelee; and it will often be the case that the most persuasive models start from an acceptance of the "unhinged," uncontrollable, and patently unreasonable nature of mental behavior. In the example above, envy—a motivational state that is written off in most economic analyses of behavior—is emphatically put forth as a possible explanation for Jim's behavior, and the role of the trainer may well be to guide Jim through a process of discovering and mapping the dynamics of his own feelings of envy toward others—of what feeds them and what foils them.

One last example of using a model as a lens upon one's self. This one features an Aikido-style maneuver, whereby the trainer makes use of a model that the trainee *himself* uses as a matter of course in his own work and persuades and co-opts the trainee to turn this model inwardly, *upon himself*, as a way of making sense of his predicament. The example is that of a forty-five-year-old investment banking executive and former operating company CEO ("Scott") who feels "overwhelmed and frustrated" by the fact that his life goals (in all domains of experience: children's education, financial net worth, social impact of his public activities, personal athletic achievement, etc.) are ever more ambitious, more expensive, and less achievable, yet ever more pressing to him personally, in the sense that he feels more rather than less compelled to expend personal energy and effort toward their achievement, on a day by day basis, and increasingly "unstable" in his pattern of activities and associations—which is something that he attributes to his sense of frustration. He feels that his own current net worth *should* in fact make him less likely to feel the sort of desperate drive for worldly achievements he believes does in fact move him, but is aware that the projects and outcomes to which he is committed have over time become less achievable and less satisfying to him—which does not stop him from borrowing against his net worth to pursue them, a pattern of leverage-accumulation-re-leverage that makes his family "edgy" and his relationship with them "tricky." As an investment executive, he has previously mused at the fact that his own life is—or "has become," although he cannot answer the question "since when?"—a "portfolio" of "projects," but he looks upon this representation as a playful metaphor—one he finds slightly annoying.

Rather than passing over this metaphor, however, suppose that Scott's coach or trainer takes it seriously—and *more* seriously, in particular, than Scott himself seems to take it. She does so by putting forth to Scott a model of the latter's life that considers each one of the domains of Scott's life experience—personal, family, business, social—as a "project"; and each such project as a European call option on the value of an underlying "asset" (spouse, business, fitness, etc.); and therefore the sum total of Scott's life as a bundle of European call options on the value of "assets" that together form the "bundle of his life's domains." Because our development candidate understands not only what a European call option is, but also *how to price it* (See Figure 21.3B) by the use of the Black-Scholes formula (Black & Scholes, 1973)—and he knows this because he frequently *uses* the formula to calculate the value of the options awarded to the executive teams of the companies he invests in—the use of the "my life as a bundle of European call options" model is highly fruitful, because the terms of the formula, the assumptions on which the formula rests, and the predictions that follow from the formula can all be made precise and applied to Scott's own life.

Once he takes (his own) metaphor seriously and accedes to using the Black-Scholes formula in order to evaluate the "value of his own life," Scott focuses on the fact that the value of a European call option goes up with the time to maturity of the option and the underlying volatility of the asset—precisely the features of the "Quixotic" projects he spends more and more time and energy engendering, nurturing, and justifying to himself and to others. Now, the assumptions that Fisher Black and Myron Scholes made when they derived their now (often used and frequently mis-used) formula are neither irrelevant nor inaccessible to Scott. The call option pricing formula rests upon the assumption that the value of the underlying asset on which the call option is defined changes as a function of time in a way that is well approximated by a geometric Brownian process. Local changes in the value of this asset are random variables, distributed according to some mean and standard deviation, which measure the volatility of the asset's value. Our life-planner is quick to understand that the option-holder is assumed, within this model, to have no significant effect upon the probability that the value of the assets of his life will take on one value or another. The implication for this is that, in spite of his allure as a "wildly successful financier and executive"—one which he has a stake in cultivating and living up to—he nevertheless feels—or acts as if he feels—powerless to impact the value of the "projects" that make up his life. Even though he appears from the outside—and, from a "social" perspective—to be "in control of his own life"—a model that seems to predict *much* about his inner life and outward behavior can only be valid if he in fact *does not* feel in control of his life's works. He comes to suspect that the "strife" within his life is not a consequence of his externally imposed predicaments, but an intendedly and consciously pursued goal ("volatility"), which is a *cause* of the outward semiology of his life. He also understands that the pursuit of increasingly far-sighted and "over-the-horizon" projects is not a consequence of the fact that he has "done all one can hope to accomplish by the age of xx in this field"—a narrative he would use as a customary form of self-medication—but rather a characteristic of his own value function, which is shaped by a generative model of "life as a portfolio of call options."

This is one case in which self-understanding—even counter-intuitive and illuminating self-understanding—does not necessarily lead to an immediate solution—behavioral or even conceptual. The subject in this case looks with some contempt on an "alternative" model of one's life's work (Figure 21.3B), wherein goals are hierarchically organized, ranging from superordinate ("having built this company up to $XX in revenues at the end of five years") to subordinate ("recruiting, hiring, and motivating executive team, articulating and communicating vision within six months"), to sub-subordinate ("securing the first-large paying customer by the end of next month")—and so forth. He sees the *prima facie* advantage of this model of his life over one that represents his domains of experience as a portfolio of options on asset over whose intrinsic value his actions have no reliable effect and understands that representing his life as a nested hierarchy of objectives, goals, and "dreams" increases his level of control and sense of "agency"; but, he is, at the same time, distrustful of the intrinsic value associated with the higher level goals that he can imagine for himself, ranging from financial to personal and relational ones. Accordingly, he looks down upon this "common sense" way of "parsing a life."

Nevertheless, the self-modeling exercise has advanced his state of consciousness significantly, as he is ready to consider that states and conditions that he had previously thought to be exogenous, "beyond my control" and accidental (by *some* definition of accidentality) may in fact have been generated by his own ways of being, which in turn arose from his choice of a particular kind of self-understanding. And, he is open to re-think his life's work in terms of different and potentially more promising self-models. One example that seems particularly promising to him is based on a "Nietzschean equilibrium" concept, which works as follows: A life will be in Nietzschean equilibrium if the subject's actions are such that he would be willing to take them even if he had to live his very same life over and over again in infinite perpetuity. I call it "Nietzschean equilibrium" because it is based on Nietzsche's suggestion that "we should live our lives as if we are fated to re-live them again forever." Under this injunction, no action is worth undertaking—regardless of its consequences—if the action in question is not something that one would do over and over again, forever, in the same circumstances. Because he understands that his choice of a self-model is likely to shape his actions even if he succeeds in pretending that no such choice is necessary, our subject is encouraged enough, at this point, to engage in the self-experimentation required to understand whether or not he can bring his own life in tune with a self-model he consciously and conscientiously chooses.

The mathematical precision of the "life model" that the trainer uses to understand—and to get the trainee to understand—the trainee's own dispositions may suggest that such model-centric interventions may not be conducive to a textured understanding of the emotional and visceral "underbelly"

Figure 21.3B

Self-Model: Use Black Scholes Option Pricing Formula for European Call option to calculate implicit value that subject places on own life . . .

$$V(C) = N(d_1)S - N(d_2)Ee^{-rT};\ d_1 = \frac{1n(S/E) + (r + \sigma^2/2)T}{\sigma\sqrt{T}};\ d_2 = d_1 - \sigma\sqrt{T}.$$

Where, $V(C)$ = value of call option interest rate; S = price of underlying stock; E = exercise price
r = risk-free interest rate;
T = time to maturity; $N(d)$ = probability that a randomly drawn number from normal distribution will be less than d;
σ = standard deviation of annualized compound ROR

"More realistic" model says that value of an option goes up with variance and time to maturity of the project on which value of equity is based.

So, if $V(C)$ is a good model for the implicit value that trainee attaches to his life:

a. Subject will seek out projects with longer time to maturity;
b. Subject will seek out projects with higher levels of uncertainty/risk.

Moreover, $V(C)$ is also the value of a levered asset, with debt to equity ratio $S/(E-S)$, something that subject "knew" as a manager but did not know as a human.

of the trainee's behavior. In fact, quite the opposite is the case. Model-centered interventions are meant to more closely illuminate the emotional and visceral substructures of the trainee's ways of being, by providing useful metaphors and imagery that will help the trainee achieve the right level of "distance" from affectively "hot" states. This distance will serve the purpose of having the trainee achieve a level of self-understanding that is not coerced or distorted by the emotions, moods, and sensations that together make up "everyday life"—impervious as it often is to efforts at self-transformation.

We have come far in understanding what self-understanding can do if it is "pitched" at the right level of precision, pressed with the right level of rigor, and enforced with the right level of commitment, but we are still far from seeing the prescriptive self-transformational power of self-modeling. For this, we need to go even deeper into dissecting the space-time cone that we call "a life" by the use of representations detailed enough to show up both its wounds *and* possible remedies and therapies. We need to delve into the discipline of *model-based self-experimentation and self-manipulation*, which will, in conjunction with model-based self-understanding, supply the right basis for self-transformation projects.

How It (Really) Works—Sophistries Aside

Onto the interventions, then, with all of the caveats that accounts of in-depth case studies should carry with them: Make inferences judiciously and carefully! Do not over-generalize! Stay attuned to the particular even as you seek for the universal! and, of course: Enter at your own risk!—for leaving might not be as simple as you think.

Case 1. A forty-one-year-old executive: "I cannot speak my own mind in top management team meetings." The trainee is aware of the fact that she does not speak truth to power (in this case: the CEO and the rest of his executive team) in situations in which doing so would be advantageous for the entire executive team and the rest of the company. She recalls several "sub-optimal" decisions the executive team as a whole made that could have been avoided or improved upon had the executive team internalized information and arguments that (a) she could have made, but did not, (b) they would have been likely to heed, conditional upon her having made them and (c) heeding them would likely have led them to make a better decision, which they were not likely to have made otherwise. The trainee is convinced, then, that a difference in her behavioral blueprint would actually "make a difference," and we are squarely in the land of "differences that make a difference" that are the stuff of causally efficacious causal models. The trainee has significant insight into the mechanisms by which she fails to say that which she knows she has most reason to say, at the right time, in the right tone, to the right people, with the right feeling and for the right reasons—Aristotle's definition of the higher human faculty of reason. In her own words (uninformed by any prior discussion of *mauvaise foi*, to boot): "I lie and then lie to myself I did not lie"—to cover up the pregnant silence that results when she does not say that which she knows she should; and, "I use fuzzy language to dissimulate the real issue, and work hard to avoid being shown up."

The trainer offers up two models of "what goes on inside the moment" when she turns away from speaking truth to power at the right place-time (Figure 21.4). The first model is a commonsense, everyday, man-on-the-street's version of "how action happens" (Model 1). In it, a human creature deliberates upon the available options, estimates the costs and benefits of her alternatives, chooses the alternative with the highest net expected payoff (the costs and benefits of speaking up or shutting up), plans its action (says the following words in this tone and intensity to these people), commits to a course of action (opens mouth and begins forming intelligible oral noises), allows the resulting intention to percolate and rise up inside itself (requisite motor neurons begin to fire), and then acts (speaks). Everything, moreover, happens under the often grim light of consciousness. (Perhaps the reader is beginning to internalize what "behavioral microscopy" means, and causal consequences of using microscopic causal maps to inform behavior). In the second model (Model 2; Figure 21.5), things happen a bit differently. In this model, an intention (avert gaze, start doodling with a piece of paper, at exactly the time when one could have most propitiously spoken) forms without conscious awareness of it, which follows just before—and sometimes just after—action; whereupon the mind races to produce explanations of the action sequence ("I was distracted," "It was not worth saying anyhow") that could well function as justifications (to others, as well as to the creature herself), and could form the basis for the "white lies" that the creature tells herself—and resents herself for—afterwards (when it is, unfortunately, far too late).

The trainee is intrigued, and the trainer capitalizes on the split second of openness that accompanies the subjective experience of "feeling intrigued" to introduce the trainee to a highly subversive—and slightly embarrassing, to many who understand its implications—experimental finding dating back to the work of Libet in the late 1970s (Figure 21.4; Libet, Wright, Feinstein, & Pearl, 1979), which suggests that Model 2 (awareness follows intention and even action) rather than Model 1 (conscious deliberation and planning precede intention and action) is a better (more reliably valid) explanation for behavioral patterns observed in most humans.

Figure 21.4 Case Study 1

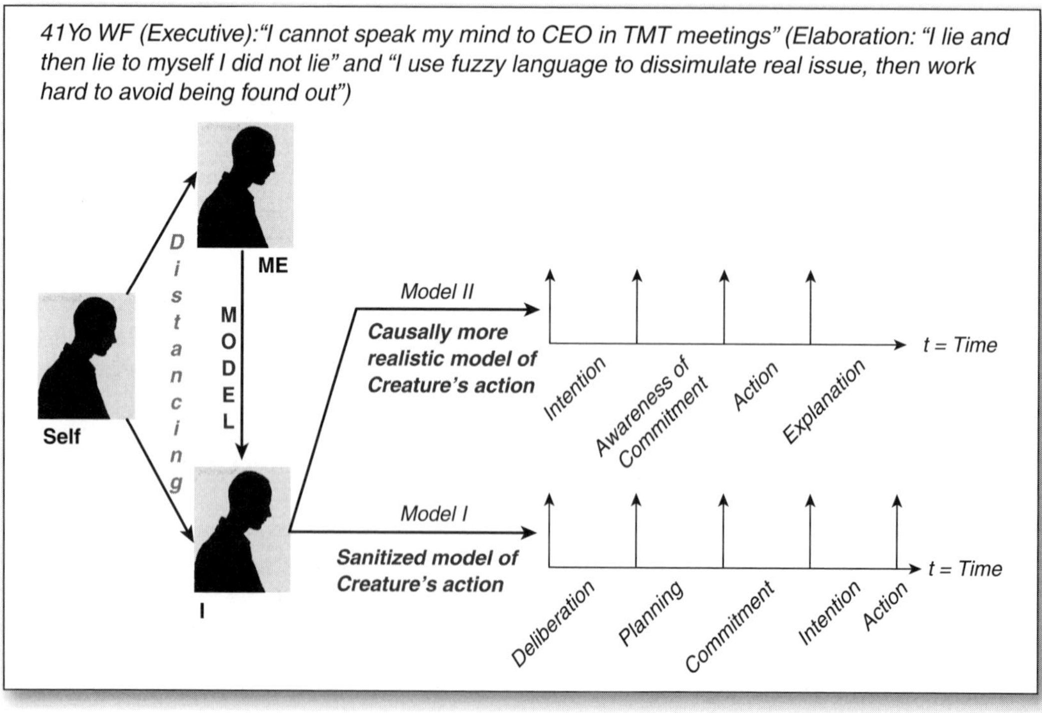

Figure 21.5 Basis for More Realistic Model 2

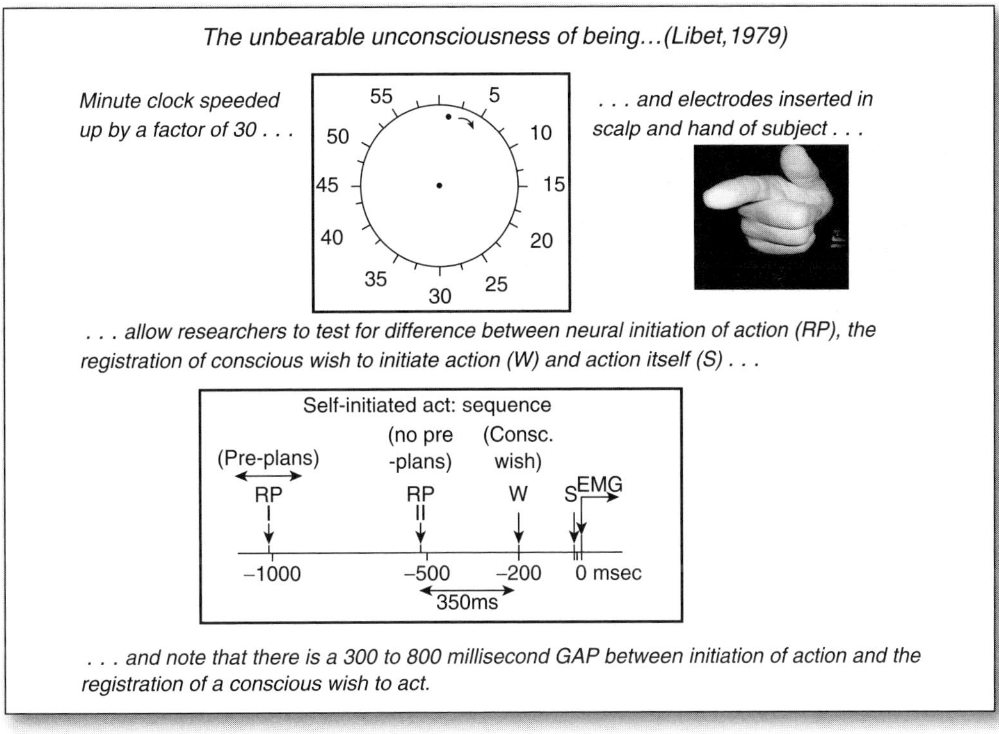
The unbearable unconsciousness of being...(Libet, 1979)
Minute clock speeded up by a factor of 30 . . .
55
5
10
15
20
25
30
35
40
45
50
. . . and electrodes inserted in scalp and hand of subject . . .
. . . allow researchers to test for difference between neural initiation of action (RP), the registration of conscious wish to initiate action (W) and action itself (S) . . .
Self-initiated act: sequence
(Pre-plans)
(no pre -plans)
(Consc. wish)
RP
I
RP
II
W
S
EMG
–1000
–500
–200
0 msec
350ms
. . . and note that there is a 300 to 800 millisecond GAP between initiation of action and the registration of a conscious wish to act.

The trainee registers that there is a gap (lasting, on average, about *350 milliseconds*, or, a third of a second: by now, "behavioral microscopy" should have acquired real meaning for the reader) between the initiation of an action—in her case, an action that precludes her from speaking out—and her conscious awareness of that action. She registers her surprise at the result, as well as her disappointment at the human condition; and, in the next breath, begins to ask about implications for freedom of the will and the like, an all-too-deeply entrenched idea in the Western mind that rears its head at just the right moment; whereupon the trainer seizes once again on the moment of internal openness of the trainee and informs her that Libet himself was puzzled and disconcerted at the implications of his own experimental findings (which he thought were valid) for the freedom of the will of the self (in which he believed) and, being a resourceful thinker rather than a dustbowl empiricist, posited that free will is exercised by the human subject via a "veto pathway," whereupon the mind can reject courses of action, but not initiate them. The trainer furthermore suggests—following an insight due to Roy Baumeister and his colleagues (Heatherton & Baumeister, 1996), suitably adapted to the case at hand, that the will—which is the seat and source of that all important, freedom preserving veto right—is like a muscle that can be depleted through exhaustion (the trainee's eyes light up, as she is, indeed, even less likely to try to speak up when she is tired) but also built up through exercise; and he suggests (Figure 21.6) two such sets of self-manipulations ("interventions" or "exercises") that the trainee can undertake as a way of getting herself to produce an all things considered desirable behavior.

The first set comprises self-manipulations based on systematic self-denial; by the

Figure 21.6 Case Study 1 Interventions

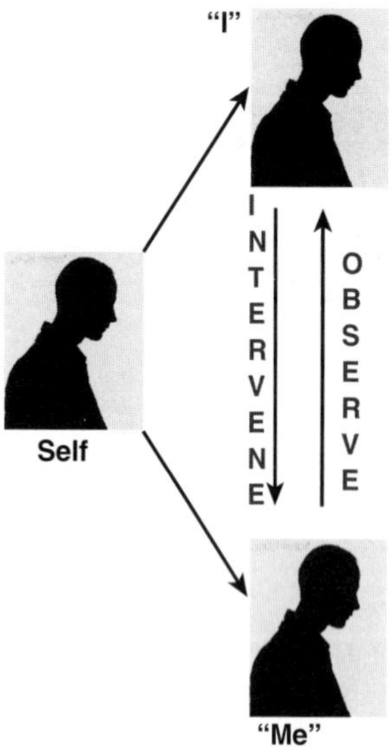

Intervention I

Increase t^{NP}_{RP} *(−500 ms) −*t_W *(-200 ms) by developing "VETO PATHWAY." Do this by implementing a "DO THE OPPOSITE" behavioral routine for 3 weeks:*

IF HUNGRY, DRINK
IF THIRSTY, READ
IF TIRED, GO FOR A RUN

RESULT: CREATURE remains silent when it feels tempted to lie or dissimulate in TMT context

Intervention II

Increase t^{PP}_{RP}*(−1000 ms) −*t_W *(-200 ms) by developing "will muscle." Do this by practicing perceptual switches in a bistable image with a metronome at faster and faster speeds.*

RESULT: CREATURE records 10 instances (out of 17 occasions) in which it provides negative feedback to TMT members (including CEO)

implementation of a "do-the-opposite" heuristic: "if feeling hungry, do not eat, but, rather, drink"; "if feeling thirsty, do not drink, but, rather, read something"; and so on, for a period of one to three weeks. If the trainee's will is indeed like a muscle, and if this muscle is in some way related to the "veto" function of conscious awareness, and if her ability to speak up is related to her ability to inhibit herself from doing something that kinematically and physiologically precludes her from speaking up, then building up this muscle should increase her ability to speak up. (There are a lot of "if's" here, but, each step of the inference chain is now plausible to the trainee and she is motivated to do *something* that changes her way-of-being.)

The second set of self-manipulations is more subtle and sounds "easier" to carry out, but relies on the same underlying presumed mechanism of the will. It is based on the insight that bi-stable images (such as that displayed in Figure 21.7) that have the property that they can be perceived in any one of at least two different ways (seal, donkey's head in the case of this particular image) can for the basis of a set of interventions aimed at increasing one's control over one's ability to exercise conscious control of an unfolding motivational process. The key to the exercise is to realize that, while "most" people can end up seeing (especially after some coaxing) both images, and most people who can experience the markings on the paper as one of at least two possible images will in fact experience "spontaneous" switching from one image to another, *very few* people, without practice, can in fact switch *at will* between the two images. Moreover, very few of those who can switch at will can vary the *rate* at which they switch—which means (multiplying "very few" by "very few") that very few humans will exhibit, without training, the "meta-control" by which they can control the process by which they control their conscious awareness of a sense perception.

Figure 21.7 Bi-stabel Image Used to Train Willful Control of Behavior

Moreover, if the will to switch is a form of "the will" and if the said "will" has the "muscle property," then, the trainer reasons, and the trainee agrees, the capacity to change the rate at which one switches between the possible images can itself be built up, through practice of the right kind, and should lead, by the "will as muscle" argument, to a sort of "cross-training" of the will, whereby the trainee's ability to do that which she has reason to do in the heat of the moment will increase with her capacity to switch perceptions of a bi-stable image, and to change the rate at which she switches. All that is left for the trainer to supply is a piece of training apparatus, which in this case is a *metronome*, with the usual markings that go from *Grave* through *Vivace* to *Presto*, and which the trainee can use to gradually force herself to switch between "high level" perceptions of "low level" visual imagery at higher and higher rates, or at variable rates.

After three weeks of self-reported engagement with *both* sets of self-manipulations, the trainee reported an increased ability to concentrate on cognitively demanding tasks in the presence of "white noise" in the environment, enhanced affect (as evidenced also by reports of acquaintances and family), and a decreased propensity to rumination. She reported on the results of attempting to voice dissent, concern, disengagement, tension, or apprehension in situations in which she perceived a high level of group cohesion around a decision she considered to be suboptimal as follows: On seven of twelve instances of outright disagreement, which she considers to have been exactly the kinds of situations that would in the past have led her to assent, she voiced "concern" with the likely end result of the group deliberation process, and "apprehension" about the bases on which the decision was made. In five of those seven instances, she reported taking time within the meeting to reconstruct, in some detail, the basis of her concerns and the possible remedies that the group as a whole could and should consider. In three of these five instances of "protracted dissent," she registered success in persuading the group to re-consider the basis of their decisions, and to agree to a modified plan of action. Finally, in two of these last three instances, the group's final decision was changed from what it would have been *sine* her intervention, and in ways that were causally related to the outcome of the group's deliberation on the decision that was triggered by her dissent and objection. Her (perceived and self-reported) self-efficacy in voicing dissent in a causally impactful and productive way rose "dramatically" as a result of the interventions, and she assessed that the causal efficacy of the interventions were causally related to the fact that understood and agreed with the causal model that generated them. Moreover, even though she agreed that the causal model of "the will and its veto power" was *one* of several ways in which she could have interpreted and understood herself, she nevertheless thought that the causal power of this causal model to produce changes in her negative feedback-giving behavior was based on the fact that she had "embraced" the self-concept of "chooser/decider/agent" that was embedded in the model.

> *We have seen the enemy, and it is us.* —*Walt Kelley's Pogo*

Case II. A thirty-year-old "high potential" manager: "I just cannot get myself to lose the last XX lbs." It is important for complicated and sophisticated interventions to be given a chance to work—or fail—on "simple" cases, cases in which other interventions have been tried and tested, and cases in which the probability of failure on the basis of base rates for other interventions is quite high. And this is precisely the setting of the next case, of a mid-level high potential manager who found herself unable to produce the behaviors required to achieve (a) a higher level of personal physical fitness, and (b) a weight loss of at least 20 lbs, both without the use of special or custom diets, nutritional supplements, weight loss pills, or other, even more invasive measures, such as the surgical removal of fat tissue from target areas such as the abdomen and the gluteal muscles—all of which she had previously considered and rejected. It was clear from the beginning of the intervention that the trainee wanted to focus on a combination of dieting and exercise as a means to producing the desired effect, and that had furthermore isolated the latter part of the day as the "failure point" in her attempt to do so: She had been for some time "unable" to replace a high-calorie "anxious eating" meal at around 6 pm with a workout or a run. The trainee was introduced to two models of personal discounting of future value, based, respectively, on traditional approaches in finance theory ("present value calculation using exponential discounting," Model I in Figure 21.8) and on newer "behavioral economics" (Ainslie, 2001; Laibson, 1997) and animal behavior (Green & Myerson, 2005) models of impulsiveness. The "rational" discounting model (Model I) posits that if an agent values a future option (weight loss, better fitness, with the value denoted by V_{LW}, or, the value of lower weight) more highly than another (indulging in the pleasure of compulsive eating to calm nerves, with the value denoted by V_E, or, the value of eating) at some point in the future, then he or she will also value that option more highly right now, where "right now," obviously, could be anywhere in time. For this so-called exponential discounter, there is no problem of self-control or self-command. He or she does what he or she has most reason to do, on time, every time. By contrast, the "impulsive creature" (Model II) is described by a value function that is best described by a hyberbolic curve, exhibiting sharp peaks corresponding to "impulsive preferences." The subjective "feel" of the hyperbolic discounting curve is rendered by the situation in which the trainee (at 7 a.m.) "decides it is in her all things considered best interest" to go to the gym and work out at 6 p.m., spends the entire day anticipating that she will indeed go to the gym and work out at 6 p.m., and "suddenly" at 5:45 p.m., upon arriving at home, makes herself a large, high-calorie sandwich and kicks back in the sofa to watch the evening news, which she does (sandwich in hand) until it is "too late" to go to the gym. The same discouraging pattern repeats itself day in and day out, and the subject is increasingly discouraged about her ability to "keep her commitments"—even if these commitments are to herself alone.

The trainee was encouraged to "play" with both models as ways of (a) *interpreting and understanding* her own behaviors, and (b) *intervening to change and transform* these behaviors by playing around with behaviors that correspond to or influence the values of the variables of the model. Having settled on Model II as a self-interpretation schema, the trainee proceeded to model her own impulsiveness by closely monitoring the "crossover" time between the value of working out (the "larger-later" value) and the value of enjoying a sandwich in the comfort of her sofa (the smaller sooner

Figure 21.8 Case Study 2

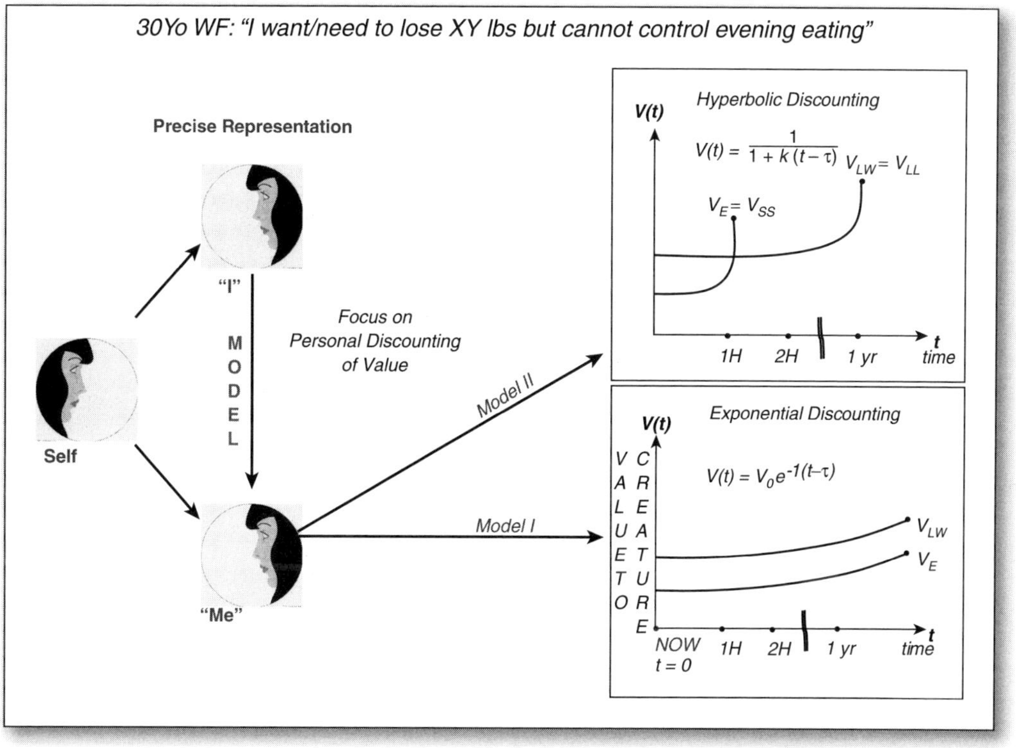

value): the crossover time (which she pegged at around fifteen to thirty minutes before the time at which she would have gone to the gym) is the time at which her will "flips" and she changes from a state of "commitment" to a state of "giving in to temptation"—which she later regrets, but can "do nothing" about. The trainee is then asked to come up with "control schemes" for manipulating her own behavior in ways that advance her all things considered interests, on the basis of the model of hyperbolic discounting she now understands to be a useful representation of her way-of-being. She *herself* derives several alternatives forms of self-control, ranging from "public commitment to go to the gym"—which, she reasons, will increase the cost of staying home and watching television by an amount proportional to the shame she will feel at having broken a public commitment—to the articulation of a "personal principle" that enjoins her from breaking her own commitments, to an attempt to "control her own mind" at the precise cross-over point between her "two selves" (the couch potato and disciplined committed individual), to devising a personal routine in the neighborhood of the crossover point (in this case, not returning home at all and going for a short walk in the neighborhood of the gym) that makes it impossible for her to engage in the reprehensible practice of fixing herself a sandwich, to purchasing substitutes for the sandwich (low-calorie meal supplement) that lower the value of the "smaller-sooner" reward. She tabulates the results of using each one of these alternative interventions and settles upon the most productive measure (or, in this case, combination of measures). In the process, she loses twelve pounds in the course of eight weeks, on the basis of sustaining a combination of routines and substitutes for the smaller-sooner reward as the preferred method of self-control. Six-month follow-up reveals that she has kept the routine, dropped the substitute, and lost an additional eight pounds of unwanted weight.

There are two characteristics of this case that merit special attention, as they relate directly to the effectiveness of the model-based approach to development. The first is that the trainee is *not* given any prescriptive "to-do's." She is not told *how* to act in order to achieve her ends. Rather, she is given a *self-model* that acts as a schema for self-interpretation and self-understanding, and as a subsequent blueprint for self-experimentation and self-manipulation, to the end of self-transformation. She then deductively *derives* injunctions and "to-do's" for herself from the *descriptive* propositions of the model and the *normative* requirements of her own behavioral transformation goals. At every step of the way, she *chooses* both to represent herself using the model in question and to *press* on and derive the prescriptive injunctions that follow from her normative goals and the

Figure 21.9 Case Study 2: Model-Based Structured Interventions

AIM: To make personal discounting function emulate exponential discounting

1. $\sum_n$ *(hyperbolic f'ns) ~ exp. f'n, n large*

   Think of choice as being between:

   "I am a glutton/slob" (eating) vs. "I am about to get slimmer" (not eating)

   ↓ OBSERVE EFFECT

   2 days of not eating after 7 pm;
   relapse

2. *Decrease V_{ss} by making public commitment (boyfriend, best friend), which decreases V_{ss} by cost of embarrassment*

   ↓ OBSERVE EFFECT

   1 day abstinence and secretive eating
   and lying to boyfriend, best friend

3. *"Mind control" /Attention control*

   Try not to think of eating/direct mind away from eating

   ↓ OBSERVE EFFECT

   None and frustration

4. *Decrease Vss by non-fattening substitute and incompatible routine (gym)*

   ↓ OBSERVE EFFECT

   12 lb weight loss after 2.5 months

descriptive model. The second is that the set of (self-)control strategies that she arrives at are *sophisticated* from a computational and modeling perspective. They have, in fact, all been *derived* from the properties of hyperbolic discounting curves (Ainslie, 2001; Moldoveanu, 2010) using functional modeling techniques. And, although it is not altogether out of the question that the trainee was sophisticated enough—from a cognitive and computational perspective—to arrive at these self-control strategies *from first principles*—i.e., from the basic functional form that she was convinced that her own "temporal discounting function" followed—it is more likely the case that the model that she understood and internalized as a representation of something essential about her way of being functioned as a map and a blueprint that guided her intuition, even though the precise contents of that intuition were not fully penetrable to her.

Weight loss and healthy living are, of course, worthwhile objectives, but not quite the stuff of leadership. Nevertheless, the example speaks to an issue that *is* central to leadership situations, and that is the broad and thorny problem of self-control and self-command. "Managing oneself" has been pointed to (notably, by Peter Drucker [2005]) as an essential component of managing others, and for good reason: If leadership has something to do with influencing or causing others to forego immediate personal benefit in order to contribute to the output of a team, a group, or an organization, and if providing a personal example and model of desired behavior is one of the leader's most powerful tools, then self-control and self-command should represent powerful components of the leader's own personal toolkit, for it is by foregoing one's own immediate self-interest that one can most likely and credibly induce others to do the same. Self-models of impulsiveness and impulse control and self-command, then, should then become part of the leader's training and set of personal technologies for intervening upon the world in the same way in which business planning and constrained optimization are part of the manager's training and personal technologies.

IN WHAT SENSE IS THIS "LEADERSHIP DEVELOPMENT"?

The title of this paper prominently features the phrase "leadership development," and the author has gone on at some length to unpack and explicate "self-understanding," "self-experimentation," "self-manipulation," and "self-transformation" with nary a passing remark being given to "leadership"; so the reader may be forgiven for wondering what is going on. Granted that "leadership by example" and "managing oneself" are accepted components of a leader's "way of being," with many vivid examples cited to support this view of matters: Napoleon "won" the battle of Marengo, the story goes, by personally taking the French flag into a deadly pocket at the foot of a bridge that had almost been taken by the enemy, defying the fire of musket and cannon and thereby inducing his own officers to attempt one more—and eventually victorious—charge that resulted in the bridge being taken back and the battle being won by the armies of the First Republic. I could, therefore, rely on common sense, the force of appeals to intuition, and persuasive examples that self-transformation is essential to leadership—indeed, that it is the "rate limiting step" or the "muscle" of leadership in the same way in which the abductors of the hip are the muscles that limit the ultimate speed that a sprinter can attain.

I prefer, however, to remain consistent to my own stance in this paper and to give a *model-based rationale* for the critical link between self-transformation and leadership. The model comes from the field of organizational economics, and specifically from the work of Bengt Holmstrom (1982) and Bernard Hermalin (1998), and attempts to establish, via a set of deductions from more or less intuitive (albeit pessimistic, as is the habit with economists) first principles the effectiveness of leadership by example. Holmstrom argued that teams of self-interested individuals working together to achieve a collaborative outcome are irretrievably beset by problems of moral hazard. Each individual knows that her own output will contribute to that of the team as a whole, which will in turn depend on it, but at the same time realizes that, if her manager cannot perfectly observe and monitor her effort level, she is better off sloughing off the work onto other team members—thus minimizing her personal cost—and claim into the payoff of the work of the team as a whole. The problem is not alleviated by the realization by *some* team members that *many other* team members will "free-ride" upon the work of a few committed individuals—for that only slants their own cost benefit calculation more heavily in the direction of shirking: They will have to work even harder to make up for the free riders, while the expected value of the benefit to the team as a whole is lower. In the (rather diminished) world of the economic analysis of work teams and organizations, the problem goes away only with perfect monitoring (by the manager who by now is more of an automaton than a leader)—but that is a costly measure, and the costs of "perfect monitoring" will come right out of the value of the output of the team as a whole. Now, leadership can be construed as the phenomenon by which an individual reliably and consistently solves this starkly put problem of moral hazard, and induces changes in the behaviors of other members of a team, group, organization, institution, or society away from socio-temporally narrow self-optimization and toward the furthering of a common and worthwhile objective. Hermalin (1990) models the "leader's problem" as the problem of "judiciously using hidden information to solve the problem of hidden action."

Let me unpack. The moral hazard problem in teams is a problem of hidden action: Because the leader cannot observe the actions of the followers and the latter know this, they will shirk or act in narrowly self-interested ways when they can; and they almost always can. The leader can issue commands, injunctions, orders, and the like, but, absent an effective monitoring system for measuring compliance with such commands, her utterances are causally impotent. Suppose, however, that the leader *leads by example*, and herself follows all of her own dicta, orders, arguments, and injunctions: she "walks her own talk," even and particularly in situations it is not in her own narrowly construed self-interest to do so. Then, argues Hermalin, she will credibly convey to the rest of the team, group, organization, institution, or society a valuable piece of *private information* regarding the value to the group as a whole of following her words. Because she "speaks by doing," her words reveal information to the group that had previously been hidden. Hence, argues Hermalin, the revelation of private information can trump the unobservability of hidden action in problems of moral hazard in teams. And, even in this stark and dour "model of leadership," collaboration toward the achievement of a common goal that transcends the personal goals of the individual members is possible. Now—I argue—if leadership is to be identifiable, then it must be related to the reliable production of a *change* in the behavior of a group or a team by the actions of an individual—the leader. Such change is rare but precious: It can lead armies to turn battles around, bankrupt organizations to become market leaders, and lambs to become lions—all without the decimation or replacement of the "followers." For such outcomes to be achieved, however, the change must be lasting: It must be a transformation. The leader, then, is a *transformational* agent: She transforms the behavior of the group, often by transforming the behavior of individual members of the group. Now—and this is the last step in this last "modeling" exercise—*self*-transformation is that process by which the leader credibly indices her followers to themselves *transform*, and hence it is a critical component—and perhaps the rate limiting step—of the leadership function.

Leadership, Hard and Soft

I want to conclude with a short excursus on the semantics of the words *hard* and *soft* in leadership research and development. We speak of "hard skills" in management and management science as those skills associated with set-theoretic, decision-theoretic, or optimization-based modeling of behaviors and situations, or with the financial modeling of business opportunities, business models, and new markets. We speak of soft skills as the "people skills" associated with "leadership"—hard pressed as we often are to articulate them to the same level of precision to which we can specify their "hard" counterparts. On the other hand, we share a deep intuition about the fact that "leadership is hard"—in the straightforward sense that is *not an easy thing to do*. At the same time, we seem to be oblivious to the tension between the two meanings of "hard" that are used in parallel—or, perhaps it is a case of Sartre's *bad faith* rearing its head among those who should know better: They choose to have forgotten the fact that they have ignored the *double entendre*.

I have attempted to turn this state of affairs on its head, and to show through examples how the "hard science" of decision-theoretic, mathematical, and even financial models can be productively used to make progress on the "hard problem" of leadership development, thus unifying the two senses of "hard" in the process. Few will argue that self-transformation is not "hard"—just as few will argue that producing decision theoretic models of one's own behaviors, thoughts, and feelings and using these models as self-tracking and self-transformation tools is not "hard." The model-based approach to leadership development makes clear the extent to which engaging in one "hard" venture will help one make progress on another "hard" venture. It makes the "ontology of leadership" precise by exposing the link between self-understanding and action, and in particular by laying bare the relationship between self-understanding and the perceptual constraints of leadership (Erhard, Jensen, Zaffron, & Granger, 2010). It aims to produce what I believe will be a massively useful dialogue between builders of "hard science" models and practitioners and developers of the "hard-to-do" skills of leadership.

Of course, whether or not this dialogue will materialize depends sensitively upon the degree to which a number of people working in different fields are willing to themselves engage in a self-transformation project whose end, by now, has, I believe, become visible. In particular, what a disciplined deployment of the model-based approach to leadership development requires is *cross-training* of leadership trainers in both the practice of a first-person understanding of the subject ("Verstehen") and in the practice of the precise articulation of one's understanding of the perceptual, physiological, emotional, visceral, cognitive, and meta-cognitive states of a human creature ("modeling"). Such cross training is challenging precisely because the logic of specialization in academia has driven the soft-skilled teachers of "hard" leadership to live and work in different social and geographical spaces from those inhabited by the hard-skilled modelers of human behavior, and to develop different ways of being, communicating, and interacting with those whom they "research" and "teach." The payoff to such cross-training, however, is palpable: Just imagine how much more precise Freud could have been in his case analyses if he had possessed the decision-theoretic apparatus for the analysis of individual behavior developed by his contemporary Frank Ramsey; or, the depth of insight that a contemporary practitioner of family therapy could glean from a textured understanding of the incentive structures of families due to someone like Gary Becker. Progress in model-centered leadership development will, then, be commensurate with the degree to which the "hard" skills of modeling and the "soft" skills of understanding will be co-located not only in the same "department" or "consultancy," but in the same person—who will thereby become a more potent transformation agent.

References

Ainslie, G. (2001). *Breakdown of will.* New York: Cambridge University Press.

Argyris, C. (2006). Private communication to author.

Black, F., & Scholes, M. (1973). The pricing of contingent options and corporate liabilities. *Journal of Political Economy, 81,* 637–654.

Drucker, P. (2005). Managing oneself. *Harvard Business Review, 83*(1), 100–109.

Erhard, W., Jensen, M.C., Zaffron, S., & Granger, K.L. (2010). Introductory reading for being a leader and the effective exercise of leadership: An ontological model (Harvard NOM Research Paper 09-022 and Barbados Group Working Paper 08-01). Boston, MA: Harvard Business School Negotiations, Organizations and Markets Unit.

Freud, S. (1979). *Civilization and its discontents.* New York: Penguin. Original work published 1931

Green, L., & Myerson, J. (2004). A discounting framework for choice with delayed and probabilistic rewards. *Psychological Bulletin, 130,* 769–792.

Heatherton, T., & Baumeister, R. (1996). Self-regulation failure: An overview. *Psychological Inquiry, 7,* 1–15.

Heidegger, M. (1963). *Bring and time.* (Trans. J. MacQuarrie). San Francisco, CA: Harper Collins. Original work published 1927

Hermalin, B. (1998). Toward an economic theory of leadership: Leading by example. *American Economic Review, 88,* 1188–1206.

Holmstrom, B. (1982). Moral hazard in teams. *Bell Journal of Economics, 13,* 324–340.

Laibson, D. (1997). Golden eggs and hyperbolic discounting. *Quarterly Journal of Economics, 83,* 443–477.

Libet, B., Wright, E.W., Jr., Feinstein, B., & Pearl, D.K. (1979). Subjective referral of the timing for a conscious sensory experience: A functional role for the somatosensory specific projection system in man. *Brain, 102,* 193–224.

Moldoveanu, M.C. (2010). *Inside man: The discipline of modeling human ways of being.* Palo Alto, CA: Stanford University Press.

Nietzsche, F. (1967) *Thus spake Zarathustra.* (J. Vogt, Trans.). New York: Basic Books. Original work published 1891

Popper, K.R. (1983). *Realism and the aims of science.* London: Routledge

Sartre, J.-P. (1996). *Being and nothingness.* (H.E. Barnes, Trans.). New York: Random House. Original work published 1945

Wittgenstein, L. (1923). *Tractatus logico-philosophicus.* Cambridge, UK: Cambridge University Press.

Wittgenstein, L. (1953). *Philosophical investigations.* (G.E. Anscombe, Trans.). New York: MacMillan.

22

LEARNING TO LEAD

A Pedagogy of Practice

◆ Marshall Ganz

Harvard Kennedy School of Government and Hauser Center for Non-Profit Organizations

◆ Emily S. Lin

Harvard University

In this chapter we argue that we can teach leadership using a pedagogy of practice. We can teach leadership by practicing leadership, aligning the content of what we teach with the way in which we teach it. We describe principles of this pedagogy, share a curricular framework, and cite examples drawn from a diversity of contexts in classrooms, workshops, campaigns, and organizations. We understand leadership as a practice of accepting responsibility for enabling others to achieve shared purpose under conditions of uncertainty. As teachers we create conditions of uncertainty by requiring our students to accept responsibility for leading a project rooted in their values, intended to achieve a specific goal within a specified time and that requires the collaboration of others. We "enable" them to achieve purpose in this context by providing behavioral, conceptual, and emotional scaffolding combined with critical reflection and cross-contextual learning. Just as a result of effective leadership can be the cascading development of more leadership, our pedagogy generates teaching capacity among our students—an approach that we suggest will equip us to meet the challenges of an uncertain, fragmented world in a more sustainable, interdependent way.

The storm: Is knowledge changed when it is applied?

Let us imagine a pilot, and assume that he had passed every examination with distinction, but that he had not as yet been at sea. Imagine him in a storm; he knows everything he ought to do, but he has not known before how terror grips the seafarer when the stars are lost in the blackness of night; he has not known the sense of impotence that comes when the pilot sees the wheel in his hand become a plaything for the waves; he has not known how the blood rushes to the head when one tries to make calculations at such a moment; in short, he has had no conception of the change that takes place in the knower when he has to apply his knowledge (Kierkegaard, 1941, pp. 35–36).

❖❖❖

As Kierkegaard's image of the first moments in which a novice helmsman must take the helm in a storm suggests, learning leadership is far more challenging than learning about leadership. While some doubt leadership can be learned, viewing it as a matter of DNA, others doubt that it can be taught, especially in a classroom. Where, when, and how—except "on the job"—can we learn to deal with the challenge Kierkegaard describes? But if, as the passage suggests, the essence of leadership is the emotional, behavioral, and strategic capacity to meet unexpected, novel, and ambiguous challenges, isn't this what we need to teach? (Bruner, 1986). We argue that leadership can be taught with pedagogy that itself entails leadership, aligning the content of what we teach with the way we teach it. We describe principles of this pedagogy, share a curricular framework, and cite examples drawn from a diversity of contexts in classrooms, workshops, campaigns, and organizations.

Leadership: Head, Hands, and Heart

Leadership is the practice of accepting responsibility to enable others to achieve shared purpose under conditions of uncertainty. As a practice, not a position, leadership does not require formal authority. Authority can be an asset, but can also be a constraint (Heifetz, 1994). Nor is leadership use of coercive force to secure compliance, "authorized" or not (Burns, 1978). We exercise leadership through the interaction of five core practices: building relationships committed to a common purpose; translating values into sources of motivation through narrative; turning resources into the capacity to achieve purpose by strategizing; mobilizing and deploying resources as clear, measurable, visible action; and structuring authority so as to facilitate the effective distribution of leadership (Ganz, 2010). Because coaching is an important way of "enabling" others to deal with "uncertainty," learning to coach, especially in heuristic problem-solving, is central to learning to lead (Ormrod, 2008).

LEARNING PRACTICE

As a practice, leadership is learned experientially, combining "heart, head, hands" or, as described at West Point, "being, knowing, and doing."[1] Because we cannot learn to use our hands in new ways without

[1]The West Point formulation is one of "Be, Know, Do"—development of the values that shape who I want to be, the concepts the enable me to understand where I want to go, and the skills to get there.

using our hands in new ways, learning requires the courage to risk action . . . and failure . . . again and again . . . just as learning to ride a bike requires the courage to get on, fall, persist, and adapt (Schein, 2004). Deep experiential learning requires conceptualization—hypothesizing, testing, reflecting, and re-hypothesizing (Gandhi, 1957; Kolb, 1984; Zull, 2002)—as opposed to the mastery of abstract concepts to be "applied" (Gardner, 1992). Learning how, when, and where to use—or innovate—new skills requires an understanding of their purpose, clarity as to conditions under which they are useful, and the imagination to adapt them to novel contexts and contents. And the relational content of leadership in particular requires developing the self-awareness to distinguish between one's own actions, the actions of others, and their interaction (Langer, 1997).

LEARNING LEADERSHIP PRACTICE

If we are to teach leadership as practice, we must create conditions in which leadership can be practiced. One way we do this is requiring students to accept responsibility for working with others to achieve a valued goal by the end of a specified learning period. They sum up their mission as "I am organizing __ (people)__ to __(outcome)_ by __(strategy) __ because __ (story)." They work with others to achieve this objective by using the five core practices: creating shared values, building relational commitments, structuring authority, strategizing outcomes, and taking action (see Figure 22.1).

Practically, we structure learning as five modules, each of which focuses on a core practice. Each module begins with a verbal explanation, often aided by visuals, followed by modeling, often by the instructor, with the support of videos or role-play. Students put these skills into practice immediately with peers with whom they share responsibility for a group outcome, which, in turn, lays a foundation for the next module. Students debrief results by articulating their "key learnings" and "plusses" (what worked) and "deltas" (what could be improved).

The first core leadership practice is based on the skill of public narrative that is used to access the motivational content of the values that inspire one's call to action, values shared by one's "constituency," and a challenge to those values that requires urgent action (Ganz, 2010). The second core leadership practice is based on the skill of one-on-one meetings and house

Figure 22.1 The Five Core Practices of Leadership

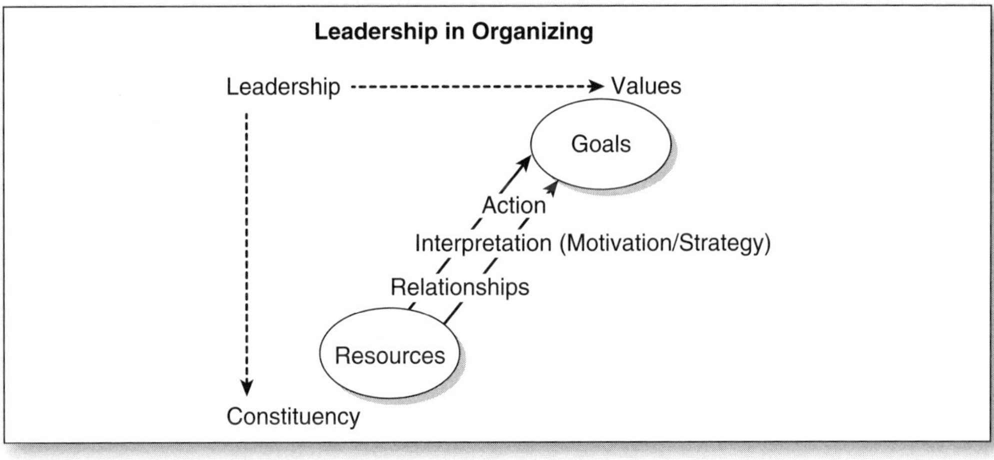

meetings used to forge mutual relationships based on commitments of resources to shared interests. The third core leadership practice is based on the skill of structuring team leadership around a shared purpose, clear norms, and interdependent roles. The fourth core leadership practice is based on the skill of strategizing turning one's resources into the power to achieve objectives. The fifth core leadership practice is based on the skill of mobilizing and deploying resources in action (Hackman & Oldham, 1976).

Participants commit to a deadline by which time they will achieve their outcome and key thresholds (peaks) along the way—enactment of what Stephen Jay Gould called "time as an arrow," the rhythm of change, in contrast with "time as a cycle," the rhythm of continuity (Gould, 1987). This campaign mode facilitates the mobilization of resources needed to achieve a final outcome in the course of achieving the outcome, making the road while walking it. Such a temporal dynamic recognizes that efforts to change the status quo usually begin with far fewer resources than are ultimately needed (see Figure 22.2).

Although we teach the five modules sequentially, the fact that each subsequent module not only introduces new information, but also alters understanding of what went before, shows that core leadership practices are interdependent, not additive. Our approach is in the spirit of what David Perkins (2009) calls teaching the "whole game"—a metaphor for how we learn to play baseball, for example. We do not master batting first, then throwing, then running, but rather learn to play the whole game, refining particular skills as needed. With leadership, teaching the whole game means enabling participants to experience the interplay of all the elements with which they will be working as early on in the process as possible, albeit in a very rudimentary way. So when we return to work on a particular skill in a given module, our understanding of it remains embedded in the experience of their combination.

In teaching the "whole game" it is important to distinguish between a "model" and a "framework," a distinction recognized in the difference between algorithmic and heuristic problem solving (Ormrod, 2008). It is not our intent to specify a formula that students are expected to apply to address the uncertain, evolving, and surprising kind of challenges that Kierkegaard describes. Rather, the

Figure 22.2 Structuring Campaigns

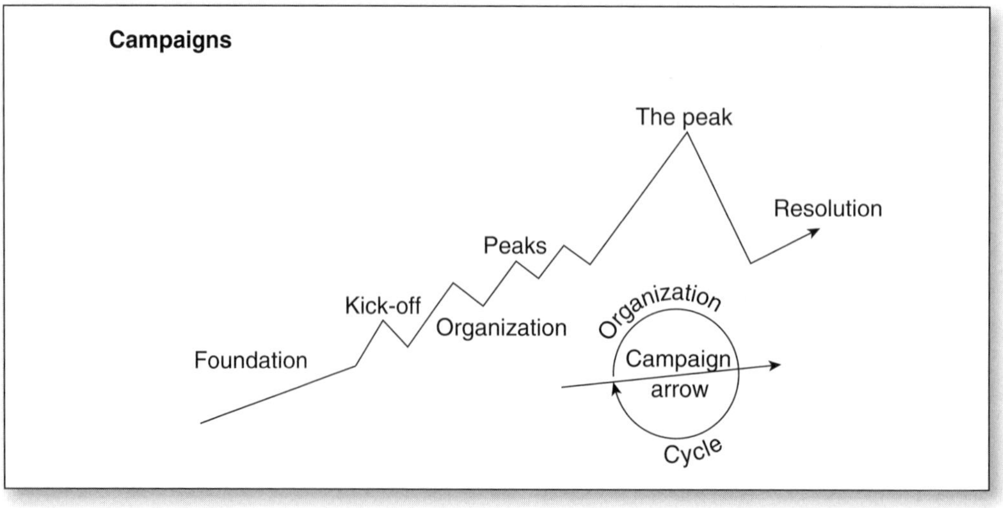

intent is to equip students with questions to ask to learn how to address the challenge they face. The experience, then, that we hope to create is not only one that requires making use of all five core practices, but one in which they must learn to bring sufficient clarity to enable action in circumstances in which outcomes, resources, and context are quite unclear. Success is not in "knowing the answer," but, rather, in learning how to "craft a solution."

One way we teach the whole game at the Kennedy School is with a six-hour introductory exercise in which students participate during the second week of a twelve-week course.

THE ORGANIZING SKILLS SESSION: THE "WHOLE GAME" IN SIX HOURS

"Did you see me? Standing up in front of all those people? I did it!" Those words, spoken by Kate, a master's student, came from a changed person. Six hours before, Kate had been insisting that she was not a leader, hated public speaking, and was just along for the ride. She was an early childhood educator and direct service provider and had entered graduate school hoping to learn how to help children better, not to be a hero. She had been invited to attend one of our bi-annual one-day organizing "skills sessions," held primarily for students enrolled in organizing classes at Harvard, but open to a larger network.

On February 6, 2010, Kate joined over 120 graduate students, fellows, and undergraduates from Harvard University, the University of Massachusetts, Tufts University, the College of the Holy Cross, and Providence College for a six-hour introduction to leading an organizing campaign. Fueled by donuts, coffee, and a potluck smorgasbord, these students participated in a crash course in the five core leadership practices—relationships, narrative, structure, strategy, and action. Each skill was introduced conceptually, modeled, then practiced and debriefed.

Kate's experience began with a one-on-one meeting with an undergraduate from Providence College. Learning that they were both passionate about equity in early childhood education, the two then found another pair of students who wanted to teach literacy. They shared their personal narratives to establish a base of shared values to motivate action. They became a team for a day by setting norms for themselves, specifying roles and agreeing on a shared purpose with respect to child literacy. They then strategized how to turn their very limited resources—especially time—into a meaningful specific outcome. They would collect fifty books in one hour by situating themselves in front of Curious George Goes to Wordsworth, a children's bookstore, and ask shoppers to buy an extra book. The books would be donated to a child literacy program in the housing development where Kate volunteered. They then acted by investing ninety minutes learning how to address shoppers, ask for their help, and "close the deal" with a book donation.

Collectively, in multiple such mini-campaigns that culminated in ninety minutes of action, the 120 workshop participants raised $1,215 for causes ranging from food for children in Haiti to literacy programs; collected 1,120 signatures on petitions on topics as diverse as supporting a bill protecting tenants' rights, establishing "Kids' Nights" in Harvard Square businesses, and reducing greenhouse gases; and collected eighty "onesies" for infants in Haiti—none of which they had planned to do when they arrived six hours before. In the final debrief of the day, one member of each team stood up and described their team's experience and learning. Fired up by her team's success, and cheeks still pink from the chill outside, Kate stood up to announce to a packed room that they had not only reached their goal of fifty books, they had surpassed it.

"Whole game" experiences, ranging from one-day skills sessions to three-day workshops to semester long campaigns, help students learn how each core practice interacts with the others to produce the final result. They are almost always surprised by what they can accomplish with focused effort engaging others over a short amount of time. This prepares students for greater complexity, scale, and scope, which, in a fractal kind of pattern, retain the shape of the original (Perkins, 2008).

PEDAGOGY AS PRACTICE

Pedagogy as practice takes experiential learning a step further: We teach leadership by practicing leadership. This requires a learning venue in which we, as instructors, "accept responsibility for enabling others to achieve purpose in the face of uncertainty." We base this approach on requiring students to take responsibility for a project rooted in their values, intended to achieve a specific goal within a specified time (day, workshop, semester) that they may or may not achieve, and that requires engagement of others. The risk of failure is real, consequential, and transparent. Similarly we make our pedagogy as transparent as we can, invite adaptation, and, using probing and targeted questions, coach—rather than instruct—students in their development of each of the five practices.

Because developing the leadership of others is so central to the practice of leadership as we teach it, we use a "cascaded learning" approach to create opportunities for "learners to become teachers." We coach students to coach others, even as they receive coaching. As they develop their coaching skills, they learn to facilitate their own teams, then become coordinators of teams of facilitators, then project managers of teams of coordinators. In our own university classes each year, we recruit graduate students to become teaching fellows, responsible for the learning of some twenty new students the following year. Teaching fellows often become collaborators on workshops, projects, and campaigns in the "real world." This approach has enabled us to introduce our leadership pedagogy in a widely diverse range of settings around the globe (see Appendix 22.1).

One example of how cascading leadership development can play out is in our work on immigration reform in 2009. In collaboration with the Center for Community Change and the New Organizing Institute, we participated in an effort to organize a grassroots base for reform in key states across the country.

CASCADED LEARNING: THE FIGHT FOR IMMIGRATION REFORM

In late summer 2009, immigration reform advocates determined a need for renewed mobilization of local support in key legislative districts. On August 28, thirty youthful advocates—fifteen from Florida and fifteen from Colorado—gathered outside Miami for a three-day workshop to launch this effort, based on our leadership practice pedagogy. In this first workshop, the presentation, facilitation, and coaching were provided by experienced trainers, most of whom were former students. Three weeks later, the fifteen Florida trainees had applied their learning to organize another three-day workshop of 175 young people who, deployed as thirty-six leadership teams, organized fourteen actions across Florida in which 1,350 people participated to launch the campaign. By the second training, three of the fifteen original trainees had begun serving as presenters, five as coaches, and all in key leadership roles. Colorado followed a similar pattern. Encouraged by this success, a second "train the trainers" workshop was held in Washington, DC, in November, attended by one hundred young people from five more states: North Carolina, California, Nevada, New York, and Ohio. One workshop of thirty young people at the end of August had launched a twelve-state "movement building network" that was the backbone of a sustained campaign, culminating in a demonstration of some 200,000 in Washington, DC. Although not enough to achieve the sought-after legislative victory, this approach not only created capacity and developed leadership, but equipped participants with the skills to continually adapt what they had learned to new challenges.

Cascaded learning works as both a means of building resources in the learning environment as well as modeling the type of leadership development that participants are working to learn. As scholars of "situated cognition" report, learning happens most effectively when activity, concept, and culture work interdependently, as what people learn is perhaps more a product of the "ambient culture" than of explicit teaching (Brown, Collins, & Duguid, 1989; Stigler & Hiebert, 1998). Our pedagogy aims to create a culture of teaching and learning in which teachers do not only teach about leadership, but exercise leadership themselves.

Four Learning Structures: Projects, Scaffolds, Reflections, and Contexts

PROJECT-FOCUSED LEARNING

If, as teachers, we model leadership by enabling our students to achieve purpose in the face of the uncertainty of their projects, then students begin to learn leadership through their experience of commitment to an organizing project. Students thus enjoy an opportunity to learn their "practice" in interaction with real constituents, yet with access to coaching, feedback, and instruction. In classrooms, the project requires commitment to an outcome by the end of the semester. In campaigns, the outcome is tied to ongoing work, a first step. In workshops, outcomes vary but may be as straightforward as finding a way in which participants can support each other's learning.

Creating conditions in which participants must take initiative to acquire the information, skills, relationships, or other resources they need to achieve a goal encourages learning (Gardner, 1992). In the case of leadership, it is the substance of what is being learned. Because the project is conducted in the "real world," many more factors are outside a student's control than is the case with a simulation or role-play, and "real" results involving "real" people are at stake. While these factors introduce uncertainty into the project context, they also enable the student to exercise autonomy in deciding how to deal with that uncertainty. This autonomy, when linked with a task that is both "significant" and that has identifiable boundaries on which one receives real feedback, engages the student's sources of intrinsic motivation, long associated with higher quality and more adaptive, more effortful work (Hackman & Oldham, 1976).

AN ORGANIZING PROJECT: ORGANIZING A TENANTS' ASSOCIATION

Diane was a veteran community organizer whose organizing leadership project focused on engaging residents of a low-income housing development to get involved in a local redevelopment process. In a traditional classroom project, Diane may have ended up conducting a needs assessment, interviewing a few residents, and writing a proposal for the creation of a tenants' association to address their issues. We, however, encouraged Diane to turn her interviews into a series of one-on-one meetings, intended to identify and recruit members of a leadership team who, in turn, would recruit twenty residents to attend a meeting launching a tenants' association–a project with a measurable outcome that required the collective commitment of others. This project was clearly more risky than writing a paper, and Diane was not certain it was doable. Additionally, she was nervous about imposing her "vision," as a white upper-class woman who did not live in the development, on the residents, who were largely African American.

As she moved forward with her project, Diane found herself frustrated with the slowness of change and the failure of her two primary "allies" in the development to show enthusiasm for the idea of holding a meeting, or to deliver on other ideas. They failed to show up for meetings with her, seemed distracted by other concerns, and did not connect her with anyone else who seemed to have interest in making change in the neighborhood. Ultimately, Diane was unable to organize a leadership team or a meeting and was not able to complete her project within the timeframe of the class.

In a typical classroom, the results of a project like Diane's might be evaluated as a failure to complete the work, and hence, a failure of the student. The student might then learn to avoid risking interdependence with others in the future. We treat failure, however, not as "judgmental," a reflection of a person's capacity, but as strategic, an experience from which one can learn (Sitkin, 1992). Students thus move from an understanding of leadership as a natural gift to understanding it as practice they can develop (Dweck, 2008). We ask, "What could be done differently to create the capacity you needed? How could you have developed better relationships or selected people with whom to develop a relationship more wisely? How could you have motivated your leadership team's commitment?" The answers to these questions are more often found to be rooted in emotional barriers than conceptual ones, e.g., fear of the risk of being rejected, of seeming too "pushy," of being thought "odd," etc. In turn, coaching a person in this kind of challenge requires emotional resources more than conceptual ones. Students who learn to practice leadership with coaching in how to engage with the emotional risk can learn to "lean in" to the pain of failure, emerging better prepared and more willing to engage with future challenges.

Objections to teaching leadership in this way may grow out of a hesitancy to require students to commit the requisite resources. Opportunities for focused learning are time-bound (e.g., a semester-long course) and resource constrained (e.g., financial resources go to books and materials, not project overhead). Students have other classes—or jobs—outside the scope of the project. On the other hand, "real" projects that motivate real commitment can, in turn, generate new resources.

One test of the readiness of students to commit the required time, energy, and effort played out in the 2010 launch of a fourteen-week distance-learning version of our course, part of Harvard's Executive Education program, in which participants commit to a leadership project that has impact on their real-life work. Each week, participants were required to attend one ninety-minute live online lecture or discussion section and to commit at least four to five hours to coursework and field work. Skeptics of high-commitment distance learning argue that working students already have too much on their plate. But we found that requiring more commitment up front screened out those less prepared to learn and engaged participating students' sense that they were doing meaningful work, resulting in higher levels of participation. While the typical Executive Education distance learning class usually drops to a 50 percent attendance rate at on-line meetings over the course of the semester, our course consistently had 85–95 percent attendance throughout. At the time of this writing, campaigns started by alumni of the course to reform health care in England, reduce corruption in Serbia, and support political mobilization in the Middle East have achieved significant victories, and graduates from Serbia, Jordan, and multiple states in the United States have returned to act as teaching assistants for the next iteration of the course.

SCAFFOLDED LEARNING

Learning new skills requires venturing beyond the limits of one's perceived competence—a step both exciting and frightening, and one that requires motivational, conceptual, and behavioral resources. Scholars describe this uncharted territory as a "zone of proximal development"—a space between what an individual will do on their own and what they will undertake with the encouragement of another—parent, teacher, or coach (Vygotsky, 1978).[2] Just as one must fall to learn to keep one's balance on a bicycle, "training wheels" can, for a time, help a learner acquire courage to face the moment when they must come off. The pedagogical challenge is deciding when such "scaffolding" provides productive support, and when it inhibits development. We offer scaffolding for the hands (behavioral), for the head (intellectual), and for the heart (motivational) (Hackman & Wageman, 2005).

As intellectual scaffolding we offer a conceptual framework linking each core leadership practice with the others in an interdependent whole. Our intent is to provide a framework, not a formula, however. In his discussion of learning, Thich Nhat Hanh (1993) recounts a parable in which the Buddha asks his disciples about the wisdom of a man who built a raft to cross a raging river, only to drag it around with him for the rest of his life in gratitude for the job it had done in that time and place. In the spirit of heuristic problem solving, our learning framework can serve as a "raft": a way to focus on critical tools, attend to key questions, observe interactions among key elements, and share a common language to learn from each other's experience. But, like any framework, ours is only a hypothesis, not a recipe, and requires constant testing, evaluation, and adaptation.

The emotional scaffolding available—in addition to the fact that we root projects in the participants' values—comes through a coach, facilitator, or peer learner. Leadership requires one to find sources of the courage to risk uncertainty, ambiguity, and novelty (Peterson, 1999). Values can be such a source, not as abstract ideas, but as emotional—or moral—resources. When confronted with a novel challenge, our impulse to retreat to the safety of what we

[2]While most conceptualizations of the zone of proximal development define it as the distance between what an individual "can" do on his own and what he "can" do with assistance, we understand ability ("can") as being intimately linked with belief and motivation ("will").

know, or, at least, what can reduce our anxiety, means we avoid learning what we need to learn to adapt ourselves, and encourage others to adapt, to the challenge. On the other hand, throwing ourselves headlong into the breach can guarantee failure. We learn best when we can balance the risk of exploration with enough security that we can find the courage to take the risk (Marcus, 2002). Eliciting our students' narratives, for example, may require probing, yet empathetic, questioning by a coach to encourage them to risk the vulnerability required for learning. An even more emotionally challenging aspect of "enabling" others can be asking for specific, clear, and unambiguous commitments. We scaffold students' engagement with this challenge by having them practice "the ask" in front of their peers, often with real-time coaching, and always followed by a debrief of the student's internal process in deciding when and how to make the ask. Unless students find their way through these more challenging aspects of social interaction, they will justify the anxiety that inhibits them by rejecting the framework, blaming the environment, or otherwise avoiding the work.

Finally, we provide behavioral scaffolding by modeling what we are teaching in the way we teach. We also use explicit role-playing exercises, such as practicing the art of getting commitments, for students to experience the practice, observe others, and get feedback on their performance in a safe learning environment. Most important, however, we create opportunities that require students to practice newly acquired skills in the real world with feedback, and support, from peers and instructors, as in the full day "organizing skills" workshop described above.

The student-dubbed "hot seat" is one pedagogical technique that exemplifies how conceptual, emotional, and behavioral scaffolding come together in our teaching practice. In the hot seat exercise, a student receives coaching on his or her project or practice in a focused, targeted way in front of the other learners. This creates an instant moment of narrative in which the class focuses on how the student will handle the challenge, not only in terms of the specifics of their project, but of being coached in front of the entire class. It thus yields conceptual learning (for example, the importance of having clear, measurable outcomes), but also emotional learning, enabling the person being questioned to learn he or she can handle the pressure. Finally, it provides behavioral scaffolding, providing those watching with a model of how to ask the tough questions. In fact, after having been in the hot seat, students often can be found to be more confident coaching others. Having been pushed out of her comfort zone into a place of uncertainty, the hot seat participant realizes that she has made a developmental leap with a little pain and a lot of learning, and is encouraged to help others on her team do the same.

BRIGET GANSKE: THE VIEW FROM THE "HOT SEAT"

One day in the first few weeks of my Public Narrative class, Professor Ganz was describing how we would coach each other in telling our Stories of Self, Us, and Now. There was a palpable sense of apprehension in the classroom; it felt like a daunting task to succinctly describe the challenges we'd gone through ourselves, choices we'd made, and the passions that were leading us to do work we cared about—in two minutes—let alone help other students, mostly strangers, do the same.

Suddenly, Professor Ganz asked, "Is Briget Ganske here today?" He had never called anyone out like this before, and people looked around curiously. I tentatively raised my hand.

Professor Ganz smiled and asked, "Briget, why are you called to do what you're called to do?" The whole room grew silent. I felt hundreds of eyes watching me as my face grew hot. Stalling for time, I repeated slowly, "Why am I called to do what I'm called to do?" Called to do? I felt I was thirteen again, forgetting my lines in the school play. Professor Ganz was nodding, calling me to answer.

"Uh," I fumbled, starting to say something about being at the Graduate School of Education and how I was a photographer and loved teaching young people. My voice sounded far away and unfamiliar. "Why do you like teaching?" Ganz asked. I started saying something abstract about the importance of education. "Where did you grow up?" Ganz asked, bringing me back to my real experience, of growing up in Iowa. "What do your parents do? Was education important to them?" A string of questions began leading me to describe my parents' medical and political careers and how I learned about service and the democratic process through delivering yard signs and listening to people at town hall meetings. "And photography?" Ganz asked, pulling out of me stories of learning to use my grandparents' camera, inspirational teachers I had, and my own experience staring an after-school program in New York City. Again and again, Ganz asked, "Why? Why did you make that choice? What was that experience like?" I recalled stories I had forgotten or hadn't thought relevant to tell but now saw as important vignettes illustrating who I was and what mattered to me.

After what felt like a re-living of my whole life (but was probably only ten minutes), Ganz thanked me and turned his attention to the rest of the class. "What am I doing?" he asked, "besides putting her on the spot." Everyone laughed. "You're giving her coaching," someone called out. What had been an abstract and slightly scary concept had been brought to life, and I had survived.

During the remainder of the class, my heartbeat slowed its to normal rate and I grew more and more glad I hadn't run away; it was as if I were more clearly seeing my life, the close-up details and the overall composition. In photographic terms, I had gained focus, a focus that helped me connect with others in a way that my previously blurry story had not. After class, dozens of people came up to me, saying things like, "I'm from Iowa!" "My parents were politically active too." "I'm a photographer as well." "I'm a big supporter of arts in education." Suddenly, the class of strangers had become real people, people with stories–like myself. I realized that the story of us had already begun and the story of now was starting to form.

CRITICAL REFLECTION

Among the challenges of teaching leadership are assumptions students bring with them about familiar skills that may serve perfectly well in private life, but not in public life—such as how to build relationships. While scholars of learning emphasize the need to engage prior knowledge explicitly when building new knowledge (Bransford, Brown, & Cocking, 1999; Strike & Posner, 1985), unexamined assumptions about leadership are especially challenging. Although few people may have prior knowledge about, for example, quantum physics, everyone has theories about how to build relationships, tell stories, and strategize outcomes. The "schemata" we develop to organize our understanding of the world enable and constrain (Fiske & Taylor, 1991). They enable us to make sense of things, generalize, make choices, draw conclusions, and act. But, as stereotypes, they can inhibit clarity of perception, cause us to see what we expect to see, and make it difficult for us to learn.

One way we try to address this challenge is by modeling "mindful learning": bringing transparency to our assumptions to free us from their constraints, allowing us to develop more useful theory (Langer, 1987). We model this not with third-person case studies, but by debriefing students' own experience of learning verbally with others, in shared writing, and in class presentations. A major focus of debriefing is what worked (plusses), what could have worked better (deltas), and what was learned. The intent is to turn challenges into learning opportunities as opposed to judgments on one's capacity or worth (Dweck, 2008). By concluding each class, presentation, or workshop with "plusses and deltas" we invite students to partner with us in "testing" the assumptions that guide their learning. To circumvent the power of negative bias, we begin by asking students to identify what worked well; what facilitated their learning (plusses). We then ask students to identify improvements that could be made (deltas). We do this with the entire group, encouraging people to speak up, and recording the results on posters or a blackboard. Once one opens up this process, however, one has to follow through by making useful improvements in the teaching, which models how assumptions, when questioned, can be adjusted. At the same time, the practice shifts responsibility for learning away from the instructor alone to a responsibility shared by the class, as students' comments change from "you could do this" to "we could do this." Processes of shared reflection and open evaluation encourage students to accept the vulnerability required to learn from their failures as well as from their successes.

CROSS-CONTEXTUAL LEARNING

Deep understanding of practice requires learning how to distinguish what is particular to a given context or content from what is core to the integrity of a process. For example, when it comes to building relationships, cultures vary widely in their rituals of expectation, encounter, and follow-up. But relationships themselves grow out of reciprocal exchange between parties, commitments reaching beyond a single exchange, and the possibility of future utility, growth, or learning. Similarly, strategic conventions differ widely, but the hypothesizing of outcomes based on choices one makes about current activity does not. And the telling of stories, perhaps the most highly contextualized practice of all, is based on a widely shared framework of plot, character, and moral. Understanding this dynamic enables one to focus on the questions that can discern genuinely unique factors salient to a particular situation in which one finds oneself. This can clarify the difference between "one way" to do a thing, and factors without which that "thing" will not happen.

One way we address this challenge is to situate learning in cross-contextual settings (Bernstein, 1971). In our distance-learning course, for example, we structured an interactive learning venue in which ninety-three students from eighteen countries participated. Students from Serbia, England, and Spain, for example, observed over live video as a fellow student from Amman organizing a national teachers' association modeled relationship building with a student from elsewhere in Jordan, who was himself focused on business development. This experience was cited repeatedly by students as one of the most useful examples of leadership practice that they had seen. By learning across contexts, participants began to understand elements of the skills that are not local to a particular project or even a particular culture, such as the emotional difficulty and significance of eliciting mutual commitment. In similar fashion, in our spring 2010 Kennedy School organizing class, ninety-two students used a common framework to work on eighty-four different projects, several of which were the main focus of discussion each week. In this way a capacity to connect intimate detail of particular circumstances—the trees—with a broader vision of the whole—the forest—that is so important for strategic thinking can be developed even as one learns specific skills.

Conclusion

In this chapter we argue that leadership not only can be but, in fact, *is* taught in classrooms, communities, campaigns, and associations—and that it could be done much better. We've specified some ways to structure this kind of learning. We hope our work contributes to a move away from leadership development as a process of selecting extraordinary individuals, giving them extraordinary opportunities, and expecting extraordinary things from them. One alternative is to understand leadership development—and leadership itself—as a practice of accepting responsibility for enabling others to achieve purpose in the face of uncertainty, a practice that itself develops new leaders. Given the increasing uncertainty of life in our rapidly changing world, growing fragmentation, and increasing stratification, the need for leadership is greater than ever. We hope our pedagogy can help equip us to meet this challenge in a better, more interdependent way.

APPENDIX 22.1: Where We Teach Leadership

COURSES AND SEMINARS

MLD 355: Public Narrative: Self, Us, Now

MLD 356: Public Narrative: Conflict, Continuity, Change

MLD 377: Organizing: People, Power, Change

MLD 327: Moral Leadership: Self, Other, and Action

Social Studies 98fu: Practicing Democracy: Leadership, Community & Power

Faith & Leadership in a Fragmented World

Leadership, Organizing, & Action: Leading Change (distance learning)

Achieving Excellence in Community Development (AECD)

COMMUNITY PRACTICE CAMPAIGNS

Organizing for Health Project: organizing community health reform efforts across the United States.

National Health Service (UK) Project: organizing health practice reform

California School Employees Association (CSEA) Project: union leadership development

Jordan Organizing Project: training community organizers

Syria Leadership Development Project: developing youth leadership

Center for Community Change: immigration policy reform

Episcopal Public Narrative Project: lay leadership development

WORKSHOPS

C.S. Mott Foundation: training community organizers in public narrative

American Federation of State, County, and Municipal Employees (AFSCME): organizer training

Middle East Women's Initiative (Harvard Kennedy School): organizer training

Leadership for the Twenty-First Century (Harvard Kennedy School): organizer training

Latino Leadership Initiative (Harvard Kennedy School): organizer training

Columbia Institute (Toronto): community, political, union organizer training

References

Bernstein, B. (1971). *Class, codes and control: Theoretical studies towards a sociology of language.* London: Routledge.

Bransford, J.D., Brown, A.L., & Cocking, R.R. (Eds.) (1999). *How people learn: Brain, mind, experience, and school.* Washington, D.C.: National Academy Press.

Bruner, J. (1986). Two modes of thought. In *Actual minds, possible worlds* (pp. 11–25). Cambridge, MA: Harvard University Press.

Burns, J.M. (1978). *Leadership.* New York: Harper Row.

Dweck, C. (2008). *Mind set.* New York: Ballantine Books.

Fiske, S., & Taylor, S.E. (1991). *Social cognition.* New York: McGraw-Hill.

Gandhi, M. (1957). *An autobiography: The story of my experiments with truth.* Boston, MA: Beacon Press.

Ganz, M. (2010). Leading change: Leadership, organization, and social movements. In N. Nohria & R. Khurana (Eds.), *Handbook of leadership theory and practice* (pp. 509–550). Boston, MA: Harvard Business Press.

Gardner, H. (1992). *The unschooled mind.* New York: Basic Books.

Gould, S.J. (1987). *Time's arrow, Time's cycle: Myth and metaphor in the discovery of geological time.* Cambridge, MA: Harvard University Press.

Hackman, J. R., & Wageman, R. (2005). A theory of team coaching. *Academy of Management Review, 30,* 269–287.

Hackman, R., & Oldham, G.R. (1976). Motivation through the design of work: Test of a theory. *Organizational Behavior and Human Performance, 16*(2), 250–279.

Heifetz, R. (1994). *Leadership without easy answers.* Cambridge, MA: Belknap Press.

Kierkegaard, M.S. (1941). *Thoughts on crucial situations in human life* (D.F. Swenson, Trans., & L.F. Swenson, Ed.). Minneapolis, MN: Augsburg Publishing House.

Kolb, D. (1984). *Experiential learning: Experience as the source of learning and development.* New Jersey: Prentice-Hall.

Langer, E. (1987). *Mindfulness.* Cambridge, MA: Perseus.

Langer, E. (1997). *The power of mindful learning.* Cambridge, MA: Perseus Books.

Marcus, G. (2002). *The sentimental citizen: Emotion in democratic politics.* University Park: Penn State University Press.

Nhat Hanh, T. (1993). The raft is not the shore. In *Thundering silence: Sutra on knowing the better way to catch a snake* (pp. 30–33). Berkeley, CA: Parallax Press.

Ormrod, J.E. (2008). *Educational psychology: Developing learners.* New Jersey: Prentice Hall.

Perkins, D. (2008). Beyond understanding. In R. Land, J.H.F. Meyer, & J. Smith (Eds.), *Threshold concepts within the disciplines* (pp. 3–20). Rotterdam: Sense Publishers.

Perkins, D.N. (2009). *Making learning whole: How seven principles of teaching can transform education.* San Francisco, CA: Jossey-Bass.

Peterson, J. (1999). *Maps of meaning: The architecture of belief.* New York: Routledge.

Schein, E.H. (2004). *Organizational culture and leadership.* San Francisco, CA: Jossey-Boss.

Sitkin, S. (1992). Learning through failure: The strategy of small losses. *Research in Organizational Behavior, 14,* 231–266.

Snook, S. (2004). Be, know, do: Forming character the West Point way. *Compass, A Journal of Leadership, 1*(2), 16–19.

Strike, K. A., & Posner, G. J. (1985). A conceptual change view of learning and understanding. In L. H. T. West & A. L. Pines (Eds.), *Cognitive structure and conceptual change* (pp. 211–231). New York: Academic Press.

Vygotsky, L.S. (1978). *Mind in society: The development of higher psychological processes.* M. Cole, V. John-Steiner, S. Scribner, & E. Souberman, (Eds.). Cambridge, MA: Harvard University Press.

Zull, J. (2002). *The art of changing the brain: Enriching the practice of teaching by exploring the biology of learning.* Sterling, VA: Stylus.

SECTION IV

CONTEXT

23

TEACHING LEADERSHIP WITH THE BRAIN IN MIND

Leadership and Neuroscience at CIMBA

◆ Al H. Ringleb

CIMBA Business Programs, University of Iowa, Consortium of Universities for International Studies

◆ David Rock

NeuroLeadership Group/CIMBA

Bolstered over the past decade by the advent of affordable and effective brain-imaging technology, neuroscience research is beginning to influence how leadership scholars both think about the brain and view the contribution neuroscience can make to furthering our understanding of leadership generally and to teaching leadership more specifically. Based on this research, readily available technology capable of measuring an individual's psychological data in real-time has the potential to make significant contributions to leadership-learning environments, particularly as it relates to students gaining an experiential understanding of the fundamental relationship between cognition and emotion. In this article the authors look at how such technology and the neuroscience research that supports its use are impacting learning environments at CIMBA, an international MBA program located in Italy and headed by the University of Iowa. At CIMBA, MBA students are wired up and measured using nonintrusive, wireless technology to support a broad range of learning events and activities from traditional classroom discussions and team-based exercises to specifically designed emotion elicitation business simulations. Although leadership is just at the beginning stages of teaching and developing leaders with the brain in mind, the authors are encouraged by the observed results and motivated by the opportunities for further research.

> *Oddly, despite B schools' scientific emphasis, they do little in the areas of contemporary science that probably hold the greatest promise for business education: cognitive science and neuroscience.*
>
> —Bennis and O'Toole (2005, p. 104)

Imagine an MBA program where students wear a device throughout the day that wirelessly, continuously, and unobtrusively collects, transmits, and stores their neurophysiological data for concurrent and later analyses. Classrooms where students not only observe the professor's presentation, but where both professors and students are able to observe their neuro-physiological (emotional) responses as they learn, engage in discussions, and participate in team activities together. Student consulting projects where the same data are collected and analyzed in assessing progress toward personal development goals, whether the student is within the walls of the school or at the client's site. Workshops where a student learns both the emotional and skill components of a particular leadership competency by confronting a variety of simulations designed to elicit the emotion commensurate with the leadership competency being taught—again, measured wirelessly, continuously, and unobtrusively and transmitted to an analysis team and the student's personal development coach. Something for the future? In reality, the technology is readily available now and this learning environment currently exists at CIMBA, an international MBA program located in Italy and headed by the University of Iowa.

Readily available neurobiofeedback technology has the potential to significantly impact the way in which we teach and develop leaders (Johnson, Boehm, Healy, Goebel, & Linden, 2010). Within the traditional ***Being-Knowing-Doing*** framework (Hesselbein & Shinseki, 2004), a successful "leader" learns skills (***Knowing***) and makes them actionable or operationally effective (***Doing***), all under the assumption that both leader and followers manifest at will the appropriate emotional and mental states (***Being***). Through observation and experience, we found traditional, informational or epistemological, skills-building approaches particularly deficient in ***Being***, the development component needed to guide, support, and assist learners to reach a deeper psychological understanding of both *their* values, emotions, behaviors, and thinking and *those of others*. In searching for ***Being*** development alternatives, our experiences moved us outside the confines of the major disciplines whose "theories" were then defining the traditional informational (and other) approaches to leadership development.

In this article, we provide an overview of the leadership and leadership development instructional approach we have developed based on the experiences, observations, insights, and thinking generated by our search for an effective ***Being*** component of leadership. An important part of that journey was an exploration and assessment of ***Being*** components within other systems and the research that supported them. While it was evident that ***Being's*** importance was very much understood and appreciated, its express inclusion and effectiveness in the leadership development experience was clearly constrained by the technology available to the theorists at the time they developed their systems. It was not difficult to envision a traditional leadership theorist asking himself or herself: "How would our leadership development system be different if we could actually measure emotion?" Through our various experiences, we found a viable solution at the intersection of neuroscience and social psychology, overlaid it onto more traditional approaches to leadership and leadership development, and created an approach that makes use of neurobiofeedback technology based on neuroscience research to explicate a leader's emotions. We begin by providing an overview of the core neuroscience and social psychology research and conceptual tools that support the approach, and some of the history that brought us to understand and appreciate the contributions they could make toward an effective leadership learning experience.

I. The Basic Foundation and Its History

While we fully appreciated both the importance of technically competent leaders and the ability of the classroom to deliver that competency, in the late 1990s we decided to move beyond traditional classroom-based leadership education with the intent to bring more process (***Doing***) and behavior (***Being***) into the leadership learning equation. To assist and guide us, we actively involved social psychologists, instructional psychologists, cognitive scientists, neuroscientists, leadership scholars, business leaders, coaches, and others. Social psychologists identified both the core psychological components upon which leadership as a social event would function most effectively and the role emotion plays in influencing the success of such events. Neuroscience was identified as a natural science upon which leadership as a struggling social science could seemingly be built or rebuilt, with neuroscientists assisting in connecting emotion and, more importantly, the measurement of emotion and its consequences to the efficacy of leadership events. Instructional psychologists provided us with insight into the most effective learning environments to replicate the emotions being generated by leadership as a social event. With the assistance of this eclectic group of thinkers, leadership at CIMBA came to mean understanding leader and follower minds with attention to neuroscience theories and research in order to better develop leaders for the effective ***practice*** of leadership and management.

LEADERSHIP AND NEUROSCIENCE

Through the late 1990s and early 2000s, the underlying subtleties and complexities of human interactions due to *individual differences* in the efficiency and sensitivity of brain structures were increasingly becoming understood and appreciated by neuroscientists working in cooperation with social psychologists. Much of this new comprehension was flowing from a rapid expansion in research on the biological underpinnings of social processes driven by the advent of functional neuro-imaging and other technologies. In this light, we observed and experienced several significant learning enhancements to be had from reframing traditional leadership and leadership development theories and concepts through the lens of neuroscience.

We first saw that neuroscience provided evidence-based, "hard" science to assist in the explanation of the ***Being*** component of leadership, which traditionally had been considered "soft" or a "soft" science. As a "soft" science, the ***Being*** component's contribution to effective leadership was understood but was typically "held constant" as being beyond the purview of traditional business education and training. But research in neuroscience would change that practice. Second, by taking neuroscience's findings identifying the active, biological "ingredients" of leadership and relating those findings meaningfully to the learner, the efficacy of those teaching efforts was significantly improved. Neuroscience provided a science-based vehicle for setting out for the learner the *What, Why, and How* of leadership—moving leadership and leadership development beyond its traditional classroom-based focus on the *What.* Learners enjoyed, were in fact drawn to, learning about their brain, as well as their ability to expressly direct its attention and its impact on leadership practices. Third, neuroscience provided the necessary scientific rigor to promote the discovery of new and important insights into the leadership mental process going forward, with some of those insights supporting existing theory and others suggesting consideration of alternatives. Finally, and perhaps most importantly, neuroscience greatly assisted us in understanding how to effectively measure emotion and along with it the objective evidence to guide us in working to understand individual differences in performance and well-being—fundamental for improving leadership competencies.

LEADERSHIP AS A SOCIAL EVENT

Our first encounter with neuroscience involved a neurobiologist who brought us to the realization that leadership is a ***social*** event. She and other neurobiologists argue persuasively that many of the adaptive challenges facing our earliest ancestors were social in nature, with those most able to solve survival problems and adapt to the social environment the most likely to reproduce and pass along their genes. Given that belonging to a social group had considerable value, the human brain was clearly motivated to evolve dedicated neural mechanisms acutely sensitive to social context, especially to any signals that group membership was somehow endangered. The brain understood that social rejection meant death and must be avoided to survive.

With this realization, we focused on understanding the underlying psychological components necessary to support leadership as a social event. We understood that being a good group member involves an awareness of one's thinking, feelings, behavior, and emotions with the ability to alter any of those to satisfy group standards or expectations. Social psychologists showed us that this awareness implies the human need for at least four psychological components, the failure of any of which can lead to undesirable outcomes and being ostracized from the social group: self-awareness, social awareness, threat/reward circuitry, and self-regulation.

Individuals need self-awareness to reflect on their emotions and behaviors to judge and evaluate them against group norms. Social awareness, or *theory of mind*, provides an individual with the ability to infer the mental states of others (particularly those within the individual's social group), to empathize with them to be able to predict their judgments, emotions, behaviors, and actions. The notion of social awareness implies that the individual understands and appreciates that they are the objects of continuous social group evaluation, which in turn necessitates knowing that others are fully capable of making such evaluations and acting upon them. The human brain's evolution further responded to this social awareness need by providing dedicated circuitry for detecting inclusionary status. The brain's threat detection circuitry continuously monitors our social environment for any signals or other evidence of possible group exclusion. Once the circuitry senses that the individual's actions have or may violate group standards and that others group members are evaluating them negatively, the individual needs the self-regulatory ability to rectify the situation and re-establish or maintain group status. The individual needs to inhibit impulses and control thoughts, actions, and emotions to change according to social context.

Against this evolutionary framework, we ultimately placed considerable importance on individual self-regulation and the ability to control impulses. From a leadership and leadership development perspective, those "impulses" are generated by the individual's brain threat/reward circuitry responding to social environment stimuli (real or perceived) (Gordon, 2008). We saw those "impulses" as being different individual-to-individual and generated by something we referred as SCARF events—generated by real or perceived stimuli in the social environment affecting the individual's status, certainty, autonomy, relatedness, and/or fairness (Rock, 2008). How an individual's SCARF "stressors" are managed depends upon the individual's self-regulatory circuitry (control-related prefrontal cortex) and the rate at which the individual depletes available brain energy in activating and engaging that circuitry. Within the development context, this further implies the need to assess and measure both an individual's SCARF profile and his or her self-regulatory ability in creating both an effective leadership development plan for the individual and the appropriate intervention strategy to bring about the desired goals and objectives set out in that plan.

By piecing together and testing relevant neuroscience and social psychology research findings the basic foundation of our instructional and developmental system took a definitive form. In essence, the system functions upon the following three core components (on the basis of our current observations, individual growth and development seem to proceed to a significant degree in the same order):

1. **Explicit understanding of emotion** (Barrett, 2006; Gooty, Connelly, Griffith, & Gupta, 2010; Izard, 2009, 2010);
2. **Self-regulation** (Bauer & Baumeister, 2011; Hooker, Gyurak, Verosky, Miyakawa, & Ayduk, 2010; Lieberman, 2009); and,
3. **The ability to effectively call upon cognitive resources regardless of one's emotion or mental state in order to enhance performance and well-being** (Farb et al., 2007; Gross & John, 2003; Gyurak et al., 2009; Lutz, Slagter, Dunne, & Davidson, 2008; Ochsner & Gross, 2005; Zeidan, Johnson, Diamond, David, & Goolkasian, 2010).

We found that the technology allowed us to both develop and test our understanding of emotional and mental states, and to assist in developing mindfulness, a necessary ingredient in strengthening self-regulation (Farb et al., 2010; Jha, Stanley, Kiyonaga, Wond, & Gelfand, 2010). From a source of information standpoint, and as the opening quote to this article also illustrates, we were surprised at the dearth of interest in applications of neuroscience among leadership and organizational behavior scholars. We were equally surprised at the science of emotion, particularly in the seemingly divergent ways in which various disciplines sought to deal with it. Leadership and organizational behavior, for example, readily acknowledged its existence but basically held it constant (Gooty, Gavin, & Ashkanasy, 2009). Sports psychology, on the other hand, seemed to have a sense of urgency in understanding the emotion-performance relationship (see, e.g., Hanin, 2007). It was when we realized the fundamental role played by emotion in effectively teaching and developing leaders and began to explore emotion's dimensions with the technology that we came to understand why.

LEADERSHIP AND EMOTION

It has been nearly 60 years since Skinner (1953, 1974) declared that emotion—*that what [is] felt or introspectively observed* (Skinner, 1974, p. 18)—was on the list of ***fictional*** causes to which an individual's behavior is commonly ascribed. The *Managed Heart* (Hochschild, 1983) and *Emotional Intelligence* (Goleman, 1995) among other publications brought the discussion of leadership emotion into the open, and served to assist both practitioners and academics in overcoming a seemingly unwritten reluctance to acknowledge the contribution of emotions to the mix of what constitutes the effective practice of leadership. Over the past two decades, leadership scholars have expressly recognized the importance of emotion and emotion regulation in effective leadership and have begun to define its core elements and components (Gooty et al., 2010). This attention on leader emotion parallels the growing attention placed on emotion in neuroscience, psychology, and organizational behavior over the same time period.[1]

In contrast to traditional social science research, the use of brain imaging has served to fortify our understanding of core concepts and their applications by providing us with a "hard science" understanding of the neural circuitry involved in emotion, emotion regulation, and cognition (e.g., Gyurak et al., 2009). As a consequence, neuroscience allows us to better understand and appreciate the role emotion plays in leadership practice, guiding and assisting in the selection and application of more effective tools and techniques in developing leaders.

Transferring that understanding of emotion in a practical sense to leadership students presented its own unique challenges. We soon learned that emotion scholars regardless of their discipline were confronting the same challenge, with relatively little consensus on the most appropriate approach. Our international learning environment made it evident from the onset that the use of English language labels was not going to produce the results we were looking for, particularly in light of the fact that descriptive labels for emotions can easily generate lists of 200 "emotion" words or more.

Furthermore, unconscious differences in individual SCARF profiles were revealed in attempts to gain agreement on the meaning and application of emotion definitions as they applied to situations a leader would commonly encounter in the workplace. To both simplify emotion identification and make that simplification operational, we moved to labeling emotion by ***color***, based on its physiological and brain state properties (see Figure 23.1 for our emotion color-coding scheme). For example, fear became a "red zone" emotion and was characterized by its physiological and brain chemical properties (for example, simply speaking, elevated heart rate and increased levels of cortisol), its corresponding reduction in available cognitive resources, and reliance on hardwired or habitual responses to the stimuli (again, real or perceived).

Rather than experiencing "fear," an individual was said to be experiencing a "red zone" emotion, with a variety of other emotions capable of generating a similar "recipe." By contrast, when attentive and focused on learning, thinking, or creating, an individual was said to be experiencing a "green zone" emotion, characterized by a moderate heart rate and lower levels of cortisol. As stress increases, an individual moves from a "green-zone" to a "blue-zone" to a "yellow-zone" to a "red-zone" emotional state with corresponding changes in physiology and brain chemicals making up the "recipe." With primary emphasis on available cognitive resources, both pleasant and unpleasant emotions are seen as generating the same "green" to "red" emotion/cognition pathway (but with differing brain chemicals defining the "recipe").

---

[1]Professor Carroll Izard (2010) perhaps best summarizes the growing interest in emotion and emotion regulation:

Only three decades ago . . . it was difficult to find books and empirically based journal articles on emotion. Now we have a cornucopia of emotion books—amazon.com has 347,272 titles, and it is not unusual for a university library to have more than 400 scholarly books on the topic. Today there are at least five scientific journals with "emotion" in their titles and there are many more that publish research on emotion, resulting altogether in 2,732 articles in the past decade. There appears to be more agreement on the significance of emotion and much greater acceptance of its place in science than was evident 25 years ago. (Izard, 2010, p. 363)

Figure 23.1 CIMBA Emotion Color-Coding System

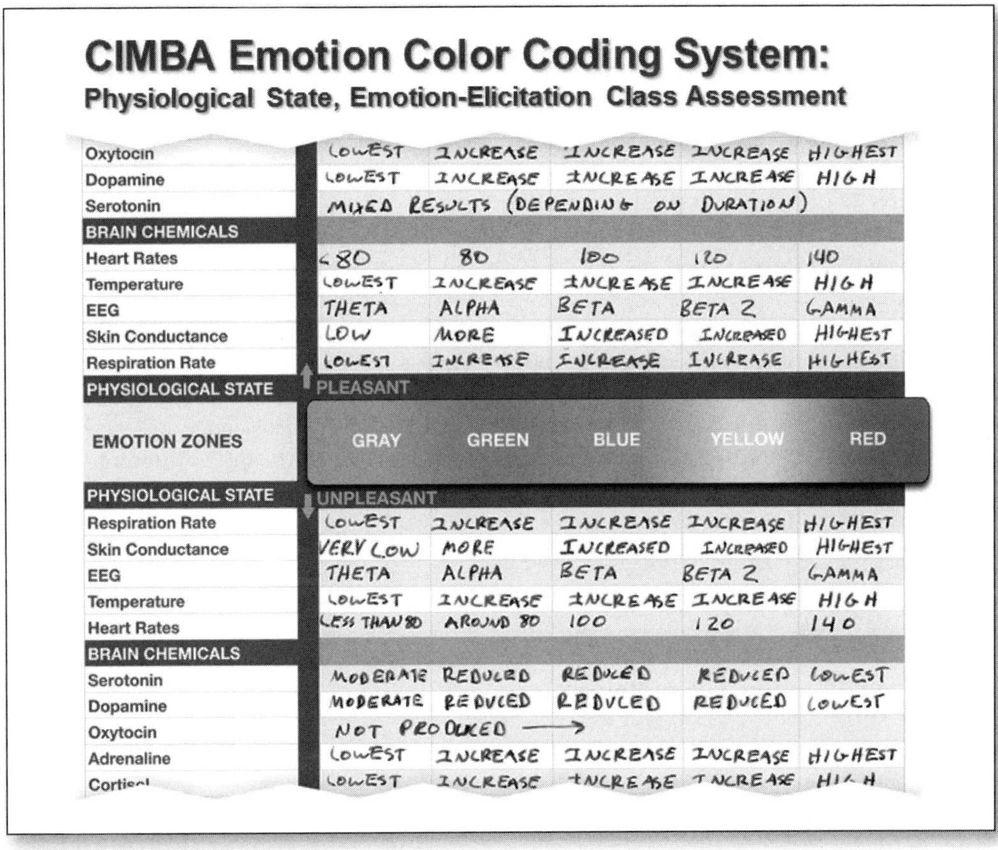
CIMBA Emotion Color Coding System:
Physiological State, Emotion-Elicitation Class Assessment
Oxytocin | LOWEST | INCREASE | INCREASE | INCREASE | HIGHEST
Dopamine | LOWEST | INCREASE | INCREASE | INCREASE | HIGH
Serotonin | MIXED RESULTS (DEPENDING ON DURATION)
BRAIN CHEMICALS
Heart Rates | <80 | 80 | 100 | 120 | 140
Temperature | LOWEST | INCREASE | INCREASE | INCREASE | HIGH
EEG | THETA | ALPHA | BETA | BETA 2 | GAMMA
Skin Conductance | LOW | MORE | INCREASED | INCREASED | HIGHEST
Respiration Rate | LOWEST | INCREASE | INCREASE | INCREASE | HIGHEST
PHYSIOLOGICAL STATE | PLEASANT
EMOTION ZONES | GRAY | GREEN | BLUE | YELLOW | RED
PHYSIOLOGICAL STATE | UNPLEASANT
Respiration Rate | LOWEST | INCREASE | INCREASE | INCREASE | HIGHEST
Skin Conductance | VERY LOW | MORE | INCREASED | INCREASED | HIGHEST
EEG | THETA | ALPHA | BETA | BETA 2 | GAMMA
Temperature | LOWEST | INCREASE | INCREASE | INCREASE | HIGH
Heart Rates | LESS THAN 80 | AROUND 80 | 100 | 120 | 140
BRAIN CHEMICALS
Serotonin | MODERATE | REDUCED | REDUCED | REDUCED | LOWEST
Dopamine | MODERATE | REDUCED | REDUCED | REDUCED | LOWEST
Oxytocin | NOT PRODUCED →
Adrenaline | LOWEST | INCREASE | INCREASE | INCREASE | HIGHEST
Corti | LOWEST | INCREASE | INCREASE | INCREASE

This approach to emotion recognition greatly simplified the way in which we taught emotion recognition, from both self and social awareness perspectives. In a "wired" classroom environment (defined below), individuals were baselined against emotion elicitation films identified by social psychology research to produce specific emotions (see, e.g., Gross & Levenson, 1995). Based on students' knowledge from prior classes on neuroscience and the brain, they were confronted with a range of pleasant and unpleasant emotions as expressed by facial expressions, voice intonation, and body language drawn from prior social psychology research. In each case, students were asked to identify the emotion being elicited on the basis of its physiological and brain state "recipe." The intent of the experience was to fully develop an "emotion recognition color chart" with the expectation that from that point forward emotions and emotional states would be defined by their color. By mindfully paying attention to their own physiology and that of others, this approach served to activate and make operational students' notions of self-awareness and social awareness, and thereby enhance each individual's understanding of the impact of emotion on performance through the brain's threat/reward circuitry.

THE USE OF TECHNOLOGY

A fundamental difference between the social- and neuro-science approaches to examining leadership issues is in the research tools they bring to bear on topics of interest—both inside and outside the laboratory. ***Inside*** the laboratory, neuroscientists use a variety of technologies, most predominately the fMRI (see Figure 23.2 for a list of common tools used in neuroscience), in seeking to identify the brain region or regions involved in a mental task or process of interest. With fMRI, the relevant parts of the subject's brain identify themselves by essentially "lighting up" when engaging in a designed mental task or process.

Looking over the shoulder of the neuroscientists, we observed defined social interactions that social science research had concluded produce similar observable behavioral responses; neuroscience research, however, showed that the interactions actually rely on different underlying brain mechanisms. fMRI data allowed the neuroscientists to distinguish between those two underlying brain mechanisms, something difficult to do using traditional social science behavioral methods. Similarly, but in the opposite direction, fMRI data allowed the neuroscientists to identify mental processes expected to *not* rely on the same brain mechanisms, when in fact they actually do.

The determination of a subject's mental state is another important area applicable to leadership understanding where social science and neuroscience research tools can deliver significantly different results.

Figure 23.2 Brain-Imaging Technologies

Brain-Imaging Technologies

Magnetic Resonance Imaging (MRI)

MRI shows detailed anatomical images. It is sometimes referred to as an "X-ray for soft tissues."

Diffusion MRI (Diffusion Imaging, Tractography)

Used to reveal the brain's "long-distance" neural connections by tracking water molecules, which diffuses along the lengths of the axons more readily than escaping through their fatty coating.

Functional Connectivity MRI (Resting State MRI)

Like the Diffusion MRI, it reveals "long-distance" neural connections by measuring spontaneous fluctuations in different brain regions, revealing the extent to which they are communicating.

Functional MRI (fMRI)

Exhibits changes in blood supply within the brain, which are assumed to correlate with neural activity during designed mental tasks and processes.

Positron Emission Tomography (PET)

Produces anatomical images to test how organs are functioning by detecting gamma rays emitted by a nuclear substance (tracer) introduced into the body.

Electroencephalogram (EEG)

Uses electrodes attached to the scalp to detect electrical activity in the brain.

fMRI data allow the neuroscientist to infer a subject's mental state by looking at the subject's benchmarked brain activity. To gain the same information in the social sciences, the experiment is often interrupted and the subject is asked, "How do you feel?" to determine mental state. This difference in experimental design is significant because the subject may not want to report mental state, or may not remember accurately what state he or she was in before the researcher asked. Perhaps more importantly to the validity of the underlying experiment, the act of simply responding to the question (a response unrelated to the experiment itself) may bring about an important change in current mental state thereby impacting subsequent responses to experimental stimuli. (In developing leaders, this distinction takes on new meaning when in a coaching session an individual is asked to either discuss a journal entry describing an [emotional] event or to examine the applicable neurobiofeedback data. Neuroscience has shown that the act of writing down, and thereby "labeling," the event's emotion has the effect of reducing the emotion's significance [Ochsner & Gross, 2005]; neurobiofeedback technology provides actual data on its significance [Johnson et al., 2010).]

With regard to technologies ***outside*** the laboratory, neuroscience connected the dots between an individual's brain and the body's physiological states. As illustrated in Figure 23.3, brain states observable by an fMRI are also measurable via heart rate, heart rate variability, skin conductance, EEG, and ECG[2]—with all but the EEG currently being measurable wirelessly and unobtrusively outside the laboratory.[3] After initial tests established the efficacy of using these neurobiofeedback measures to study leadership and leadership development, we began to look for viable technology to bring to the classroom. Our decision criteria included cost, durability, precision, intrusiveness, and functionality both inside and outside the classroom/laboratory. With limited options ranging in cost from a few hundred to several thousand dollars, we elected to adapt a SUUNTO performance measurement instrument from the field of sport. We found the SUUNTO td6 device along with its group support equipment and software to meet our basic decision criteria. Once we integrated the device into our classroom environment, the results were immediate and obvious. From a mindfulness standpoint, and in combination with our emotion color-coding system, students became much more aware of their emotional physiology and that of others.

The SUUNTO system involves a chest strap in which sensors are imbedded and a "watch" that displays a variety of data at the user's discretion in real-time. The watch has the capability to record up to five hours of data, which can then be downloaded and analyzed by the SUUNTO software. Alternatively, data can be captured by a computer loaded with SUUNTO software along with an attached antenna. The SUUNTO software allows heart rate data for up to 72 users to be projected for public observation simultaneously in real-time

[2]**Electrocardiograph** (*ECG,* or **EKG** [from the German *Elektrokardiogramm*]) is a diagnostic tool that measures and records the electrical activity of the heart over time, captured and externally recorded by skin electrodes. Our current wireless system relies on just two points of measure, and therefore has been of limited usefulness to date.

[3]"Hardwired" measurement devices rely on physical wires running from the sensors to a recording and/or display device, inhibiting user movement and basically confining assessments to the laboratory. Wireless technology operates through a chest strap that houses the sensors and a display device worn on the wrist of the user. Data can be recorded by the display device outside the laboratory or by a computer fitted with an antenna and accompanying software inside the laboratory. Both hardwired and wireless neurobiofeedback systems are "noninvasive" in the sense that no break in the skin is created to secure the requisite data. Wireless systems are "nonintrusive" relative to hardwired technologies in the sense that other than the possibility of some (often initial) discomfort from the chest strap, the device does not interfere with user movement or other activities, making them ideal for the classroom and other leadership development events.

(with other data captured but not presented). The SUUNTO system allows us to calibrate each individual's heart rate according to our emotion recognition color-coding system so that the projected panel of individual data shows "green-zone" for everyone when a professor begins a class and all students are attentive.

Both the success of this experiment and the limitations of the SUUNTO software led us to design and build our own system.[4] SUUNTO, for example, did not have the expectation that the data would be further downloaded and analyzed independent of their software, nor aggregated in a group format. Our new system prototype involves an independent third component in addition to the chest-strap and watch/display. This third component can be a Smartphone, iPad, or other similar device with the ability to collect data from the chest-strap (expanded from heart rate and heart rate variability to include skin conductance, a basic EKG measure, movement, and respiration), analyze it in real-time, and send the appropriate data to both the watch/display and/or to a main server via the Internet. At the server level, the data are analyzed against the greater database and the individual's data. According to prescribed algorithms, the individual and/or the individual's coach can be informed of any action needed in real-time. In initial assessment and measurement stages of an

Figure 23.3

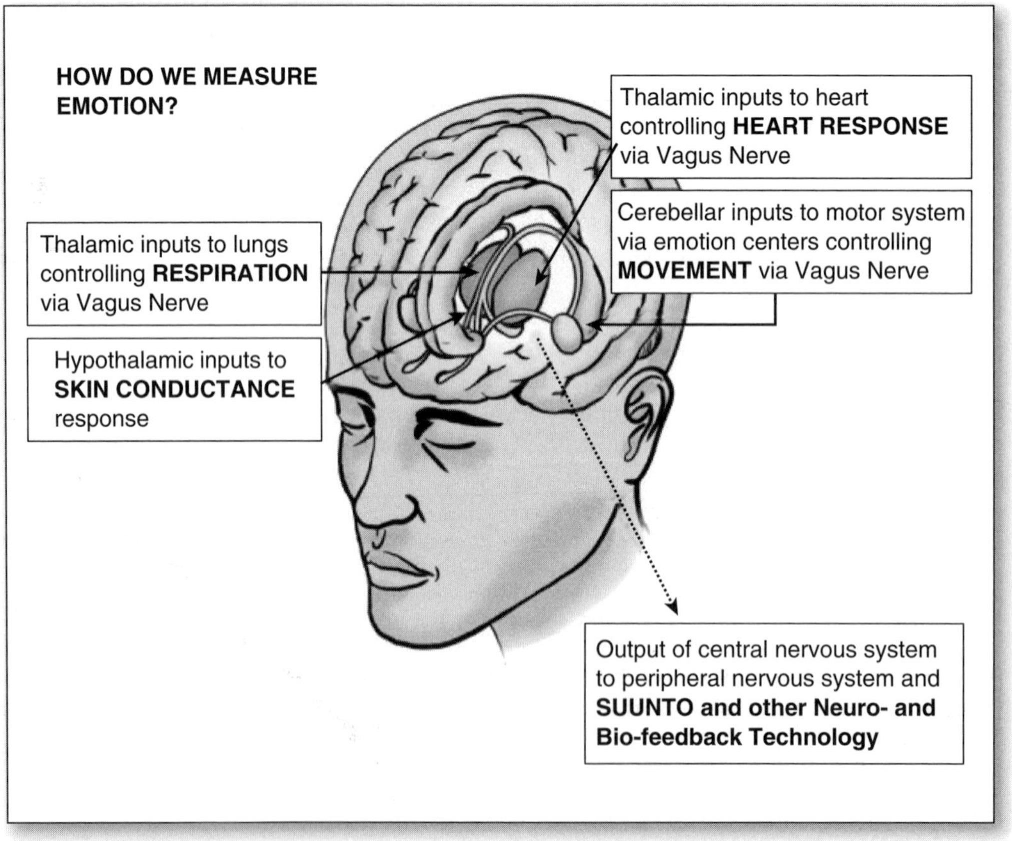
HOW DO WE MEASURE EMOTION?
Thalamic inputs to heart controlling HEART RESPONSE via Vagus Nerve
Cerebellar inputs to motor system via emotion centers controlling MOVEMENT via Vagus Nerve
Thalamic inputs to lungs controlling RESPIRATION via Vagus Nerve
Hypothalamic inputs to SKIN CONDUCTANCE response
Output of central nervous system to peripheral nervous system and SUUNTO and other Neuro- and Bio-feedback Technology

[4]Discussions with SUUNTO about a "SUUNTO Leadership Development Classroom" showed us that their primary focus was justifiably on the known sport performance improvement market.

individual's leadership development journey, the data collected are used to construct the individual's development plan template and to specify to the coach the most appropriate intervention strategy.

NEUROSCIENCE AND LEADERSHIP LEARNING ENVIRONMENTS

Neuroscience also influenced the structure of our leadership learning environments. In our experience, when it came to our ***Knowing*** component, the traditional classroom proved to be the most effective learning environment. The classroom-based, informational learning/assimilation process provided direct instructional guidance to the learner. For the ***Doing*** and ***Being*** components, we found a minimally guided, experiential learning environment supplemented with the support of our process facilitators and leadership development coaches to be far more effective. (For example, with specific regard to leadership the key was to produce an understanding of emotion through a designed experience, event, or activity.) Any effort on our part to alter this basic formula—using, for example, the classroom to instruct students on effective leadership behavior or an experiential learning environment to learn leadership axioms, theorems, principles, and formulas—detracted significantly from the student learning experience. As with many aspects of leadership and leadership development, it was through neuroscience that we came to understand and appreciate why.

As educational psychology moved into the early 2000s, insights from neuroscience were beginning to impact and reshape thinking. Instructional psychologists began to place increased attention on human cognitive architecture—specifically, examining the relationship between working and long-term memory, and learning. Relying on this line of thinking, a specific work that most confirmed our approach to leadership-learning environments was Prof. David C. Geary's *Educating the Evolved Mind* (Geary, 2007). Geary was the first to draw a distinction between ***biologically primary*** and ***biologically secondary*** information and thereby resolve the ongoing dispute regarding instruction design within educational psychology (essentially a dispute over the efficacy of experiential learning[5]). Geary's thesis argues persuasively why learners acquire some information easily and unconsciously (which he labeled as being "biologically primary" information or knowledge) whereas other information can be acquired only through considerable conscious effort, often requiring external motivation ("biologically secondary"). Examples of biologically primary knowledge are listening to and speaking our first language, recognizing faces, using general problem-solving techniques, and engaging in basic social relations, all of which are acquired easily outside of educational contexts; explicit instruction is unnecessary for effective learning. From a neurobiology, evolutionary standpoint, the acquisition of such knowledge was and is essential for survival—as we discussed previously, the brain is clearly motivated to evolve neural connections receptive to such information. Under Geary's thesis, both the ***Doing*** and ***Being*** components of leadership constitute biologically primary knowledge best acquired

---

[5]According to Professor John Sweller (2008), an educational psychologist best known for formulating cognitive load theory:

> David C. Geary's distinction between biologically primary and biologically secondary information constitutes an advance that is rare in our discipline. For researchers in instructional psychology, the distinction adds a major piece of the jigsaw puzzle on which we are all working. In the process, Geary has provided a theoretical framework that has the potential to resolve important issues with profound instructional implications.(p. 214)

in a minimally guided, experiential learning environment.

In contrast, biologically secondary knowledge is associated with more advanced learning, learning that one would associate with a particular discipline or subject matter. As such, Geary's thesis asserts persuasively that we have not evolved to acquire biologically secondary knowledge openly, but that learners acquire such knowledge relatively slowly and with conscious effort through explicit instruction. The vast majority of knowledge acquired by learners through educational institutions consists of biologically secondary knowledge. As in other programs, biologically secondary knowledge is largely acquired by students through classroom instruction at CIMBA. Within this instructional psychology paradigm, there is relatively little difference among leadership training and development approaches with regard to the manner in which students acquire biologically secondary leadership knowledge. Most serious programs rely on traditional student-teacher classroom environments to transmit specific discipline-based knowledge. However, it is in the acquisition of biologically primary knowledge that approaches to leadership differ significantly.

The importance of understanding emotion coupled with Geary's thesis guided us to develop experiential learning opportunities to elicit specific emotions—to best assist participants in acquiring biologically primary leadership knowledge. Our basic premise was to assist individuals in identifying their most influential SCARF elements (their SCARF profile) and the activities within their business day most likely to be affected by their particular SCARF "stressors." Our principal assessment and measurement vehicles are emotion elicitation films and simulations, developed professionally, and baselined against existing emotion elicitation research (e.g., Gross & Levenson, 1995). In addition, we are continuing to experiment with a variety of more active, participative events including "wired" indoor and outdoor leadership experiences and activities, contemporaneous acting workshops, and others.

II. The Neurobiofeedback Leadership Classrooms

From the onset, it was our intent to fully integrate a leadership and leadership development system throughout a traditional MBA program. CIMBA's beautiful location in Italy gave us the ability to attract extraordinarily talented people from a variety of fields, the majority with expertise quite divergent from that typically found in traditional business schools. Our express focus on leadership and leadership development coupled with considerable system flexibility has allowed us to develop and test leadership tools and techniques at a much more determined pace than would be possible at a traditional business school. As an unforeseen consequence of the manner and purpose for which CIMBA was originally created, the organization has focused on student results, and not on the publications it could generate.

In its simplest form, the CIMBA approach to leadership adds neurobiofeedback technology to the traditional approach to leadership and leadership development. The neurobiofeedback technology is fully integrated into all learning environments to capture performance emotion data for the express purpose of improving participant performance and health. The neurobiofeedback technology and accompanying training and development methodology allows CIMBA to expressly generate and measure defined emotion elicitation events and experiences, moving participants beyond traditional skills or content-focused development to an understanding of underlying emotions and their impact on behavior, cognition, and performance—in a word, *Being*.

ASSESSMENT AND MEASUREMENT CLASSROOMS

Assessment and measurement begins prior to MBA content classes with LIFE (Leadership Initiative For Excellence), a two-and-a-half day, highly intensive, experiential self-learning experience. The ultimate goal of LIFE is to deepen and broaden participant understanding of the importance of the relationship between emotion, behavior, and cognition, and how the ability to effectively manage that relationship impacts performance. It begins with a detailed overview of the latest NeuroLeadership concepts, and the neuroscience and social psychology research that supports it. Each subsequent LIFE module raises a designed workplace emotion, reveals how that emotion drives behavior, and shows how it impacts participant and group performance. Through a practical understanding of how the brain works in such situations, each module illustrates experientially how the participant can learn to become cognizant of and then better control emotions to manifest a more effective behavior and improve performance, health, and well-being. During these modules, participants wear the latest SUUNTO performance measurement instruments, which provide real-time feedback on brain performance by measuring body physiology.

Although it is not made known expressly to the participants, the LIFE trainers systematically create a strongly negative SCARF environment (low engagement) and then a strongly positive SCARF environment (high engagement) as an integral part of the LIFE experience. Participant cognition is baselined just prior to the beginning of their LIFE experience and then measured during both the low-engagement environment (consistently found to be statistically lower than baseline) and the high-engagement environment (consistently statistically higher). After each LIFE module, the LIFE "Professor" guides participants in understanding experientially the cognitive consequence of allowing their brain to dictate the behavioral reaction to the SCARF element the module portrayed—versus taking cognitive control of their emotions and rationally calling upon a more effective behavior or mental state. The comparison provides the participant with the determination, desire, and hardiness necessary for the demanding CIMBA personal development journey they are about to undertake.

With the intent to develop key participant emotion-behavior-performance baselines, participants continue the assessment process by completing selected traditional psychometric instruments and then move to assessments unique to the CIMBA system. Participants are asked to engage in a variety of emotion-eliciting events common to the stressful environment that interacting and working with others often creates. The interest is in understanding the emotion the stimuli elicit, the behavior manifested, and how that behavior impacts the participant's performance. SUUNTO and additional, more sophisticated technologies provide neurobiofeedback data on the participant's mental state. Statistical comparisons are made between distinct stimulant environments on participant self-regulatory ability and on each of the five SCARF "stressors" identified by neuroscience and social psychology. The assessments assist in determining emotion-behavior-performance baselines with the results compared against psychometric instrument results for consistency. Ultimately, the data collected are analyzed and used to construct the participant's development plan template and to specify to the coach the most appropriate intervention strategy to be used in bringing about the plan's goals and objectives.

NEUROBIOFEEDBACK IN THE TRADITIONAL MBA CLASSROOM

At CIMBA, leadership content (***Knowing***) is biologically secondary knowledge and as such is delivered in a traditional classroom setting. A primary distinction between CIMBA and other programs is that the classroom learning environment for leadership content as well as all other MBA content courses (e.g., classes on accounting, economics, finance, marketing, production, etc.) are "wired" classrooms. That is, all students wear SUUNTO measurement technology with their basic physiological data displayed on a large projected panel. After a period of individual student calibration, appropriate adjustments are made so that comparisons can be made on emotional color rather than on far less relevant, absolute heart rate comparisons. For example, one student may have an attentive brain heart rate of 50 beats per minute and another student 85 beats per minute. As the professor enters the classroom, he or she expects to find those numbers but in each case the emotion color code displayed will be green—designating a "green-zone" emotion state for both students. In fact (unless a student is day-dreaming about a favorite beach or restaurant experience), the professor would expect to find the entire panel green for the class once the calibration process is complete (a period of one to two months, with intermittent adjustments normally required). After each major class, the data are reviewed by the coaches to see if there is a need for extraordinary action or inquiry based on a particular student's physiological response to a classroom activity or event.

While the majority of MBA professors are trained in the system, the intent is to involve them largely indirectly in leadership development. Still, professors actively see how students differ in responses to various classroom discussions, group activities, and project presentations—making them an important source of confirming information regarding student progress toward development plan goals and objectives. In fact, with their interest peaked by the technology, it is not uncommon for professors to both request their own measurement device and to begin to look for classroom activities more likely to take advantage of the new measurement technology. With regard to students, the use of the technology in the traditional classroom is a mandatory ingredient in their implicit mindfulness training, assisting them in becoming more and more aware of their physiology and that of others in a variety of circumstances, both emotional and cognitive.

LEADERSHIP COMPETENCY CLASSROOMS

After assessment and measurement, the participant and his or her coach establish a development plan from the template provided by analysis of the data collected. Depending upon the "Data-Driven" coaching intervention strategy suggested by the assessments, that plan schedules data collection, online neuro-based training provided by *My Brain Solutions*, "challenge" tests, and coaching sessions. The CIMBA approach to coaching differs somewhat from traditional coaching systems in its greater reliance on physiological data. In many cases, the elusiveness of the root cause behind the participant's leadership "issue" is the participant's lack of conscious awareness of the emotion or mental state a debilitating workplace stimulus (stress, fear of social ostracism, anger) is creating. The situation is often further compounded by the participant's self-regulatory brain circuitry (observed through participant behavior and responses within traditional coaching systems, as well as through neurobiofeedback assessment and measurement data by our coaches), which if insufficiently developed is unable to control emotion and thus draw up the appropriate behavior. By coaching to the participant's neurobiofeedback data, Data-Driven coaching not only works to make the participant's underlying brain state visible and understandable, it also provides an objective, quantifiable basis for measuring participant improvement. In addition—and as dictated by the participant's needs and assessments—the development plan provides a list of suggested Leadership Competency Workshops, which are separate and distinct from the MBA content courses.

CIMBA defines "leadership competency" quite specifically. A person has a "Leadership Competency" only after having gained mastery over both the appropriate mental state and the appropriate skill making up the competency. In addition to being a wired classroom, a leadership competency classroom may also make use of more sophisticated, neurobiofeedback technologies and data assessments and display. In teaching a specific skill for the purpose of addressing a leadership competency, the workshop design involves an overview of the SCARF emotion anticipated, designed emotion elicitation events involving the competency, an overview of the neuroscience involved, and then the skill component. Under the neuroscience principle "neurons that fire together, wire together," the skill and its corresponding emotion are taught together. In the event an individual registers a SCARF response of concern during an emotion elicitation event, the coach is informed so that it can be assessed against the individual's development plan. For example, consider teaching the leadership competency conflict management. A person who has difficulty managing the emotions associated with conflict will not likely be able to implement skills a traditional conflict management course would teach until the emotional side of conflict has been addressed. In our system, students first visit the emotion of conflict through a series of emotion elicitation simulations. The skills instruction that follows encompasses both the technical aspects of conflict management and the lessons learned about the emotion of conflict from those simulations. Coaches are informed of those students identified as having a sensitivity of concern so that specific issue can be further addressed in a coaching forum.

III. Preliminary Results and Challenges

An advantage of the CIMBA approach to leadership and leadership development is its reliance on data derived from its neurobiofeedback assessment system, a system established on a foundation of neuroscience and social psychology research. To get a sense of the impact and sustainability of neurobiofeedback-based leadership and personal development intervention strategies, consider the biofeedback for four participants presented in the Figure 23.4. The four participants were being "challenge" tested through a specially designed, emotion elicitation business simulation. (CIMBA trained one of the participants: can you determine which one?) After the simulation, each of the participants was asked about a specific event that took place during the simulation: "What was your emotion, what behavior did it manifest, and how did it impact your performance?" Importantly, all four participants reported being "calm," a response at odds with the data. This lack of self-awareness is a common result and emphasizes the importance of neurobiofeedback and Data-Driven coaching if the intent is long-term, sustainable change. (Answer: upper left-hand corner.)

CIMBA has several ongoing studies looking at both the short- and longer-term consequences of its intervention strategies. At the very core of the CIMBA development theory is the importance of self-regulation. The CIMBA neurobiofeedback assessment system determines with remarkable precision whether a person is an "A" (low ability to self-regulate), "B" (moderate ability to self-regulate), or "C" (significant self-regulatory ability). Against a very large database, and in most cases highly statistically significant, the results show that a person identified as being in the "A" category has challenges they do not need to face. The challenges facing "A"s, along with the emotions they will experience and the behaviors that will manifest, impact their workplace and life environments, adversely affecting both productivity and health. Demanding situations significantly increase stress; dramatically reduce memory, attention, and planning abilities; increase negativity; reduce communication; and significantly lower resilience. As stress levels

Figure 23.4 Four-Person "Challenge" Test Biofeedback

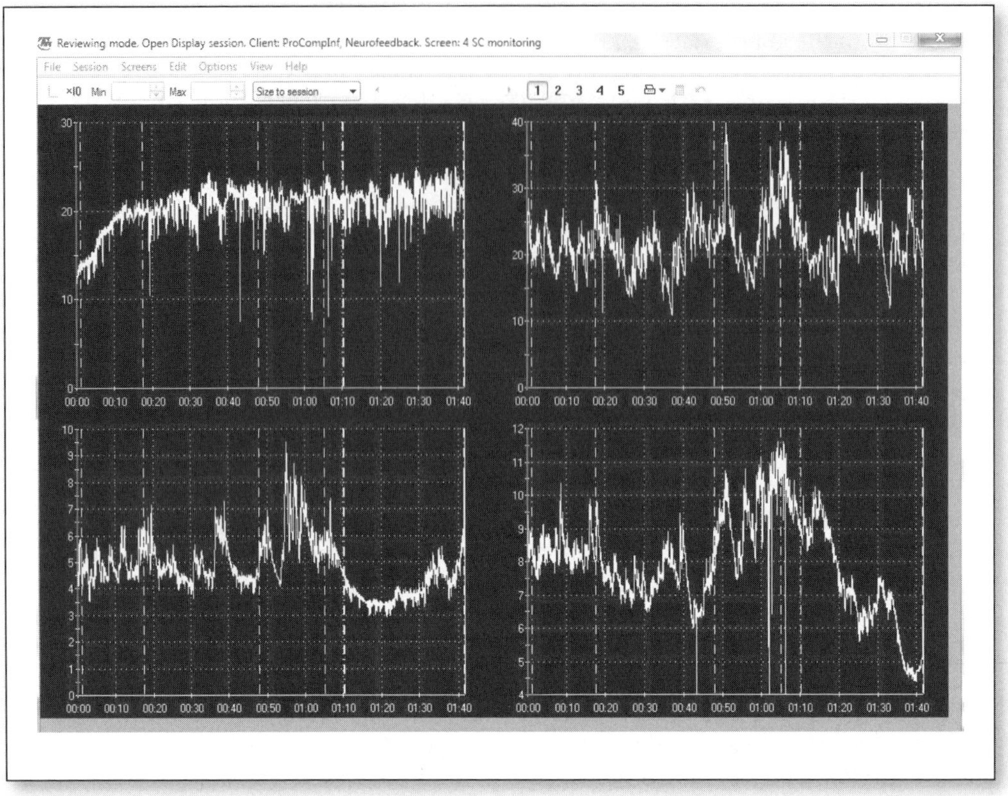

rise, both creativity and the ability to sustain high-level thinking decline, adversely impacting creative problem-solving in difficult situations and the ability to multitask in less demanding ones. Cognitive companies such as consulting and accounting companies will find a temporary solution by over-training these "A" individuals, so that as stress levels increase their brains move to "hardwired," robotic responses to tasks at hand—until boredom and/or lifestyle conflicts cause them to quit (or, their negativity brings about their dismissal). Strong anecdotal evidence indicates that this quit pattern follows a two-year cycle unless either the individual develops or is seen as having developed an indispensable skill, or a serious, provocative event or experience causes them to examine himself or herself more closely. Many follow up the event or experience by electing to seek assistance through a coach, mentor, friend, or family member (or, in appropriate cases, a therapist).

The CIMBA approach to leadership and leadership development emphasizes the importance of assessing the functional relationship between an individual's performance (and health) as defined by his or her ability to self-regulate emotions that can adversely affect behavior, negatively impact cognition, and undermine skill effectiveness. Thriving organizations are driven by their mental capital—healthy employees whose brains are functioning at their best: employees who can think clearly, are positive, resilient, and can collaborate optimally with colleagues and customers. CIMBA internal studies on a database of more than 1,000 people show statistically significant increases of more than 10 percent in both emotional resilience and positivity bias, considered key indicators in traditional psychometric instrument measurements for self-regulation.

More than 10 years of conversations with HR directors in leading companies worldwide clearly shows that the vast majority of companies, in particular those companies where employee cognition is its primary product, hire employees on the basis of IQ, or some similar proxy for human intelligence. On its face, this is fully understandable: Every company wants technically competent employees, managers, and leaders. Those same conversations, however, provide an even more interesting insight: Those same companies almost universally fire employees on the basis of EQ (Emotional Intelligence Quotient) and RQ (Rational Intelligence Quotient)—employees who have made poor personal or professional decisions that cast serious doubt on their ability to meet company expectations. With RQ being statistically correlated with EQ, with both being direct functions of self-regulation, and with both RQ and EQ showing no discernible statistical relationship with IQ within ranges relevant to leaders and managers, the importance of focusing developmental resources on identifying and assisting "A"s seems obvious.

IV. Conclusion

In 1997 there were some 10 neuroscience studies based on fMRI data arguably relevant to explaining personal behavior; in 2010 there were nearly 10 per day. Virtually every major discipline from the arts to the sciences is being impacted by neuroscience and its findings. The teaching and development of leadership is no exception. Although neurobiofeedback technology is still in a laboratory state, the situation is evolving at a rapid rate. We are beginning to more precisely assess and measure individual performance and identify the brain functions holding individuals back from achieving their full potential. Importantly, those same hard data are allowing us to better tailor intervention strategies to assist, challenge, and support individuals in overcoming their personal barriers to effective leadership. With the ability to assess, measure, and understand emotion and its consequences on cognition and creativity, neuroscience is assisting us in creating better leaders than we could before it appeared on the horizon. While we are just at the beginning of teaching leadership with the brain in mind, we are inspired by the real results we see in the classroom, and excited by the opportunities for further research in this area.

References

Barrett, L. F. (2006). Solving the emotion paradox: Categorization and the experience of emotion. *Personality and Social Psychology Review, 10*(1), 20–46.

Bauer, I. A., & Baumeister, R. F. (2011). Self-regulatory strength. In K. D. Vohs & R. F. Baumeister (Eds.), *Handbook of Self-Regulation: Research, Theory, and Applications* (pp. 64–82). New York: The Guilford Press

Bennis, W., & O'Toole J. (2005). How business schools lost their way. *Harvard Business Review, 83*(5), 96–124.

Farb, N.A.S., Anderson, A.K., Mayberg, H., Bean, J., McKeon, D., & Segal, Z.V. (2010). Minding one's emotions: Mindfulness training alters the neural expression of sadness. *Emotion, 10*(1), 25–33.

Farb, N. A. S., Segal, Z. V., Mayberg, H., Bean, J., McKeon, D., Fatima, Z., & Anderson, A. K. (2007). Attending to the present: Mindfulness meditation reveals distinct neural modes of self-reference. *Social Cognitive and Affective Neuroscience, 2,* 313–322.

Geary, D. C. (2007). Educating the evolved mind: Conceptual foundations for an evolutionary educational psychology. In J. S. Carlson & J. R. Leven (Eds.), *Educating the evolved mind: Conceptual foundations for an evolutionary educational psychology* (pp. 1-99). Charlotte, NC: Information Age Publishing, Inc.

Goleman, D. (1995). *Emotional intelligence: Why it can matter more than IQ*. New York: Bantam Books.

Gooty J., Connelly, S., Griffith J., & Gupta A. (2010). Leadership, affect, and emotions: A state of the science review. *The Leadership Quarterly, 21*(6), 979–1004.

Gooty, J., Gavin, M., & Ashkanasy, N. M. (2009). Emotions research in OB: The challenges that lie ahead. *Journal of Organizational Behavior, 30*, 833–838.

Gordon, E. (2008). NeuroLeadership and integrative neuroscience. *NeuroLeadership Journal, 1*, 74–80.

Gross, J., & Levenson, R. W. (1995). Emotion elicitation using films. *Cognition and Emotion, 9*, 87–108.

Gross,J. J., & John,O. P. (2003). Individual differences in two emotion regulation processes: Implications for affect, relationships, and well-being. *Journal of Personality and Social Psychology, 85*(2), 348–362.

Gyurak, A., Goodkind, M. S., Madan, A., Kramer, J. H., Miller, B. L., & Levenson, R. W. (2009). Do tests of executive functioning predict ability to down regulate emotions spontaneously and when instructed to suppress? *Cognitive, Affective, & Behavioral Neuroscience, 9*(2), 144–152.

Hanin, Y. L. (2007). Emotions in sports: Current issues and perspectives. In G. Tenenbaum & R. C. Eklund (Eds.), *Handbook of Sports Psychology* (pp. 31–58). New York: John Wiley & Sons Publishers.

Hesselbein, F., & Shinseki, E. K. (2004). *Be-Know-Do: Leadership the Army way*. San Francisco, CA: Jossey-Bass.

Hochschild, A. R. (1983). *The managed heart: commercialization of human feelings*. Berkeley, CA: University of California Press.

Hooker, C. I., Gyurak, A., Verosky, S. C, Miyakawa, A., & Ayduk, Ö. (2010). Neural activity to a partner's facial expression predicts self-regulation after conflict. *Biological Psychiatry, 67*, 406–413.

Izard, C. E. (2009). The many meanings/aspects of emotion: Definitions, functions, activation, and regulation, *Emotion Review, 2*(4), 363–370.

Izard, C. E. (2010). Emotion theory and research: Highlights, unanswered questions, and emerging issues. *Annual Review of Psychology, 60*, 1–25.

Jha, A. P., Stanley, E. A., Kiyonaga, A., Wond, L., & Gelfand, L. (2010). Examining the protective effects of mindfulness training on working memory capacity and affective experience. *Emotion, 10* (1), 54–64.

Johnson, S. J., Boehm, S. G., Healy, D., Goebel, R., & Linden, D. E. J. (2010). Neurofeedback: A promising tool for the self-regulation of emotion networks. *NeuroImage, 49*, 1066–1072.

Lieberman, M. D. (2009). The brain's breaking system (and how to use your words to tap into it). *NeuroLeadership Journal, 2*, 9–14.

Lutz, A., Slagter, H. A., Dunne, J. D., & Davidson, R. J. (2008). Attention regulation and monitoring in meditation. *Trends in Cognitive Sciences, 12*, 163–169.

Ochsner, K. N., & Gross, J. J. (2005). The cognitive control of emotion. *Trends in Cognitive Science, 9*, 242–249.

Rock, D. (2008). SCARF: A brain-based model for collaborating with and influencing others. *NeuroLeadership Journal, 1*, 44–52.

Skinner, B. F. (1953). *Science and human behavior*. New York: The Free Press.

Skinner, B. F. (1974). *About behaviorism*. New York: Alfred A. Knopf, Inc.

Sweller, J. (2008). Instructional implications of David C. Geary's evolutionary educational psychology. *Educational Psychologist, 43*(4), 214–216.

Zeidan, F., Johnson, S. K., Diamond, B. J., David, Z., & Goolkasian, P. (2010). Mindfulness meditation improves cognition: Evidence of brief mental training. *Consciousness and Cognition, 19*, 597–605.

24

THE COMPANY COMMAND PROFESSIONAL FORUM

Peer-to-Peer Leadership Development in the US Army

◆ Tony Burgess
US Army

This chapter explores peer-to-peer leadership development in the US Army's "Company Command" professional forum. Through the lens of teaching leadership, the author and cofounder of the forum introduces the idea that the ongoing experiences of the "students" (company commanders) is the learning curriculum, and the students learn from each other as they engage in conversation about their experiences. This chapter provides specific examples of how learning in such a community can be increased through well-designed learning interventions; in fact, it is these interventions that bring the informal learning system to life. The chapter finishes with a deep dive into the core-group phenomenon, which is the story of a smaller, socially connected, and committed group of members that emerges to serve the community. Without this smaller group of informal leaders, the community would dry up, and there would be no learning. A key insight is that one must cultivate and sustain a vibrant core group in order to have a vibrant learning community.

The Company Command forum teaches us that leaders who engage in such a professional forum will become more effective and they will in turn grow more effective organizations. They will learn to be better leaders.

❖ ❖ ❖

This book is about teaching leadership, so it is through that frame that we'll continue to look in this chapter. When we think about teaching leadership it is usually in the context of a classroom or some kind of course or, perhaps, a workshop. But what happens when the "students" are several thousand geographically dispersed US Army company commanders whose best "teachers" are each other?[1] In 2000, when a small band of junior officers in the US Army created www.CompanyCommand.com, our goal was to connect company commanders with each other so that we could share our ideas and experiences. Online, we could foster peer-to-peer connections and conversations that cut across the army structure, not limited by geography or the formal organization. We describe ourselves as a growing network of leaders who are deeply committed to exceptional leadership at the company level. We believe, even more strongly now after a decade of experience, that leaders who engage in such a professional forum will become more effective and will grow more effective organizations. They will learn to be better leaders.

Background and Context

Nate Allen and I were great friends at West Point and five years out of the Academy we were assigned as company commanders in the 25th Infantry Division in Hawaii where we also happened to be next-door neighbors. We spent a lot of time together on our front porches, or lanais as we call them in Hawaii, talking. In those front-porch conversations, we often talked about what was happening at work, with a heavy emphasis on growing exceptional units and serving the soldiers we had the privilege to lead. We shared our best ideas (what was working), acted as sounding boards for each other, and brainstormed ways to navigate leadership challenges as we faced them. Along the way we realized that our front-porch conversations were making us better leaders. Talking about company command was having a practical impact for us and our units. This basic insight—that talking with peers about what we are doing and are learning improves our effectiveness—set the conditions for what would follow.

In February 2000, we purchased the URL www.companycommand.com and, with a band of 8–12 like-hearted commanders that included a Web-savvy West Point classmate named Steve Schweitzer, we launched an online version of those front-porch conversations. Key to our early success was a grass-roots marketing campaign leveraging our extended personal network—friends located all over the army that we recruited to act as point men. These point men helped seed the website or, as we began to call it, the *forum*, with quality content, and they effectively spread the word. It was exciting! Company commanders *loved* it and joined the movement by the bucket load.

Why the overwhelmingly positive response? First, CompanyCommand.com spoke with a distinct voice—informal, passionate, positive—and, as the authors of *The Cluetrain Manifesto* underscore about voice on the emerging web, it was "human" as opposed to the typical bureaucratic corporate speak that everyone was used to (Levine, Locke, Searls, & Weinberger, 2001). Second, it was by and for the people, as opposed to being built by the organization for the employees. Third, it was peers sharing their ideas based on and in the context of their actual experiences, as opposed to context-stripped bullet comments. On CompanyCommand.com you got the whole story, in the raw, including the subtle nuances and meaning that get lost when you "harvest out" the key lessons. Finally, the content was rocking good and the ability to follow up with the authors (your peers) was right there, a click away; being engaged in the conversation meant you were being exposed to cool ideas and people that directly impacted your effectiveness as a company commander. Yes, like the Hawaiian front-porch conversation, only on a much larger scale.

There was some pushback from senior leaders in the army, which typically sounded like, "How is this information vetted?" and "What if someone shares something that is wrong?" And there were a small number of Colonels who felt threatened enough to give us a piece of their mind. Overall, though, the response from "higher HQ" was positive. General Shinseki, the Chief of Staff of the Army (CSA) at the time, was overheard directing his subordinates to "stay out of their way." He inherently saw the value of leaders informally connecting with each other, and he understood the bureaucratic tendency to spoil grass-roots innovation. Critical to gaining support from senior leaders was the clear alignment between the values of the forum and the values of the larger organization. An altruistic and deep commitment to training and taking care of soldiers, a passion for growing combat-effective teams, and an overarching drive to develop ourselves and our subordinate leaders were the values that seeped out of the online space—values that resonated with the army's senior leaders. And it was immensely helpful that the Colonels and Generals had all one day been platoon leaders and company commanders. Advocates like General Gordon Sullivan, former CSA, reacted by saying, "I sure wish we had this when I was a captain in Vietnam."

But this is a story of grass-roots collective action. Like the Nike mantra, we just did it. We didn't ask for permission because we never thought we needed permission. The army profession is not only the senior leaders; rather, it is all of us—each of the committed members of the profession, all with a responsibility to advance its collective effectiveness. Having said that, our success quickly brought us to a point where we needed the support of the organization or face burnout. Within two years of launch, which included rolling out a separate forum for platoon leaders (the Platoon Leader forum), it became obvious that the venture needed resources. We were not in a position to continue paying for everything out of pocket and doing all the work on our free time.

Although we had appreciated General Shinseki's directive to stay out of our way, we now needed somebody to help us on our way. We explored several options to include creating a non-profit organization to provide support. We also reached out to the senior leaders at West Point, the United States Military Academy, where we were assigned by this time. They came along side us and endorsed the creation of a research center that we would lead, focused on leader development and organizational learning in the context of professional learning communities. Our mission was to improve leader effectiveness of company commanders and platoon leaders in the army by connecting them with each other inside an informal learning system—and to share what we learned about how to do this with the rest of the army. Pete Kilner, a Company Command forum founding member and a long-term leader of the research center, recalls that the dean of the Academic Board, Brigadier General Dan Kaufman, on the day that the new center was officially approved, looked him square in the eye and said, "If you do things the same way the army already does them, you're wasting my time. If you don't fail sometimes, you're not being creative enough. If you don't fundamentally change the way the army educates its leaders, you will have betrayed my trust. So, good luck and have fun!" How's that for an exhortation?

Resourcing for the center has evolved. Four personnel slots were initially taken out of hide at West Point, a bold decision by Brigadier General Kaufman in a zero-sum personnel environment. These personnel slots were eventually backfilled by the Department of the Army.[2] West Point provides the brick and mortar and basic infrastructure for the center, while the research funds have come almost entirely from Department of the Army grants that the center competes for annually. In part based on the example of the Company Command and Platoon Leader forums, the Army's Combined Arms Center (CAC) at Fort Leavenworth took on the role of creating professional forums for dozens of other jobs in the army. The West Point team serves as a research and development arm for CAC and, in turn, CAC pays for annual software licenses and provides two forum facilitators.

What Actually Happens in the Company Command Forum?

Having described how the Company Command forum was established, let me now turn to the main storyline of this chapter, which is the idea of creating and cultivating an informal learning system to connect people, so that they can become more effective leaders (in the context of their work in the army profession). This chapter introduces the idea that the ongoing experiences of the "students" comprise the curriculum and that they learn from each other as they engage in conversation about those ongoing experiences. Moreover, the storyline provides an example of how opportunities for learning can be increased through well-designed informal learning interventions.

The front-porch conversation metaphor is easy to understand. We create a place on the Web for leaders to connect with each other in conversation about what matters to them in the context of their professional roles leading soldiers. A foundational assumption that drives us is the idea that the cutting-edge knowledge of the army resides in the minds of leaders at the tip of the spear—leaders in the experience right now (Dixon, Allen, Burgess, Kilner, & Schweitzer, 2005). Connecting those leaders in conversation with each other, as well as with those who will follow in their footsteps, improves the effectiveness of those who participate. Topics of conversation in the Company Command (CC) forum run the gamut from the technical and somewhat mundane one minute to the broader leadership question the next. As I type this chapter, a new company commander named Joseph has asked a question about policy letters:

> I have a question: Is there any Army regulation which gives commanders the authority to create their own command policies, other than those prescribed by Army Regulation 600-20? I mean, AR 600-20 specifies certain command policies that all commanders are required to have, but does it or any other regulation grant commanders the authority to create other command policies of their choosing, or is that a practice that is dictated purely by precedence? Can I create a command policy for anything that is not against other regulations or policies, or do I have more limitations? Can I, for instance, make a command policy that states that everyone in my company must read a book every week? Be vegetarian? I've been reviewing the command policies that I've inherited. There are many areas of my company that I would like to improve, to make my company better in my time as commander, and I would like to make some of my improvements in the form of command policies, so I've been trying to research regulations or manuals which govern command policies, to find: the correct use of command policies, my authorities and limitations, and the correct format of command policies. So far my search has not been very fruitful.

This thread is just getting under way. There are seven responses, several recommending that Joseph make sure his policy letters are reviewed by his Judge Advocate General's (JAG) Corps office and that his First Sergeant and boss understand and support them. There is some debate about whether any policy letter can be punitive, and one experienced company commander who has an informal leadership role within the CC forum takes it upon herself to contact a couple JAG officers offline to get their input on the legal authority that a policy letter carries. One member jokes about a unit he was in where he had to read 70 plus policy letters and sign to acknowledge he had read and understood them. His joking subtly introduces the idea that having too many policy letters rings of legalism and doesn't go over well with soldiers. Then, another experienced commander and informal leader in the forum jumps in with this:

> Joseph: I'm going to play the devil's advocate role here, so bear with me. Beyond the absolute bare minimum (like the use of "bear" and "bare"?) that you are dictated by regs [regulations] to have, do you need any additional "policy" letters at the company level? Is that the most effective way to influence soldiers? Might one way to improve your company be to throw out all the extra policy letters? I think your question is a really good one, and if we get multiple viewpoints into the conversation, I think we are all going to learn something as a result. Thanks for starting this off!

The informal leader reframed the conversation—in a positive, appreciative way—from "how to use command policies" to "why you create them in the first place." Members are invited to think about the effects they want to achieve as a leader. Is there another way to achieve the desired outcome that will be more effective in the long term? This conversation is part of the leadership curriculum, grounded in the lived experience of the members who are seeking to become more effective leaders.

Another question comes from Tommy, a future company commander:

> My question deals with calendars/training schedules. My current Battalion Commander is trying to push DTMS [training management software]. We all see the value in it, but our higher HQ is not using it. How do we get a higher HQ to conform to what the Army is supposed to be doing?

And Jamie posts a third question on the same day and titles it, "End of Tour Award Drama":

> Have you ever been ordered to write an award you know is wrong? Our CO [commanding officer] is on leave, which makes me CO again for the fourth time this tour initially in Iraq and now Kuwait. Some of these individuals do not deserve awards and I won't sign my name to it, but someone else might, and I believe it will negatively impact the rest of the troops. This is my 4th deployment. I've seen some that don't deserve awards get them, but never on this level.

What appears to start out as a question about calendars and training schedules turns quickly to a common leadership challenge: How do you influence your higher headquarters? And Jamie's situation is similar to but more values laden than Tommy's. Members respond to these questions by sharing their own experiences. Josh, for example, explains to Jamie how he was in a similar situation with awards and took a hard stance only to lose the argument and, in the process, to severely strain his relationship with his boss, his key subordinate leaders, and the soldier who got the award in the end. Another member recommends that Jamie choose his battles wisely and to keep in mind that, as Josh described, "You could lose your ability to take care of your soldiers on future issues that come up because you have lost your credibility over something that might not be as important as it appears right now." Finally, another member reminds Jamie that he's not in it alone and recommends that he reach out to his First Sergeant, a seasoned sister company commander, or even his boss—with humility—for coaching on this issue.

This front-porch conversation has largely defined the Company Command forum. However, by 2007 we were on the sidelines watching the likes of Twitter and Facebook develop new, exciting ways for people to connect with each other. We felt uniquely positioned to integrate the best new technologies into the army context, and so we began to seek funding and to think deeply about the kinds of features and capabilities that would complement the front-porch conversation and reinforce our vision for connecting leaders. We needed to take action on something we already knew: To be on the cutting edge requires continuous innovation and never-ending experimentation.

Professional Forums 2.0

In 2008, with sponsorship from the Army Chief Information Officer, we secured a research grant and began developing and integrating Web 2.0–style features and design. We named the redesigned learning system "MilSpace," which included both the Platoon Leader and the Company Command forums along with a suite of Web 2.0–style features. One of the features that immediately took off was the status update (aka micro blog), which we named SITREP—army lingo for situation report, a term that resonates with army leaders (see Figure 24.1). The question we ask members is, "What are you doing/learning today? SITREP, over." We believe that answering this question regularly, in the context of a professional community, creates value for both the person answering it and the broader community that reads it. Moreover, we believe that regularly answering that question will begin to positively influence what professionals are doing and learning.

Figure 24.1 Actual SITREP Examples

Andrew is packing for redeployment.

Andrea is loving life.

Thomas is "Hard pressed on my right. My center is yielding. Impossible to maneuver. Situation excellent, I am attacking." –Ferdinand Foch at the Battle of the Marne.

Brett is planning a CFLX and studying for Jumpmaster School.

Jason is working on hand receipts.

Jamie is writing end-of-tour awards.

Rebecca is at AMEDD CCC.

Sean is working NCOERs, inventories, USRs, taskings, pre-deployment training, LBE, Hail and Farewell, & my daughter's dance class this evening. Smile, it could be worse.

Jeff is downrange, Afghanistan… improving the Afghan police.

Nicholas is moving to Bragg next week.

Michael is bringing CrossFit to Korea.

Brian is preparing to take command of an HR Company Rear D.

David is almost 100 days into command. From day 1 to now is almost like night and day. "Until you have walked a mile in another man's shoes, you just don't know."

Charles is fighting at the forward edge of freedom…Assassins!

Chalmus prepping 4 deployment again.

James is back from Iraq.

Jeremie is in the middle of inventories.

When SITREPs are submitted, they post onto a member's personal page, becoming a micro-journal and a catalyst for reflection on the member's experience. Not only that, but friends and mentors can track a member and provide direct feedback through the form of "Liking" or "Commenting" on a SITREP. SITREPs also post into MilSpace Tracker, an activity feed of everything happening across the MilSpace system. This visibility of SITREPs can impact the learning of members who become aware of what others are doing and learning. For example, I posted a SITREP stating that I was putting together a book of Afghanistan lessons learned from the commanders in the 506th Infantry Regiment (the Currahees, made famous in the *Band of Brothers* HBO miniseries). Within minutes, a current company commander on the ground in Afghanistan emailed me: "I am in Afghanistan. I have your last *Afghan Lesson Learned* book that the unit I replaced left for me. I saw your SITREP, and I'm wondering when I can get my hands on the new one?" Within a week, we mailed him a hard copy of the new book. He was connected to the hard-earned insights of dozens of commanders who had just finished a year-long combat tour not too far from where he was currently serving, and with the book came access to the contributors, because their email addresses were included with the book.

Figure 24.2 provides another example, with identifying information removed, of a SITREP with a comment from an experienced member. William was not necessarily looking for help, but because he took the time to describe what he was doing, members connected him to content that might be relevant to his current experience. Similarly, when another member posted, "Changing command in Iraq," a leader in the forum could direct him to a great article and set of discussions on the unique challenges of changing command while deployed.

Furthermore, the SITREP feature lowers the barrier to participation and engagement in the forum. Members who might have hesitated to engage in a discussion thread in the Company Command forum feel less threatened when they are posting a SITREP to their personal space. Matthew, for example, wrote, "Trying to find COC [change of command] brief powerpoints to help make one for upcoming COC." Eleven minutes later, Tim, serving as a new commander in the same battalion but who had yet to meet Matthew, commented, "Just sent some stuff to your Fort Drum email. Hope that helps." Matthew had never posted anything in the CC forum, but the SITREP was easy and low threat.

Finally, the SITREP feature opens up the possibility for members to be more personal, for that human voice, a la *Cluetrain* (Levine et al., 2001), to come out in the forum in a way that it just doesn't otherwise. In the process of writing this chapter, I asked a current platoon leader named

Figure 24.2 Example SITREP With Comment

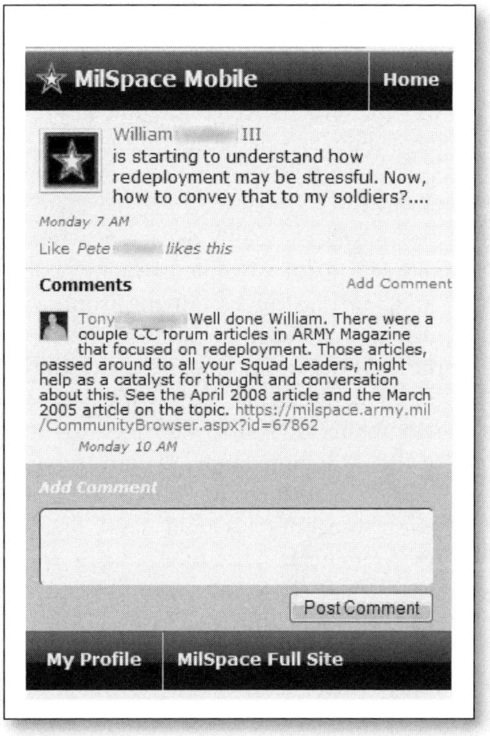

Tim what he thought of SITREP. He responded from Balad, Iraq:

> I have to be honest, when I first saw the "What are you doing/learning today?" I immediately thought to myself that this was the Army's feeble attempt at creating a military safe facebook or twitter. I had absolutely no intent on ever using the feature. However, I started viewing the milspace "wall" or activity board and saw a lot of updates from people doing various things ranging from griping, to mundane, to pointless (such as the majority of my updates :)) to things that I could either help with, such as researching SOP's, to figuring out how to be a maintenance PL, to reading "XYZ" or researching "ABC." If I could assist someone, I would send them a quick email. If what others were doing was of interest to me I would research, read, or look into it—I'm a sucker for personal and professional development. I then started to update my own SITREP to try and elicit a response from others. On Facebook, I couldn't necessarily post my happiness of my 14-year old daughter's boyfriend's family moving away—because she would see it, and then I'd have to buy her something expensive to make it up to her (teenage girls you know). But, by posting it as a SITREP I was not only looking for an outlet to express my joy, but hoping to elicit a response, which I received, in the form of tips from someone else who had a teenage daughter. I also use SITREPs as a litmus test, of sorts. I post something that I'm doing, and I get a few comments or "likes," and I know that I'm not alone or I'm on the right track.

Although, as I mentioned, the mainstay of the forums has always been the front porch conversation, members have posted over 5,000 SITREPS in the last year, actually edging out conversation in terms of numbers of posts. SITREPs are personal; they foster a sense of community and a sense of connectedness—and, they absolutely trigger professional learning.

Designed Learning Interventions

One thing we know is that design of the online space is critical—and we have designed our space with three primary effects in mind: (1) to connect members with each other and to relevant content; (2) to be a catalyst for conversation; and (3) to foster a sense of professional community. Those three design elements create a structure that is conducive to learning in many types of environments to include an online community. The SITREP feature, situated in the context of a professional community, is helping achieve the desired effects, and it is fostering learning. One way you could look at it is in terms of a designed learning intervention. Three additional learning interventions that I will discuss here are the CC Jam and ARMY Magazine, the MilSpace Leader Challenge, and the Pro-Reading Challenge.

CC JAM AND ARMY MAGAZINE

Once a month, the forum's core team crafts an engaging question about a relevant topic and emails it out to all members of the Company Command forum; we call it the CC Jam.[3] Our desire is for the CC Jam to be a catalyst for thought and conversation across the army and for company commanders to learn and become more effective as a result. Last month's question was especially succinct:

> SUBJECT: CC JAM, "Leader or Manager?"
>
> We pride ourselves on being leaders, but what we really need these days are managers. Agree? Disagree?

This one struck a chord, inciting passionate, long responses. The conversation continues but, as of today, there are 83 replies totaling 12,000 words. In the conversation, members disagree with each other but do it respectfully; the tone is positive. Members often acknowledge another member's reply and provide positive feedback to those they appreciate. They consult the literature (both army doctrine and the broader academic and managerial literature) to advance our understanding of this topic. Although many members make strong arguments one way or the other, at the end of the day there is no pat answer to the question and no real consensus achieved. As we describe in our book *Company Command: Unleashing the Power of the Army Profession*, a good conversation causes some participants to see new connections in what they already know, provides them insight into other members' reasoning, broadens their perspective, helps them question their own assumptions, and highlights gaps between their views and those of other professionals (Dixon et al., 2005, pp. 57–58). We note, "Conversations transform the thinking of the company commanders involved in them . . . cause participants to think, and it is this internal thinking process that creates insights for those involved in the conversation" (p. 58).

Another memorable CC Jam was titled, "Do you follow a stupid order?" We wrote up the Jam like this (and, yes, it was true):

> Last month, I was sitting with a group of future platoon leaders, listening to a division commander talk about leadership challenges in combat. At one point, he paused and said, "Ok, what about when you get a stupid order. What do you do? Do you follow a stupid order?"
>
> Most of us can probably think of a not-so-bright order that we've issued ourselves, so this isn't about pointing the finger. But this is a legitimate question and one that we think would be valuable to discuss as a profession.
>
> Have you been in a situation when an order didn't seem to make sense? What were your options? What was at stake? What did you do?

There were 60 replies to this CC Jam, most of them personal stories relating "stupid order" experiences. The overall theme that emerged is that professional officers obey legal orders but have obligations to provide the boss feedback and alternative options when the order is "not so bright." However, what also emerges in the stories is that life is complex and, despite the espoused value of obedience, leaders sometimes "do what it takes" to keep their soldiers safe; and this willingness to go around the boss emerges in organizations where the boss doesn't listen or is judged to be incompetent over time.

The CC Jams create a lot of activity and opportunities to learn in the forum. Sometimes, though, like at the end of a great in-person conversation, you find yourself wanting a little more, wanting the conversation not to simply fade away. We considered different ways to more effectively "close out" a conversation. What we decided to do was to translate the monthly CC Jams into the form of a magazine article—to organize the online conversation, to hone it down to 3,000 or so words, and to present it as a conversation by and for company commanders. In March of 2005, the Association of the United States Army (AUSA) created a home for this monthly article in their ARMY Magazine—what became the Company Command Column.

There are a number of positive effects of doing the monthly article. It definitely closes out the conversation with a positive bang. And the magazine deadline motivates us and helps us to be more disciplined about launching an engaging CC Jam every month and then following up to organize it into an article. (If you are like us, a solid deadline can be a great way to make sure you get things done.) Moreover, the article serves as a catalyst for us to connect with the contributors, who always review their own input and decide if they want it to appear in an article that will be read outside of the member-only forum. This is a back-and-forth process that includes asking for permission, additional information, and even photographs to make the article more interesting. As a result, we get to know many of the active participants in the forum in a way we would not otherwise, and both the process and having their contribution published in a hard-print magazine fosters in them a new regard for the forum. Finally, this activity means that the wider army—to include senior army leaders—gains access to some of the best content in the forums. Tens of thousands more leaders are exposed to a unique "learning curriculum" and gain a sense of appreciation for the forum, even if they are not eligible to be members. Reading some of the article titles, depicted in Figure 24.3 below, may further reinforce the cumulative positive impact of this activity and a sense for how it serves as a part of the informal leadership curriculum.

THE MILSPACE LEADER CHALLENGE

Another learning intervention is the MilSpace Leader Challenge, an interactive, video-based vignette that features a dilemma-type scenario that a leader has experienced (see Figure 24.4 for a screen shot of the website). We have said that actual leadership experience is what develops us the most, and challenging experiences are the best leader development curriculum—especially when you include reflective conversation about those experiences. The Leader Challenge concept builds on this idea. We ask leaders in combat to tell us stories on videotape about their most challenging experiences—hard hitting, dilemma-type situations that weren't necessarily covered in their training. We then bring those video clips into the online community and ask members to put themselves in the leader's shoes and to succinctly respond: "What are your considerations . . . What would you do?" (in 500 characters or less). When members submit a response, they then gain access to the responses of all those who have taken the challenge, as well as to the "rest of the story" video in which the protagonist describes what he or she did—not "the answer" but, rather, what actually happened.

The following examples will give you a better feel for what these leader challenge

Figure 24.3 ARMY Magazine Company Command Article Titles

"Preparing for Command" "Giving Up Command" "Redeployed, Now What?"

"Making Sense of Killing" "Leadership and the Death of a Soldier" "Leading Up"

"Why Bother With the Media?" "Combined Action in Afghanistan"

"The Art of Rewarding Soldiers" "Zero KIAs as an Organizational Goal?"

"Force Protection From the 'Hidden Wounds' of War" "Second Guessing Our Decisions"

"Understanding What Causes Combat Stress, PTSD, & What Leaders Can Do"

"Switching Gears in the Counterinsurgency Fight" "Leading Our Soldiers to Fight With Honor"

"Iraqi Security Forces Galvanized Into Action" "Is Training Management Still Relevant?"

Figure 24.4 Leader Challenge Design

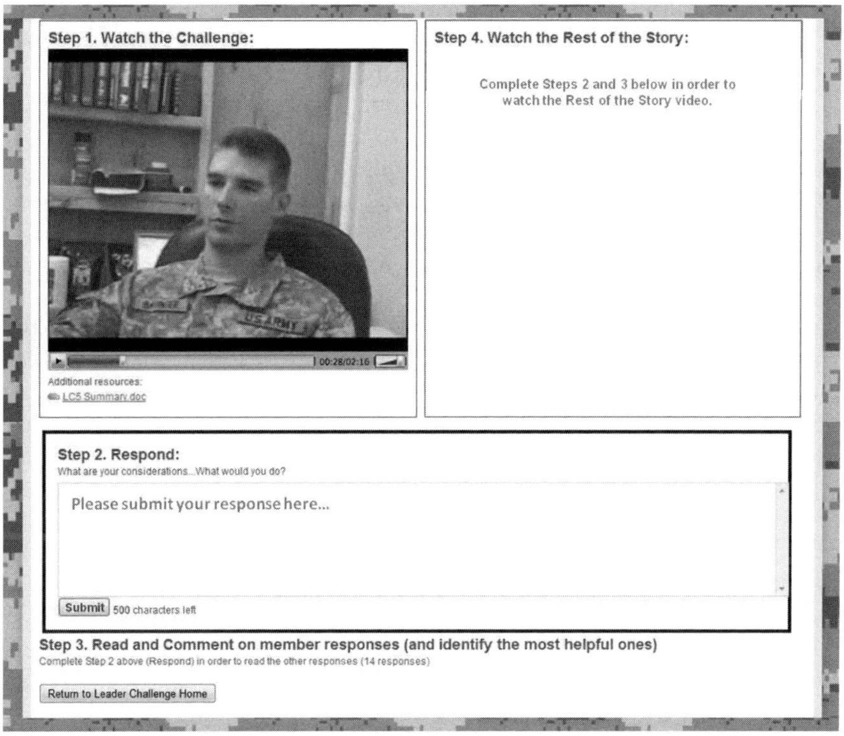

vignettes are like. As you read them, imagine a young army leader telling the story on videotape from the front lines:

> My best friend Robbie was killed by an IED. That night was a long and emotional night.
>
> The very next morning, LTC Jones called me in to tell me I was moving from the battalion operations office down to take over Robbie's platoon, IMMEDIATELY!

> We were high up in the mountains observing a favorite enemy ambush location. Are those insurgents on the rooftop, or are they innocent goat herders? I see a weapon; yes, that looks like a weapon. Do you see the weapon?
>
> My forward observer sitting next to me says, "Yes, I'm pretty sure that is a weapon!"
>
> We are too far away to engage with direct fire, and I can't make radio communications with our mounted patrol that is coming up the road any minute. This is the same spot where one of our guys was killed last week. Crap, what am I going to do?

> Once we passed the 8-month mark, I started witnessing my 2nd squad leader growing more and more risk averse. One morning in the chow line I overheard PFC Jones talking about how they sat in a building for eight hours instead of patrolling—something that, if true, is at odds with what the squad leader reported in his patrol debrief.

> Coming back from an all-night foot patrol, SGT Hollings was hit by an IED. He didn't make it. After getting him

MEDEVAC'd out, I began thinking about what I was going to tell the platoon once we got back to our base. Then, the commander called and gave me a direct order to clear the nearest village, where the guys who put in the IED could be located—a mission that would easily take eight hours. My guys were out of food and water, were already physically smoked, and they were pissed off about SGT H. He was easily the men's favorite team leader, and there's no way those people [Iraqis] didn't know something about that IED. Then my trusted platoon sergeant tells me, "Sir, there is no way we can do this mission. Look at the guys!" At that point, my company commander called again to find out why I wasn't moving to the village. What do I do?

These are the challenging experiences that our junior leaders in the army are having. Situated in the Company Command and Platoon Leader forums, the leader challenge stories become a cutting-edge leader-development curriculum.

One practice that has worked well for us is to ask a set of very experienced leaders to respond to a new leader challenge so that each newly published challenge starts out with a dozen or so exceptional responses. I have personally found reading experienced leaders' responses to be the most developmental part of the experience because, invariably, those responses are nuanced and laced with insight and deeper meaning.

As participants read through other members' responses, they can vote those responses "Helpful" as well as "Comment" on them. This wisdom-of-crowds effect helps bubble the most helpful responses to the top of the list. Moreover, when you receive a "Helpful" vote or a "Comment," a notification email lets you know. We designed the notification to positively reinforce your participation and to invite you back into the experience. Figure 24.5 provides an example.

Figure 24.5 Leader Challenge Auto-Notification Email Example

EMAIL SUBJECT: Your leader challenge response was spot on

EMAIL BODY: William xxxxx likes your response to LC2 "Combat Leadership" -- and just marked it as "HELPFUL." This means your response will bubble to the top of the responses and will be read by more members.

Your LC2 response: Considerations: black on food and water, the Soldiers may be physically at their limit, routes are "black" so vehicular support is an issue, just had a soldier killed, and the platoon isn't fully read in on what is happening. Given that the AO was controlled by AQI, I don't think a hasty reaction will yield results (not wise). I would ask to move back to the COP to resupply and reorganize/plan. If the answer is "No," I would establish an ORP, talk to the PLT, assess/plan before just launching.

--Now, go back into the Leader Challenge to read William xxxxx's response and to help identify other "HELPFUL" responses:

[hyperlink to this Leader Challenge]

Notice that we include the actual text of the member's response to the leader challenge; we know that members will read and reflect on their response as a result, and the hyperlink invites them back into the leader challenge space to read and comment on others' responses. This way, the learning experience is extended beyond the few minutes that it took to take the challenge initially. This process has the potential to shift the learning curve for leaders so that they arrive in the actual experience at a different level of preparation.

Leaders can engage in Leader Challenges to develop themselves and, as many leaders are doing, they can use Leader Challenges to develop their teams of leaders. Ari, a current company commander, serving in Iraq as I write, shared this about how he used the MilSpace Leader Challenges during his unit's preparation for the combat deployment:

> I like the Leader Challenges because they force you to very succinctly explain a difficult choice. I found them to be a good tool to generate conversation with my lieutenants about battlefield ethics. The first one that we all did I assigned as homework, and the next two we did at work where I applied a short time hack to force them to quickly choose and explain themselves. Using the basic construct of the MilSpace Challenges, my 1SG and I developed additional scenarios based on my NCO's previous combat tours, which we used with all the soldiers in the unit. As a result, we were able to talk about ethics in general, and I was able to lay out my own expectations. We all know that a commander cannot be everywhere at all times, and I want my subordinates to make the appropriate judgment decisions when called upon to do so.

This example conveys that leaders are not only leveraging MilSpace Leader Challenges for their own development and that of their subordinate leaders, but they are also applying the methodology in ways that are making their entire organization more effective.

The Leader Challenges have also been well-received by cadets in ROTC and at West Point who are, among other things, all preparing to be commissioned as army lieutenants and to lead soldiers. Kim, a current army platoon leader, was introduced to the Platoon Leader forum and Leader Challenges while she was a cadet at West Point. She writes:

> I've been a platoon leader for 7 months now. Working through the "Leader Challenges" helped teach me how to assess a situation from every angle. This has set me apart from my peers, and, as a 2nd Lieutenant, my company commander has come to respect me and trust that I'll get things done. He's having me become the XO when we deploy because they trust my decision making capabilities. The PL forum teaches you how to think through a situation and also introduces you to more of the military way of thinking.

For the first time in history, officer apprentices are able to listen in and engage in the ongoing conversation of the army profession before they are commissioned. The conversation in the forum and engagement in leader challenges becomes a living curriculum, grounded in the cutting-edge experiences of actual platoon leaders. By engaging in the forum, cadets learn how "to be" officers in a way that was not possible before. And they depart West Point, like Kim, further along the learning curve and better equipped to be exceptional leaders.[4]

THE PRO-READING CHALLENGE

The basic concept of the Pro-Reading Challenge is for teams of leaders to read and talk about developmental books with each other. We invite company commanders to take on this challenge, and we give them the resources to do it. Those who respond to the challenge select a book, and we send them free copies to read with their lieutenants. We then establish a space in the online forum for them to talk about the book.

Over the last six months, we've shipped 266 books. But the design of the Pro-Reading Challenge allows it to reach further than the realms of the leaders who visibly participate. We affix a sticker to the inside front cover of the books, communicating that the book belongs to the profession and for the officer to sign it and pass it on to another leader once it has been read, creating a chain of reading with a positive, "pay-it-forward" ripple effect. And because part of the discussion happens in the online space, thousands of MilSpace members gain visibility of what would otherwise be completely hidden to the profession. Each participating commander serves as a positive role model when it comes to leveraging professional reading to develop their leaders and to make their team more effective.

When we launch a commander's pro-reading page, we begin by posting a question for the commander: "To kick off your forum, I'll throw out a two-part question for you. Why did you choose this book, and what do you hope your leaders get out of reading it?" Stephen, the most recent commander to participate, selected the book *Ghost Wars* by Steve Coll (2004). Stephen is focused on preparing his leaders for another deployment to Afghanistan. Here is his kickoff response:

> I read this book prior to deploying to Afghanistan and again while I was there. The historical aspects it provided on Afghanistan and the different ethnic sects helped me understand the background on many of the people I interacted with daily. It hit home for me one day while I was in a large meeting room with an Afghan corps commander, many brigade and battalion commanders, and their US counterparts. There was a large mural of Ahmed Shah Massood, the Tajik military hero from the war with the Soviet Union. Being that the majority of higher level officers were from the north, many were Tajik, I understand why next to a mural of Hamid Karzai there was another of Massood, who was killed on SEP 10, 2001.
>
> It also helped me understand how Al Qaeda was able to gain a foothold in the country. I learned that Osama bin Laden was conducting stability and support operations (SASO) back during the Russian occupation by building hospitals in Khost and Paktika provinces, which I could relate to because I was in both.
>
> Lastly, many of the main players we hear about these days were around during the Mujahedeen days—e.g., Haqqani and Hekmayter—now lead the most dangerous Taliban networks, HQN and HIG.
>
> This is a good book for company-level leaders to read prior to deployment and it is worth revisiting during deployment. I haven't read many books on the history of Afghanistan, but I would guess this is about as good a history book as we need. Platoon leaders need to understand what's going on around them with the social fabric of society and the cultural aspects of the Afghan military to be effective. One day, when he's partnered with an Afghan company and he sees Tajiks and Pashtuns fighting each other, he'll have a better understanding that it's not because one of them got a little more chow at the mess hall, it's probably due to a long-standing grudge.

Another commander, Heath, selected *Words for Warriors*, by Colonel Ralph Puckett (2007). Here is his kickoff response:

> Thank you, indeed, for this program—and the opportunity! I decided to run with Colonel Puckett's book for one big reason: Alignment of training philosophy and values.

Our company has pretty much done a facelift of senior leaders. With minimal train-up time until we have a National Training Center rotation and, ultimately, deployment, I don't have the luxury of developing leaders the way I'd like to. This book, along with my emphasis on specific training goals, really drives home a lot of the thought processes, behind-the-scene actions, and development for my leaders.

I spoke with some of my personal mentors and some of the mentors from this site about "philosophy-type" versus "how-to-type" books as a first book to go with. There are reasons to do both types first. Colonel Puckett really incorporates both in his writing. It seemed that this was just the best choice.

I really want my leaders to get passionate, absolutely 100% in love with their soldiers. It will be then that they will sacrifice their own energies to best prepare our Soldiers for the fight. It is obvious that Colonel Puckett is passionate about his soldiers; he is what "Right" looks like, and worth attempting to emulate.

If you are like me, reading through these responses makes you want to read the books. Now picture the impact on the lieutenants. Picture the effect on the other MilSpace members who will read these notes.

Company commanders typically spend several weeks discussing the book, combining both online and face-to-face discussions. Most have found it effective to ask a series of questions in the online forum, perhaps one a week, which everyone has to reply to, and then to meet periodically in person to talk about it. The online conversation serves as a primer for the in-person conversation, which is richer and more engaging as a result. Additional techniques that commanders have employed include rotating the role of conversation facilitator and closing the activity out by having each participant summarize their key takeaways from the book.

In order to get a sense for what actually happens in the Company Command forum, we have looked at four examples: SITREPs, the CC Jam, the Leader Challenge, and the Pro-Reading Challenge. The ongoing experiences of the "students" *is* the learning curriculum. And it is the learning interventions, designed to connect leaders in conversation about those experiences, that bring the informal learning system to life.

Core Group

Reflecting on the story of the Company Command forum in light of this book's main topic, teaching leadership, it occurs to me that there are two different stories to tell. One is the story of company commanders in general—regular members who engage in the online forum and become more effective leaders as a result. We have been primarily talking about this group so far. A second story actually makes the first story possible but is less obvious. It is the story of a smaller, socially connected, and committed group of members that emerges to serve the community. Without this smaller group, the community would dry up, and there would be no learning. As we will see, this smaller group of members has a broader leadership curriculum, and its members learn more even as they create the conditions that allow the larger community to learn. Using the teaching metaphor, we could describe these members as the "honors" class.

In any social system, especially an informal or volunteer-based system, there are varying degrees of participation. A snapshot at one point in time typically reveals a large number of people who are nominally active (or peripheral), and progressively smaller numbers of people who are more active and especially active. The smaller, especially active group within the system has been called the core group. This pattern of a small, core group taking responsibility for the majority of activity within the system is pervasive in just about every informal social system. Wenger,

McDermott, and Snyder (2002) describe the core group as one of three main levels of participation in a community of practice:

> The first [of three levels of participation] is a small core group of people who actively participate in discussions, even debates, in the public community forum. They often take on community projects, identify topics for the community to address, and move the community along its learning agenda. **This group is the heart of the community.** As the community matures, this core group takes on much of the community's leadership, its members becoming auxiliaries to the community coordinator. But this group is usually rather small, only 10 to 15 percent of the whole community. (p. 56, emphasis added)

You find this pattern of participation in churches, community-based organizations, and online communities—and it is the pattern we have seen in the Company Command forum.

If you would, please take a minute to stop reading and to think about a time in your life when you became involved as a volunteer in some kind of informal social system. Over time, you became increasingly involved to the point where you may have even found yourself in a leadership role within the group. Your example might be church-related, the Boy Scouts, a Parent Teacher Association (PTA), or, perhaps, a committee at your work that you volunteered for and in which, over time, you found yourself serving a leadership role. You didn't magically start in this leadership role. What is the story of your journey from the periphery to the core? What were the key events and inflection points that altered your trajectory on this journey to a place of leadership? As we gain insight into this process, we gain understanding about how to cultivate and sustain vibrant core groups and, therefore, vibrant learning communities.

When we originally created the Company Command forum, a team of 8–12 of us worked energetically behind the scenes to be catalysts for connections and conversation, to create great content, and to foster a sense of professional community. We called ourselves the CC Team; we were the core group. We were all volunteers, running on passion, pride of creation, and a deep commitment to give back and to make a difference. Over time, CC Team members moved on and others stepped up to undertake leadership roles in the forum.

We intuitively understood that the core group was critical to success, and, as the "coordinators," we began to more deliberately focus on growing the team. We began convening, for example, annual gatherings of the CC Team to build relationships; to create shared understanding of purpose, vision, and values; and to equip new team members in their roles as volunteer leaders in the forum. We started reading and discussing a book at least once a year (our annual CC Team Pro-Reading Challenge), with our most recent book being *Switch: How to Change Things When Change Is Hard*, by Chip and Dan Heath (2010). We have quarterly team phone calls, communicate in a "team-only" part of the online forum, encourage each other, wear CC hats, and drink out of CC mugs.

Becoming a Leader: Moving From the Periphery to the Core

If indeed the success of the larger community is contingent upon the vitality of the core group, we wanted to better understand the process whereby members of the community moved from a peripheral level of participation to becoming leaders in the community. In my research, I explored this process by studying individual core group members' stories of becoming community leaders, which we now call "becoming" stories.

The becoming journey includes a mutually reinforcing pattern of participation and connection, where participation is an observable act in the online forum (e.g., asking a question or engaging in an online conversation) and connection is a thread of affiliation between two members, a relationship. Participation and connection are co-creative. Participation creates connection, which deepens participation—and vice versa. This process begins with the initial interaction and it is continuous thereafter, with a positive, cumulative effect over time. "Acts" of participation increase and connections between people thicken into relationships. The initial connection typically includes a warm welcoming as well as acknowledgment and appreciation of the other's participation. One CC Team member, Martin, who was a company commander in Iraq at the time, describes his experience:

> One of the guys wrote me and said, "Hey, saw your post—it's good stuff; we're glad to have you; welcome aboard; we think you're gonna enjoy the website, etc., etc." And then I wrote him back and said, "Well, thanks for such a warm welcome," you know, and we started a little conversation about who I was and what the website was about, and then they just came right out and said . . . "Hey, we're looking for somebody to run the Aviation site. Are you interested?" And I allowed as how I wasn't sure how much time I could dedicate to it being as how we were deployed, but, yes, I was definitely interested in doing it, and it kind of grew from there.

As we see in this interview excerpt, another step in the prototypical becoming journey is that at some point in the iterative cycle of participation and connection, the future core group member is invited to take greater responsibility in an area that matches well with his or her background and passion. Our assumption is that company commanders who become active members of the online forum have experience with and passion for certain aspects of command. It is therefore our goal to discover the person's talent/passion, and then to give the person a platform to more fully be his or her self—and to more fully bring themselves to the community. Roy, another CC Team member, provides valuable insight into how this can occur:

> And it was at that point that Tommy contacted me and sent me an email saying, "Hey, I saw your post, I looked at your dog tag [member profile]. I really think you are somebody that we would benefit from having on our team. Are you in a position to contribute to the profession?" . . . And so Tommy and I had a phone conversation; we talked about different places to contribute, different ways to contribute . . . [We] finally settled that I would jump into the Soldiers and Families [topic] . . . I felt strongly about the topic because in my experience it was something that really mattered to soldiers and it was one of those intangibles that really made a difference in how prepared your soldiers were and how prepared they felt . . . Soldiers and Families was a place where I felt that I could advance the level of knowledge and the level of discussion that was present and it was an area where I felt that I could really make a difference . . .

Inviting members to undertake a leadership role serves as an invitation for them to take additional responsibility, and it grants them permission to take more initiative. Roy reflects on how the invitation to a leadership role influenced the nature of his participation:

> [Without having a role], I think I would have been active but I would not have taken any type of leadership or organizational role because I simply would not have felt the confidence to do that. I

> certainly felt like I had a responsibility to do it, but without that conversation, without that outreach from another team member and that empowering of, "We want you to take this part of it," I would not have felt that I had the authority to do the kinds of things like reaching out to team members and saying, "Hey, we want you on board, we think you're a great person" etc. So, yeah, I don't think I would have been anywhere near as engaged in CompanyCommand as I have been over the last two years.

Thus, we see that having a leadership role—and especially one that is aligned with the member's talents and expertise—plays an important role in the becoming process.

Of note, the becoming story does not end with taking on a leadership role; rather, that moment is a key inflection point in that member's trajectory. Undertaking a leadership role is not the end state but rather a catalyst for a richer experience. The iterative process of participation and connection continues, with the quality of those interactions growing—creating a cumulative, positive effect on the person. If the initial interaction and participation/connection cycle is the key to growing a core group, it is the series of positive (and reinforcing) experiences that happen to a person after they assume a leadership role that are vital to sustaining the core group.

Meaning Sustains the Core Group

We have looked at the process whereby members of the CC forum move from the periphery to the core, but why do they do it? What motivates them to volunteer and to continue giving of themselves when they don't have time for the things they already have piled on their plates? Recall your own example of becoming involved as a volunteer in some informal group. Perhaps your story goes something like this:

> I discovered the group through a friend who was a real advocate for what they were doing. She invited me to attend a meeting and to share my own perspective on the issues. I met several like-minded people and developed a relationship with one of the founding leaders who invited me to take on a specific assignment and then that led to this and, before I knew it, I was leading a project myself.

With your own example in mind, I'd like you to consider this: **As you reflect back on your time being part of that team—your experiences, the work you did, etc.—what did it mean to you to be involved like that? You invested a lot of time and energy into that effort. I'm wondering what drove you, what caused you to invest so much of yourself?** In our answers to these questions we begin to tease out key insights about why core group members volunteer to do more than they have to, why they become leaders, and why they sustain their leadership.

> The big insight that emerged in my study of CC team members is that their experience as core group members is meaningful to them, and it is the meaningful nature of their iterative experiences as active members of the core group that motivates them to continue to participate. More practically, however, I discovered that there were specific aspects of their experience as core group members that they found especially meaningful: making a contribution, connecting with other people, and becoming more effective personally. For us, this was a breakthrough insight! It led to a definition for meaningful action in an informal social system: An action, situated in the purposeful context of the community of practice, is meaningful to me when (1) I make a tangible contribution to a valued other and/or the community (**to contribute**); (2) I become more socially connected and achieve greater solidarity

> with other members (**to connect**); or (3) I become more personally effective (**to develop personally**). (Burgess, 2010)

All three are meaningful as they relate to the purpose of the CC forum, which is to improve the effectiveness of company commanders and to advance the practice of company command. To clarify this important point, *contribution*, *connection*, and *personal development* are purposeful in that they all relate directly back to the work to which these leaders have committed themselves: being army professionals. The members' *contribution* is situated in the context of helping army company commanders become more effective as well as advancing the profession more generally. The members' *connection* occurs in the context of relationships with people that share their professional aspirations; and the members' *personal development* is situated in the context of becoming more effective army leaders. In this way, meaning is situated in purpose.

We often ask ourselves, "How can we increase member participation?" However, a more productive question might be: "What can be done to increase the frequency and quality of member experiences, in terms of the meaningfulness of those experiences, as perceived by the members?" One way of framing this shift is in terms of leadership: a shift away from leadership as influence, toward leadership as meaning-creation. We could define leadership in an informal social system as a process whereby members foster the creation of meaning for each other. And based on what we've learned, it is possible to be more specific:

> Leadership is a process whereby members (1) create opportunities for each other to make tangible contributions, (2) cultivate a more socially connected network of members, and (3) develop each other.

Acts of leadership cultivate a vibrant core group and directly serve the purpose of the larger social system, which, in the case of the Company Command forum, is to increase company commander effectiveness.

This new understanding changes the way that we (the CC Team) see what is happening in the CC forum. When Bill asks a question in the forum, we appreciate it because it creates opportunities for John to contribute and to connect with Bill. Members of the core group reach out and invite other experienced members to respond to the question not only because we want to serve Bill, but also because we know that answering his question will be valuable to the question answerer. We watch for emerging leaders, we reach out to them and get to know them, and we invite them to bring themselves to the table and to take concrete action. We encourage feedback and closing the loop so that contributors gain a sense of the tangible impact they are making for others and the profession. We are intentional about creating exciting developmental experiences for each other and especially experiences that involve two or more doing something tangible together. We expose each other to cutting-edge people and ideas. In the process, we begin to satisfy our deep desire to connect with each other, to give back, and to learn and become more effective leaders.

As I mentioned earlier, we started with a core group of 8–12 volunteers. Although the number of overall forum members has skyrocketed to over 10,000, the number of fully engaged CC team members has stayed relatively static (15–25). There has been a continuous flow of new leaders emerging as others transition out of an active role; those who transition out remain on as part of the looser network of alumni, which, after ten years, numbers around 150 or so. That is 150 army officers who have matriculated through a leadership curriculum that the formal organization has absolutely zero awareness of. One hundred and fifty leaders who are more effective and who are more satisfied and who are sharing what they've learned with their subordinate leaders as they advance through the ranks into positions of greater influence in the army. From the perspective of teaching leadership, this "honors" class graduates from the ranks of the active CC Team better equipped to lead than they otherwise would have been and better connected to a network of like-hearted peers, a band of brothers, that are likewise committed to serving their soldiers and growing combat-effective organizations.

Conclusion

This book is about teaching leadership, so it is through that lens that we have looked at the Company Command forum. We introduced the idea that leadership can be taught outside the formal organizational structure. This is not a story about informal leaders in an organization so much as it is a story about an informal organization, a grassroots learning network, that was created inside the formal organization and exists to improve the effectiveness of its members. And, because these members are also "official" leaders in the formal organization (company commanders), the formal organization becomes more effective as a result of their improved effectiveness. Moreover, we have seen that intentionality of process and designed learning interventions situated in the informal network—interventions that are not part of the formal army organization—are critical to the success of the formal organization. The experience of the Company Command Forum teaches us that leaders who engage in vibrant professional forums will become more effective and they will in turn grow more effective organizations. They will learn to be better leaders.

Notes

1. A company (also battery, troop, detachment) is an organizational unit in the US Army comprised of about 100 soldiers. A captain with anywhere from five to eight years of service in the army leads this organization for an average of eighteen months as the company commander. This is the first level of leadership granted full command authority, which includes the authority to administer the Uniform Code of Military Justice (UCMJ). Due to the nature of the current operating environment—complex and rapidly evolving—power and responsibility are being increasingly delegated to the company level. The decentralized nature of modern warfare, combined with a significant increase in technological capabilities, has resulted in company commanders having more responsibility and power than ever before. Finally, every soldier in the army is assigned to a company. Thus, an initiative that improves the effectiveness of company commanders is strategic.

2. Current staffing at West Point includes two lieutenant colonels (PhDs), a rotating junior officer with recent experience commanding troops, and a technologist who plays an enormous role in the continuous development of the software. The team is working to add a research assistant to the official books.

3. To read more about the process of crafting and facilitating a priority conversation (aka "jam"), see Chapter 9, "Making the Most of Online Conversation" in our book *Company Command: Unleashing the Power of the Army Profession* (Dixon et al., 2005).

4. For research on the effectiveness of the leader challenge as a learning intervention, see Chris Miller, et al., "Leader Challenge: A Platform, for Training and Developing Leaders" (2009); for the theoretical underpinning informing the leader challenge process, see Sternberg et al., *Practical Intelligence in Everyday Life* (2000).

References

Burgess, A. (2010). From the periphery to the core: Understanding the process whereby members of a distributed community of practice become leaders of a community (and what the experience means to them). In A. Green, M. Stankosky, & Vandergriff (Eds.), *In search of knowledge management: Pursuing primary principles* (pp. 287–331). Bingley, UK: Emerald Group Publishing Limited.

Coll, S. (2004). *Ghost wars: The secret history of the CIA, Afghanistan, and bin Laden, from the Soviet invasion to September 10, 2001.* New York: Penguin Press.

Dixon, N. M., Allen, N., Burgess, T., Kilner, P., & Schweitzer, S. (2005). *Company command: Unleashing the power of the army profession.* West Point, NY: Center for the Advancement of Leader Development & Organizational Learning.

Heath, C., & Heath, D. (2010). *Switch: How to change things when change is hard.* New York: Broadway Books.

Levine, R., Locke, C., Searls, D., & Weinberger, D. (2001). *The Cluetrain manifesto: The end of business as usual.* New York: Perseus.

Miller, C., Self, N., & Garven, S. (2009). Leader challenge: A platform for training and developing leaders. Paper presented at the Interservice/Industry Training, Simulation, and Education Conference (I/ITSEC).

Puckett, R. (2007). *Words for warriors: A professional soldier's notebook.* Tucson, AZ: Wheatmark.

Sternberg, R., Forsythe, G., Hedlund, J., Horvath, J., Wagner, R., Williams, W., Snook, S., & Grigorenko, E. (2000). *Practical intelligence in everyday life.* Boston, MA: Cambridge University Press.

Wenger, E., McDermott, R., & Snyder, W. (2002). *Cultivating communities of practice: A guide to managing knowledge.* Boston, MA: Harvard Business Press.

25

CITY YEAR

Developing Idealistic Leaders Through National Service

◆ Max Klau

City Year

City Year is a national service organization that engages young adults of all backgrounds, ages 17–24, in a demanding year of full-time citizen service. As tutors, mentors, and role models, these diverse young leaders help children stay in school and on track, and transform schools and communities across the nation. This chapter presents City Year's comprehensive leadership development model, designed to unleash the full potential of this challenging long-term service experience to transform idealistic young adults into effective, engaged, and inspiring civic leaders. City Year's leadership development model, *The Flame of Idealism*, includes a four-part focus on immersive organizational culture (context), civic identity ("Be"), civic capacity ("Know"), and civic action ("Do"). The organization thoughtfully integrates a powerful strategy for changing the *outer world* of communities in need (through service) with a sophisticated model of changing the *inner world* of our young adult volunteers (through leadership development). The result is a holistic and comprehensive leadership development program that develops young adults into idealistic civic leaders through the experience of having those young adults provide service that measurably impacts the nation's high school dropout crisis.

❖ ❖ ❖

Introduction

City Year unites young adults of all backgrounds, ages 17–24, for a demanding year of full-time citizen service. As tutors, mentors, and role models, our diverse young leaders—known as "corps members"—help children stay in school and on track, and transform schools and communities across the nation. Our program is founded on the belief that young people can change the world; we view the energy and idealism of America's youth as a national resource with the potential to transform our nation's most pressing public problems.

City Year was launched as a 50-person summer pilot program in Boston in 1988. The founders, Michael Brown and Alan Khazei, were social entrepreneurs eager to prove the viability of the concept of national service. More than two decades later, the organization has grown to a $65 million organization operating in 21 U.S. cities and engaging 1,750 corps members annually. Along the way, City Year played a pivotal role in the creation and expansion of AmeriCorps, a government initiative that to date has engaged more than 500,000 young people in a year of full-time citizen service. With the founding of international City Year sites in Johannesburg, South Africa (in 2005), and London, England (in 2010), it is clear that the organization is catalyzing a global citizen service movement.

From the beginning, Brown and Khazei recognized that a national service experience represented a uniquely powerful context for developing civic leaders. Inspired by Joseph Campbell's (1993, 2008) writings on the power of myth and the "hero's journey" they believed that a year of full-time service could serve as a "civic right of passage" for all young adults: a transformational experience with the power to usher each volunteer across the threshold of assuming his or her full rights and responsibilities as American citizens.

Brown and Khazei also saw the multifaceted nature of year of service as another factor that made the experience a uniquely powerful context for developing leaders. Like military service, corps members from wildly diverse backgrounds have the opportunity to come together and work effectively as a team to address a critical national challenge. Like a service learning experience, corps members learn about a critical social issue, engage in front-line service focused on addressing that issue, and deepen their learning through reflection. Like a full-time job, corps members work full days and are held accountable for fulfilling clear responsibilities and expectations. Like school, corps members spend time in educational sessions focused on issues related to civic engagement, leadership development, and educational reform. Because of the intense, immersive ways that it challenges corps members to develop their head (knowledge), heart (empathy), and hands (skills and experience) in equal measure, City Year could provide a uniquely comprehensive and multifaceted leadership development experience.

City Year's Theory of Leadership Development

> *City Year taught me how to use every experience and piece of knowledge as a step toward becoming a stronger, wiser, and more socially aware person.*
>
> —Sylvia, Corps Member

City Year's theory of leadership is deeply influenced by the thinking of the well-known civic leaders in American history. For example, we agree with Martin Luther King Jr.'s well-known assertion that "Everyone can be great, because anyone can serve." Inherent in King's statement is a refutation of the "great man" theory of leadership and a belief in the civic power of all citizens—including young adults who may be years away from holding positions of formal power and authority in society.

We have also been inspired by Robert Kennedy's sentiments, delivered during a speech in South Africa in 1966, when that country was still deeply mired in the policy of apartheid:

> It is from numberless diverse acts of courage and belief that human history is thus shaped. Every time a person stands up for an ideal or acts to improve the lot of others, he or she sends out a tiny ripple of hope, and crossing each other through many centers of energy and daring, those ripples create a mighty current that can strike down event the strongest walls of oppression and resistance.

Here, again, is an implicit theory that informs City Year's leadership development efforts: Large numbers of individual citizens, each engaged in his or her own seemingly limited effort to make positive change, can have a massive cumulative impact on a pressing public problem.

Our leadership development model is also influenced by eastern philosophy. For example, the *Tao Te Ching* highlights water as a powerful metaphor for social change. Water seeks the lowest level and therefore touches and connects all things; it flows around what cannot move, makes good things grow, acts as a solvent on things that are stuck, and puts out fires—such as the anger that too often consumes change agents and the causes they are passionate about (City Year, 2004;Tzu, 2006). Water is therefore an ideal metaphor for the "servant leader" who leads through service, example, and assistance, rather than through power and authority (Greenleaf, 2002).

City Year's leadership development work is also grounded in a fundamental belief in the transformational power of idealism, which we define as the belief that you can change the world, and the passion, skills, and courage to do it. We understand that many of the 20th century's most oppressive systems and intractable challenges—Jim Crow segregation in America, colonialism in India, apartheid in South Africa are a few examples—have been transformed through the collective and non-violent effort of large numbers of citizens. Those citizens were idealistic in their belief that the world could be made better, as well as in their belief that they themselves could play a role in making that change happen. Because we know that history proved those idealists to be right on both fronts, City Year seeks to put the idealism of a new generation to work to address the most pressing challenges we face in the 21st century.

Finally, City Year recognizes the interconnected nature of social change and individual transformation. Our tagline is "give a Year. change the World.", and we believe that changing the world has two dimensions: changing the *outer world* through service, and changing the *inner world* of our corps members through leadership development. We have always maintained a dual focus on both of these elements of our work, and strive always to strike a powerful "both/and" integration of the two. We recognize that a high-impact service experience is the essential element of transformational leadership development, and a transformational leadership development experience is the essential element in empowering our corps members to provide high-impact service. Through a clear understanding of the nature of the outer and inner challenges we seek to address, we are able to maximize the change that we create through a year-long national service experience.

City Year has distilled all of these ideas into a conceptual model of leadership development intended to fully capture both the spirit of idealism that informs our work and the depth of the transformation that we aspire to create in our corps members. Inspired by our colleagues engaged in military service,* City Year has embraced the U.S. Army's "Be, Know, Do" model of leadership development (Hesselbein & Shinseki, 2004) and adapted it to our purpose. Like the military, we ask each of our corps members to grapple with three important questions:

1. Who do I want to BE?
2. What do I need to KNOW?
3. What can I DO to effect change?

As we will explain in the pages below, we have created thoughtful, intentional systems to develop our corps members in each of these three domains.

Recognizing the interdependent nature of service, idealism, individual transformation, and organizational culture, however, we have chosen to conceptualize the "Be, Know, Do" model as a ***Flame of Idealism,*** with these three developmental experiences nested one inside the other and grounded in our unique culture. A visual representation of the model is as follows (Figure 25.1).

An overview of the concepts included in the Flame of Idealism is as follows:

DO is the outermost level of the flame (think of this as the part of the flame that touches the outer world). This dimension

Figure 25.1 The Flame of Idealism

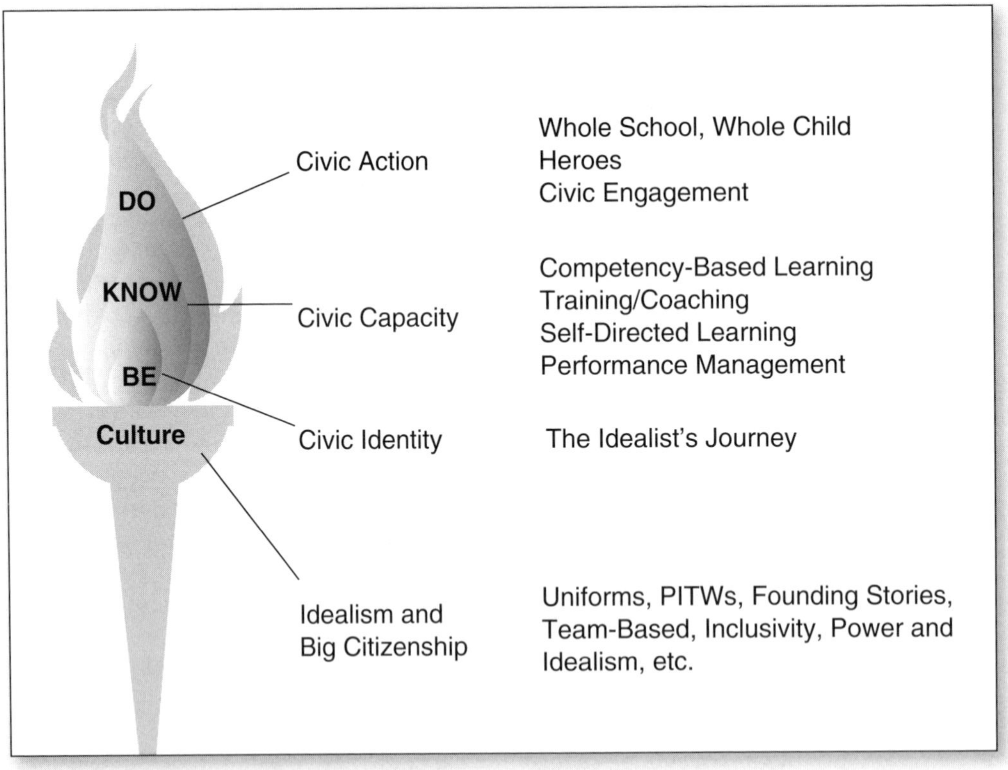

Source: Reprinted with permission © City Year.

*In particular, we are indebted to Colonel Robert Gordon III, our former Senior Vice President for Civic Leadership, for introducing this military framework to our civilian service efforts.

of our leadership development experience is about giving our corps members the opportunity to take *civic action* in their communities; we develop this dimension by providing each corps member with the opportunity to complete 1,700 hours of front-line, grass-roots service delivering one of our three service models. The vast majority of our corps members deliver our Whole School Whole Child school service model, while a minority delivers our "Heroes" youth leadership programs or serves on civic engagement teams that plan and execute large-scale physical service projects.

Nested within the outermost DO dimension is the **KNOW** level. This dimension of our leadership development experience is focused on developing the *civic capacity* of our corps members through trainings, coaching, self-directed learning opportunities, and a performance management process built around six civic leadership competencies.

At the innermost level—nested inside the DO and the KNOW—is the **BE** component. This dimension of our leadership development experience is focused on developing the *civic identity* of our corps members through a guided reflection experience. Our curriculum, *The Idealist's Journey,* gives corps members the opportunity to reflect as individuals and in small groups on deep questions of purpose, meaning-making, and leadership development over the course of a challenging service experience.

Finally, the entire flame of idealism is fueled by City Year's unique **CULTURE**, which has been intentionally designed to cultivate, magnify, and focus the idealism of our corps members while developing them into "big citizens," actively involved in the civic life of their community and nation.

As the model makes clear, City Year provides a comprehensive and multifaceted leadership development experience to each of our corps members. Our approach is simultaneously focused on behavior, cognition, identity, and context, and integrates a sophisticated understanding of the inherently interconnected and interdependent nature of those four elements. To state it as simply as possible, City Year believes that *what we do* is influenced by *what we know*, what we know is influenced by *who we are*, and all three of these dimensions are influenced by the *organizational culture in which we are immersed.* With this conceptual framework, we are able to powerfully integrate and align a wide variety of seemingly disparate leadership development tools, concepts, processes, and practices.

From Theory to Practice: How City Year Cultivates the Flame of Idealism

FUEL FOR THE FLAME: CITY YEAR'S CULTURE OF IDEALISM

> *These students need hope. They need to believe they too deserve more. Because of what they see in corps members, they can now see potential in themselves. I call upon all of my peers—the young people of this nation—to join me in creating a new national tradition that helps fulfill the American Dream for everyone in our great society: a year of service.*
>
> —Steven, Corps Member

From the very beginning, City Year's founders recognized the need to create a practical, usable, immersive, and idealistic civic culture.* By intentionally creating an organizational culture that allowed corps members to quickly embrace a

*Stephanie Wu, a founding staff member currently serving as Senior Vice President and Chief Program Design and Evaluation Officer, has played a critical role in City Year's culture work over the years. She has influenced the invention and design of many cultural tools and rituals, and has led the organization's efforts to teach, standardize, and continue to improve the culture across multiple sites as City Year has grown.

shared identity as idealists, City Year sought to rapidly transform a diverse group of strangers into a cohesive, effective, and inspiring service corps. A culture that built relationships across lines of difference while providing corps members with leadership skills would also serve to develop the social capital of each corps member, empowering them to become lifelong "big citizens" actively engaged in the civic life of their community and nation.

Over the course of two decades, the ongoing effort to develop this one-of-a-kind immersive civic culture has resulted in the accumulation of a wealth of leadership development-related tools, concepts, rituals, and best practices. A brief overview is as follows:

Power and Idealism. City Year culture includes conceptual frameworks designed to provide each corps member with a clear understanding of how we think about these two subjects that are so central to the work we do every day:

Power: City Year has identified four qualities that idealists must possess in order to be effective:

1. ***Spirit***—Demonstration of enthusiasm, passion, and energy that generates motivation
2. ***Discipline***—Maintenance of self-control and direction of one's energy toward achieving a goal
3. ***Purpose***—Focus on motivation, mission, and goals
4. ***Pride***—Demonstration of commitment, dignity, self-worth, and confidence in all you do

Idealism: City Year believes that effective idealists must master the following four abilities:

1. ***Imagine***—Seeing the world and its problems as they really are and only then imagining a profound change for the better
2. ***Recruit***—Through vision and hard work, recruiting resources and people to your cause
3. ***Transform***—Executing on your vision, in the process changing yourself, those you've recruited, and the community you are serving
4. ***Inspire***—Through execution of your vision, encouraging others to imagine and act as well

Everything our corps members do should be done with BOTH *power* AND *idealism*; the two concepts are inextricably linked and mutually reinforcing. Corps members learn these conceptual frameworks within their first days at City Year; the clarity and focus they provide empower each corps member to become a more engaged, effective, and collaborative idealistic leader.

Inclusivity. City Year embraces inclusivity as a core value. We see service as the "common ground" that can unite diverse citizens who might otherwise never have the opportunity to encounter each other in a substantive way. Our recruitment efforts are focused on ensuring that each year's cohort of corps members reflects the full diversity of American society, and our focus on team-based service delivery ensures our corps members will spend their days working closely with individuals of different colors, creeds, backgrounds, and work styles.

Uniforms. By having all corps members serve in uniform, City Year seeks to create a sense of unity, shared purpose and values, and a commitment to a cause larger than any individual. The red or yellow jacket, khaki pants, and Timberland boots worn by every corps member are an integral—and highly visible—element of the organizational culture. The City Year uniform is symbol of a full-time commitment to service that makes every corps member immediately identifiable in the communities in which he or she serves. Each time a corps member puts on the uniform, he or she accepts the responsibility to serve as a representative of the values and mission of national service in general and City Year in particular. They recognize that their daily actions will reflect on everyone who has ever worn the uniform before them, and everyone who will ever wear the uniform after they graduate from the corps.

Founding Stories. City Year has pulled together a collection of stories, legends, quotations, and sayings from different cultures and communities that speak powerfully to the core values that inform our culture of idealism. These stories have been collected to serve as a reservoir of wisdom and inspiration intended to keep our corps members—and the entire organization—inspired and connected to the fundamental motivations of our civic work. The MLK ("Everyone can be great") and RFK ("Ripples") quotes and the "Water" metaphor presented above are included in this collection of stories; other examples include the following:

> ***"The Starfish Story":*** This founding story highlights the value of *perseverance*. It tells the tale of a girl who stumbles upon a beach covered with thousands of starfish that have been washed ashore during a storm. When she begins throwing individual starfish back into the sea, she is challenged by onlookers who ask, "Why bother? You can't possibly make a difference!" She responds by throwing another starfish back into the ocean and declaring, "I made a difference to that one!"
>
> ***"Mocassins"***: This founding story highlights the value of empathy. It presents a Native American prayer that states: "Great spirit, grant that I may never criticize my brother or sister until I have walked the trail of life in their moccasins."
>
> ***"Ubuntu":*** This founding story highlights the value of *unity*. It presents a word from the Zulu language spoken in South Africa; it means: *I am a person through other people. My humanity is tied to yours.*

City Year has currently compiled a collection of twenty-one similar sayings, concepts, and stories, and actively weaves these Founding Stories into the fabric of the organizational culture.

Power Tools. A Power Tool is an inclusive, accountable structure for mobilizing diversity. This set of tools—accumulated through two decades of creativity and experimentation by both staff and corps—allows groups of corps members and staff to work together more effectively. Examples include the following:

> ***Hands Up:*** This tool serves to quickly quiet a large group in order to begin a meeting or event. When a group of corps members are talking among themselves, anyone in the group can raise their hand. Once others notice the raised hand, they are expected to stop talking and raise their hand as well. In an instant, a loud, unfocused room is transformed into a silent collection of individuals with hands raised, quietly waiting for a program to formally begin.
>
> ***Strong Circles:*** This tool serves to powerfully mobilize a small- to medium-sized group of corps members. When information needs to be shared, participants stand shoulder-to-shoulder in a tight, perfectly formed circle, with no one inside and no one outside the circle. Because everyone is fully included in the circle, everyone is able to participate equally and share information effectively.
>
> ***Spirit Break:*** This tool connects corps members, for a brief moment, through a symbolic physical gesture and focused thought. At the end of any meeting, check-in, or event, participants gather together and put one hand into the center of the group. Someone suggests a word to break on (for example, "Unity!" or "Power!"); then, at the leaders mark, everyone counts "1, 2, 3" and yells the

agreed-upon word loudly while raising their hands to the sky. Borrowed from the world of team sports, the spirit break brings inspirational and meaningful closure to a meeting, gathering, or event.

Over the course of two decades, a long list of Power Tools has accumulated at City Year, and the collection continues to grow as best practices are created at individual sites and then shared with the network. These tools allow even very large numbers of corps members to collaborate quickly and efficiently, using techniques that have been intentionally designed to keep each individual energized, engaged, and inspired.

PITWs. "PITW" is an acronym for "Putting Idealism to Work." A PITW is an individual tip or technique for getting things done effectively; the organization has currently accumulated 181 such tips or techniques. Here is an example:

> **PITW #1: Challenge cynicism—wherever you find it.** The first step toward putting idealism to work is to reject cynicism and embrace idealism. All successful human endeavors—from breakthrough inventions like the telephone to great social leaps forward like the civil rights movement—begin with the assumption that change is possible. Nothing is more destructive today than the growth of cynicism, a pervasive negativity—an habitual scoffing—that ridicules positive initiative, questions everyone's motives, and assumes the worst in people and institutions. Cynicism is the enemy of positive change because it discourages creative thinking—and destroys both the belief that change is possible and the will to act. Like a corrosive cancer of the human spirit, cynicism has become so pervasive that recognizing and standing up to cynicism—especially in everyday conversation and thinking—is now a major act of courage and belief. Learn to recognize cynicism, in all its forms. Challenge cynicism everywhere, especially within City Year itself.

Rituals. City Year's culture is saturated with rituals intentionally designed to ensure that every day is filled with activities that inspire idealism and to keep corps members connected to the stories and tools described above. For example, on a regular basis corps members do physical training (jumping jacks, calisthenics, etc.) in a public space in their community, providing a visceral experience of demonstrating spirit, discipline, purpose, and pride. Every meeting and conference call at City Year begins with a brief ritual in which participants are invited to share "ripples" created by their service. In this way, the "ripples" founding story comes alive through an activity that provides corps members with regular opportunities to reflect on the ways that their work is making positive change. Team meetings regularly occur in strong circles and end with an energetic spirit break.

Corps members often don't understand the purpose or the benefits at first, but by continually enacting these rituals, our members come to appreciate the way our rituals inspire idealism and build community. By performing these rituals from day one and sustaining them throughout the year, corps members are developed into idealistic leaders who have internalized our cultural values and achieved excellence at working effectively in inclusive teams.

As the Flame of Idealism model makes clear, however, the culture described here is only one component of a comprehensive leadership development experience. Our culture fuels the flame by providing a full-immersion context in which we seek to develop the civic identity ("Be"), civic capacity ("Know"), and civic action ("Do") of each of our corps members.

Implementing BE, KNOW, DO and the Flame of Idealism

As previously stated, City Year borrowed the "Be, Know, Do" leadership development framework from the U.S. Army; the succinct three-word phrase presents the distilled essence of that institution's many decades of thinking about effective leadership development. "Be, Know, Do" refers to an experience that simultaneously focuses on identity, cognition, and behavior; each dimension is important and plays a critical role the leadership development process.

City Year has embraced "Be, Know, Do" both because of its conceptual clarity and power, and because we are eager to build bridges between the distinct but related worlds of military and civilian service. We have adapted the model in important ways, however, to ensure that it captures our unique focus on idealism, service, and personal transformation.

An overview of the ways that we develop our corps members in each of these three dimensions is as follows.

DO: PROVIDING OPPORTUNITIES FOR CIVIC ACTION THROUGH HIGH-IMPACT SERVICE IN SCHOOLS

> *Every day, my fellow corps members and I are at our schools before the first bell rings to greet students and we stay until the last child leaves our after-school program. We are tutors, mentors and role models. We serve because nearly 40 percent of students in Boston drop out of high school.*
>
> —Paul, Corps Member

As we have made clear, the DO dimension of our model is focused on civic action; we develop our corps members in this dimension by giving them the opportunity to complete ten months of front-line, grassroots service. We conceptualize this element of our leadership development model as the outermost level of the flame—the part that touches the outer world.

Over the course of two decades, our corps members have engaged in a myriad array of different service experiences. In recent years, however, City Year has standardized the service we provide across all our sites in an ambitious effort to demonstrate the power national service possesses to make a measurable impact on a significant public problem. Specifically, we are laser-focused on strategically addressing the nation's high school drop out crisis (see City Year, 2010).

In many of our nation's cities, less than 50 percent of students who enter high school graduate; as a result, more than one million students drop out of school annually. The results of this failure rate are devastating, both to the young adults who give up on school and to their communities. Dropouts are more likely than high school graduates to be unemployed, in poor health, living in poverty, on public assistance, and single parents with children who drop out of school. On average, they earn more than $1 million less over a lifetime than do college graduates. They are three times more likely to be unemployed and disengaged from civic live, and are eight times more likely to be in prison or jail than college graduates.

Fortunately, recent research has emerged from Johns Hopkins University that sheds valuable light on the high school dropout crisis. Of the more than one million youth that drop out from school each year, we know that 50 percent of the nation's dropouts come from only 12 percent of the high schools, which are located predominantly in urban, high-poverty, minority communities. Research also tells us that as early as 6th grade, students begin to demonstrate signs that they are likely to drop out. These signs are called "Early Warning Indicators" (EWIs), and they consist of poor attendance, poor behavior, and poor course performance in math or English. When a student in an urban public school exhibits even one of these indicators when they are in 6th grade, that student has a 75 percent chance of dropping out (MacIver, Durham, Plank, Farley-Ripple, & Balfanz, 2008).

City Year's service efforts are deeply informed by this clarity regarding the scope and scale of the high school dropout crisis.

Since the founding of the organization, a significant percentage of our corps members have served in schools, and we have known for some time that the relationships that our corps members develop with students in schools are uniquely powerful. These relationships provide an experience of "reciprocal transformation" (Nakkula & Ravitch, 1997): The students are transformed by the encounter with a caring, inspiring "near peer" role model and mentor, and the corps members are transformed by the experience of providing that support to children and youth. Again and again, corps members have stated that the most important, enduring element of their City Year experience was the opportunity to positively impact the life of a student in need.

The high school dropout research suggested an intriguing opportunity for maximizing the impact City Year could have through these transformational relationships. Because of the highly clustered nature of the problem, we realized that a relatively limited number of corps members deployed strategically to the feeder systems to the most problematic high schools could make a disproportionate impact on the dropout crisis. Furthermore, by having those corps members work specifically with students identified as exhibiting an Early Warning Indicator, and providing service tailored to address that indicator, City Year can maximize its impact on the problem. In other words, by providing the *right service* to the *right students* in the *right schools*, our corps members can make a measurable impact on this serious national challenge.

City Year has developed a school service model called "Whole School Whole Child" designed to do just that. Working in partnership with school districts, teams of corps members are deployed to feeder schools in a pattern carefully chosen to maximize their impact. In the schools where they work, teams of corps members work in close partnership with the school staff and administration to provide academic support focused on addressing the EWIs, run afterschool programs, and promote positive school climate through initiatives like morning greeting (the team cheers on students as they arrive at school every morning) and schoolwide literacy events. Significantly, we partner with schools to collect student-level data to measure the progress our corps members are making with each of their students, allowing us to meaningfully assess our impact and adapt service interventions based on progress reports.

City Year's focus on delivering this research-based, sophisticated service represents a new era for our organization and the national service movement as a whole. For the first time, our corps members have the opportunity to deliver service informed by a detailed understanding of a serious public challenge, and they are able to receive regular, ongoing feedback regarding the impact they are having on each student they serve. We implement the **DO** dimension of our leadership development model by empowering our corps members to take civic action by delivering this strategic, high-impact service model for the duration of their City Year.

KNOW: DEVELOPING OUR CORPS MEMBERS' CIVIC CAPACITY

> *I have gained more skills and learned more lessons working at City Year than I have at any other job. The leadership, time management, planning, and team building skills that I acquired are so valuable to me now and will remain valuable assets to me in the future.*
>
> —Jed, Corps Member

City Year recognizes that everything our corps members *do* is influenced by what they *know*; that is why we conceptualize the KNOW dimension as nested within the DO dimension of the Flame of Idealism. We develop the civic capacity of our corps members in the following ways: training, coaching, self-directed learning, and performance management. An overview of each element is as follows.

Training. Training is an integral part of the City Year experience. The corps members begin the year with a three to four week training period called *Basic Training Academy* (this includes a *Basic Training Retreat*—a 2–3 day off-site retreat providing a powerful community-building and educational experience). We give them the opportunity to step away from service for a week in the middle of the year for another full week of training called *Advanced Training Academy*. Most Fridays are set aside as *Leadership Development Days*, creating a space for ongoing training as well as community building and service planning time.

Within this structure, corps members receive training on City Year's history, culture, rules, and regulations. Equally important, they receive in-depth training focused on the school-based service they provide throughout the year. They learn how to effectively tutor students in literacy and math, how to implement behavior management systems, how to run engaging afterschool programs, how to plan family engagement and school-wide positive school climate events, and more. We continue to revise and update these trainings in an ongoing effort to maximize the impact each corps member is able to achieve through their service.

Coaching. As we have stated, our corps members serve in teams that range in size from eight to twelve. Each team is managed by a Program Manager (PM), City Year's front-line staff who oversees one to two teams over the course of the year. In addition, each team has a Team Leader (TL)—a Senior Corps Member who has returned for a second year of service and who assists the PM in providing support to the team. This management structure is a critical component of the City Year leadership development model. Corps Members work closely with the TLs on a daily basis, and PMs play a major role in guiding each individual—and each team—through a challenging year of service.

Given the critical role that PMs and TLs play in the corps member experience, City Year's staff training model includes a strong focus on being an effective coach. Our PMs and TLs learn how to provide appropriate levels of support over the course of the year, recognizing that the needs of a corps member two weeks into the year are dramatically different from the needs of that same corps member six months later.

City Year applies its core value of inclusivity not only to people but also to the conceptual frameworks we pull together in an effort to optimize the coaching experience we are able to provide to our corps members. Staff receive training in models like situational leadership (Blanchard, Zigarmi, & Zigarmi, 1999) and facilitative leadership (Interaction Associates, 1997) and are often exposed to multiple training sessions run by an array of content experts offering their own unique framework for coaching and management. By presenting our staff with this diverse array of theories and models related to coaching, we seek to ensure that our corps members are powerfully guided through their year embedded in multiple coaching relationships that provide an optimal balance of challenge and support.

Self-Directed Learning. City Year recognizes that providing too much structure and guidance to each corps member can inadvertently engender passivity and conformity in the very individuals we aspire to develop into self-motivated, outspoken civic leaders. For this reason, we balance a strong focus on coaching with opportunities for each corps member to engage in self-directed learning. For example, in the middle of the year, we ask each corps member to create their own "Personal Learning Edge Challenge" (we call it a "P.L.Edge"), in which they develop a service-related initiative they find personally meaningful, and to set clear goals related to that initiative. Each corps member then has the opportunity before the end of the year to implement this self-selected and self-designed challenge.

It's an opportunity for each corps member to connect with his or her own sense of purpose and mission, and learn from the experience of undertaking what is essentially a small-scale social entrepreneurship initiative. In this way, we enrich the service experience teams provide to their schools while providing each corps member with a meaningful opportunity to engage in self-directed learning.

Performance Management. City Year's Performance Management Process (PMP) is built around six civic leadership competencies, distilled from 20 years of experience with training idealistic young adults to become effective civic leaders. The six competencies are:

1. Team Collaboration & Leadership
2. Communication
3. Successful Relationship Development
4. Problem Solving & Decision Making
5. Executes to Results
6. Civic Knowledge & Industry Insight

Each competency includes a detailed set of learning outcomes, as well as a "Technical Challenge List"—a set of specific challenges, arranged in five levels of difficulty (from "Basic/Beginner" to "Exceptional Performer"), that presents increasingly difficult tasks corps members can complete to demonstrate their skills related to each competency (for a sample of the way competencies are presented in the PMP, see Appendix 25.1). Corps members review these competencies in Performance Review meetings with their Program Manager that occur once at the beginning of the year, once in the middle of the year, and again at the end of the year.

At the middle of the year and again at the end of the year, corps members are rated on their demonstration of skills levels related to each competency; they can receive anywhere from a zero to a five, based on the five levels of difficulty presented in the technical challenge lists. The six ratings are then added up and divided by six to generate each corps members' Civic Competency Point Average (CCPA). The CCPA is City Year's metric for assessing corps member demonstration of skills related to these six civic competencies, and our goal is to have at least 75 percent of all corps members graduating with a CCPA of 3.0 (the "standard performer" difficulty level) or higher.

BE: DEVELOPING OUR CORPS MEMBERS' CIVIC IDENTITY

> *In my mind, the Idealist's Journey is one of the most potent symbols of the way City Year strives to develop its corps members, not just as civically engaged, inclusive changemakers, but as committed, servant leaders—leaders of integrity and conscience, leaders whose very presence speaks their message. It symbolizes to me how City Year inspires each of its corps members to keep growing, to keep evolving, to become his or her best self.*
>
> —Lindsey, Senior Corps Member

One of City Year's Founding Stories is Gandhi's well-known assertion that "You must be the change you wish you see in the world." City Year recognizes that everything our corps members *do*, and everything they *know*, is influenced by *how they are being* as they deliver their service. For this reason, we conceptualize BE as the innermost dimension of the flame, nested within the DO and KNOW levels of the flame. Recognizing the critical role this dimension plays in the leadership development experience of each individual, City Year seeks to develop civic identity by giving each corps member regular opportunities to reflect deeply on the matter of *who they are and how they are being* as they do their service over the course of their City Year.

City Year accomplishes this through a leadership development curriculum called *The Idealist's Journey*. Inspired by Joseph Campbell's (2008) well-known "hero's journey" framework, *The Idealist's Journey* asks each corps member to understand their year of service as a journey of personal transformation. By asking each corps member to view their experiences through this mythic, heroic lens, we invite each corps member to access the full transformational potential of a challenging year of service.

The *Journey* presents a framework borrowed directly from Joseph Campbell. It asks our corps members to view their year as having three stages:

1. ***Departure***, in which the idealist leaves behind a familiar, comfortable home to embark upon a journey into mysterious terrain.
2. ***Road of Trials***, in which the idealist faces trials and challenges that profoundly test his or her character. In ways that the idealist scarcely understands at the time, she or he is powerfully transformed by each challenge along the journey.
3. ***Return***, in which the idealist returns to his or her homeland able to share the new strength, knowledge, and wisdom earned through confronting the challenges of the journey.

Informed by this three-stage structure, the *Journey* presents a series of carefully sequenced, guided reflection questions that provides each corps member with the opportunity to pay close attention to their inner life over the course of their City Year. For example, in the Departure stage, corps members are asked to craft a personal leadership mission statement that articulates their highest aspirations for the type of leader they want to be during their City Year (the text of the mission statement exercise is presented in Appendix 25.2). Two examples of mission statements written by corps members are as follows:

> As a leader, I dedicate my life to the propagation of world peace, and the happiness of all living beings. I fundamentally believe that in order for this to happen, I start by creating peace within my own life. My happiness and inner peace, rather, inner light, will shine through to my friends, family, loved ones, students, community, and eventually, the world.

> As a leader, I will strive to appreciate the individual differences and characteristics among all people. Through spreading and sharing this appreciation of differences, I hope to strengthen the human race rather than divide it.

Months later, in the midst of the Road of Trials, corps members are given the opportunity to revisit their mission statements, and reflect on the degree to which they are living up to their own aspirations for themselves as leaders. Then, in the Return stage at the end of the year, they are given a final opportunity to reflect on how well they lived their mission over the course of their City Year.

The *Journey* guides each corps member through twenty such reflection exercises over the course of the year. Other questions ask each idealist to craft personal goals for the year, identify their "dragon to slay" (the highly personal challenge that most limits his or her ability to lead powerfully), and reflect upon the challenges he or she has with giving and receiving aid on the journey. The curriculum also integrates concepts from beyond the boundaries of Campbell's hero's journey framework. For example, we have integrated several ideas from the *Anatomy of Peace* model developed by the Arbinger Institute (2000, 2006); this framework asks corps members to reflect deeply on how they relate to their peers, manage conflict, and honor the basic humanity of others. The curriculum also presents relevant ideas from adaptive leadership theory, such as "getting to the balcony," "giving the work back to the group," and recognizing the difference between technical and adaptive challenges (Heifetz, 1994, 2002).

An overview of how this curriculum is integrated into the corps member experience is as follows:

Over the course of their City Year, corps members come together for one-hour "Idealist's Journey Sessions" that occur once every other week. For these sessions, corps members are brought together in small groups that are facilitated by Senior Corps Members (or, at some sites, Program Managers). The sessions have a clear structure designed to integrate a dual focus on both individual and small-group reflection. They begin with ten minutes of individual reflection focused on one of the reflection exercises in the Idealist's Journey curriculum; the next ten minutes are devoted to a small-group discussion of that exercise. Because the curriculum is used across the network, all 1,750 corps members move through this sequenced series of reflection questions at roughly the same time, ensuring a standardized leadership development experience across the network.

Facilitators send a clear message that these sessions are "challenge by choice," meaning that nobody will ever be forced to reveal information that they prefer to keep private. We have found that there is great value in talking *about* concepts like mission statements or "dragons to slay" without forcing individuals to share their mission or dragon. In this way, we create a safe space in which corps members have an opportunity to reflect on the inner challenges of developing as a leader while comfortably managing their own boundaries regarding how much of their own personal experience that want to share with the group.

The next 30 minutes of the Idealist's Journey Session are dedicated to a reflection exercise called "Leadership Learning Session." For this exercise, a member of the group presents a leadership-related challenge or question to the group, and the group consults with the presenter on how best to address or understand the challenge. The goal here is to create a space in which the personal struggles and questions of the group are placed at the center of a peer leadership learning conversation. To optimize the power of this conversation, we provide corps members with a "Presentation Development Process." This process is adapted from groundbreaking work done by an organization called The Right Question Project* that for 20 years has been helping marginalized communities learn how to advocate for themselves by learning how to craft empowering and incisive questions. We also provide facilitators with a dozen tools and techniques they can draw upon as they facilitate these conversations to support their efforts to make these sessions a valuable learning experience.

For corps members, these sessions provide a significant and meaningful learning experience. The sessions create a space that allows the corps members to step away from the demands of changing the outer world through their service and focus their attention for a while on the challenges of changing the inner world through an exploration of their own leadership development challenges. The Presenters develop the capacity to look inward to identify a personally meaningful struggle or question, and have a chance to hone their skills at crafting that inner challenge into a clear, concise, compelling presentation that invites valuable support and insight from their peers. The other participants in the group learn how to effectively provide thoughtful, useful feedback intended to both support and challenge their peers. Over time, individuals in the group come to see each other as valuable learning partners, and develop norms of sharing struggles and challenges instead of trying to muddle through difficult situations in isolation. Also, the facilitators of the group get an invaluable leadership development experience, as the challenge of helping others to become better leaders inevitably compels each facilitator to engage with that work in a rigorous way as well.

The final ten minutes of this hour are set aside for revisiting past presentations and for handling administrative issues related to

*www.rightquestion.org

the next session (e.g., clarifying who is scheduled to present at the next session). In this way, the sessions allow for powerful group learning over time. Each group is able to access its own history on a regular basis and build upon the cumulative learning that occurs through an ever-expanding collection of shared group discussions.

Each element of these Idealist's Journey Sessions has been thoughtfully designed to powerfully develop the civic identity of our corps members. The *Journey* curriculum provides concepts and language that invites each corps member to access the mythic, heroic dimension of their service experience. It also provides a series of sequenced reflection exercises designed to guide each corps member through the inner work of leadership development via a carefully designed reflection process. Finally, each Idealist's Journey Session opens up a space in the corps member experience designed to give each corps member an opportunity to step away from the demands of service and explore the inner life of a practicing civic leader in partnership with a group of peers. In these ways, City Year seeks to maximize the leadership development that happens over the course of a year of national service by thoughtfully developing the innermost BE dimension at the heart of the Flame of Idealism.

Outcomes: Measuring the Impact of Our Leadership Development Model

Given the multifaceted nature of our leadership development model, it is appropriate that we employ a diverse array of outcome metrics and assessment strategies in our efforts to measure the impact of our work. An overview of these outcome measures and strategies is as follows.

MEASURING THE DO: SERVICE IMPACT METRICS

City Year measures the outcomes of our service (the DO dimension of our leadership development model) via a comprehensive array of service impact metrics. Given our focus on the Early Warning Indicators (attendance, behavior, and course performance in math and English), we collect student-level data related to each EWI. We focus on tracking student attendance rates, behavior-related metrics like the number of detentions and suspensions for each student, and—of course—academic performance in math and English. All of these student-level data are regularly compiled to provide a snapshot of the overall number of students demonstrating EWIs at each school. (For a sample of service impact metrics gathered during the 2009–2010 program year, see Appendix 25.3.)

MEASURING THE KNOW: SKILL DEVELOPMENT AND ONGOING TRAINING IMPROVEMENT

As explained above, City Year has developed a Performance Management Process built around six civic leadership competencies. The clarity of our service model and the standardization of our efforts across the network has allowed us to develop a sophisticated process for assessing skill development by having corps members track completion of increasingly difficult tasks. Ratings (which are essentially achievement levels) for all six competencies are averaged to generate each corps member's Civic Competency Point Average (CCPA), which serves as City Year's metric for assessing skill development related to our six competencies over the course of the year.

MEASURING THE BE: ASSESSING THE JOURNEY'S IMPACT

City Year assesses the impact of the Idealist's Journey curriculum by asking corps members to complete survey questions focused on the goals of the curriculum. In our mid-year and end-of-year corps member surveys, we ask corps members to rate the degree to which the Journey helped them to

- Reflect on their experiences at City Year
- Provide better service
- Learn from their peers
- Develop as a leader
- Connect with their sense of purpose

These data provide an overview of the quality and impact of the Journey experience at each site and across the network as whole. Naturally, given the Journey's focus on personal meaning making, we supplement this information with rich qualitative data gathered from interviews and focus groups with corps members, senior corps members, and staff involved in the Journey. In this way, we gain a deep understanding of how the curriculum influences the way each of these stakeholder groups understands and manages the meaning of its service experiences.

MEASURING CULTURAL IMPACT: CITY YEAR AND THE DEVELOPMENT OF BIG CITIZENS

The final element of our leadership development model is City Year's one-of-a-kind culture, which has been carefully designed to fuel idealism, develop the social capital of corps members, and foster a lifetime of sustained civic leadership (see Khazei, 2010). A recent study conducted by Policy Studies Associates—a leading research firm—demonstrated that on every established major indicator of civic engagement, City Year alumni excel (Anderson & Fabiano, 2007):

Voting: When compared with the voting behavior of 18- to 40-year-olds in the national population, City Year alumni were 45% more likely to vote.

Volunteering: Nearly 70% of City Year alumni volunteer 10 hours a month, making them 65% more likely to be engaged in volunteer activities than similarly situated individuals in the national population.

Leadership: At least 90% of alumni reported that their City Year experience contributed to their ability to lead others.

Diversity: More than 90% of alumni reported that their City Year experience contributed to their ability to work as part of a team and work with people from diverse backgrounds.

Civic Involvement: Three-quarters of alumni reported that City Year contributed to their ability to solve problems in their communities.

Membership: More than 75% of City Year alumni belong to a community group or civic organization, compared with 29% of similarly situated members of the national population.

Education: 81% of alumni completed additional school after City Year, including 83% of alumni who came to City Year without a GED or high school diploma

Relevance Beyond City Year

In the context of this collection of best practices in leadership education, City Year provides a unique perspective. The number of organizations working in the national service space is limited, especially when compared with more established and traditional sectors like business, government, and education. In an effort to give readers some sense of how the practices described here might be relevant beyond the boundaries of the national service movement, we offer these thoughts on the most unique elements of our model and how they might be applied in different contexts.

THE POWER OF CULTURE

As this chapter makes clear, City Year has been incredibly thoughtful and intentional in its effort to create and sustain a unique organizational culture of idealism. Over the course of two decades, City Year has collected, invented, adapted, and refined a collection of practices, rituals, concepts, and stories that make our values come alive on a daily basis for everyone at the organization. While our particular emphasis on idealism may not be applicable to other organizations working in other sectors, our thoughtfulness about culture may offer lessons that are relevant far beyond the boundaries of national service.

At many organizations, culture is an afterthought. Instead of being deliberately designed and cultivated, it is allowed to develop organically in ways that are neither mindful nor productive. Instead of being an essential, aligned, and powerful element of the leadership development experience of an organization, it is simply irrelevant. Or—more problematically—an unintentional culture can actually serve to undermine the lessons, messages, and values espoused by an organization in its leadership development model.

For these reasons, City Year's culture provides lessons that are generalizable far beyond the unique context in which we work. At your organization, what would it look like to make organizational values live and breathe in powerful ways at every meeting or event? What practices and rituals could be integrated into daily life at the organization that would keep all staff focused on core values in engaging and meaningful ways? What stories could be told that give organizational values vivid color and life? And when could they be shared?

In their research on companies that have far outlasted their competition, Jim Collins and Jerry Porras (1994) highlight strong, values-based "cult-like" cultures as a prominent feature of long-lasting organizations. Clearly, City Year's ongoing effort to identify and enact thoughtful answers to questions of organizational culture represents a best practice with relevance beyond our organization's work in the national service space.

DEVELOPING THE BE

The other unique element of the City Year model is our effort to create a thoughtful, powerful system around the "Be" dimension of our "Be, Know, Do" leadership development model. Many organizations—especially those in the non-profit and education spaces—claim to care deeply about *how their leaders are being*, not just *what those leaders are doing*. When you look at the systems, structures, and experiences these organizations have created, however, they are often completely focused on the "Do" and the "Know" elements. The assumption (usually unstated and unexamined) appears to be that transformation at the "Be" level will simply happen as a natural by-product of mastering all the skills and competencies that leaders are compelled to demonstrate at the "Do" and "Know" levels of leadership development.

Of course, numerous leadership development scholars and practitioners have thought deeply about this element of leadership development. Many leadership development programs are powerful because they give individuals an opportunity to step out of their normal environments and reflect on these types of questions in places like conference centers or off-site retreats. It is rare, however, to find spaces for reflection on the "Be" that are integrated into organizational cultures, and rarer still to find such spaces informed by a thoughtful, guided reflection experience grounded in an understanding of the inner work of leadership development.

We therefore believe that City Year's work around the "Be" dimension of leadership development is unique, and has relevance far beyond the boundaries of our work with young people engaged in national service. Any organization seeking to address a major public problem must struggle with the challenge of sustaining idealism and personal purpose in the face of seemingly intractable challenges. Our efforts to open up spaces devoted to reflection on the inner work of leadership development represents a promising frontier for any organization that aspires to shine a beacon of light and hope onto problems that are by definition mired in darkness and despair.

Conclusion

> *City Year has given me a place to stand so I can change the world.*
>
> —Aaron, Corps Member

Michael Brown and Alan Khazei founded City Year more than two decades ago out of a deep conviction that a year of national service had the potential to be a uniquely powerful context for developing civic leaders. They believed that a year-long service experience could harness the energy and idealism of young people to effectively address critical community needs—and the experience of providing that service could be a profoundly transformational and life-altering leadership development experience for the volunteers themselves. Brown and Khazei dedicated themselves to demonstrating the viability of that idea, and to creating a culture and experience designed to maximize the transformational impact of a year of full-time service. Twenty years later, the organization has clearly demonstrated the validity of this founding vision.

Any long-term service experience is likely to make an impact on both the community served and the volunteer providing the service. However, City Year's dual focus on promoting clearly defined change in both the outer world (through service) and the inner world (through leadership development) provides a framework for unleashing the full transformational potential of a year of national service. Through a clear understanding of the scope and scale of the high school dropout crisis, City Year has been able to craft a focused, strategic, and high-impact service model that promises to meaningfully address the high school dropout crisis on a national scale. Through a sophisticated understanding of the interconnected and interdependent nature of behavior, cognition, identity, and organizational culture, City Year's model of leadership development promises to maximize the personal transformation that occurs in our corps members while they deliver that service. By preserving a dual focus on maximizing the impact of both our service and our leadership development efforts, City Year is developing a generation of effective, empowered, and idealistic leaders while making a measurable impact on a critical national problem.

Finally, by cultivating, magnifying, and focusing the flame of idealism in each of our corps members, City Year seeks to fulfill the full promise and potential of American democracy. In his 1910 essay *The Moral Equivalent of War*, William James argues that national service has the potential to both channel and magnify the civic passion of American citizens, suggesting that "it is only a question of blowing on the spark until the whole population gets incandescent." From Ronald Reagan's "shining city on a hill" to George H. W. Bush's "thousand points of light" to John F. Kennedy's declaration that "the torch has been passed," America's civic leaders have repeatedly spoken of our democracy as source of light in a world threatened by darkness.

We envision a generation of civic leaders—in America and across the globe—lighting up their communities with flames of idealism burning bright as they work together to address the most pressing problems of the 21st century. As we seek to make this vision a daily reality, our efforts are inspired by the following lines from John F. Kennedy's inaugural address:

> The energy, the faith, the devotion which we bring to this endeavor will light our country and all who serve it—and the glow from that fire can truly light the world.

Appendix 25.1

Sample Competency from Corps Member Performance Management Document

Team Collaboration and Leadership
WSWC Corps Member Version

Teamwork is one of City Year's core values and your service year is a head first dive into the power of a team. You will learn first hand your strengths and areas of growth as a team member when you are charged with accomplishing your service goals together. Being an effective and contributing team member helps set the groundwork for you to be an effective team leader—both skills you will continue to polish throughout your life as an agent of social change!

1) Increased ability to be an effective and contributing team member

By the end of the year you will be able to:

• Exercise respectful, responsive and participatory communication within a diverse team • Display the attitude and behaviors that foster a sense of team cohesion and help to build healthy working relationships amongst team members, including initiating and participating in proactive problem solving • Contribute equal effort in completing collective goals and meeting responsibilities on time to the best of your ability •Take on increasingly demanding leadership roles within the team and support and encourage others as they take on roles that challenge their skill level within a team setting.

2) Increased ability to effectively lead a diverse team

By the end of the year you will be able to:

• Effectively facilitate team exercises and activities that encourage inclusive participation and meaningful contribution from diverse team members • Apply situational leadership practices in reacting and responding to team needs by adapting the leadership approach to meet team needs at any given time • Delegate responsibilities to team members and demonstrate an ability to effectively support team members to successfully complete assigned responsibilities. • Demonstrate an increased ability to effectively respond to and proactively manage conflict amongst team members.

(Continued)

(Continued)

Technical Challenge: Suggested Activities
You Can Undertake to Demonstrate Your Skill

Level 1: Basic/ Beginner	Read about City Year's culture of idealism in the Idealist's Handbook
	Consistently meet all City Year attendance and standard expectations
	Contribute to discussion during an Idealist's Journey discussion
Level 2: Advanced Beginner	Facilitate a team brainstorming session or debrief of an event
	Take a monthly leadership role (leading planning times/daily circles. PMOM)
	Lead an afterschool activity for one week
Level 3: Standard Performer	Lead a team meeting
	Serve as a Project Coordinator for an internal service day or internal CY event
	Lead a team in a site service initiative (ex: school food drive)
Level 4: Advanced Performer	Become a Young Heroes or City Heroes Team Leader for a year.
	Develop and plan WSWC event, Starfish Corps graduation
	Apply to be a Senior Corps Member
Level 5: Exceptional Performer	Become a leader/coordinator for a City Year site wide event or program (ex. Servathon, Global Youth Service Day)
	Serve as Director of Spring Camps
	Create your own:

Source: Reprinted with permission © City Year.

Appendix 25.2

Mission Statement Exercise Text from the Idealist's Journey

Leadership Mission Statement Exercise

Idealistic leaders are connected to both their deepest sense of purpose and their highest aspirations for who they want to be in the world. For this reason, our first step in developing you into an idealistic leader involves asking you to strive personally for that clarity and focus. This short, clear statement should capture the essence of what you want to do in the world. Guidelines for writing your leadership mission statement are as follows:

- It should begin with the phrase, "As a leader, I...."
- In its final form, it should be no more than 1-3 sentences long
- It should represent a vision that you could not possible complete or achieve; this is a mission you will always be working towards, but never arriving at
- Similarly, it should not include specific tasks, or quantifiable goals ("As a leader I teach three classes a day."). We'll get to goals later, but a mission statement is bigger than any one specific task or goal
- Finally, your mission statement should be larger than your involvement with City Year. You are bigger than any role or job you hold, and we encourage you to connect with that deeper sense of purpose. Your mission should articulate the purpose we hope you will express not only in your work us this year, but also outside of your professional role and far into the future.

Here are some examples:

"As a leader, I will strive to appreciate the individual differences and characteristics among all people. Through spreading and sharing this appreciation of differences, I hope to strengthen the human race rather than divide it."

-Mollie, Senior Corps Member

"As a leader, I dedicate my life to the propagation of world peace, and the happiness of all living beings. I fundamentally believe that in order for this to happen, I start by creating peace within my own life. My happiness and inner peace, rather, inner light, will shine through to my friends, family, loved ones, students, community (Pittsburg), and eventually, the world."

-Erik, Senior Corps Member

Take some time to craft a statement that you feel to be authentic, honest, and accurate. This mission will guide you through the trials you will encounter in the year ahead.

My leadership mission statement:

____
____
____
____

Source: Reprinted with permission © City Year.

Appendix 25.3

Sample Service Impact Data

The following data is meant to provide an overview of the types of data City Year collects to measure the impact of our service.

Service Partner Surveys

Note: End-year results from 2009-2010 Teacher and Principal/ Liaison surveys (K-9), based on 1-5 scale.

Sample Teacher Survey Results

My corps members have helped foster a positive environment for learning: **92% agree** (n=920)

My corps members have helped my students feel more motivated to learn: **88% agree** (n=963)

Sample Principal/ Liaison Survey Results

Corps members are positive role models: **95% agree** (n=274)

I am satisfied with the overall experience of having City Year in the school: **96% agree** (n=277)

Sample Student Surveys:

Note: % of students grades 3-9 rating often/ almost always (5 pt scale: 1=Hardly ever, 5=Almost always); according to 2009-2010 end-of-year survey.

City Year helps me learn: **80% agree** (n=4,413)

City Year helps me believe I can succeed: **80% agree** (n=4.438)

Attendance Data

Note: n=331; Based on start to end-of-year data from pilot programs at six City Year sites, grades 6-9 (2009-2010).

55% reduction in students with less than 90% attendance as a result of City Year's attendance support activities

Literacy Data

Note: n=1,691; based on data from ten City Year sites, grades K-5. Data has been aggregated from ten different assessments, using grade-level benchmarks.

90% of all students tutored by City Year improved raw literacy scores

Sample Site Level Data

Chicago
Note: Students grade K-5. Based on STEP assessment (n=379).

81% of students tutored by City Year improved on the standard literacy assessment from start to mid-year

Washington, DC
Note: Based on increases in proficiency in levels on the DIBELS literacy assessments. City Year students n=49. Non-City Year students n=133.

Percentage of students increasing one or more reading levels:

City Year students: 61%

Non-City Year students: 39%

Source: Reprinted with permission © City Year.

References

Anderson, L., & Fabiano, L. (2007). *The City Year experience: Putting alumni on the path to lifelong civic engagement.* Washington, DC: Policy Study Associates.

Arbinger Institute. (2000). *Leadership and self-deception: Getting out of the box.* San Francisco, CA: Berrett Koehler.

Arbinger Institute. (2006). *The anatomy of peace: Resolving the heart of conflict.* San Francisco, CA: Berrett Koehler.

Balfanz, R., Herzon, L., & Neild, R.C. (2007). An early warning system. *Educational Leadership, 65*(2), 28–33.

Blanchard, K., Zigarmi, D., & Zigarmi P. (1999). *Leadership and the one minute manager: Increasing effectiveness through situational leadership.* New York: William Morrow.

Campbell, J. (1993). *Myths to live by.* New York: Penguin.

Campbell, J. (2008). *The hero with a thousand faces.* Novato, CA: New World Library.

City Year (2004). *Founding stories.* Boston, MA: Author.

City Year (2010). *Scaling City Year's impact: Growth plans to reach 50% of the off-track students in City Year's 20 US locations.* Boston, MA: Author.

Collins, J., & Porras, J. (1994). *Built to last: Successful habits of visionary companies.* New York: HarperBusiness.

Greenleaf, R. (2002). *Servant leadership: A journey into the nature of legitimate power and greatness.* Mahwah, NJ: Paulist Press.

Heifetz, R. (1994). *Leadership without easy answers.* Cambridge, MA: Belknap Press of Harvard University Press.

Heifetz, R. (2002). *Leadership on the line: Staying alive through the dangers of leading.* Boston, MA: Harvard Business School Press.

Hesselbein, F., & Shinseki, E. (2004). *Be Know Do: Leadership the army way.* San Francisco, CA: Jossey-Bass.

Interaction Associates. (1997). *Facilitative leadership: Tapping the power of participation.* Boston, MA: Author.

Khazei, A. (2010). *Big citizenship: How pragmatic idealism can bring out the best in America.* Philadelphia, PA: Public Affairs.

MacIver, M., Durham, R., Plank, S., Farley-Ripple, E., & Balfanz, R. (2008). *The challenge of on-time arrival: The seven-year flight paths of Baltimore's sixth graders of 1999–2000.* Baltimore, MD: Johns Hopkins and Morgan State Universities.

Nakkula, M., & Ravitch, S. (1997). *Matters of interpretation: Reciprocal transformation in therapeutic and developmental relationships with youth.* San Francisco: Jossey-Bass.

Tzu, L. (2006). *Tao Te Ching.* (Steven Mitchel, Trans.). New York: Harper Perennial Modern Classics. (Original work published approximately 80 BC–10 AD.)

26

PROJECT GLOBE

Global Leadership and Organizational Behavior Education

◆ Marcus W. Dickson and Ariel Lelchook

Wayne State University

◆ Mary Sully de Luque

Thunderbird School of Global Management

◆ Paul J. Hanges

University of Maryland

In this chapter, we target instructors who are going to teach about leadership across cultures, probably to graduate students in MBA, PhD, or EMBA programs in Management, Organizational Psychology, or related fields. We briefly describe Project GLOBE, the largest study of leadership across cultures conducted to date. Our discussion includes a variety of criticisms of GLOBE, as well as summaries of the published responses to those critiques. We then focus on what we see as the big question: the universality and the cultural contingency of specific approaches to leadership. The relationship between specific cultural values and preferred leadership styles are also reviewed. We identify and answer questions about GLOBE that have often emerged from students in our teaching about the project, and describe for instructors how to use these questions in ways that promote students' understanding of the leadership and culture connection. We conclude by discussing the data from the project, and offer suggestions for using GLOBE data and results to facilitate student exploration about leadership and culture.

❖ ❖ ❖

As researchers who have been involved with Project GLOBE for many years, we have often written about the findings of the project, or the analyses employed in the project. Three of the authors have been engaged with GLOBE for over a decade each, and so we've presented and written extensively about the project.

In this chapter, though, we get to take a different approach—we get to discuss the use of GLOBE as a teaching tool. While there are ways to use GLOBE to discuss a variety of methodological and statistical issues, especially around multi-level analyses, our concern in this chapter is on using GLOBE to help teach about leadership in a global context. As Bass (1990) and others have noted, a substantial majority of the writing about leadership in the last fifty years has been written by North Americans, and then perhaps has been extended to consider how it might vary in other cultural contexts. Considering the cultural variation and universality identified in Project GLOBE and the systematic relationships between cultural characteristics and preferences for several different styles of leadership can be particularly useful in addressing the assumption that "leadership is leadership" or that "people want the same things all over the world" that we have at times encountered in our teaching about global leadership. More importantly, the results in GLOBE open the door for discussion around the variety of ways in which cultural variations and culturally variant leadership preferences manifest themselves, helping to prepare leaders for in-depth exploration of specific regions' or specific societies' typical/modal leadership styles.

Our presumed audience for this chapter is instructors who are going to teach about leadership across cultures, probably to graduate students in MBA, PhD, or EMBA programs in Management, Organizational Psychology, or related fields. We assume a reasonable prior knowledge of the dimension-based approach to assessing culture (e.g., Hofstede, 1980, and GLOBE), of leadership theory, and at least some prior knowledge of Project GLOBE, as well as access to House et al. (2004), the first GLOBE book.

We start off by describing GLOBE sufficiently to allow an instructor to describe the project to students. We identify and address several criticisms of GLOBE, and then focus on the big question that students generally have when talking about leadership across cultures—the universality of specific approaches to leadership. Several other potential questions about GLOBE that often emerge in conversations with students follow. Once students have generated questions, they may want to explore the answers on their own. In other words, if an instructor wanted to get his or her students to actually mess around with the GLOBE data set, or to examine the items, what possibilities are available to them? Thus, we conclude by discussing the data from the project, and how to use GLOBE data and results to facilitate student exploration.

So with our somewhat facetious title to this chapter, we do not disavow GLOBE's original title, but instead of focusing on "Global Leadership and Organizational Behavior Effectiveness," we focus on Global Leadership and Organizational Behavior *Education*—using GLOBE to teach culture, leadership, and the interaction between the two. To begin to achieve that goal, we'll first provide a brief overview of the project, to facilitate teaching about Project GLOBE itself. As with any study, it is important to understand how a project was executed in order to understand the extent to which its results can be seen as legitimate. Thus in this section, we'll provide both information about the project and suggestions on how to teach about the project.

What Is Project GLOBE, and How Might I Teach About It?

Project GLOBE is a multi-phase, multi-method study of leadership and culture around the world. The first phase of GLOBE focused on the creation of research instruments to measure leadership and societal and organizational culture. (For purposes of this chapter, we focus on the development of the leadership scales, with lesser reference to the development of the culture scales.) In GLOBE Phase II, the psychometric properties of the scales were replicated through a wide-ranging, multi-industry data collection phase. Together, these two phases created the basis for the first two GLOBE books (Chhokar, Brodbeck, & House, 2007; House, Hanges, Javidan, Dorfman, & Gupta, 2004). The third and current phase of this research program presents a comprehensive study of the strategic leadership effectiveness of specific CEO leader behaviors on top management team attitudes and firm performance in twenty-four cultures (see early studies by Sully de Luque, Washburn, Waldman, & House, 2008; Waldman et al., 2006, as well as the upcoming book by House, Sully de Luque, Dorfman, Javidan, & Hanges, 2011).

HOW DID GLOBE START?

The initial notion of Project GLOBE surfaced from discussions regarding the global relevance of charismatic leadership theory. In summer of 1991, GLOBE's Principal Investigator, Robert House, developed the idea of a global research program, focused on culturally contingent aspects of leadership and organization practices. House initially organized Project GLOBE as a small coordinating group (Robert House, Paul Hanges, Mike Agar, & Marcus Dickson) and a large group of Country Co-Investigators (CCIs) who gathered data and helped interpret the data in the context of (in most cases) their own native cultures. Over the next few years, two multi-national pilot studies were conducted, with an international gathering of the Coordinating Team and CCIs held between the two pilot studies to interpret the results of the first study and to make revisions in anticipation of the second.

A key outcome of the international gathering of Coordinating Team and CCIs was the recognition that several non-western leadership items needed to be added to the questionnaires. In addition, the GLOBE researchers devoted a considerable amount of time to defining the construct of *leadership* to reflect their myriad perspectives. From this, an operational definition of organizational leadership emerged: *the ability of an individual to influence, motivate, and enable others to contribute toward the effectiveness and success of the organizations of which they are members* (House & Javidan, 2004).[1] Additionally, following this meeting the GLOBE Coordinating Team grew in size to become a truly international team. Thus, after two pilot studies and the international gathering, six second-order leadership factors had been empirically identified, in addition to twenty-one first-order leadership subscales, as well as the nine GLOBE culture scales.[2] Definitions for both the culture and leadership dimensions are shown in Figures 26.1 and 26.2 (Javidan et al., 2006).

---

[1]Also debated was the definition of *culture*, which was ultimately defined as the "shared motives, values, beliefs, identities, and interpretations or meanings of significant events that result from common experiences of members of collectives that are transmitted across generations" (House & Javidan, 2004).

[2]In the present chapter, we focus on the six second-order leadership factors. Full details of the twenty-one first-order factors, as well as the nine GLOBE culture scales, are available in House et al., 2004.

Figure 26.1 GLOBE Culture Dimension Definitions

Performance Orientation. The degree to which a collective encourages and rewards (and should encourage and reward) group members for performance improvement and excellence. In countries like the United States and Singapore that score high on this cultural practice, businesses are likely to emphasize training and development; in countries that score low, such as Russia and Greece, family and background count for more.
Assertiveness. The degree to which individuals are (and should be) assertive, confrontational, and aggressive in their relationships with others. People in highly assertive countries such as the United States and Austria tend to have can-do attitudes and enjoy competition in business; those in less assertive countries such as Sweden and New Zealand prefer harmony in relationships and emphasize loyalty and solidarity.
Future Orientation. The extent to which individuals engage (and should engage) in future-oriented behaviors such as delaying gratification, planning, and investing in the future. Organizations in countries with high future oriented practices like Singapore and Switzerland tend to have longer term horizons and more systematic planning processes, but they tend to be averse to risk taking and opportunistic decision making. In contrast, corporations in the least future oriented countries like Russia and Argentina tend to be less systematic and more opportunistic in their actions.
Humane Orientation. The degree to which a collective encourages and rewards (and should encourage and reward) individuals for being fair, altruistic, generous, caring, and kind to others. Countries like Egypt and Malaysia rank very high on this cultural practice and countries like France and Germany rank low.
Institutional Collectivism. The degree to which organizational and societal institutional practices encourage and reward (and should encourage and reward) collective distribution of resources and collective action. Organizations in collectivistic countries like Singapore and Sweden tend to emphasize group performance and rewards, whereas those in the more individualistic countries like Greece and Brazil tend to emphasize individual achievement and rewards.
In-Group Collectivism. The degree to which individuals express (and should express) pride, loyalty, and cohesiveness in their organizations or families. Societies like Egypt and Russia take pride in their families and also take pride in the organizations that employ them.
Gender Egalitarianism. The degree to which a collective minimizes (and should minimize) gender inequality. Not surprisingly, European countries generally had the highest scores on gender egalitarianism practices. Egypt and South Korea were among the most male dominated societies in GLOBE. Organizations operating in gender egalitarian societies tend to encourage tolerance for diversity of ideas and individuals.
Power Distance. The degree to which members of a collective expect (and should expect) power to be distributed equally. A high power distance score reflects unequal power distribution in a society. Countries that scored high on this cultural practice are more stratified economically, socially, and politically; those in positions of authority expect, and receive, obedience. Firms in high power distance countries like Thailand, Brazil, and France tend to have hierarchical decision making processes with limited one-way participation and communication.
Uncertainty Avoidance. The extent to which a society, organization, or group relies (and should rely) on social norms, rules, and procedures to alleviate unpredictability of future events. The greater the desire to avoid uncertainty, the more people seek orderliness, consistency, structure, formal procedures, and laws to cover situations in their daily lives. Organizations in high uncertainty avoidance countries like Singapore and Switzerland tend to establish elaborate processes and procedures and prefer formal detailed strategies. In contrast, firms in low uncertainty avoidance countries like Russia and Greece tend to prefer simple processes and broadly stated strategies. They are also opportunistic and enjoy risk taking.

Source: From Javidan, M., Dorfman, P.W., Sully de Luque, M.F., & House, R.J. (2006). In the eye of the beholder: Cross cultural lessons in leadership from Project GLOBE. *Academy of Management Perspectives*, February, 67–90.

Figure 26.2 GLOBE Leadership Dimension Definitions

Charismatic/Value-Based. A broadly defined leadership dimension that reflects the ability to inspire, to motivate, and to expect high performance outcomes from others on the basis of firmly held core beliefs. Charismatic/value-based leadership is generally reported to contribute to outstanding leadership. The highest reported score is in the Anglo cluster [6.05]; the lowest score in the Middle East cluster [5.35 out of a 7-point scale].
Team-Oriented. A leadership dimension that emphasizes effective team building and implementation of a common purpose or goal among team members. Team-oriented leadership is generally reported to contribute to outstanding leadership (highest score in Latin American cluster [5.96]; lowest score in Middle East cluster [5.47]).
Participative. A leadership dimension that reflects the degree to which managers involve others in making and implementing decisions. Participative leadership is generally reported to contribute to outstanding leadership, although there are meaningful differences among countries and clusters (highest score in Germanic Europe cluster [5.86]; lowest score in Middle East cluster [4.97]).
Humane-Oriented. A leadership dimension that reflects supportive and considerate leadership but also includes compassion and generosity. Humane-oriented leadership is reported to be almost neutral in some societies and to moderately contribute to outstanding leadership in others (highest score in Southern Asia cluster [5.38]; lowest score in Nordic Europe cluster [4.42]).
Autonomous. This newly defined leadership dimension, which has not previously appeared in the literature, refers to independent and individualistic leadership. Autonomous leadership is reported to range from impeding outstanding leadership to slightly facilitating outstanding leadership (highest score in Eastern Europe cluster [4.20]; lowest score in Latin America cluster [3.51]).
Self-Protective. From a Western perspective, this newly defined leadership dimension focuses on ensuring the safety and security of the individual. It is self-centered and face saving in its approach. Self-protective leadership is generally reported to impede outstanding leadership (highest score in Southern Asia cluster [3.83]; lowest in Nordic Europe [2.72]).

Source: Adapted from Javidan, M., Dorfman, P.W., Sully de Luque, M.F., & House, R.J. (2006). In the eye of the beholder: Cross cultural lessons in leadership from Project GLOBE. *Academy of Management Perspectives*, February, 67–90.

WHAT HAPPENED IN PHASE II?

In Phase II, the GLOBE team consisted scientists, with 145 of these serving as CCIs.[3] This team collected and analyzed data from approximately 17,000 managers from 951 organizations in sixty-two societies. The sample from each culture consisted of middle managers in at least two of three industries: telecommunications services, food processing, and financial services. The three industries were selected because they commonly exist in most countries regardless of economic development and offer some variability in industry type.

The validation process confirmed that the leadership and culture scales displayed acceptable psychometric properties as well

[3]Many of these researchers continue to be engaged in GLOBE's ongoing, programmatic research.

as construct validity when compared within a nomological network (Hanges & Dickson, 2004). The culture and leadership scores aggregated to the society level of analysis were subsequently ranked for the sixty-two societies. This information allows for a comparison of societies on each dimension.

The primary conclusion of Phase II was that cultures can be differentiated based on the attributes and behaviors that culture members rate as either facilitating or inhibiting effective leadership, and that this differentiation varies systematically based on the pattern of endorsement of the various culture scales. In other words, leadership preferences vary around the world, and culture predicts leadership preference. Building on the social information processing perspective on leadership (e.g., Lord & Maher, 1991; O'Connell, Lord, & O'Connell, 1990; Shaw, 1990), GLOBE referred to the shared leadership perceptions within each culture as Culturally endorsed implicit Leadership Theories (CLTs).

Finally, in order to provide a more parsimonious way of considering the range of data, the GLOBE data for the sixty-two societies were analyzed to establish a set of ten regional clusters (Gupta & Hanges, 2004), conceptually similar to the work by Ronen and Shenkar (1985). Gupta and Hanges note that this clustering approach provides a "convenient way of summarizing intercultural similarities as well as intercultural differences" (p. 178), providing great utility for both training and research (Javidan et al., 2006). The cultures included in GLOBE's Phase II and their respective clusters are shown in Figure 26.3.

Figure 26.3 Countries and Clusters Included in the GLOBE Study

Cluster Name	*Countries*
Anglo	Australia, Canada, England, Ireland, New Zealand, South Africa (white sample), United States
Latin Europe	France, Israel, Italy, Portugal, Spain, Switzerland (French-speaking)
Nordic Europe	Denmark, Finland, Sweden
Germanic Europe	Austria, Germany (former East), Germany (former West), Netherlands, Switzerland (German-speaking)
Eastern Europe	Albania, Georgia, Greece, Hungary, Kazakhstan, Poland, Russia, Slovenia
Latin America	Argentina, Bolivia, Brazil, Columbia, Costa Rica, Ecuador, El Salvador, Guatemala, Mexico, Venezuela
Sub-Saharan Africa	Namibia, Nigeria, South Africa (black sample), Zambia, Zimbabwe
Middle East	Egypt, Kuwait, Morocco, Qatar, Turkey
Southern Asia	India, Indonesia, Iran, Malaysia, Philippines, Thailand
Confucian Asia	China, Hong Kong, Japan, Singapore, South Korea, Taiwan

What Are the Major Criticisms of GLOBE?

Although there has been passionate debate on the GLOBE cultural dimensions (see Graen, 2006; Hofstede, 2006; House, Javidan, Dorfman, & Sully de Luque, 2006; House, Javidan, Dorfman, Hanges, & Sully de Luque, 2006; Tung & Verbeke, 2010), less attention has been given to the GLOBE leadership research. The vast majority of the literature focusing on the GLOBE leadership dimensions has been distinctly supportive of the research process and findings (Aycan, 2008; Grisham & Walker, 2008; Liddell, 2005; Yan, 2005).

The GLOBE leadership research is not without criticisms, however—some very vocal and very strong. In teaching about GLOBE's leadership findings, we would encourage instructors to have their students read about GLOBE, perhaps starting with the Den Hartog et al. (1999) article and then some specific chapters from House et al. (2004), including Chapter 2 (by House & Javidan) providing an "Overview of GLOBE," Chapter 3 (by Javidan, House, & Dorfman), "A Nontechnical Summary of GLOBE Findings," Chapter 6 (by House & Hanges), which reviews "Research Design," Chapter 8 (by Hanges & Dickson) on "The Development and Validation of the GLOBE Culture and Leadership Scales," and Chapter 21 (by Dorman, Hanges, & Brodbeck) on "Leadership and Cultural Variation: The Identification of Culturally Endorsed Leadership Profiles." Then allow the students to generate their own list of criticisms of the project, and ask them to generate specific details about those criticisms—not just "I don't think the scales are valid," but instead "I have questions about the validity of the scales because . . . " In generating a list of criticisms, your students are likely to identify most or all of the following, and maybe a few others. After identifying them, your students might find reading the critiques cited here useful, as well as the responses from GLOBE, where they exist.

SAMPLE AND EXTRAPOLATIONS TO SOCIETIES

Several criticisms of the GLOBE leadership research have centered on the sample used and the extrapolations made to societies (Graen, 2006; Hofstede, 2006). Specifically, since some countries in the GLOBE Phase II sample have sizable subcultures (e.g., China, India, the United States), it is questionable whether the samples used in GLOBE in any country are representative of that entire country. Indeed, demarcated cultural boundaries may not be reflected through national borders. To this, Graen (2006) notes "little can be concluded about the many variables that may be responsible for national means of these samples, much less differences between means of several national samples" (p. 97). In the GLOBE research, the CCIs were directed to sample the dominant business sectors of their societies when collecting data. For each country, samples were to be comparable on the dominant effects that influence cultures (e.g., language, religion, history, ecological factors). To address this issue, House and colleagues (2006) note that "GLOBE uses the terms 'societies' and 'societal culture' instead of 'country' or 'nation' to indicate the complexity of the culture concept and because in several instances we sampled two subcultures from a single nation" (p. 104). Examples of separate subcultures included population samples from black and white South Africa, former East and former West Germany, as well as French- and German-speaking Switzerland.

THE USE OF MIDDLE MANAGERS

Another critique relates to the sampling of middle managers. Criticizing the GLOBE leadership research, Hofstede (2006) states that "measuring leadership from survey answers by leaders is, in my eyes, a debatable approach. If you want to find out about the quality of a product, do you ask the producer or the consumers?" (p. 884). However, it was precisely because of the view they have as producers and consumers that middle managers were selected for this research. Indeed, middle managers are leaders of some and followers of others (Javidan et al., 2006). Although Graen (2006) suggests that GLOBE employed a convenience sample, the middle manager sample was a deliberately selected middle manager sample. With the intent of testing implicit leadership at the cultural level, House and colleagues (2006) note "such a test requires an appraisal of how leadership is perceived and evaluated in each culture in general rather than administering a self-assessment or reporting on a specific leader" (p. 104).

CONSTRUCT AND METHODOLOGICAL VALIDITY

A final critique of the GLOBE leadership research centers on matters of construct and methodological validity (Graen, 2006; Hofstede, 2006). Although a complete review of the statistical rigor that address these criticisms is beyond the scope of this discussion (for comprehensive reviews see Hanges & Dickson, 2004, 2006; Javidan et al., 2006), several methodological issues should be noted. Using a sample of middle managers permits generalizability about the subcultures of middle managers in the three industries studied. This increases the internal validity since the units of analysis are carefully delineated and internally homogeneous, hence comparable (Hanges & Dickson, 2004). These procedures were designed to avoid common source bias to help ensure the construct validity of GLOBE scales (House & Hanges, 2004).

Additionally, these scales were assessed for external validity. One procedure to minimize response bias contamination is to implement multiple methodologies to measure the same constructs. GLOBE researchers used unobtrusive measures to accomplish this. Content analysis of text was conducted with the GLOBE culture scales that revealed well-founded support of the quantitative results (Gupta, Sully de Luque, & House, 2004). With respect to all the scales, utilizing other source information gathered separately, such as media analysis, individual and focus group interviews, archival data, and other national surveys (e.g., World Values Survey), discriminant and convergent validity was shown providing evidence for the construct validity of the measures (Javidan & Hauser, 2004). As House and colleagues (2006) note, "this was of utmost importance, because construct validity provides essential information about the integrity of the constructs measured by the GLOBE scales" (p. 103). Ultimately, the utility of the GLOBE leadership scales is found both in their robust psychometric properties and just as importantly in their capability to emphasize implicit leadership theories cross-culturally.

What Does Project GLOBE Tell Us About Whether Leadership Is Universal or Culturally Contingent?

One of the most frequent and broadest questions that students ask about Project GLOBE is whether it answers the question of whether there is one thing that around the world is considered to be effective leadership. They want to know because if there is a single leadership style that is likely to be successful across all cultures, then expatriate training and management of culturally diverse groups becomes infinitely less complex than if different leadership styles and behaviors are necessary across cultural contexts (e.g., Dickson et al., 2001). Several researchers have tried to address this issue, including Robie and colleagues (2001), who assessed data from Personnel Decisions International's (PDI) PROFILOR—a multisource managerial performance feedback system—to try to determine whether there are managerial skill dimensions that are consistently seen as critical across cultures. Using a sample of seven European countries and the United States, Robie et al.

found that two of the PROFILOR's managerial skill dimensions—"drive for results" and "analyze issues"—were consistently endorsed across cultures, though several other dimensions did not. As in many studies, Robie and colleagues found inconsistent results about the universality of leadership styles across cultures.

This assessment gets more complicated, however, when we realize that the term "universal" can mean a great many different things (Bass, 1997; Lonner, 1980), and it is important to be clear about what is meant by the term. We find it helpful to rely on Lonner's (1980) descriptions of different types of universality, including:

- The simple universal—a phenomenon that is constant all across the world. In data terms, a simple universal occurs when means do not vary across cultures;
- The variform universal—when a general principle holds constant across cultures but the enactment differs from culture to culture. In data terms, culture is a moderator;
- The functional universal—when within-group relationships between variables are constant across cultures. In data terms, within-country correlations between variables do not vary across cultures.

Bass (1997) took this one step further in discussing leadership across cultures, and introduced another conceptualization of universality:

- The variform functional universal—when consistent relationships between two variables are found in every culture, but the magnitude of the relationship changes from culture to culture.

Bass (1997) was concerned about identifying an additional way to think about universality because he was assessing whether transformational leadership (Bass, 1985) was universally effective. He concluded that it is, based on three criteria:

1. there is a consistent hierarchy of correlations across cultures, such that transformational leadership correlates most strongly with important outcomes, with contingent reward leadership less strongly correlated, various management-by-exception approaches still less strongly correlated, and laissez-faire leadership least correlated with important leadership outcomes;
2. there is a "one-way augmentation effect"—in other words, in a hierarchical regression, when you enter transformational leadership after transactional leadership, transformational always accounts for additional variance in predicting important leadership outcomes, but when transformational leadership is entered first, transactional leadership does not account for additional variance; and
3. "in whatever the country, when people think about leadership, their prototypes and ideals are transformational" (p. 135).

Interestingly, GLOBE has contributed to the field of leadership studies recognizing that "variform and variform functional universals can be simultaneously universal and culturally contingent in a predictable way, as when the variation in the enactment of a common characteristic or the strength of a common relationship is determined by measurable characteristics of the cultures" (Dickson, Den Hartog, & Mitchelson, 2003, p. 734). Relating specifically to Bass' (1997) assertions about the universality of transformational leadership, GLOBE data suggest that some components (*visionary* and *inspirational*) of their analog of the transformational/charismatic leadership style were in fact universally preferred across cultures, while others (*self-sacrificial*) were not universally preferred. Further, given the culture-level variability that can exist within a variform-functional universal, GLOBE also found that the variability in both the universal and the non-universal aspects of the transformational/charismatic leadership style could be predicted based on the cultural values of the society (Dorfman, Hanges, & Brodbeck, 2004). Thus, the data suggest that Bass (1997) was right when he suggested that transformational leadership is universal, but that he only had part of the story.

The universality versus cultural contingency of other aspects of leadership was also tested within GLOBE. Specifically, GLOBE standardized scores at the country cluster level of analysis, and then tested to see whether the cluster scores differed significantly from each other for each of the six second-order leadership factors. One aspect of these findings partially re-printed from House et al. (2004) is shown in Figure 26.4.

This shows that for some dimensions of leadership (Team-Oriented and Autonomous), there are no significant differences in the extent to which these are valued across the country clusters.[4] The other four second-order leadership factors, however, are significantly differently endorsed across the ten country clusters, suggesting that these should not be considered to be universally endorsed approaches to leadership. While it may seem strange, for example, to those in the Anglo cluster (highest endorsers of Charismatic/Value-Based Leadership) that not everyone *equivalently* endorses charismatic leadership, or to those in Germanic Europe (highest endorsers of Participative Leadership) that not everyone *equivalently* endorses Participative Leadership, these styles of leadership are endorsed significantly differently across the clusters (though in some cases the differences are between high endorsement and very high endorsement).

In teaching about these differences in the endorsement of leadership styles, it may be useful to turn to the series of figures presented in Chapter 21 of House et al. (2004). Slides based on these figures (Figures 21.1 through 21.10) are available in PowerPoint format at the web address listed in this chapter's appendix. They show the leadership scores for each cluster in a circumplex model. We have structured this file to allow instructors to superimpose one cluster atop another, highlighting the magnitude of the differences between, as well as the variability in scores within, clusters. These slides may be especially useful in discussing the universal and contingent aspects of leadership. Students often find the nuances of universal leadership to be challenging to understand especially if it is their first introduction to these concepts.

Teaching the concepts of universal and contingent leadership can challenge students' assumptions about how effective leadership is defined. Some students may only be familiar with how leadership is viewed within their own culture and assume that all cultures value the same leadership traits. Thus, it may be helpful to first teach the concept of culturally contingent leadership values. After students are introduced to the idea of culturally contingent leadership values the various nuances of what is meant by "universal" can be introduced. Introducing the various nuances of universal leadership will further challenge students' ideas of effective leadership and will likely change how they view what is meant by the term "universal," even applied to constructs other than leadership. Using the PowerPoint slides will provide practical examples of how concepts can be either culturally contingent or "universal."

[4]Using raw data (rather than the standardized-within-cluster data presented above), the lack of significant difference—or universality of level of endorsement—holds true for Autonomous leadership, though not for Team-Oriented leadership.

Figure 26.4 Ranking of Societal Clusters Using Relative (i.e., Standardized) Country Cluster Scores

Charismatic/ Value-Based	Team Oriented	Participative	Humane Oriented	Autonomous	Self-Protective
highest	*highest*	*highest*	*highest*	*highest*	*highest*
Anglo Germanic Europe Nordic Europe Southern Asia L. Europe L. America	Southern Asia[a] E. Europe Confucian A. L. America Sub-Sahara Af. L. Europe Nordic Europe Anglo Middle East Germanic Europe	Germanic Europe Anglo Nordic Europe	Southern Asia Anglo Sub-Sahara Af. Confucian A.	Germanic Europe[b] E. Europe Confucian A. Nordic Europe Southern Asia Anglo Middle East L. Europe Sub-Sahara Af. L. America	Middle East Confucian A. Southern Asia E. Europe L. America
Confucian A. Sub-Sahara Af. E. Europe		L. Europe L. America Sub-Sahara Af.	Germanic Europe Middle East L. America E. Europe		Sub-Sahara Af. L. Europe
Middle East		Southern Asia E. Europe Confucian A. Middle East	Nordic Europe L. Europe		Anglo Germanic Europe Nordic Europe
lowest	*lowest*	*lowest*	*lowest*	*lowest*	*lowest*
Charismatic/ Value-Based	**Team Oriented**	**Participative**	**Humane Oriented**	**Autonomous**	**Self-Protective**

Abbreviations

L. – Latin A. – Asia Af. – Africa E. – Eastern

Note: The placement of each societal cluster below a leadership dimension indicates the relative importance of this dimension compared with the other leadership dimensions within a particular societal cluster. For example, the Anglo cluster is the highest in rank for Charismatic/Value-Based leadership, indicating that this leader dimension was extremely important (relative measure) in comparison to the other five leadership dimensions within the Anglo cluster. The size of the relative score for each societal cluster is this compared to the size of the relative scores for other societal clusters. Using the Tukey HSD analysis, clusters in the top band are significantly different from those in the bottom band. The clusters in the middle band are placed between these extremes for heuristic purposes. Societal clusters within each block are not significantly different from each other.

[a, b]Societal clusters in these columns are ranked in order; however, there are no significant differences among them in each column.

Source: Adapted from House et al. (2004).

Some Other Potential Questions From Students About Project GLOBE

The next part of the chapter addresses several other potential questions from students regarding Project GLOBE and how it can be used to teach leadership. In courses designed for global managers the information from Project GLOBE can be used to teach them how to adapt to other cultures. Different countries' culture scores and culture cluster memberships can be examined to help identify the differences and similarities between cultures. In courses designed to teach about the fundamentals of cross-cultural leadership, GLOBE can be used to provide information on how countries differ in values and how that affects which leadership attributes and behaviors are seen as effective in different countries.

HOW CAN WE USE THE RESULTS?

The results from Project GLOBE can be used in many ways. The findings from the study can be used to understand differences and similarities between or within cultures in perceptions of leadership styles and effectiveness. However, care should be taken in how the results are examined to ensure appropriate types of comparisons are being made (e.g., is the unit of analysis the aggregated societal-level responses or the ten regional clusters?). The results can be used to help managers and executives work with others from different cultures or to develop cross-cultural training programs to help the transfer of knowledge (Javidan, Stahl, Brodbeck, & Wilderom, 2005).

The ability for leaders to make comparisons between their own cultures and other cultures can help leaders remain open-minded (Javidan & Dastmalchian, 2009). Understanding other cultures is necessary in the ever-increasing global economy. In developing the list of leadership items the focus was to create a comprehensive list of behaviors, attributes, and characteristics based on several leadership theories (Javidan & Dastmalchian, 2009). Thus, the results from GLOBE provide information on a vast number of leadership attributes and behaviors that allow a wide-range of cross-cultural comparison of the leader attributes and behaviors that are seen as desirable and effective.

There are different types of information than can be obtained from Project GLOBE. When teaching leaders how the data from Project GLOBE can be used to help them navigate a global economy, they can be taught to use the GLOBE results to examine country and cluster information, compare the culture profiles of two or more countries, examine country or cluster information on the profiles of outstanding leadership, and compare the profiles of outstanding leadership between two or more countries (Javidan & Dastmalchian, 2009). For example, when comparing two societies such as Russia and Denmark, knowing Russia is high on the cultural dimension of power distance and that Denmark is low on power distance will help a leader recognize that in Russia obedience toward superiors is expected; however, in Denmark more equality is expected between individuals that are high in power and individuals that are low in power (Javidan & Dastmalchian, 2009). Leadership profiles provide information on what is viewed as effective leadership in the various countries and culture clusters.

As a leader working in another country or with people from other cultures, success may depend on the ability to appreciate the leader characteristics valued by people in other cultures. Results from GLOBE indicate that cultural values can predict leadership profiles. For example, societies that have high scores on Performance Orientation, Gender Egalitarianism, or Humane Orientation are more likely to desire Participative Leaders, while societies that have high scores on Uncertainty Avoidance and Power Distance are more likely to disfavor Participative Leaders (House et al., 2004, p. 47).

The nine cultural dimensions in GLOBE are aspects of a country's culture that distinguish it from other countries and societies. The six leadership dimensions are leader attributes and behaviors that people from all cultures can recognize. These cultural and leadership dimensions are important because many leadership differences found among cultures have their origins in the implicit leadership beliefs that stem from different cultural values (Javidan et al., 2006). Knowledge of a society's score on the nine cultural dimensions provides insight into the leadership attributes and behaviors valued by the society. However, while scores on the cultural dimensions will provide a good starting point to understand a society's leadership values, it is important to remind students that knowledge of a society's score on cultural dimensions does not immediately reveal the exact leadership profile valued by the society. Each culture has a unique combination of scores on the nine cultural dimensions.

In summary, the results of Project GLOBE support the argument that leadership values, or the strength of the relationship between leadership values and what is viewed as effective leadership, can be identified from the cultural dimensions. In a practical application of this research, teaching students how to use the data obtained in Project GLOBE will help them understand leadership attributes and behaviors valued in cultures other than their own. Being aware of cultural values that are strongly endorsed within a society will help managers identify leadership practices that are strongly associated with effective leadership and strongly associated with inhibiting effective leadership.

What Are the Major Take-Away Points on Leadership From GLOBE?

As we are in an increasingly global context, executives and managers face new and evolving leadership challenges. As people from different cultures are in more contact, there is a need to increase understanding between various cultures and develop successful cross-cultural business relationships. One of the benefits of Project GLOBE in teaching leadership is the availability of data from sixty-two societies that were included as part of the project (Javidan & Dastmalchian, 2009). While this list of societies is not exhaustive, it does provide the most comprehensive examination of cross-cultural leadership to date.

Not all managerial practices are universally acceptable (Javidan, Dorfman, Sully de Luque, & House, 2006). GLOBE has helped leaders or managers identify which practices from their own culture are acceptable or unacceptable in cultures that are unlike their own, while noting the leader attributes that will direct leaders to succeed in other cultures. The study suggests that there are some leader behaviors, attributes, and characteristics that are universally desirable (e.g., being motivational, dynamic, honest, and decisive) and some that are universally undesirable (e.g., being a loner, egocentric, irritable, and ruthless; Dorfman & House, 2006). There are other leader behaviors that are culturally contingent—which are valued in certain countries and cultures, but not in others (e.g., being individualistic, status-conscious, or a risk taker; Javidan et al., 2006).

The results from Project GLOBE also suggest that even some of the universally desirable or undesirable attributes may be enacted distinctively in different cultures. Javidan and colleagues (2006) provide many useful examples, including that while both Americans and Brazilians value respect for a manager, they have different expectations for behaviors that constitute respect. Brazilians typically prefer formal relationships between leaders and subordinates, while Americans typically prefer an open environment where there is mutual respect and opportunity for subordinates to debate with their subordinate. Formality in the American culture may be seen as not being open to suggestions by subordinates; however, in Brazilian culture it will generally be viewed as a manager appropriately treating people according to their position. Behavior that is viewed as a friendly debate between a manager and subordinate in American culture may be viewed as aggressive behavior by a manager in Brazilian culture. Thus, while both cultures value "respect," the behaviors associated with respect may differ (Javidan et al., 2006).

The identification of universally desirable and undesirable leadership characteristics suggests that there are both similarities and differences between societies. Leaders and managers can build on the similarities between their culture and other cultures when addressing differences in desired leadership behaviors. While the general advice to recognize that cultural differences exist and to respect them is better than assuming all societies share the same values, GLOBE can be used to teach leaders how to determine what specific behaviors and actions will be viewed as acceptable in different cultures.

GLOBE data can be used to learn about other cultures; however, they can also be used to teach leaders about their own culture. Teaching leaders how to communicate the similarities and differences between cultures can help them identify common ground to build future relationships, and dismiss misunderstandings between their own culture and their host culture (Javidan et al., 2006). Teaching about the nine cultural dimensions and six leadership dimensions identified in Project GLOBE can help leaders gain a better understanding of their own culture. This may help leaders realize that beliefs they hold about effective leadership, which may in fact be specific to their own culture and are not universal.

While adapting to other cultures may at times be useful, leaders do not necessarily have to automatically adopt an entirely new leadership approach to become more effective in another culture (Javidan et al., 2006). However, leaders should make informed decisions about when they will adapt and what they will retain from their own leadership style. If leaders prefer a style different from one typically used in a host culture they should clearly explain their rationale to employees in the host culture. The information from GLOBE can help leaders (a) explain their approach to leadership in cultures other than their own, (b) identify how their approach is similar and different from leadership approaches typically seen as effective in another culture, and (c) understand why they prefer a particular leadership approach.

Are There Specific Attributes That It Would Be Helpful for Global Leaders to Have?

To succeed globally, leaders must address cross-cultural challenges. While there are some leadership attributes that are universally desirable or undesirable, many are culturally dependent. Global leaders need to be able to adapt to other cultures, have a global mindset, and be able to endure amid ambiguity (Javidan et al., 2006). There are many factors that should be considered when adapting a leadership style to be more effective in other cultures. Maintaining a global mindset is important because it will be helpful for the leader to remember that differences in leadership relate to differences in cultural values, social systems, and societal norms. Each culture has unique combinations of cultural values and expectations that influence what is seen as effective leadership. When teaching about global leadership and how to adapt to other cultures it may be helpful to remind leaders that the process of adapting to other cultures may be stressful and difficult. Being able to tolerate ambiguity will be important as leaders identify similarities and differences between their own culture and other cultures. Adapting to differences will not necessarily be easy and being able to tolerate misunderstandings and uncertainty will help a leader prevail in another culture.

The Data From Project GLOBE Were Collected in the Mid-1990s. Are the Results From the Study Still Applicable Today?

When asked this question, we are reminded of a sub-heading in Hofstede and Peterson (2000), which succinctly sums up those authors' response to similar questions. They start one section of their chapter with a heading reading "Old data? Older cultures!" (p. 412). There have in fact been a number of studies conducted for the purpose of determining whether societal-level values and preferences change dramatically over a short period of time, and the general finding has been that, while change can and does occur, societies typically change at a relatively slow pace (e.g., Kolman, Noorderhave, Hofstede, & Dienes, 2003; Merritt, 2000; Søndergaard, 1994). This suggests that such data are likely to continue to be meaningful descriptions of those societies for a significant period of time.

These findings can be extended to the leadership data from Project GLOBE. For the most part, societal leadership preferences will likely remain relatively static over time and the data collected from Project GLOBE will provide meaningful information to managers and executives that interact with clients or colleagues from different cultures. However, even if there is reason to believe the data collected as part of Project GLOBE may be outdated, the cross-cultural leadership framework presented in GLOBE (the twenty-one leadership dimensions and six second-order leadership factors) are likely to continue to be valid to identify similarities and differences in perceptions of effective leadership between cultures.

How Can I Use the GLOBE 2004 Data to Facilitate Student Learning About Leadership?

As indicated earlier, we believe that students will benefit in their understanding of culture and how it affects leadership by incorporating the GLOBE databases into the classroom. We believe—and the educational data support—the old saying often attributed as a Chinese proverb, "Tell me and I'll forget; show me and I may remember; involve me and I'll understand." To this end, we have tried to find ways to facilitate student exploration of GLOBE leadership data by making several data files available to instructors for downloading. Specifically, we have added several files to the web address listed in the appendix. This webpage already contains a variety of useful information about Project GLOBE such as PDF versions of the original GLOBE surveys that can be downloaded and used to provide students with context for the data files.

For this chapter, we have added six data files to this website. Specifically, we have added an Excel file that has the leadership data averaged to the country level for all the six GLOBE higher order leadership scales as well as the twenty-one first-order leadership scales. A comma-delimited file of this information is also available on the website. In addition to the GLOBE leadership scales, we also have Excel and comma-delimited files for society averages of the separate GLOBE leadership items and files for the GLOBE culture scales, again averaged to the country level, posted on this website.

GLOBE Learning Exercises

The GLOBE leadership scales data can be used to provide students with first-hand experience regarding country differences that affect whether leadership styles are perceived to benefit or inhibit effective leadership. For example, it is widely believed in the United States that participative leadership is beneficial in the United States. Thus, students may be quite surprised to explore the GLOBE data and find that there are countries that rated participative leadership as ineffective or even harmful to effective leadership. Students could then generate hypotheses regarding factors that might explain this societal variety in perceived effectiveness of leadership attributes. In the 2004 book, GLOBE demonstrated the explanatory power of societal culture to account for these leadership rating differences. However, the students may generate other hypotheses and so new variables can be entered into the data and the explanatory power of these variables can be explored (e.g., GNP, level of development, religious beliefs). This analysis can be repeated with the first-order leadership scales. The societal differences on these scales were not reported in the 2004 book and so this more detailed exploration of leadership would be an excellent follow-up exercise after exploration of the second-order factors.

Another exercise would be for the students to discuss how to best conceptualize leadership differences across societies. In other words, is it practical to acknowledge that each society differs in their desired leadership attributes beyond what was examined in GLOBE? Or is there practical utility in only paying attention to leadership differences that are a function of the GLOBE societal clusters? (Gupta & Hanges, 2004; Gupta, Hanges, & Dorfman, 2002). Students could explore how much variability there is in leadership styles for countries within each cluster as opposed to variability in leadership styles for societies from different clusters. This exercise can lead to a discussion of expatriate managers and the extent to which cultural similarity might facilitate adaptive expatriate assignments. Further, this exercise tends to lead into a discussion of the boundary conditions of social science research and how various organizational interventions and practices (e.g., mergers and acquisitions, transfer of technology, human resource practices) may or may not be successfully implemented across societies.

Finally, the files containing the individual leadership items provide the most flexibility for the individual instructor. For example, students could identify individual leadership items that are culturally contingent as opposed to culturally universal. Also, this data set does not limit students to replicating the GLOBE 2004 findings. Rather, students could identify their own themes among the items and explore the extent to which these leadership attributes vary across cultures. For example, while not part of the original intent of the GLOBE study, Resick, Hanges, Dickson, and Mitchelson (2006) reviewed the items in the GLOBE survey and created several different measures of ethical leadership. Resick and colleagues (2006) reported on the differences across societies on these different ethical leadership measures. These researchers subsequently validated these ethical leadership measures in that they found that these measures were related to the United Nation's corruption index (Resick, Mitchelson, Dickson, & Hanges, 2009).

In sum, there are several exercises that can be developed with the GLOBE data that can improve students' understanding of leadership and the effect of culture on this variable as well. Allowing students to "mess around" with the data directly will likely enhance their understanding of the strengths and the limitations of Project GLOBE, and of the influence of societal culture on organizational leadership preferences.

Conclusions

In 1997, Mark Peterson and the late Jerry Hunt raised a cry of alarm about what they believed to be an American bias in cross-cultural leadership research. Mellahi (2000) went further with this concern and looked at how managers from different parts of the world are taught about leadership when they pursue MBAs in Western countries. Focusing specifically on Asian, Arab, and African managers in MBA programs in the UK, Mellahi found Western leadership values to be significantly emphasized while indigenous leadership values were neglected, leading the non-British MBA students to interpret these indigenous leadership values as being unimportant.

We agree that these are serious concerns, and they make the teaching of leadership across cultures challenging. Those teaching leadership in some parts of the world or in some educational settings may find that their students have very limited experience with—and perhaps stereotypical views of—people in other cultures and their views and preferences related to leadership. In other parts of the world or in other educational settings, students may be well-traveled or have very extensive knowledge of cultures other than their own. In both types of settings, a data-driven approach to discussions of cultural similarity and variation provides, in our experience, the best approach for promoting understanding and breaking down of preconceptions. Project GLOBE provides the opportunity to take such a data-driven approach in teaching about leadership across cultures.

In the present chapter, therefore, we have attempted to provide support to and ideas for instructors who wish to approach issues of leadership across cultures in a more culturally complete manner with a data-driven approach.

References

Aycan, Z. (2008). Cross-cultural approaches to leadership. In P.B. Smith, M.F. Peterson, & D.C. Thomas (Eds.), *The handbook of cross-cultural management research* (pp. 219–238). Thousand Oaks, CA: Sage.

Bass, B. (1990). *Bass and Stogdill's handbook of leadership: Theory, research, & managerial applications.* New York: Free Press.

Bass, B. M. (1997). Does the transactional-transformational leadership paradigm transcend organizational and national boundaries? *American Psychologist, 52*, 130–139.

Chhokar, J.S., Brodbeck, F.C., & House, R.J. (2007). *Culture and leadership across the World: The GLOBE book of in-depth studies of 25 societies.* Mahwah, NJ: Lawrence Erlbaum.

Den Hartog, D., House, R. J., Hanges, P. J., Ruiz-Quintanilla, S. A., Dorfman, P. W., & 170 co-authors. (1999). Culture-specific and cross-culturally generalizable implicit leadership theories: Are attributes of charismatic/transformational leadership universally endorsed? *The Leadership Quarterly, 10,* 219–256.

Dickson, M. W., Den Hartog, D. N., & Mitchelson, J. K. (2003). Research on leadership in a cross-cultural context: Making progress, and raising new questions. *The Leadership Quarterly, 14,* 729–768.

Dickson, M.W., Hanges, P.J., & Lord, R.M. (2001).Trends, developments, and gaps in cross-cultural research on leadership. In W. Mobley & M. McCall (Eds.), *Advances in global leadership*, vol. 2 (pp. 75–100). Stamford, CT: JAI Press.

Dorfman, P.W., Hanges, P.J., & Brodbeck, F.C. (2004). Leadership and cultural variation: The identification of culturally endorsed leadership profiles. In R.J. House, P.J. Hanges, M. Javidan, P.W. Dorfman, & V. Gupta (Eds.), *Culture, leadership, and organizations: The GLOBE study of sixty-two societies* (pp. 669–713). Thousand Oaks, CA: Sage.

Dorfman, P.W., & House, R.J. (2004). Cultural influences on organizational leadership: Literature review, theoretical rationale, and GLOBE Project goals. In R.J. House, P.J. Hanges, M. Javidan, P.W. Dorfman, & V. Gupta (Eds.), *Culture, leadership, and organizations: The GLOBE study of sixty-two societies* (pp. 51–73). Thousand Oaks, CA: Sage.

Graen, G. (2006). In the eye of the beholder: cross-cultural lesson in leadership from project GLOBE: A response viewed from the third culture bonding (TCB) model of cross-cultural leadership. *Academy of Management Perspectives, 20*(4), 95–101.

Grisham, T., & Walker, D.H.T. (2008). Cross-cultural leadership. *International*

Journal of Managing Projects in Business, 1(3), 439–445.

Gupta, V., & Hanges, P.J. (2004). Regional and climate clustering of social cultures. In R.J. House, P.J. Hanges, M. Javidan, P.W. Dorfman, & V. Gupta (Eds.), *Culture, leadership, and organizations: The GLOBE study of sixty-two societies* (pp. 78–218). Thousand Oaks, CA: Sage.

Gupta, V., Hanges, P.J., & Dorfman, P.W. (2002). Cultural clusters: methodology and findings. *Journal of World Business, 37*, 11–15.

Gupta, V., Sully de Luque, M.F., & House, R.J. (2004). Multisource construct validity of GLOBE scales. In R.J. House, P.J. Hanges, M. Javidan, P.W. Dorfman, & V. Gupta (Eds.), *Culture, leadership, and organizations: The GLOBE study of sixty-two societies* (pp. 152–172). Thousand Oaks, CA: Sage.

Hanges P., & Dickson, M. (2006). Agitation over aggregation: Clarifying the development of and the nature of the GLOBE scales. *The Leadership Quarterly*, 17, 522–536.

Hanges, P.J., & Dickson, M.W. (2004). The development and validation of the GLOBE culture and leadership scales. In R.J. House, P.J. Hanges, M. Javidan, P.W. Dorfman, & V. Gupta (Eds.), *Culture, leadership, and organizations: The GLOBE study of sixty-two societies* (pp. 122–151). Thousand Oaks, CA: Sage.

Hofstede, G. (1980). *Culture's consequences: comparing values, behaviors, institutions, and organizations across nations*. Beverly Hills, CA: Sage.

Hofstede, G. (2006). What did GLOBE really measure? Researchers' minds versus respondents' minds. *Journal of International Business Studies, 37*, 882–896.

Hofstede, G., & Peterson, M. F. (2000). Culture: National values and organizational practices. In N. M. Ashkanasy, C. Wilderom, & M. F. Peterson (Eds.), *Handbook of organizational culture and climate* (pp. 401–416). Thousand Oaks, CA: Sage.

House, R. J., Hanges, P. J., Javidan, M., Dorfman, P. W., Gupta, V., & GLOBE Associates. (2004). *Leadership, culture and organizations: The Globe study of sixty-two societies*. Thousand Oaks, CA: Sage.

House, R., Javidan, M., & Dorfman, P. (2001). Project GLOBE: An introduction. *Applied Psychology: An International Review, 50*, 489–505.

House, R.J., & Hanges, P.J. (2004). Research design. In R.J. House, P.J. Hanges, M. Javidan, P.W. Dorfman, & V. Gupta (Eds.), *Culture, leadership, and organizations: The GLOBE study of sixty-two societies* (pp. 95–101). Thousand Oaks, CA: Sage.

House, R.J., Hanges, P.J., Javidan, M., Dorfman, P.W., & Gupta, V. (2004) *Culture, leadership, and organizations: The GLOBE study of sixty-two societies*. Thousand Oaks, CA: Sage.

House, R.J., & Javidan, M. (2004). Overview of GLOBE. In R.J. House, P.J. Hanges, M. Javidan, P.W. Dorfman, & V. Gupta (Eds.), *Culture, leadership, and organizations: The GLOBE study of sixty-two societies* (pp. 9–26). Thousand Oaks, CA: Sage.

House, R.J., Javidan, M., Dorfman, P., & Sully de Luque, M. (2006). A failure of scholarship: Response to George Graen's critique of GLOBE. *Academy of Management Perspectives*, 3, 37–42.

House, R.J., Quigley, N.R., & Sully de Luque, M.F. (2010). Insights from Project GLOBE: Extending Global Advertising Research through a Contemporary Framework. *International Journal of Advertising*, 29, 111–139.

Javidan, M., & Dastmalchian, A. (2009). Managerial implications of the GLOBE project: A study of sixty-two societies. *Asia Pacific Journal of Human Resources, 47*, 41–58.

Javidan, M., Dorfman, P.W., Sully de Luque, M.F., & House, R.J. (2006). In the eye of the beholder: Cross-cultural lessons in leadership from Project GLOBE. *Academy of Management Perspectives, 20*(1), 67–90.

Javidan, M., & Hauser, M. (2004). The linkage between GLOBE findings and other cross cultural information. In R.J. House, P.J. Hanges, M. Javidan, P.W. Dorfman, & V. Gupta (Eds.), *Culture, leadership, and organizations: The GLOBE study of sixty-two societies* (pp. 95–101). Thousand Oaks, CA: Sage

Javidan, M., House, R.J., Dorfman, P., Hanges, P.M., & Sully de Luque, M. (2006). Conceptualizing and measuring cultures and their consequences: A comparative review of GLOBE's and Hofstede's approaches. *Journal of International Business Studies*, 37, 897–914.

Javidan, M., Stahl, G. K., Brodbeck, F., & Wilderom, C. P. M. (2005). Cross-border transfer of knowledge: Cultural lessons from Project GLOBE. *Academy of Management Executive, 19,* 59–76.

Kolman, L., Noorderhaven, N. G., Hofstede, G., & Dienes, E. (2003). Cross-cultural differences in Central Europe. *Journal of Managerial Psychology, 18,* 76–88.

Liddell, W.W. (2005). Project GLOBE: A Large Scale Cross-Cultural Study of Leadership. *Problems and Perspectives in Management, 3,* 5–9.

Lonner, W. J. (1980). The search for psychological universals. In H. C. Triandis & W. W. Lambert (Eds.), *Handbook of cross-cultural psychology* (Vol. 1, pp. 143–204). Boston: Allyn and Bacon.

Lord, R., & Maher, K.J. (1991). *Leadership and information processing: linking perceptions and performance.* Boston, MA: Unwin-Everyman.

Mellahi, K. (2000). The teaching of leadership on UK MBA programmes: A critical analysis from an international perspective. *Journal of Management Development, 19,* 297–308.

Merritt, A. (2000). Culture in the cockpit: Do Hofstede's dimensions replicate? *Journal of Cross-Cultural Psychology, 31,* 283–301.

O'Connell, M. S., Lord, R. G., & O'Connell, M. K. (1990, August). *Differences in Japanese and American leadership prototypes: Implications for cross-cultural training.* Paper presented at the meeting of the Academy of Management, San Francisco.

Peterson, M. F., & Hunt, J. G. (1997). International perspectives on international leadership. *The Leadership Quarterly, 8,* 203–231.

Resick, C.J., Hanges, P.J., Dickson, M.W., & Mitchelson, J.K. (2006). A cross-cultural examination of the endorsement of ethical leadership. *Journal of Business Ethics, 63,* 345–359.

Resick, C.J., Mitchelson, J.K., Dickson, M.W., & Hanges, P.J. (2009). Culture, corruption, and the endorsement of ethical leadership. In W.H. Mobley, Y. Wang, & M. Li (Eds.), *Advances in global leadership,* vol. 5 (pp. 113–144). Bingley, UK: Emerald Books.

Robie, C., Johnson, K.M., Nilsen, D., & Hazucha, J.F. (2001). The right stuff: Understanding cultural differences in leadership performance. *Journal of Management Development, 20,* 639–650.

Ronen, S., & Shenkar, O. (1985). Clustering countries on attitudinal dimensions: A review and synthesis. *Academy of Management Review, 10,* 435–454.

Shaw, J. B. (1990). A cognitive categorization model for the study of intercultural management. *Academy of Management Review, 15,* 626–645.

Søndergaard, M. (1994). Hofstede's consequences: A study of reviews, citations, and replications, *Organizational Studies, 15,* 447–456.

Sully de Luque, M.F., Washburn, N., Waldman, D.A., & House, R.J. (2008). Unrequited profits: The relationship of economic and stakeholder values to leadership and performance. *Administrative Science Quarterly, 53,* 626–654.

Tung, R.L., & Verbeke, A. (2010). Beyond Hofstede and GLOBE: Improving the quality of cross-cultural research. *Journal of International Business Studies, 41,* 1259–1274.

Waldman, D., Sully de Luque, M., Washburn, N., House, R., & colleagues. (2006). Cultural and leadership predictors of corporate social responsibility values of top management: A study of fifteen countries. *Journal of International Business Studies,* 37, 823–837.

Yan, J. (2005). A cross cultural perspective on perceived leadership effectiveness. *International Journal of Cross Cultural Management, 5*(1), 49–66.

Appendix 26.1: Article Suggestions and Access to Files

The following articles are ones we would recommend that instructors especially consider when teaching about GLOBE's leadership results.

Den Hartog, D., House, R. J., Hanges, P. J., Ruiz-Quintanilla, S. A., Dorfman, P. W., & 170 co-authors. (1999). Culture specific and cross culturally generalizable implicit leadership theories: Are attributes of charismatic/transformational leadership universally endorsed? *The Leadership Quarterly, 10,* 219–256.

This is the first major article to appear describing the results of the GLOBE study, including both the culture and leadership results. The large number of co-authors raises interesting discussions with students around what is necessary to execute a project of this size, and how collaborators are recognized.

House, R., Javidan, M., & Dorfman, P. (2001). Project GLOBE: An introduction. *Applied Psychology: An International Review, 50,* 489–505.

This article provides exactly what the title suggests—an introduction to the project.

Javidan, M., Stahl, G.K., Brodbeck, F., & Wilderom, C.P.M. (2005). Cross-border transfer of knowledge: Cultural lessons from Project GLOBE. *Academy of Management Executive, 19*(2), 59–76.

This article uses GLOBE to discuss why it is important to consider cross-cultural differences in leadership. An example of an ineffective transfer of leadership knowledge is provided when cross cultural differences are not accounted for.

Javidan, M., Dorfman, P.W., Sully de Luque, M.F., & House, R.J. (2006). In the eye of the beholder: Cross-cultural lessons in leadership from Project GLOBE. *Academy of Management Perspectives, 20*(1), 67–90.

This article provides four hypothetical examples of an American manager in other cultures and provides examples of how GLOBE data can be used to address cultural differences and some of the processes involved in adapting to other cultures.

Javidan, M., & Dastmalchian, A. (2009). Managerial implications of the GLOBE project: A study of sixty-two societies. *Asia Pacific Journal of Human Resources, 47,* 41–58. DOI: 10.1177/1038411108099289

This article focuses on the practical implications that can be obtained from the GLOBE data. It provides a summary of the culture and leadership dimensions as well as how managers can apply the information.

Files referred to in this chapter can be found at http://www.bsos.umd.edu/psyc/hanges.

27

LEADERSHIP ACCELERATION AT GOLDMAN SACHS

◆ Shoma Chatterjee, Cary Friedman, and Keith Yardley

Goldman Sachs

In 1999, the year Goldman Sachs became a public company, the firm began an exploration and debate of how best to develop leaders with the highest potential to take on strategically important roles. Tailoring the initiative to the needs and constraints of the audience—ultra-pragmatic managing directors in a fast-changing, 24 × 7 industry with little time to spare away from client service—was a formidable challenge. This chapter details the origins of the Leadership Acceleration Initiative (LAI) at Goldman Sachs while providing a candid assessment of its strengths and limitations. Over the years, LAI has evolved into a context-driven experience where leaders connect with each other, contribute to the firm's strategic objectives, and hone their commercial instinct while exploring their leadership impact. The flexible architecture of the LAI allows the program to align with the firm's strategic priorities and leadership needs.

In 2000, the year after Goldman Sachs became a public company, the firm's executive team created the Pine Street Leadership Development Group. Pine Street was borne out of the dual imperatives to keep the apprenticeship model alive as the firm grew larger around the world and to transfer leadership lessons, cultural values, and business practices to successive generations of leaders.

Shortly after the creation of Pine Street, the firm began an exploration and debate of how best to develop leaders with the highest potential to take on strategically important roles in the future. More specifically, what type of leadership programming would work for this audience, in this industry context, and at this firm? Tailoring the program to the needs and constraints of the audience—ultra-pragmatic managing directors in a fast-changing, 24 × 7 industry with little time to spare away from client service—was a formidable challenge.

This chapter describes the origins and components of the Leadership Acceleration Initiative (LAI) at Goldman Sachs and provides a candid assessment of its strengths and limitations. Over the last eight years, the LAI has evolved into a context-driven experience where leaders connect with each other, contribute to the firm's strategic objectives, increase their commercial instinct, and enhance their personal impact.

The Roots of Leadership Development at Goldman Sachs

> *"Don't run leadership courses when the markets are open, and remember we're a global firm so the markets are always open somewhere."*

For the first 130 years of Goldman Sachs' existence, on-the-job learning and mentorship by respected senior leaders were the primary vehicles for leadership development. This apprenticeship model was deeply embedded into the firm's culture and served its purposes. However, when the firm went public in 1999, growth into new markets and geographies became the primary strategic imperative. The resultant growth plans necessitated a drastic increase in the workforce and a proliferation of new leadership positions around the world.

When key positions were created or became available in new geographies, the same short-list of potential successors was presented to senior leadership each time. When senior leadership was asked about issues that kept them up at night, their response was consistent: "Do we have the people in place or the talent in the pipeline to run the firm effectively?" The overarching belief was that while the requisite talent was somewhere in the firm, a more systematic and scalable way to identify, develop, and produce leaders was a critical precondition for sustainable growth.

The Pine Street Leadership Development Group, the team of internal Goldman Sachs professionals charged with developing the firm's partner and managing director population, was confident that it could become a strategic lever for the executive office to drive organizational change and development. Whatever shape the leadership program took would have to complement the apprenticeship model and account for the sea change inherent in going from a flat, non-hierarchical culture that eschewed "stars" to one signaling a small number of leaders that were somehow "chosen" on the basis of their potential.

The firm had grown to a size and scale where most other organizations had programmatic efforts in place to identify and develop key talent. Goldman Sachs, unlike most other firms, prided itself on not implementing "programs for program's sake." Indeed, many senior leaders were convinced that the apprenticeship model worked quite well and if any change was needed, perhaps it was a large scale development program available to the nearly one thousand managing directors at the firm at that time. In addition, many had a deep respect for specialization and struggled to define the incentive to broaden and develop leadership skills beyond those required to be an effective banker, trader, or other functional expert.

While Pine Street benchmarked and gathered best practices, it became clear that the team would need a bespoke solution for Goldman Sachs. The research revealed that job-based assignments and experiences played the most meaningful role in developing leaders, and that successful leadership development highlighted the 70/20/10 rule, where 70 percent of the development occurs through action, interaction, and relationships; 20 percent through feedback and coaching; and the last 10 percent through topical skills or classroom training. While widely accepted in leadership practice today, the 70/20/10 concept was fairly novel in the late 1990s and fit well with the action-bias and time-constrained characteristic of leaders at the firm.

Pine Street's proposed model incorporated all of the critical aspects of the 70/20/10 method of development—job-based learning, feedback, coaching, networking, and training—in a way that would minimize the time that participants had to spend offline or away from their desks. In order to create the meaningful experience required to achieve the program's goals, those selected to participate would have to commit to an intensive and comprehensive twelve-month initiative. When Pine Street professionals met with the firm's senior leaders to assess the feasibility of launching a program of this duration, one partner looked on quizzically and said, "I would suggest you don't run courses when the markets are open and remember, we're a global firm so the markets are always open somewhere." There were many skeptics who questioned how those selected to participate would carve out the necessary time and what the incentive would be for their managers to have them involved in such a daunting program on top of an already demanding day job.

While other firms outside of the financial services industry had the luxury of being able to take participants offline for three to four weeks or months at a time to focus solely on their leadership development programs, such an option would be anathema to Goldman Sachs' culture.

An even bigger road block was to determine who would be selected to participate. The idea of nominating participants was perceived by many to be counter-cultural in a firm that heretofore had rewarded teamwork and openly discouraged a "star" system. It was also "unnatural" for senior members of Goldman Sachs to invest their time in something they had previously considered to be soft skills training.

To aid the change management and socialization challenge, the Pine Street Group recruited two members of its advisory board to champion its efforts. These two board members believed in the LAI concept and ultimately were able to convince one of the firm's Vice Chairs to serve as the program's overall sponsor. Along with the CEO and COO, the Vice Chair was most interested in potential outcomes to identify and accelerate the development of leaders who understood how the firm worked and who would be able to move into key seats over time. The development of an appropriate methodology was left in the hands of Pine Street.

The Vice Chair's key role as the program's sponsor was integral to gaining acceptance for the selective nomination process. Traditionally, the firm has recognized performance through promotion and differentiated compensation. Such an untraditional program represented a visible and public signaling of its high performers. In addition, divisions were asked to select senior people, which implied that they would be spending less time executing trades or doing deals. In his role as program sponsor, the Vice Chair sent a message to all of the Global Division Heads that underlined his sponsorship of Pine Street's inaugural leadership acceleration initiative. He emphasized that this would be "the most intensive of Pine Street's offerings, and you should focus on those with the greatest leadership potential. While the program will require a special commitment, participants will remain fully engaged in their day jobs."

When the nominations were submitted, the Vice Chair played an active role in reviewing the nominees to determine if they fit the desired profile. In the case of one candidate, the Vice Chair noted that, "while he is clearly the best in the world at what he does, I don't have a sense for what other roles he could play at the firm. If this is truly about acceleration then I'd like his division head to call me and explain what role he is supposedly being accelerated to take on." With that, the individual was removed from the list. It became clear this program was not about gratifying egos or awarding consolation prizes to elevate someone's stature. As one senior leader who was involved in the nomination process said, "MD LAI is not meant to be used as a lifetime achievement award but rather we use it to make an investment in our highest potential leaders."

Things became even more complex once the names were chosen. The nomination process presented challenges for the firm's most senior leaders as there were many high-potential performers who were perhaps as qualified as those selected. Soon enough, they would be making their way to their manager's office to ask why they were not chosen to be in the program. In one instance, one co-head of a business was nominated while the other co-head was not. The unselected co-head questioned whether the one chosen was being viewed as having a higher trajectory and inquired whether he should be seeking opportunities elsewhere within the firm. The issue of how best to communicate and explain the concept of "high potential" in a culture of high performers was thorny at best. However, it created the opportunity for sustained coaching and education of senior leaders on how best to manage expectations and have career development conversations.

Current Architecture of Leadership Acceleration Initiatives

> *"Most financial services firms do not have a layer of general managers. If you don't have much natural mobility in a firm of specialists, you need creative ways of giving people the breadth of experience and relationships outside their daily setting."*

The last eight years for the LAI program have been marked by iterative adaptation, constantly evolving to meet the needs and strategy of the firm and the constraints and demands of the audience.

While the original LAI was twelve months in duration, it is currently a six-month program as participants felt a tighter time frame would enhance their experience and maintain momentum for the action learning projects that they undertake. Over the years, the action learning component—primarily composed of strategic taskforce assignments sanctioned by the firm's leaders—have become more substantive and central to the experience. Similarly, the definition of "high potential" gets refined each year. MD LAI focuses on a select group of high-performing MDs who have the potential to fill key seats and build businesses or expand Goldman Sachs' global footprint (normally within one to three years of the program). The tightness of the definition aids in creating a shared urgency and experience both for the participants and the organization.

COMPONENTS OF THE LAI EXPERIENCE

Each spring, the MD LAI program commences with sixty managing directors (out of roughly 1,800 in the firm) attending a global launch event that is supported by the firm's senior leadership. The LAI experience consists of seven components, generally split into the 70/20/10 allocation:

1. Entry poll

In keeping with the feedback-intensive and adaptive nature of the program, Pine Street gathers the pulse of each year's participants through an entry poll designed to gauge their top leadership challenges, the specific skills they would like to develop, and their aspirations at the firm. This information is used throughout the program to tailor the group and individual sessions.

2. Global launch and immersion experience

The global launch is a one-and-one-half-day event designed to set the tone and expectations for the next six months. This is the first time all of the participants meet as a global class as well as hear from program sponsors, divisional leaders, external thought leaders, and taskforce clients. A significant portion of the launch is devoted to learning about their specific taskforce assignment and meeting their taskforce teams. The MD LAI launch typically culminates in an immersion trip to the battlefields of Gettysburg, Pennsylvania, or Normandy, France. LAI participants have also traveled to the United States Military Academy at West Point to take part in a negotiations simulation. There they were divided into convoy teams and tasked with entering a foreign village to negotiate with local leaders (played by Army faculty) to ensure safe passage of needed supplies. The goal of these immersion experiences is primarily to implant a language of leadership among participants in a memorable manner. For example, at Normandy, participants debated the strategy that shaped the war-planning process, how information was gathered, how decisions were made, communicated, modified, the effect of individual motivation on decision making, and the role of chance and luck. Further, through facilitator led after-action reviews, participants immediately apply these lessons to current business situations. A secondary, but very important, long-term goal is that through these historically stimulating environments, group-based work and time together away from the office result in new relationships and networks being formed across the organization.

3. 360 feedback and coaching

While Goldman Sachs has a firm-wide 360 performance review system, the 360 feedback gathered through LAI is focused on leadership acumen and used only for developmental purposes. Therefore, the feedback does not impact a participant's performance rating or compensation. This results in a more candid, direct, and actionable level of feedback for the participant. After the feedback is aggregated, each participant meets with a coach to discuss, clarify, and crystallize a focused leadership action plan for the remainder of the program. Participants continue to receive coaching to support their action plans throughout the program.

4. Senior leader roundtables

Leveraging the firm's oral history and storytelling culture, senior leader roundtables provide a forum for leaders to share their career inflection points, decision-making process, and business priorities with the participants. Typically, Senior Leader Roundtables occur one to two times a month during the LAI and last approximately ninety minutes. To maximize interactivity and dialogue, senior leaders are advised to kick off the discussion and speak for no more than twenty to thirty minutes. They are asked to address three topics: (1) an overview and strategic direction of their current business, (2) highlights and trajectory of their career path, and

(3) specific leadership and career navigation advice for the participants. The last two topics often provide the most "teachable moments" as they often address issues participants may be reluctant to surface. For example, how does one say "no" when offered a new career opportunity? What does one do when they feel their career has stalled or how does one recover from pitfalls? One senior leader recounted the story of being too blunt during a key firm-wide meeting. As one gets more senior in the organization, the level of candid feedback tends to decrease. So, others did not tell the senior leader that she was being perceived as insensitive and as a result, may have severed a few relationships. Later, the senior leader actively sought feedback from her peers while clarifying the intent of her words and repairing her peer relationships. Another leader recounted a time earlier in his career when his trading strategy was resulting in losses. At the end of the week, he met with his manager to discuss how to recover. The manager tested him on his thinking and assured him that his strategy was sound. As he left his manager's office, he recalled his parting advice: "splash some water on your face," he said, "because you are a leader now, people are watching you, and if your team sees that shade of red on your face, they will panic."

5. Skills training

Through the years, the most prevalent training need has been executive communications. Expert coaches work with individuals on honing their presence, influence, and gravitas relevant to their role at the firm. In addition to communications, personal productivity and time management sessions have also been part of the program offering.

6. Taskforces and action learning

Perhaps the most important and most demanding element of LAI, the strategic taskforce assignments, feed the action-bias of both the firm and the participants. Each project is staffed based on both client needs and participant development goals. Senior partners of the firm serve as clients while a group of five to eight participants focuses on addressing a critical and real time business challenge. The sourcing process starts months before the launch of the program as the Pine Street team meets with divisional and functional leaders as well as Management Committee members.

Taskforce topics typically fall into four categories: (1) Opportunities to improve the firm's service to clients, shareholders, or investors; (2) New market, product/service, acquisition opportunity or pricing model; (3) Opportunities to improve the firm's risk management and governance; and (4) Assessment and recommendations to strengthen the firm's culture. Examples from recent years range from assessing new market opportunities or acquisitions; solutions to better serve distinct client segments; and approaches to engage and communicate the work of the firm to external stakeholders.

Each taskforce must be sponsored by a partner or senior leader of the firm who is responsible for affecting change or implementing the recommendations. The importance of sourcing actual projects that reflect the firm's priorities cannot be understated. It also limits the scalability of the program as any firm has a finite number of priorities that can be feasibly moved to action within the next year. However, the team has learned that general benchmarking or market sizing exercises do not make for optimal taskforces as the participants view them as "make work projects" that deter from their jobs. To help Pine Street staff the projects, sponsors provide input on the types of skills, background, and knowledge that would be beneficial.

During the global launch of the program, participants receive project briefs and bios of their sponsor/stakeholders. The Pine Street team along with external coaches provide sessions on project management and team building. Appendix 1 provides the general guidance on timeframes. While the teams are encouraged to put in a few hours each week toward their taskforce project, as with any group assignment, the lion's share of the work occurs before the midpoint presentation and before the final deliverable. The team members negotiate among themselves on scope, responsibilities, and timeframes.

At the end of the engagement, participants are reviewed by both taskforce clients and peers. Taskforce clients assess the teams' recommendations based on intellectual rigor, commercial instinct, and feasibility of implementation. They are also asked for observations on each member's leadership impact. Peers are asked to rate each other on the following criteria: setting direction/showing initiative, creativity, results orientation, teamwork, strengths, and development opportunities. Inevitably, there are one or two participants who are unable to contribute in the manner of their peers but this issue is often minimized due to the sponsor attention and peer "pressure" inherent in the projects.

The primacy of these action learning projects cannot be overestimated. As one alumnus noted, "Most financial services firms do not have a layer of general managers. If you don't have much natural mobility in a firm of specialists, you need creative ways of giving people the breadth of experience and relationships outside their daily setting."

7. Global Close

The six-month experience ends with a celebratory but intense closing event, the highlight of which is an opportunity for MD LAI participants to interact with firm executives and the Goldman Sachs Board of Directors while discussing the recommendations of their taskforce projects. As one participant noted, "I appreciated the depth of questions asked by Board members. They showed a willingness to invest time and patience in understanding the complexity of issues we face." The Board, in turn, has a line of sight to the high-potential talent at the firm as well as an opportunity to engage them in meaningful discussions.

While the themes and the taskforce/action learning projects change each year with the firm's strategy and the shifting industry landscape, LAI has three consistent and equally important objectives:

- Enhance participants' knowledge of key firm issues and businesses outside their own function
- Provide participants with a thorough assessment of their leadership skills and the coaching to maximize their leadership impact at the firm
- Broaden participants' relationships among their peers and with senior leaders of the firm

The objectives underscore the critical success factors of leadership at Goldman Sachs' commercial results as well as role modeling the culture and values of the firm, wearing a firmwide and "silobusting" hat, and finally, relationships—an indispensable currency in a relatively flat, matrixed, growing organization and the cultural glue of an institution.

THEORETICAL UNDERPINNINGS OF THE LAI APPROACH

The previous sections described the components of the program and the contextually important nature of senior leader engagement. The selection of these components and their sequence was based on three primary assumptions: *a bias for action*; *leadership as a contact sport*; *leaders connecting with leaders*.

Assumption #1: A bias for action. At the core of the approach is a strong belief in the 70/20/10 formula that is attributed to Eichinger and Lombardo (2007) of the Center for Creative Leadership.

The primary driver of the 70 percent is the strategic taskforce project whose design has been heavily influenced by the Action Reflection Learning (ARL) methodology. Pine Street's interpretation of ARL is that participants learn new (leadership) skills through working on live organizational challenges. At the center of the learning theory is that adults learn best through a reflective process in small groups that have a deep appreciation of questioning (vs. listening to a lecture) as the core way to learn. There is strong belief in the wisdom of the founder of Action Learning, Reg Revans (1982), who said there can be no learning without action and no action without learning. To be more specific, ARL in our MD LAI program encourages our participants to learn at five levels (Rimanoczy & Turner, 2008):

1. *The operating business level.* Participants learn to develop strategic thinking and problem solving skills by being required to provide recommendations to address a real life business challenge and/or opportunity.
2. *The organizational development level.* Participants learn how to navigate a new network of relationships in the firm in order to solve a real-life business challenge and/or opportunity.
3. *The team-working level.* Participants learn to work on cross-functional teams, in which no member has a defined leadership role.
4. *The professional competency level.* Participants learn new skills and technical knowledge.
5. *The personal mindset level.* Participants learn to view the world from different perspectives.

Assumption #2: Leadership development is a contact sport and happens through repeated contact with key stakeholders. Specifically, Goldsmith and Morgan (2004) demonstrated that the most important variable in the design of a leadership development program to the achievement of positive long-term change was the participants' ongoing interaction and follow-up with colleagues. It is the interaction with colleagues, rather than a coach, trainer, consultant, or academic guru, that was most important. According to the authors, "leaders who discussed their own improvement priorities with their co-workers, and regularly followed up with these co-workers, showed striking improvement." Our belief in this assumption is such that participants are promised that any feedback data that are collected from their co-workers and the development plans that they construct through direct discussion with their coach and manager will be used for development purposes only. This promise we believe creates enough psychological safety for participants to discuss vulnerabilities and areas for personal growth.

Assumption #3: The third assumption is something that has been in Goldman Sachs' culture for over a hundred years, but more recently academic research has emerged to give it a language. The theoretical area is one of social networks. Research from this field demonstrates that numerous ties across a firm are an important factor for information sharing and innovation, though simply more connectivity is not better. It is therefore better for organizations to tie their network building efforts with the core value proposition of the firm. Our program strengthens what Cross, Liedtka, and Weiss (2005) labeled "Customized Response Networks." Characteristics of a customized response network include where individuals are rapidly drawn together to define a client's problem or business opportunity, and coordinate their relevant expertise to solve the problem. For these networks to be built it requires connectivity across business and geographical boundaries, requires trust in others' expertise and a culture where the norm is of generalized reciprocity. It is because of this belief in the importance of customized networks that the programs are designed to be extremely interactive across functional areas, geographies, and levels across the firm.

Assessment, Strengths, and Limitations

> *"Through the program, I had the simple realization that maybe leadership cannot be taught but it can definitely be learned. My thinking has expanded from 'how can I be the best research analyst' to 'how can I generate value for the firm, where are we going in the years ahead, and who should I be talking to about it.'"*

As with leadership programs in all institutions, Pine Street aims to gauge feedback and the impact of its LAI. Key metrics include the following:

- Over 350 managing directors are graduates of the MD LAI program.
- The Kirkpatrick Model consists of four levels of training evaluation: (1) reaction—how the learners react to the content and process based on post-program surveys, (2) learning—how much the learners gained in terms of knowledge and skills, (3) behavior—how the training was applied on the job, and (4) results—returns in terms of savings, revenues, efficiency, morale, etc. At the first and simplest level of the Kirkpatrick model of evaluation, the post-program participant feedback has risen consistently since the inception. In recent years, MD LAI has scored on average 4.7 on a 5-point scale. The rise in scores is primarily attributable to the focus on improving the quality, sponsorship, and action-orientation of the taskforce projects.
- At the second and third levels, participants have indicated that learning occurred primarily in three areas:

1. Firm strategy and expertise—and more importantly, how they can leverage this expertise to improve their business performance and serve their clients. In a professional services firm, knowing the individuals who possess specific domains of knowledge is a clear advantage. One MD LAI participant had a meeting with a key client in the consumer products industry. During their meeting, the conversation turned to how the growth of the middle class in Latin America would fuel the client's long-term strategy. The MD LAI participant recalled that one of her teammates in her MD LAI taskforce project focused on emerging and growth markets in the region. She called her former teammate from her client's office and was able to provide frontline insights from the region. In her words, "the LAI experience makes a big firm feel like a small community because we go through a shared experience in a compressed timeframe while forging relationships with individuals we may not have come across otherwise."
2. Improved ability and willingness to manage and support a team of diverse peers to deliver results in a difficult assignment in an unfamiliar and often uncomfortable subject area. As one trader recounted, "I have enhanced my confidence in tackling new challenges, which will be key as we currently live in a time of rampant uncertainty in our industry. Our project's scope was open-ended and vague. While we were nervous and,

at times, frustrated, the broadening of our horizons beyond our functions has been illuminating. I think most of us have come to appreciate the breadth and depth of the organization and the fact that as we grow more senior in our roles, challenges have less to do with technical matters and more to do with adaptation."

3. Exercising leadership voice, presence, and influence. While many of the participants are good presenters and communicators, they soon learn to differentiate between communications and leadership communications. "Leadership communications is different in that it has to create change or motivate others to do something differently and give something extra. Often it is about influencing without authority and we have to do this many times over, especially while working with our peers in the taskforces."

- At level four, behavior change and the holy grail of "ROI" have been difficult to measure outside of anecdotal evidence and due to the short length of the program. However, positive client feedback on the commercial impact of taskforce recommendations, the overwhelming demand for places in the program, and the willingness of senior leaders to engage as faculty are all indicators of the firm's acceptance of significant ROI.
- Over fifty taskforce projects have been completed.
- The 2010 MD LAI program alone engaged 180 senior leaders as faculty, mentors, or taskforce sponsors. This number does not include the firm "luminaries" that host networking events.
- Retention rates for LAI graduates have exceeded those of their peers at the firm. The small size of each participant class allows Pine Street to track the progression of individuals as they are promoted or take on greater roles at the firm. These rates have also exceeded those of peers who have not gone through the program. However, though there is correlation, it is erroneous to attribute causation of participant success to a six-month LAI program, especially since the participants were high-performing and high-potential when they entered.
- The demand for the seats in the program exceeds supply by a factor of at least four or five.

STRENGTHS OF THE PROGRAM

The primary strength of the program is its commerciality and pragmatism—each component is designed to make the participants more successful at this firm, at this time, and in this industry. This strength keeps most questions about ROI at bay since the relevance of building networks and relationships in a global organization, focusing on solving critical business issues in taskforces, and learning from frontline leaders is unquestionable and obvious. In fact, the value of the taskforce recommendations, given that the top talent of the firm is engaged in providing consulting services, would be in the millions of dollars if measured. Also, business disruption is minimized since the participants continue in their daily roles while participating in LAI.

The class composition, the key themes for the program, and the taskforce projects are intrinsically linked to the firm's strategic priorities and the current industry landscape, and thus add to the commerciality dimension. For example, given the firm's current emphasis on growth and growing markets, the 2010 class composition was decidedly composed of leaders who are growing businesses at home and in high-priority geographies. Similarly, many of the 2010 taskforces focused on assessing growth opportunities or on how the firm can set the highest standards of ethics, transparency, and client focus across its business activities.

Secondly, through the discussion forums and the taskforce projects arise a shared understanding of the firm's strategic priorities among its leaders and its key talent. Additionally, the cultural tenets and success factors of the firm have been methodically passed on to all graduates of LAI. The value of this institutional glue cannot be underestimated.

Third, the architecture of the program bridges the traditional dialectic between leader development and leadership development as the elements build and strengthen both human capital and sociocultural capital in the organization (Day, 2001).

Fourth, the exhaustive candidate vetting process in the LAI program results in increased visibility of the firm's talent pipeline and their respective development trajectories. Pine Street allots a given number of slots to each division and region based on the current strategy of the firm and the size and leadership needs of each division and region. Then, each of the eight divisions and three regions within Goldman Sachs reaches out to its business functions and industry sectors to ask for their high-potential candidates. A long list of candidates bubbles up to divisional leadership (division heads and their operating committees) where each candidate is vetted again based on the performance and potential relative to their peers within the division. As a final step in the process, the Executive Office often applies a firm-wide optic to vet the candidates that each division puts forth.

Finally, and perhaps most importantly, the sponsorship of the Executive Office, the CEO and President in particular, has been unwavering over the years and through leadership changes. Their involvement ranges beyond leading sessions and sharing personal experiences and includes reviewing candidate nominations, framing critical firm-wide issues for taskforce projects, providing one-on-one advice to participants, and inviting the Goldman Sachs Board of Directors to meet the participants and hear their final taskforce recommendations.

LIMITATIONS OF THE APPROACH

Scalability is a major limitation of the highly tailored and high-touch LAI approach. While the firm wishes to maintain the aspirational and selective rigor of the program, there have been discussions to double the size of the LAI class as the firm pursues growth markets around the world. However, this increase in scale would tax the capacity of the organization to produce meaningful taskforces, dilute the leader to participant ratio as well as the intimate and relational flavor of the program.

Second, while the 360-degree feedback emanating from the program produces more candid and instructive feedback than the firm's performance review process, and we do capture through the peer feedback process those participants who naturally emerge as leaders during the taskforce project cycle, this information is not shared beyond the LAI participants and their manager. Though the information would serve as valuable inputs to the firm's succession or other talent management processes, we believe that changing our development-only program philosophy would alter the willingness of feedback respondents to provide such candid responses when completing the peer-to-peer feedback process.

Third, the short timeframe as well as the commercial thrust of the program leaves little opportunity for personal or team reflection on broader and more philosophical leadership issues. Similarly, the strategic taskforces and leadership discussions of the LAI program impose a twelve- to eighteen-month optic, reflecting the traditional short-term focus of Wall Street culture. There is little exploration of scenarios or issues beyond the next one to two years.

Perhaps the most important lesson learned from Goldman Sachs' Leadership Acceleration Initiatives is that they are as much of a change management effort as an exercise in program design. The tenets of gaining sponsorship, getting buy-in, and adapting to the audience's context each and every year have been fundamental to their popularity and institutionalization. The current post-crisis environment in the financial services industry has started a new round of discussion and debate on how the LAI can be used to create leaders for "the new normal"—leaders who can apply additional rigor in decision-making, thrive despite uncertain and fluid markets, and engage a broad array of external stakeholders in the work of the firm. Ultimately, having the Leadership Acceleration Initiative experience and platform to build on is viewed as a valuable asset in a firm so focused on developing its leaders.

References

Cross, R., Liedtka, J., & Weiss, L. (2005). A practical guide to social networks. *Harvard Business Review, 83*(3), 124–132.

Day, D.V. (2001). Leadership development: A review in context. *Leadership Quarterly, 11*, 581–613.

Eichinger, M.M., & Lombardo, R.W. (2007). *Career architect development planner*, (4th ed.). Minneapolis, MN: Lominger International.

Goldsmith, M., & Morgan, H. (2004). Leadership is a contact sport: The follow-up factor in management development. *Strategy & Business, 36*, 70–79.

Revans, R.W. (1982). *The origin and growth of action learning*. Brickley, UK: Chartwell-Bratt.

Rimanoczy, I., & Turner, E. (2008). *Action-reflection-learning: Solving real business problems by connecting learning and earning*. Mountain View, CA: Davies-Black Publishing.

Appendix 27.1: Taskforce Participant Reference Guide

TIMING	*TEAM'S ROLE*	*SUCCESS FACTORS*
Beginning of June (60–90 minutes)	Meet with sponsors/clients to kick-off project Understand strategic context of the project Get relevant start-up information and contacts for team's due diligence activities Ask clients how best to communicate with them over the course of the project Pine Street will liaise with both you and the client throughout the project	Understand the scope—specifically what to include and exclude from your analysis Team should decide on roles and responsibilities based on each person's strengths Choose 1–2 team members to serve as program managers Team should decide on meeting schedule and communication norms
Mid-June (weekly meeting/call with day-to-day client contact)	Conduct due-diligence/research activities Analyze initial findings On average, this will take a few hours of time each week	Continue to focus the scope of the team Contact Pine Street if any issues arise Do as much work upfront as possible in case there is slippage later
July/August (Mid-Point Presentation)	Schedule a mid-point progress review with client Review initial findings and preliminary conclusions with client	Be candid about progress to date Ask them what you should start, stop, or emphasize?
Mid-September/ Mid-October (60–90 minutes) Final Presentation	Team will provide final presentation and deliverable Most if not all team members should be present (in person or via teleconference)	Present your findings crisply—have a point of view (this is not an academic research project) Make recommendations as actionable as possible More than one person should present the final deliverable
End of October (30 minutes)	Pine Street will gather feedback from you on each of your team members Pine Street will provide feedback on you from your team members and clients	Provide candid feedback on team members

28

DEVELOPING INTERDEPENDENT LEADERSHIP

◆ Charles J. Palus, John B. McGuire, and Chris Ernst
The Center for Creative Leadership

The most important challenges we face today are interdependent: They can only be solved by groups of people working collaboratively across boundaries. In this chapter we offer four practical arts for teaching and developing the forms of interdependent leadership required to meet these challenges. Behind these four arts is an ontology of leadership we refer to as the *DAC framework*, based in the three essential leadership outcomes of shared *direction*, *alignment*, and *commitment*. DAC is produced (that is, leadership can be created) through three epistemologies, the *leadership logics* of *dependence*, *independence*, and *interdependence*. The four arts represent the four social levels at which people create shared DAC: *society*, *organization*, *group*, and *individual* (the SŌGI Model). All four levels are engaged in developing interdependent leadership. The first art is developing leadership from the *inside-out*, working with the subjective meaning-making (the core values, beliefs, identity, emotions, intuition, imagination, and leadership logics) of each individual. At the group level, the art is *boundary spanning* across horizontal, vertical, demographic, geographic, and stakeholder boundaries. At the organizational level the art is *creating headroom*, working with the required time, space, risk-taking, learning, and modeling to "lift up" the entire *leadership culture* to a new order of thought and action. Finally the art of *dialogue* in society and across all the SŌGI levels uses collaborative inquiry and creative conversations to create wise and effective direction, alignment, and commitment about the challenges that matter most.

❖❖❖

Introduction: A Declaration of Interdependence

We hold this truth to be self-evident: The natural world, our lives, our work, and our collective well-being are *interdependent*. Everything is, or will be, connected.

In 1998, Pulitzer prize-winning Harvard biologist E.O. Wilson revived the concept of *consilience*: Knowledge on all subjects is fundamentally unified. The enlightenment thinkers had it right in knowing a lot about everything, he argued. Today's specialists know a lot about a little—a counterproductive approach in a world where science and art and everything in between stem from the same roots and grow toward the same goals. The issues that vex humanity can be solved only by integrating fields of knowledge.

> Only fluency across the boundaries will provide a clear view of the world as it really is, not as it appears through the lens of ideology and religious dogma, or as a myopic response solely to immediate need. (Wilson, 1998)

Advances in Internet and collaboration technologies have dismantled many of the physical boundaries that once prevented people from working together. Yet, as physical boundaries are removed, the boundaries that still exist in human relationships remain, in sharp and jagged relief. Against this shifting leadership landscape the enormous challenges we face—climate, war, disease, prosperity, justice—can only be solved by groups working collaboratively together (Johansen, 2010).

We need a new kind of leadership, one more concerned with solving big challenges for all our futures than with winning the next political battle that the other group loses. We need a *declaration of interdependence* (McGuire, 2010).

It's already happening. In the world today there is an evolution in leadership thought. Leadership is increasingly becoming a process shared by people throughout an organization or society rather than a responsibility of just a few individuals at the top.

Intentional transformation to a leadership culture of interdependence is feasible under the right circumstances. The United States began as a *dependent* culture—a group of colonies under the authoritarian rule of the king. Rebelling against this oppression, colonists developed more *independent* minds. The U.S. Constitution expresses a form of *interdependence* that uses authority and compromise as tools within a broader vision of collaboration, new frontiers, and further transformation.

Collaborative work uses dialogue, not debate, to understand deeply the challenges we face. Collaboration generates multiple options and integrates the best ones into sustainable solutions. Compromise gives us incremental progress and there is a role for that. Collaboration is a creative process that combines perspectives into something new.

So how do you teach that? How can interdependent leadership be developed?

This chapter explores the theory and practice of effective leadership education and development in an increasingly interdependent world.

We begin by rethinking the source of leadership. Instead of thinking of leadership capability as located only within individuals, we also think of it within a much larger domain—as people together creating shared *direction, alignment, and commitment* (DAC) in all sorts of interesting and potentially generative ways. In our own research and practice over the last twenty years, this has been a liberating idea, opening the door to new possibilities for developing more collaborative, connected, adaptive, and vital—*interdependent*—forms of leadership.

The practices by which people create shared direction, alignment, and commitment can be observed at four levels within a continuum described by the SŌGI Model—society, organization, group, and individual. SŌGI (pronounced SŌ′-jee) specifies the sources of leadership—that is, the beliefs and practices that result in DAC—and the levels necessary for evaluating the outcomes of leadership development (Hannum, Martineau & Reinelt, 2007; Martineau & Hoole, in press; Wilber, 2000; Yammarino & Dansereau, 2008).

Our aim in this chapter is to support real-world change through leadership development. We explore the feasibility for developing more advanced leadership cultures. We describe four practical arts for leadership development, keyed to SŌGI, and how to use them in moving *toward* (not always *to*) interdependent leadership.

The first art is *dialogue* in society, using collaborative inquiry and creative conversations to create wise and effective direction, alignment, and commitment around the challenges that matter most. The second art is *creating headroom* at the organizational level, working with the required time, space, risk-taking, learning, and modeling to "lift up" the entire leadership culture to a new order of thought and action. At the group level, the art is *boundary spanning* across horizontal, vertical, demographic, geographic, and stakeholder boundaries. Finally there is the art of developing leadership from the *inside-out*, working with the subjective meaning-making (the core values, beliefs, identity, emotions, intuition, imagination, and leadership logics) of each individual.

A New Ontology of Leadership

How one teaches or develops leadership depends on one's ontological commitment, that is, on what one believes leadership to be at its foundation. Historically the field of leadership has been committed to a foundation that Warren Bennis refers to as a *tripod*: "a leader or leaders, followers, and a common goal they want to achieve" (Bennis, 2007, p. 3). This commitment typically results in a focus on developing the character, competencies, and skills of individuals in "leader" roles. Much good has come of this commitment, and yet it is has become limiting to those seeking paths to more interdependent leadership.

We work from a leadership ontology in which the essential entities are three *outcomes*: (1) *direction*: widespread agreement in a collective on overall goals, aims, and mission; (2) *alignment*: the organization and coordination of knowledge and work in a collective; and (3) *commitment*: the willingness of members of a collective to subsume their own interests and benefits within those of the collective.

With the tripod ontology, it is the presence of leaders and followers interacting around their shared goals that marks the occurrence of leadership. With an outcomes-based ontology, it is the presence of direction, alignment, and commitment (DAC) that marks the occurrence of leadership. From this ontology we obtain two useful definitions: *Leadership* is the production of direction, alignment, and commitment. *Leadership development* is the expansion of a collective's capacity to produce direction, alignment, and commitment (Drath et al., 2008).

SŌGI

The capabilities for producing DAC reside within and across the four levels of social scale previously introduced as SŌGI: society, organization, group, and individual. The *societal* level includes relationships among organizations and their value webs, entire fields and industries, regional cultures, and global society (Ospina & Foldy, 2010 Quinn; & Van Velsor, 2010). The *organizational* level includes multi-part organizations and communities. The *group* level includes smaller sub-collectives such as divisions, functions, teams, workgroups, and task forces. The *individual* level addresses the personal domain, including the qualities and subjective viewpoints of individual leaders, followers, and members.

These four levels represent a continuous spectrum of human activity. One level shades into the next, and all levels can be identified as vital in any scenario in which DAC is produced. SŌGI helps us embrace the entire domain of leadership and its impacts, including yet going beyond the individual leader. Our research and experience suggest that attention to processes and outcomes at all four levels are necessary for developing interdependent leadership.

THREE LEADERSHIP LOGICS

Put a large assortment of people in a room and ask them to describe effective leadership. You will get three types of replies, signaling three underlying *leadership logics* (McGuire, Palus, & Torbert, 2007). Each is a comprehensive way of "knowing leadership," an epistemology for knowing what DAC is and how it is produced (Drath, 2001; McCauley et al., 2006). We call these three leadership logics *Dependent*, *Independent*, and *Interdependent* (Figure 28.1).

Constructive developmental psychology shows that people grasp these logics in a lifelong sequence, as stages of development. Each stage represents a transformation in epistemology. Later logics are more complex. They can successfully embrace more environmental complexity, in part, because they have the advantages of altitude and hindsight. Later stages transcend and include the earlier stages, which remain available as "objects" or tools within the new more comprehensive logic (Cook-Greuter, 1999; Kegan, 1994; Torbert, 2004; Wilber, 2001). One cannot be intentionally interdependent without first having absorbed the basic lessons of dependence and independence.

The three leadership logics can be seen as operating at and shaping each level of SŌGI. For individuals, the logics are expressed by how one relates to others and gets work done. For groups, it shows up as

Figure 28.1 The Three Leadership Logics

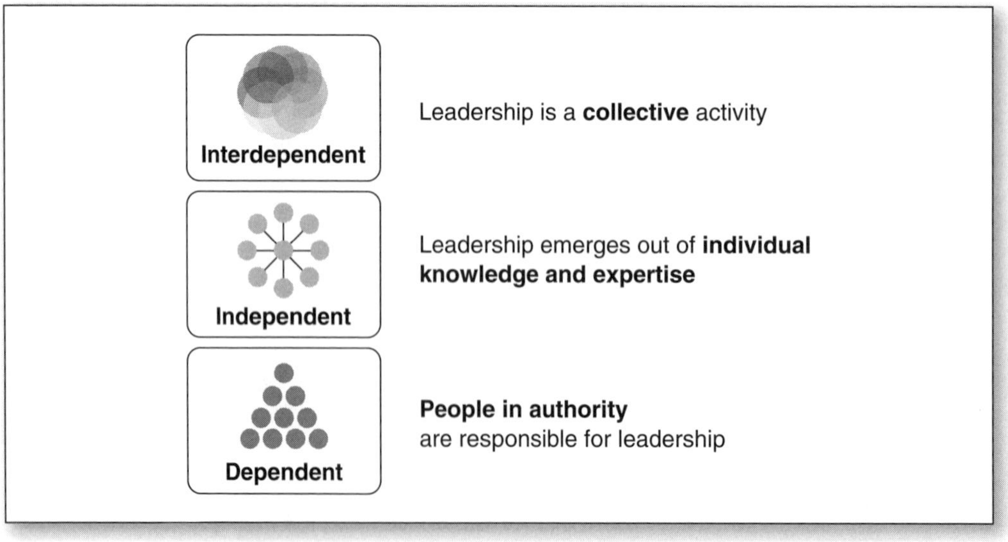
Interdependent
Leadership is a **collective** activity
Independent
Leadership emerges out of **individual knowledge and expertise**
Dependent
People in authority are responsible for leadership

behavioral norms about power, control, and inclusion. At the organizational level, the logics shape the leadership culture, that is, the enduring pattern of shared beliefs and practices. At the level of societies, the advance of civilization itself depends on first attaining, then transcending, the logic of dependent leadership (Fukayama, 2011; Turchin, 2007).

We believe that the leadership cultures of groups and organizations, being the huge, operational "middle" of SŌGI, are critical in this shift toward interdependent leadership. Let's look at what we mean by leadership culture.

Understanding and Transforming Leadership Culture

> *"This was as traditional a culture as you could find. In a couple of years we have started changing the culture from comfort and conformity to responsibility, commitment and interdependence. Our results have gotten better in a tough period of the economy."*
>
> —Vance Tang, CEO, KONE Americas

Culture matters. Culture sets norms on everything in an organization: how to share bad news, whether to take risks, whether and how people are developed and promoted, how people interact with one another, how problems are solved. When people say "it's just the way things are around here," they're talking about culture (McGuire & Rhodes, 2009).

Where strategy meets culture, culture always wins (see Figure 28.2). Organizations seeking to grow and adapt in the face of complex challenges in turbulent times—like now—cannot get there by the purely technical approaches of restructuring and reengineering. Lack of culture development is why 66 percent to 75 percent of organizational change initiatives fail.

Figure 28.2 Culture Eats Strategy for Breakfast

Leadership culture is the self-reinforcing web *of individual and collective beliefs and practices* in a collective (group, organization, community, etc.) for producing the outcomes of shared direction, alignment, and commitment.

Beliefs unconsciously drive decisions and behaviors, and repeated behaviors become leadership practices. Leadership cultures can be understood in terms of the three essential leadership logics (Figure 28.3) as they guide collectives of people creating direction, alignment, and commitment (Drath, Palus, & McGuire, 2010).

Dependent leadership cultures are characterized by practices driven by the belief that only people in positions of authority are responsible for leadership. This assumption may lead to organizations that emphasize top-down control and deference to authority. In general, dependent cultures can be thought of as "conformer" cultures.

Independent leadership cultures are characterized by practices driven by the belief that leadership emerges from a variety of individuals based on knowledge and

Figure 28.3 Three Forms of Leadership Culture

	Direction	**Alignment**	**Commitment**
	How will we decide on a shared direction?	How will we coordinate our work so that it fits together?	How will we maintain commitment to the collective?
 **Interdependent**	Agreement on direction is the result of **shared exploration** and the **emergence** of new perspectives.	Alignment results from **ongoing mutual adjustment** among **system-responsible** people.	Commitment results from **engagement in a developing** community.
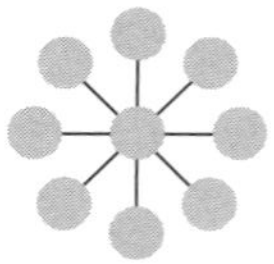 **Independent**	Agreement on direction is the result of **discussion, mutual influence,** and **compromise**.	Alignment results from **negotiation** among **self-responsible** people.	Commitment results from **evaluation of the benefits for self** while benefiting the larger community.
 **Dependent**	Agreement on direction is the result of willing **compliance** with an authority.	Alignment results from **fitting into** the expectations of the **larger system**.	Commitment results from **loyalty** to the source of authority or to the community itself.

expertise. This assumption may lead to decentralized decision-making, high demand for individual responsibility, and competition among types of experts. In general, independent cultures can be thought of as "achiever" cultures.

As with dependent leadership cultures, there are limits to the capability for independent leadership cultures to produce DAC. When the clients or customers of such a collective demand more fully integrated service across the various disciplines and areas of expert knowledge, the value of maintaining independence is called into question. When the environment in which the collective operates grows in complexity beyond the scope of any given area of expertise, negotiation and compromise may not produce the degree of integrated action needed. A deeper sense of togetherness—interdependence—is required.

Interdependent leadership cultures are characterized by practices driven by the belief that leadership is a collective activity that requires mutual inquiry and learning (McCauley et al., 2008). This assumption may lead to the widespread use of dialogue, collaboration, horizontal networks, valuing of differences, and a focus on learning. In general, interdependent cultures can be thought of as collaborative cultures. Other characteristics associated with interdependent cultures include the ability to work effectively across organizational boundaries, openness and candor, multi-faceted standards of success, and synergies being sought across the whole enterprise. Interdependent cultures are successful in adapting to rapid changes in which it is necessary to work inter-systemically, internally as well as with external partners and collaborators across the value web.

As with individuals, leadership cultures gain capability as they ascend from dependent to independent to interdependent. Each stage is more capable of dealing with more ambiguity and complexity than the previous one. The rule of transcend and include applies: The previous stage is included in the capability of the new one. Like climbing stairs, each step remains as a platform as we take the next one.

It's easy to be carried away by enthusiasm for interdependence as ideal for every case. It's not. There are highly successful dependent, independent, and interdependent organizations in business, government, and NGOs. Pockets of dependent, independent, and interdependent environments can and do exist in all organizations. Even a predominately interdependent culture, unless it is a small group of like-minded individuals, is likely to exhibit all three leadership logics. For example, an organization that provides mental health services might exhibit a dependent culture in its support staff, an independent culture among its case workers, and an interdependent culture in its relations among these parts and with external stakeholders.

With only a small fraction of individuals and social systems measuring at the interdependent stage of development (Kegan, 1994; McCauley et al., 2006; Torbert, 2004), leadership development requires meeting people where they are. Often the starting place is a *dependent* epistemology and the first stage of the journey is toward *independence*.

FOUR ARTS FOR DEVELOPING INTERDEPENDENT LEADERSHIP

Each level of SŌGI provides leverage points for development. There are particular arts, or practices, for working well and wisely at each level. We describe four such arts, one at each level. We have found these four to be essential for teaching and developing interdependent leadership.

Think of the SŌGI levels as like nested "Russian dolls," with society on the outside, surrounding everything, and with the individual at the core (Figure 28.4). The Western tradition of leader development (based in the tripod ontology) is to begin with the individual and work outward. The Eastern tradition says that society determines the individual. An integrated

Figure 28.4 Four Arts for Developing Interdependent Leadership

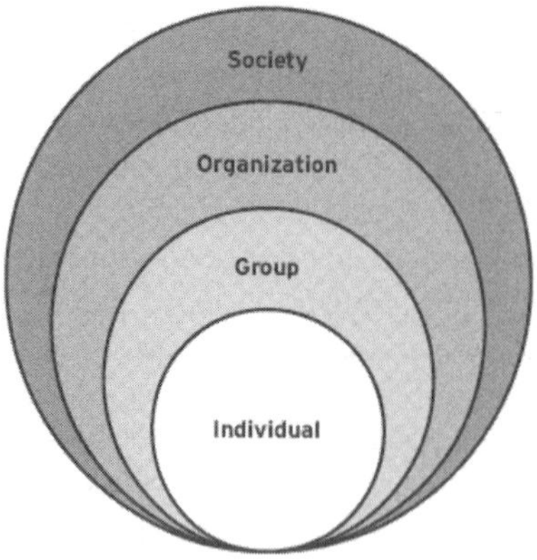

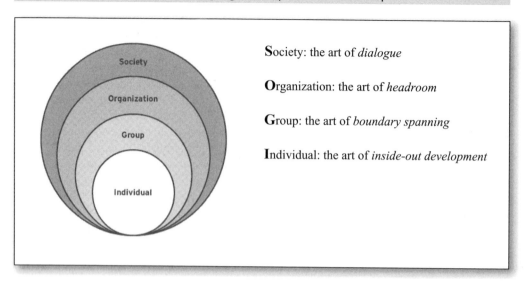

Society: the art of *dialogue*

Organization: the art of *headroom*

Group: the art of *boundary spanning*

Individual: the art of *inside-out development*

approach, using the four arts, works at multiple levels at the same time. Here, we discuss the arts in the SŌGI order, starting with society, a gentle breaking of the honorable but limiting Western habit of "starting with the individual." At the same time the Russian doll analogy reminds us that people inhabit each level. People create DAC. People make it all work.

THE ART OF DIALOGUE

In conversations at all levels of society (in which direction, alignment, and commitment are created), conflict and misunderstandings abound. The practices of dialogue offer a variety of ways to reflect on unquestioned assumptions and difficult topics, and to find common ground and new frontiers amid seemingly vast differences. In dialogue, people learn to ask more and better questions, pay more careful attention, and explore the perspectives of others. Dialogue helps explore "hot spots" (conflicting or polarizing points of view) without smoothing them over, in a way that builds shared meaning (Beer & Eisenstat, 2004; Bohm, 1990; Dixon, 1998; Isaacs, 1999; McGuire & Palus, 2003;).

This is a tall order. Dialogue can be difficult to teach or facilitate. We have found an approach that usually works well, at least as a starting place. We call this methodology *mediated dialogue*, or *putting something in the middle* (Palus & Drath, 2001). What is put in the middle of the conversation, initially, are two kinds of things: first, a shared challenge with associated questions, and then, some tangible objects used to explore the questions. The objects serve as metaphors and symbols. They can be artifacts, souvenirs, mementos, or representations. The objects are also places to project and then explore feelings, viewpoints, and responses to the questions. Each object creates an inviting and playful right-brain focus for attention, imagination, story telling, perspective taking, and co-inquiry. Emotional hot spots are projected onto the objects, and channeled through the metaphors, rather than being pointed directly "at" others. It helps that people are physically handling the artifacts in the here and now. When people have experienced dialogue this way, they can then be coached to generalize from the tangible objects to abstract "objects" in which the "something in the middle" is the problem or challenge itself.

Photographic images are ideal objects for conducting mediated dialogue. We have invented a tool called Visual Explorer for this purpose, but almost any diverse and interesting photo collection can work (Palus & Horth, 2002, 2007, 2010). Images in the middle help people connect across all kinds of boundaries including differences in spoken language and national culture. We like to tell the story of the blind man who participated in such a dialogue—and became a leader for that period—by hearing descriptions of the images, asking questions, choosing one, and engaging the metaphors verbally and through the mind's eye.

The art of dialogue became a cornerstone for our work with Lenoir Memorial Hospital. Lenoir is a regional hospital facing enormous challenges, including new for-profit competitors, rapidly advancing technology, and large shifts in patient demographics. The hospital was limited by their largely dependent culture, based in conformance to rules and regulations, with a steep management hierarchy. Some subcultures had developed more independent mindsets: doctors, nursing, and hospital operations all had their own different right answers, but none of them really understood the others.

Our work with Lenoir focused on helping to evolve their leadership culture toward collaboration and agility. We began with the senior leadership team, who labored with a host of unexamined issues. In one session we shared organizational survey data including the Denison Organizational Culture Survey (Denison, 1997), a team survey, and a customized questionnaire. To help them process the data and get past their deference to authority and risk-avoidance, we used Visual Explorer. The were able to explore their dilemmas, surface the strong emotions they were biting back, tell the truth, and get to the root of things.

Here's how we did that.

First we asked each team member to make notes about two questions: *What stands out for me in the data? What creative competency do I personally bring to the challenges we face?* Next, we asked each person to choose two Visual Explorer images (which were spread around the room). One image was to represent or illustrate their answer to each question. Then, we asked them to look closely at each image and write down their answers and insights. During this entire process we played instrumental jazz and asked them not to talk. Right brain thinking kicked in. They relaxed a little. Finally the entire group sat in a circle, no table. Each person first described the image itself, then talked about why they picked the image and what it meant to them. To each image, the others responded with their own observations of the image, and their own connections and meanings given the question. Typically, and often profoundly, one person saw something in the image no one else has noticed. With each image, and question, it was clear that there was more than one valid perspective and more than one right answer. What stood out for this group was: *possibility* . . . *core values* . . . *upward energy* . . . and also . . . *disconnection* . . . *dissonance between senior managers and directors* . . . *a thread of fear and blame in the interviews*.

After using the images, they continued in the deepened conversation. They gave and received feedback from each other on specific behaviors. A senior member of the clinical staff faced up to a powerful operations manager. An HR person bravely and fearfully challenged the CEO's assumptions. The objects in the middle—the images—leveled the playing field and enabled collaborative conversation. In what turned into a raucous expression of relief, they named all the "sacred cows"—the nagging issues that bothered everyone and yet had previously been undiscussable. This experience launched the change leadership team into its pursuit of a collaborative, customer-focused hospital.

The other question we posed and talked about—*What creative competency do I personally bring to the challenges we face?*—supported an appreciative and optimistic outlook in the conversation, and points directly to the *art of inside out*, to which we will return shortly.

Afterward, we made a slide show of the images overlaid with key insights in their own words. We played it the next morning to remind them of the process and insights (Figure 28.5, the theme of fear). Because this client is a long-term partner, they have reviewed these graphics on multiple occasions to reflect on their journey.

The immediate outcomes were greater trust and openness. The practice of dialogue spread to include everyone in the hospital, and eventually included patients and families, partners, suppliers, neighbors and community—their "society." For example, one director said the Patient Safety Committee "would have been just one more committee, playing it safe, and everybody deferring to who's in charge. Instead we tried collaborating. Now, people from different functions trade the chairman role. Everybody owns all the problems, there are no priority silos. Conflict is okay now. We often ask ourselves, 'Is there more than one right answer?'—that works!"

THE ART OF HEADROOM

Headroom is our term for the time and space created to enable people to begin to think and act differently, together, in service of intentionally developing the leadership culture. Headroom allows people, as they work together, to grow a bigger mind—to embrace the larger and more complex leadership logic of interdependence. Headroom means raising the ceiling of potential, making room for new actions, thoughts, and beliefs.

Developmental stages tend to be self-reinforcing, and therefore stable. For example, authoritarian beliefs tend to beget the same, and a dependent leadership culture

Figure 28.5 An Artifact From Mediated Dialogue Using Visual Explorer

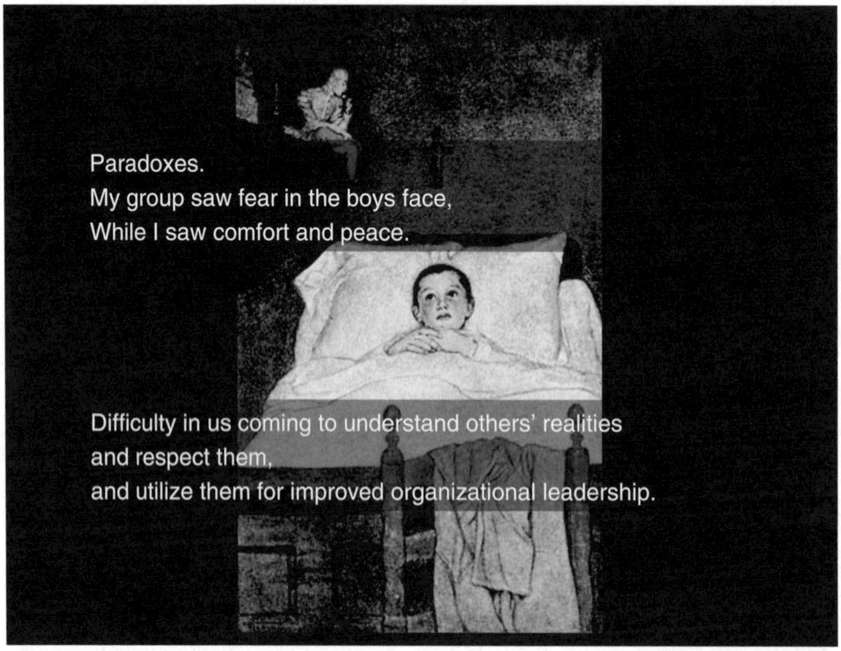

tends to remain so. Therefore some type of practice field is needed to allow people to break out of these old habits and question assumptions. Making headroom is the creation of these on-the-job experiences. It means intentionally enacting the desired culture here and now.

A key practice is public learning. Moving expressly beyond the rules of the current culture, leaders practice taking risks in groups and public forums. They discuss mistakes, aspirations, flaws, and barriers. Undiscussables (Argyris, 1990) become discussable.

When Louis Gerstner transformed IBM from its silos and fiefdoms, he didn't do it just one leader at a time. He created headroom for integration around customer needs. For example, he challenged the company's top two hundred executives to reach out to at least five customers for face-to-face, problem-solving visits. Moving into the discomfort and vulnerability of direct contact with customers revealed the need for a services-led, customer-focused culture. As he later said, "I came to see in my time at IBM that culture wasn't just one aspect of the game. It is the game" (Gerstner, 2002).

Sustained development toward an interdependent culture requires a vanguard of interdependent individuals, and those who seek to be. Transformation, and headroom, requires players in key positions. C-suite executives must "go first" to enact the desired leadership culture. Change in the culture depends on this group getting on board early, raising their own levels of development, learning from their own successes and missteps. They must practice learning in their own teams before taking it to the middle to engage the entire organization in more interdependent ways.

Our client KONE Americas provides a good illustration.

For nearly one hundred years, KONE has been a global leader in the elevator and escalator industry. In 2007 KONE Americas was fourth in the industry, with great opportunities to improve, and focused more on internal operations than customer needs. What most alarmed new CEO Vance Tang was the general acceptance with being a market follower. He expected more—and he viewed leadership development and culture change, ultimately focused on the customer, as the best way to get there.

KONE Americas is now in transformation toward interdependent leadership.

The CEO and senior vice president of human resources at KONE talk about the importance of a journey versus a set of programs:

SVP HR Chuck Moore: "I was charged as the HR leader to build this so-called program—the roadmap. I was quite certain that I knew the answer in terms of the training plan and program around leader development. But as I listened to CCL talk about leadership strategy and transformation I had an epiphany. I realized that we're not talking about a program, or even about HR owning the development. For this to work, our senior leadership had to own it. Our executive team had to design and to develop and to deliver this experience and development opportunity with our people. This was really different and all about the culture journey."

CEO Vance Tang: "I was comfortable that we didn't have a clear path that I could share with my colleagues and peers about how we were going to achieve this because I knew the team had to take ownership of the ideas and approach. We had to appreciate that changing ourselves came first in changing the culture. We had to slow down to power up. We had to experience change together, within our team first. So we changed how we worked together. That was a huge step for us because we were very operationally focused. We knew how to get things done, but we needed to be more strategic. This was different. We had to discover, collectively, together, interdependently. We had to become a true high-performing team."

In our initial multi-day engagement with the KONE Americas executives we facilitated a discovery process. Working side by side with them, we assessed their strategic needs and alignment, measured the culture, introduced the art of dialogue, and tested their ability and willingness to engage in making headroom. In their fourth dialogue, on the last day, they raised the ceiling and began to put previously undiscussed but important issues on the table. They took personal risks, built trust, re-aligned team process, and made commitments about new collaborative ways of working.

A few months later CCL facilitated the annual meeting of the top one hundred leaders. For one session we used the *fishbowl* tool. The executives sat in a small half-circle in the middle of the meeting and talked to one another about their own experiences so far in experimenting with dialogue. The rest of the top one hundred observed the discussion and then talked about what they heard. The fishbowl format is a small and concentrated example of what it's like to make headroom. The benefit of the fishbowl is to expose only a few senior people to the risks of public learning. Thrilling to some, confusing to many, the executives introduced this process in the earliest phase of transformation to set new expectations.

By the next year's top one hundred meeting everyone had advanced well beyond confusion and awkwardness. KONE's leaders had accepted new learning tools and understood how new beliefs and practices would advance the culture.

During that year the CCL team became true partners with the top team. In monthly executive meetings, our role was to observe, reflect, and facilitate leadership development within the context of business issues.

By mid-year the team had skillfully developed collaborative mindsets. They practiced both-and thinking, well beyond their previous either-or, achiever orientation. They moved from focusing on dozens of operational initiatives to placing emphasis on a few strategic areas key for the enterprise. They expanded participation to include non-executive players into the strategy teams. It is noteworthy that the CEO chaired the strategy team that became the focus for developing the leadership culture and capability.

They initiated the development of core beliefs as a platform for building enterprise wide headroom. For example, their customer-driven belief was defined as *customer-driven*:

> We consider the customer first in every decision we make and everything we do. We actively work to understand our customer's needs and desires. We serve our customers the way they want to be served, with impeccable integrity. We are each 100 percent responsible for customer satisfaction and outcomes. We collaborate to deliver the best services and solutions for every one of our customers.

After a year's work, KONE was ready to take headroom into the middle of the organization. Realizing that their technicians held 70 percent of customer relationship time, these senior leaders initiated engagement with all branches. During one meeting, for example, the regional SVP used dialogue and storytelling to create headroom for public learning. Several seasoned mechanics told safety stories: "*They used to just give us a bag of safety stuff, but now they tell us what it is and how to use it, and they follow-up, they ask on the job, 'where are your gloves and glasses?'—you can tell they really care about this, now that they believe in it.*"

The SVP engaged the technicians: "*You—everyone of you in this room all have authority, my complete authority to stop work anytime you believe you are in unsafe conditions . . . do you hear this? You can stop work anytime!* (rapt attention, heads nodding, verbal affirmations). . . . *and just as you are now responsible for these collaborative behaviors—so am I. If you see me or any of our senior leaders not living these beliefs, I invite you to call me on it—let's have a discussion. We can talk about this anytime.*"

Leader development often focuses on individuals with the most authority and power. The development of interdependence calls for more, because by definition an interdependent leadership culture potentially includes everyone in the organization. As culture change proceeds, the development of individuals with the most authority and power becomes just one facet of a comprehensive transformation of the collective beliefs and practices.

In creating headroom at KONE Americas it took the executive team only a few days to commit to developing a "slow down to power up" mindset, and a few more days to agree on core beliefs. It took another year to learn, practice, and transform into a strategic, collaborative team while engaging the top hundred leaders. Now, the headroom at the top is extending deep into the organization. As a result, during one of most challenging economic environments in history, customer satisfaction has more than tripled, employee engagement has increased by over 30 percent, and the financial results improved dramatically. KONE's top priority of employee safety has reached industry leadership levels (McGuire & Tang, 2011).

THE ART OF BOUNDARY SPANNING

Within the vast domain of SŌGI are many social boundaries. Boundaries can separate people into groups of "us" and "them," resulting in conflict, and the fragmentation of direction, alignment, and commitment. Boundaries can also be frontiers with fertile intersections that lead to new possibilities.

The art of boundary-spanning can be taught. Recent research shows that effective boundary-spanning leadership is possible with the right frameworks, strategies, practices, and tactics (Cross & Thomas, 2009; Ernst & Chrobot-Mason, 2010; Ernst & Yip, 2009;). There are five kinds of social boundaries to consider:

Vertical: Rank, class, seniority, authority, power

Horizontal: Expertise, function, peers, competitors

Stakeholder: Partners, constituencies, value chain, communities

Demographic: Gender, religion, age, nationality, culture

Geographic: Location, region, markets, distance

Effective spanning is accomplished through six practices within a sequence of three strategies (Figure 28.6). The objective, in leadership terms, is the creation of direction, alignment, and commitment across boundaries in service of a larger vision or goal.

Our team at CCL facilitated a series of leadership development experiences culminating in a boundary-spanning workshop between the senior leadership teams of two very different government departments. Let's call them the Department of Blue and the Department of Green. These two teams and their organizations—with very different leadership cultures—were just beginning an important and urgent joint mission.

There were three main objectives for the participants:

1. Understand interdependent culture and boundary-spanning concepts.
2. Apply these concepts to develop a shared vision, common language, and unified set of goals and metrics.
3. Accelerate development of the interdependent environment between Blue and Green.

The design of the day-long session follows the sequence of the three strategies and six practices for boundary spanning, with Managing Boundaries in the morning, Forging Common Ground in the afternoon, and Discovering New Frontiers in the evening.

Figure 28.6 Boundary-Spanning Strategies and Practices

Strategy	Practices	Definition (with outcomes in italics)
1. Managing Boundaries taps into the power of differentiation and the need for distinctiveness, divergence and uniqueness within groups	Buffering 	Monitor and protect the flow of information and resources across groups to *define boundaries and create safety*
	Reflecting 	Represent distinct perspectives and facilitate knowledge-exchange across groups to *understand boundaries and foster respect*
2. Forging Common Ground taps into the power of integration and the need for unity, convergence, and belonging across groups	Connecting 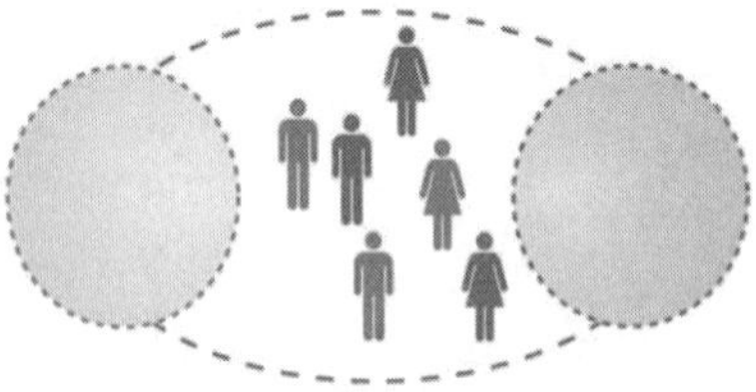	Link people and bridge divided groups to *suspend boundaries and build trust*
	Mobilizing 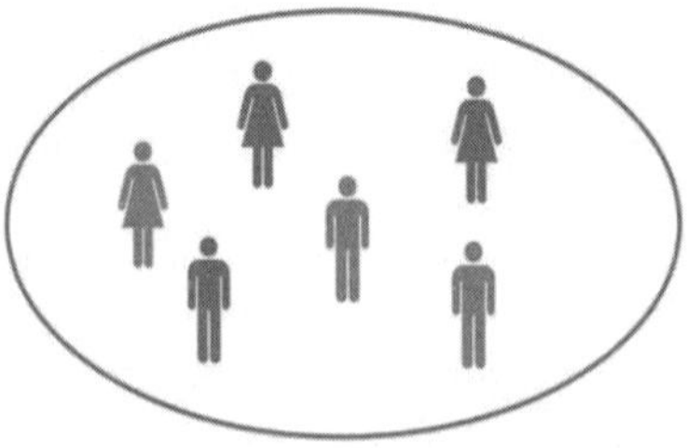	Craft common purpose and shared identity across groups to *reframe boundaries and develop community*

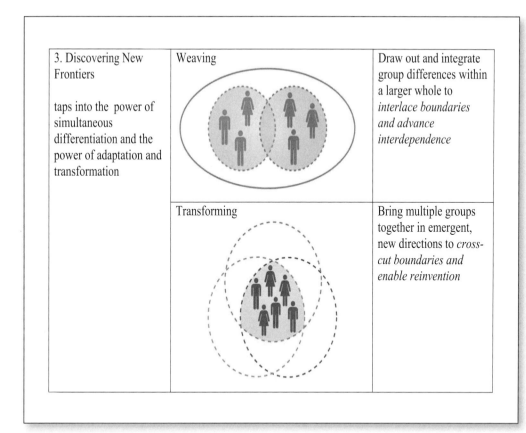

3. Discovering New Frontiers taps into the power of simultaneous differentiation and the power of adaptation and transformation	Weaving 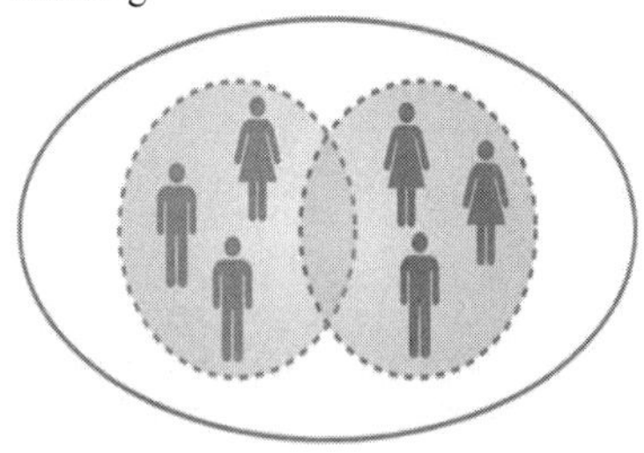	Draw out and integrate group differences within a larger whole to *interlace boundaries and advance interdependence*
	Transforming 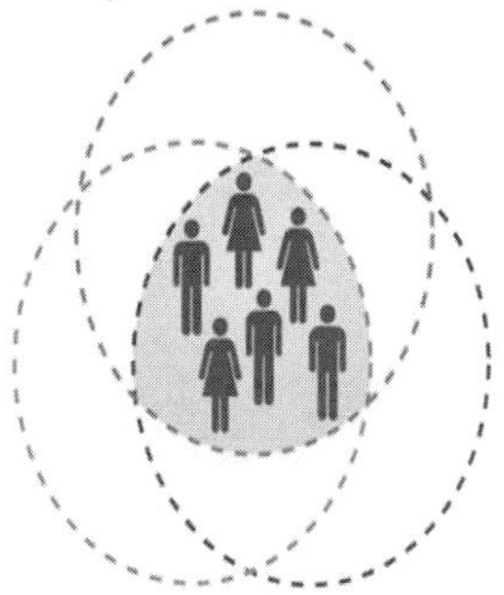	Bring multiple groups together in emergent, new directions to *cross-cut boundaries and enable reinvention*

Prior to the day of the session, there was a period of *discovery* that included interviews and conversations individually and in groups with participants in order to clarify the history, present state, and the future desired states of the leadership cultures.

During the morning session, the design focused on differentiating the boundaries between the two organizations through the practice of *buffering*. The two groups (Green and Blue) were in different classrooms. The course of instruction was the same for both groups: "*Today we begin by meeting in each organization separately in order to clarify and explore your unique organizational needs, cultures, and environments.*" A brief time was spent putting the idea of boundary-spanning leadership in a broader set of concepts including organizational transformation, strategic leadership, change management, and the three types of leadership culture.

The first activity involved creating a shared vision of achievement within each group. Each participant wrote a headline of an article they would like to see sixteen months in the future to highlight the positive results of their work together. The article could appear in any publication of their choice. The headlines and themes were shared and discussed. Later, when the Blue and Green groups came together in the afternoon, the headlines were posted for all to see.

The next activity further defined ("buffered") each organization. We used the Leadership Metaphor Explorer (LME) tool *to explore the leadership culture each group currently has and what culture is needed in the future to achieve mission objectives.* LME is a deck of eighty-three cards, each one containing a unique metaphor for leadership consisting of a drawing and a label (several illustrative cards are depicted below in Figure 28.7). The cards are laid out on a table in the back of the room. Each person is asked to browse the cards and choose two that best represent their thoughts on two different questions:

> First card: **What is the leadership culture like now** at the Department of Blue (or Green) as you face the challenges of implementing policy in this environment?
>
> Second card: **What will the leadership culture need to be like** to achieve success in the next sixteen months?

Group members shared and discussed their "Now" cards, then their "Future" cards. After that, facilitators created a PowerPoint collage of the thematic card images. For both the Blue and Green groups, the pattern of card selections reflected a desired shift toward more interdependent and collaborative leadership cultures.

The final morning activity presented the concepts, strategies, and practices for working successfully across organizational boundaries. Using the Boundary Explorer tool (a deck of twenty-one cards) we illustrated the boundary-spanning leadership model. Each group assessed their own effectiveness in working across different kinds of boundaries. More specifically, they identified which boundaries they work across *Best*—i.e., vertical, horizontal, stakeholders, demographic, or geographic—as well as those they work across the *Worst.*

The "best and worst" self-assessments were revealing. The two groups were practically mirror images of each other. What Blue saw itself as worst in, Green sees itself best in—and vice versa. One important implication of this finding is that the strength of one could offset the weakness of the other when working collaboratively together.

Next, the Blue and Green groups turned to the practice of *reflecting*—to understand the inter-group boundary by sharing cross-organizational perspectives. For this, we used the technique of fishbowl dialogue. In this variation, the top leader of each group sat in the middle of the room along with a facilitator/interviewer. The focus of their dialogue was on key insights from the morning sessions: *How does each group view themselves and their leadership challenges?* All the others, from both of the groups, sat in an outside circle and practiced active listening. After twenty minutes, the two top leaders finished their dialogue

Figure 28.7 Sample Cards From the Leadership Metaphor Explorer

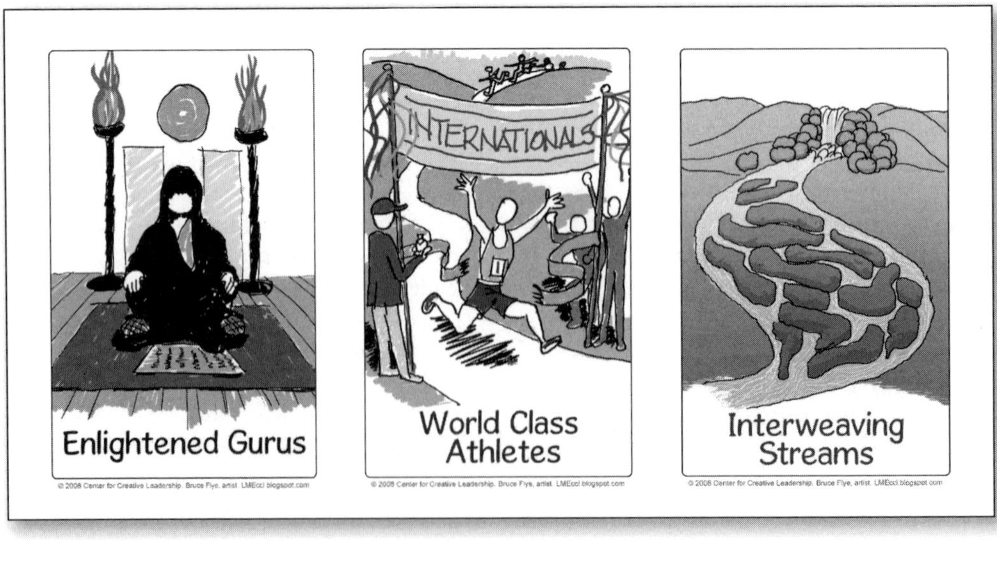

and become listeners and the dialogue shifted to all those who had been listening. The group talked about what they just heard from their top leaders, how they see themselves, and how each group now sees the other. It's often quite insightful to debrief the experience of the fishbowl itself: *What was it like for subordinates to talk about what they heard from their bosses, in front of their bosses? What was it like to discuss your own group in front of the other group?*

The next activity introduced the practice of *connecting*—suspending boundaries by building cross-organizational relationships. With the goal of sharing leadership commitments and building relationships, each participant was asked to take out the "future" Leadership Metaphor card they had selected earlier and *"identify a leadership trait that represents your personal commitment to creating the future leadership culture. What is the type of leadership you will model for others?"* An activity of "speed networking" followed in which participants used their card and trait as a way of introducing themselves to ten or so people from the counterpart organization in just ten minutes.

Next, Blue and Green were directed in the practice of *mobilizing*—reframing boundaries by crafting shared vision. Members of the Blue and Green groups were instructed to sit intermixed among tables. Each table was asked to create a vision statement about their collaborative work, encompassing the themes and patterns identified from both morning sessions. For reference, the news headlines from the morning are posted around the room. Each table group then wrote a single headline representing their vision and three metrics of how they would measure success in accomplishing the headline. Table representatives then provided brief reports to the others about their headlines/metrics.

The concluding activity of the session on forging common ground is introduced this way: "*Given your shared headline, what are the challenges that might get in your way? What obstacles are you facing to creating an effective Team of Teams? Write all your challenges on the blank butcher paper [posted on walls]—everything that could potentially get in the way of realizing your headlines. Use direction, alignment, and commitment as a frame for the challenges.*" Once the challenges were posted, each participant voted (using sticky dots) for the "top three" challenges he or she viewed as most important. The six challenges receiving the most votes overall become the focus of the next session.

The final session was about the boundary-spanning strategy of *discovering new frontiers*. Two activities allowed participants to bring the maximum diversity of their experience and expertise to bear on developing innovative solutions in service of key challenges.

First, the groups focus on the practice of *weaving*—interlacing boundaries by combining unique experience and expertise in service of solving a joint challenge. In this activity, the top six challenges they just identified were posted next to six tables. Participants moved to the table that posed the challenge that interests them the most, while also maintaining mixed representation at each table. They were asked to write down ideas and innovative approaches to the challenge. In ten-minute rotations, participants "table hopped" to build upon and add to the posted ideas—retaining one convener at each table. When time was up, everyone voted on the best near-term and long-term solutions for each challenge and the groups reported the results.

Using a similar process, Blue and Green explored how to span boundaries by reinventing external stakeholder relationships—the final practice of *transforming*. External stakeholders may include, for example, specific customers, suppliers, governmental agencies, NGOs, or partners in a value chain. The senior leaders of

Blue and Green identified six specific external stakeholders on which they wanted the larger group to focus. Repeating the table-hopping technique, participants went to a table focused on one particular external stakeholder (who are typically not in the room, but, depending on the design, they could be). They were told: *"As a 'Team of Teams' what are your challenges in spanning boundaries with these external stakeholders? How could these challenges be transformed into new solutions? Move to a table with the particular external stakeholder that interests you the most."* Facilitated to ensure mixed groups at each table, participants identify as many challenges as possible that are specific to that stakeholder group. They also identify as many solutions as possible, and a representative from each provides a brief report to all others on their favorite solution.

THE ART OF INSIDE-OUT DEVELOPMENT

The core Russian doll in the SŌGI model is the individual person. There are two necessary and complementary ways to help people develop at the individual level. One way is to view people as resources with certain competencies and traits. This is an objective view "from the outside-in." Since the Industrial Age many organizations have focused on the outside-in dimension under the banner of scientific management. Another way is to engage people according to their core values, beliefs, identity, emotions, intuition, imagination, and leadership logics. This is a subjective approach starting "from the inside-out." Inside-out then becomes plural and cultural as people share experiences, beliefs, and values.

An outside-in perspective is full of objects and things. It's all stuff you can point to, including people. It is scientific and empirical. It is a comfortable zone for most of us, removed and manageable.

Inside-out is different terrain. Inside-out is the province of subjective experience. This internal territory feels private. The degree that we are unsure, unaware, or potentially embarrassed by it is the degree of risk and vulnerability we face in its exposure. You have to dive in without really knowing what lies under the surface. This inner self, times billions, is the engine of human creativity and progress in a complex, volatile, and uncertain world.

One of the most powerful ways of developing from the inside-out is through feedback intensive programs and processes (King & Santana, 2010). Individuals gain self-awareness of their beliefs and behaviors through their own active inquiry, within small groups, based on 360-degree feedback, personality assessment, experiential exercises, and coaching. Inside-out development only occurs if the outside-in pressures to conduct appraisal and advancement are removed.

Inside-out development occurs when individuals "learn to learn" the lessons of their own experiences and begin to internalize those lessons as a part of their identities (Yip & Wilson, 2010).

One of the most universal and effective ways we have found to learn the lessons of experience and practice the art of inside-out development is through storytelling. Stories build human connections, from the inside out. Storytelling is a remarkably portable and efficient method, quickly adaptable to almost any context.

Stories have the advantage of connecting with every level of leadership logic. Stories can convey norms and foster conformity. Stories are powerful components of individual identity and can foster independence. Stories reveal connections, complex relations, and transformation, and can foster interdependence. Stories can reveal the hidden dimensions of an organization and are essential for managing and leading change (Denning, 2000). Just as a tribe, village, or nation uses myths and legends to describe how and why transformation happens, leaders can craft stories for the same purposes (Nissley, 2003; Sewerin, 2009;).

Noel Tichey, business professor at the University of Michigan, says that effective stories in leadership contexts answer three kinds of questions: "Who am I?" "Who are we?" and "Where are we going?" "Who am I" stories are the foundation for the other kinds of stories, lending them a core of values and beliefs. "Who are we?" stories are great for group retreats and times of planned reflection and re-aiming, re-enforcing shared identity. In organizations with strong leadership cultures, "where we are going?" stories are told and lived every day (Tichey, 1997).

In our workshops we use various kinds of *developmental storytelling* (Lipman, 1999; McAdams, 1997; Whyte, 2002). Developmental stories focus on incidents in one's own life that were moments of change or great insight—*Who am I?*

Here is one version that works well with a group that already trusts each other. Done near the beginning of a workshop, it helps people be present, and to ground them in their own gut-level, inside-out experience of transformation. Eight to twelve people participate in each group and there can be several groups. The setup goes like this:

> *This is a way to get to know the people in your group (team).*
>
> *This is a way for you to develop yourself as a transformative leader from the inside-out.*
>
> *Each one of us has many experiences and memories that make us who we are.*
>
> *I am going to ask each of you to think of a particular story of when you changed in some important way.*
>
> *You are free to choose which story to tell, if any, and which parts. What is said in this room stays in this room.*
>
> *In Round 1 share your story, two minutes each.*
>
> *In Round 2 respond to one or more of the stories you just heard.*
>
> *Let's find the stories. One will come to mind as the one you want to tell. Relax, pay attention to your breath and sit comfortably. Look back over the past ten years. Were there were any incidents in the last decade that were an eye-opening moment, a time when your perception changed in any important way? [pause] Now go back another decade. Anything come to mind? [pause] Go back another decade, pause and check your memories. What was happening? [pause] If you can, go even further, into your childhood. You are young, with your family or friends. Something changed for you. What memories come in? [pause] Now zero in on one story. Recall in detail what happened. Who else or what else is there with you? What did you discover?*

Each participant is asked to tell their story. Listeners, too, are guided. They are asked to quietly observe what is going on, giving the speaker your full attention. If distracted by their own thoughts, they are reminded to simply acknowledge it and go back to listening.

In one workshop with forty executives, this process brought out many stories, including:

- At twelve years old, I played in a soccer tournament. All my focus was to win, to be the best. We took second, and I saw a kid there with cancer. It really got my attention. My father was emotional—that was the only time I'd ever seen that. It gave me perspective and balance on what is really important in life.

- As a northern girl I spent summers with grandparents in the segregated south. They brought me to a swimming pool, and I thought how lucky we were to have our own pool. It was not until the end of summer that I learned why we could not go to the public, segregated pool.

- I learned about fear and love, both in just three hours. It was spring on the lake, we were kids, and without permission we took a boat out, way out. A storm came up and we lost control. We were stuck out there for a long time, really scared, not sure what would happen. When my father got to us he didn't say anything—but he got his hands on me—and he just held onto me in relief and love. I think about that now with my son.

We then ask people in each group to reflect on each other's stories—the emotional core, the images, the word choices and the values or beliefs that emerge. This group saw a few themes:

- The basic human connections that are made or missed, and the impact that has on our sense of self
- Failure and success, and the relativity of achievement in the larger context of life
- Judgment and forgiveness, and how beliefs and values shift over time as our experience changes our perspectives
- Compassion increases through trials, understanding emerges from tribulation

By hearing a little of someone's story you can see what drives them. This enriches a working relationship and establishes what we have in common.

What's your story? Who are you?

A CAVEAT

Feasibility for quickly adopting interdependent leadership varies tremendously. Most leaders would say that an advanced culture is desirable—but talk is cheap. It is essential to honestly judge the practicality of transformation toward interdependence. For example, management-heavy, divisionalized hierarchies are often saddled with highly dependent leadership cultures. These organizations survive as conformance-based institutions, continue to dominate markets by their size or strong barriers to entry, or they become targets of consolidation. Senior executives reflect this conservative mindset of the organization and developing them is a long-term prospect. Inside-out practices are not tolerated. Boundaries are rigid. Headroom for new leadership logics does not exist. Dialogue exists strictly behind closed doors, and relationships to the broader society are transactional. Interdependent leadership is not going to be developed in such organizations anytime soon.

Within such cultures the most feasible approach is assist sub-cultures in exercising more achievement-oriented independent logics, tied to high priority deliverables. Tying change to specific outcomes will protect the "greenhouse" in which headroom for change is occurring.

PUTTING IT ALL TOGETHER

A hierarchy of cultures exists. Each successive culture is increasingly capable of dealing with complexity, velocity, and uncertainty. Each successive culture fosters "bigger minds" of the people in the culture. The first step in putting it all together is to analyze the gap between the current culture and the one required by the business strategy. This analysis examines the interplay between business strategy, leadership strategy, the few essential organizational and leadership capabilities. It also looks at the requirements of inside-out change leadership in balance with outside-in change management.

For example, questions about the leadership strategy trigger questions about the do-ability of the business strategy—which in turn triggers deeper inquiry about the leadership and organizational capabilities.

What are the relationships between what we say we'll do and the realistic capability we have to do it? Can we actually execute this brilliant strategy with today's collective leadership mindset? Given our leadership culture what kind of DAC can we realistically expect? Are we setting ourselves up for failure? Should we re-think our strategy based on what's real to expect? Beyond the current strategy, it is essential to build the leadership capability necessary to not only meet rapidly evolving conditions, but also to anticipate the next emergent strategies.

By conducting this kind of *discovery* about themselves and the organization, senior leaders begin to test their headroom-making ability. They confront themselves around issues of ownership and the trust required to succeed in serious change efforts (Marshall, 1995, 1999). They begin to learn about the relationships between collective leadership capability and key business requirements. This can feel like an overthrow of the ruling class to some. To others it means intentionally leading an enterprise transformation. One size does not fit all, and there are no reliable recipes. A contested "revolution" can drag on for years whereas the willing and ready transformers can often succeed more quickly. Thorough discovery at the front end can save a great deal of time and investment in the longer run. Discovery starts a learning process about the interrelated factors of change management and change leadership (Figure 28.8), which gains momentum as it spirals outward from senior leadership into the middle of the organization and beyond.

Once the hard work of discovery has taken place, the four arts can be adapted for all kinds of situations where development toward interdependence is desirable. As a practical matter, we spend much of

Figure 28.8 Change Leadership and Change Management

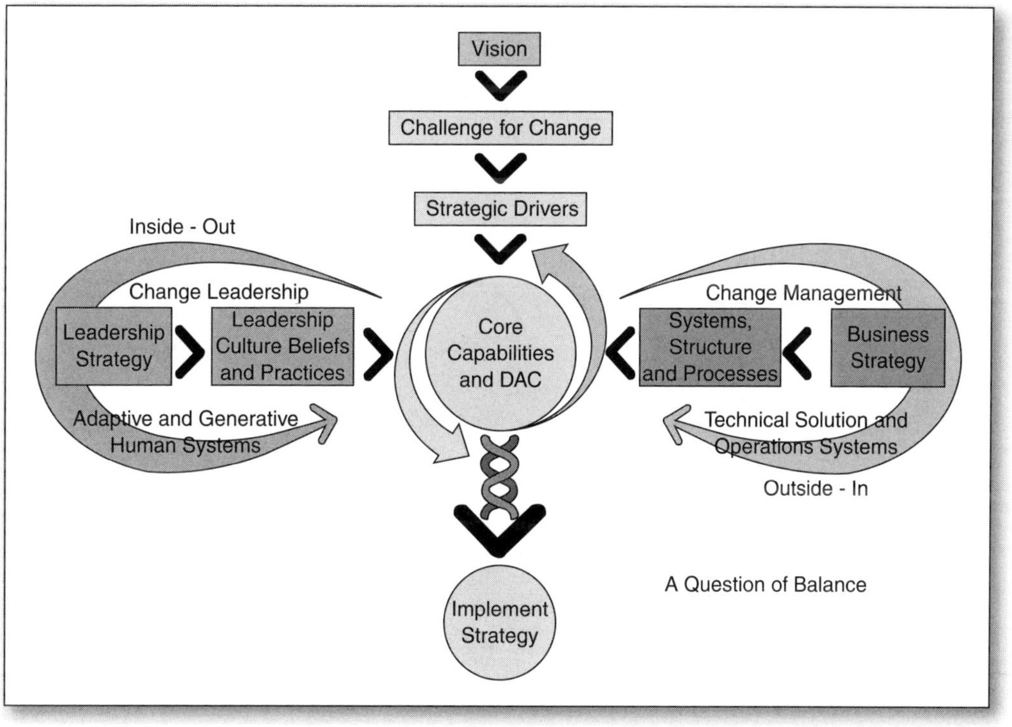

our time in mid- to large-size corporations, guiding and coaching our clients in change leadership. Our aim is to develop the kind of leadership culture required by the client's business strategy and to thus increase their probability of successful strategy execution. We, and our clients, are finding that most business strategies now require leadership development toward interdependence if they are to be successful. This is a practical pursuit requiring collaborative capability. Let's look at how to make that happen.

The client's dilemmas of leadership development can be compared to a complex Game. The idea at any point in the Game is to make good moves, while learning to play the game along the way. In this analogy, there are the *Players*, the *Game Board*, and the *Game* itself (Figure 28.9).

The Players are everyone in the leadership culture, including constituencies in the external network and the broader society.

The Game Board is the strategic landscape of where you are, where you are going, and how your expanding leadership mindset will get you there.

The Game is played across the enterprise, using the four arts with simple, accessible tools to develop leadership while doing the work of the organization.

THE PLAYERS

Everyone in the interdependent organization is potentially a part of the leadership culture—everyone is a player. But, short of interdependence, senior leaders typically launch the Game. So, we begin at the top to determine whether the players in charge are up to the challenge.

We assess, either formally or subjectively, the leadership logics in use within the executive team. The executive team needs critical mass of two or three influential members who are at least beginning to develop personal leadership logics beyond independence. Many executive teams do not. In

Figure 28.9 Putting It All Together

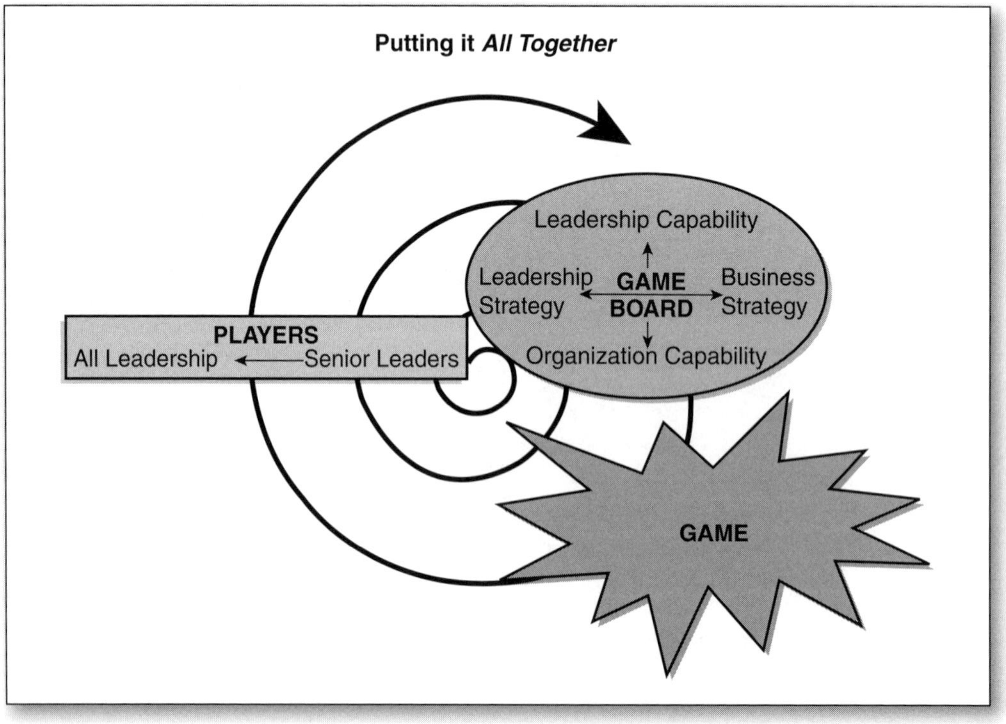

such cases strengthening rather than transforming the culture is recommended.

This requires judgment and experience. Even small experiments can indicate the will to progress or not.

To illustrate, we offer two examples.

The executives at Asia Electronics (details disguised) had the "double double" goal of doubling their revenue *and* market share in two years. Their strategy included re-branding while reengineering across their supply chain, with a new leadership university aimed at creating a learning organization. This strategy required a center of gravity in an interdependent leadership logic. However the center of gravity of the team, as represented by the CEO, the Chief Talent Officer, and many of the business unit vice presidents, was *dependent* leadership: *Command the organization and people will follow*. This executive team was unlikely to develop sufficiently in the short run. We assessed the feasibility of this leadership transformation as improbable.

On the other hand, the executives at Enterprise Inc. (details disguised) had a team with a strong core of independent-minded leaders, with a more interdependent logic already gaining influence. They sought nothing less than industry leadership across a balanced scorecard. They were convinced that company-wide transformation to an interdependent leadership culture was required to achieve this vision. This team had the advantages of key players ready to advance themselves, a willingness to practice on themselves first, and the gumption to lead the change into the middle of the organization and beyond.

If leaders expect culture change in others, they must first begin to change themselves. Delegation of culture change is a non-starter. Culture is not an object or a system "out there"; it is something internal, "in here." We often tell our clients, "You are *in* the culture and the culture is *in* you, and in a very real way you *are* the culture. You can't change the culture without changing yourself."

There are a few key criteria that can be explored as signals about readiness of senior leadership to pursue interdependence:

Time sense—Is time seen as a resource or constraint? Can they "slow down to power up?

Control—Are they willing and able to share control?

Headroom—Can they create headroom for themselves and others?

THE GAME BOARD

While working with the players at the top we focus attention on the Game Board consisting of business strategy, leadership strategy, and the key work areas in which to practice and implement these strategies. *Leadership strategy* is the identification of the required culture, strategic drivers, and the critical few leadership capabilities—informed by SŌGI and thus including but going beyond individual leader competencies—that define the focus of development as required for business strategy execution (Beatty & Byington, 2010; Hughes & Beatty, 2005; Pasmore & Lafferty, 2009).

We spend time getting to know the senior players by having them confront these key game-board questions in open and honest ways: What is the business strategy? What is the existing leadership capability? What is the leadership strategy to build the required capability to produce DAC in support of the business strategy?

Honest assessment and discussion of these issues advances the business strategy outcomes, the development of the executives, and, over time, the leadership culture of the organization. The game board, in effect, is mapped out and then continuously re-created through collective learning processes.

THE GAME

The Game consists of developing the core organizational capabilities required to execute current strategy, while dealing with complex challenges and generating the next emergent strategy. First, we introduce collaborative leadership tools and skills so senior leaders can get a handle on them. Then we apply them to real, strategic work and develop organization-wide leadership capabilities. Unlike competency training, this approach focuses on how leadership is practiced and developed collectively. We call this approach *action development*. Working together, people practice the art of headroom in public learning forums. They span multiple boundaries as they collaborate across groups. And they practice inside-out engagement to bring their higher values and passions to bear on real work. A very dynamic game!

Conclusion

We see people everywhere who are eager to play the game of interdependent leadership. They see the value of leading in new ways, but are often unsure of how to begin or how to get traction. The process isn't simple, or one-size-fits-all. Even so, we've identified five steps that build toward interdependent leadership at the organizational level:

1. *Discover*. Initiate the learning process through assessment of the level of leadership culture and capability required by the business strategy.
2. *Develop Strategy*. Understand the nature of the game and its key elements. Focus on the relationship between leadership strategy and business strategy and the role of leadership in building organizational capability.
3. *Develop the Players*. Practice the four arts first with the senior players.
4. *Set Up the Game Board*. Align the leadership and business strategies, and integrate human capability requirements with the key work of the organization. Rearrange, re-create, and reassess the game board as senior players learn and gain new skills and perspectives.
5. *Play the Game*. Take the four arts to the middle, and then everywhere, in the organization. Now, leadership is developing, while the real work of the organization is getting done.

Developing interdependent leadership within and between societies, organizations, groups, and individuals is a complex process, a leadership version of four-dimensional chess—playing on multiple boards all at once. It's a challenge we cannot ignore. Our interdependent world requires nothing less than interdependent leadership.

References

Argyris, C., Putnam, R., & Smith, D. (1985). *Action science: Concepts, methods, and skills for research and intervention.* San Francisco, CA: Jossey-Bass.

Beatty, K.C., & Byington, B. (2010). Developing strategic leadership. In C.D. McCauley, E. Van Velsor, & M.N. Ruderman (Eds.), *The Center for Creative Leadership Handbook of Leadership Development*, (3rd ed.). San Francisco: Jossey-Bass.

Bennis, W.G. (2007). The challenges of leadership in the modern world: An introduction to the special issue. *American Psychologist, 62*(1), 2–5.

Bohm, D. (1990). *On dialogue*. Ojai, CA: David Bohm Seminars.

Cook-Greuter, S. (1999). Postautonomous ego development: A study of its nature and measurement. Doctoral Dissertation. Cambridge, MA: Harvard Graduate School of Education.

Cross, R.L., & Thomas, R.J. (2009). *Driving results through social networks: How top organizations leverage networks for performance and growth.* San Francisco: Jossey-Bass.

Denison, D.R. (1997). *Corporate culture and organizational effectiveness, 2nd Edition.* Ann Arbor, MI: Denison Consulting.

Denning, S. (2000). *The springboard story: How storytelling ignites action in knowledge-era organizations*. Burlington, MA: Butterworth Heinemann.

Dixon, N.M. (1998). *Dialogue at work: Making talk developmental for people and organizations*. London: Lemos & Crane.

Drath, W.H. (2001). *The deep blue sea: Rethinking the source of leadership*. San Francisco, CA: Jossey-Bass.

Drath, W.H., McCauley, C.D., Palus, C.J., Van Velsor, E., O'Connor, P.M.G., & McGuire, J. B. (2008). Direction, alignment, commitment: Toward a more integrative ontology of leadership. *Leadership Quarterly, 19*, 635–653.

Drath, W.H., & Palus, C.J. (1994). *Making common sense: Leadership as meaning-making in a community of practice*. Greensboro NC: Center for Creative Leadership.

Drath, W.H., Palus, C.J., & McGuire, J.B. (2010). Developing interdependent leadership. In C.D. McCauley, E. Van Velsor, & M.N. Ruderman (Eds.), *The Center for Creative Leadership Handbook of Leadership Development*, (3rd ed.). San Francisco: Jossey-Bass.

Ernst, C., & Chrobot-Mason, D. (2010). *Boundary spanning leadership: six practices for solving problems, driving innovation, and transforming organizations*. New York: McGraw-Hill Professional.

Ernst, C., & Yip, J. (2009). Boundary spanning leadership: Tactics to bridge social identity groups in organizations. In T.L. Pittinsky (Ed.), *Crossing the divide: Intergroup leadership in a world of difference* (pp. 89–99). Boston: Harvard Business School Press.

Fukayama, F. (2011). *The origins of political order: From prehuman times to the French revolution*. New York: Farrar, Straus and Giroux.

Hannum, K.M., Martineau, J.W., & Reinelt, C. (Eds.). (2007). *The handbook of leadership development evaluation*. San Francisco, CA: Jossey-Bass & CCL.

Hughes, R.L., & Beatty, K.C.(2005). *Becoming a strategic leader: Your role in your organization's enduring success*. San Francisco: Jossey-Bass.

Isaacs, W. (1999). *Dialogue and the art of thinking together*. New York: Random House.

Johansen, B. (2009). *Leaders make the future: Ten new leadership skills for an uncertain world*. San Francisco, CA: Berrett-Koehler Publishers.

Kegan, R. (1994). *In over our heads: The demands of modern life*. Cambridge, MA: Harvard University Press.

King, S.N., & Santana, L.C. (2010). Feedback-intensive programs. In C.D. McCauley, E. Van Velsor, & M.N. Ruderman (Eds.), *The Center for Creative Leadership Handbook of Leadership Development*, (3rd ed.). San Francisco: Jossey-Bass.

Lipman, D. (1999). *Improving your storytelling: Beyond the basics for all who tell stories in work or play*. Atlanta, GA: August House Publishers, Inc.

Marshall, E.M. (1995). *Transforming the way we work*. AMACOM, New York.

Marshall, E.M. (1999). *Building trust at the speed of change*. New York: AMACOM, American Management Association.

Martineau, J.M., & Hoole, E. (in press). Evaluation methods. In D.V. Day, (Ed.), *The Oxford Handbook of Leadership and Organizations*. Oxford: Oxford University Press.

McAdams, D.P. (1997). *The stories we live by: Personal myths and the making of the self*. New York: Guilford Press.

McCauley, C.D., Drath, W.H., Palus, C.J., O'Connor, P.M.G., & Baker, B.A. (2006). The use of constructive-developmental theory to advance the understanding of leadership. *Leadership Quarterly, 17*, 634–653.

McCauley, C. D., Palus, C. J., Drath W. H., Hughes, R. L., McGuire, J. B, O'Connor, P. M. G., & Van Velsor, E. (2008). *Interdependent leadership in organizations: Evidence from six case studies*. CCL Research Report no. 190. Greensboro, NC: Center for Creative Leadership.

McGuire, J.B. (January 28, 2010). *Leaders we need with mind's afire*. Editorial, The Washington Post.

McGuire, J. B., & Palus, C. J. (2003). Conversation piece: Using dialogue as a tool for better leadership. *Leadership in Action. 23*(1), 8–11.

McGuire, J.B., Palus, C.J., & Torbert, W.R. (2007). Toward interdependent organizing and researching. In A.B., Shani, et al. (Eds.), *Handbook of Collaborative Management Research* (pp. 123–142). Sage Publications.

McGuire, J.B., & Rhodes, G. (2009). *Transforming your leadership culture*. San Francisco, CA: Jossey-Bass.

McGuire, J.B., & Tang, V. (February, 2011). *Fighting the complexity conspiracy*. Forbes. com.

Nissley, N. (2003). Fictionalization and imaginative "restoryation": In A.B.VanGundy & L. Naiman (Eds.), *Orchestrating collaboration at work: Using music, improv, storytelling, and other arts to improve teamwork* (pp. 199–202). San Francisco: Jossey-Bass.

Ospina, S., & Foldy, E. (2010). Building bridges from the margins: The work of leadership in social change organizations. *Leadership Quarterly, 21*(2), 292–307.

Palus, C. J., & Drath, W. H. (2001). Putting something in the middle: An approach to dialogue. *Reflections, 3*(2), 28–39.

Palus, C.J., & Horth, D.M. (2002). *The leader's edge: Six creative competencies for navigating complex challenges*. San Francisco, CA: Jossey-Bass.

Palus, C.J., & Horth, D.M. (2007). Visual explorer. In P., Holman, T., Devane, & S. Cady, (Eds.), *The change handbook: The definitive resource on today's best methods for engaging whole systems* (pp. 603–608). San Francisco, CA: Berrett-Koehler Publishers.

Palus, C.J., & Horth, D.M. (2010). *Visual explorer facilitator's guide*. Greensboro, NC: The Center for Creative Leadership.

Pasmore, B., & Lafferty, K., (2009). Developing a leadership strategy. Center for Creative Leadership white paper series.

Quinn, L., & Van Velsor, E. (2010). Developing globally responsible leadership. In C.D. McCauley, E. Van Velsor, & M.N. Ruderman (Eds.), *The Center for Creative Leadership Handbook of Leadership Development* (3rd Ed.). San Francisco: Jossey-Bass.

Sewerin, T. (2009). *Leadership, teams and coaching*. Malmo, Sweden: Tertulia Books.

Tichey, N.M. (1997). *The leadership engine: How winning companies build leaders at every level*. New York: Harper Business.

Torbert, B., & Associates. (2004). *Action inquiry: The secret of timely and transforming leadership*. San Francisco, CA: Berrett-Koehler.

Turchin, P. (2007). *War and peace and war: The rise and fall of empires*. New York: Plume.

Whyte, D. (2002). *Crossing the unknown sea: Work as a pilgrimage of identity*. New York: Riverhead Trade.

Wilber, K. (2000). *Integral psychology*. Boston, MA: Shambala.

Wilson, E. O. (1998). Back from chaos. *Atlantic Monthly, 281*(3). Retrieved August 30, 2010, from http://www.theatlantic.com/past/docs/issues/98mar/eowilson.htm

Yammarino, F.J., & Dansereau, F. (2008). Multilevel approaches to leadership. *The Leadership Quarterly, 19*(2), 135–141.

Yip, J., & Wilson, M.S. (2010). Learning from experience. In C.D. McCauley, E. Van Velsor, & M.N. Ruderman (Eds.), *The Center for Creative Leadership Handbook of Leadership Development* (3rd Ed.). San Francisco: Jossey-Bass.

29

DEVELOPING BUSINESS INNOVATORS WHO INTEGRATE PROFITABILITY AND SOCIAL VALUE

◆ Nancy McGaw
Aspen Institute, Business and Society Program

Expectations for the role that business can and should play in society are changing, creating greater demand for business leaders who are attentive to the independency of business success and social and environmental progress. This article outlines a new leadership development program, inaugurated by the Aspen Institute Business and Society Program in 2009, specifically designed to help meet this demand. This First Movers Fellowship Program brings together a select group of high-potential, mid-career business professionals who, we believe, are already acting as social intrapreneurs in their companies, creating new products, services, and management innovations that achieve greater profitability and positive social and environmental impacts. The program's objective is to strengthen their capacity to innovate and lead change in their companies. In turn, we believe they can help their companies develop competitive advantage by more effectively integrating social and environmental value into core strategic priorities. The article discusses the genesis of the program, the rationale for its design and pedagogy, the target audience, and the key components of the fellowship experience.

It also presents early positive findings from an independent program evaluation and highlights challenges ahead.

"Time out in the midst of chaos" is how one individual described the First Movers Fellowship Program launched by the Aspen Institute Business and Society Program (Aspen BSP) in 2009. "A window and a mirror" is another. "Development accelerator" is a third. Each of these assessments was offered by one of the Fellows in the inaugural class.

The fellowship program is designed for a specific type of business professional: exceptional innovators in for-profit companies—the First Movers—who are helping their companies grow in ways that produce financial results **and** contribute to our collective well-being. They are individuals acting on the conviction that business can leapfrog the competition by embracing innovations that achieve financial success and social and environmental value. Like Peter Drucker, they dare to imagine that "Every single social and global issue of our day is a business opportunity in disguise" (Cooperrider, 2008).

The need today to develop business leaders with these capacities is great. To meet global competitive pressures and changing public expectations, there is increased urgency in companies to adapt and innovate and to do so with attention to the footprint they are leaving on communities and the planet. Companies already have experts in their midst, the First Movers, whose efforts are helping their organizations meet these pressures and expectations. At present, however, we believe they are an under-recognized and under-developed pool of talent. The First Movers Fellowship endeavors to change that equation.

The fellowship experience offers selected individuals a chance to become part of a community of business men and women who share a passion about their work and belief in the new possibilities for business. It also serves as an innovation lab where Fellows develop the skills to realize their vision and succeed even when they have to work against organizational impediments to change. By identifying these First Movers and offering them a tailor-made development experience, we hope to encourage them to be even more daring and inventive and to become more effective leaders and champions for change within their companies and across industries. The ultimate goal of the program is audacious: to nurture and empower individuals who can improve the way the world does business so that the business sector lives up to its full potential as a contributor to a sustainable society.

The program design reflects a view prevalent within the Aspen Institute that open dialogue can be a powerful learning experience if it is structured to call on the knowledge and experience of the participants in the room. As a result, presentations in the required seminars are few, and plenty of time is allotted for Fellows to help each other identify challenges and work through them. Various readings, assigned in advance of the convenings, offer context for discussion. Fellowship projects, designed and executed by each Fellow, serve as a focal point for learning.

Our inaugural class of sixteen Fellows, announced in April 2009, successfully completed their fellowship the following year. As of this writing, the second class of Fellows is actively involved in the fellowship experience, and we are recruiting the third. Fellows in the first two classes are diverse. They come from many companies in different industries, including Best Buy, Colgate-Palmolive, Dow Chemical, IBM, IDEO, Method, Microsoft, MetLife, Pick n Pay, State Street Global Advisers, and WalMart. Ethnicity, years of experience, and age vary, although most Fellows are in their thirties and forties. The Fellows have come from nine countries and have a wide range of functional responsibilities, among them purchasing; leadership development; design, brand, risk, general, and executive management; and sustainability. What the Fellows have in common is enthusiasm for exploring possibilities for integration of financial, social, and environmental value; a conviction that they have as much to learn as they do to teach; humility about their own accomplishments; and unbridled eagerness to work with a group of individuals who share their passion for this kind of business innovation.

This chapter situates the fellowship in the context of changing expectations about the role business plays in society and summarizes what we have learned to date about the First Movers themselves. It also tells the story about how and why we came to develop the fellowship program and provides an overview of the program and the rationale for the program design and pedagogy. Included throughout are highlights from the independent evaluation that was conducted during the first, pilot year of the program.[1]

Changing Expectations for Business

For years, leaders in business and academia have been calling for a fundamental mind shift in business, to encourage the sector to pay far greater attention to the interdependency of business success and social progress. A few references are illustrative. As early as 1984, R. Edward Freeman wrote *Strategic Management: A Stakeholder Approach,* a seminal work (reissued by Cambridge University Press in 2010) that contributed to our understanding of the importance of relationships among stakeholders for achieving business success.[2] In the past decade many more voices have been raised. In 2002, for example, three pioneering business leaders collaborated to produce *Walking the Talk: The Business Case for Sustainable Development* (Holliday, Schmidheiny, & Watts, 2002). Three years later, the managing partner at McKinsey (Davis, 2005) called for a new implicit social contract that recognizes the obligations, opportunities, and advantages for both business and society. In the following year, in the pages of the *Harvard Business Review*, companies were urged to reevaluate the relationship between their corporate strategy and society and move beyond thinking of "corporate success and social welfare as a zero sum game" (Porter & Kramer, 2006). At the end of the decade, the same publication included a call from leading strategist Gary Hamel who argued for no less than the reinvention of management, exhorting managers to "ensure that the work of management serves a higher purpose" (Hamel, 2009). Even more recently, in their cover article on how to fix capitalism, Porter and Kramer offered further perspectives on the imperative of creating "shared value" to achieve business success (Porter & Kramer, 2011).

[1]The objectives of the evaluation were to track the effectiveness of the program in achieving the intended personal and organizational impacts; to provide real time feedback; and to assess the sustainability of the program over time. The evaluator was present as an observer at all three seminars and participated in the program's design team. The evaluation report is based on three Fellows' surveys, three rounds of Fellows' interviews; a survey of thought partners; interviews with thought partners after the completion of the program; interviews with members of the design team after the completion of the program; program assignments and other documents. The evaluation was conducted by Shari Cohen, PhD, Intersections Resources.

[2]Through a faculty pioneer awards program, over the years Aspen BSP has conferred "lifetime achievement" awards on several faculty, including R. Edward Freeman, who have taught thousands of business school students and provided a theoretical basis for rethinking this mindset in business. (Information about recipients of these awards is available at www.facultypioneers.org.)

Since 1999 Aspen BSP has been examining what this mind shift would mean in practice. In that year we organized the first of several convenings of leadership development experts from corporations and academia to ask two fundamental questions: If we want business to produce results that take financial, social, and environmental impacts into account, what kind of leaders do we need? And, how do we develop individuals with these capabilities?

Over the ensuing decade we continued to bring experts together to examine how exemplary business leaders, at all levels of the firm, manage complex and interdependent social, financial, and environmental dynamics and thus achieve results that create long-term value for the firm's diverse constituencies. These conversations have taught us a great deal about the kinds of leadership development experiences most effective for meeting the needs of such leaders (McGaw, 2005). Although we have been inspired by many of the pioneering efforts in the field, we believe that leadership programs typically available to these business professionals do not fully address their needs. Thus, we have come to realize that companies are not taking full advantage of a valuable resource already within their midst.

Social Intrapreneurs: Emergence of a New Business Resource

The kinds of business leaders referenced above generally fit an entrepreneurial profile. They see opportunities where others don't because they bring characteristics typically associated with entrepreneurs: "inspiration, creativity, direct action, courage, and fortitude" (Martin & Osberg, 2007). A key driver for them is their desire to make a direct connection between their personal aspiration to make a difference and their professional endeavors. Fellows often recount the early formation of personal commitments to address social inequities or environmental challenges that sprang from experiences living abroad or working with community groups. However, unlike some of their peers who have escaped business to join non-profits or start mission-based social enterprises, they have made a strategic choice to stay in mainstream, often very large, companies as the best way for achieving maximum impact.

These individuals are, in effect, social **intra**preneurs. Like the exceptional performers described in *How to Be a Star at Work*, these individuals are "blazing trails in the organization's white spaces" (Kelley, 1998). But the white spaces they are looking for in their companies are places where they can create new products, services, business models, or processes that achieve greater profitability **and** positive social and environmental impacts. As they do so, they are helping their companies take leadership roles in this complicated arena.

Only recently has there been any focused attention on understanding the characteristics of this group (Grayson, McLaren, & Spitzeck, 2011).[3] While some social intrapreneurs have public profiles (Sustainability, 2008), most work below the radar in corporations and certainly don't have *social intrapreneur* or First Mover designations on their business cards. The most effective of these intrapreneurs know their companies well. They are respected by superiors and peers for the quality of their work. Because of their track record, they can get a hearing even among skeptics. However, they often have to swim upstream and work against the odds. Many tell us that they are constrained within their companies by risk-averse cultures that favor the status quo and fear failure. Moreover, because most social intrapreneurs are recommending metrics that go beyond short-term financial results, they are constrained by skepticism about the business case for the kinds of innovations they espouse.

[3]Debra Meyerson, with her research on "tempered radicals," was an early contributor to our understanding of such innovators in business (Meyerson, 2001).

To find candidates for this program, we reach out to hundreds of individuals who know us well and understand the type of business men and women we are looking for. The recruitment and selection process for this program runs about five months (see Figure 29.1). We stress that we are looking for mid-career business professionals recognized as high-potential talent in their companies who have demonstrated passion and capacity for working at the intersection of business growth and positive social and environmental change. We also make it clear that ideal candidates come from core business functions within their companies: finance, marketing, design, leadership and organizational development, etc. Moreover, we emphasize that successful candidates will have a new idea or business opportunity they urgently want to implement in their companies that will move the company further into the zone where business growth and social well-being intersect. These ideas form the basis for the next-stage innovation projects that they work on during their fellowships.

As we assess candidates, we consider their:

- Track record of innovation, coupled with a sense of humility about their accomplishments;
- Enthusiasm for learning from others and commitment to supporting other Fellows;
- Willingness to reflect honestly and openly on their personal objectives and aspirations;
- Comfort with a program that is largely self-directed;
- Ability to meet the requirements of the fellowship (attending the seminars, working with thought partners, paying the fellowship fee);
- Access to executive decision makers in their companies.

Figure 29.1

First Mover Selection Process	
Nominations	A candidate must be nominated by someone familiar with his or her work (no self-nominations).
Initial Screening	Individuals working in government, in non-profit organizations or social enterprises are excluded.
Phone interviews with staff	Aspen staff interview promising candidates and decide whether to offer the candidate an application form.
Applications	Candidates selected for next round indicate possible scope of their projects and potential thought partners and indicate their willingness to meet fellowship requirements.
Phone interviews with Fellows	Fellows in current and previous classes are asked to schedule a conversation with candidates to assess their fit.
Design Team Review and final selection	Based on application and feedback from interviews, program staff present profiles of semi-finalists to Design Team, which makes the final selection. In this process we strive to build a diverse group in terms of gender, ethnicity, geographic location, industry, company, and type of project.

As the selection process continues, we take a close look at the nature of the project that the Fellow intends to undertake during the fellowship. We are looking for projects that are innovative, feasible, closely aligned with the core strategic priorities of his or her company, and potentially game-changing for the company/industry.

The First Movers Fellowship Experience: Meeting the Needs of Social Intrapreneurs

Realizing there are few leadership programs available for high-potential professionals who fit the social intrapreneur profile, we sought to develop a distinctive program with this type of business professional in mind. To do so, we called on the lessons gained from dialogues with leadership development experts about the most effective ways to develop leaders with the will and ability to find innovative pathways to achieving business success that integrate profitability and social value. To help envision and implement the fellowship, we established a small design team with deep expertise in innovation and leadership development.[4]

What emerged is a program with several basic elements. First of all, the program gives Fellows access to a powerful and selective network of exceptionally talented and diverse colleagues. These individuals come together for three mandatory seminars, twelve days in total, held at Aspen Institute conference centers or other retreat facilities. Designing and implementing a "next stage innovation project" is a requirement of the fellowship. Each project must be based on a compelling idea about a new product, service, process, or business model that would help the Fellow's company move toward greater strategic integration of some critical social or environmental objective. Fellows are selected, in part, on the basis of their early stage project proposals. We look for projects that have game-changing potential and that are closely related to a company's core strategic priorities. Figure 29.2 shows a sample of the kinds of work Fellows undertake during their fellowship.

Figure 29.2

Sample Fellowship Projects *Fellows are required to undertake a "next stage innovation" project as part of their fellowship experience. Examples of the kind of game-changing innovations they are working on are presented below.*
Mentor small scale farmers and entrepreneurs in Southern Africa so they can connect to the market as suppliers to Pick 'n Pay and other retailers in that country
Foster collaboration across the dairy industry supply chain to create systemic, sustainable value; then work with all players in the system (farmers to retailers) to enable transformation
Grow enrollment in Walmart's new Lifelong Learning Program, making it more affordable and convenient for employees to attend college and complete a degree while also working at the company
Scale the Corporate Service Corps, a leadership and business development program at IBM that gives top performing employees the skills to function effectively in a globally integrated, smarter planet
Develop sustainability as a competency for Method's supply chain partners, pursuing an ultimate goal of zero waste manufacturing in cleaning supplies
Build sustainable business models at Best Buy that transform lives by enabling underserved communities to access the benefits of a digitally connected world
Make Autodesk into a "Living Lab" to build and validate new software solutions that accelerate the greening of buildings and infrastructure

Fellows are also expected to select at least two thought partners, generally from within their own companies, to work with them throughout the fellowship.[5] Thought

[4]The design team includes Robert Adams and David Sluyter, The Fetzer Institute; Matthew Breitfelder, BlackRock; Shari Cohen, Intersections Resources; Fred Dust, IDEO; Mary Gentile, Babson College; Nancy McGaw, Sarah Rienhoff, and Judith Samuelson, Aspen Institute Business and Society Program.

[5]The individuals whom Fellows invite to serve as thought partners represent a range of functional responsibilities within their companies. Sample titles are illustrative: Vice President, Strategic and Executive Communications; Chief Marketing Officer; Head of US Product Engineering; Chief Technology Coordinator; Executive Vice President, Strategic Insights & Analysis.

partners serve in many capacities: they help the Fellows build support within the company for their innovations; serve as sounding boards and skeptics; and challenge Fellows' thinking in productive—and often disruptive—ways. Their involvement also makes it more likely that lessons learned by the Fellows will be leveraged within their companies and that the fellowship will therefore have deeper organizational impact. Fellows' experiences working with thought partners have been mixed, but many report that even a limited amount of time with these individuals can produce "small bites of nourishment" that can lead to very big breakthroughs. Moreover, they come to understand that even if an executive declines the opportunity to be involved, the ask itself is powerful. One Fellow reported that he kept approaching senior executives to find his partners. Initially, many said they couldn't do it, but all said "keep me posted on your progress." The impact of that response is tremendous. Even before he started the fellowship, he had already built a network of support within his company. This network has paid off for him in remarkable ways.

Each of the program elements noted above is important, but what really distinguishes the program from other leadership development programs, along with its singular focus on social intrapreneurs, is the interweaving throughout the program of the four thematic building blocks: *Innovation, Leadership, Reflection, Community*. Each of these is discussed in greater detail below.

Innovation. We sought to develop a program that would serve as an innovation lab where Fellows develop the skills they need to make next stage innovations real and successful in their organizations. Emphasis on this particular building block of the program arises from a simple premise: that the most effective way to ensure the adoption of a new management mindset is through the path of innovation. Every company understands the imperative to innovate. Still, many ignore the powerful innovations that are being launched by employees who are finding ways to integrate financial success with positive social and environmental impacts.

First Movers who are the focus of this program are often not identified as innovators by their colleagues. Sometimes they don't even see themselves in that light. Being designated an Aspen First Mover Fellow gives them a new perspective on their work and calls attention within their company to their efforts. What Fellows have told us is that simply having this imprimatur gives them "wind at their back." It validates their corporate contribution and makes them eager to hone their capacity to innovate.

The fellowship seminars help Fellows learn and practice a range of innovation tools and methods so they can better conceptualize and implement game-changing innovations within their firm. Fellows are introduced to the concept of design thinking as one broad framework for developing their capacity for innovation. Design thinking, as defined by Tim Brown, CEO of IDEO, is "a discipline that uses the designer's sensibility and methods to match people's needs with what is technologically feasible and what a viable business strategy can convert into customer value and market opportunity" (Brown, 2008). With its human-centered tenets, a focus on what is possible, and a recognition that a new social contract is required if all are to thrive in an interconnected world, design thinking is an approach that has great utility for those trying to create business models, products, and services that will achieve positive financial outcomes and social and environmental benefits as well (Brown, 2009).

Design thinking essentially helps the Fellows zoom out and in: to study the system in which they work to better understand and position their own endeavors and also to examine the specifics of these endeavors. Thus, it provides a pathway for Fellows to become more systematic in their thinking. We cover a range of design thinking topics. For example, in the seminars there is a session on helping Fellows discover the ecosystem of their organizations. As they do so, they consider the myths that empower and constrain innovation at their companies. They map the official and unofficial channels for innovation and become more intentional about finding ways to get things done. Looking at the system in this way is eye-opening for the Fellows. As one said, he now sees "all the avenues, contributors, obstacles, and gatekeepers and the multiple channels for innovation versus established protocols."

Fellows are also encouraged to step back and examine the problem or situation that they are trying to address. They come to realize that defining a problem correctly is critical for figuring out the solution. They learn techniques for reframing problems and explore the assumptions that are behind the approaches they are taking in their project work. They ask, for example, how might others see the problem they are working on? What constraints could they add to the framing of the problem that might result in greater clarity? Where is the silver lining in the situation as they see it? In collaboration, Fellows ask themselves these questions to reframe and rethink the situations they are trying to address. As a result of this exercise and others, many Fellows revise their projects significantly throughout the fellowship and enhance their chances for success. "My ability to reframe issues and challenges and to help others do so," reports one Fellow, "has made me more effective in the company."

Studying pilots and prototyping, a concept at the heart of design thinking, is the focus for other sessions. Fellows find these discussions help them position their work more effectively since piloting and prototyping is often perceived as less risky for a company. It also provides a framework that explicitly anticipates rapid adaptation and learning. One Fellow in the inaugural class indicated that as a direct result of describing her ambitious project as a pilot, she gained the financial support of a powerful partner. Fellows also explore the kinds of metrics they can use to value the impact of their projects and make the case for adoption of new ideas (Boston College, 2009).

Leadership. Often social intrapreneurs work against corporate norms and accepted habits of practice. Even those who work in environments that are hospitable to change struggle with the usual impediments to new thinking: dismissive bosses, corporate inertia, short-term planning horizons. The seminars help Fellows explore ways to lead change in their organizations and to build the political and social capital they need to succeed. Fellows and their thought partners confirm the effectiveness of this aspect of the program. At the end of the fellowship, Fellows report much greater confidence and appetite to take on leadership roles, and their supervisors agree. As one noted, for example, the Fellow he worked with could now "lead sustainability efforts at the company more autonomously."

We encourage Fellows to look at storytelling as a powerful leadership tool. They see that stories engage listeners much more effectively than presentations of facts and data. Stories also give the storyteller a chance to paint a picture of possible futures that others need to imagine if they are to become part of a change initiative. Fellows are given multiple opportunities to practice this art. Throughout the fellowship, they share stories with each other about strategies they have used for bringing others on board. By telling stories of past successes and naming the strengths they have relied on to achieve results, they become more aware of the personal qualities they bring to current challenges. They think about "coding and decoding": how to frame ideas for different audiences and to listen more actively. The impact is significant. As one Fellow commented, "I realized I had to start engaging with others in conversations rather than being the one to propose the solution." Doing so has helped him achieve corporate buy-in—and a promotion. Another Fellow said she had never realized "the validity that stories had in the work environment," and she is now using them extensively to engage colleagues.

Fellows also examine the role of experimentation and failure in innovation. One Fellow said he learned that success and failure are "twins." One moment you are leading an effort and making great progress; everybody is enthusiastic and on board with next steps in the process of implementing an innovative idea. A minute later, momentum is stalled by some new challenge, a powerful detractor, or simply organizational inertia. To be a leader, Fellows come to understand that they have to be prepared for both eventualities, and that failure can offer critical and ultimately empowering lessons. Perhaps ironically, they also consider how to "cope" with success. Robert Redford's admonition to "return to zero" every time you achieve success served as a touch point for the Fellows. Redford, an acknowledged disruptive innovator in the film industry, argues for the need to "commit yourself to some new sacrifice and some new risk" with each success or risk being lulled into complacency (Meyerson & Fryer, 2002).

Reflection. Over the years in discussions with leadership development experts and with social intrapreneurs themselves, we have heard repeatedly that individuals are more likely to stay the course—even when obstacles abound—if they connect their work to their own deeply held values. So we unabashedly state that seminar objectives include an intentional focus on life's big questions. We give Fellows the opportunity to wrestle with these questions, to reflect on the meaning of life and work and develop a compelling sense that there is a link between their projects and their deeper sense of personal purpose.

We also share the Giving Voice to Values (GVV) approach to dealing with values conflicts when they arise in the workplace.[6] GVV is an innovative curriculum for developing the skills, knowledge, and commitment required to implement values-based leadership. Rather than a focus on ethical *analysis*, the *GVV* curriculum focuses on ethical *implementation* and asks the question: "What if I were going to act on my values? What would I say and do? How could I be most effective?" Although speaking up about ethical issues is often envisioned as learning how to say "no," to resist the pressure to violate one's values, GVV is presented to the Fellows as a tool that can also help them use an "affirmative Voice" to generate support for their values-driven initiatives. Fellows are encouraged to think about how to reframe and script possible conflicts in their own workplaces and realize that taking control of that narrative is a particularly powerful tool in voicing and enacting values (Gentile, 2010). Although positioned here as a core component of the First Mover emphasis upon Reflection, the seven principles at the heart of GVV link back to Leadership, Innovation, and Community as well. For example, the story of GVV's origin and development is shared as an example of the use of "piloting" to launch and fuel innovation. And the emphasis upon peer coaching and upon building and practicing influence skills tie directly and respectively to Community and Leadership.

In advance of the first seminar, the Fellows rarely anticipate the impact these reflection activities will have for them. One Fellow's reaction illustrates this point. In the first of the three fellowship seminars, we travel from the Aspen conference facility to a spectacular site in the Rockies, have dinner, and tell stories around a campfire.

[6]Giving Voice to Values (www.GivingVoiceToValues.org) was developed by Dr. Mary Gentile with founding partners the Aspen Institute and the Yale School of Management. The program is now based at and supported by Babson College. Conventional ethics training is often centered on helping students figure out what is "right." GVV takes a different approach. It is designed to give people tools so that they can act with confidence and conviction when they know what is right.

The assignment for the evening is to share a story of a moment, or the period of time, when clarity about life purpose emerged for you and gave you a sense of what you are supposed to do for the rest of your life. As we wrapped up a recent seminar week in Aspen, one of the Fellows confessed that when she was packing for the seminar, dealing with the stress of organizing work and arrangements for a young child so she could be away from home for a week, she complained to her husband about this particular part of the program. It made her wonder why she had decided to commit, since time spent in this way seemed so extraneous to her immediate concerns. At the end of the seminar, however, she reported to the group that the campfire experience and the emotionally honest stories that were told in this beautiful setting were transformative for her and actually had enormous impact on the way she planned to approach work when she returned to the office.

This focus on reflection is consistent with findings that support the notion that leaders who become more self-aware and conscious of the world around them become better leaders (Mirvis, 2008). Most Fellows come from companies where reflection is rarely a part of daily work life so it is not surprising that they are skeptical about the impact these practices can have on their effectiveness and level of engagement.

To encourage reflection, we include poetry and essays as an important part of the readings that Fellows do throughout the fellowship.[7] Excerpts from *A Hidden Wholeness: The Journey Toward an Undivided Life* have special relevance for the Fellows who strive to bring their whole selves to work (Palmer, 2004). Acknowledging and exploring the divide they often feel between their professional and personal personae allows them to imagine and then live a greater integration. This alignment is empowering. They speak of feeling "renewed, refreshed, emboldened." Greater engagement and commitment not only reenergizes them but, they say, serves as inspiration for their colleagues as well.

Community. The professional life of a social intrapreneur can be a lonely one. They often work alone, lacking support for their ideas and feeling out of sync with supervisors and colleagues. So we knew that establishing a strong bond among the Fellows had to be a central focus for the program. Thus, we choose the class with extreme care and then strive to create an environment that contributes to relationship building. Our objective is to help the Fellows connect with and learn from a group of innovators who will remain a lifelong source of inspiration, encouragement, collaboration, and support.[8]

When we evaluate candidates we look for people with a collaborative, generous spirit. We only select Fellows who are eager not only to achieve their own goals but to work hard to help others achieve theirs. We want Fellows to find themselves in the midst of a diverse group of exceptional business people who are accomplished, daring, and humble. Community building begins as soon as the class is announced. A joint press release focuses on the cohort of Fellows so that the public—and especially colleagues in

[7]Examples of poems included in the program include Mary Oliver's "The Summer Day," Chuan Tzu's "The Woodcarver," and Denise Levertov's "Witness."

[8]As we are in the very early years of the program, we don't yet know to what extent we will achieve this objective. Many efforts are underway to keep the Fellows engaged. They are asked to participate in the selection process of new Fellows by nominating and interviewing candidates. They are invited to join conference calls. When opportunities arise, we invite them to present their work to various audiences. Program staff collect and send updates to Fellows. The independent evaluator conducts follow-up interviews. Reunions happen when Fellows are in the same cities; and there are plans for a reunion for the first two classes in 2012.

the Fellows' own companies—can see the breadth of the experience represented within the class. A First Movers section on the Aspen Institute website offers a full profile of each Fellow and a hint of the scope of work each will undertake during their tenure as a Fellow.

Quickly into the first seminar, Fellows acknowledge the growing bonds among the Fellows and express relief as they realize they are no longer alone. Realizing the potential that resides in the community for support and mutual understanding, Fellows are highly motivated to connect personally and professionally. And being part of this group spurs Fellows to be more daring in their own companies. As one Fellow said, he was inspired to push harder because he didn't want "to let the group down."

During the twelve days the group is together during the program, there is plenty of time for Fellows to interact, offer feedback on challenges, and learn about each other's initiatives. Sessions are dialogue—not presentation—based. The first two hours of each seminar are devoted to stories. Themes from these opening stories are picked up and threaded through the rest of the sessions. In the first seminar, for example, we typically ask each Fellow to provide an introduction by responding to the following question:

> *Reflecting on your own experience, if you were asked to highlight one exceptional story of innovation when you were working at your best to realize an objective that achieved business growth and achieved a positive social or environmental impact (e.g., it also served as a force for peace, or green value creation, or poverty eradication, or community well-being), what real-life story would you tell? Be sure to tell us what personal strengths were particularly critical for achieving this success.*[9]

In subsequent seminar sessions, in conference calls between sessions, and informally throughout the program, Fellows provide updates on project progress, coach each other on overcoming challenges, and celebrate wins—big and small. Over time, the sharing of joys and challenges binds them in a friendship that we expect will extend well beyond the conclusion of the formal fellowship period.

Looking Ahead

As we arrive at the mid-point of our second class of Fellows, we know we are just beginning our own learning journey. There is so much more we need to explore about the social intrapreneurship phenomenon and the kinds of experiences that help these innovators thrive within business. So far, however, we believe we are on the right track. As the independent evaluator of this program wrote about the first pilot year, "At its best, the fellowship program helped the first class of Fellows become bolder, think bigger, develop tools to succeed as change makers, and establish meaningful relationships with peers from other companies. It also helped them make step changes in their own leadership and in projects of strategic significance to their companies and industries."[10]

There are many challenges ahead for this work. To name a few: developing a useful database to track long-term impacts of the program; strengthening the connections with the thought partners; improving the rigor of project development, especially

---

[9]This question and other aspects of the seminar agenda draw heavily on the scholarship associated with Appreciative Inquiry, an approach to organizational change (Cooperrider, Whitney, & Stavros, 2008).

[10]Final unpublished evaluation report prepared by Shari Cohen, PhD.

between seminars; sustaining connections to program alumni; facilitating the development of teaching case studies of individual projects and Fellows so that the lessons of their experiences can be shared with students who aspire to become First Movers.

The Fellows have generously advised us about ways to strengthen the program and we are acting on many of these suggestions. For example, we now ask thought partners to complete an online survey after the first seminar rather than before (as we did with the first class) so that Fellows can use the responses to help them communicate more effectively with these individuals. We schedule conference calls more frequently between seminars and now rely more on the expertise of the Fellows in these sessions. And we are working diligently to meet the challenge of keeping the Fellows connected within and across classes. We know that these connections are critical to the long-term success of the program and that they can't be achieved by dedicated staff time alone, although that resource is essential. The Fellows themselves have to take the lead. Early evidence suggests Fellows have the will and determination to do so, but only time will tell if the Fellowship lives up to its full potential.

We will know we have succeeded in achieving the objectives of this program when we see evidence that the Fellows have risen to greater levels of leadership and influence; that their fellowship projects have paved the way for greater integration of financial, social, and environmental value in their companies and industries; and that the network of Fellows has been built, creating a critical mass of leaders across industries who can collectively begin to change the way business is done. Along the way, we'll watch a number of indicators to be sure we are on the right path: size and depth of the candidate pool; additional nominees from participating companies

Figure 29.3

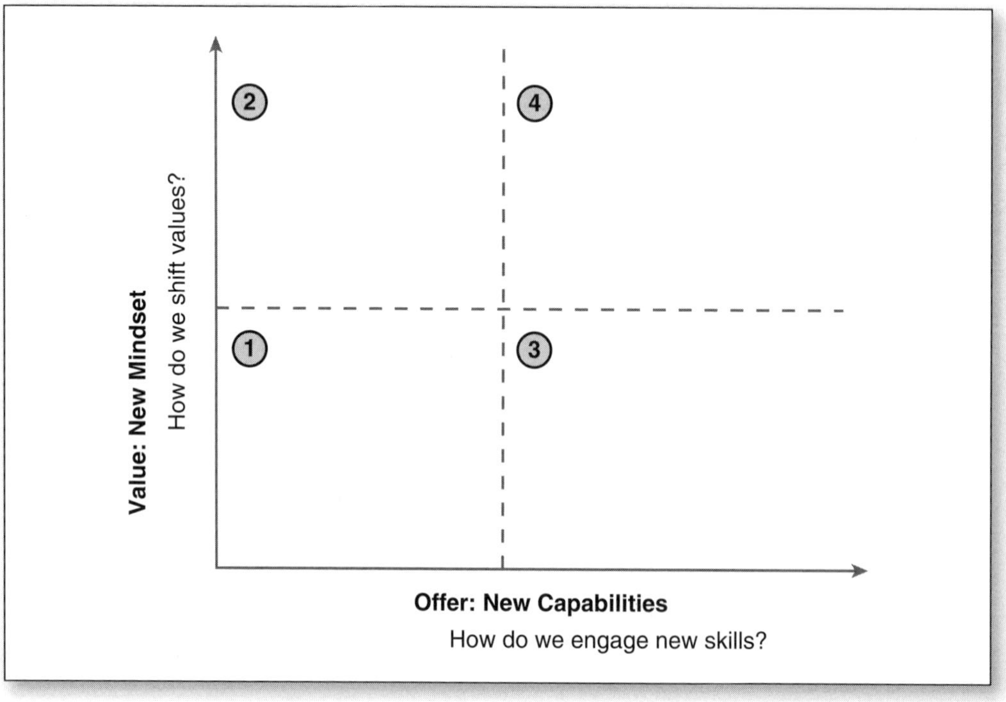

and from the Fellows themselves; satisfaction levels measured in evaluation interviews and surveys; career progression of the Fellows; number of viable and innovative collaborations across companies launched by Fellows.

The impetus to make headway on all these fronts is great. We believe that calling attention to the contributions of social entrepreneurs and helping them implement the game-changing innovations they are undertaking has significant, positive implications for how quickly and effectively businesses move toward greater integration of financial, social, and environmental value.

The promise of the program is demonstrated by the results of a simple exercise that we ask Fellows to complete. With their project in mind, we invite them to place a pin on a graph.[11] (See Figure 29.3.)

The location of the pin is meant to represent their best assessment of where their companies fall on two dimensions related to the implementation of social and environmental innovations. The vertical axis represents corporate mindset. Moving up the graph shows the extent to which a company values these innovations and considers them core to strategy. The horizontal axis represents capabilities. Moving along this axis indicates the ability of companies to implement these new innovations. The results of the exercise in both classes are telling. In each class, a significant majority of Fellows placed their pin in the second quadrant on the graph: high values, relatively low capabilities.

Fellows' perceptions demonstrate what we believe to be true: Many companies understand the critical need to integrate greater concern for social and environmental impacts into their core strategic priorities, but they lack the know-how to execute. Our objective with the First Movers Fellowship is to help individuals within business who have particular expertise and commitment in this regard take their companies much more quickly along the capabilities continuum. By doing so, they will be raising the bar for defining business success.

References

Boston College Center for Corporate Citizenship. (2009). *How virtue creates value for business and society.* Chestnut Hill, MA.

Brown, T. (2008). Design thinking. *Harvard Business Review, 86, (6)*, 84–92.

Brown, T. (2009). *Change by design: How design thinking transforms organizations and inspires innovation.* New York: HarperCollins.

Cooperrider, D. (2008). Sustainable innovation. *BizEd*, 7(4), 32–38

Cooperrider, D., Whitney, D., & Stavros, J.M. (2008). *Appreciative inquiry handbook for leaders of change* (2nd ed.). Brunswick, OH: Crown Custom Publishing Inc. and San Francisco, CA: Berrett-Koehler Publishers, Inc.

Davis, I. (2005). What is the business of business? *McKinsey Quarterly, 3*, 104–113.

Freeman, R.E. (1984). *Strategic management: A stakeholder approach.* Boston, MA: Pitman.

Gentile, M. (2010). *Giving voice to values: How to speak your mind when you know what's right.* New Haven and London: Yale University Press.

Grayson, D., McLaren, M., & Spitzeck, H. (2011). Social intrapreneurship: An extra force for sustainability. Doughty Center for Corporate Responsibility, Occasional Paper. Cranfield University School of Management.

Hamel, G. (2009). Moon shots for management. *Harvard Business Review, 87*(2), 91–98.

Holliday C., Jr., Schnidheiny, S., & Watts, P. (2002). *Walking the talk: The business case for sustainable development.* San Francisco, CA: Berrett-Koehler.

Kelley, R.E. (1998). *How to be a star at work: Nine breakthrough strategies you need to succeed.* New York: Three Rivers Press.

[11]The exercise and the graph were developed by Fred Dust, IDEO.

Martin, R., & Osberg, S. (2007). Social entrepreneurship: The case for definition. *Stanford Social Innovation Review*, Spring.

McGaw, N. (2005). Developing leaders for a sustainable global society. *Strategic HR Review*, *4*(6), 32–35.

Meyerson, D.E. (2001). *Tempered radicals: How people use difference to inspire change at work.* Boston, MA: Harvard Business School Publishing.

Meyerson, D.E., & Fryer, B. (2002). Turning an industry inside out: A conversation with Robert Redford. *Harvard Business Review, 80*(5), 57–61.

Mirvis, P. (2008). Executive development through consciousness-raising experiences. *Academy of Management Learning & Education, 7*(2), 173–188.

Palmer, P.J. (2004). *A hidden wholeness: The journey toward an undivided life.* San Francisco, CA: Jossey-Bass.

Porter, M.E., & Kramer, M.R. (2011). Creating shared value. *Harvard Business Review, 89*(1/2), 62–77.

Porter, M.E., & Kramer, M.R. (2006). Strategy & society: The link between competitive advantage and corporate social responsibility. *Harvard Business Review, 84*(12), 78–92.

Sustainability Ltd. (2008). *The social intrapreneur: A field guide for corporate changemakers.*

30

RE-DEVELOPING LEADERS

The Harvard Advanced Leadership Experiment in Even Higher Education

◆ Rosabeth Moss Kanter
Harvard Business School

Leadership development is best realized as a lifelong, evolving process, yet it is a process desperately needed to respond to the changing needs of every area of society and the global environment (health, education, environment, economic opportunity, etc.). In 2006, three professors from Harvard Business School began to develop a new curriculum—in partnership with other schools within the University—to try to incubate leaders who could address these problems.

The Advanced Leadership Fellowship program was conceived in order to drive change and enhance the public well-being by means of educating leaders from a wide variety of backgrounds in a cross-disciplinary, university-wide initiative at Harvard to realize the goal of educating leaders who can make a difference in this world. This chapter outlines the fundamental history, purpose, and design of the Advanced Leadership program, and how the program may contribute to solving global problems by providing effective and informed leadership.

❖ ❖ ❖

The Harvard Advanced Leadership innovation in leadership development, still an experiment, began with the grand goal of creating a movement that could sweep the world. The goal was based on an equally grand vision that someday leadership and leadership development would become a fully lifelong process. We imagined the possibility that, after twenty to twenty-five years of hard work, experienced leaders ready to shift their focus from their income-earning years would consider where to go to school to prepare for their next phase of service, to move from being merely great leaders to being truly advanced leaders. We also felt strongly that the world desperately needs more and better leaders to fill gaps, create new coalitions, and harness new technology to improve education, health, communities, economic opportunity, and the environment. Because established institutions are falling short, a new supply of leaders is needed, particularly those with experience that could be directed to purpose-based ends.

There is a great deal packed into this vision: a new stage of higher education; an effort to build and deploy a leadership force of seasoned leaders who can tackle challenging societal problems that require institutional, not merely organizational or interpersonal, capabilities; a cross-disciplinary collaboration among university professional school faculty to integrate areas of knowledge (or at least find the intersections among them); and a response to a dramatic demographic shift that makes possible later-in-life service careers with new dimensions of leadership.

For all the grandeur of this vision for the long term, the execution is modest in the short term. The experiment at Harvard to be described in this chapter is in the early "proof of concept" phase, the number of leaders involved to date is small, and the projects they are undertaking are barely beginning. After several years of organizing and planning, twenty faculty members from five professional schools have guided the process of finding and educating fifty-five experienced leaders coming to Harvard as Advanced Leadership Fellows, in three calendar-year cohorts (2009, 2010, 2011), along with thirteen officially registered accompanying Partners, some highly accomplished leaders themselves. The long prior experience of these leaders means that we were working on "re-development" rather than development per se.

Yet, even with a short experiment-in-progress with a relatively small numbers of leaders, we have generated ideas and learning that can be useful to scholars and practitioners of leadership development, whether or not they wish to replicate our model:

- A budding definition of the difference between great and advanced leadership
- The centrality of substance in leadership development: why a research university?
- Education in context: the importance of life-stage and situation-appropriateness
- Professional identities as facilitators or inhibitors of later-stage learning, and identity shifts
- The leadership model reflected in the design and creation of a university innovation

This chapter will provide an overview of the Advanced Leadership Fellowship educational program. We will cover its history, rationale, and design, and make some observations about the re-development and re-deployment of already-accomplished leaders.

History and Broad Guiding Principles

Depending on the eventual success of this very new experiment, the story might someday be called "The Miracle on the

Charles River." The hatching of the idea and creation of the prototype took place during some of the most difficult days for the university: the premature exit of a president and a year's gap before a new president took office and a severe financial crisis that required cutting budgets significantly and freezing hiring. Moreover, the organization itself was known for its principle of "every tub on its own bottom," a metaphor adopted well before the idea of silos became popular in management theory. But we mention this context only in passing. Regardless of crises, the initiative still must prove itself on its own terms as a contribution to the university as well as to leadership re-development. The story starts in 2005, although there were precursors in slightly earlier discussions.

In 2005, Harvard Business School faculty members Rosabeth Moss Kanter, Rakesh Khurana, and Nitin Nohria (now Dean) began to discuss the opportunity presented by three intersecting phenomena:

1. **An evolving university concerned with its societal mission.** Universities have created new schools when societal change has revealed knowledge gaps, giving rise to new fields and education in new professions. There has been little change in the basic forms and offerings of universities since the 1980s, despite the emergence of new technologies in a globalizing world and questions about the relevance of universities. Many research universities have been under pressure to contribute to their surrounding communities, add service learning for students, and translate their research into practice.

2. **A global problem agenda that requires the development of new cross-profession knowledge and leadership competencies.** In the early twenty-first century, a set of global societal challenges have become more visible, yet efforts to address them have often stalled. Problems such as poverty, global health, basic education, or environmental quality are systemic in nature, have political as well as technical dimensions, and tend to require cross-sector and cross-profession collaboration. But there is a knowledge gap about how to develop and implement solutions, which should be filled by integrative research and educational innovation.

3. **Changing demographics.** A longer life-cycle and healthier aging have produced a demographic revolution in the developed world, especially North America, Western Europe, Japan, Singapore, and China. Demographic changes create new challenges, such as pension finance, but they can bring potential solutions. Studies show that accomplished leaders are increasingly interested in service in the productive years following their primary income-earning years—especially solving problems such as those outlined above. This is an enormous group that will only grow larger. Many in this group seek meaningful contributions rather than income, but there is an absence of established pathways. The opportunity this population presents has not been addressed by higher education.

Each issue represents a problem, but their intersection represents an opportunity. Universities could potentially create new graduate/professional schools to educate experienced leaders who wish to tackle societal and global problems in their next phase of life. Such third-stage schools (following undergraduate and graduate/professional schools) could offer more than retraining for transitions to new careers, although they could also serve that purpose. Rather, third-stage schools could set a distinctive intellectual agenda by focusing on the knowledge required to lead social institutions and address global challenges.

That was the starting premise. But to build support for any new idea, it helps to use the currency of the institution—in this case, a written product that was rigorously researched and footnoted. The White Paper introducing the rationale for an Advanced Leadership program, called "Moving Higher Education to the Next Stage," was circulated broadly throughout the university for discussion and reactions and provided to key deans and published as a Working Paper in October 2005. The feedback helped refine the concept but also identified faculty members who would potentially help lead the development of a pilot initiative.

The early stages of refining the idea and developing a pilot program were guided by theories, frameworks, and findings about innovation in established organizations, self-organized change, and social movements. Consciously or unconsciously, the founding faculty members were reinforcing ideas and tools that would later be taught to Advanced Leadership Fellows about institutional change, thus, in Silicon Valley parlance, "eating our own dog food."

There were two important early decisions about guiding principles, one of which initially slowed down the creation of the program but proved to be a very important investment essential for success, and the second which came in handy later.

The first principle was interdisciplinary, cross-sector collaboration, and shared ownership. This innovation had to be collectively owned across diverse, relatively independent professional schools. Without ownership by faculty at all the key professional schools, it would never realize its potential as an integrative entity or be able to offer to its target population of experienced leaders the kind of education and development they should have. This was challenging. It is always easier to work through established channels, but innovations rarely present themselves in the existing boxes on organization charts. At a decentralized university with powerful professional schools, it is much easier to get things done by working inside one silo than to mount a program across silos. But through individual and group meetings, leaders from the faculty of five professional schools, and ties to a sixth, came together to share and test ideas about the content and shape of this new stage of higher education.

The first group invited to join discussions were senior faculty with credibility and ability to persuade their own deans. Those interested voted with their feet and volunteered their time. There were breakfast meetings every few weeks in a noisy but central restaurant. There was an intimate dinner with former Treasury Secretary Paul O'Neill, a former CEO and health reform advocate, that inspired a new faculty member to commit. A presentation to a faculty seminar hosted by Social Enterprise at the Business School but with a broad university invitation list brought additional offers to help. A pro bono team from Monitor Group produced market research information that attracted many faculty members to a presentation. Bonds were also forged in adversity; phone conferences after running against university barriers (including the financial crisis) solidified belief in the vision and determination to get the program up and running.

Initial internal funding for part-time staff and expenses reflected the collaboration. Small amounts of seed money came from Office of the President, Harvard Business School; the Center for Public Leadership at Harvard Kennedy School; and eventually Harvard Law School.

The second principle was to try to get one of everything that the founding team might want later into the first prototype. That is tricky and sometimes paradoxical, but important. Doing this would avoid the classic problem of operationalizing goals and then losing sight of the broad vision while wallowing in concrete details. Also, to gain support for the idea, it was important to point out familiar elements so that audiences could understand it, while also making clear in every communication that the idea was different. The faculty team learned to reiterate the vision and not compromise on trying to reflect everything in the first iteration—representation of every school; a mix of all professions; a program element dealing with every key social challenge or institution, diversity of eventual Fellows by geography, gender, race, interest; funding sources—individual, corporate, and foundation gifts, payment by Fellows of their costs, etc.

As faculty group meetings began in earnest in 2006, the thought was to develop collaborative research and publications, then create a teaching program. Faculty members enjoyed the rich substantive discussions about issues that cut across many sectors and professions, such as childhood obesity or clean water. Many ideas for case studies surfaced. One that came to fruition involved a case study on Benjamin Hooks, a former judge and civil rights leader, and his founding of the Children's Health Forum later in life, guided by three tenured faculty members representing Harvard Law School, Harvard Business School, and Harvard School of Public Health, and employing students from each school. But it became clear that dates on calendars drive everything, and so does teaching. The faculty group concluded that it was essential to find the right organizational home and vehicle and then get started with the teaching program that demonstrated that there was indeed a receptive market and a way to run the program while faculty still carried out their responsibilities to their own schools.

Bottom-up, self-organized, as a coalition of volunteers, and without a single administrative home—this was not a recipe for viability. Meanwhile, the university president resigned, and the interim president for a year was not ready to authorize new initiatives. A few alternatives were explored, but faculty wanted to get moving. With support from a deputy provost inspired by the idea, a proposal and business plan were created to make the group an official "inter-faculty initiative" (IFI) under the Provost. The faculty worked creatively to develop sub-innovations to make possible a robust and complete educational program without requiring faculty to develop entirely new courses for this purpose, which would have been impossible.

Authorized as IFI under the Provost's office in July 2007, the Advanced Leadership Initiative (ALI) was ready to plan the prototype. The informal coalition became a formal governing board. Workshops at Harvard Business School and Harvard Law School alumni reunions in the fall of 2007 showcased Advanced Leadership and identified a few possible interested Fellow candidates.

As an IFI pilot program, everything had to be developed from scratch: logo, letterhead, office space, messages, policies, staffing, support systems, IT, connection with the professional schools, selection and invitation process, financial systems, etc. Though small and called a pilot, this was indeed like creating an entirely new and different school. The Working Paper had proposed a two-year program, but market feedback indicated that shorter was more viable, at least initially. It was decided to run the program as a year-long affiliation; for reasons to be discussed later, it was also decided, but only after considerable debate, to run it by calendar year rather than academic year, to better suit the target population of leaders.

With the hiring of the first full-time staff member in January 2008, the new ALI team crafted messages, designed a brochure (which became a uniting document), and began the process of hand-recruiting candidates to become Fellows—a designation for the leaders being "re-developed" that carried an honorific. Drafting the brochure required systemization of the program offerings as well as the statement of concrete goals and the setting of dates.

Fellows are expected to meet three main criteria:

- a minimum of twenty to twenty-five years of leadership accomplishments, with a track record of innovation;
- a motivation to make a difference on some of society's most challenging problems;
- an understanding of the value that engaging with a university could have

> as preparation for their transition from a primary focus on income-earning careers to their next years of service.

Because of the guiding principle discussed above, that the first prototypes had to send the right signals, it was important to have senior leaders who would have brand-name value for ALI. Of course, those are the very people in the most demand who might not think that they needed to "go back to school" (to use the phrase we avoided). We knew that in an aspirational society, it is best to start with the top, because the middle will follow, but that it is impossible to start with lower standards and move up. This made initial recruitment very challenging. Recruitment of fellows for the inaugural year was managed through informal networks. The first two commitments came in late March and early April 2008. The first was a respected doctor and entrepreneur referred by a faculty member. The second was a Fellow sponsored by IBM, based on a relationship with another faculty member.

By the time the 2009 program began, there were fourteen 2009 Fellows along with four officially registered accompanying partners (see below), plus a base of sponsors and donors that covered at least one of every main type. The 2010 cohort consisted of twenty-two Fellows and five Partners, plus five Senior Advanced Leadership Fellows from the 2009 cohort who stayed on to complete their projects (making clear that eventually the two-year option might work). The 2011 cohort, just underway, includes nineteen Fellows, four Partners, and nine Senior Advanced Leadership Fellows (some with Partners).

Creating Life-Stage Appropriate Leadership Development

The whole university, with its rich array of fields, disciplines, research efforts, and programs, was seen as the best arena for developing advanced leaders—not through any single entity or course, but as an environment in which Fellows could connect ideas and make connections that would not only enhance their skills but also make it more likely that they would undertake high-impact projects. We were interested in helping them ramp up, think bigger, tackle significant issues, and do it with more competence, increasing the likelihood for impact. We saw that individual efforts could be joined, so that over time, the network of Fellows and former Fellows could multiply their impact.

There is little guidance about how to design education for this life stage, when people are seeking not a job but a legacy. The analogy of "going back to school" is tempting to use but can create problems and tensions. After all, the target population consists of people who have already gone to school. Many have MDs, PhDs, JDs, and other advanced degrees. They have proven themselves in their professions and careers. They have families and a wide range of commitments even beyond formal jobs. And they could as easily be teachers as learners.

Thus, the Advanced Leadership Fellowship was explicitly designed to be appropriate to the late-career life stage and stature of the Fellows. This also was seen as a way to motivate them to be active learners, since they would be treated with full respect for their accomplishments. Several elements also proved to be helpful for faculty schedules, since the faculty were volunteers, although they tended to create administrative complexities. But the faculty board always put pedagogy and program considerations first, rather than be driven to fit the administrative structures and processes already in place at the university. There were several main design considerations.

Calendar year. Universities work on an academic year that is familiar earlier in life, from the primary grades through professional schools, but does not fit the way most adults live their lives or conduct their careers. Even in organizations that operate on a fiscal-year basis, where fiscal years start and finish in the middle of the calendar year, many people still time their transitions or exits to the calendar year, e.g., December 31. Therefore, the program operates on a calendar year, January–December. Orientation, called Introduction to Harvard, would be a Thursday–Saturday in mid-December, giving Fellows the opportunity to engage with the university before they start so they can begin the calendar year (i.e., winter) term with knowledge of the university. The official end to the Fellowship year is the end of classes in December, although the final symposium at which Fellows present their project thinking to a public audience is held in late November.

Front-end-loaded. In a fast-paced world where people have many opportunities and new information is created rapidly and transmitted rapidly there is a tendency to seek time compression on nearly everything. A common question asked by the first rounds of candidates for the Advanced Leadership Fellowship was how short can the program be, what is the minimum time for participation? For the first round, we decided to "frontload" the main formal program activities into the first 4–5 months, so that fellows would get the formal education first and could feel some sense of satisfaction about what they're learning early. This also turned out to have important pedagogical value because fellows could develop a shared platform of knowledge as well as have their individual thinking stimulated before defining a project, which by its nature requires independent study and individualized relationships with student and faculty. (Interestingly, as the year unfolded, many fellows asked why the program wasn't designed to be longer, stating their desire to spend more time learning at Harvard and working out their projects—one reason for naming Senior Advanced Leadership Fellows who can be affiliated for a second year in a lighter way.)

Partners. By the end of their primary income-earning years, people who have had demanding careers are often interested in connecting closely again with their spouses or partners for their next phase of service. Thus, the program is family-friendly. Certainly spouses and, in some cases, other family members are included in a few activities from time-to-time. But the program also provides an option for Fellows to be accompanied by a fully registered Partner who can do everything the Fellows do (but without an expectation of creating an independent project). The Partner might work jointly with the Fellow and do many things in parallel or the Partner may pursue his or her own agenda at the university. Occasionally, Partners may find themselves working jointly with Fellows other than their own spouse, in areas of mutual interest.

External obligations. At this life stage, experienced leaders have many other obligations, even in the absence of a full-time job. These include commitments commensurate with their stature, such as memberships on boards of directors. Fellows in certain professions may also have ongoing commitments to long-term clients even though this may be at a reduced level. Thus, the program must have sufficient flexibility and make activities efficient to attend as much as possible while at the same time hoping that fellows will be in residence on campus as much as possible in order to take advantage of courses and work with students.

Mentoring. Another element of being life-stage appropriate is to acknowledge the fellows' experiences and accomplishments. Some have advanced degrees already. They are experts in their field. They could as easily be teachers themselves. So, the program needs to emphasize what they have to offer to students and faculty, as well as what they might learn. Fellows must be treated as teachers as well as learners. The program emphasizes the expectation that all Fellows will be available to students and will assemble and guide student teams, both in the interest of their own projects and also to serve as role models and coaches to students.

Balancing structure and flexibility. Executive education programs tend to structure and schedule every moment of their participants' time, but that is not appropriate for a program like this that intends to open access to intellectual resources and opportunities rather than march people through a fixed curriculum. Fellows come with a wide variety of interests, and even when they have a main area of focus, they can benefit from a serendipitous encounter with an area of knowledge they had not previously considered. Furthermore, while people at the top of most professions are accustomed to highly structured activities filling their calendars, they also do not want to be told what to do—they want to feel in control. Thus, the program has core elements for all Fellows to participate in together but also offers a great deal of choice; depending on a Fellow's agenda, the mix of activities and the modes of learning will vary. The program also leaves open the possibility that Fellows will organize activities on their own, according to their preferences. They can determine, individually or in groups, other faculty they might wish to contact or others ways to communicate. At the same time, they are encouraged to avoid the "activity trap" of filling every moment with an activity, in order to leave time for reading and reflection. Balancing structure and flexibility is a continuing challenge, because some people will always demand that more things get done for them, while others will resent having too much done to them.

The Educational Goal: Advanced Leadership Competencies

What is "advanced" leadership? The term is clearly a play on words, signifying in part the advanced career stage from which the target population is drawn. But "advanced" also reflects the strong higher-order skills required to lead in complex, unbounded societal and institutional settings where goals are unclear, there are multiple stakeholders, and there is no clear authority.

Our pedagogical goal was to create a mix of experiences, mostly in the classroom but also including reflection and other experiential modes, that would address a comprehensive set of advanced leadership competencies. These were identified by a team of the core faculty before the first cohort began and introduced to each cohort periodically through the program as a basis for self-reflection and discussion. The specific concepts and accompanying frameworks or tools are covered in the Advanced Leadership Seminar sessions (or, in some cases, through subject-matter courses), so that every Fellow is exposed to the ideas. In some cases they are also the basis for workshops that facilitate experiential understanding. Interactions with students from diverse background, field visits, and the occasional summer internship add a dimension. The competencies include:

- Understanding purpose, values, principles; productive social change, good work, good outcome; collective definitions of success; what is worth doing and from whose point of view; the perspective of the ultimate beneficiary
- Mastering relevant subject matter knowledge at an appropriate, feasible level, connecting actions to facts, to domain-specific factors; examining problems and potential solutions from the perspective of recent best knowledge in a number of fields—e.g., life sciences, physical sciences, social sciences, engineering, economics, etc.; how to know what questions to ask, when/how to rely on experts
- Diagnosing root causes, intersecting layers of issues, and system dynamics;

seeing the broad context, mapping systems/ecosystems to see connections; behavioral clues and system trajectories, e.g., self-fulfilling prophecies, self-fueling cycles, success momentum ("winning streaks"), decline cycles ("losing streaks"); elements of systemic change to guide sustainable transformations

- Understanding relevant aspects of legal frameworks, legislative processes, rules enforcement processes, electoral dynamics, public resources and their allocation, interest groups and their influence; determining when to use tools of the law to intervene, support change, or prevent negative changes; how to access and use legal tools
- Understanding drivers of public behavior and public opinion, including values, history, culture, and languages; within countries and in a cross-border, global environment
- Picking targets for action: whether public policy, a demonstration program, grass-roots organizing or consciousness-raising; and what kinds of action make sense given starting point, goals, and tactics/resources necessary for each; the wide repertoire of intervention possibilities
- Determining the organizational or action vehicle: whether to work through an existing organization or create a new one, whether to stand-alone or use coalitions, whether to emphasize one-time or discrete events or build a continuing organization—with awareness of the challenges and tradeoffs of each choice
- Understanding the differences (and similarities) among sectors (business, government, civil society; for-profit, public, non-profit, sectors), and the sources and role of capital (financial, intellectual), e.g., resource mobilization and from what entities, how; resource allocation, compensation, and the implications for management and motivation
- Determining whether, how, when to convene others as individuals (including network models) or via organizations (including membership models), and to influence them so that their actions reinforce rather than cancel each other—e.g., establishing collective goals or definitions of change among disparate individuals or organizations pursuing specific agendas
- Identifying stakeholders, interest groups, opinion leaders, resource-holders, beneficiaries, competitors; political mapping of players, roles, and relationships; when and how to collaborate with competitors
- Building coalitions across organizations for action toward similar goals, especially Grand Coalitions of independent organizations with their own constituencies; how to organize, via appropriate tactics; negotiations; barriers and how to overcome them; finite time-oriented goals (campaigns) or ongoing effort to hang together
- Developing standards, governance, accountability, and performance metrics for complex multi-layered partnerships and progress on complex issues
- Understanding and orchestrating the rhythm of change, phases of change: seeing context, finding needs/opportunities; creative new approaches; visions and themes; initial backers and supporters; working teams; problems of middles; celebrating and building on early wins; diagnosing resistance to change and making converts ("the change agent's rule of thirds")
- Enhancing individual/personal skills in pattern recognition and system

diagnosis, in influence without sole authority, in communicating across cultures within countries and in a cross-border, global environment, and in micro-interpersonal engagement including running effective meetings and taking actions appropriate to the stage of development of relationships/groups

- Cultivating integrative thinking and "contextual intelligence"; ability to articulate a "theory of the system" that encompasses many forces and variables, ties together the perspective and interests of multiple stakeholders, shows connections and common interests, that points to powerful but non-obvious possibilities for intervention; use of stories and narratives
- Cultivating empathy and "emotional intelligence": cognitive awareness, ability to see the system from various points of view; authentic inquiry before advocacy; ability to surface, understand, suspend own assumptions/biases; ability to respect differences and transcend them via a common framework, goal, common definition of the situation and of success

This list covers both macro understanding of direction-setting for big, complex, unbounded systems, and micro understanding of leading people individually and in groups. Our assumption is that successful leaders will have mastered most of these competencies through career experience, so that the Advanced Leadership Fellowship can focus more on the cognitive side of new knowledge. But the "refreshers" and heightened self-awareness turned out to be critical for some. We could also see gaps. Systems thinking, stakeholder awareness, contextual intelligence, and emotional intelligence tended to be gaps for many Fellows. In the West Point language (per Scott Snook) or "being, knowing, and doing," the competencies list stresses "knowing," encourages awareness of "being," and provides a way for the Fellows to begin the process of "doing," per their project plans.

Program Design and Flow

The program can be thought of as involving two main dimensions: "vertical" deep dives into subject matter; and a "horizontal" thread of core education about advanced leadership competencies culminating in project planning. The elements of the program unfold over time according to a theory of the order in which topics should be introduced and the rhythm of the year. Thus, it is extremely important to look at the program as a whole, because its effectiveness depends on the reinforcement of knowledge and skills that come in a variety of forms throughout the year.

Harvard regular course audits. Fellows can audit almost any course at the university, with the instructor's permission, for either term when they are affiliated. Courses are considered a major program element, even though Fellows spread out to many schools to find areas of study. Fellows identify courses of interest and pursue them with individual agendas.

Core course: The Advanced Leadership Seminar. The core course is a horizontal uniting activity. It consists of almost-weekly three-hour classroom sessions and longer workshops of four to fifteen hours designed to provide knowledge and experience around the advanced leadership competencies. The core course runs from February–May and for two days in September. There are three modules: systems, sectors, and intervention modes; strategies and tactics, including individual leadership and social entrepreneurship; and moving into action, with project identification, stakeholder analysis, and change management frameworks. The course has a full curriculum with readings and case studies; the seminar chairs generally ask faculty from around the university to teach or participate in particular sessions in order to maximize Fellows' exposure to faculty. In mid-May sessions, Fellows are asked to produce a short statement of the domain for their project, and there is also a cross-cohort idea exchange, coinciding with the return of past Fellows to campus. At the September sessions, Fellows' project ideas are expected to be deeper and more developed, in preparation for presenting their project plans at the Fellows' Final Symposium, open to the public, in late November.

Think Tanks. The program takes three vertical deep dives into subject matter involving societal challenges through two- to three-day "Think Tanks," focused on the domains of education, health, and communities or environment. They are held in the winter term, at intervals of two to five weeks from March through late April or early May. Each is the equivalent of a course in length and substance, but takes the form of a mini-conference with discussion, aimed at identifying current practice, leadership gaps, and opportunities for advanced leaders and new interventions. Think Tanks provide Fellows an opportunity for learning (and sometimes presenting, if they are already experts) alongside faculty, students, outside experts, and guests. Even though the sectors and issues are different, and each Think Tank is a stand-alone event generating significant content, it becomes clear that the issues of societal and institutional change cut across all Think Tanks. Advanced leadership competencies are also introduced into the discussions. Think Tanks bring theories to real problems and also help Fellows make connections with experts, which has often led to additional opportunities for Fellows and their projects through these relationships.

Field experiences. Once Fellows begin to think about their projects, in May, the program makes an effort to offer field visits that can further connect the theories, frameworks, and problem identification with the real-world work of practitioners attempting to grapple with these issues, as well as first-hand knowledge of what the problems look like on the ground. These are short, facilitated visits to organizations and communities, in various parts of the world.

Independent study. Once Fellows have identified project domains and built a base of relationships with faculty and students, they are expected to organize their time for the second half of the year around their independent (or small group) work on developing their projects over the summer and into the fall. This is their opportunity for research, in the library or in the field. Some Fellows hire students for the summer to assist them or are ready for a project team in the fall. Fellows are encouraged to do the work of project development individually, since this will be the product they carry with them to make a difference in the world after the Harvard program. Independent study culminates with a presentation of their project or business plan at the late November Fellows' final symposium. They are also expected to produce an analytic paper.

Engaging With the Program: Fellows' Behavior and Experiences

The program came to life as the 2009 and 2010 Fellows audited classes, attended weekly seminar, participated in Think Tanks, worked on project ideas, and created their own informal learning opportunities, working with faculty and students. One Fellow lived with students in a Harvard house (dormitory).

The degree of engagement varied from a full load of four courses for two terms, plus the core seminar and Think Tanks, to participation in only the core program. The faculty encouraged Fellows to take full advantage of all elements, including coursework. However, there was no necessary correlation between time on campus and either perceived learning or the quality of the project.

We had to tread carefully. For one thing, faculty authority could not be established in the same way it can with students at earlier career stages. Getting demanding leaders with a sense of accomplishment and entitlement to "meet requirements" in a new program requiring a long time commitment—a year—is very difficult. The faculty group held high standards and expected Fellows to adhere to them, but not everyone in the first two cohorts proved to be able or willing to meet them. No matter how often expectations were communicated by faculty leaders, there were still occasional misunderstandings or pushback from Fellows who wanted to go beyond program boundaries or challenge university policies. Like all new ventures, rapid prototyping was the norm in the beginning rather than a full blown script that everyone could follow.

Overall, the Fellows were eager to learn, and gracious and generous contributors to the university. The major ways they engaged will be outlined first, and then the challenges presented by a few of them, which caused the faculty to tighten selection criteria.

POSITIVE ENGAGEMENT: THE VALUE OF EXPERIENCE

Faculty members found the Fellows generally a pleasure to teach and were motivated to work with them, because experienced leaders bring some unique things to the educational table when they decide to affiliate with a university.

1. *Pattern recognition.* They absorbed a great deal of information quickly. They were able to conceptualize and apply frameworks, sometimes faster than graduate students.
2. *High standards and a willingness to work.* For the most part, they wanted to know what was required, and they were eager to do a good job. They sought faculty feedback. They valued what faculty members had to offer and found something they could learn. (There were a few exceptions, of course—a few Fellows who wanted to seize control themselves or did not want to meet expectations, thinking they did not need to.)
3. *Willingness to be challenged, even in firmly held beliefs or mental models.* The length of the program and the degree of dialogue in the Seminar and Think Tank made this likely for even the most dogmatic Fellows. Fellows who had succeeded with a particular toolkit began to see that their toolkit could be enlarged, or that a top-down style would not be effective in other contexts, so they became more open to bottom-up organizing.
4. *Openness to learning from the young.* With their accomplishments already established, they had less to prove and were more secure in their own achievements, so they were willing to engage young students and listen to them.
5. *Deep experience.* Their experience provided analogies they could draw on in discussions and that influenced their ability to find a pathway toward a solution for a perplexing societal challenge. For example, a Fellow who had become a master of retail logistics over twenty-five years could see the application of that experience to solving food waste and hunger problems.
6. *A wealth of connections.* Many Fellows were affluent, but all of them were respected, if not rich, and could transfer those connections to create benefits for the program, faculty, students, and their projects. Some had convening power.

These benefits of years of experience can be summarized in three C's—capabilities, connections, and cachet (which is sometimes translated into "cash" by those who equate experience with affluence).

IDENTITY AND BEHAVIOR CHANGE

Although the program was not designed to provide personal coaching, career counseling, or behavior change, in fact the length of time and number of encounters did provoke change in identities and behavior. Some absorbed messages of the program, found a new reference group in social entrepreneurs, or were smart enough to see the reactions they provoked in peers and faculty. In one case, a Fellow wrote a faculty leader partway through the year that he had found the program personally transforming. He realized that the hierarchical, command-and-control style that was common in his profession and had worked well for him did not work at a university and therefore would not work externally in the communities he hoped to influence and contribute to. Another Fellow, who had worked at a large corporation as a top executive, began to refer to himself as a "social entrepreneur." Some Fellows took to their new identities quickly, but over time even those who were more distant began to be absorbed into the process of learning and reflection. They became more open over time. The peer group turned out to be a very valuable anchor—in some cases, too much so, in that Fellows began to feel that everyone had to communicate or have social events with everyone else, which also led to "group think" in which Fellows with a different view kept quiet while the loudest voices dominated.

ENGAGEMENT DIFFICULTIES

A few people found the university a challenging setting and were less able to cope with its uncertainty, ambiguity, and complexity. A Fellow from the first cohort approached registrars of some schools with demands rather than requests, and failed to ask questions. One was frustrated that the mode to which he was accustomed was not well-received and kept pushing to be put in charge without checking facts. A few demanded services beyond what was promised or was feasible and were unwilling to take initiative—which is not what the faculty members expected of reputed leaders. Faculty board members discussed patterns, in order to refine the selection process to screen out those who would have difficulty engaging with the university.

"Trained incapacity" could be one explanation, in that people had to unlearn styles that had worked well for them in the past and that they thought were essential for their success. One hypothesis stems from Fellows' past occupations. Among the most critical and contentious, whether in classroom discussions or beyond, were lawyers—although this was not true of all lawyers, and as we have said throughout, the numbers are too small for valid tests. The operating mode tends to be case by case (not context-oriented) in adversarial fashion; lawyers are generally arguing about something and trained to take a hard position against another equally hard position. The nature of legal writing fosters details-orientation in which the exact words matter, not the intentions. Because lawyers often serve as advisers, they can develop a self-image as a definitive voice on issues, and they feel self-assured about probing the weakness in others' arguments.

A second group of Fellows with engagement difficulties, or who misinterpreted the university, also had some occupational characteristics in common. A few who were anxious without structure wanted to organize the Fellows' peer group and serve as facilitators, making that group loom larger than the surrounding opportunities for courses and widespread engagement. These were largely people from corporate staff roles, whose jobs had been concerned with facilitation on behalf of others and whose stock in trade were not their own ideas but their support for others. They tended to look primarily at their peer group and not the context and thus were likely to want to challenge university policies ostensibly on behalf of the group.

ENGAGEMENT SUCCESSES

Among the Fellows in the first two cohorts, those who made the transition to a university well, saw immediate value in Fellowship, and were least critical were physicians. Even the least-engaged of the physicians were highly positive. A possible explanation is that the occupation is evidence-based, not argument-based. Although the medical hierarchy does not necessarily encourage teamwork, those physicians who are motivated to be leaders to change the health system, yet did not get leadership concepts or training in medical school, soak this up. Advanced leadership concepts give them tools and frameworks. Furthermore, their underlying humanitarian orientation motivates them to absorb ideas that will get results, so they like models from other sectors.

Another group for whom the fellowship and university experience is smoother are those who have been CEOs. Among those in the first cohorts, the chiefs were less authoritarian initially than the lawyers. Perhaps the explanation is that they tend to be open to new information and will change their minds when they get it. Pragmatism, not dogmatism, is associated with success of those responsible for large organizations; they need to know the latest ideas. They either get results or not. Furthermore, they have led large numbers of people and have learned to steer a course among competing views or competing interpretations of information. They are likely to feel positive about anyone who is a source of useful information. They have learned to be multi-functional and cross-disciplinary. They have had to motivate and inspire people. They might have their own theories but their self-image is not bound up with being the thought leader, so they are willing to ask questions, listen, and learn.

Of course, with small numbers, this analysis is not only anecdotal but stereotypical. Still, this is a provocative beginning for further exploration. Experienced leaders differ from earlier-stage subjects of leadership development. Their modes of operating stemming from the positions they hold and the central tendencies of their professions have had longer reinforcement and more time to harden. Re-developing leaders requires encouraging unlearning and identity change.

Output: Project Plans

The ambition for this program goes beyond a satisfying learning experience for potential advanced leaders. They are expected to engage with the intellectual resources of the university to produce projects of significance that can serve as a central focus for their next productive years. This means a plan for action that will unfold over the next several years, rather than a finished product such as a doctoral dissertation—although a few Fellows' projects take the form of books or films. By the time Fellows complete their year, they should have a project idea or business plan that can be developed further on their own. Those Fellows invited to continue as Senior Advanced Leadership Fellows must have projects ready for further development in which one or more faculty members has an interest with the potential for high impact, which could benefit from additional time and would contribute to the university, a school, or a line of work.

The faculty look upon this the way venture capitalists look at their investments: as a portfolio. Perhaps 20 percent of the Fellows' projects will have significant impact, 40 percent will make a more modest contribution, 20 percent will have a small but positive impact, and the remaining 20 percent might never get off the ground. With the reasoning, the Advanced Leadership Initiative has made good investments, with a sufficient pipeline of well-developed projects already turned into product or services with solid impact potential.

In the 2009 cohort:

- A mass audience film on patient safety, *Chasing Zero*, which aired on the Discovery Channel and was then used as the basis for a toolkit for hospital boards to improve quality and reduce medical errors. The toolkit is ready for mass dissemination.
- A book on the water problem and actions to solve it, *Running Out of Water*, co-authored by a Fellow who convinced a Harvard engineering professor to include her to ensure translation into policy and practice. The Fellow is using this platform for advocacy and might start an organization on advocacy for change in water policies.
- A model for college financing for students from disadvantaged communities and a non-profit organization that is running its first pilot programs.
- A series of products designed to teach ethics to middle school students and their families by using new media, including a video game.
- A non-profit organization focused on attracting American investment to Africa as a means to increase leadership capacity in Africa.
- Continuing work on deployment of education for primary care physicians in the developing world.

In the 2010 cohort:

- A for-profit venture to develop smartphone apps around nutrition, to improve food choices and health, with an accompanying non-profit to bring the benefits to public schools and communities.
- A for-profit venture to bring low-cost alternative energy through solar cells to Africa, starting with Liberia.
- A model for after-school "study halls" to encourage reading and advance literacy, based on a single program that will be rolled out in other communities.
- A model for faith organizations to be community conveners, bringing social innovation and social change to cities across the income divide, with a demonstration in place in a southern U.S. city.
- A plan for a non-profit retail chain in urban "food deserts" as a solution for adjacent problems of food waste, hunger, and nutrition.
- A project to use IT to bring an evidence basis to traditional Chinese medicine, thereby improving medical practice and health.
- Plans to work with an existing literacy program to bring the program to additional sites and add a legal literacy component by developing children's books about rights and the justice system.
- A book on teamwork in medicine and the development of leadership skills in physicians and medical students, plus collaboration on a course for medical students.

The cross-cohort idea exchanges (discussed earlier) and Think Tanks in which past Fellows participate are designed to identify synergies or connections among Fellows' projects. Several Fellows are supporting one another's projects, serving on advisory boards or making connections.

Side Benefits: Enriching the University

Interviews with Fellows and input from faculty members (broadly, not just the governing boards) indicate that the Fellows' presence at the university and class participation through audits create value for faculty members, although it should be said that this is also the result of faculty interactions with one another across disciplines and professional schools in the process of thinking about advanced leadership and social entrepreneurship. Faculty members have been stimulated to create new educational materials and even whole courses because of these various interactions. Fellows add the voice of experience to class discussions, and even faculty members who had told Fellows to be silent auditors (because students are graded on class participation) came to welcome Fellows' contributions to dialogues or the resources Fellows represented in terms of connections and ideas. In some cases, relationships are on-going, continuing beyond the Fellowship year in mutually enriching ways.

For students, Fellows serve not only as role models, but they are more active mentors. Fellows are told that mentoring students is one of their responsibilities, but there is no enforcement mechanism, so this is strictly voluntary. Yet it has worked well in all cases in which Fellows have been actively engaged with the full educational program. Fellows coach students for business plan contests, hire and pay students as research assistants, offer summer internships, help them find jobs or funding for their ventures, and sometimes provide professional services—such as a lawyer who helped a student non-profit startup.

Fellows can enrich the university in other ways, including through their projects, which might bring new capabilities or financial support to the various schools. For example, a Fellow has secured grant money for the Graduate School of Education to host a conference on personalized learning. Another Fellow, as mentioned above, is collaborating with faculty from Harvard Business School and Harvard Medical School to develop a course on leadership and teamwork in medicine for medical students.

Assessment: Progress Toward Success

The Advanced Leadership program is a new initiative, just two cohorts old at the time of this writing, with numbers too small to permit a full-blown evaluation and time too short to determine the post-program impact of Fellows and their projects. Furthermore, like many education and development programs, a selection bias makes it hard to attribute outcomes to the program itself. Would these cohorts of experienced leaders have done the same thing without the opportunity provided by Harvard? And was the value primarily in the time to reflect, the identity shift, the influence of peers, or the formal components of the program?

Advanced Leadership at Harvard is still in its pilot proof-of-concept phase, with one replication of the initial model. But as a proof of concept, a few things have been demonstrated:

- There is a market. Experienced leaders will sign up for a year at a university, many will cover their own program and residential costs, and a subset will stretch the year into two years. These leaders come from many professions and parts of the world. They were serious about education. They did the coursework and reading, and they interacted effectively with students.
- This innovation can get started in a large, complex, traditional university. The founding faculty team faced skepticism and overcame it. They set

high standards, commensurate with the university's own, and were able to meet them.

- Faculty can execute effectively with a demanding group of leaders. Interviews with Fellows indicated that 100 percent would do it again and recommend the program to others—even the few who grumbled about something or had suggestions for the future.

- Faculty can collaborate across schools, professions, and disciplines. This "Miracle on the Charles River" took an enormous amount of voluntary faculty time, energy, and effort—largely unpaid but highly applauded. An inspiring vision and the potential for development of new intellectual capital prove to be powerful motivators.

- Faculty leaders can provide models for other leaders. The development of this innovation required putting our own theories to work, in an authentic way. What we teach is what we do.

The opportunity at Harvard can be an opportunity for the world. The next steps for this initiative include a review at Harvard in the spring of 2011 to determine the future. At the same time, the faculty leadership is working on dissemination of the ideas and the innovation itself. In June 2011, there will be a pilot Advanced Leadership road show in the international crossroads community of Miami: a global conference to encourage the identification of greater numbers of advanced leaders, a taste of the Advanced Leadership core seminar to spread ideas and tools, and a workshop for higher education leaders to discuss the potential for them to create similar programs at their own institutions.

We believe in the unique power of institutions of higher education to give birth to professions via professional schools. Lawyers once were apprentices reading the law in small offices. Physicians once were barbers. About one hundred years ago, the world's second business school and first MBA was invented by five people in the basement of the Harvard economics department. With history behind us, we look to the future. We hope that someday advanced leaders will have the same opportunity at many colleges and universities to become professional about the way they work on social and environmental problem-solving, with the confidence and commitment to excellence that comes from their educational credentials.

AUTHOR INDEX

SUBJECT INDEX

ABOUT THE EDITORS

Scott Snook is currently a Senior Lecturer at the Harvard Business School. He graduated with honors from West Point and was commissioned in the US Army Corps of Engineers where he served in various command and staff positions for over twenty-two years, earning the rank of Colonel before retiring in 2002. He has led soldiers in combat. Among his military decorations are the Legion of Merit, Bronze Star, Purple Heart, and Master Parachutist badge. He has an MBA from Harvard Business School, where he graduated with High Distinction as a Baker Scholar. Dr. Snook earned his Ph.D. from Harvard University in Organizational Behavior winning the Sage-Louis Pondy Best Dissertation Award from the Academy of Management for his study of the Friendly Fire Shootdown in Northern Iraq. Until July of 2002, Colonel Snook served as an Academy Professor in the Behavioral Sciences and Leadership Department at the United States Military Academy. He also directed West Point's Center for Leadership and Organizations Research as well as its joint Master's Program in Leader Development.

Professor Snook's book, *Friendly Fire* was selected by the Academy of Management to receive the 2002 Terry Award. He has also co-authored a book that explores the role of "common sense" in leadership titled, *Practical Intelligence in Everyday Life,* available from Cambridge University Press (2000). He received the 2010 Emerald LiteratiNetwork Outstanding Paper Award. Professor Snook has shared his leadership insights in formal executive education programs at Harvard and with numerous corporate audiences around the world.

Professor Snook's research and consulting activities include leadership, leader development, leading change, organizational systems, and culture.

Nitin Nohria became the tenth dean of Harvard Business School on 1 July 2010. He previously served as co-chair of the Leadership Initiative, Senior Associate Dean of Faculty Development, and Head of the Organizational Behavior unit.

His intellectual interests center on human motivation, leadership, corporate transformation and accountability, and sustainable economic and human performance. He is co-author or co-editor of 16 books. His most recent, *Handbook of Leadership Theory and Practice,* is a compendium dedicated to advancing research on leadership based on a colloquium he co-organized with Rakesh Khurana and Scott Snook during HBS's centennial celebrations.

Dean Nohria has taught courses across Harvard Business School's MBA, Ph.D., and Executive Education programs. He also served as a visiting faculty member at the London Business School in 1996.

Prior to joining the Harvard Business School faculty in July 1988, Dean Nohria received his Ph.D. in Management from the Sloan School of Management, Massachusetts Institute of Technology, and a B. Tech. in Chemical Engineering from the Indian Institute of Technology, Bombay (which honored him as a Distinguished Alumnus in 2007).

Rakesh Khurana is the Marvin Bower Professor of Leadership Development at the Harvard Business School. He is also the Master of Cabot House at Harvard College. He received his B.S. from Cornell University and his A.M. and Ph.D. from Harvard University.

Professor Khurana's research uses a sociological perspective to focus on the processes by which elites and leaders are selected and developed. He has written extensively about the CEO labor market with a particular interest on: the factors that lead to vacancies in the CEO position; the factors that affect the choice of successor; the role of market intermediaries such as executive search firms in CEO search; and the consequences of CEO succession and selection decisions for subsequent firm performance and strategic choices.

Continuing with his focus on business elites, his most recent book, *From Higher Aims to Hired Hands: The Social Transformation of American Business Schools and the Unfulfilled Promise of Management as a Profession* (2007: Princeton University Press), chronicles the evolution of management as a profession, with particular focus on the institutional development of the MBA.

Khurana is now working on a new research project examining business leadership in the context of globalization and its implications for democratic capitalism.

ABOUT THE CONTRIBUTORS

José Luis Alvarez is a Professor of Business Policy at ESADE, a Visiting Professor at INSEAD since 2001, and at Cambridge University's Judge Business School. Since the beginning of his career he has taught courses on both leadership and on "power and influence in organizations" for both MBA and executive education, including Advanced Management Programs.

His research interest has always been related to the interface between leadership studies and organizational theory, especially the neo-institutional school. His dissertation was on the origins and diffusion of managerial ideologies, which he followed up on afterwards with the support of the European Science Foundation, studying the spread of business education and knowledge in Europe.

In recent years his work has centered on the evolution of the jobs and roles of top managers in complex structures, and their impact on corporate politics and governance. He has published part of this research in the book *Sharing Executive Power: Roles and Relationships at the Top* (Cambridge University Press).

Recently he has initiated a research program on the theory of executive action, exploring whether new ways of structuring and governing organizations demand new orientations to action beyond the ones Weber and Parsons proposed.

Professor Alvarez holds degrees in Law and Philosophy from the University of Barcelona, an MBA from IESE Business School, and an MA and a PhD in Organizational Behavior from the Harvard Business School, where years later he taught the "Power and Influence" elective as Visiting Professor. His research has been published in the *European Management Journal*, *Organization Studies*, *Organizations*, *Corporate Governance*, *Journal of Organizational Behavior*, *MIT Sloan Management Review,* and he has authored and published several books. He also likes to write about politics in the European press.

Deborah Ancona is the Seley Distinguished Professor of Management at the MIT Sloan School of Management, and Faculty Director of the MIT Leadership Center. Deborah's research into how successful teams operate has highlighted the critical importance of "managing outside the team's boundary as well as inside it." This research has led directly to the concept of X-Teams as a vehicle for driving innovation within large organizations. Her book, *X-Teams: How to Build Teams That Lead, Innovate, and Succeed,* was published by Harvard Business School Press in June 2007.

Deborah's work has also focused on the concept of "distributed leadership," and the capabilities needed to foster creative leadership at every level within organizations. This work was highlighted in the *Harvard Business Review*, "In Praise of the Incomplete Leader," February 2007.

In addition to *X-Teams*, Deborah's studies of team process and performance have also been published in the *Administrative Science Quarterly*, the *Academy of Management Journal*, *Organization Science*, and the *Sloan Management Review*. Her previous book, *Managing for the Future: Organizational Behavior and Processes* (South-Western College Publishing, 1999, 2005) centers on the skills, processes, and structures needed in today's diverse and changing organizations.

Deborah received her BA and MS in psychology from the University of Pennsylvania and her PhD in management from Columbia University.

Deborah has served as a consultant on leadership and innovation to premier companies such as W.L. Gore, Li & Fung, Cisco, Merrill Lynch, Newscorp, Nike, BP, and HP. Her work has been highlighted in the *Financial Times*, *Time Magazine*, and the *Washington Post.*

Jeffrey Anderson is an Associate Dean at the University of Chicago Booth School of Business. In this role, he has responsibility for the leadership development activities for full-time MBA students, including the ground-breaking Leadership Effectiveness and Development (LEAD) program. Mr. Anderson also teaches classes on leadership as a part of the school's Executive Education curriculum.

Mr. Anderson is also a partner and co-founder of The Chatham Group, an association of experienced business executives who provide strategic advice and individual coaching to senior business leaders worldwide. Mr. Anderson has worked for more than a decade with senior executives in a wide variety of industries including distribution, consumer products, oil and gas, automotive, financial services, manufacturing, and telecommunications.

Before starting The Chatham Group, Mr. Anderson held executive roles in finance, operations, corporate development, and international business with RR Donnelley & Sons Company, a leading provider of commercial printing, distribution, and marketing communication services.

He is a Board Member and Trustee of The Danish Home of Chicago and has served as Chairman of The Night Ministry and as a member of the audit committee of The City of Lake Forest.

Mr. Anderson received a BA in economics and accounting with high honors from Carthage College and a MBA with honors from The University of Chicago. He is a frequent speaker on topics related to executive leadership including "Creating Powerful and Effective Impressions," "Relationship Building," and "Understanding What Teams Really Want From Their Leader."

Colonel Tony Burgess, a faculty member at the United States Military Academy (West Point, New York), is the cofounder of the Company Command forum and part of the team that created the MilSpace professional development system—a grassroots learning system that connects platoon leaders and company commanders across the Army with each other in an ongoing conversation about leading soldiers and growing combat-effective teams. Tony graduated from West Point in 1990 and was commissioned as a second lieutenant of Infantry. He has served in the 82nd Infantry Division (Airborne) and the 25th Infantry Division (Light). He holds a master's degree in leader development and counseling from Long Island University (2000) and a doctorate of science in engineering management from the George Washington University (2006) where he focused his research on leadership within informal social systems and, specifically, the core group phenomenon in communities of practice. Tony has co-authored two books: *Taking the Guidon: Exceptional Leadership at the Company Level* (2001) and *Company Command: Unleashing the Power of the Army Profession* (2005). Tony continues to serve platoon leaders and company commanders in his role with the U.S. Army's Center for the Advancement of Leader Development and Organizational Learning at West Point.

Shoma Chatterjee is a Vice President at Goldman Sachs with its Pine Street Leadership Development Group. Pine Street serves the partners and managing directors of Goldman Sachs, as well as senior executives at select external client organizations. Her current focus areas include leadership acceleration initiatives for high potentials as well as targeted executive development programs for managing directors, partners, women, and diverse professionals. Her functional expertise includes strategy formulation and implementation, change management, and executive communications and influence. Prior to joining the firm, Shoma had over 15 years of management consulting experience at various firms including Deloitte Consulting and CSC Index. She also has significant experience in the public sector as consultant to the United Nations in complex humanitarian emergencies in Bosnia and Kosovo and as head of the talent and succession management function at the Federal Reserve Bank in Chicago. Shoma earned an MBA from Columbia Business School, a master's in International Affairs from Columbia's School of International and Public Affairs (SIPA), and a bachelor of science from Northwestern University. While at Columbia, she was the Managing Editor of the *Journal of International Affairs*.

Louis S. Csoka, PhD, President and Founder, APEX Performance, has designed, developed, and implemented Leader Development programs with primary focus on sustained peak performance. He is a leading expert in the application of sport and performance psychology to the development of mental skills for exceptional performance. He has been recently developing new and innovative ways to apply the latest discoveries from the new science of the brain to the education and training of critical mental skills for leadership and peak performance. Currently, Dr. Csoka is the Lead Consultant for the U.S. Army's program for establishing Army Centers for Enhanced Performance (ACEP) throughout the Army. Previously as SVP for Human Resources in a $6B global manufacturing company, Dr. Csoka led the transformation of the company's human resources function. Other roles have included Director of Research at The Conference Board and 21 years on the West Point faculty in the Department of Behavioral Sciences and Leadership as Professor of Psychology and Leadership. In this capacity, he created and directed the first ever Performance Enhancement Center at West Point. He served for 28 years in the U.S. Army and led units in Germany, Holland, Korea, and as a Combat Commander in Vietnam. Dr. Csoka is a graduate of the U.S. Military Academy at West Point and holds an MS and PhD from the University of Washington.

Thomas DeLong is the Philip J. Stomberg Professor of Management Practice in the Organizational Behavior area at the Harvard Business School. Before joining the Harvard Faculty, DeLong was Chief Development Officer and Managing Director of Morgan Stanley Group, Inc., where he was responsible for the firm's human capital and focused on issues of organizational strategy, talent management, organizational change, and leadership development.

At Harvard, Professor DeLong teaches MBA and executive courses focused on managing human capital, organizational behavior, leadership, and career management. DeLong serves as course head for the required course on Leadership and Organizational Behavior. He has designed MBA courses focusing on managing human capital in high performance organizations and strategic issues in professional service firms.

DeLong teaches globally in a myriad of executive programs as well as executive courses on campus. He also chairs the senior leadership program for Novartis and chairs the executive course for educational leaders interested in enhancing teaching through participant-centered learning.

DeLong consults with leading organizations on the process of making transformational change. His latest book, *Flying Without a Net: Turn Fear of Failure Into Fuel for Success*, has recently been published by Harvard Business Review Press.

He co-authored two books focused on leading professional service firms, *When Professionals Have to Lead: A New Model for High Performance* (Harvard Business School Press, 2007) and *Professional Services: Cases and Texts* (McGraw-Hill/Irwin 2003). DeLong has coauthored two *Harvard Business Review* articles, "Let's Hear It for B Players" and "Why Mentoring Matters in a Hypercompetitive World."

Professor DeLong received his undergraduate and master's degrees from Brigham Young University and his PhD from Purdue University in Industrial Supervision. He received a post-doctoral fellowship from Massachusetts Institute of Technology.

Marcus W. Dickson is currently Professor of Organizational Psychology and Associate Chair in the Department of Psychology at Wayne State University in Detroit, Michigan, USA. He completed his master's thesis and doctoral dissertation at the University of Maryland under the supervision of Drs. Rick Guzzo and Paul Hanges, respectively. He served as a member of the Project GLOBE Coordinating Team for nearly a decade, filling a variety of roles, including several years as Co-Principal Investigator. His work has appeared in a number of prestigious outlets, including *Journal of Applied Psychology, The Leadership Quarterly, Applied Psychology: An International Review, Handbook of Organizational Culture and Climate*, and many others. He currently edits a column for the Society of Industrial-Organizational Psychology's (SIOP's) journal *TIP* focusing on teaching Industrial-Organizational Psychology, and been recognized with SIOP's Award for Distinguished Contributions in Teaching, as well as the President's Award for Excellence in Teaching by Wayne State University. He has taught leadership and global leadership in a variety of settings, including undergraduate, master's, executive master's, and doctoral levels.

James Emery is Research Director of the Fuqua/Coach K Center on Leadership and Ethics and an Instructor in Management and Organizations at Duke University's Fuqua School of Business. His research and teaching interests in leadership and learning emerged from years of management consulting work with health care organizations. Jim is currently working on research projects examining the causes and effects of personal loyalty in leader-follower relationships, how college experiences affect student leadership development, and inspirational leadership. He is also part of an interdisciplinary research team funded by a grant from the Department of Veterans Affairs to explore how to improve patient transfer processes. Jim has been an executive educator and leadership coach with for-profit corporations, non-profit organizations, and government agencies. Jim received his PhD and MBA in Business Administration from the Fuqua School of Business, Duke University. He also holds a BS in Mechanical Engineering from Virginia Tech.

Werner H. Erhard is an original thinker whose ideas have transformed the effectiveness and quality of life for millions of people and thousands of organizations. While known by the general public for the est Training and the Forum of the 1970s and 1980s, his models have been the source of new perspectives by thinkers and practitioners in fields as diverse as philosophy, business, education, psychotherapy, emerging country development, medicine, conflict resolution, and community building. He lectures widely, and has served as consultant to various corporations, foundations, and governmental agencies. Erhard was acknowledged in *Forbes Magazine's* 40th Anniversary issue as one of the major contributors to modern management thinking, and is a recipient of the Mahatma Gandhi Humanitarian Award.

Chris Ernst is a senior faculty member at the Center for Creative Leadership, specializing in developing more collaborative approaches to leadership. Chris has served in multi-year expatriate roles in Asia and Europe, leads cross-functional and multicultural teams, and researches, designs, and facilitates leadership interventions in diverse industries crossing the regions of Africa, Asia, Europe, Middle East, and North and South America. Out of this varied experience, Chris holds the conviction that spanning boundaries is critical in an interdependent world, yet appreciates firsthand that collaborating across our differences is hard work. Currently, Chris is a core faculty member in CCL's Organizational Leadership Practice, focusing on developing integrative leadership solutions across individuals, groups, organizations, and society worldwide. Previously, he served as Research Director, Asia-Pacific, with responsibility for the start-up of CCL's Research and Innovation group located in Singapore. Chris is widely published in articles, book chapters, the popular press, and is co-author of two books, *Boundary Spanning Leadership: Six Practices for Solving Problems, Driving Innovation, and Transforming Organizations* (McGraw-Hill Professional) and *Success for the New Global Manager: How to Work Across Distance, Countries and Cultures* (Jossey-Bass/Wiley). Chris holds a PhD in industrial and organizational psychology from North Carolina State University.

Cary Friedman serves as the global chief operating officer of the Pine Street Leadership Development Group at Goldman, Sachs & Co. He focuses on leadership development and organizational effectiveness for the firm's partners and managing directors, as well as senior executives at external client organizations. Cary's current focus areas include overall leadership of several of Pine Street's key initiatives, including the Managing Director Leadership Acceleration Initiative (an experiential learning-based initiative for high-potential leaders), the firm's Global Executive Coaching Program, the Partner Orientation Program, and select leadership programs for external clients. Cary is also engaged in the creation of several innovative programs pertaining to the development of the leadership pipeline in the emerging markets. Topics of his research include best practices in the expatriation and repatriation of senior talent; best practices for integrating, developing and ensuring the long-term success of senior–level external hires; and best practices in maximizing the effectiveness of co-headships. His publications include "Coaching at Goldman Sachs: An Inside Look" in *Profiles in Coaching – The 2004 Handbook of Best Practices in Leadership Coaching* (Morgan, Harkins, & Goldsmith, Editor). Cary joined Goldman Sachs in 1998 and was a founding member of the Pine Street Leadership Development Group. He has had numerous speaking engagements at major national conferences and serves as a guest lecturer at several leading universities. He holds a bachelor of science from Cornell University.

Marshall Ganz grew up in Bakersfield, California, where his father was a Rabbi and his mother, a teacher. He entered Harvard College in the fall of 1960. He left a year before graduating to volunteer with the 1964 Mississippi Summer Project. He found a "calling" as an organizer for the Student Nonviolent Coordinating Committee, and, in the fall of 1965, joined Cesar Chavez in his effort to unionize California farm workers. During sixteen years with the United Farm Workers he gained experience in union, political, and community organizing, became Director of Organizing, and was elected to the national executive board on which he served for eight years. During the 1980s, he worked with grassroots groups to develop new organizing programs and designed innovative voter mobilization strategies for local, state, and national electoral campaigns. In 1991, in order to deepen his intellectual understanding of his work, he returned to Harvard College and, after a 28-year "leave of absence," completed his undergraduate degree in history and government. He was awarded an MPA by the Kennedy School in 1993 and completed his PhD in sociology in 2000. As lecturer in public policy at the Kennedy School of Government, he teaches, researches, and writes on leadership, organization, and strategy in social movements, civic associations, and politics. He has published in the *American Journal of Sociology, American Political Science Review, American Prospect, Washington Post, Los Angeles Times,* and elsewhere. His newest book, *Why David Sometimes Wins: Leadership, Organization and Strategy in the California Farm Worker Movement* was published in 2009, earning the Michael J. Harrington Book Award of the American Political Science Association. He was awarded an honorary doctorate in divinity by the Episcopal Divinity School in 2010.

Bill George is a professor of management practice at Harvard Business School, where he has taught leadership since 2004. He is the author of four best-selling books: *7 Lessons for Leading in Crisis*, *True North: Discover Your Authentic Leadership, Finding Your True North: A Personal Guide,* and *Authentic Leadership.*

Mr. George is the former chairman and chief executive officer of Medtronic. He joined Medtronic in 1989 as President and Chief Operating Officer, was Chief Executive Officer from 1991–2001, and Chairman of the Board from 1996 to 2002. Earlier in his career, he was an executive with Honeywell and Litton Industries and served in the U.S. Department of Defense.

Mr. George currently serves as a director of ExxonMobil and Goldman Sachs, and also recently served on the board of Novartis and Target Corporation. He is also currently a trustee of Carnegie Endowment for International Peace, World Economic Forum USA, and the Guthrie Theater. He has served as chair of the board of Allina Health System, Abbott-Northwestern Hospital, United Way of the Greater Twin Cities, and Advamed.

Mr. George received his BSIE with high honors from Georgia Tech, his MBA with high distinction from Harvard University, where he was a Baker Scholar, and honorary PhDs from Georgia Tech and Bryant University. During 2002–03 he was professor at IMD International and École Polytechnique in Lausanne, Switzerland, and executive-in-residence at Yale School of Management.

He has been named one of the "Top 25 Business Leaders of the Past 25 Years" by PBS; "Executive of the Year—2001" by the Academy of Management; and "Director of the Year—2001–02" by the National Association of Corporate Directors. Mr. George makes frequent appearances on television and radio, and his columns are published in the *New York Times, Wall Street Journal, Business Week,* and *Fortune.*

He and his wife Penny split their time between Cambridge and Minnesota, where Penny runs their family foundation and is deeply involved in integrative medicine. They have two sons: Jeff George, who lives in Munich, Germany, with his wife Renee Will and daughter Dylan; and Jon George, MD, who lives in San Francisco with his wife Jeannette Lager, MD, and son Freeman.

Rob Goffee, Professor of Organisational Behaviour, London Business School, is trained as a sociologist and has worked at London Business School for over twenty-five years. His interest in and experience of leadership comes from his research and teaching; from the leadership roles he has filled at the School (as Director of several flagship executive programmes; Chair of the Organisational Behaviour Group; Faculty Director of Executive Education; Director of the Innovation Exchange; Deputy Dean; and Member of the Governing Body); and from running — with Gareth Jones — the consulting firm Creative Management Associates.

Rob's work has spanned a variety of organizational contexts ranging from an early interest in entrepreneurship and family firms; through middle managers and their careers; the corporate culture of large global organizations; and more recent work on the peculiar challenges of leading clever people.

Rob has led executive development interventions all over the world, working with executives in a variety of industries. Consulting clients have included Anglo-American, Axa, Electronic Arts, Heineken, IHG, KPMG, Lloyds, LVMH, MLIM, Nestle, Roche, Singapore Airlines, and Unilever.

This work has been a constant reminder that leadership always varies according to context; and that hierarchical achievement or position should not be confused with leadership.

Rob has published ten books and more than seventy articles in the areas of entrepreneurship, managerial careers, organization design, leadership, and corporate culture. His recent books with Gareth Jones include *The Character of a Corporation; Why Should Anyone Be Led By You?;* and *Clever-Leading Your Smartest Most Creative People. His articles with Gareth feature in Harvard Business Review, Leader to Leader, European Business Forum, Business Strategy Review, Management Today, People Management,* and *The Financial Times.*

He is the recipient of several teaching excellence awards and has contributed as a keynote speaker to conferences all over the world. He is twice recipient (with Gareth Jones) of the McKinsey Award for best article in *Harvard Business Review* and contributes regularly to TV and radio business programs.

Kari L. Granger is a fellow of the Center for Character and Leadership Development at the United States Air Force Academy (USAFA), a former Assistant Professor there, and currently serves as a performance consultant with Sunergos, LLC. As a decorated former military officer, Granger brings extensive field experience from leading complex logistical operations missions to combat duty in Iraq. Currently Granger is engaged in a collaborative effort to address the challenges of reintegration facing service members returning from hardship deployments. Granger is a Distinguished Graduate of USAFA with a BS in Human Factors and an MA from the University of New Mexico in Education Leadership.

Carol Hall is Professor of Human Relations at the University of Nottingham, School of Education. Carol was formerly Head of School and Dean of the Faculty of Education. She has published widely in the area of human relations and learning and her books have been translated into five languages. She is an experienced coach and mentor working with leaders in both private and public sector organizations and contributes to personal development and leadership programs in both the Business School and the School of Education. She is currently working on a book focusing on creative approaches to executive coaching.

Co-founder of The Ariel Group, **Belle Linda Halpern** has developed and delivered leadership programs for executives in the U United States Europe, and Asia for the past twenty years using an innovative, experiential approach based in the performing arts. The Ariel Group helps individuals discover their authentic leadership talents and make enduring improvements in their ability to connect with others.

Since 1992, Ariel has provided transformational learning experiences to over 30,000 executives in around the globe. Ariel's leadership and communication skills training workshops have been integrated into leadership development programs at major corporations such as American Express, Google, Procter & Gamble, and KPMG, and at educational non-profits such as Teach for America. Ariel also delivers through the executive education curriculum at leading graduate schools of business, including Harvard, Darden, and Duke.

Belle has been featured in *The New York Times, Fast Company*, *The Boston Globe*, and on CNBC; is co-author of *Leadership Presence: Dramatic Techniques to Reach Out, Motivate, and Inspire* (Penguin Putnam); and is a featured keynote speaker. Currently, Belle is focused on bringing Ariel's work to school leaders in challenged populations.

Ariel's approach to leadership presence is derived from the founders' backgrounds in the performing arts. As a cabaret singer, Belle has performed in New York, Boston, San Francisco, Paris, Munich, and the hill towns of Northern Italy. Her current show *Cravings: Songs of Hunger & Satisfaction* (cravingscabaret.com) explores hunger for food, for love, for acceptance, for fame . . . and for true nourishment.

Belle has also designed a methodology for teaching singing to non-singers and has worked with students at Harvard University, Longy School of Music, and the Roy Hart Theatre in France. She co-founded tuscanyproject.com and teaches singing each summer in Italy. A Harvard University graduate, Belle lives outside of Boston with her husband, Mitch, and her children, Aviva and Lev.

Paul J. Hanges, PhD, is Professor of Industrial/Organizational Psychology and is currently the Associate Chair/Director of Graduate Studies for the University of Maryland's Psychology Department. He is also an affiliate of the University of Maryland's R. H. Smith School of Business and the Zicklin School of Business (Baruch College). Originally from New York City, Paul received his PhD from the University of Akron in 1987. His research focuses on three themes: (a) human resource practices, team/organizational diversity, and organizational climate, (b) leadership, team-processes, and cross-cultural issues, and (c) dynamical systems theory and other research methodology issues.

He has published one book and has one book pending. He has written more than 70 articles and book chapters. Paul's publications have appeared in such journals as *Advances in Global Leadership, American Psychologist, Applied Psychological Measurement, Applied Psychology: An International Review, Journal of Applied Psychology, Journal of International Business Studies*, and *Psychological Bulletin.* He is on the editorial boards of the *Journal of Applied Psychology* and *The Leadership Quarterly.* Paul is a fellow of the American Psychological Association, Association for Psychological Sciences, and the Society for Industrial/Organizational Psychology.

Kimberly Hester is a doctoral student in the industrial and organizational psychology program at the University of Oklahoma. Her research interests include creativity, innovation, and leadership.

Linda A. Hill is the Wallace Brett Donham Professor of Business Administration at the Harvard Business School. She is the faculty chair of the Leadership Initiative and has chaired numerous HBS Executive Education programs, including the Young Presidents' Organization Presidents' Seminar and the High Potentials Leadership Program. She is a former faculty chair of the Organizational Behavior unit at Harvard Business School, and she was coursehead during the development of the new Leadership and

Organizational Behavior MBA required course. She is the author of *Becoming a Manager: How New Managers Master the Challenges of Leadership* (2nd Edition) and *Being the Boss: The 3 Imperatives of Becoming a Great Leader*. Professor Hill has a book forthcoming in 2011 from Harvard Business Press on leadership for innovation. Hill has authored numerous *Harvard Business Review* articles, including "Where Will We Find Tomorrow's Leaders?" and "Winning the Race for Talent in Emerging Markets."

Professor Hill's consulting and executive education activities have been in the areas of managing change, managing cross-organizational relationships, implementing global strategy, innovation, talent management, and leadership development. Organizations with which Professor Hill has worked include General Electric, Reed Elsevier, Accenture, Pfizer, IBM, MasterCard, Mitsubishi, Morgan Stanley, the National Bank of Kuwait, Areva, and The Economist.

Professor Hill is a member of the Boards of Directors of State Street Corporation, Cooper Industries, and Harvard Business Publishing. She is a Fellow at Diamond Management & Technology Consultants, Inc. She is a trustee of the Nelson Mandela Children's Fund USA, The Bridgespan Group, and Bryn Mawr College. She is a former member of the Board of Trustees of The Rockefeller Foundation. She is also on the Advisory Board of the Aspen Institute Business and Society Program. She serves on the Editorial Board of the *Leadership Quarterly*.

Multiple award-winning executive educator and author whose teaching and research interests span the globe, **Mansour Javidan** received his MBA and PhD degrees from the Carlson School at the University of Minnesota. He is Dean of Research and Garvin Distinguished Professor, and Director of the Thunderbird Global Mindset Institute at Thunderbird School of Global Management in Arizona.

Mansour is Past President and Chairman of the Board of Directors of the GLOBE (Global Leadership and Organizational Behavior Effectiveness) Research Foundation and has been designated as an expert in global leadership by the World Bank. He is on the board of the International Leadership Association. His publications have appeared in such journals as *Harvard Business Review, Journal of International Business Studies, Strategic Management Journal, Organization Science, Academy of Management Perspectives, Leadership Quarterly,* and *Journal of Management Studies*.

Dr. Javidan is the Past Senior Editor, Global Leadership, for the *Journal of World Business*. He also served a three-year term on the editorial board of the *Academy of Management Perspectives*. Mansour has lived and worked in 25 countries around the world. He has worked closely with executives in many global companies such as Accenture, Dow Chemical, Walmart, Cummins, Exxon Mobil, LG Electronics, Petronas, TransCanada Pipelines, and Telstra.

Michael C. Jensen, the Jesse Isidor Straus Professor of Business, Emeritus, at Harvard Business School, is widely respected as a leading financial economist, organization theorist, the intellectual father of private equity, and for advancing the theory and practice of managerial compensation and corporate governance. Jensen is the creator of Agency Theory (with Bill Meckling) and Jensen's Alpha (a widely-used portfolio performance measure); he co-founded the *Journal of Financial Economics* and the Social Science Research Network (SSRN). Jensen has an MBA and PhD in economics from the University of Chicago. He was given the "Morgan Stanley–American Finance Association 2009 Award for Excellence in Financial Economics."

Gareth Jones's career has spanned both the academic and business worlds. He began as a university academic in Economic and Social Studies at the University of East Anglia before moving to the London Business School, where he joined the Organisational Behaviour Group, directing the School's Accelerated Development Programme.

Thereafter he was appointed as Senior Vice President for Polygram's global human resources, where his responsibilities covered more than thirty countries. In 1996 he reverted to academia when he became the BT Professor of Organisational Development at Henley where he also served on the Board of Governors. His most recent job was as Director of Human Resources and Internal Communications at the BBC. He is currently Visiting Professor at the Instituto de Empresa, Madrid, and at INSEAD, Fontainebleu. He is also a Fellow of the Centre for Management Development at London Business School.

He has published several books with co-author Rob Goffee including *The Character of a Corporation: How Your Culture Can Make or Break Your Business*, *Why Should Anyone Be Led by You?* and most recently, *Clever: Leading Your Smartest, Most Creative People* by Harvard Business School Press.

Why Should Anyone Be Led By You? is the winner of the prestigious McKinsey Award for the best article in *Harvard Business Review* and "Leading Clever People" was runner-up for the 2008 McKinsey Award. "Managing Authenticity" also appeared in an *HBR* article and other highly successful articles have been published in the *European Management Journal* and *Human Relations.*

Gareth's research interests are predominately in organizational design, culture, leadership, and change. He is a founding partner of Creative Management Associates (CMA), a consultancy focused on organizations where creativity is a source of competitive strength. He also serves on the Editorial Advisory Board of *People Management Magazine.*

For further information visit www.whyshouldanyonebeledbyyou.com.

Rosabeth Moss Kanter holds the Ernest L. Arbuckle Professorship at Harvard Business School, where she specializes in strategy, innovation, and leadership for change. Her strategic and practical insights have guided leaders of large and small organizations worldwide for over twenty-five years, through teaching, writing, and direct consultation to major corporations and governments. The former Editor of *Harvard Business Review* (1989–1992), Professor Kanter has been repeatedly named to lists of the "50 Most Powerful Women in the World" (*Times of London*), and the "50 Most Influential Business Thinkers in the World" (Accenture and Thinkers 50 research). In 2001, she received the Academy of Management's Distinguished Career Award for her scholarly contributions to management knowledge, and in 2002 was named "Intelligent Community Visionary of the Year" by the World Teleport Association, and in 2010 received the International Leadership Award from the Association of Leadership Professionals. She is the author or co-author of eighteen books. Her latest book, *SuperCorp: How Vanguard Companies Create Innovation, Profits, Growth, and Social Good*, a manifesto for leadership of sustainable enterprises, was named one of the ten best business books of 2009 by Amazon.com.

She has received twenty-three honorary doctoral degrees, as well as numerous leadership awards and prizes for her books and articles; for example, her book *The Change Masters* was named one of the most influential business books of the twentieth century (*Financial Times*). Through Goodmeasure Inc., the consulting group she co-founded, she has partnered with IBM on applying her leadership tools from business to other sectors; she is a Senior Advisor for IBM's Global Citizenship portfolio. She advises CEOs of large and small companies, has served on numerous business and non-profit boards including City Year, the urban "Peace Corps" now focused on addressing the school dropout crisis, and national or regional commissions including the Governor's Council of Economic Advisors. Before joining the Harvard Business School faculty, she held tenured professorships at

Yale University and Brandeis University and was a Fellow at Harvard Law School, simultaneously holding a Guggenheim Fellowship.

She is Chair and Director of the Advanced Leadership Initiative of Harvard University, a collaboration across the professional schools to help successful leaders at the top of their professions apply their skills to addressing challenging national and global problems in their next stages of life.

Barbara Kellerman is the James MacGregor Burns Lecturer in Public Leadership at Harvard University's John F. Kennedy School of Government. She was the Founding Executive Director of the Kennedy School's Center for Public Leadership, from 2000 to 2003; and from 2003 to 2006 she served as the Center's Research Director. Kellerman has held professorships at Fordham, Tufts, Fairleigh Dickinson, George Washington, and Uppsala Universities. She also served as Dean of Graduate Studies and Research at Fairleigh Dickinson, and as Director of the Center for the Advanced Study of Leadership at the Academy of Leadership at the University of Maryland.

Kellerman received her BA from Sarah Lawrence College, and her MA, MPhil, and PhD (1975, in Political Science) degrees from Yale University. She was cofounder of the International Leadership Association (ILA), and is author and editor of many books including *Leadership: Multidisciplinary Perspectives; The Political Presidency: Practice of Leadership*; and *Reinventing Leadership: Making the Connection Between Politics and Business*. She has appeared often on various media outlets and has contributed articles and reviews to the *New York Times*, the *Washington Post*, the *Boston Globe*, the *Los Angeles Times*, and the *Harvard Business Review*.

Her most recent books are *Bad Leadership: What It Is, How It Happens, Why It Matters* (2004); a co-edited (with Deborah Rhode) volume, *Women & Leadership: State of Play and Strategies for Change* (2007); *Followership: How Followers Are Creating Change and Changing Leaders* (2008), and *Leadership: Essential Selections on Power, Authority, and Influence* (2010).

Kellerman was ranked by *Forbes.com* as among "Top 50 Business Thinkers" (2009) and by *Leadership Excellence* in top 15 of 100 "best minds on leadership" (2008–09). Her next book on leadership/followership will be published in 2012 by HarperCollins.

Manfred F. R. Kets de Vries holds the Raoul de Vitry d'Avaucourt Chair of Leadership Development at INSEAD, France, Singapore, and Abu Dhabi. In addition, he is the Director of INSEAD's Global Leadership Center. He is also the Distinguished Professor of Leadership Development Research at the European School of Management and Technology in Berlin. He has held professorships at McGill University, the Ecole des Hautes Etudes Commerciales, Montreal, and the Harvard Business School, and he has lectured at management institutions around the world. He is the author, co-author, or editor of more than thirty books and three hundred articles. His books and articles have been translated into twenty-seven languages. He is program director of INSEAD's top management program "The Challenge of Leadership," and the Scientific Director of the program "Consulting and Coaching for Change." Kets de Vries is a consultant on organizational design and strategic human resource management to leading European, U.S., Canadian, Australian, African, and Asian companies. As an educator and consultant he has worked in more than forty countries. He is a member of seventeen editorial boards. He has been elected a Fellow of the Academy of Management. He is also the recipient of the International Leadership Association Lifetime Achievement Award for his contributions to leadership research and development. The *Financial Times, Le Capital, Wirtschaftswoche*, and *The Economist* have judged Manfred Kets de Vries one of the leading thinkers on management.

(e-mail: manfred.ketsdevries@insead.edu; website: www.ketsdevries.com).

Max Klau is the Director of Leadership Development at City Year, a national service program headquartered in Boston, Massachusetts. Since joining the organization in 2006, his efforts have focused on leveraging a challenging year of full-time citizen service as a transformational leadership development experience. Max received his EdD in Human Development and Psychology from the Harvard Graduate School of Education in 2005; his studies focused on civic leadership education. An alumnus of four service programs, he has completed two years of service in Israel and led service trips to Israel, Honduras, Ghana, and the Ukraine. He has edited a journal focused on youth leadership and has contributed articles about leadership development to the *Washington Post* and *Harvard Business Review*.

Stacey R. Kole is Deputy Dean for the Full-time MBA Program and Clinical Professor of Economics at Chicago Booth. Her research interests include policies and practices that dictate behavior within organizations and its relation to firm performance. Before joining Chicago Booth in 2004, she served as member of the faculty and Associate Dean for MBA Programs at the University of Rochester's Simon School of Business.

Deputy Dean Kole's published research includes "Workforce Integration and the Dissipation of Value in Mergers: The Case of USAir's Acquisition of Piedmont Aviation," with Kenneth Lehn, in *Mergers and Productivity*, published by the National Bureau of Economic Research; "Deregulation and the Adaptation of Governance Structure: The Case of U.S. Airlines Industry," with Kenneth Lehn published in the *Journal of Financial Economics*; and "The Complexity of Compensation Contracts" in the *Journal of Financial Economics*.

Prior to her career in academics, she was a financial economist in the Office of Economic Analysis at the U.S. Securities and Exchange Commission.

Deputy Dean Kole received a PhD in economics from the University of Chicago, an MA in economics from the University of Chicago, and a BA in economics from the University of Rochester.

Konstantin Korotov is Associate Professor at ESMT—European School of Management and Technology in Berlin, Germany, where he also is a founder of the Center for Leadership Development Research. He received his PhD in Management at INSEAD. His research interests include leadership development, executive transitions, leadership coaching, career development, and executive education. He is the author, co-author, or co-editor of a dozen academic and practitioner articles on leadership development, five books, and multiple book chapters and case-studies. He is program director of ESMT's bestselling "Leading People and Teams" executive education program, and the convener of the ESMT's Coaching Colloquium—a global research and practice development forum for leadership coaches. Korotov also teaches in the ESMT's "Developing Leaders: Theoretical Foundations and Practical Tools" open-enrollment program, ESMT, EMBA, and MBA programs, and multiple customized executive education programs. Among his executive education clients are Deutsche Telekom, Lufthansa, E.On, ThyssenKrupp, Allianz, Deutsche Bank, Rosatom, Gazprom, Ernst & Young, Xerox, RWE, McDonald's, etc. He is also a global leadership development consultant and coach. Prior to Korotov's academic career, he held a director's position at Ernst & Young (e-mail: konstantin.korotov@esmt.org; websites: www.korotov.com; www.esmt.org).

Joseph LeBoeuf is a retired Army Colonel, formerly the Deputy Head of the Department of Behavioral Sciences and Leadership at the United States Military Academy at West Point, currently serving as a Professor of the Practice of Management, Fuqua School of

Business, Duke University, and holds an Adjunct Professor appointment in the Sanford School of Public Policy. He teaches one core and two elective courses in Leadership and Management in the Fuqua School of Business, and an undergraduate course on military leadership. Joe is also the Faculty Advisor to the Coach K Center on Leadership and Ethics Leadership Fellows program. He teaches in and serves as an executive coach in Duke Leadership program, and has been a leadership educator and consultant for many business and governmental organizations. He has been a contributing author on a number of books and other publications for the United States Military Academy and the US Army to include FM1, The Army, FM 22-100, Army Leadership, US Army's Concept for Officership, and a chapter in the book *Future of the Army Profession* (McGraw-Hill, 2003). Most recently, he was co-author for publications on two year-long studies: *Developing Leaders of Character at the U.S. Air Force Academy: From "First Contact" to Commissioning,* and *Junior Officer Leadership Development Research BOLC 1: ROTC.* His research and writings have also appeared in *Military Review, The Teaching of Sociology*, and the *Journal of Consulting Psychology.* Professor LeBoeuf's academic education includes a BS in Engineering from West Point, a master's in Engineering Psychology and PhD degree in Industrial/Organizational Psychology from the Georgia Institute of Technology. He is also a graduate of the U.S. Army's two signature educational institutions: Command and General Staff College and Army War College.

Ariel Lelchook completed her master's thesis under Dr. Marcus Dickson and is a doctoral candidate in Industrial-Organizational Psychology at Wayne State University. Her work has appeared in *Personality and Individual Differences, Journal of Occupational and Organizational Psychology*, and *Human Relations.* Her research and teaching interests include leadership and leadership in a global context.

Emily S. Lin is a Research Associate at the Hauser Center for Non-Profit Organizations at Harvard University and is pursuing a PhD in Applied Child Development at Tufts University. Since 2008, she has worked with Marshall Ganz as a researcher, teaching fellow, and workshop facilitator and coach for public narrative and organizing. Her research focuses on the relationship between learning and the development of self- and community efficacy and leadership, particularly around collaborative data-driven decision-making and values-driven action. She is currently studying these processes within communities engaged in comprehensive education reform efforts, in collaboration with America's Promise Alliance and the Institute for Applied Research in Youth Development at Tufts University.

She received her EdM in the Technology, Innovation, and Education program at the Harvard Graduate School of Education as a Catherine B. Reynolds Fellow in Social Entrepreneurship. Prior to that, she spent a year starting youth programs for the Village Bicycle Project in Ghana, West Africa, then taught engineering, robotics, and programming to young people for several years at Machine Science, Inc. She graduated from Harvard College in 2003 with a joint concentration in Physics and Astronomy and Astrophysics.

Nancy McGaw is deputy director of the Business and Society Program at the Aspen Institute and creator/director of the Aspen Institute First Movers Fellowship Program. The fellowship program, launched in 2009, is designed to be an innovation lab and leadership development opportunity for exceptional business professionals who have demonstrated an ability and passion for imagining new products, services, and management innovations that achieve profitable business growth and positive social and environmental impacts. The vision of the program is that, over time, nurturing a critical mass of innovators across companies will help ensure that business lives up to its full potential to operate in a way that contributes to our collective well-being. In creating this program, in close collaboration with a gifted design team, she built on wisdom collected over a number of years from leadership development experts who participated in dialogues she organized at the Aspen Institute.

In her role as deputy director, she leads research initiatives to identify trends in corporate leadership and management education, including Beyond Grey Pinstripes, a global database and alternative ranking of MBA programs; CasePlace.org, an online resource to help faculty integrate social, ethical, and environmental issues into their teaching and research; MBA student attitude research; and research into the relationship between business value and values.

In addition to her experience for the last ten years at the Aspen Institute, her perspective on leadership has been enriched, among other things, by nearly two decades of work in commercial banking, a love of literature, motherhood, and five years living overseas in Japan and England. She has a BA from Michigan State University and an MA from the Nitze School of Advanced International Studies at Johns Hopkins University.

John B. McGuire is a senior faculty member and leader in the Center for Creative Leadership's (CCL) Leadership Culture Transformation practice, specializing in interdependent forms of leadership. Prior to joining CCL, John's two decades of business and organizational experience crossed a broad array of sectors, industries, and senior management positions. These experiences led to the core belief that most organizations require transformational leadership today in order to face the rising complexity unfolding in all our tomorrows. At CCL, he specializes in organizational leadership and building future-ready capability and capacity across the leadership culture to drive business results. John holds to the maxim: Best in class business strategies require best in class leadership strategies. John has leveraged his background and has advanced the singular belief that addressing the leadership culture is the common, missing link in facing change and complexity. Where others assumed culture not to be a feasible lever for development, John founded CCL's transformation practice centered on change leadership that transforms both leadership beliefs and practices simultaneously. His focus on applied research and practical experience in partnering with client organizations has led to advancing feasible development methods that increase the probability of success in change management. This practice brings not just solid theory, but proven practical solutions that have helped organizations in industries such as healthcare, manufacturing, services, and government and non-profit sectors to transform themselves toward more collaborative, interdependent leadership cultures. John currently balances his ongoing research and development work with client engagements in which he guides executive teams through the process of building interdependent leadership capability. By concentrating first within their teams, executives enhance their credibility and skills to target and advance transformation throughout their organizations. Recent example publications include the book *Transforming Your Leadership Culture* published by Jossey-Bass, and *Change Your Mind Before You Change Your Company* in Forbes.com. Other current publications include articles in *Harvard Business Review, CEO Magazine, The Washington Post, Leadership Quarterly,* select book chapters, and the CCL White Paper series. John holds masters' degrees from Harvard and Brandeis Universities, and he has received a variety of excellence awards acknowledging his contributions.

Andrew Meikle's career began in 1988 when he was one of only twelve contracted athletes in the original Uncle Toby's Ironman Series. Whilst he enjoyed considerable success as an ironman, the podium proved mostly elusive, and so began a quest to fully understand the dynamics of human high performance and what sets the highest achievers apart.

Andrew's research began in the obvious place—among those within the Ironman world who were consistently placing in the top three—and now comprises research and interviews with thousands of high achievers in the fields of sport, science, medicine, academia, the arts, politics, the military, and even faith; including such people as Everest mountaineer Sir Edmund Hilary, leader Nelson Mandela (in conjunction with Centre for the Mind), Olympic gold medallist Carl Lewis, evolutionary biologist Dr. Richard Dawkins, Japanese samurai master Nishioka Sensei, Commanding Officer British Army General Patrick Cordingley, seven times world champion surfer Layne Beachley, Nobel Peace Laureate Dr. Shirin Ebadi, Chief of the Australian Defence Force General Peter Cosgrove, and many leading CEOs.

For over a decade this research has continued and evolved to include not only individual high achievers but also "high performance environments"—those places or events where the very best are stretched to their limits: the Juilliard School in New York, Australian Institute of Sport, English National Ballet, Royal College of Music in London, Harvard Business School, Massachusetts Institute of Technology (MIT), Japanese Samurai Masters, leading scientific teams, NASA's Phoenix Mars Mission, the British Royal Opera House, and many others.

The end result is one of the largest banks of data of this kind in the world.

Andrew's research has been applied in organizations such as Accenture, Cisco, Coca-Cola, Fletcher Building, GlaxoSmith Kline, Luxottica Retail, McDonald's, Microsoft, Olympic Sporting Teams, and many more.

Henry Mintzberg is Cleghorn Professor of Management Studies at the Desautels Faculty of Management at McGill University in Montreal, where he have been since graduating with a doctorate from MIT in 1968, with stints in between at other universities in Canada, the United States, France, and England. For the past 25 years, he has been half time at McGill, he is also a founding partner of CoachingOurselves.com, which enables teams of managers to develop themselves and their organizations in their own workplaces.

Mintzberg devotes himself largely to writing and research. In 2004 he published *Managers not MBAs*, in 2007 *Tracking Strategies*, and in 2009 *Managing*. He is completing a monograph entitled *Managing the Myths of Health Care* and now working on an electronic pamphlet entitled *Balancing Society . . . radical renewal beyond Smith and Marx*.

On the teaching side, he has worked for much of the past fifteen years, in collaboration with colleagues from Canada, England, France, India, Japan, China, and Brazil to develop new approaches to management education and development.

Mintzberg may spend his public life dealing with organizations, but he prefers to spend his private life escaping from them. He does this on a bicycle (preferably on quiet roads in Europe), up mountains, and in the Laurentian wilderness of Canada atop skates, snowshoes, or cross-country skis, or else during summertime in a canoe.

Mihnea Moldoveanu is the Marcel Desautels Professor of Integrative Thinking at the Rotman School of Management at the University of Toronto, where he also serves as the Associate Dean for the Global MBA program and the Director of the Desautels Centre for Integrative Thinking. Professor Moldoveanu has been a member of the faculty at the Rotman School since 1999, and has served as the Director of the Desautels Centre for Integrative Thinking since 2002. He is the Founder, past CEO, and Chief technical officer of Redline Communications, Inc., manufacturer of the world's first operational 4G system, and a public company headquartered in Toronto. Moldoveanu is the co-author (with Nitin Nohria) of *Master Passions: Emotion, Narrative and the Development of Culture* (MIT Press, 2002) and more recently of *Inside Man: The Discipline of Modeling Human Ways of Being* (Stanford University Press, 2011). He is one of Canada's Top 40 under 40 for 2008.

Michael D. Mumford is the George Lynn Cross Distinguished Research Professor of psychology at the University of Oklahoma where he directs the Center for Applied Social Research. He received his doctoral degree from the University of Georgia in 1983 in the fields of organizational psychology and psychometrics. Dr. Mumford is a fellow of the American Psychological Association (divisions 3, 5, 10, 14), the Society for Organizational Psychology, and the American Psychological Society. He has written more than 270 articles on creativity, leadership, planning, and ethics. He has served as senior editor of *The Leadership Quarterly*, and is on the editorial boards of the *Creativity Research Journal*, the *Journal of Creative Behavior*, *IEEE Transactions on Engineering Management*, *The International Journal of Creativity and Problem Solving*, and *Ethics and Behavior*. Dr. Mumford has served as principal investigator on grants totaling more than $30 million from the National Science Foundation, the National Institutes of Health, the Department of Defense, the Department of State, and the Department of Labor. He is a recipient of the Society for Organizational Psychology's M. Scott Myer award for applied research in the workplace.

James O'Toole is the Daniels Distinguished Professor of Business Ethics at the University of Denver's Daniels College of Business.

Previously, at the University of Southern California's business school he held the University Associates' Chair of Management, served as Executive Director of the Leadership Institute, and edited *New Management* magazine.

O'Toole's research and writings have been in the areas of leadership, philosophy, ethics, and corporate culture. He has addressed dozens of major corporations and professional groups, and has over one hundred published articles. Among his sixteen books, *Vanguard Management* was named "One of the best business and economics books of 1985" by the editors of *Business Week*. His latest books are *Creating the Good Life* (2005), *The New American Workplace* (with Edward Lawler, 2006), *Transparency* (with Warren Bennis and Daniel Goleman, 2008), and *Good Business* (editor, with Don Mayer, 2010).

O'Toole received his Doctorate in Social Anthropology from Oxford University, where he was a Rhodes Scholar. He served as a Special Assistant to Secretary of Health, Education and Welfare, Elliot Richardson, as Chairman of the Secretary's Task Force on Work in America, and as Director of Field Investigations for President Nixon's Commission on Campus Unrest. He has served on the Board of Editors of the *Encyclopaedia Britannica* and as editor of *The American Oxonian* magazine. From 1994–97 O'Toole was Executive Vice President of the Aspen Institute and later Mortimer J. Adler Senior Fellow at the Institute. He also has served as Chair of the Booz/Allen/Hamilton Strategic Leadership Center.

O'Toole has won a Mitchell Prize for a paper on economic growth policy. Recently, he was named one of the "100 most influential people in business ethics" by the editors of *Ethisphere,* one of "the top 100 thought leaders on leadership" by *Leadership Excellence* magazine, and author of one of the "hundred most influential business articles" by the editors of *Strategy+Business.*

Charles J. (Chuck) Palus, PhD, is a senior faculty member at the Center for Creative Leadership (CCL), responsible for research, innovation, and product development, specializing in interdependent leadership. Chuck is the founder and manager of CCL Labs, an innovation lab whose inventions include Visual Explorer, Leadership Metaphor Explorer, and Boundary Explorer. Chuck first entered the field of leadership development as a chemical engineer with the DuPont Company, responsible for the manufacture of polymer products, learning firsthand that quality is a social achievement. Chuck earned his PhD in adult developmental psychology from Boston College and designed and facilitated leadership development programs for the Hurricane Island Outward Bound School. At CCL these developmental ideas took root in *Making Common Sense: Leadership as Meaning Making in a Community of Practice,* and *Evolving Leaders: A Model for Promoting Leadership Development in Programs.* His book *The Leader's Edge: Six Creative Competencies for Navigating Complex Challenges* received the annual Best Book Award from The Banff Centre for Leadership Development in Calgary. He has researched, partnered, and published widely on the topic of interdependent leadership and is a contributor to the *CCL Handbook of Leadership Development* and the *CCL Handbook of Coaching.* Chuck is advisor to the Research Center for Leadership in Action at New York University, and to the Global Leadership and Learning Initiative at Columbia University, and is a member of the Teaching Leadership Community of the Harvard Business School.

David Peterson is a doctoral student in the industrial and organizational psychology program at the University of Oklahoma. His research interests include creativity, innovation, and leadership.

Gianpiero Petriglieri, MD, is Affiliate Professor of Organisational Behaviour at INSEAD in Fontainebleau, France. His areas of interest include leadership, team dynamics, experiential learning, and unconscious processes in individuals, groups, and organizations. His research explores the features that make leadership development effective and meaningful; managers' use of business school courses to shape personal and professional identities; the influence of unconscious factors in leadership; and the emotional dilemmas of high potential managers. Over the last decade, he has contributed to refining a unique approach to experiential leadership development currently used within Business School and organizations in the private and public sectors.

At INSEAD, Professor Petriglieri teaches "Organisational Behaviour I" in the MBA and directs the "Management Acceleration Programme," the school's flagship executive program for emerging leaders. He also designs and directs customized leadership development programs for multinationals in a number of industries including professional services, FMCG, fashion, building materials, and pharmaceuticals. He consults to a range of organizations on the design and implementation of programs for developing effective and responsible leaders. Prior to joining INSEAD, he was Visiting Professor at Copenhagen Business School, where he received teaching awards in the MBA and Executive MBA, and contributed regularly to executive education programmes, and to the MBA, at IMD International in Lausanne, Switzerland.

Professor Petriglieri received a Medical Doctorate and a specialization in Psychiatry from the University of Catania Medical School, Italy, and a diploma in Advanced Organizational Consultation from the Tavistock Institute of Human Relations in London. He has practiced as a psychotherapist and often serves on the staff of group relations conferences in Europe and the United States. He is past President of the International Transactional Analysis Association (ITAA) and a member of the A.K. Rice Institute for the Study of Social Systems.

Following his education at universities in the UK and USA, **Richard Richards** worked in management, training, and leadership development in the hospitality industry while living in the United States, Germany, Egypt, Kuwait, Saudi Arabia, and Hong Kong. He gained additional leadership, organizational development, and facilitation skills while leading teams in Australia, Korea, Israel, China, Mariana Islands,

Germany, Chile, Argentina, and Mexico. In his own consulting practice, he developed and produced training materials, industrial videos, and internal communications materials for leaders, managers, and employees internationally.

While living in the United States he has reconnected with theater, studying improvisation at Second City in Chicago and has worked as an actor on the stage, in voice-over and in film, and continues to write and perform. For 13 years he owned a for-profit art gallery that more closely resembled a struggling non-profit—a valuable but expensive "alternative MBA."

His most recent degree from DePaul University focused on "The Use of Theatre to Describe, Understand and Modify People's Perceptions and Behavior," foreshadowing his relationship with The Ariel Group and his work in leadership development.

Over the years, he has been connected with a number of social causes, including community arts projects, developmentally disabled adults, and theater companies that have focused on a variety of different communities including GLBT youth, immigrant communities, and the formerly incarcerated. He is currently on the Board of a collaborative theater project dedicated to healing, public awareness, and social change through empowering the voices of formerly incarcerated people and their loved ones.

In his current role of VP of Learning Design at The Ariel Group, he has been able to bring together many aspects of his previous work (paid and unpaid) in creating experiential learning opportunities that develop leadership presence, a critical skill set for all leaders.

Al H. Ringleb received his PhD in economics from Kansas State University and his JD from the University of Kansas. He is the Executive Director and founder of the nonprofit Consortium of Universities for International Studies, an organization of 40+ U.S. universities headed by the University of Iowa. Dr. Ringleb is also president and founder of CIMBA (Consortium Institute for Management and Business Analysis), a research, training, and development organization located in Asolo, Italy. Through the University of Iowa, and in cooperation with the Consortium, CIMBA offers a leading international MBA in Asolo, and a leadership and personal development focused undergraduate study abroad program at its academic campus in Paderno, Italy. In combination with its strategic partners, CIMBA offers a cutting edge, neuroscience-based, leadership development system to both its academic and executive clients. With Dr. David Rock, Dr. Ringleb is a co-founder of the NeuroLeadership Institute, co-editor of the *NeuroLeadership Journal* and, in conjunction with his research and development efforts at CIMBA, heads the NeuroLeadership Laboratory. In 2007, CIMBA hosted the first-ever NeuroLeadership Conference in Asolo, attracting leading neuroscientists and leadership development practitioners from around the globe.

His most recent academic research interests are in the areas of leadership and leadership development. He is particularly interested in the leadership applications of recent and ongoing research in neuroscience and social psychology, which are being driven by rapid advances in brain-imaging technology. In cooperation with CIMBA's strategic partners, Dr. Ringleb's research and development teams are developing wireless neurobiofeedback technology and assessment algorithms for use in the CIMBA leadership development system. He has published over seventy-five professional articles, books, and technical reports in leading business management, economic, and legal journals, including the *Academy of Management Journal, Journal of Political Economy,* and the *Journal of Legal Studies.*

Issac Robledo is a doctoral student in the industrial and organizational psychology program at the University of Oklahoma. His research interests include creativity, innovation, and leadership.

David Rock coined the term *NeuroLeader*ship and co-founded the NeuroLeadership Institute, a global initiative bringing neuroscientists and leadership experts together to build a new science for leadership development. He co-edits the *NeuroLeadership Journal* and heads up an annual global summit. He has written or co-written many of the central academic and discussion papers defining the NeuroLeadership Field.

David is also the founder and CEO of RCS, a global consulting and training firm with operations in 24 countries. Academically, David is on the faculty and advisory board of Cimba, an international business school based in Europe. He is a guest lecturer at universities in 5 countries including Oxford University's Said Business School, and on the board of the BlueSchool, a new educational initiative in New York City. He received his professional doctorate in the Neuroscience of Leadership (by published works) from Middlesex University in March 2010.

David is the author of *Personal Best*, (Simon & Schuster, 2001), *Quiet Leadership* (Harper Collins, 2006), *Coaching with the Brain in Mind* (Wiley & Sons, 2009), and *Your Brain at Work* (HarperBusiness, 2009). He lives between New York City and Sydney, Australia, with his wife and two young daughters.

Sanyin Siang is the Executive Director of the Fuqua/Coach K Center on Leadership and Ethics at Duke University's Fuqua School of Business. Since its inception, the center has been recognized as a premier leadership and ethics center through its distinguished advisory board, strategic partnerships with other leading universities and organizations, innovative MBA and executive leadership development programs, and a successful annual leadership conference. Sanyin has been an executive educator and leadership coach with for-profit corporations, non-profit organizations, and government agencies. Her experience in mentoring, strategic planning, board development, strategic partnerships, coupled with an entrepreneurial mindset has helped organizations and executives identify gaps and develop programs for a rapidly changing marketplace. Sanyin's thought pieces and research have been published in journals such as *Science, DNA and Cell Biology*, and *Science and Engineering Ethics*. She is co-editor of a special issue of the *Leader to Leader* journal (co-published by Wiley & Sons). Her board service has included the Executive Committee of the National Board of Duke University Children's Health Center, editorial board of *Clinical Researcher*, and the Editorial Boards for the American Bar Association's Science & Technology Law Section and The Professional Ethics Report of the American Association for the Advancement of Science. She received her MBA in Business Administration and BSE in Biomedical Engineering from Duke University.

Sim B. Sitkin is Professor of Management and Faculty Director of the Fuqua/Coach K Center on Leadership and Ethics at Duke University's Fuqua School of Business. He is also Founding Partner of Delta Leadership, Inc. and Professor of Organization Science at the Free University of Amsterdam. His research, teaching, and consulting focus on leadership and control systems and their influence on how organizations and their members become more or less capable of change and innovation. He has published widely on the effects of formal and informal organizational control systems and leadership on risk taking, accountability, trust, learning, change, and innovation. His latest book is *Control in Organizations* (co-edited with Laura Cardinal and Katinka Bijlsma-Frankema) published by Cambridge University Press. Sim is Deputy Editor of *Behavioral Science and Policy*. His previous service has included the Academy of Management Board of Governors, *Organization Science* Senior Editor, and *Journal of Organizational Behavior* Associate Editor. Sim has worked as a consultant and executive educator with many large and small corporations, non-profit and government organizations worldwide. Sim received his PhD in organizational behavior from Stanford Business School, EdM in educational administration from Harvard Graduate School of Education, and BA in psychology from Clark University.

Ken Starkey is Professor of Management and Organisational Learning and Director of Research at Nottingham University Business School where he was previously Director of the Executive MBA program and Head of School. Ken is a Fellow of the Sunningdale Institute of the National School of Government, a Fellow of the British Academy of Management, and the author of a number of reports on the future of management research and management education commissioned by the Foundation for Management Education and the UK Department of Trade and Industry. He has written 12 books and 100+ academic papers on the challenges of modern management.

He works for public and private sector organizations, increasingly on the challenges of sustainable management. He is currently writing a book on the implications of the economic crisis for leadership and management philosophy and practice.

Mary Sully de Luque is an Assistant Professor of Management and is a Research Fellow at the Thunderbird School of Global Management. Before joining Thunderbird, she spent three years as a Senior Fellow in the Wharton School at the University of Pennsylvania, with Professor Robert House, working on the Global Leadership and Organizational Effectiveness (GLOBE) Project. She is currently co-facilitating the GLOBE Phase Three Project, which is a 24-country study of CEO strategic leadership effectiveness. She teaches Global Leadership, Cross-cultural Management and Global Human Resource Management in MBA, EMBA and graduate-level business programs.

Her current lines of research examine the influences of culture in the areas of leadership, the effects of feedback processes in the work environment, and international talent management. Sully de Luque has presented her research at international conferences and she has published in such journals as *Administrative Science Quarterly, Academy of Management Review, Journal of International Business Studies,* and *Academy of Management Perspective*, as well as many book chapters.

Additionally, Dr. Sully de Luque has also served as the faculty co-director of Project Artemis and the Goldman Sachs 10,000 Women Project in Afghanistan, Pakistan, and Peru, which provides business education to women entrepreneurs in these countries. She holds a PhD in Organizational Behavior from the University of Nebraska, and her BA in Communication Studies from Creighton University. Prior to finishing her formal education, she worked as an aide for two United States Senators.

Michael Useem is Professor of Management and Director of the Center for Leadership and Change Management at the Wharton School of the University of Pennsylvania. He has completed several studies of corporate organization, ownership, governance, restructuring, leadership, and teamwork. He is co-author of *The India Way: How India's Top Business Leaders Are Revolutionizing Management* (Harvard Business Press, 2010); co-author and co-editor of *Learning From Catastrophes* (Wharton School Publishing, 2009); author of *The Go Point: When It's Time to Decide* (Random House, 2006); and author of *The Leadership Moment: Nine True Stories of Triumph and Disaster and Their Lessons for Us All* (Random House, 1998), *Investor Capitalism: How Money Managers Are Changing the Face of Corporate America* (HarperCollins, 1996), *Executive Defense: Shareholder Power and Corporate Reorganization* (Harvard University Press, 1993), *The Inner Circle: Large Corporations* *and the Rise of Business Political Activity in the U.S. and U.K.* (Oxford University Press, 1984). His articles have appeared in the *Administrative Science Quarterly*, *Fortune*, *Harvard Business Review*, *McKinsey Quarterly*, *New York Times*, and elsewhere. His university teaching includes MBA and executive-MBA courses on leadership and change, and he offers programs on leadership, teamwork, governance, and decision making for managers in the United States, Asia, Europe, and Latin America. He also works on leadership development and governance with many companies and organizations in the private, public, and non-profit sectors, including American Express, Minsheng Bank (China), Cisco, Fidelity, Google, IBM, ICICI Bank (India), Intel, Johnson & Johnson, Microsoft, Morgan Stanley, Travelers, U.S. Department of Justice, U.S. Marine Corps, World Economic Forum, and other organizations. Email:useem@wharton.upenn.edu.

Keith Yardley is a Vice President at Goldman Sachs with its Pine Street Leadership Development Group. Pine Street serves the partners and managing directors of Goldman Sachs, as well as senior executives at select external client organizations. His current focus areas include design of Partner development initiatives, co-hosting leadership programs for the firm's clients, and internal advisory services. His functional expertise includes behavioral assessment, coaching, talent management, and process facilitation. Prior to joining Goldman Sachs in 2007, Keith was a senior vice president for HSBC Global Markets and Banking based in New York designing learning, coaching, diversity, employee engagement and succession management projects. Before that he worked for HSBC in Hong Kong delivering the implementation of performance management and talent identification solutions across their Asia operations. He was previously at Kiddy & Partners from 1997 to 2000, a London-based business psychology firm specializing in assessment and talent management across a number of industry sectors. Keith earned his PhD in behavioral decision making from the center for decision research at Leeds University Business School, UK. He is a registered Chartered Psychologist with the British Psychological Society.